American Prisoners of War
Held at
Portsmouth, Stapleton,
Gibraltar and Malta
during the War of 1812

Heritage Books by the Society of the War of 1812
in the State of Ohio:

Transcribed by Harrison Scott Baker

*American Prisoners of War Held at Bermuda,
Cape of Good Hope and Jamaica During the War of 1812*

*American Prisoners of War Held at Barbados,
Newfoundland and New Providence During the War of 1812*

*American Prisoners of War Held at Halifax
During the War of 1812, Volume I and II*

Transcribed by Eric Eugene Johnson

American Prisoners of War Held at Chatham During the War of 1812

American Prisoners of War Held at Dartmoor During the War of 1812

*American Prisoners of War Held in Montreal
and Quebec During the War of 1812*

*American Prisoners of War Held at Plymouth
During the War of 1812*

*American Prisoners of War Held at Portsmouth,
Stapleton, Gibraltar and Malta during the War of 1812*

*American Prisoners of War Held at Quebec
During the War of 1812, 8 June 1813–11 December 1814*

*American Prisoners of War Paroled at Dartmouth,
Halifax, Jamaica and Odiham During the War of 1812*

*American Sea Fencibles in the War of 1812:
United States Sea Fencibles, State Sea Fencibles*

Black Regulars in the War of 1812

Black Regulars and Militiamen in the War of 1812

Forgotten Americans Who Served in the War of 1812

Ohio and the War of 1812: A Collection of Lists, Musters and Essays

Ohio's Regulars in the War of 1812

Heritage Books by the Society of the War of 1812
in the State of Maryland:

Maryland Regulars in the War of 1812
Transcribed by Eric Eugene Johnson; Foreword by Christos Christou

American Prisoners of War

Held at
Portsmouth, Stapleton, Gibraltar and Malta
during the War of 1812

Transcribed by
Eric Eugene Johnson

Society of the War of 1812
in the
State of Ohio

HERITAGE BOOKS
2019

HERITAGE BOOKS
AN IMPRINT OF HERITAGE BOOKS, INC.

Books, CDs, and more—Worldwide

For our listing of thousands of titles see our website
at
www.HeritageBooks.com

Published 2019 by
HERITAGE BOOKS, INC.
Publishing Division
5810 Ruatan Street
Berwyn Heights, Md. 20740

Copyright © 2019 Society of the War of 1812 in the State of Ohio

All rights reserved. No part of this book may be reproduced or transmitted in any form or by any means, electronic or mechanical, including photocopying, recording or by any information storage and retrieval system without written permission from the author, except for the inclusion of brief quotations in a review.

International Standard Book Number
Paperbound: 978-0-7884-5886-6

- Table of Contents -

Introduction	1
The Honored Dead	7
Portsmouth	
Alphabetical listing of names	9
Numeric listing by prisoner number	121
Crew listing	137
Stapleton	
Alphabetical listing of names	157
Numeric listing by prisoner number	185
Crew listing	190
Gibraltar	
Alphabetical listing of names	197
Numeric listing by prisoner number	243
Crew listing	253
Malta	
Alphabetical listing of names	263
Numeric listing by prisoner number	267
Crew listing	268

Introduction

This is a transcription of American prisoner of war records from the U.S. Navy, privateers and merchant vessels (plus civilians) who were captured and then interned by the British Empire at the Portsmouth or the Stapleton prisoner of war depots in England, or in the prisoner of war facilities located at either Gibraltar or Malta in the Mediterranean Sea during the War of 1812.

This volume was compiled from copies of the *General Entry Book of American Prisoners of War* ledgers of the British Admiralty made by the Public Records Office in London, Great Britain (ADM 103 series). The *General Entry Book* (GEB) records are composed of lines for the recording of names and personal information of those incarcerated. The record of each prisoner is found on two facing pages. The clerk making the entries wrote the page number on the upper right-side corner of each page.

The names and information of ten men can be found on each double page for the Americans interned at the Portsmouth Depot, nine men per double page for the Stapleton Depot, and twenty-five men per double page for the Gibraltar and Malta facilities.

Prisoner of War Facilities

Microfilm	POW facilities	Dates	Number of prisoners
ADM 103/342	Portsmouth	Jul 1812 – Sep 1813	1,170
ADM 103/343	Portsmouth	Oct 1813 – Jun 1814	339
ADM 103/144	Gibraltar	Aug 1812 – Feb 1815	752
ADM 103/226	Malta	Nov 1812 – Mar 1813	55
AMD 103/409	Stapleton	Dec 1812 – Apr 1814	421
Total			2,737

Below are the column headers from the GEB ledgers used at the Portsmouth and the Stapleton Depots. Titles in brackets, "[" and "]", indicates that the transcriber has changed the column headers from the original to a more meaningful header. Some of the columns have been eliminated in this book while other columns have been combined.

Column 1 – Number
   Each prisoner of war arriving at a prisoner facility was assigned a number.

Column 2 – By what Ship or how taken [How taken]
   This column lists the Royal Naval ship or privateer which captured the prisoner. Also included in this column are the men who gave themselves up as a prisoner, who were impressed by the Royal Navy, taken ashore or captured by the Royal Army.

Column 3 – Time when [When Taken]
   The date the prisoner was taken into custody.

Column 4 – Where Taken
   This column lists the location of capture which could indicate latitudes and longitudes if at sea, a port, or a geographic region or location.

Column 5 – Name of Prize [Prize Name]
   The name of the ship or vessel of the prisoner of war, or if from land forces, the name of the regiment or service.

Column 6 - Whether Man of War, Privateer, or Merchant Vessel [Ship Type]
   The type of ship or vessel, that is: man of war (warship), revenue cutter, privateer, letter of marque, merchant vessel, or prize of a privateer. Land forces indicate regular army, volunteers or militia.

Column 7 – Prisoner's Names [title not used]

2 Introduction

The prisoner names given in the GEB are first name then last name, e.g. John Smith, but in this book the last name is given first then the first name.

Column 8 – Quality [title not used]
This column gives the rank of the prisoner. In addition to naval, privateer and merchant vessel ranks, there are also civilians, merchants, supercargoes and passengers found in these records.

Column 9 – Time when received into custody [Date Received]
The date when a prisoner arrived at a prisoner facility.

Column 10 – From what ship, or whence received [From what ship]
The location of the prisoner before being received at the current prisoner of war facility. This could be the capturing ship, the ship that transported the prisoner to England, a hospital, another prison facility or parole location.

Column 11 – Place of Nativity [Born]
Lists the birth place of a prisoner.

Column 12 – Age
The age of the prisoner in years, most likely, from his last birthday.

Columns 13 through 18 are not used in this book [Race]
These columns indicate the height, hair color, color of eyes, type of complexion and any body marks (including tattoos) or wounds of a prisoner. Included in these physical descriptions are the races of non-Caucasians, which are Black, Negro, Mulatto, Creole or Chinese. The author has created a new column entitled Race to indicate non-Caucasians.

Columns 19 through 32 are not used in this book
The personal items of a prisoner were inventoried upon arrival at a prisoner of war facility and the required missing items were replaced. These items include hammocks, beds, straw mattresses, cushions, blankets, hats, jackets, waistcoats, trousers, shirts, shoes, stockings and handkerchiefs.

Columns 33 through 35 have been combined into a single entry [title not used]
This new column indicates when a prisoner died at a prisoner facility, when he escaped from a prisoner facility, when he was discharged to another prison facility, or when he was released and sent back to the United States.

Column 33 – Exchanged, Discharged, Died or Escaped [Field not used]
"E" or "R" indicates that the prisoner escaped from the parole location while "D" indicates that he was discharged. "DD" indicates that he died while assigned to a parole location.

Column 34 – Time When [Field not used]
Contains the date of the event from column 33.

Column 35 - Whither, and by what order if discharged. [Field not used]
This column shows the place or ship that the prisoner was sent when he was discharged from the prison facility. Orders were given by the His Majesty's Transport Board.

The above form was used by all of the British prisoner of war facilities for Americans in England during the War of 1812. The British also used four other forms to record the activities of alien prisoners of war. A slightly different form was used in the Empire for prisoners of war. This second form did not include a place of nativity, age, race, and prisoner's personal items. The Gibraltar and the Malta prisoner of war facilities used this second form to record he American prisoners.

The third form was used to record the names and personal information of those prisoners of war who were transferred between a prisoner of war facility and a hospital.

The fourth form was a weekly report to record the deaths of prisoners who had died during the previous week, and it was also used to record those prisoners who escaped. The form includes the prisoner's number in General Entry Book, name and sometimes birthplace and age, quality (rank), name of the prisoner's ship (or regiment), date of death and cause of death.

The final form was for prisoners of war who were paroled in a village or city near a prisoner of war facility. These men were officers, warrant officers, and some seaman and civilians. Civilians also included American women and children who were captured by the British. This form is similar to the first form except that there was no space allowed for clothing and bedding.

Portsmouth

The Royal Navy's Portsmouth Naval Base was the home of one of the three prisoner of war prison ship facilities in England used during the War of 1812 to house American prisoners of war. The facility had been used since 1796 to intern French prisoners of war during the Napoleonic Wars. The other two prison ship facilities were located at Plymouth and at Chatham.

In 1813, there were fourteen prison hulks at Portsmouth, which were housing 9,337 French prisoners and a growing number of American prisoners. These ships were the *Prothee, Crown, San Damaso, Vigilant, Guildford, San Antonio, Vengeance, Veteran, Suffolk, Assistance, Ave Princessa, Kron Princessa, Waldemar,* and *Negro*.

The American prisoner of war ledgers for Portsmouth has 1,509 entries but fourteen men were listed twice and three men who had arrived at this facility had died in route. They still had their names added to the ledgers. A total of 1,492 living men were interned at Portsmouth.

The majority of the men had either been captured by the British on the high seas or had given themselves up for internment instead of serving on British ships. This last group of men were either impressed American seamen or those who had volunteered to serve on British ships.

A total of six men had died at Portsmouth. One man was released for being a British subject, two were released and sent to London (no reasons were given), two men were transferred to Ashburton on parole, twenty-eight men were sent to Odiham on parole and seven men were sent to Reading on parole. Ashburton, Odiham and Reading were cities in which senior American naval officers were permitted to live instead of being assigned to a prison ship.

Sixteen percent of the men were African-Americans, for a total of 239 men. The majority of the Americans were interned at Portsmouth for less than thirty days. The last group of men arrived at Portsmouth and they were immediately sent to Plymouth on the same day. 1,414 Americans were sent to Chatham while thirty men, the last group, were sent to Plymouth.

Gibraltar

The Gibraltar prison depot operated as an American prisoner of war facility between 12 Aug 1812 and 14 Mar 1815. The ledger book for this camp has 786 entries but thirty-six prisoner numbers were not used and two prisoners were never assigned prisoner numbers.

At least twenty-two Americans were entered twice in this ledger book. It appears that these men were released back to their ships to work as maintenance men until their ships were disposed of. Once they were no longer needed for this duty, they were sent back to the prison facility and issued a new prisoner number. There were approximately 752 individual Americans interned at Gibraltar.

The first group of prisoners were men whose ships happened to be in Gibraltar's harbor when word was received that war had broken out. Most of the other men were captured on merchant ships off Lisbon, Portugal or Cadiz, Spain. Other men were taken in the ports in the western Mediterranean Sea. Only three American ships, that were captured by the British, were privateers.

Two of the men interned by the British were labeled as Englishmen, one American was released on parole, one died, and there were no recorded escapes. Of the remaining men, all were sent to England in 1813 except forty in 1814 and three in 1815. There are no indications in the ledger that Gibraltar used a prison ship to house the prisoners.

Malta

It is not known if the American prisoners of war were interned in either a military prison or a prison ship on the island of Malta. There were fifty-five Americans interned at this facility. The facility operated between 17 Nov 1812 and 3 May 1814. All of the men, except three who died, were sent to England.

Most of the men gave themselves up from British warships or merchant ships. The crew from one privateer and one merchant vessel were captured and sent to this facility.

Stapleton Depot

The Stapleton Depot, outside of Bristol, England, had over 5,000 French prisoners of war and only 421 Americans during the War of 1812. This depot was organized into three prisons with a third of the Americans assigned to each prison.

This facility was built in 1782 to house 800 Spanish and Dutch prisoners of war. In 1794, there were over 1,000 French prisoners and by 1800 this figure had increased to 2,900 prisoners. The depot was rebuilt in 1805 to house 5,000 prisoners. It was closed in 1815.

Three hundred and ninety-one Americans arrived from the prison ships located at Plymouth in two groups, one on 7 July 1813 and the other on 11 July 1813. Americans who gave themselves up or who were captured in the ships in the vicinity of Bristol started to arrive at this depot on 2 December 1812.

A total of 421 Americans were interned at this facility, of which, six died, nine escaped, and twenty-six enlisted in the British naval service. There were seventy-four African-Americans at this prison facility.

Of the foreign nationals captured with the Americans, three Portuguese, one Prussian, one Dane and three Swedes were released and sent to their government's consuls in England. On 13 and 16 June 1814, the remaining 369 Americans were sent to Dartmoor Depot.

The penmanship in these ledgers was very good. The spelling of non-familiar names was done phonetically.

Any errors or omissions are regretted and are the fault of the transcriber.

Eric Eugene Johnson

President (2008-2011)
Society of the War of 1812 in the State of Ohio

Registrar General (2017-   )
General Society of the War of 1812

Abbreviations

HM – His Majesty
HMS – His Majesty's Ship
HMT – His Majesty's Transport
MV – Merchant Vessel
MW – Man of War
P – Privateer
US – United States
USRM – United States Revenue Marine

Also, standard state name abbreviations

The locations in Maine are listed as MA and not ME. During the War of 1812, Maine was still a part of Massachusetts.

- In memory of those who did not return -

The Honored Dead

Portsmouth

Bearbere, John
Bessey, Jonas
Davy, William (alias Davis)
Drew, William
Halmore, Henry Michael
Harris, George
Plur, Henry
Unknown American
Weed, Ebenezer

Gibraltar

Moro, Henry

Malta

Chapman, Enoch
Wampo, Nathaniel
Wilson, Thomas

Stapleton

Dunn, John
Francis, Joseph B.
Michel, Jacob
Swatt, David
Watson, Isaac

- Those who die in service to the United States should not be forgotten –

Portsmouth Depot

Adzard, Thomas - Seaman - Number: 1098 - How taken: Gave himself up from HM Ship-of-the-Line Berwick - Date received: 5 Oct 1813 - From what ship: HM Ship-of-the-Line Achille - Born: Rhode Island - Age: 22 - Discharged on 17 Oct 1813 and sent to Chatham on HM Store Ship Weymouth.

Albet, John - Seaman - Number: 629 - How taken: Gave himself up from HM Guardship Royal William - Date received: 3 Feb 1813 - From what ship: HMS Royal William - Born: New Jersey - Age: 22 - Race: Black - Discharged on 11 Mar 1813 and sent to Chatham on HM Store Ship Abundance.

Albro, George - Seaman - Number: 762 - How taken: Gave himself up from HM Ship-of-the-Line Blake - Date received: 1 Apr 1813 - From what ship: HMS Blake - Born: Newport - Age: 33 - Discharged on 3 Apr 1813 and sent to Chatham on HM Transport Chatham.

Aldridge, Richard - Seaman - Number: 1293 - Prize Name: Mary, prize to the True Blooded Yankee - Ship type: MV - How taken: HM Ship of-the-Line Bellerophon - When taken: 16 Dec 1813 - Where taken: off Land's End - Date received: 22 Dec 1813 - From what ship: HMS Bellerophon - Born: Lancaster, PA - Age: 24 - Discharged on 26 Dec 1813 and sent to Chatham on HMS Frigate Nemesis.

Alexander, Robert - Seaman - Number: 596 - How taken: Gave himself up from HMS Dapper - Date received: 31 Jan 1813 - From what ship: HMS Dapper - Born: Salem, MA - Age: 19 - Discharged on 10 Jun 1813 and sent to Chatham on HM Frigate Arethusa.

Alfos, Robert (alias Lucas) - Seaman - Number: 996 - How taken: Gave himself up from HM Sloop Acorn - Date received: 17 Aug 1813 - From what ship: HMS Acorn - Born: Philadelphia - Age: 22 - Discharged on 21 Sep 1813 and sent to Chatham on HM Ship-of-the-Line Queen.

Allen, Barnes - Seaman - Number: 163 - Prize Name: Baltimore - Ship type: P - How taken: HM Transport Diadem - When taken: 7 Oct 1812 - Where taken: S. Andera - Date received: 3 Nov 1812 San Antonio - From what ship: HMS Diadem - Born: Baltimore - Age: 33 - Discharged on 19 Feb 1813 and sent to Chatham on HM Store Ship Dromedary.

Allen, David - Seaman - Number: 1190 - Prize Name: Fire Fly of Gloucester - Ship type: MV - How taken: HM Frigate Revolutionnaire - When taken: 19 Oct 1813 - Where taken: at sea - Date received: 9 Nov 1813 - From what ship: HMS Revolutionaire - Born: Gloucester - Age: 20 - Discharged on 26 Dec 1813 and sent to Chatham on HM Ship of-the-Line Diomede.

Allen, Elihu - Seaman - Number: 308 - Prize Name: Catherine - Ship type: MV - How taken: HM Frigate Leonidas - When taken: 31 Dec 1812 - Where taken: off Ireland - Date received: 31 Dec 1812 - From what ship: HM Ship-of-the-Line Northumberland - Born: New Bedford - Age: 18 - Discharged on 4 Mar 1813 and sent to Chatham on HM Ship-of-the-Line Queen.

Allen, Henry - Gunner's Mate - Number: 449 - Prize Name: Sword Fish - Ship type: P - How taken: HM Ship-of-the-Line Elephant - When taken: 28 Dec 1812 - Where taken: at sea - Date received: 14 Jan 1813 - From what ship: HMS Elephant - Born: Salem - Age: 23 - Discharged on 11 Mar 1813 and sent to Chatham on HM Store Ship Abundance.

Allen, John - Boy - Number: 892 - Prize Name: Prompt - Ship type: MV - How taken: Chance, privateer - When taken: 28 May 1813 - Where taken: Bay of Biscay - Date received: 24 Jun 1813 - From what ship: HM Frigate Unicorn - Born: Boston - Age: 14 - Discharged on 2 Jul 1813 and sent to Chatham on HM Frigate Tribune.

Allen, Peter - Boatswain - Number: 250 - Prize Name: King of Rome - Ship type: P - How taken: HM Brig Wolverine - When taken: 13 Dec 1812 - Where taken: at sea - Date received: 27 Dec 1812 - From what ship: HMS Wolverine - Born: Port Garlett, Spain - Age: 32 - Discharged on 19 Feb 1813 and sent to Chatham on HM Store Ship Dromedary.

Allen, William - Seaman - Number: 372 - Prize Name: Mariner - Ship type: MV - How taken: HM Brig Lyra - When taken: 15 Dec 1812 - Where taken: off Bilboa, Spain - Date received: 3 Jan 1813 - From what ship: HM Frigate Fox - Born: Newburyport - Age: 19 - Discharged on 4 Mar 1813 and sent to Chatham on HM

Ship-of-the-Line Queen.

Allen, William - Seaman - Number: 931 - Prize Name: Tender of the True Blooded Yankee - Ship type: P - How taken: HM Ship-of-the-Line Fame - When taken: 24 Jun 1813 - Where taken: at sea - Date received: 1 Jul 1813 - From what ship: HM Brig Hope - Born: Newburyport - Age: 25 - Discharged on 2 Jul 1813 and sent to Chatham on HM Brig Scorpion.

Alley, Jacob - Seaman - Number: 17 - Prize Name: USRM Cutter James Madison - Ship type: MW - How taken: HM Frigate Barbadoes - When taken: 22 Aug 1812 - Where taken: at sea - Date received: 12 Oct 1812 San Antonio - From what ship: HM Ship-of-the-Line Polyphemus - Born: Boston - Age: 24 - Discharged on 19 Feb 1813 and sent to Chatham on HM Frigate Ulysses.

Andermach, John - Boy - Number: 365 - Prize Name: Three Brothers - Ship type: MV - How taken: HM Brig Bermuda - When taken: 9 Dec 1812 - Where taken: off St. Valery - Date received: 2 Jan 1813 - From what ship: HM Prison Ship Assistance - Born: Achim, Prussia - Age: 10 - Released on 16 Jan 1813 and sent to London.

Anderson, Aaron - Seaman - Number: 700 - Prize Name: Calcutta - Ship type: East Indian Ship - How taken: Two Brothers, privateer of Guernsey - When taken: 23 Nov 1812 - Where taken: at sea - Date received: 24 Feb 1813 - From what ship: HM Brig Escort - Born: Newburn, NY - Age: 18 - Discharged on 6 Mar 1813 and sent to Chatham on HMS Frigate Alexandria.

Anderson, Andrew - Seaman - Number: 18 - Prize Name: USRM Cutter James Madison - Ship type: MW - How taken: HM Frigate Barbadoes - When taken: 22 Aug 1812 - Where taken: at sea - Date received: 12 Oct 1812 San Antonio - From what ship: HM Ship-of-the-Line Polyphemus - Born: Savannah, GA - Age: 26 - Discharged on 19 Feb 1813 and sent to Chatham on HM Frigate Ulysses.

Anderson, Henry - Seaman - Number: 821 - Prize Name: Ajax, prize to the Privateer Governor Tomkins - Ship type: MV - How taken: HM Frigate Revolutionnaire - When taken: 10 Apr 1813 - Where taken: at sea - Date received: 13 May 1813 - From what ship: HMS Revolutionaire - Born: North Carolina - Age: 20 - Discharged on 17 May 1813 and sent to Chatham on HMS Impeleux.

Anderson, James - Seaman - Number: 857 - How taken: Gave himself up from HM Frigate Leonidas - Date received: 22 Jun 1813 - From what ship: HM Ship-of-the-Line Vigo - Born: Long Island - Age: 39 - Discharged on 2 Jul 1813 and sent to Chatham on HM Frigate Tribune.

Anderson, John - Mate - Number: 1176 - How taken: Detained at Fareham by the officers on Impress Service - Date received: 17 Oct 1813 - From what ship: Fareham Rendezvous - Born: Washington, NC - Age: 29 - Discharged on 17 Oct 1813 and sent to Chatham on HM Transport Malabar No. 352.

Anderson, John - Captain - Number: 103 - Prize Name: HM Brig Richmond - Ship type: MV - How taken: Detained by Court of Admiralty - When taken: 31 Jul 1812 - Where taken: Portsmouth harbor - Date received: 16 Oct 1812 San Antonio - From what ship: HM Brig Richmond - Born: Aberdeen, Scotland - Age: 25 - Discharged on 27 Oct 1812 and sent to Chatham on HM Guardship Royal Williams.

Anderson, John - Seaman - Number: 1384 - Prize Name: Pilate - Ship type: P - How taken: Victoria, privateer of Guernsey - When taken: 28 Jan 1814 - Where taken: off Bordeaux - Date received: 7 Feb 1814 - From what ship: Mary from Guernsey - Born: Maryland - Age: 24 - Race: Black - Discharged on 13 Feb 1814 and sent to Chatham on HM Transport Malabar No. 352.

Anderson, Joseph - Seaman - Number: 505 - How taken: Gave himself up from HM Ship of-the-Line Diomede - Date received: 16 Jan 1813 - From what ship: HMS Diomede - Born: Baltimore - Age: 33 - Discharged on 11 Mar 1813 and sent to Chatham on HM Store Ship Abundance.

Anderson, Oliver - Seaman - Number: 19 - Prize Name: USRM Cutter James Madison - Ship type: MW - How taken: HM Frigate Barbadoes - When taken: 22 Aug 1812 - Where taken: at sea - Date received: 12 Oct 1812 San Antonio - From what ship: HM Ship-of-the-Line Polyphemus - Born: Sweden - Age: 23 - Discharged on 19 Feb 1813 and sent to Chatham on HM Frigate Ulysses.

Anderson, Thomas - 1st Mate - Number: 523 - Prize Name: Expectation - Ship type: MV - How taken: HMS Butain - When taken: 17 Dec 1812 - Where taken: at sea - Date received: 25 Jan 1813 - From what ship: HM Ship-of-the-Line Queen - Born: Philadelphia - Age: 26 - Discharged on 29 Jan 1813 and sent to Odiham on parole.

Anderton, Thomas - Seaman - Number: 476 - Prize Name: Sword Fish - Ship type: P - How taken: HM Ship-of-the-Line Elephant - When taken: 28 Dec 1812 - Where taken: at sea - Date received: 14 Jan 1813 - From what ship: HMS Elephant - Born: Marblehead - Age: 17 - Discharged on 11 Mar 1813 and sent to Chatham on HM Store Ship Abundance.

Anderton, Samuel - Prize Master - Number: 440 - Prize Name: Sword Fish - Ship type: P - How taken: HM Ship-of-the-Line Elephant - When taken: 28 Dec 1812 - Where taken: at sea - Date received: 14 Jan 1813 - From what ship: HMS Elephant - Born: Marblehead - Age: 32 - Discharged on 6 Mar 1813 and sent to Chatham on HMS Frigate Alexandria.

Andrews, John - Seaman - Number: 1114 - How taken: Gave himself up from HM Ship-of-the-Line America - Date received: 5 Oct 1813 - From what ship: HM Ship-of-the-Line Achille - Born: Charleston - Age: 27 - Race: Black - Discharged on 17 Oct 1813 and sent to Chatham on HM Store Ship Weymouth.

Andrews, John - Seaman - Number: 1116 - How taken: Gave himself up from HM Ship-of-the-Line America - Date received: 5 Oct 1813 - From what ship: HM Ship-of-the-Line Achille - Born: Alexandria - Age: 24 - Discharged on 17 Oct 1813 and sent to Chatham on HM Store Ship Weymouth.

Andrey, Alexander - Seaman - Number: 188 - Prize Name: Baltimore - Ship type: P - How taken: HM Transport Diadem - When taken: 7 Oct 1812 - Where taken: S. Andera - Date received: 10 Nov 1812 - From what ship: HMS Diadem - Born: Georgetown - Age: 30 - Discharged on 19 Feb 1813 and sent to Chatham on HM Store Ship Dromedary.

Andson, John - Seaman - Number: 231 - Prize Name: Antelope - Ship type: P - How taken: HM Brig Zephyr - When taken: 10 Dec 1812 - Where taken: at sea - Date received: 27 Dec 1812 - From what ship: HMS Zephyr - Born: Portsmouth, NH - Age: 35 - Discharged on 19 Feb 1813 and sent to Chatham on HM Store Ship Dromedary.

Angel, Silvester - Seaman - Number: 1337 - How taken: Gave himself up from HM Ship-of-the-Line Illustrious - Date received: 3 Jan 1814 - From what ship: HM Ship-of-the-Line Prince - Born: New London - Age: 26 - Discharged on 5 Jan 1814 and sent to Chatham on HM Ship-of-the-Line Poictiers.

Anthony, John - Seaman - Number: 346 - Prize Name: Experiment - Ship type: MV - How taken: HM Brig Rover - When taken: 10 Nov 1812 - Where taken: off Bordeaux - Date received: 31 Dec 1812 - From what ship: HM Ship-of-the-Line Northumberland - Born: New Orleans - Age: 28 - Discharged on 4 Mar 1813 and sent to Chatham on HM Ship-of-the-Line Queen.

Anthony, Luke - Seaman - Number: 161 - Prize Name: Baltimore - Ship type: P - How taken: HM Transport Diadem - When taken: 7 Oct 1812 - Where taken: S. Andera - Date received: 3 Nov 1812 San Antonio - From what ship: HMS Diadem - Born: New Orleans - Age: 20 - Discharged on 19 Feb 1813 and sent to Chatham on HM Store Ship Dromedary.

Antonie, John - Seaman - Number: 63 - Prize Name: Diana, prize of Privateer Decatur - Ship type: MV - How taken: HM Ship-of-the-Line Polyphemus - When taken: 14 Sep 1812 - Where taken: at sea - Date received: 12 Oct 1812 San Antonio - From what ship: HM Ship-of-the-Line Polyphemus - Born: Bradford, MA - Age: 25 - Discharged on 19 Feb 1813 and sent to Chatham on HM Frigate Ulysses.

Armstrong, Elijah - Seaman - Number: 214 - How taken: Gave himself up from HM Ship-of-the-Line Victory - Date received: 23 Dec 1812 - From what ship: HM Guardship Royal William - Born: Harford - Age: 22 - Discharged on 19 Feb 1813 and sent to Chatham on HM Store Ship Dromedary.

Armstrong, Thomas - Seaman - Number: 205 - Prize Name: Perseverance - Ship type: MV - How taken: HM Sloop Atalante - When taken: 31 Jul 1812 - Where taken: at sea - Date received: 25 Nov 1812 - From what ship: HM Guardship Royal William - Born: Wiscasset - Age: 20 - Discharged on 19 Feb 1813 and sent to Chatham on HM Store Ship Dromedary.

Armstrong, Thomas - Seaman - Number: 953 - How taken: Gave himself up from HM Ship-of-the-Line Swiftsure - Date received: 28 Jul 1813 - From what ship: HM Sloop Volentaire - Born: Lancaster, MA - Age: 25 - Discharged on 7 Aug 1813 and sent to Chatham on HM Brig Rinaldo.

Arnold, Benjamin - Marine - Number: 1450 - Prize Name: Lord Ponsonbe, prize of the Privateer Diomede - Ship type: MV - How taken: HM Brig Sappho - When taken: 27 Feb 1814 - Where taken: at sea - Date received:

31 May 1814 - From what ship: HM Ship-of-the-Line Valiant - Born: Adams, CT - Age: 23 - Discharged on 28 Apr 1814 and sent to Chatham on HM Store Ship Weymouth.

Arnold, William - Seaman - Number: 709 - Prize Name: Tom Thumb - Ship type: MV - How taken: Lion, Privateer - When taken: 15 Feb 1813 - Where taken: at sea - Date received: 24 Feb 1813 - From what ship: HM Brig Escort - Born: Baltimore - Age: 16 - Discharged on 6 Mar 1813 and sent to Chatham on HM Ship-of-the-Line Cornwall.

Arthur, Alexander - Boy - Number: 360 - Prize Name: Argus - Ship type: MV - How taken: Fancy, cutter - When taken: 19 Dec 1812 - Where taken: Bay of Biscay - Date received: 31 Dec 1812 - From what ship: HM Ship-of-the-Line Northumberland - Born: New York - Age: 15 - Discharged on 4 Mar 1813 and sent to Chatham on HM Ship-of-the-Line Queen.

Arve, Joseph - Seaman - Number: 140 - Prize Name: Gossypium - Ship type: MV - How taken: HM Sloop Goree - When taken: 15 Aug 1812 - Where taken: off Bermuda - Date received: 29 Oct 1812 - From what ship: HM Ship-of-the-Line Ardent - Born: New Orleans - Age: 25 - Discharged on 19 Feb 1813 and sent to Chatham on HM Store Ship Dromedary.

Ashfield, Henry - Seaman - Number: 897 - Prize Name: Weasel - Ship type: MV - How taken: Foxhound, privateer - When taken: 25 May 1813 - Where taken: Bay of Biscay - Date received: 24 Jun 1813 - From what ship: HM Frigate Unicorn - Born: New York - Age: 19 - Discharged on 2 Jul 1813 and sent to Chatham on HM Frigate Tribune.

Asten, John - Boy - Number: 490 - Prize Name: Sword Fish - Ship type: P - How taken: HM Ship-of-the-Line Elephant - When taken: 28 Dec 1812 - Where taken: at sea - Date received: 14 Jan 1813 - From what ship: HMS Elephant - Born: Boston - Age: 19 - Discharged on 11 Mar 1813 and sent to Chatham on HM Store Ship Abundance.

Attwood, Edward - Seaman - Number: 627 - How taken: Gave himself up from HM Guardship Royal William - Date received: 3 Feb 1813 - From what ship: HMS Royal William - Born: Putney, VT - Age: 25 - Discharged on 11 Mar 1813 and sent to Chatham on HM Store Ship Abundance.

Atwood, Thomas - Seaman - Number: 884 - Prize Name: Prompt - Ship type: MV - How taken: Chance, privateer - When taken: 28 Mar 1813 - Where taken: Bay of Biscay - Date received: 24 Jun 1813 - From what ship: HM Frigate Unicorn - Born: Wilmington - Age: 29 - Discharged on 2 Jul 1813 and sent to Chatham on HM Frigate Tribune.

Avery, Charles - Seaman - Number: 850 - How taken: Gave himself up from HM Bomb Vessel Strombolo - Date received: 15 Jun 1813 - From what ship: HM Sloop Helena - Born: New York - Age: 34 - Discharged on 2 Jul 1813 and sent to Chatham on HM Frigate Tribune.

Babb, Benjamin - Seaman - Number: 621 - How taken: Gave himself up from HM Guardship Royal William - Date received: 3 Feb 1813 - From what ship: HMS Royal William - Born: Barrington, RI - Age: 33 - Discharged on 11 Mar 1813 and sent to Chatham on HM Store Ship Abundance.

Bachelor, Benjamin - Captain - Number: 106 - Prize Name: Nancy - Ship type: MV - How taken: HM Brig Parthian - When taken: 1 Aug 1812 - Where taken: off the Needles - Date received: 16 Oct 1812 San Antonio - From what ship: HM Brig Nancy - Born: Kingston, MA - Age: 36 - Discharged on 26 Oct 1813 and sent to Odiham on parole.

Bagley, Moses - Surgeon - Number: 504 - Prize Name: Sword Fish - Ship type: P - How taken: HM Ship-of-the-Line Elephant - When taken: 28 Dec 1812 - Where taken: at sea - Date received: 15 Jan 1813 - From what ship: HMS Elephant - Born: Canada - Age: 34 - Discharged on 6 Mar 1813 and sent to Chatham on HM Ship-of-the-Line Cornwall.

Bailey, John - Seaman - Number: 902 - Prize Name: Weasel - Ship type: MV - How taken: Foxhound, privateer - When taken: 25 May 1813 - Where taken: Bay of Biscay - Date received: 24 Jun 1813 - From what ship: HM Frigate Unicorn - Born: Gloucester - Age: 22 - Discharged on 2 Jul 1813 and sent to Chatham on HM Frigate Tribune.

Baisley, Abraham - Marine - Number: 1402 - Prize Name: Yorktown - Ship type: P - How taken: HM Frigate Maidstone - When taken: 18 Jul 1813 - Where taken: Grand Banks - Date received: 16 Feb 1814 - From what ship: HM Transport Malabar No. 352 - Born: New York - Age: 22 - Discharged on 28 Apr 1814 and sent to Chatham on HM Store Ship Weymouth.

Bakeman, Ely - Seaman - Number: 1141 - Prize Name: Hepsey - Ship type: MV - How taken: HM Brig Zenobia - When taken: 22 Jun 1813 - Where taken: Lisbon - Date received: 6 Oct 1813 - From what ship: HM Sloop Kingfisher - Born: Massachusetts - Age: 25 - Discharged on 17 Oct 1813 and sent to Chatham on HM Transport Malabar No. 352.

Baker, Henry - Seaman - Number: 29 - Prize Name: USRM Cutter James Madison - Ship type: MW - How taken: HM Frigate Barbadoes - When taken: 22 Aug 1812 - Where taken: at sea - Date received: 12 Oct 1812 San Antonio - From what ship: HM Ship-of-the-Line Polyphemus - Born: Norfolk - Age: 28 - Discharged on 19 Feb 1813 and sent to Chatham on HM Frigate Ulysses.

Baker, John - 2nd Mate - Number: 524 - Prize Name: Expectation - Ship type: MV - How taken: HMS Butain - When taken: 17 Dec 1812 - Where taken: at sea - Date received: 25 Jan 1813 - From what ship: HM Ship-of-the-Line Queen - Born: Salem, MA - Age: 26 - Discharged on 11 Mar 1813 and sent to Chatham on HM Store Ship Abundance.

Baker, Robert - Seaman - Number: 1083 - How taken: Gave himself up from HM Ship-of-the-Line Hibernia - Date received: 1 Oct 1813 - From what ship: HM Ship-of-the-Line Barham - Born: Virginia - Age: 29 - Discharged on 17 Oct 1813 and sent to Chatham on HM Store Ship Weymouth.

Baker, Robert - Seaman - Number: 1057 - How taken: Gave himself up from HM Ship-of-the-Line Hibernia - Date received: 19 Sep 1813 - From what ship: HM Brig Imogen - Born: Virginia - Age: 29 - Discharged on 29 Sep 1813 and sent to Chatham on HM Transport Chatham.

Ball, John - Seaman - Number: 198 - How taken: Gave himself up from HM Frigate Argo - Date received: 25 Nov 1812 - From what ship: HMS Argo - Born: Rhode Island - Age: 21 - Discharged on 19 Feb 1813 and sent to Chatham on HM Store Ship Dromedary.

Banta, John - Seaman - Number: 795 - How taken: Gave himself up from HM Ship-of-the-Line Sterling Castle - Date received: 16 Apr 1813 - From what ship: HMS Sterling Castle - Born: New Jersey - Age: 31 - Discharged on 27 Apr 1813 and sent to Chatham on HM Sloop-of-War Bonne Citoyenne.

Baptiste, John - Seaman - Number: 428 - Prize Name: Brunswick - Ship type: MV - How taken: HM Frigate Iris - When taken: 16 Dec 1812 - Where taken: at sea - Date received: 10 Jan 1813 - From what ship: HM Guardship Royal William - Born: New Orleans - Age: 26 - Race: Black - Discharged on 6 Mar 1813 and sent to Chatham on HMS Frigate Alexandria.

Barber, John - Seaman - Number: 546 - Prize Name: Rossie - Ship type: MV - How taken: HM Frigate Dryand - When taken: 7 Jan 1813 - Where taken: at sea - Date received: 25 Jan 1813 - From what ship: HM Ship-of-the-Line Queen - Born: Gravesend, England - Age: 27 - Discharged on 11 Mar 1813 and sent to Chatham on HM Store Ship Abundance.

Barber, Major - Seaman - Number: 1138 - Prize Name: Maydock - Ship type: MV - How taken: HM Brig Rebuff - When taken: 16 Jun 1813 - Where taken: St. Mary's - Date received: 6 Oct 1813 - From what ship: HM Sloop Kingfisher - Born: North Carolina - Age: 22 - Race: Mulatto - Discharged on 17 Oct 1813 and sent to Chatham on HM Transport Malabar No. 352.

Barford, James - Seaman - Number: 1481 - How taken: Gave himself up from HMS Nerias - Date received: 28 May 1814 - From what ship: HM Transport Akbar - Born: Philadelphia - Age: 26 - Discharged on 2 Jun 1814 and sent to Plymouth on HMS Growler.

Bark, David - Seaman - Number: 630 - How taken: Gave himself up from HM Guardship Royal William - Date received: 3 Feb 1813 - From what ship: HMS Royal William - Born: Providence - Age: 23 - Race: Black - Discharged on 11 Mar 1813 and sent to Chatham on HM Store Ship Abundance.

Barnes, William Smith - Quartermaster - Number: 1362 - Prize Name: Elbridge Gerry - Ship type: P - How taken: HM Frigate Crescent - When taken: 16 Sep 1813 - Where taken: at sea - Date received: 1 Feb 1814 - From what ship: HM Frigate Sybille - Born: Connecticut - Age: 41 - Discharged on 13 Feb 1814 and sent to Chatham on HM Transport Malabar No. 352.

Barnett, John - Seaman - Number: 196 - How taken: Sent into custody by order of the commander in chief - Date received: 22 Nov 1812 - From what ship: HM Guardship Royal William - Born: Fairfax, VA - Age: 27 - Discharged on 19 Feb 1813 and sent to Chatham on HM Store Ship Dromedary.

Baron, Peter - Seaman - Number: 1273 - Prize Name: Pomona, prize of Privateer Prince Neuchatel - Ship type: MV - How taken: HM Frigate Ethalion - When taken: 14 Dec 1813 - Where taken: at sea - Date received: 22 Dec 1813 - From what ship: HMS Ethalion - Born: New Orleans - Age: 26 - Discharged on 26 Dec 1813 and sent to Chatham on HM Ship of-the-Line Diomede.

Barrett, George - Seaman - Number: 813 - How taken: Gave himself up from HM Ship-of-the-Line Tigre - Date received: 24 Apr 1813 - From what ship: HM Fire Ship Spitfire - Born: Lancaster - Age: 39 - Discharged on 27 Apr 1813 and sent to Chatham on HM Sloop-of-War Bonne Citoyenne.

Barrett, James - Seaman - Number: 652 - How taken: Gave himself up from HM Sloop Albacore - Date received: 3 Feb 1813 - From what ship: HMS Albacore - Born: Delaware - Age: 27 - Discharged on 11 Mar 1813 and sent to Chatham on HM Store Ship Abundance.

Barry, John - Seaman - Number: 150 - Prize Name: William - Ship type: MV - How taken: HM Brig Recruit - When taken: 29 Aug 1812 - Where taken: at sea - Date received: 29 Oct 1812 - From what ship: HM Ship-of-the-Line Ardent - Born: Savannah, GA - Age: 65 - Race: Black - Discharged on 19 Feb 1813 and sent to Chatham on HM Store Ship Dromedary.

Barry, Peter - Seaman - Number: 1159 - How taken: Gave himself up from HM Ship-Sloop Jalouse - Date received: 9 Oct 1813 - From what ship: HM Sloop Stork - Born: Salem - Age: 39 - Race: Black - Discharged on 17 Oct 1813 and sent to Chatham on HM Transport Malabar No. 352.

Bartholf, Nicholas - Seaman - Number: 870 - Prize Name: Tiger - Ship type: MV - How taken: HM Brig Scylla - When taken: 22 Mar 1813 - Where taken: Bay of Biscay - Date received: 24 Jun 1813 - From what ship: HM Frigate Unicorn - Born: New York - Age: 20 - Discharged on 2 Jul 1813 and sent to Chatham on HM Frigate Tribune.

Bartis, John - Cook - Number: 882 - Prize Name: Prompt - Ship type: MV - How taken: Chance, privateer - When taken: 28 Mar 1813 - Where taken: Bay of Biscay - Date received: 24 Jun 1813 - From what ship: HM Frigate Unicorn - Born: New Orleans - Age: 26 - Race: Black - Discharged on 2 Jul 1813 and sent to Chatham on HM Frigate Tribune.

Bartlett, George B. - Sailing Master - Number: 503 - Prize Name: Sword Fish - Ship type: P - How taken: HM Ship-of-the-Line Elephant - When taken: 28 Dec 1812 - Where taken: at sea - Date received: 15 Jan 1813 - From what ship: HMS Elephant - Born: Marblehead - Age: 31 - Discharged on 11 Mar 1813 and sent to Chatham on HM Store Ship Abundance.

Bartlett, John - Seaman - Number: 1398 - Prize Name: Elbridge Gerry - Ship type: P - How taken: HM Frigate Crescent - When taken: 13 Nov 1813 - Where taken: off St. Johns - Date received: 16 Feb 1814 - From what ship: HM Transport Malabar No. 352 - Born: New Hampshire - Age: 23 - Discharged on 28 Apr 1814 and sent to Chatham on HM Store Ship Weymouth.

Bartlett, Robert - Cook's Mate - Number: 1280 - Prize Name: Growler - Ship type: P - How taken: HM Brig Electra - When taken: 7 Jul 1813 - Where taken: off St. Johns - Date received: 22 Dec 1813 - From what ship: HM Ship of-the-Line Bellerophon - Born: Philadelphia - Age: 26 - Race: Black - Discharged on 26 Dec 1813 and sent to Chatham on HMS Frigate Nemesis.

Barton, Elijah - Seaman - Number: 120 - Prize Name: Hannibal - Ship type: P - How taken: MV Patent - When taken: 24 Sep 1812 - Where taken: off Bermuda - Date received: 28 Oct 1812 - From what ship: MV Patent - Born: Westchester, NY - Age: 20 - Discharged on 19 Feb 1813 and sent to Chatham on HM Store Ship Dromedary.

Basset, Gorum - Seaman - Number: 1488 - Prize Name: Indian Lass, prize of Privateer Grand Turk - Ship type: MV - How taken: HM Transport Akbar - When taken: 20 Apr 1814 - Where taken: at sea - Date received: 28 May 1814 - From what ship: HMS Akbar - Born: Barnstable - Age: 23 - Discharged on 2 Jun 1814 and sent to Plymouth on HMS Growler.

Bassett, William - Seaman - Number: 1404 - Prize Name: Treaser - Ship type: P - How taken: HM Frigate Boreas - When taken: Unknown - Where taken: at sea - Date received: 16 Feb 1814 - From what ship: HM Transport

Malabar No. 352 - Born: Philadelphia - Age: 29 - Race: Black - Discharged on 28 Apr 1814 and sent to Chatham on HM Store Ship Weymouth.

Bates, Joseph - Seaman - Number: 1107 - How taken: Gave himself up from HM Ship-of-the-Line Swiftsure - Date received: 5 Oct 1813 - From what ship: HM Ship-of-the-Line Achille - Born: Massachusetts - Age: 21 - Discharged on 17 Oct 1813 and sent to Chatham on HM Store Ship Weymouth.

Baurs, Francis - Seaman - Number: 943 - Prize Name: Tender of the True Blooded Yankee - Ship type: P - How taken: HM Ship-of-the-Line Fame - When taken: 24 Jun 1813 - Where taken: at sea - Date received: 1 Jul 1813 - From what ship: HM Brig Hope - Born: New Orleans - Age: 20 - Discharged on 2 Jul 1813 and sent to Chatham on HM Brig Scorpion.

Baxter, John - 1st Mate - Number: 79 - Prize Name: HM Ship-of-the-Line Ganges - Ship type: MW - How taken: Detained by Court of Admiralty - When taken: 31 Jul 1812 - Where taken: Portsmouth harbor - Date received: 16 Oct 1812 San Antonio - From what ship: HM Ship-of-the-Line Ganges - Born: Yalmouth - Age: 25 - Discharged on 26 Oct 1813 and sent to Odiham on parole.

Bayman, James - Seaman - Number: 569 - Prize Name: Rossie - Ship type: MV - How taken: HM Frigate Dryand - When taken: 7 Jan 1813 - Where taken: at sea - Date received: 25 Jan 1813 - From what ship: HM Ship-of-the-Line Queen - Born: Vermont - Age: 21 - Race: Black - Discharged on 11 Mar 1813 and sent to Chatham on HM Store Ship Abundance.

Beachman, George - Carpenter - Number: 323 - Prize Name: Independence - Ship type: MV - How taken: HM Frigate Medusa - When taken: 9 Nov 1812 - Where taken: off St. Sebastian - Date received: 31 Dec 1812 - From what ship: HM Ship-of-the-Line Northumberland - Born: Baltimore - Age: 32 - Discharged on 4 Mar 1813 and sent to Chatham on HM Ship-of-the-Line Queen.

Bean, Amos - Seaman - Number: 595 - How taken: Gave himself up from HM Ship-of-the-Line Mars - Date received: 31 Jan 1813 - From what ship: HMS Mars - Born: Brentwood, MD - Age: 22 - Discharged on 11 Mar 1813 and sent to Chatham on HM Store Ship Abundance.

Beans, Samuel - Seaman - Number: 531 - Prize Name: Expectation - Ship type: MV - How taken: HMS Butain - When taken: 17 Dec 1812 - Where taken: at sea - Date received: 25 Jan 1813 - From what ship: HM Ship-of-the-Line Queen - Born: Virginia - Age: 34 - Discharged on 11 Mar 1813 and sent to Chatham on HM Store Ship Abundance.

Bearbere, John - Seaman - Number: 3 - Prize Name: USRM Cutter James Madison - Ship type: MW - How taken: HM Frigate Barbadoes - When taken: 22 Aug 1812 - Where taken: at sea - Date received: 12 Oct 1812 San Antonio - From what ship: HM Ship-of-the-Line Polyphemus - Born: North Carolina - Age: 25 - Died on 28 May 1813.

Beazley, Edward - Seaman - Number: 526 - Prize Name: Expectation - Ship type: MV - How taken: HMS Butain - When taken: 17 Dec 1812 - Where taken: at sea - Date received: 25 Jan 1813 - From what ship: HM Ship-of-the-Line Queen - Born: Kent Island - Age: 22 - Discharged on 11 Mar 1813 and sent to Chatham on HM Store Ship Abundance.

Beck, William - Seaman - Number: 640 - How taken: Gave himself up from HM Guardship Royal William - Date received: 3 Feb 1813 - From what ship: HMS Royal William - Born: Portsmouth, NH - Age: 47 - Discharged on 11 Mar 1813 and sent to Chatham on HM Store Ship Abundance.

Beckett, William - Seaman - Number: 292 - Prize Name: Hibernia - Ship type: MV - How taken: Taken up on shore - When taken: 18 Oct 1812 - Where taken: Liverpool - Date received: 31 Dec 1812 - From what ship: HM Ship-of-the-Line Northumberland - Born: Virginia - Age: 28 - Race: Black - Discharged on 4 Mar 1813 and sent to Chatham on HM Ship-of-the-Line Queen.

Beckner, Henry - Seaman - Number: 246 - Prize Name: Antelope - Ship type: P - How taken: HM Brig Zephyr - When taken: 10 Dec 1812 - Where taken: at sea - Date received: 27 Dec 1812 - From what ship: HMS Zephyr - Born: Brunswick, NJ - Age: 21 - Discharged on 19 Feb 1813 and sent to Chatham on HM Store Ship Dromedary.

Beckwith, James - Seaman - Number: 1323 - How taken: Gave himself up from HMS Scopard - Date received: 25 Dec 1813 - From what ship: HMS Scopard - Born: Maryland - Age: 25 - Discharged on 26 Dec 1813 and sent to Chatham on HMS Frigate Nemesis.

Beecher, William Palmer - Seaman - Number: 885 - Prize Name: Prompt - Ship type: MV - How taken: Chance, privateer - When taken: 28 Mar 1813 - Where taken: Bay of Biscay - Date received: 24 Jun 1813 - From what ship: HM Frigate Unicorn - Born: New Haven - Age: 16 - Discharged on 2 Jul 1813 and sent to Chatham on HM Frigate Tribune.

Benjamin, Everard - Prize Master - Number: 1296 - Prize Name: Mary, prize to the True Blooded Yankee - Ship type: MV - How taken: HM Ship-of-the-Line Bellerophon - When taken: 16 Dec 1813 - Where taken: off Land's End - Date received: 22 Dec 1813 - From what ship: HMS Bellerophon - Born: Connecticut - Age: 23 - Discharged on 26 Dec 1813 and sent to Chatham on HMS Frigate Nemesis.

Benjamin, James - Seaman - Number: 527 - Prize Name: Expectation - Ship type: MV - How taken: HMS Butain - When taken: 17 Dec 1812 - Where taken: at sea - Date received: 25 Jan 1813 - From what ship: HM Ship-of-the-Line Queen - Born: Philadelphia - Age: 23 - Discharged on 11 Mar 1813 and sent to Chatham on HM Store Ship Abundance.

Benjamin, Joseph - Seaman - Number: 619 - How taken: Gave himself up from HM Guardship Royal William - Date received: 3 Feb 1813 - From what ship: HMS Royal William - Born: Philadelphia - Age: 34 - Race: Black - Discharged on 6 Mar 1813 and sent to Chatham on HM Ship-of-the-Line Cornwall.

Benjamin, Polasskie - Seaman - Number: 757 - Prize Name: Pallas - Ship type: MV - How taken: HM Brig Rebuff - When taken: 23 Jan 1813 - Where taken: Cadiz - Date received: 1 Apr 1813 - From what ship: HM Ship-of-the-Line Blake - Born: Stratford, CT - Age: 17 - Discharged on 3 Apr 1813 and sent to Chatham on HM Transport Chatham.

Benn, William - Seaman - Number: 847 - How taken: Gave himself up from HM Ship-of-the-Line Malta - Date received: 15 Jun 1813 - From what ship: HM Sloop Helena - Born: Petersburg, VA - Age: 34 - Discharged on 2 Jul 1813 and sent to Chatham on HM Frigate Tribune.

Benner, Lewis - Seaman - Number: 348 - Prize Name: Experiment - Ship type: MV - How taken: HM Brig Rover - When taken: 10 Nov 1812 - Where taken: off Bordeaux - Date received: 31 Dec 1812 - From what ship: HM Ship-of-the-Line Northumberland - Born: Baltimore - Age: 22 - Race: Mulatto - Discharged on 4 Mar 1813 and sent to Chatham on HM Ship-of-the-Line Queen.

Bennymans, John - Seaman - Number: 755 - How taken: Gave himself up from HM Ship-of-the-Line Sterling Castle - Date received: 30 Mar 1813 - From what ship: HMS Sterling Castle - Born: Wilmington - Age: 29 - Discharged on 3 Apr 1813 and sent to Chatham on HM Transport Chatham.

Bensin, Leven - Seaman - Number: 831 - How taken: Gave himself up from HM Ship-of-the-Line Sterling Castle - Date received: 5 Jun 1813 - From what ship: HM Guardship Royal William - Born: Baltimore - Age: 33 - Race: Mulatto - Discharged on 10 Jun 1813 and sent to Chatham on HM Frigate Arethusa.

Benson, Jonas - Seaman - Number: 829 - How taken: Gave himself up from HM Frigate North Star - Date received: 26 May 1813 - From what ship: HMS North Star - Born: Maryland - Age: 23 - Discharged on 10 Jun 1813 and sent to Chatham on HM Frigate Arethusa.

Benster, John - Seaman - Number: 416 - Prize Name: Otter - Ship type: MV - How taken: HM Ship-Sloop Jalouse - When taken: 1 Dec 1812 - Where taken: at sea - Date received: 10 Jan 1813 - From what ship: HM Guardship Royal William - Born: Virginia - Age: 23 - Discharged on 6 Mar 1813 and sent to Chatham on HMS Frigate Alexandria.

Berry, John - Seaman - Number: 101 - Prize Name: HMS Eos - Ship type: MW - How taken: Detained by Court of Admiralty - When taken: 31 Jul 1812 - Where taken: Portsmouth harbor - Date received: 16 Oct 1812 San Antonio - From what ship: Eos - Born: Kingston, MA - Age: 18 - Race: Colored - Discharged on 19 Feb 1813 and sent to Chatham on HM Frigate Ulysses.

Berry, John - Seaman - Number: 832 - How taken: Gave himself up from HMS Juniper - Date received: 5 Jun 1813 - From what ship: HM Guardship Royal William - Born: Massachusetts - Age: 31 - Discharged on 10 Jun 1813 and sent to Chatham on HM Frigate Arethusa.

Berry, Joseph - Seaman - Number: 557 - Prize Name: Rossie - Ship type: MV - How taken: HM Frigate Dryand - When taken: 7 Jan 1813 - Where taken: at sea - Date received: 25 Jan 1813 - From what ship: HM Ship-of-the-Line Queen - Born: Baltimore - Age: 18 - Discharged on 11 Mar 1813 and sent to Chatham on HM Store Ship Abundance.

Berry, Joseph - 1st Mate - Number: 520 - Prize Name: Columbia - Ship type: MV - How taken: HMS Butain - When taken: 17 Dec 1812 - Where taken: at sea - Date received: 25 Jan 1813 - From what ship: HM Ship-of-the-Line Queen - Born: Philadelphia - Age: 32 - Discharged on 22 Feb 1813 and sent to Ashburton on parole.

Bessey, Jonas - Seaman - Number: 268 - Prize Name: King of Rome - Ship type: P - How taken: HM Brig Wolverine - When taken: 13 Dec 1812 - Where taken: at sea - Date received: 27 Dec 1812 - From what ship: HMS Wolverine - Born: Bridgewater - Age: 22 - Died on 13 Feb 1813.

Bessom, Nicholas - Seaman - Number: 485 - Prize Name: Sword Fish - Ship type: P - How taken: HM Ship-of-the-Line Elephant - When taken: 28 Dec 1812 - Where taken: at sea - Date received: 14 Jan 1813 - From what ship: HMS Elephant - Born: Marblehead - Age: 20 - Discharged on 11 Mar 1813 and sent to Chatham on HM Store Ship Abundance.

Best, John - Seaman - Number: 650 - How taken: Gave himself up from HM Sloop Albacore - Date received: 3 Feb 1813 - From what ship: HMS Albacore - Born: New Jersey - Age: 27 - Discharged on 11 Mar 1813 and sent to Chatham on HM Store Ship Abundance.

Bird, David - Seaman - Number: 1423 - Prize Name: Hannah - Ship type: MV - How taken: HM Ship-of-the-Line Conquestador - When taken: 15 Jan 1814 - Where taken: at sea - Date received: 1 Mar 1814 - From what ship: HMS Helicone - Born: Falmouth - Age: 29 - Discharged on 28 Apr 1814 and sent to Chatham on HM Sloop Favorite.

Bishop, Edward - Seaman - Number: 877 - Prize Name: Dick - Ship type: MV - How taken: HM Brig Dispatch - When taken: 17 Mar 1813 - Where taken: Bay of Biscay - Date received: 24 Jun 1813 - From what ship: HM Frigate Unicorn - Born: New York - Age: 27 - Discharged on 2 Jul 1813 and sent to Chatham on HM Frigate Tribune.

Bissel, Samuel W. - Seaman - Number: 1144 - Prize Name: Hepsey - Ship type: MV - How taken: HM Brig Zenobia - When taken: 22 Jun 1813 - Where taken: Lisbon - Date received: 6 Oct 1813 - From what ship: HM Sloop Kingfisher - Born: Connecticut - Age: 22 - Discharged on 17 Oct 1813 and sent to Chatham on HM Transport Malabar No. 352.

Bistie, Asaph - Seaman - Number: 607 - Prize Name: Sword Fish - Ship type: P - How taken: HM Ship-of-the-Line Elephant - When taken: 20 Dec 1812 - Where taken: at sea - Date received: 1 Feb 1813 - From what ship: HM Frigate Hermes - Born: Limington - Age: 24 - Discharged on 11 Mar 1813 and sent to Chatham on HM Store Ship Abundance.

Bitters, John - Seaman - Number: 528 - Prize Name: Expectation - Ship type: MV - How taken: HMS Butain - When taken: 17 Dec 1812 - Where taken: at sea - Date received: 25 Jan 1813 - From what ship: HM Ship-of-the-Line Queen - Born: Philadelphia - Age: 23 - Discharged on 11 Mar 1813 and sent to Chatham on HM Store Ship Abundance.

Black, John - Seaman - Number: 461 - Prize Name: Sword Fish - Ship type: P - How taken: HM Ship-of-the-Line Elephant - When taken: 28 Dec 1812 - Where taken: at sea - Date received: 14 Jan 1813 - From what ship: HMS Elephant - Born: Salem - Age: 20 - Race: Colored - Discharged on 11 Mar 1813 and sent to Chatham on HM Store Ship Abundance.

Black, William - Seaman - Number: 425 - Prize Name: Brunswick - Ship type: MV - How taken: HM Frigate Iris - When taken: 16 Dec 1812 - Where taken: at sea - Date received: 10 Jan 1813 - From what ship: HM Guardship Royal William - Born: Providence - Age: 24 - Discharged on 6 Mar 1813 and sent to Chatham on HMS Frigate Alexandria.

Blackman, Moses - Seaman - Number: 900 - Prize Name: Weasel - Ship type: MV - How taken: Foxhound, privateer - When taken: 25 May 1813 - Where taken: Bay of Biscay - Date received: 24 Jun 1813 - From what ship: HM Frigate Unicorn - Born: Boston - Age: 40 - Discharged on 2 Jul 1813 and sent to Chatham on HM Frigate Tribune.

Blake, Charles - Seaman - Number: 600 - Prize Name: Sword Fish - Ship type: P - How taken: HM Ship-of-the-Line Elephant - When taken: 20 Dec 1812 - Where taken: at sea - Date received: 1 Feb 1813 - From what ship:

HM Frigate Hermes - Born: Newbury - Age: 16 - Discharged on 11 Mar 1813 and sent to Chatham on HM Store Ship Abundance.

Blankenship, Charles - Seaman - Number: 15 - Prize Name: USRM Cutter James Madison - Ship type: MW - How taken: HM Frigate Barbadoes - When taken: 22 Aug 1812 - Where taken: at sea - Date received: 12 Oct 1812 San Antonio - From what ship: HM Ship-of-the-Line Polyphemus - Born: Rochester, MA - Age: 23 - Discharged on 19 Feb 1813 and sent to Chatham on HM Frigate Ulysses.

Blazon, Stephen - Seaman - Number: 707 - Prize Name: Tom Thumb - Ship type: MV - How taken: Lion, Privateer - When taken: 15 Feb 1813 - Where taken: at sea - Date received: 24 Feb 1813 - From what ship: HM Brig Escort - Born: Baltimore - Age: 23 - Discharged on 6 Mar 1813 and sent to Chatham on HM Ship-of-the-Line Cornwall.

Bloomdose, John - Seaman - Number: 1440 - Prize Name: HMS Devon Transport No. 15, prize of Privateer Bunker Hill - Ship type: MV - How taken: HM Brig Fly - When taken: 21 Jan 1814 - Where taken: at sea - Date received: 1 Mar 1814 - From what ship: HMS Helicone - Born: Albany - Age: 23 - Discharged on 28 Apr 1814 and sent to Chatham on HM Brig Cordelia.

Bocalt, John (alias Bogard) - Seaman - Number: 385 - How taken: Gave himself up from HM Ship-of-the-Line Salvador del Mundo - Date received: 10 Jan 1813 - From what ship: HM Guardship Royal William - Born: Kings County, MD - Age: 37 - Discharged on 4 Mar 1813 and sent to Chatham on HM Ship-of-the-Line Queen.

Boite, Julius Pierre - Marine - Number: 1469 - Prize Name: Bunker Hill - Ship type: P - How taken: HM Frigate Pomone & HM Frigate Cydnus - When taken: 4 Mar 1814 - Where taken: French coast - Date received: 11 Apr 1814 - From what ship: HMS Ship-on-the-Line San Domaso - Born: Angrand, France - Age: 46 - Discharged on 28 Apr 1814 and sent to Chatham on HM Store Ship Weymouth.

Booder, Jacob - Seaman - Number: 458 - Prize Name: Sword Fish - Ship type: P - How taken: HM Ship-of-the-Line Elephant - When taken: 28 Dec 1812 - Where taken: at sea - Date received: 14 Jan 1813 - From what ship: HMS Elephant - Born: New York - Age: 21 - Race: Black - Discharged on 11 Mar 1813 and sent to Chatham on HM Store Ship Abundance.

Booth, Thomas - Seaman - Number: 631 - How taken: Gave himself up from HM Guardship Royal William - Date received: 3 Feb 1813 - From what ship: HMS Royal William - Born: Maryland - Age: 27 - Discharged on 11 Mar 1813 and sent to Chatham on HM Store Ship Abundance.

Borwer, Frederick (alias Brenere) - Seaman - Number: 698 - Prize Name: Calcutta - Ship type: East Indian Ship - How taken: Two Brothers, privateer of Guernsey - When taken: 23 Nov 1812 - Where taken: at sea - Date received: 24 Feb 1813 - From what ship: HM Brig Escort - Born: Albany, NY - Age: 27 - Discharged on 6 Mar 1813 and sent to Chatham on HMS Frigate Alexandria.

Boston, John - Seaman - Number: 1456 - Prize Name: Soley - Ship type: MV - How taken: HM Brig Derment - When taken: 21 Jan 1814 - Where taken: at sea - Date received: 9 Apr 1814 - From what ship: HM Ship-of-the-Line Leyden - Born: Salem - Age: 36 - Discharged on 28 Apr 1814 and sent to Chatham on HM Store Ship Weymouth.

Boston, Robert - Seaman - Number: 88 - Prize Name: HM Frigate Janus - Ship type: MW - How taken: Detained by Court of Admiralty - When taken: 31 Jul 1812 - Where taken: Portsmouth harbor - Date received: 16 Oct 1812 San Antonio - From what ship: HM Frigate Janus - Born: Lyman, MA - Age: 22 - Discharged on 19 Feb 1813 and sent to Chatham on HM Frigate Ulysses.

Botrell, John - Pilot - Number: 919 - Prize Name: Tender of the True Blooded Yankee - Ship type: P - How taken: HM Ship-of-the-Line Fame - When taken: 24 Jun 1813 - Where taken: at sea - Date received: 1 Jul 1813 - From what ship: HM Brig Hope - Born: New Orleans - Age: 30 - Discharged on 2 Jul 1813 and sent to Chatham on HM Brig Scorpion.

Bowden, Benjamin - Master's Mate - Number: 1300 - Prize Name: Growler - Ship type: P - How taken: HM Brig Electra - When taken: 7 Jul 1813 - Where taken: off St. Johns - Date received: 22 Dec 1813 - From what ship: HM Frigate Hyperion - Born: Marblehead - Age: 21 - Discharged on 26 Dec 1813 and sent to Chatham on HMS Frigate Nemesis.

Bowden, William - Seaman - Number: 1284 - Prize Name: Growler - Ship type: P - How taken: HM Brig Electra - When taken: 7 Jul 1813 - Where taken: off St. Johns - Date received: 22 Dec 1813 - From what ship: HM Ship-of-the-Line Bellerophon - Born: Marblehead - Age: 17 - Discharged on 26 Dec 1813 and sent to Chatham on HMS Frigate Nemesis.

Bowie, Henry - 2nd Mate - Number: 271 - Prize Name: Antelope - Ship type: P - How taken: HM Brig Zephyr - When taken: 10 Dec 1812 - Where taken: at sea - Date received: 29 Dec 1812 - From what ship: HMS Zephyr - Born: Yorktown - Age: 35 - Discharged on 19 Feb 1813 and sent to Chatham on HM Store Ship Dromedary.

Bowker, Nicholas - Seaman - Number: 985 - Prize Name: Jane, prize of the Privateer Snap Dragon - Ship type: MV - How taken: HM Frigate Crescent & HM Ship-of-the-Line Bellerophon - When taken: 28 Jun 1813 - Where taken: at sea - Date received: 9 Aug 1813 - From what ship: HM Sloop Hazard - Born: Massachusetts - Age: 40 - Discharged on 13 Aug 1813 and sent to Chatham on HM Brig Cadmus.

Boyd, Andrew - Seaman - Number: 1139 - Prize Name: Hepsey - Ship type: MV - How taken: HM Brig Zenobia - When taken: 22 Jun 1813 - Where taken: Lisbon - Date received: 6 Oct 1813 - From what ship: HM Sloop Kingfisher - Born: Maryland - Age: 22 - Discharged on 17 Oct 1813 and sent to Chatham on HM Transport Malabar No. 352.

Boyd, Jesse - Seaman - Number: 1367 - How taken: Gave himself up from HM Ship-of-the-Line Malta - Date received: 4 Feb 1814 - From what ship: HM Frigate Bombay - Born: Pennsylvania - Age: 32 - Discharged on 19 Feb 1814 and sent to Chatham on HM Ship-of-the-Line Prince.

Boyd, John - Seaman - Number: 553 - Prize Name: Rossie - Ship type: MV - How taken: HM Frigate Dryand - When taken: 7 Jan 1813 - Where taken: at sea - Date received: 25 Jan 1813 - From what ship: HM Ship-of-the-Line Queen - Born: New York - Age: 36 - Discharged on 11 Mar 1813 and sent to Chatham on HM Store Ship Abundance.

Boyd, John - Seaman - Number: 1025 - How taken: Gave himself up from HM Frigate Bombay - Date received: 7 Sep 1813 - From what ship: HM Frigate Unicorn - Born: North Carolina - Age: 40 - Discharged on 21 Sep 1813 and sent to Chatham on HM Ship-of-the-Line Queen.

Boyd, John - Seaman - Number: 213 - How taken: Gave himself up from HM Frigate Loire - Date received: 14 Dec 1812 - From what ship: HM Guardship Royal William - Born: Kennebunk - Age: 20 - Discharged on 19 Feb 1813 and sent to Chatham on HM Store Ship Dromedary.

Boyd, Stephen (alias Steffen Beale) - Seaman - Number: 1088 - Prize Name: Hindostan - Ship type: MV - How taken: HM Brig Zenobia - When taken: 25 Jun 1813 - Where taken: off Lisbon - Date received: 1 Oct 1813 - From what ship: HM Ship-of-the-Line Barham - Born: Hamburg - Age: 30 - Discharged on 17 Oct 1813 and sent to Chatham on HM Store Ship Weymouth (see Prisoner Number 1063).

Boyd, Stephen (alias Steffen Beale) - Seaman - Number: 1063 - Prize Name: Hindostan - Ship type: MV - How taken: HM Brig Zenobia - When taken: 25 Jun 1813 - Where taken: off Lisbon - Date received: 19 Sep 1813 - From what ship: HM Brig Imogen - Born: Hamburg - Age: 30 - Discharged on 29 Sep 1813 and sent to Chatham on HM Transport Chatham (see Prisoner Number 1088).

Bradford, George - 2nd Lieutenant - Number: 1316 - Prize Name: Elbridge Gerry - Ship type: P - How taken: HM Frigate Crescent - When taken: 16 Sep 1813 - Where taken: at sea - Date received: 22 Dec 1813 - From what ship: HM Frigate Hyperion - Born: Plymouth, MA - Age: 30 - Discharged on 26 Dec 1813 and sent to Chatham on HMS Frigate Nemesis.

Brady, Jason - Seaman - Number: 544 - Prize Name: Rossie - Ship type: MV - How taken: HM Frigate Dryand - When taken: 7 Jan 1813 - Where taken: at sea - Date received: 25 Jan 1813 - From what ship: HM Ship-of-the-Line Queen - Born: Baltimore - Age: 23 - Discharged on 11 Mar 1813 and sent to Chatham on HM Store Ship Abundance.

Brainard, Richard - Seaman - Number: 625 - How taken: Gave himself up from HM Guardship Royal William - Date received: 3 Feb 1813 - From what ship: HMS Royal William - Born: Chatham - Age: 23 - Discharged on 11 Mar 1813 and sent to Chatham on HM Store Ship Abundance.

Bramblecome, David - Seaman - Number: 282 - Prize Name: Cornelia - Ship type: MV - How taken: HM Brig

Zenobia - When taken: 14 Aug 1812 - Where taken: Western ocean - Date received: 31 Dec 1812 - From what ship: HM Ship-of-the-Line Northumberland - Born: Marblehead - Age: 38 - Discharged on 19 Feb 1813 and sent to Chatham on HM Store Ship Dromedary.

Branch, Anthony - Seaman - Number: 1075 - How taken: Gave himself up from HM Ship-of-the-Line Centaur - Date received: 1 Oct 1813 - From what ship: HM Ship-of-the-Line Barham - Born: Lancaster - Age: 25 - Discharged on 17 Oct 1813 and sent to Chatham on HM Store Ship Weymouth.

Branch, Anthony - Seaman - Number: 1041 - How taken: Gave himself up from HM Ship-of-the-Line Centaur - Date received: 10 Sep 1813 - From what ship: HMS Centaur - Born: Lancaster, PA - Age: 26 - Discharged on 29 Sep 1813 and sent to Chatham on HM Ship-of-the-Line Barham.

Branham, Stephen - Seaman - Number: 225 - Prize Name: Antelope - Ship type: P - How taken: HM Brig Zephyr - When taken: 10 Dec 1812 - Where taken: at sea - Date received: 27 Dec 1812 - From what ship: HMS Zephyr - Born: Philadelphia - Age: 30 - Discharged on 19 Feb 1813 and sent to Chatham on HM Store Ship Dromedary.

Branton, James - Seaman - Number: 511 - How taken: Gave himself up from HMS Renealous - Date received: 22 Jan 1813 - From what ship: HMS Renelous - Born: Philadelphia - Age: 27 - Discharged on 11 Mar 1813 and sent to Chatham on HM Store Ship Abundance.

Bray, Zachariah - Seaman - Number: 609 - Prize Name: Sword Fish - Ship type: P - How taken: HM Ship-of-the-Line Elephant - When taken: 20 Dec 1812 - Where taken: at sea - Date received: 1 Feb 1813 - From what ship: HM Frigate Hermes - Born: Salem - Age: 20 - Race: Black - Discharged on 11 Mar 1813 and sent to Chatham on HM Store Ship Abundance.

Brenton, York - Seaman - Number: 628 - How taken: Gave himself up from HM Guardship Royal William - Date received: 3 Feb 1813 - From what ship: HMS Royal William - Born: Somerset, MA - Age: 32 - Race: Black - Discharged on 11 Mar 1813 and sent to Chatham on HM Store Ship Abundance.

Brewster, Sturges - Passenger & Farmer - Number: 272 - Prize Name: Antelope - Ship type: P - How taken: HM Brig Zephyr - When taken: 10 Dec 1812 - Where taken: at sea - Date received: 29 Dec 1812 - From what ship: HMS Zephyr - Born: Fairfield - Age: 23 - Discharged on 31 Dec 1812 and sent to Odiham on parole.

Brickum, James - Carpenter - Number: 1395 - Prize Name: Pilate - Ship type: P - How taken: Victoria, privateer of Guernsey - When taken: 28 Jan 1814 - Where taken: off Bordeaux - Date received: 7 Feb 1814 - From what ship: Mary from Guernsey - Born: Virginia - Age: 25 - Race: Mulatto - Discharged on 13 Feb 1814 and sent to Chatham on HM Transport Malabar No. 352.

Bridges, Philip - Prize Master - Number: 441 - Prize Name: Sword Fish - Ship type: P - How taken: HM Ship-of-the-Line Elephant - When taken: 28 Dec 1812 - Where taken: at sea - Date received: 14 Jan 1813 - From what ship: HMS Elephant - Born: Marblehead - Age: 30 - Discharged on 6 Mar 1813 and sent to Chatham on HMS Frigate Alexandria.

Briggs, Bolon - Seaman - Number: 923 - Prize Name: Tender of the True Blooded Yankee - Ship type: P - How taken: HM Ship-of-the-Line Fame - When taken: 24 Jun 1813 - Where taken: at sea - Date received: 1 Jul 1813 - From what ship: HM Brig Hope - Born: Virginia - Age: 31 - Race: Black - Discharged on 2 Jul 1813 and sent to Chatham on HM Brig Scorpion.

Brightman, Joseph - Quartermaster - Number: 302 - How taken: Gave himself up from HM Ship-of-the-Line San Josef - When taken: 31 Dec 1812 - Date received: 31 Dec 1812 - From what ship: HM Ship-of-the-Line Northumberland - Born: Boston - Age: 36 - Discharged on 4 Mar 1813 and sent to Chatham on HM Ship-of-the-Line Queen.

Brill, John - Boy - Number: 905 - Prize Name: Weasel - Ship type: MV - How taken: Foxhound, privateer - When taken: 25 May 1813 - Where taken: Bay of Biscay - Date received: 24 Jun 1813 - From what ship: HM Frigate Unicorn - Born: New York - Age: 13 - Discharged on 2 Jul 1813 and sent to Chatham on HM Frigate Tribune.

Brimmer, John - Seaman - Number: 478 - Prize Name: Sword Fish - Ship type: P - How taken: HM Ship-of-the-Line Elephant - When taken: 28 Dec 1812 - Where taken: at sea - Date received: 14 Jan 1813 - From what ship: HMS Elephant - Born: New York - Age: 37 - Discharged on 11 Mar 1813 and sent to Chatham on HM Store

Ship Abundance.

Broden, Norman - Seaman - Number: 686 - Prize Name: Rachael - Ship type: MV - How taken: HM Schooner Herring - When taken: 8 Feb 1813 - Where taken: at sea - Date received: 20 Feb 1813 - From what ship: HMS Herring - Born: Marblehead - Age: 18 - Discharged on 6 Mar 1813 and sent to Chatham on HM Ship-of-the-Line Cornwall.

Brooks, Edward - Seaman - Number: 141 - Prize Name: Gossypium - Ship type: MV - How taken: HM Sloop Goree - When taken: 15 Aug 1812 - Where taken: off Bermuda - Date received: 29 Oct 1812 - From what ship: HM Ship-of-the-Line Ardent - Born: Baltimore - Age: 22 - Race: Black - Discharged on 19 Feb 1813 and sent to Chatham on HM Store Ship Dromedary.

Brooks, John - Seaman - Number: 959 - How taken: Gave himself up from HM Ship-of-the-Line Leviathan - Date received: 31 Jul 1813 - From what ship: HMS Leviathan - Born: Newford, NC - Age: 34 - Discharged on 7 Aug 1813 and sent to Chatham on HM Brig Rinaldo.

Brown, Elisha - Seaman - Number: 783 - How taken: Gave himself up from HM Frigate Franchise - Date received: 1 Apr 1813 - From what ship: HM Ship-of-the-Line Blake - Born: Georgetown - Age: 25 - Discharged on 3 Apr 1813 and sent to Chatham on HM Transport Chatham.

Brown, Francis - Seaman - Number: 1167 - Prize Name: Russian merchant vessel - How taken: Taken out of the HM Ship-of-the-Line Neptune - When taken: 28 Sep 1813 - Where taken: Cork - Date received: 12 Oct 1813 - From what ship: HM Brig Hope - Born: Pennsylvania - Age: 28 - Race: Mulatto - Discharged on 17 Oct 1813 and sent to Chatham on HM Transport Malabar No. 352.

Brown, George - Seaman - Number: 1047 - How taken: Gave himself up from HM Ship-of-the-Line Ocean - Date received: 14 Sep 1813 - From what ship: HM Brig Savage - Born: Rhode Island - Age: 35 - Discharged on 29 Sep 1813 and sent to Chatham on HM Ship-of-the-Line Barham.

Brown, Isaac - Seaman - Number: 1045 - How taken: Gave himself up from HM Brig Shearwater - Date received: 14 Sep 1813 - From what ship: HM Brig Savage - Born: Bucks County - Age: 30 - Race: Black - Discharged on 29 Sep 1813 and sent to Chatham on HM Ship-of-the-Line Barham.

Brown, James - Seaman - Number: 974 - How taken: Gave himself up from HM Ship-of-the-Line Caledonia - Date received: 31 Jul 1813 - From what ship: HMS Leviathan - Born: Maryland - Age: 30 - Discharged on 13 Aug 1813 and sent to Chatham on HM Brig Cadmus.

Brown, John - Seaman - Number: 336 - How taken: Gave himself up from HM Brig Goldfinch - When taken: 27 Nov 1812 - Date received: 31 Dec 1812 - From what ship: HM Ship-of-the-Line Northumberland - Born: Boston - Age: 34 - Discharged on 4 Mar 1813 and sent to Chatham on HM Ship-of-the-Line Queen.

Brown, John - 2nd Mate - Number: 409 - Prize Name: Otter - Ship type: MV - How taken: HM Ship-Sloop Jalouse - When taken: 1 Dec 1812 - Where taken: at sea - Date received: 10 Jan 1813 - From what ship: HM Guardship Royal William - Born: Marblehead - Age: 24 - Discharged on 6 Mar 1813 and sent to Chatham on HMS Frigate Alexandria.

Brown, John - Quarter Gunner - Number: 1211 - Prize Name: Elbridge Gerry - Ship type: P - How taken: HM Frigate Crescent - When taken: 16 Sep 1813 - Where taken: at sea - Date received: 16 Nov 1813 - From what ship: HM Sloop Talbot - Born: Charleston, SC - Age: 22 - Discharged on 26 Dec 1813 and sent to Chatham on HM Ship of-the-Line Diomede.

Brown, Joseph - Sailing Master - Number: 1216 - Prize Name: Growler - Ship type: P - How taken: HM Brig Electra - When taken: 7 Jul 1813 - Where taken: at sea - Date received: 16 Nov 1813 - From what ship: HM Sloop Talbot - Born: Marblehead - Age: 29 - Discharged on 26 Dec 1813 and sent to Chatham on HM Ship of-the-Line Diomede.

Brown, Joseph - Seaman - Number: 958 - How taken: Gave himself up from HM Ship-of-the-Line Swiftsure - Date received: 28 Jul 1813 - From what ship: HM Sloop Volentaire - Born: Old Providence - Age: 32 - Race: Black - Discharged on 7 Aug 1813 and sent to Chatham on HM Brig Rinaldo.

Brown, Mark - Seaman - Number: 963 - How taken: Gave himself up from HM Ship-of-the-Line Leviathan - Date received: 31 Jul 1813 - From what ship: HMS Leviathan - Born: Maryland - Age: 28 - Discharged on 7 Aug 1813 and sent to Chatham on HM Brig Rinaldo.

Brown, Sawyer - Seaman - Number: 1330 - How taken: Gave himself up from HM Ship-of-the-Line Invincible - Date received: 27 Dec 1813 - From what ship: HMS Frigate Nemesis - Born: New York - Age: 37 - Race: Black - Discharged on 27 Dec 1813 and sent to Chatham on HMS Frigate Nemesis.

Brown, Seth - Seaman - Number: 938 - Prize Name: Tender of the True Blooded Yankee - Ship type: P - How taken: HM Ship-of-the-Line Fame - When taken: 24 Jun 1813 - Where taken: at sea - Date received: 1 Jul 1813 - From what ship: HM Brig Hope - Born: Bristol - Age: 23 - Discharged on 2 Jul 1813 and sent to Chatham on HM Brig Scorpion.

Brown, Thomas - Seaman - Number: 1156 - How taken: Gave himself up from HM Frigate Orpheus - Date received: 7 Oct 1813 - From what ship: HM Frigate Spartan - Born: New Jersey - Age: 31 - Discharged on 17 Oct 1813 and sent to Chatham on HM Transport Malabar No. 352.

Brown, William - Seaman - Number: 664 - How taken: Gave himself up from HM Frigate Ulysses - Date received: 7 Feb 1813 - From what ship: HMS Ulysses - Born: Boston - Age: 25 - Discharged on 6 Mar 1813 and sent to Chatham on HM Ship-of-the-Line Cornwall.

Brown, William - Seaman - Number: 1498 - How taken: Returned into custody from HMS Leyden - Date received: 4 Jun 1814 - From what ship: HM Ship-of-the-Line Leyden - Born: Boston - Age: 28 - Discharged on 30 Jun 1814 and sent to Plymouth on HM Brig Steady.

Bryant, Moses - Seaman - Number: 815 - How taken: Gave himself up from HM Service - Date received: 9 May 1813 - From what ship: HM Guardship Royal William - Born: Middleburg, MA - Age: 23 - Discharged on 17 May 1813 and sent to Chatham on HMS Impeleux.

Buddington, Asa - Seaman - Number: 508 - How taken: Gave himself up from HM Frigate Stag - Date received: 20 Jan 1813 - From what ship: HMS Stag - Born: New London - Age: 47 - Discharged on 11 Mar 1813 and sent to Chatham on HM Store Ship Abundance.

Buel, Jeremiah - Seaman - Number: 1277 - Prize Name: US Schooner Growler - Ship type: MW - How taken: Sir James Yeo's Squadron - When taken: 11 Aug 1813 - Where taken: Lake Ontario - Date received: 22 Dec 1813 - From what ship: HM Frigate Ethalion - Born: New Haven - Age: 25 - Discharged on 26 Dec 1813 and sent to Chatham on HM Ship of-the-Line Diomede.

Buffington, James - Master & Passenger - Number: 1162 - Prize Name: Russian merchant vessel - How taken: Taken out of the HM Ship-of-the-Line Neptune - When taken: 28 Sep 1813 - Where taken: Cork - Date received: 12 Oct 1813 - From what ship: HM Brig Hope - Born: Salem - Age: 43 - Discharged on 17 Oct 1813 and sent to Chatham on HM Transport Malabar No. 352.

Bumpus, Asa - Seaman - Number: 806 - How taken: Gave himself up from HMS Nempis - Date received: 21 Apr 1813 - From what ship: HM Guardship Royal William - Born: Wareham, MA - Age: 23 - Discharged on 27 Apr 1813 and sent to Chatham on HM Sloop-of-War Bonne Citoyenne.

Bunker, Thomas - Seaman - Number: 1009 - Prize Name: Fame - Ship type: MV - How taken: HM Ship of-the-Line Cressy - When taken: 20 Jul 1813 - Where taken: at sea - Date received: 18 Aug 1813 - From what ship: HMS Cressy - Born: Nantucket - Age: 58 - Race: Black - Discharged on 21 Sep 1813 and sent to Chatham on HM Ship-of-the-Line Queen.

Burke, Charles - Seaman - Number: 1061 - How taken: Gave himself up from HM Ship-of-the-Line Hibernia - Date received: 19 Sep 1813 - From what ship: HM Brig Imogen - Born: Charleston, SC - Age: 50 - Race: Mulatto - Discharged on 13 Oct 1813 to HM Brig Avon.

Burke, James - Seaman - Number: 262 - Prize Name: King of Rome - Ship type: P - How taken: HM Brig Wolverine - When taken: 13 Dec 1812 - Where taken: at sea - Date received: 27 Dec 1812 - From what ship: HMS Wolverine - Born: Boston - Age: 18 - Discharged on 19 Feb 1813 and sent to Chatham on HM Store Ship Dromedary.

Burke, John - Seaman - Number: 1356 - How taken: Gave himself up from HM Ship-of-the-Line Bulwark - Date received: 28 Jan 1814 - From what ship: HMS Bulmark - Born: Washington - Age: 25 - Discharged on 13 Feb 1814 and sent to Chatham on HM Transport Malabar No. 352.

Burnham, David - Seaman - Number: 653 - How taken: Gave himself up from HM Sloop Albacore - Date received: 3 Feb 1813 - From what ship: HMS Albacore - Born: Ipswich, MA - Age: 50 - Discharged on 11 Mar 1813 and sent to Chatham on HM Store Ship Abundance.

Burnham, John - Seaman - Number: 677 - How taken: Gave himself up from HM Brig Bold - Date received: 14 Feb 1813 - From what ship: HMS Bold - Born: Boothbay, MA - Age: 22 - Discharged on 6 Mar 1813 and sent to Chatham on HM Ship-of-the-Line Cornwall.

Burns, George - Seaman - Number: 388 - Prize Name: Empress - Ship type: MV - How taken: HM Brig Rover - When taken: 30 Nov 1812 - Where taken: at sea - Date received: 10 Jan 1813 - From what ship: HM Guardship Royal William - Born: New York - Age: 26 - Discharged on 4 Mar 1813 and sent to Chatham on HM Ship-of-the-Line Queen.

Burton, William - Seaman - Number: 763 - How taken: Gave himself up from HM Ship-of-the-Line Blake - Date received: 1 Apr 1813 - From what ship: HMS Blake - Born: Kent County - Age: 52 - Discharged on 3 Apr 1813 and sent to Chatham on HM Transport Chatham.

Busson, John - Seaman - Number: 788 - Prize Name: Dick - Ship type: MV - How taken: HM Brig Dispatch - When taken: 17 Mar 1813 - Where taken: at sea - Date received: 3 Apr 1813 - From what ship: Prussian Ship Argo - Born: Baltimore - Age: 21 - Discharged on 3 Apr 1813 and sent to Chatham on HM Transport Chatham.

Butler, George - Seaman - Number: 435 - How taken: Gave himself up from HM Ship of-the-Line Cressy - Date received: 11 Jan 1813 - From what ship: HMS Cressy - Born: Charlestown - Age: 45 - Race: Colored - Discharged on 6 Mar 1813 and sent to Chatham on HMS Frigate Alexandria.

Butler, Thomas - Seaman - Number: 804 - How taken: Gave himself up from HM Ship-of-the-Line Plantagenet - Date received: 21 Apr 1813 - From what ship: HM Guardship Royal William - Born: Cambridge, MA - Age: 23 - Discharged on 27 Apr 1813 and sent to Chatham on HM Sloop-of-War Bonne Citoyenne.

Butler, Thomas - Seaman - Number: 1357 - How taken: Gave himself up from HM Ship-of-the-Line Bulwark - Date received: 28 Jan 1814 - From what ship: HMS Bulmark - Born: Maryland - Age: 37 - Discharged on 13 Feb 1814 and sent to Chatham on HM Transport Malabar No. 352.

Butts, Joseph W. - Seaman - Number: 1043 - How taken: Gave himself up from HM Ship-of-the-Line Centaur - Date received: 10 Sep 1813 - From what ship: HMS Centaur - Born: Boston - Age: 23 - Discharged on 29 Sep 1813 and sent to Chatham on HM Ship-of-the-Line Barham.

Byer, Peter - Seaman - Number: 868 - Prize Name: Tiger - Ship type: MV - How taken: HM Brig Scylla - When taken: 22 Mar 1813 - Where taken: Bay of Biscay - Date received: 24 Jun 1813 - From what ship: HM Frigate Unicorn - Born: Boston - Age: 27 - Discharged on 2 Jul 1813 and sent to Chatham on HM Frigate Tribune.

Caban, Samuel - Seaman - Number: 701 - Prize Name: Calcutta - Ship type: East Indian Ship - How taken: Two Brothers, privateer of Guernsey - When taken: 23 Nov 1812 - Where taken: at sea - Date received: 24 Feb 1813 - From what ship: HM Brig Escort - Born: Salem - Age: 30 - Discharged on 6 Mar 1813 and sent to Chatham on HM Ship-of-the-Line Cornwall.

Cadwell, Samuel - Seaman - Number: 869 - Prize Name: Tiger - Ship type: MV - How taken: HM Brig Scylla - When taken: 22 Mar 1813 - Where taken: Bay of Biscay - Date received: 24 Jun 1813 - From what ship: HM Frigate Unicorn - Born: New York - Age: 19 - Discharged on 2 Jul 1813 and sent to Chatham on HM Frigate Tribune.

Caine, Enoch - Seaman - Number: 714 - How taken: Gave himself up from HM Ship-of-the-Line Tigre - Date received: 25 Feb 1813 - From what ship: HMS Tigre - Born: Philadelphia - Age: 35 - Race: Colored - Discharged on 6 Mar 1813 and sent to Chatham on HM Ship-of-the-Line Cornwall.

Calder, John H. - Seaman - Number: 859 - Prize Name: Tiger - Ship type: MV - How taken: HM Brig Scylla - When taken: 22 Mar 1813 - Where taken: Bay of Biscay - Date received: 24 Jun 1813 - From what ship: HM Frigate Unicorn - Born: New York - Age: 22 - Discharged on 2 Jul 1813 and sent to Chatham on HM Frigate Tribune.

Caldwell, Abraham - Seaman - Number: 1022 - How taken: Gave himself up from HM Ship-of-the-Line Scipion - Date received: 7 Sep 1813 - From what ship: HM Frigate Unicorn - Born: Pennsylvania - Age: 36 - Discharged on 21 Sep 1813 and sent to Chatham on HM Ship-of-the-Line Queen.

Caleb, Lewis - Seaman - Number: 1348 - How taken: Gave himself up from HMS Muros - Date received: 26 Jan 1814 - From what ship: HMS Muros - Born: New Orleans - Age: 25 - Race: Black - Discharged on 13 Feb 1814 and sent to Chatham on HM Transport Malabar No. 352.

Calleb, Lewis - Seaman - Number: 1408 - How taken: Gave himself up from HMS Muros - Date received: 16 Feb 1814 - From what ship: HM Transport Malabar No. 352 - Born: New Orleans - Age: 25 - Race: Black - Discharged on 28 Apr 1814 and sent to Chatham on HM Store Ship Weymouth.

Campbell, James - Seaman - Number: 980 - How taken: Gave himself up from HMS Voluntaire - Date received: 31 Jul 1813 - From what ship: HM Ship-of-the-Line Leviathan - Born: New York - Age: 36 - Discharged on 13 Aug 1813 and sent to Chatham on HM Brig Cadmus.

Campbell, John - Seaman - Number: 770 - Prize Name: Miser Merchant Ship - How taken: Taken from the HM Transport Mariner No. 146 - Date received: 1 Apr 1813 - From what ship: HM Ship-of-the-Line Blake - Born: Boston - Age: 26 - Discharged on 3 Apr 1813 and sent to Chatham on HM Transport Chatham.

Campbell, Nicholas - Seaman - Number: 1026 - How taken: Gave himself up from HM Frigate Bombay - Date received: 7 Sep 1813 - From what ship: HM Frigate Unicorn - Born: Albany - Age: 30 - Discharged on 21 Sep 1813 and sent to Chatham on HM Ship-of-the-Line Queen.

Campbell, William - Cook - Number: 1431 - Prize Name: Minerva - Ship type: MV - How taken: HM Ship-of-the-Line Conquestador - When taken: 19 Jan 1814 - Where taken: Bay of Biscay - Date received: 1 Mar 1814 - From what ship: HMS Helicone - Born: Charlestown - Age: 27 - Race: Black - Discharged on 28 Apr 1814 and sent to Chatham on HM Sloop Favorite.

Camsure, Dominick - Passenger & Surgeon - Number: 1265 - Prize Name: Dart - Ship type: P - How taken: HM Frigate Niger & HMS Fortunee - Where taken: at sea - Date received: 19 Dec 1813 - From what ship: HMS Fortunee - Born: New Orleans - Age: 28 - Discharged on 26 Dec 1813 and sent to Chatham on HM Ship of-the-Line Diomede.

Cannon, Thomas - Seaman - Number: 1354 - How taken: Gave himself up from HM Ship-of-the-Line Bulwark - Date received: 28 Jan 1814 - From what ship: HMS Bulmark - Born: New York - Age: 30 - Discharged on 13 Feb 1814 and sent to Chatham on HM Transport Malabar No. 352.

Cappel, John - Seaman - Number: 898 - Prize Name: Weasel - Ship type: MV - How taken: Foxhound, privateer - When taken: 25 May 1813 - Where taken: Bay of Biscay - Date received: 24 Jun 1813 - From what ship: HM Frigate Unicorn - Born: Newport - Age: 18 - Discharged on 2 Jul 1813 and sent to Chatham on HM Frigate Tribune.

Carebo, Henry - Seaman - Number: 40 - Prize Name: USRM Cutter James Madison - Ship type: MW - How taken: HM Frigate Barbadoes - When taken: 22 Aug 1812 - Where taken: at sea - Date received: 12 Oct 1812 San Antonio - From what ship: HM Ship-of-the-Line Polyphemus - Born: Orleans - Age: 36 - Discharged on 19 Feb 1813 and sent to Chatham on HM Frigate Ulysses.

Carmon, James - Seaman - Number: 581 - How taken: Gave himself up from HM Frigate Ulysses - Date received: 26 Jan 1813 - From what ship: HMS Ulysses - Born: Philadelphia - Age: 22 - Discharged on 11 Mar 1813 and sent to Chatham on HM Store Ship Abundance.

Carney, William - Seaman - Number: 658 - How taken: Gave himself up from HM Guardship Royal William - Date received: 6 Feb 1813 - From what ship: HMS Royal William - Born: Boston - Age: 48 - Race: Black - Discharged on 6 Mar 1813 and sent to Chatham on HM Ship-of-the-Line Cornwall.

Caroline, Tobias - Seaman - Number: 366 - How taken: Gave himself up from HM Ship-of-the-Line Orion - Date received: 2 Jan 1813 - From what ship: HM Prison Ship Assistance - Born: Albany, NY - Age: 30 - Race: Black - Discharged on 4 Mar 1813 and sent to Chatham on HM Ship-of-the-Line Queen.

Carr, Richard - Seaman - Number: 337 - Prize Name: on shore - How taken: HM Battery Princess - When taken: 5 Aug 1812 - Where taken: Liverpool - Date received: 31 Dec 1812 - From what ship: HM Ship-of-the-Line Northumberland - Born: Charlestown - Age: 29 - Discharged on 4 Mar 1813 and sent to Chatham on HM Ship-of-the-Line Queen.

Carr, Samuel - Seaman - Number: 417 - Prize Name: Otter - Ship type: MV - How taken: HM Ship-Sloop Jalouse - When taken: 1 Dec 1812 - Where taken: at sea - Date received: 10 Jan 1813 - From what ship: HM

Guardship Royal William - Born: New York - Age: 30 - Discharged on 6 Mar 1813 and sent to Chatham on HMS Frigate Alexandria.

Carrel, Michael - Seaman - Number: 494 - Prize Name: Sword Fish - Ship type: P - How taken: HM Ship-of-the-Line Elephant - When taken: 28 Dec 1812 - Where taken: at sea - Date received: 14 Jan 1813 - From what ship: HMS Elephant - Born: Marblehead - Age: 21 - Discharged on 11 Mar 1813 and sent to Chatham on HM Store Ship Abundance.

Carter, Enoch - Seaman - Number: 1439 - Prize Name: HMS Devon Transport No. 15, prize of Privateer Bunker Hill - Ship type: MV - How taken: HM Brig Fly - When taken: 21 Jan 1814 - Where taken: at sea - Date received: 1 Mar 1814 - From what ship: HMS Helicone - Born: Middleton - Age: 37 - Discharged on 28 Apr 1814 and sent to Chatham on HM Brig Cordelia.

Carter, Henry - Seaman - Number: 1425 - Prize Name: Harvest, prize of Privateer Bunker Hill - Ship type: MV - How taken: HM Brig Orestes - When taken: 21 Jan 1814 - Where taken: at sea - Date received: 1 Mar 1814 - From what ship: HMS Helicone - Born: New York - Age: 26 - Race: Mulatto - Discharged on 28 Apr 1814 and sent to Chatham on HM Sloop Favorite.

Carter, Thomas - Seaman - Number: 945 - Prize Name: Tender of the True Blooded Yankee - Ship type: P - How taken: HM Ship-of-the-Line Fame - When taken: 24 Jun 1813 - Where taken: at sea - Date received: 2 Jul 1813 - From what ship: HM Brig Hope - Born: Troy, NY - Age: 25 - Discharged on 7 Aug 1813 and sent to Chatham on HM Brig Rinaldo.

Caesar, James - Seaman - Number: 1161 - How taken: Gave himself up from HM Hospital Ship Trent - Date received: 9 Oct 1813 - From what ship: HM Sloop Stork - Born: Charleston - Age: 28 - Race: Mulatto - Discharged on 17 Oct 1813 and sent to Chatham on HM Transport Malabar No. 352.

Castor, Charles - Seaman - Number: 430 - Prize Name: Columbia - Ship type: MV - How taken: Unknown British warship - Where taken: at sea - Date received: 10 Jan 1813 - From what ship: HM Guardship Royal William - Born: Batavia - Age: 19 - Race: Mulatto - Discharged on 6 Mar 1813 and sent to Chatham on HM Ship-of-the-Line Cornwall.

Chambers, Charles - Seaman - Number: 424 - Prize Name: Brunswick - Ship type: MV - How taken: HM Frigate Iris - When taken: 16 Dec 1812 - Where taken: at sea - Date received: 10 Jan 1813 - From what ship: HM Guardship Royal William - Born: Richmond - Age: 17 - Discharged on 6 Mar 1813 and sent to Chatham on HMS Frigate Alexandria.

Chambers, Joseph - 2nd Mate - Number: 573 - Prize Name: Rossie - Ship type: MV - How taken: HM Frigate Dryand - When taken: 7 Jan 1813 - Where taken: at sea - Date received: 25 Jan 1813 - From what ship: HM Ship-of-the-Line Queen - Born: New Jersey - Age: 26 - Discharged on 11 Mar 1813 and sent to Chatham on HM Store Ship Abundance.

Chandler, Henry - Seaman - Number: 392 - Prize Name: Empress - Ship type: MV - How taken: HM Brig Rover - When taken: 30 Nov 1812 - Where taken: at sea - Date received: 10 Jan 1813 - From what ship: HM Guardship Royal William - Born: Pittsfield - Age: 24 - Discharged on 4 Mar 1813 and sent to Chatham on HM Ship-of-the-Line Queen.

Chaon, Daniel - Seaman - Number: 1483 - How taken: Gave himself up from HMS Nerias - Date received: 28 May 1814 - From what ship: HM Transport Akba - Born: Boston - Age: 26 - Discharged on 2 Jun 1814 and sent to Plymouth on HMS Growler.

Chaple, Samuel (Chaplin) - Seaman - Number: 123 - Prize Name: Nancy - Ship type: MV - How taken: HM Brig Parthian - When taken: 1 Aug 1812 - Where taken: off the Needles - Date received: 29 Oct 1812 - From what ship: HM Brig Nancy - Born: Marblehead - Age: 27 - Discharged on 19 Feb 1813 and sent to Chatham on HM Store Ship Dromedary.

Charles, Philip - Seaman - Number: 1480 - How taken: Gave himself up from HM Ship-of-the-Line Elizabeth - When taken: 4 Aug 1813 - Where taken: at Malta - Date received: 25 May 1814 - From what ship: Transport Peggy - Born: Louistown - Age: 36 - Race: Mulatto - Discharged on 27 Jul 1814 and sent to the Royal Naval Hospital Haslar at Gosport.

Chase, Eliphalet - Seaman - Number: 97 - Prize Name: HMS Eos - Ship type: MW - How taken: Detained by Court of Admiralty - When taken: 31 Jul 1812 - Where taken: Portsmouth harbor - Date received: 16 Oct 1812 San Antonio - From what ship: Eos - Born: Newburyport - Age: 24 - Discharged on 19 Feb 1813 and sent to Chatham on HM Frigate Ulysses.

Chase, Nathaniel - Seaman - Number: 883 - Prize Name: Prompt - Ship type: MV - How taken: Chance, privateer - When taken: 28 Mar 1813 - Where taken: Bay of Biscay - Date received: 24 Jun 1813 - From what ship: HM Frigate Unicorn - Born: Cape Cod - Age: 21 - Discharged on 2 Jul 1813 and sent to Chatham on HM Frigate Tribune.

Chase, Nathaniel - Seaman - Number: 1000 - Prize Name: Kitty, prize of US Frigate President - Ship type: MV - How taken: Dart, privateer of Guernsey - When taken: 20 Jun 1813 - Where taken: at sea - Date received: 18 Aug 1813 - From what ship: HMS Dexterous - Born: Massachusetts - Age: 23 - Discharged on 21 Sep 1813 and sent to Chatham on HM Ship-of-the-Line Queen.

Chase, Oliver - Seaman - Number: 1183 - How taken: Gave himself up from HM Brig Racehorse - Date received: 5 Nov 1813 - From what ship: HMS Racehorse - Born: Massachusetts - Age: 29 - Discharged on 26 Dec 1813 and sent to Chatham on HM Ship of-the-Line Diomede.

Chase, Samuel - Seaman - Number: 34 - Prize Name: USRM Cutter James Madison - Ship type: MW - How taken: HM Frigate Barbadoes - When taken: 22 Aug 1812 - Where taken: at sea - Date received: 12 Oct 1812 San Antonio - From what ship: HM Ship-of-the-Line Polyphemus - Born: Harwich - Age: 27 - Discharged on 19 Feb 1813 and sent to Chatham on HM Frigate Ulysses.

Chastante, John Baptist - Merchant - Number: 189 - Prize Name: Baltimore - Ship type: P - How taken: HM Transport Diadem - When taken: 7 Oct 1812 - Where taken: S. Andera - Date received: 10 Nov 1812 - From what ship: HMS Diadem - Born: France - Age: 55 - Discharged on 11 Nov 1812 and sent to Odiham on parole.

Chattles, John - Seaman - Number: 171 - Prize Name: Baltimore - Ship type: P - How taken: HM Transport Diadem - When taken: 7 Oct 1812 - Where taken: S. Andera - Date received: 3 Nov 1812 San Antonio - From what ship: HMS Diadem - Born: Baltimore - Age: 26 - Discharged on 19 Feb 1813 and sent to Chatham on HM Store Ship Dromedary.

Chauvel, Thomas - Boy - Number: 1435 - Prize Name: HMS Devon Transport No. 15, prize of Privateer Bunker Hill - Ship type: MV - How taken: HM Brig Fly - When taken: 21 Jan 1814 - Where taken: at sea - Date received: 1 Mar 1814 - From what ship: HMS Helicone - Born: L'Amcon, France - Age: 11 - Discharged on 28 Apr 1814 and sent to Chatham on HM Brig Cordelia.

Chidsey, Abraham - Seaman - Number: 146 - Prize Name: William - Ship type: MV - How taken: HM Brig Recruit - When taken: 29 Aug 1812 - Where taken: at sea - Date received: 29 Oct 1812 - From what ship: HM Ship-of-the-Line Ardent - Born: New Haven, CT - Age: 21 - Discharged on 19 Feb 1813 and sent to Chatham on HM Store Ship Dromedary.

Chipp, Charles - Seaman - Number: 787 - Prize Name: Dick - Ship type: MV - How taken: HM Brig Dispatch - When taken: 17 Mar 1813 - Where taken: at sea - Date received: 3 Apr 1813 - From what ship: Prussian Ship Argo - Born: New York - Age: 27 - Discharged on 3 Apr 1813 and sent to Chatham on HM Transport Chatham.

Christie, John - Seaman - Number: 926 - Prize Name: Tender of the True Blooded Yankee - Ship type: P - How taken: HM Ship-of-the-Line Fame - When taken: 24 Jun 1813 - Where taken: at sea - Date received: 1 Jul 1813 - From what ship: HM Brig Hope - Born: Philadelphia - Age: 28 - Discharged on 2 Jul 1813 and sent to Chatham on HM Brig Scorpion.

Christy, William - 2nd Mate - Number: 72 - Prize Name: HM Frigate Leonidas - Ship type: MW - How taken: Detained by Court of Admiralty - When taken: 31 Jul 1812 - Where taken: Portsmouth harbor - Date received: 16 Oct 1812 San Antonio - From what ship: HM Frigate Leonidas - Born: Nantucket - Age: 24 - Discharged on 19 Feb 1813 and sent to Chatham on HM Frigate Ulysses.

Church, Benjamin - Seaman - Number: 622 - How taken: Gave himself up from HM Guardship Royal William - Date received: 3 Feb 1813 - From what ship: HMS Royal William - Born: Newport, RI - Age: 38 - Discharged on 11 Mar 1813 and sent to Chatham on HM Store Ship Abundance.

Church, Richard - Seaman - Number: 662 - How taken: Gave himself up from HM Frigate Ulysses - Date received: 7 Feb 1813 - From what ship: HMS Ulysses - Born: New York - Age: 30 - Discharged on 6 Mar 1813 and sent to Chatham on HM Ship-of-the-Line Cornwall.

Church, William - Prize Master - Number: 1491 - Prize Name: Traveler, prize of the Privateer Surprise - Ship type: MV - How taken: HM Schooner Canso - When taken: 14 May 1814 - Where taken: at sea - Date received: 1 Jun 1814 - From what ship: HMS Canso - Born: Rhode Island - Age: 34 - Discharged on 2 Jun 1814 and sent to Plymouth on HMS Growler.

Churchill, Timothy - Seaman - Number: 860 - Prize Name: Tiger - Ship type: MV - How taken: HM Brig Scylla - When taken: 22 Mar 1813 - Where taken: Bay of Biscay - Date received: 24 Jun 1813 - From what ship: HM Frigate Unicorn - Born: Massachusetts - Age: 27 - Discharged on 2 Jul 1813 and sent to Chatham on HM Frigate Tribune.

Chute, Davis - Seaman - Number: 387 - How taken: Gave himself up from HM Ship-of-the-Line Salvador del Mundo - Date received: 10 Jan 1813 - From what ship: HM Guardship Royal William - Born: Salem, MA - Age: 31 - Discharged on 4 Mar 1813 and sent to Chatham on HM Ship-of-the-Line Queen.

Clabby, Martin John - Seaman - Number: 1242 - Prize Name: British South Sea Whaler - How taken: HM Ship-of-the-Line Illustrious - When taken: 22 Oct 1813 - Where taken: at sea - Date received: 26 Nov 1813 - From what ship: HMS Illustrious - Born: Boston - Age: 24 - Discharged on 26 Dec 1813 and sent to Chatham on HM Ship of-the-Line Diomede.

Clark, Aaron - Seaman - Number: 153 - Prize Name: Lydia - Ship type: MV - How taken: HM Frigate Orpheus - When taken: 3 Sep 1812 - Where taken: at sea - Date received: 29 Oct 1812 - From what ship: HM Ship-of-the-Line Ardent - Born: Middletown, CT - Age: 21 - Discharged on 19 Feb 1813 and sent to Chatham on HM Store Ship Dromedary.

Clark, Abraham D. - 2nd Lieutenant & commander - Number: 915 - Prize Name: Tender of the True Blooded Yankee - Ship type: P - How taken: HM Ship-of-the-Line Fame - When taken: 24 Jun 1813 - Where taken: at sea - Date received: 1 Jul 1813 - From what ship: HM Brig Hope - Born: New York - Age: 29 - Discharged on 7 Aug 1813 and sent to Chatham on HM Brig Rinaldo.

Clark, George - Supercargo - Number: 276 - Prize Name: King of Rome - Ship type: MV - How taken: HM Brig Wolverine - When taken: 13 Dec 1812 - Where taken: at sea - Date received: 29 Dec 1812 - From what ship: HMS Wolverine - Born: Connecticut - Age: 31 - Discharged on 31 Dec 1812 and sent to Odiham on parole.

Clark, Jean - Seaman - Number: 152 - Prize Name: William - Ship type: MV - How taken: HM Brig Recruit - When taken: 29 Aug 1812 - Where taken: at sea - Date received: 29 Oct 1812 - From what ship: HM Ship-of-the-Line Ardent - Born: Dudley, MA - Age: 28 - Discharged on 2 Dec 1812 to HM Brig Borer.

Clark, John - Seaman - Number: 1016 - Prize Name: Fame - Ship type: MV - How taken: HM Ship of-the-Line Cressy - When taken: 20 Jul 1813 - Where taken: at sea - Date received: 18 Aug 1813 - From what ship: HMS Cressy - Born: Boston - Age: 29 - Discharged on 21 Sep 1813 and sent to Chatham on HM Ship-of-the-Line Queen.

Clark, John D. - Seaman - Number: 197 - How taken: Sent into custody by order of the commander in chief - Date received: 22 Nov 1812 - From what ship: HM Guardship Royal William - Born: New York - Age: 30 - Discharged on 19 Feb 1813 and sent to Chatham on HM Store Ship Dromedary.

Clark, William - Seaman - Number: 828 - How taken: Gave himself up from HM Frigate North Star - Date received: 26 May 1813 - From what ship: HMS North Star - Born: Philadelphia - Age: 30 - Discharged on 10 Jun 1813 and sent to Chatham on HM Frigate Arethusa.

Clarke, Alexander - Boy - Number: 105 - Prize Name: HM Brig Richmond - Ship type: MV - How taken: Detained by Court of Admiralty - When taken: 31 Jul 1812 - Where taken: Portsmouth harbor - Date received: 16 Oct 1812 San Antonio - From what ship: HM Brig Richmond - Born: Charlestown - Age: 18 - Discharged on 19 Feb 1813 and sent to Chatham on HM Frigate Ulysses.

Clarke, Arnold - Seaman - Number: 517 - How taken: Gave himself up from HM Ship-of-the-Line Tigre - Date received: 23 Jan 1813 - From what ship: HMS Tigre - Born: New Orleans - Age: 23 - Discharged on 11 Mar 1813 and sent to Chatham on HM Store Ship Abundance.

Clarke, Samuel - Seaman - Number: 738 - Prize Name: Dart - Ship type: MV - How taken: HM Brig Doterel - When taken: 5 Mar 1813 - Where taken: at sea - Date received: 21 Mar 1813 - From what ship: HMS Dotteril - Born: Alfred - Age: 28 - Discharged on 28 Mar 1813 and sent to Chatham on HM Store Ship Seaphis.

Clawson, Henry - Seaman - Number: 1268 - Prize Name: US Schooner Julia - Ship type: MW - How taken: Sir James Yeo's Squadron - When taken: 11 Aug 1813 - Where taken: Lake Ontario - Date received: 22 Dec 1813 - From what ship: HMS Elalion - Born: New York - Age: 23 - Discharged on 26 Dec 1813 and sent to Chatham on HM Ship of-the-Line Diomede.

Clawson, John (1) - Seaman - Number: 1076 - How taken: Gave himself up from HM Ship-of-the-Line Centaur - Date received: 1 Oct 1813 - From what ship: HM Ship-of-the-Line Barham - Born: Vermont - Age: 19 - Discharged on 17 Oct 1813 and sent to Chatham on HM Store Ship Weymouth.

Clawson, John (2) - Seaman - Number: 1042 - How taken: Gave himself up from HM Ship-of-the-Line Centaur - Date received: 10 Sep 1813 - From what ship: HMS Centaur - Born: Vermont - Age: 19 - Discharged on 29 Sep 1813 and sent to Chatham on HM Ship-of-the-Line Barham.

Clay, John - Seaman - Number: 803 - How taken: Gave himself up from HMS Freaja - Date received: 21 Apr 1813 - From what ship: HM Guardship Royal William - Born: New York - Age: 57 - Discharged on 27 Apr 1813 and sent to Chatham on HM Sloop-of-War Bonne Citoyenne.

Clements, Henry - Seaman - Number: 11 - Prize Name: USRM Cutter James Madison - Ship type: MW - How taken: HM Frigate Barbadoes - When taken: 22 Aug 1812 - Where taken: at sea - Date received: 12 Oct 1812 San Antonio - From what ship: HM Ship-of-the-Line Polyphemus - Born: Albany, NY - Age: 49 - Discharged on 19 Feb 1813 and sent to Chatham on HM Frigate Ulysses.

Clerk, William - Seaman - Number: 121 - Prize Name: Hannibal - Ship type: P - How taken: MV Patent - When taken: 24 Sep 1812 - Where taken: off Bermuda - Date received: 28 Oct 1812 - From what ship: MV Patent - Born: New York - Age: 19 - Discharged on 19 Feb 1813 and sent to Chatham on HM Store Ship Dromedary.

Clifford, States Laurence - Seaman - Number: 775 - How taken: Gave himself up from HM Frigate Brune - Date received: 1 Apr 1813 - From what ship: HM Ship-of-the-Line Blake - Born: Philadelphia - Age: 33 - Discharged on 3 Apr 1813 and sent to Chatham on HM Transport Chatham.

Cloutman, George - Master's Mate - Number: 448 - Prize Name: Sword Fish - Ship type: P - How taken: HM Ship-of-the-Line Elephant - When taken: 28 Dec 1812 - Where taken: at sea - Date received: 14 Jan 1813 - From what ship: HMS Elephant - Born: Marblehead - Age: 22 - Discharged on 6 Mar 1813 and sent to Chatham on HMS Frigate Alexandria.

Cloutman, Robert - 1st Lieutenant - Number: 437 - Prize Name: Sword Fish - Ship type: P - How taken: HM Ship-of-the-Line Elephant - When taken: 28 Dec 1812 - Where taken: at sea - Date received: 14 Jan 1813 - From what ship: HMS Elephant - Born: Marblehead - Age: 49 - Discharged on 6 Mar 1813 and sent to Chatham on HMS Frigate Alexandria.

Coates, S. Murray - Seaman - Number: 182 - Prize Name: Baltimore - Ship type: P - How taken: HM Transport Diadem - When taken: 7 Oct 1812 - Where taken: S. Andera - Date received: 3 Nov 1812 San Antonio - From what ship: HMS Diadem - Born: Harford County, MD - Age: 30 - Discharged on 19 Feb 1813 and sent to Chatham on HM Store Ship Dromedary.

Cobb, Samuel - 2nd Mate - Number: 431 - Prize Name: Experiment - Ship type: MV - How taken: HM Brig Rover - When taken: 21 Oct 1821 - Where taken: at sea - Date received: 10 Jan 1813 - From what ship: HM Guardship Royal William - Born: Limington, MA - Age: 28 - Discharged on 6 Mar 1813 and sent to Chatham on HMS Frigate Alexandria.

Cock, Isaac - Seaman - Number: 1020 - How taken: Gave himself up from HM Ship-of-the-Line Prince of Wales - Date received: 7 Sep 1813 - From what ship: HM Frigate Unicorn - Born: Long Island - Age: 24 - Discharged on 21 Sep 1813 and sent to Chatham on HM Ship-of-the-Line Queen.

Cocks, Isaac - Cook - Number: 273 - Prize Name: Antelope - Ship type: P - How taken: HM Brig Zephyr - When taken: 10 Dec 1812 - Where taken: at sea - Date received: 29 Dec 1812 - From what ship: HMS Zephyr - Age: 36 - Race: Black - Discharged on 19 Feb 1813 and sent to Chatham on HM Store Ship Dromedary.

Codding, Caleb - Seaman - Number: 957 - How taken: Gave himself up from HM Ship-of-the-Line Swiftsure - Date received: 28 Jul 1813 - From what ship: HM Sloop Volentaire - Born: Massachusetts - Age: 48 - Discharged on 7 Aug 1813 and sent to Chatham on HM Brig Rinaldo.

Cody, James - Seaman - Number: 856 - How taken: Gave himself up from HM Frigate Leonidas - Date received: 22 Jun 1813 - From what ship: HM Ship-of-the-Line Vigo - Born: Boston - Age: 31 - Discharged on 2 Jul 1813 and sent to Chatham on HM Frigate Tribune.

Coffin, Daniel G. - 1st Mate - Number: 71 - Prize Name: HM Frigate Leonidas - Ship type: MW - How taken: Detained by Court of Admiralty - When taken: 31 Jul 1812 - Where taken: Portsmouth harbor - Date received: 16 Oct 1812 San Antonio - From what ship: HM Frigate Leonidas - Born: Nantucket - Age: 23 - Discharged on 26 Oct 1813 and sent to Odiham on parole.

Coffin, Edward - 3rd Mate - Number: 1385 - Prize Name: Pilate - Ship type: P - How taken: Victoria, privateer of Guernsey - When taken: 28 Jan 1814 - Where taken: off Bordeaux - Date received: 7 Feb 1814 - From what ship: Mary from Guernsey - Born: Nantucket - Age: 24 - Discharged on 13 Feb 1814 and sent to Chatham on HM Transport Malabar No. 352.

Coffin, Edward - Chief Mate - Number: 275 - Prize Name: King of Rome - Ship type: MV - How taken: HM Brig Wolverine - When taken: 13 Dec 1812 - Where taken: at sea - Date received: 29 Dec 1812 - From what ship: HMS Wolverine - Born: Nantucket - Age: 23 - Discharged on 31 Dec 1812 and sent to Odiham on parole.

Coffin, James - Seaman - Number: 1122 - Prize Name: Sampson - Ship type: MV - How taken: HM Brig Rebuff - When taken: 12 May 1813 - Where taken: off Cape St. Vincent - Date received: 5 Oct 1813 - From what ship: HM Ship-of-the-Line Achille - Born: Fort Washington - Age: 28 - Discharged on 17 Oct 1813 and sent to Chatham on HM Transport Malabar No. 352.

Coffin, Joseph - Seaman - Number: 1329 - How taken: Gave himself up from HM Ship-of-the-Line Invincible - Date received: 27 Dec 1813 - From what ship: HMS Frigate Nemesis - Born: Rhode Island - Age: 29 - Discharged on 27 Dec 1813 and sent to Chatham on HMS Frigate Nemesis.

Coggins, George - Seaman - Number: 112 - Prize Name: HM Brig Nancy - Ship type: MV - How taken: Detained by Court of Admiralty - When taken: 1 Aug 1812 - Where taken: off the Needles - Date received: 17 Oct 1812 San Antonio - From what ship: W. Lindegreon, deputy marshal - Born: Surry, MA - Age: 26 - Discharged on 19 Feb 1813 and sent to Chatham on HM Frigate Ulysses.

Cole, Hutchinson A. - 2nd Mate - Number: 691 - Prize Name: Calcutta - Ship type: East Indian Ship - How taken: Two Brothers, privateer of Guernsey - When taken: 23 Nov 1812 - Where taken: at sea - Date received: 24 Feb 1813 - From what ship: HM Brig Escort - Born: North Kingston, RI - Age: 23 - Discharged on 6 Mar 1813 and sent to Chatham on HMS Frigate Alexandria.

Cole, Stephen - Seaman - Number: 910 - Prize Name: William Rathbourne - Ship type: Prize - How taken: HM Brig Charybdis - When taken: 9 Oct 1812 - Where taken: at sea - Date received: 1 Jul 1813 - From what ship: HM Frigate Tribune - Born: Sanford, MA - Age: 31 - Discharged on 2 Jul 1813 and sent to Chatham on HM Brig Scorpion.

Cole, William - Seaman - Number: 942 - Prize Name: Tender of the True Blooded Yankee - Ship type: P - How taken: HM Ship-of-the-Line Fame - When taken: 24 Jun 1813 - Where taken: at sea - Date received: 1 Jul 1813 - From what ship: HM Brig Hope - Born: Alexandria, VA - Age: 26 - Discharged on 2 Jul 1813 and sent to Chatham on HM Brig Scorpion.

Cole, William - Seaman - Number: 879 - Prize Name: Prompt - Ship type: MV - How taken: Chance, privateer - When taken: 28 Mar 1813 - Where taken: Bay of Biscay - Date received: 24 Jun 1813 - From what ship: HM Frigate Unicorn - Born: Cape Cod - Age: 23 - Discharged on 2 Jul 1813 and sent to Chatham on HM Frigate Tribune.

Coleman, Christian - 1st Mate - Number: 186 - Prize Name: Baltimore - Ship type: P - How taken: HM Transport Diadem - When taken: 7 Oct 1812 - Where taken: S. Andera - Date received: 10 Nov 1812 - From what ship: HMS Diadem - Born: Nantucket, MA - Age: 29 - Discharged on 11 Nov 1812 and sent to Odiham on parole.

Coleman, Daniel - Seaman - Number: 35 - Prize Name: USRM Cutter James Madison - Ship type: MW - How taken: HM Frigate Barbadoes - When taken: 22 Aug 1812 - Where taken: at sea - Date received: 12 Oct 1812 San Antonio - From what ship: HM Ship-of-the-Line Polyphemus - Born: Philadelphia - Age: 37 -

Discharged on 19 Feb 1813 and sent to Chatham on HM Frigate Ulysses.

Coleman, John - Seaman - Number: 408 - How taken: Taken up at Dublin - When taken: 15 Nov 1812 - Date received: 10 Jan 1813 - From what ship: HM Guardship Royal William - Born: Delaware - Age: 27 - Discharged on 28 Mar 1813 and sent to Chatham on HMS Scraphid.

Coleman, Jonathan - Seaman - Number: 367 - How taken: Gave himself up from HM Ship-of-the-Line Orion - Date received: 2 Jan 1813 - From what ship: HM Prison Ship Assistance - Born: Newark, NJ - Age: 25 - Discharged on 4 Mar 1813 and sent to Chatham on HM Ship-of-the-Line Queen.

Collins, George - Seaman - Number: 1249 - How taken: Gave himself up from HM Ship-of-the-Line Vigo - Date received: 16 Dec 1813 - From what ship: HMS Vigo - Born: Boston - Age: 27 - Race: Black - Discharged on 26 Dec 1813 and sent to Chatham on HM Ship of-the-Line Diomede.

Colwell, John - Seaman - Number: 530 - Prize Name: Expectation - Ship type: MV - How taken: HMS Butain - When taken: 17 Dec 1812 - Where taken: at sea - Date received: 25 Jan 1813 - From what ship: HM Ship-of-the-Line Queen - Born: Philadelphia - Age: 20 - Discharged on 11 Mar 1813 and sent to Chatham on HM Store Ship Abundance.

Combs, Thomas - Seaman - Number: 562 - Prize Name: Rossie - Ship type: MV - How taken: HM Frigate Dryand - When taken: 7 Jan 1813 - Where taken: at sea - Date received: 25 Jan 1813 - From what ship: HM Ship-of-the-Line Queen - Born: Maryland - Age: 37 - Discharged on 11 Mar 1813 and sent to Chatham on HM Store Ship Abundance.

Comtis, Thomas - Seaman - Number: 587 - How taken: Gave himself up from HM Ship-of-the-Line Mars - Date received: 31 Jan 1813 - From what ship: HMS Mars - Born: Marblehead - Age: 26 - Discharged on 11 Mar 1813 and sent to Chatham on HM Store Ship Abundance.

Congdon, Henry - Seaman - Number: 130 - How taken: Gave himself up from HM Ship-of-the-Line Ruby - When taken: 30 Aug 1812 - Date received: 29 Oct 1812 - From what ship: HM Ship-of-the-Line Ardent - Born: Staten Island, NY - Age: 25 - Discharged on 17 Nov 1812 and sent to Chatham on HM Guardship Royal Williams.

Conklin, Enoch - Captain - Number: 269 - Prize Name: Antelope - Ship type: P - How taken: HM Brig Zephyr - When taken: 10 Dec 1812 - Where taken: at sea - Date received: 29 Dec 1812 - From what ship: HMS Zephyr - Born: New York - Age: 42 - Discharged on 31 Dec 1812 and sent to Odiham on parole.

Conklin, Smith - Seaman - Number: 1444 - How taken: Gave himself up from HM Ship-of-the-Line Salvador del Mundo - Date received: 1 Mar 1814 - From what ship: HMS Helicone - Born: New York - Age: 21 - Discharged on 28 Apr 1814 and sent to Chatham on HM Brig Cordelia.

Conaway, Samuel - Seaman - Number: 593 - How taken: Gave himself up from HM Ship-of-the-Line Mars - Date received: 31 Jan 1813 - From what ship: HMS Mars - Born: North Carolina - Age: 53 - Discharged on 11 Mar 1813 and sent to Chatham on HM Store Ship Abundance.

Conner, Jesse - Seaman - Number: 507 - How taken: Gave himself up from HM Sloop Partridge - Date received: 17 Jan 1813 - From what ship: HMS Partridge - Born: Virginia - Age: 29 - Discharged on 11 Mar 1813 and sent to Chatham on HM Store Ship Abundance.

Conner, Michael - Seaman - Number: 1429 - Prize Name: Minerva - Ship type: MV - How taken: HM Ship-of-the-Line Conquestador - When taken: 19 Jan 1814 - Where taken: Bay of Biscay - Date received: 1 Mar 1814 - From what ship: HMS Helicone - Born: Charleston - Age: 26 - Discharged on 28 Apr 1814 and sent to Chatham on HM Sloop Favorite.

Conon, John - Seaman - Number: 1333 - How taken: Gave himself up from HM Ship-of-the-Line Invincible - Date received: 27 Dec 1813 - From what ship: HMS Frigate Nemesis - Born: New York - Age: 25 - Race: Mulatto - Discharged on 27 Dec 1813 and sent to Chatham on HMS Frigate Nemesis.

Conway, Andrew - Seaman - Number: 670 - How taken: Gave himself up from HM Brig Electra - Date received: 10 Feb 1813 - From what ship: HMS Electra - Born: Baltimore - Age: 20 - Discharged on 6 Mar 1813 and sent to Chatham on HM Ship-of-the-Line Cornwall.

Conway, Samuel - Seaman - Number: 322 - Prize Name: Taken on shore - How taken: Elizabeth, tender - When taken: 29 Oct 1812 - Where taken: Greenoch - Date received: 31 Dec 1812 - From what ship: HM Ship-of-the-Line Northumberland - Born: Salem - Age: 23 - Discharged on 4 Mar 1813 and sent to Chatham on HM Ship-of-the-Line Queen.

Cook, Silvanus - Carpenter - Number: 1207 - Prize Name: Elbridge Gerry - Ship type: P - How taken: HM Frigate Crescent & HM Ship of-the-Line Bellerophon - When taken: 16 Sep 1813 - Where taken: at sea - Date received: 16 Nov 1813 - From what ship: HM Sloop Talbot - Born: Kingston, MA - Age: 39 - Discharged on 26 Dec 1813 and sent to Chatham on HM Ship of-the-Line Diomede.

Cool, John - Seaman - Number: 817 - Prize Name: Ajax, prize to the Privateer Governor Tomkins - Ship type: MV - How taken: HM Frigate Revolutionnaire - When taken: 10 Apr 1813 - Where taken: at sea - Date received: 13 May 1813 - From what ship: HMS Revolutionaire - Born: New Orleans - Age: 27 - Discharged on 2 Jul 1813 and sent to Chatham on HM Frigate Tribune.

Coombs, Michael - Seaman - Number: 1314 - Prize Name: Growler - Ship type: P - How taken: HM Brig Electra - When taken: 7 Jul 1813 - Where taken: off St. Johns - Date received: 22 Dec 1813 - From what ship: HM Frigate Hyperion - Born: Marblehead - Age: 21 - Discharged on 26 Dec 1813 and sent to Chatham on HMS Frigate Nemesis.

Coon, John (alias John Combs) - Seaman - Number: 721 - How taken: Gave himself up from HM Guardship Royal William - Date received: 11 Mar 1813 - From what ship: HMS Royal William - Born: Pennsylvania - Age: 24 - Discharged on 28 Mar 1813 and sent to Chatham on HM Store Ship Seaphis.

Cooper, Alfred - Seaman - Number: 710 - Prize Name: Tom Thumb - Ship type: MV - How taken: Lion, Privateer - When taken: 15 Feb 1813 - Where taken: at sea - Date received: 24 Feb 1813 - From what ship: HM Brig Escort - Born: Newburyport - Age: 32 - Discharged on 6 Mar 1813 and sent to Chatham on HM Ship-of-the-Line Cornwall.

Cooper, James - Seaman - Number: 148 - Prize Name: William - Ship type: MV - How taken: HM Brig Recruit - When taken: 29 Aug 1812 - Where taken: at sea - Date received: 29 Oct 1812 - From what ship: HM Ship-of-the-Line Ardent - Born: Tolbert, MD - Age: 22 - Race: Black - Discharged on 19 Feb 1813 and sent to Chatham on HM Store Ship Dromedary.

Cooper, Thomas - Boatswain - Number: 1177 - How taken: Gave himself up from HM Frigate Nisus - Date received: 22 Oct 1813 - From what ship: HM Brig Racehorse - Born: Philadelphia - Age: 33 - Discharged on 26 Dec 1813 and sent to Chatham on HM Ship of-the-Line Diomede.

Cooper, Thomas - 2nd Mate - Number: 1347 - Prize Name: Union - Ship type: MV - How taken: Susan, East Indian Ship - When taken: 10 Jun 812 - Where taken: Sago Roads - Date received: 5 Jan 1814 - From what ship: HM Ship-of-the-Line Prince - Born: Massachusetts - Age: 34 - Discharged on 5 Jan 1814 and sent to Chatham on HM Ship-of-the-Line Poictiers.

Copasses, Matthew (alias Cabristal) - Seaman - Number: 555 - Prize Name: Rossie - Ship type: MV - How taken: HM Frigate Dryand - When taken: 7 Jan 1813 - Where taken: at sea - Date received: 25 Jan 1813 - From what ship: HM Ship-of-the-Line Queen - Born: New York - Age: 18 - Discharged on 11 Mar 1813 and sent to Chatham on HM Store Ship Abundance.

Copland, Thomas - Seaman - Number: 1129 - How taken: Gave himself up from HM Ship-of-the-Line Achille - Date received: 5 Oct 1813 - From what ship: HM Ship-of-the-Line Achille - Born: Massachusetts - Age: 29 - Race: Black - Discharged on 17 Oct 1813 and sent to Chatham on HM Transport Malabar No. 352.

Corban, Daniel - Seaman - Number: 506 - How taken: Gave himself up from HM Sloop Partridge - Date received: 17 Jan 1813 - From what ship: HMS Partridge - Born: Philadelphia - Age: 29 - Discharged on 11 Mar 1813 and sent to Chatham on HM Store Ship Abundance.

Cornelius, John - Seaman - Number: 228 - Prize Name: Antelope - Ship type: P - How taken: HM Brig Zephyr - When taken: 10 Dec 1812 - Where taken: at sea - Date received: 27 Dec 1812 - From what ship: HMS Zephyr - Born: Stettin, Prussia - Age: 38 - Discharged on 19 Feb 1813 and sent to Chatham on HM Store Ship Dromedary.

Corta, John - Cook - Number: 906 - Prize Name: Gleamer - Ship type: MV - How taken: Brothers, privateer - When taken: 2 Apr 1813 - Where taken: Bay of Biscay - Date received: 24 Jun 1813 - From what ship: HM Frigate

Unicorn - Born: New York - Age: 25 - Race: Black - Discharged on 2 Jul 1813 and sent to Chatham on HM Frigate Tribune.

Corvet, Isaac - Seaman - Number: 794 - How taken: Gave himself up from HM Frigate Loire - Date received: 14 Apr 1813 - From what ship: HMS Loire - Born: New York - Age: 31 - Discharged on 27 Apr 1813 and sent to Chatham on HM Sloop-of-War Bonne Citoyenne.

Cottril, Henry - Seaman - Number: 1151 - How taken: Gave himself up from HM Ship-of-the-Line Majestic - Date received: 7 Oct 1813 - From what ship: HM Frigate Spartan - Born: New London - Age: 53 - Discharged on 17 Oct 1813 and sent to Chatham on HM Transport Malabar No. 352.

Coullay, Andrew - Seaman - Number: 226 - Prize Name: Antelope - Ship type: P - How taken: HM Brig Zephyr - When taken: 10 Dec 1812 - Where taken: at sea - Date received: 27 Dec 1812 - From what ship: HMS Zephyr - Born: New York - Age: 31 - Discharged on 19 Feb 1813 and sent to Chatham on HM Store Ship Dromedary.

Covelle, Ephraim - Seaman - Number: 623 - How taken: Gave himself up from HM Guardship Royal William - Date received: 3 Feb 1813 - From what ship: HMS Royal William - Born: Wellfleet, MA - Age: 39 - Discharged on 11 Mar 1813 and sent to Chatham on HM Store Ship Abundance.

Cowen, William - Seaman - Number: 235 - Prize Name: Antelope - Ship type: P - How taken: HM Brig Zephyr - When taken: 10 Dec 1812 - Where taken: at sea - Date received: 27 Dec 1812 - From what ship: HMS Zephyr - Born: New York - Age: 32 - Discharged on 19 Feb 1813 and sent to Chatham on HM Store Ship Dromedary.

Cox, Daniel - Seaman - Number: 467 - Prize Name: Sword Fish - Ship type: P - How taken: HM Ship-of-the-Line Elephant - When taken: 28 Dec 1812 - Where taken: at sea - Date received: 14 Jan 1813 - From what ship: HMS Elephant - Born: Frederick, MD - Age: 38 - Race: Black - Discharged on 11 Mar 1813 and sent to Chatham on HM Store Ship Abundance.

Crawford, George - Seaman - Number: 1509 - How taken: Gave himself up from HM Ship-of-the-Line Rodney - Date received: 30 Jun 1814 - From what ship: HMS Rodney - Born: Philadelphia - Age: 45 - Discharged on 30 Jun 1814 and sent to Plymouth on HM Brig Steady.

Crocker, Silvanus - Prize Master - Number: 1291 - Prize Name: Growler - Ship type: P - How taken: HM Brig Electra - When taken: 7 Jul 1813 - Where taken: off St. Johns - Date received: 22 Dec 1813 - From what ship: HM Ship of-the-Line Bellerophon - Born: Massachusetts - Age: 32 - Discharged on 26 Dec 1813 and sent to Chatham on HMS Frigate Nemesis.

Cross, John - Seaman - Number: 237 - Prize Name: Antelope - Ship type: P - How taken: HM Brig Zephyr - When taken: 10 Dec 1812 - Where taken: at sea - Date received: 27 Dec 1812 - From what ship: HMS Zephyr - Born: Boston - Age: 21 - Discharged on 19 Feb 1813 and sent to Chatham on HM Store Ship Dromedary.

Crow, John - Seaman - Number: 1370 - How taken: Gave himself up from HM Transport William Pitt - Date received: 4 Feb 1814 - From what ship: HM Frigate Bombay - Born: Baltimore - Age: 27 - Discharged on 13 Feb 1814 and sent to Chatham on HM Transport Malabar No. 352.

Cruff, William - Seaman - Number: 50 - Prize Name: Fame, prize of Privateer Decatur - Ship type: MV - How taken: HM Ship-of-the-Line Polyphemus - When taken: 13 Sep 1812 - Where taken: at sea - Date received: 12 Oct 1812 San Antonio - From what ship: HM Ship-of-the-Line Polyphemus - Born: Marblehead - Age: 20 - Discharged on 19 Feb 1813 and sent to Chatham on HM Frigate Ulysses.

Cummings, Edward - Seaman - Number: 129 - How taken: Gave himself up from HM Ship-of-the-Line Ruby - When taken: 30 Aug 1812 - Date received: 29 Oct 1812 - From what ship: HM Ship-of-the-Line Ardent - Born: Philadelphia - Age: 35 - Discharged on 19 Feb 1813 and sent to Chatham on HM Store Ship Dromedary.

Cunningham, John - Seaman - Number: 318 - Prize Name: Taken on shore - How taken: HM Battery Princess - When taken: 27 Oct 1812 - Where taken: Liverpool - Date received: 31 Dec 1812 - From what ship: HM Ship-of-the-Line Northumberland - Born: Charlestown - Age: 23 - Discharged on 4 Mar 1813 and sent to Chatham on HM Ship-of-the-Line Queen.

Cunningham, John - Seaman - Number: 181 - Prize Name: Baltimore - Ship type: P - How taken: HM Transport

Diadem - When taken: 7 Oct 1812 - Where taken: S. Andera - Date received: 3 Nov 1812 San Antonio - From what ship: HMS Diadem - Born: Georgetown, MA - Age: 22 - Discharged on 19 Feb 1813 and sent to Chatham on HM Store Ship Dromedary.

Curtis, Enoch - Seaman - Number: 1352 - How taken: Gave himself up from HM Sloop Dauntless - Date received: 26 Jan 1814 - From what ship: HMS Dauntless - Born: Boston - Age: 37 - Race: Mulatto - Discharged on 13 Feb 1814 and sent to Chatham on HM Transport Malabar No. 352.

Dairs, William - Seaman - Number: 638 - How taken: Gave himself up from HM Guardship Royal William - Date received: 3 Feb 1813 - From what ship: HMS Royal William - Born: Baltimore - Age: 26 - Discharged on 11 Mar 1813 and sent to Chatham on HM Store Ship Abundance.

Dalliber, James - Boy - Number: 491 - Prize Name: Sword Fish - Ship type: P - How taken: HM Ship-of-the-Line Elephant - When taken: 28 Dec 1812 - Where taken: at sea - Date received: 14 Jan 1813 - From what ship: HMS Elephant - Born: Marblehead - Age: 15 - Discharged on 11 Mar 1813 and sent to Chatham on HM Store Ship Abundance.

Darrow, Aaron - Seaman - Number: 1171 - How taken: Gave himself up from HM Hospital Ship Trent - Date received: 12 Oct 1813 - From what ship: HM Brig Hope - Born: Massachusetts - Age: 24 - Discharged on 17 Oct 1813 and sent to Chatham on HM Transport Malabar No. 352.

Davenport, Russel - Seaman - Number: 1502 - How taken: Gave himself up from HM Frigate Amphion - Date received: 27 Jun 1814 - From what ship: HMS Amphion - Born: New London - Age: 33 - Discharged on 30 Jun 1814 and sent to Plymouth on HM Brig Steady.

David, Daniel - Seaman - Number: 752 - How taken: Gave himself up from HM Guardship Royal William - Date received: 26 Mar 1813 - From what ship: HMS Royal William - Born: Caroline, PA - Age: 28 - Discharged on 28 Mar 1813 and sent to Chatham on HM Store Ship Seaphis.

Davidson, John - Boy - Number: 1090 - Prize Name: Hindostan - Ship type: MV - How taken: HM Brig Zenobia - When taken: 25 Jun 1813 - Where taken: off Lisbon - Date received: 1 Oct 1813 - From what ship: HM Ship-of-the-Line Barham - Born: Charleston - Age: 17 - Discharged on 17 Oct 1813 and sent to Chatham on HM Store Ship Weymouth (see Prisoner Number 1065).

Davidson, John - Boy - Number: 1065 - Prize Name: Hindostan - Ship type: MV - How taken: HM Brig Zenobia - When taken: 25 Jun 1813 - Where taken: off Lisbon - Date received: 19 Sep 1813 - From what ship: HM Brig Imogen - Born: Charleston - Age: 17 - Discharged on 29 Sep 1813 and sent to Chatham on HM Transport Chatham (see Prisoner Number 1090).

Davies, George - Seaman - Number: 647 - How taken: Gave himself up from HM Guardship Royal William - Date received: 3 Feb 1813 - From what ship: HMS Royal William - Born: Albany - Age: 19 - Race: Black - Discharged on 11 Mar 1813 and sent to Chatham on HM Store Ship Abundance.

Davis, Daniel - Seaman - Number: 218 - How taken: Gave himself up from HM Ship-of-the-Line Aboukir - When taken: 29 Oct 1812 - Date received: 26 Dec 1812 - From what ship: HMS Abonkir - Born: Thames, MA - Age: 36 - Discharged on 19 Feb 1813 and sent to Chatham on HM Store Ship Dromedary.

Davis, Francis - Seaman - Number: 818 - Prize Name: Ajax, prize to the Privateer Governor Tomkins - Ship type: MV - How taken: HM Frigate Revolutionnaire - When taken: 10 Apr 1813 - Where taken: at sea - Date received: 13 May 1813 - From what ship: HMS Revolutionaire - Born: New Orleans - Age: 22 - Discharged on 2 Jul 1813 and sent to Chatham on HM Frigate Tribune.

Davis, George - Seaman - Number: 995 - How taken: Gave himself up from HM Sloop Sabrina - Date received: 14 Aug 1813 - From what ship: HM Ship-of-the-Line Medway - Born: New Jersey - Age: 34 - Race: Mulatto - Discharged on 21 Sep 1813 and sent to Chatham on HM Ship-of-the-Line Queen.

Davis, James - Ordinary Seaman - Number: 796 - Prize Name: Elizabeth, tender - How taken: Gave himself up from HM Guardship Royal William - Date received: 18 Apr 1813 - From what ship: HMS Royal William - Born: New York - Age: 37 - Discharged on 27 Apr 1813 and sent to Chatham on HM Sloop-of-War Bonne Citoyenne.

Davis, John - Seaman - Number: 221 - How taken: Taken out of the MV Oaks - Date received: 26 Dec 1812 - From what ship: HM Guardship Royal William - Born: Roxborough - Age: 36 - Discharged on 19 Feb 1813 and sent to Chatham on HM Store Ship Dromedary.

Davis, John - Pilot - Number: 1214 - Prize Name: Elbridge Gerry - Ship type: P - How taken: HM Frigate Crescent - When taken: 16 Sep 1813 - Where taken: at sea - Date received: 16 Nov 1813 - From what ship: HM Sloop Talbot - Born: Machias - Age: 27 - Discharged on 26 Dec 1813 and sent to Chatham on HM Ship of-the-Line Diomede.

Davis, John (alias Dairs) - Seaman - Number: 334 - Prize Name: Independence - Ship type: MV - How taken: HM Frigate Medusa - When taken: 9 Nov 1812 - Where taken: off St. Sebastian - Date received: 31 Dec 1812 - From what ship: HM Ship-of-the-Line Northumberland - Born: New York - Age: 24 - Race: Black - Discharged on 4 Mar 1813 and sent to Chatham on HM Ship-of-the-Line Queen.

Davis, Michael - Seaman - Number: 155 - Prize Name: Lydia - Ship type: MV - How taken: HM Frigate Orpheus - When taken: 3 Sep 1812 - Where taken: at sea - Date received: 29 Oct 1812 - From what ship: HM Ship-of-the-Line Ardent - Born: Middletown, CT - Age: 22 - Discharged on 19 Feb 1813 and sent to Chatham on HM Store Ship Dromedary.

Davis, Nathan - Seaman - Number: 23 - Prize Name: USRM Cutter James Madison - Ship type: MW - How taken: HM Frigate Barbadoes - When taken: 22 Aug 1812 - Where taken: at sea - Date received: 12 Oct 1812 San Antonio - From what ship: HM Ship-of-the-Line Polyphemus - Born: Gorham, MA - Age: 22 - Discharged on 19 Feb 1813 and sent to Chatham on HM Frigate Ulysses.

Davis, Nicolas - Seaman - Number: 1247 - How taken: Gave himself up from HM Brig Echo - Date received: 28 Nov 1813 - From what ship: HMS Echo - Born: Hudson - Age: 31 - Race: Mulatto - Discharged on 26 Dec 1813 and sent to Chatham on HM Ship of-the-Line Diomede.

Davis, Osborn - Seaman - Number: 1109 - How taken: Gave himself up from HM Ship-of-the-Line America - Date received: 5 Oct 1813 - From what ship: HM Ship-of-the-Line Achille - Born: New Jersey - Age: 29 - Discharged on 17 Oct 1813 and sent to Chatham on HM Store Ship Weymouth.

Davy, William (alias Davis) - Number: 1322 - How taken: Received dead for interment - Date received: 25 Dec 1813 - From what ship: HM Transport Hero No. 132 - Born: New York - Age: 35 - Race: Black - Died on 25 Dec 1813.

Dawson, John - Seaman - Number: 421 - How taken: Gave himself up from HM Hospital Ship Trent - Date received: 10 Jan 1813 - From what ship: HM Guardship Royal William - Born: Philadelphia - Age: 21 - Discharged on 6 Mar 1813 and sent to Chatham on HMS Frigate Alexandria.

Day, John - Seaman - Number: 1195 - Prize Name: Fire Fly of Gloucester - Ship type: MV - How taken: HM Frigate Revolutionnaire - When taken: 19 Oct 1813 - Where taken: at sea - Date received: 9 Nov 1813 - From what ship: HMS Revolutionaire - Born: Gloucester - Age: 30 - Discharged on 26 Dec 1813 and sent to Chatham on HM Ship of-the-Line Diomede.

Day, Thomas - Seaman - Number: 1248 - How taken: Gave himself up from HM Brig Espoir - Date received: 12 Dec 1813 - From what ship: HMS Espoir - Born: Frederick County, VA - Age: 24 - Discharged on 26 Dec 1813 and sent to Chatham on HM Ship of-the-Line Diomede.

Daymen, Celeb - Seaman - Number: 9 - Prize Name: USRM Cutter James Madison - Ship type: MW - How taken: HM Frigate Barbadoes - When taken: 22 Aug 1812 - Where taken: at sea - Date received: 12 Oct 1812 San Antonio - From what ship: HM Ship-of-the-Line Polyphemus - Born: Scituate, MA - Age: 30 - Discharged on 19 Feb 1813 and sent to Chatham on HM Frigate Ulysses.

de Peyster, Arent S. - Master - Number: 1178 - Prize Name: Monticello - Ship type: MV - How taken: HM Brig Racehorse - When taken: 12 Nov 1812 - Where taken: Cape of Good Hope - Date received: 22 Oct 1813 - From what ship: HMS Racehorse - Born: New York - Age: 31 - Discharged on 3 Nov 1814 and sent to Reading on parole.

De Soder, Bastian - Seaman - Number: 92 - Prize Name: HM Frigate Janus - Ship type: MW - How taken: Detained by Court of Admiralty - When taken: 31 Jul 1812 - Where taken: Portsmouth harbor - Date received: 16 Oct 1812 San Antonio - From what ship: HM Frigate Janus - Born: St. Michael, Portugal - Age: 28 - Discharged on 19 Feb 1813 and sent to Chatham on HM Frigate Ulysses.

Dean, Jeremiah B. - Marine Lieutenant - Number: 1361 - Prize Name: Elbridge Gerry - Ship type: P - How taken:

HM Frigate Crescent - When taken: 16 Sep 1813 - Where taken: at sea - Date received: 1 Feb 1814 - From what ship: HM Frigate Sybille - Born: Bolton, MA - Age: 24 - Discharged on 13 Feb 1814 and sent to Chatham on HM Transport Malabar No. 352.

Debarize, Francis John - Seaman - Number: 1432 - Prize Name: HMS Devon Transport No. 15, prize of Privateer Bunker Hill - Ship type: MV - How taken: HM Brig Fly - When taken: 21 Jan 1814 - Where taken: at sea - Date received: 1 Mar 1814 - From what ship: HMS Helicone - Born: Isle of France - Age: 21 - Discharged on 28 Apr 1814 and sent to Chatham on HM Sloop Favorite.

DeBuck, Cornelius - Seaman - Number: 373 - Prize Name: Mariner - Ship type: MV - How taken: HM Brig Lyra - When taken: 15 Dec 1812 - Where taken: off Bilboa, Spain - Date received: 3 Jan 1813 - From what ship: HM Frigate Fox - Born: Rostock, Prussia - Age: 36 - Discharged on 4 Mar 1813 and sent to Chatham on HM Ship-of-the-Line Queen.

Deering, William F, - Sailing Master - Number: 1290 - Prize Name: Growler - Ship type: P - How taken: HM Brig Electra - When taken: 7 Jul 1813 - Where taken: off St. Johns - Date received: 22 Dec 1813 - From what ship: HM Ship of-the-Line Bellerophon - Born: Portland - Age: 22 - Discharged on 26 Dec 1813 and sent to Chatham on HMS Frigate Nemesis.

Deistel, John - Seaman - Number: 613 - Prize Name: Sword Fish - Ship type: P - How taken: HM Ship-of-the-Line Elephant - When taken: 20 Dec 1812 - Where taken: at sea - Date received: 1 Feb 1813 - From what ship: HM Frigate Hermes - Born: Salem - Age: 35 - Discharged on 11 Mar 1813 and sent to Chatham on HM Store Ship Abundance.

Delancey, William - Seaman - Number: 240 - Prize Name: Antelope - Ship type: P - How taken: HM Brig Zephyr - When taken: 10 Dec 1812 - Where taken: at sea - Date received: 27 Dec 1812 - From what ship: HMS Zephyr - Born: Westchester, NY - Age: 16 - Discharged on 19 Feb 1813 and sent to Chatham on HM Store Ship Dromedary.

Delenne, John - 2nd Mate - Number: 733 - Prize Name: Dart - Ship type: MV - How taken: HM Brig Doterel - When taken: 5 Mar 1813 - Where taken: at sea - Date received: 21 Mar 1813 - From what ship: HMS Dotteril - Born: Hamburg, Germany - Age: 21 - Discharged on 25 Mar 1814 and sent to Reading on parole.

Demalo, Francis - Seaman - Number: 1391 - Prize Name: Pilate - Ship type: P - How taken: Victoria, privateer of Guernsey - When taken: 28 Jan 1814 - Where taken: off Bordeaux - Date received: 7 Feb 1814 - From what ship: Mary from Guernsey - Born: Philadelphia - Age: 22 - Race: Mulatto - Discharged on 13 Feb 1814 and sent to Chatham on HM Transport Malabar No. 352.

Demerie, Ephraim - Boy - Number: 1436 - Prize Name: HMS Devon Transport No. 15, prize of Privateer Bunker Hill - Ship type: MV - How taken: HM Brig Fly - When taken: 21 Jan 1814 - Where taken: at sea - Date received: 1 Mar 1814 - From what ship: HMS Helicone - Born: Paris, France - Age: 11 - Discharged on 28 Apr 1814 and sent to Chatham on HM Brig Cordelia.

Dempsey, Daniel - Boy - Number: 1196 - Prize Name: Fire Fly of Gloucester - Ship type: MV - How taken: HM Frigate Revolutionnaire - When taken: 19 Oct 1813 - Where taken: at sea - Date received: 9 Nov 1813 - From what ship: HMS Revolutionaire - Born: Gloucester - Age: 15 - Discharged on 26 Dec 1813 and sent to Chatham on HM Ship of-the-Line Diomede.

Denham, William - Seaman - Number: 632 - How taken: Gave himself up from HM Guardship Royal William - Date received: 3 Feb 1813 - From what ship: HMS Royal William - Born: New York - Age: 26 - Race: Black - Discharged on 11 Mar 1813 and sent to Chatham on HM Store Ship Abundance.

Dennis, John - Seaman - Number: 252 - Prize Name: King of Rome - Ship type: P - How taken: HM Brig Wolverine - When taken: 13 Dec 1812 - Where taken: at sea - Date received: 27 Dec 1812 - From what ship: HMS Wolverine - Born: Rhode Island - Age: 26 - Discharged on 19 Feb 1813 and sent to Chatham on HM Store Ship Dromedary.

Dennis, Thomas - Boy - Number: 77 - Prize Name: HMS Belleville - Ship type: MW - How taken: Detained by Court of Admiralty - When taken: 31 Jul 1812 - Where taken: Portsmouth harbor - Date received: 16 Oct 1812 San Antonio - From what ship: Belleville - Born: Ipswich - Age: 16 - Discharged on 19 Feb 1813 and sent to Chatham on HM Frigate Ulysses.

Dennis, Thomas - Seaman - Number: 920 - Prize Name: Tender of the True Blooded Yankee - Ship type: P - How taken: HM Ship-of-the-Line Fame - When taken: 24 Jun 1813 - Where taken: at sea - Date received: 1 Jul 1813 - From what ship: HM Brig Hope - Born: Newport - Age: 27 - Discharged on 2 Jul 1813 and sent to Chatham on HM Brig Scorpion.

Dennis, Thomas - Seaman - Number: 151 - Prize Name: William - Ship type: MV - How taken: HM Brig Recruit - When taken: 29 Aug 1812 - Where taken: at sea - Date received: 29 Oct 1812 - From what ship: HM Ship-of-the-Line Ardent - Born: Kent, MD - Age: 17 - Discharged on 19 Feb 1813 and sent to Chatham on HM Store Ship Dromedary.

Dennison, Lawson - Seaman - Number: 718 - How taken: Gave himself up from HM Frigate Niobe - Date received: 1 Mar 1813 - From what ship: HMS Niobe - Born: Vermont - Age: 23 - Discharged on 6 Mar 1813 and sent to Chatham on HM Ship-of-the-Line Cornwall.

Deselva, Manuel - Seaman - Number: 744 - Prize Name: Dart - Ship type: MV - How taken: HM Brig Doterel - When taken: 5 Mar 1813 - Where taken: at sea - Date received: 21 Mar 1813 - From what ship: HMS Dotteril - Born: Madeira, Portugal - Age: 15 - Discharged on 28 Mar 1813 and sent to Chatham on HM Store Ship Seaphis.

Deventer, William - Seaman - Number: 722 - How taken: Gave himself up from HM Frigate Niobe - Date received: 13 Mar 1813 - From what ship: HMS Niobe - Born: Philadelphia - Age: 31 - Discharged on 28 Mar 1813 and sent to Chatham on HM Store Ship Seaphis.

Deverence, Benjamin - Cooper - Number: 1308 - Prize Name: Growler - Ship type: P - How taken: HM Brig Electra - When taken: 7 Jul 1813 - Where taken: off St. Johns - Date received: 22 Dec 1813 - From what ship: HM Frigate Hyperion - Born: Salem - Age: 27 - Discharged on 26 Dec 1813 and sent to Chatham on HMS Frigate Nemesis.

Dews, William - Seaman - Number: 838 - How taken: Gave himself up from HM Frigate Melpomene - Date received: 8 Jun 1813 - From what ship: HM Guardship Royal William - Born: Savannah, GA - Age: 44 - Discharged on 10 Jun 1813 and sent to Chatham on HM Frigate Arethusa.

Dibble, Zachariah - Seaman - Number: 1369 - How taken: Gave himself up from HM Ship-of-the-Line Malta - Date received: 4 Feb 1814 - From what ship: HM Frigate Bombay - Born: Connecticut - Age: 40 - Discharged on 13 Feb 1814 and sent to Chatham on HM Transport Malabar No. 352.

Diemar, John - Seaman - Number: 1411 - Prize Name: General Kemp, prize of Privateer Grand Turk - Ship type: P - How taken: HM Brig Foxhound - When taken: 18 Dec 1813 - Where taken: at sea - Date received: 1 Mar 1814 - From what ship: HMS Helicone - Born: Marblehead - Age: 20 - Discharged on 28 Apr 1814 and sent to Chatham on HM Sloop Favorite.

Dildure, Samuel - Seaman - Number: 588 - How taken: Gave himself up from HM Ship-of-the-Line Mars - Date received: 31 Jan 1813 - From what ship: HMS Mars - Born: Princeton - Age: 21 - Discharged on 11 Mar 1813 and sent to Chatham on HM Store Ship Abundance.

Distouet, John - Captain - Number: 274 - Prize Name: King of Rome - Ship type: MV - How taken: HM Brig Wolverine - When taken: 13 Dec 1812 - Where taken: at sea - Date received: 29 Dec 1812 - From what ship: HMS Wolverine - Born: New York - Age: 47 - Discharged on 31 Dec 1812 and sent to Odiham on parole.

Dixon, Peter - Seaman - Number: 1368 - How taken: Gave himself up from HM Ship-of-the-Line Malta - Date received: 4 Feb 1814 - From what ship: HM Frigate Bombay - Born: New York - Age: 26 - Discharged on 13 Feb 1814 and sent to Chatham on HM Transport Malabar No. 352.

Dobbs, Jeremiah - Seaman - Number: 191 - Prize Name: Felix - Ship type: MV - How taken: HM Frigate Indefatigable - When taken: 13 Nov 1812 - Where taken: Portsmouth harbor - Date received: 22 Nov 1812 - From what ship: HM Frigate Gladiator - Born: New York - Age: 24 - Discharged on 19 Feb 1813 and sent to Chatham on HM Store Ship Dromedary.

Doevall, Francis - Boatswain's Mate - Number: 452 - Prize Name: Sword Fish - Ship type: P - How taken: HM Ship-of-the-Line Elephant - When taken: 28 Dec 1812 - Where taken: at sea - Date received: 14 Jan 1813 - From what ship: HMS Elephant - Born: Salem - Age: 35 - Discharged on 11 Mar 1813 and sent to Chatham on HM Store Ship Abundance.

Doliber, Joseph - 1st Mate - Number: 684 - Prize Name: Rachael - Ship type: MV - How taken: HM Schooner Herring - When taken: 8 Feb 1813 - Where taken: at sea - Date received: 17 Feb 1813 - From what ship: HMS Herring - Born: Marblehead - Age: 44 - Discharged on 6 Mar 1813 and sent to Chatham on HM Ship-of-the-Line Cornwall.

Dominico, Joseph - Seaman - Number: 68 - Prize Name: Diana, prize of Privateer Decatur - Ship type: MV - How taken: HM Ship-of-the-Line Polyphemus - When taken: 14 Sep 1812 - Where taken: at sea - Date received: 12 Oct 1812 San Antonio - From what ship: HM Ship-of-the-Line Polyphemus - Born: New York - Age: 21 - Discharged on 19 Feb 1813 and sent to Chatham on HM Frigate Ulysses.

Donaldson, Josiah - Seaman - Number: 876 - Prize Name: Dick - Ship type: MV - How taken: HM Brig Dispatch - When taken: 17 Mar 1813 - Where taken: Bay of Biscay - Date received: 24 Jun 1813 - From what ship: HM Frigate Unicorn - Born: New York - Age: 21 - Discharged on 2 Jul 1813 and sent to Chatham on HM Frigate Tribune.

Doosenberry, Richard - Seaman - Number: 1452 - Prize Name: Lord Ponsonbe, prize of the Privateer Diomede - Ship type: MV - How taken: HM Brig Sappho - When taken: 27 Feb 1814 - Where taken: at sea - Date received: 31 May 1814 - From what ship: HM Ship-of-the-Line Valiant - Born: New York - Age: 32 - Discharged on 28 Apr 1814 and sent to Chatham on HM Store Ship Weymouth.

Dorr, Edward - Prize Master - Number: 48 - Prize Name: Fame, prize of Privateer Decatur - Ship type: MV - How taken: HM Ship-of-the-Line Polyphemus - When taken: 13 Sep 1812 - Where taken: at sea - Date received: 12 Oct 1812 San Antonio - From what ship: HM Ship-of-the-Line Polyphemus - Born: Salisbury - Age: 29 - Discharged on 19 Feb 1813 and sent to Chatham on HM Frigate Ulysses.

Douglas, Charles - Seaman - Number: 571 - Prize Name: Rossie - Ship type: MV - How taken: HM Frigate Dryand - When taken: 7 Jan 1813 - Where taken: at sea - Date received: 25 Jan 1813 - From what ship: HM Ship-of-the-Line Queen - Born: Virginia - Age: 24 - Discharged on 11 Mar 1813 and sent to Chatham on HM Store Ship Abundance.

Douglas, Thomas - Seaman - Number: 429 - Prize Name: Columbia - Ship type: MV - How taken: Unknown British warship - Where taken: at sea - Date received: 10 Jan 1813 - From what ship: HM Guardship Royal William - Born: Rhode Island - Age: 25 - Race: Black - Discharged on 6 Mar 1813 and sent to Chatham on HMS Frigate Alexandria.

Dowling, Peter - Seaman - Number: 133 - How taken: Gave himself up from HM Ship-of-the-Line Ruby - When taken: 30 Aug 1812 - Date received: 29 Oct 1812 - From what ship: HM Ship-of-the-Line Ardent - Born: Wells Town, PA - Age: 24 - Discharged on 19 Feb 1813 and sent to Chatham on HM Store Ship Dromedary.

Downs, John - Boy - Number: 1379 - Prize Name: Pilate - Ship type: P - How taken: Victoria, privateer of Guernsey - When taken: 28 Jan 1814 - Where taken: off Bordeaux - Date received: 7 Feb 1814 - From what ship: Mary from Guernsey - Born: Philadelphia - Age: 10 - Discharged on 13 Feb 1814 and sent to Chatham on HM Transport Malabar No. 352.

Downs, William - Boy - Number: 1378 - Prize Name: Pilate - Ship type: P - How taken: Victoria, privateer of Guernsey - When taken: 28 Jan 1814 - Where taken: off Bordeaux - Date received: 7 Feb 1814 - From what ship: Mary from Guernsey - Born: Philadelphia - Age: 16 - Discharged on 13 Feb 1814 and sent to Chatham on HM Transport Malabar No. 352.

Drew, William - Seaman - Number: 436 - How taken: Gave himself up from HM Transport Flora - Date received: 11 Jan 1813 - From what ship: HMS Flora - Born: Edenton, NC - Age: 26 - Died on 2 Mar 1813.

Drinkwater, Andrew - Seaman - Number: 14 - Prize Name: USRM Cutter James Madison - Ship type: MW - How taken: HM Frigate Barbadoes - When taken: 22 Aug 1812 - Where taken: at sea - Date received: 12 Oct 1812 San Antonio - From what ship: HM Ship-of-the-Line Polyphemus - Born: New Yarmouth, MA - Age: 23 - Discharged on 19 Feb 1813 and sent to Chatham on HM Frigate Ulysses.

Drybourgh, James - 2nd Mate - Number: 355 - Prize Name: Argus - Ship type: MV - How taken: Fancy, cutter - When taken: 19 Dec 1812 - Where taken: Bay of Biscay - Date received: 31 Dec 1812 - From what ship: HM Ship-of-the-Line Northumberland - Born: Philadelphia - Age: 21 - Discharged on 4 Mar 1813 and sent to Chatham on HM Ship-of-the-Line Queen.

Dudley, Ephraim - Marine Sergeant - Number: 493 - Prize Name: Sword Fish - Ship type: P - How taken: HM Ship-of-the-Line Elephant - When taken: 28 Dec 1812 - Where taken: at sea - Date received: 14 Jan 1813 - From what ship: HMS Elephant - Born: East Sudbury - Age: 25 - Discharged on 11 Mar 1813 and sent to Chatham on HM Store Ship Abundance.

Duhard, Thomas - 3rd Mate - Number: 574 - Prize Name: Rossie - Ship type: MV - How taken: HM Frigate Dryand - When taken: 7 Jan 1813 - Where taken: at sea - Date received: 25 Jan 1813 - From what ship: HM Ship-of-the-Line Queen - Born: Baltimore - Age: 21 - Discharged on 11 Mar 1813 and sent to Chatham on HM Store Ship Abundance.

Duncan, Edward - Seaman - Number: 1082 - How taken: Gave himself up from HM Ship-of-the-Line Hibernia - Date received: 1 Oct 1813 - From what ship: HM Ship-of-the-Line Barham - Born: Rhode Island - Age: 38 - Discharged on 17 Oct 1813 and sent to Chatham on HM Store Ship Weymouth.

Duncan, Edward - Seaman - Number: 1056 - How taken: Gave himself up from HM Ship-of-the-Line Hibernia - Date received: 19 Sep 1813 - From what ship: HM Brig Imogen - Born: Rhode Island - Age: 38 - Race: Mulatto - Discharged on 29 Sep 1813 and sent to Chatham on HM Transport Chatham.

Dunham, Daniel - Seaman - Number: 1004 - Prize Name: Fame - Ship type: MV - How taken: HM Ship of-the-Line Cressy - When taken: 20 Jul 1813 - Where taken: at sea - Date received: 18 Aug 1813 - From what ship: HMS Cressy - Born: Massachusetts - Age: 27 - Discharged on 21 Sep 1813 and sent to Chatham on HM Ship-of-the-Line Queen.

Dunham, John - Seaman - Number: 1021 - How taken: Gave himself up from HM Ship-of-the-Line Scipion - Date received: 7 Sep 1813 - From what ship: HM Frigate Unicorn - Born: Massachusetts - Age: 20 - Discharged on 21 Sep 1813 and sent to Chatham on HM Ship-of-the-Line Queen.

Dunn, David - Seaman - Number: 901 - Prize Name: Weasel - Ship type: MV - How taken: Foxhound, privateer - When taken: 25 May 1813 - Where taken: Bay of Biscay - Date received: 24 Jun 1813 - From what ship: HM Frigate Unicorn - Born: New York - Age: 27 - Discharged on 2 Jul 1813 and sent to Chatham on HM Frigate Tribune.

Dunn, Hezekiah - Seaman - Number: 354 - Prize Name: Experiment - Ship type: MV - How taken: HM Brig Rover - When taken: 10 Nov 1812 - Where taken: off Bordeaux - Date received: 31 Dec 1812 - From what ship: HM Ship-of-the-Line Northumberland - Born: Maryland - Age: 24 - Discharged on 4 Mar 1813 and sent to Chatham on HM Ship-of-the-Line Queen.

Dunn, James - Seaman - Number: 946 - How taken: Gave himself up from HM Frigate Unicorn - Date received: 8 Jun 1813 - From what ship: HMS Eldegon - Born: Boston - Age: 30 - Race: Mulatto - Discharged on 7 Aug 1813 and sent to Chatham on HM Brig Rinaldo.

Dunning, William - Seaman - Number: 1499 - How taken: Gave himself up from HM Frigate Forth - Date received: 10 Jun 1814 - From what ship: HMS Forth - Born: Massachusetts - Age: 38 - Discharged on 30 Jun 1814 and sent to Plymouth on HM Brig Steady.

Dunslan, John - Seaman - Number: 586 - How taken: Gave himself up from HM Transport Diadem - Date received: 30 Jan 1813 - From what ship: HMS Diadem - Born: Baltimore - Age: 23 - Discharged on 11 Mar 1813 and sent to Chatham on HM Store Ship Abundance.

Dunvall, N. D. - Seaman - Number: 1066 - Prize Name: Hindostan - Ship type: MV - How taken: HM Brig Zenobia - When taken: 25 Jun 1813 - Where taken: off Lisbon - Date received: 19 Sep 1813 - From what ship: HM Brig Imogen - Born: Maryland - Age: 23 - Discharged on 29 Sep 1813 and sent to Chatham on HM Transport Chatham (see Prisoner Number 1091).

Dussing, Caesar - Seaman - Number: 287 - Prize Name: Purse - Ship type: MV - How taken: HM Frigate Armide - When taken: 29 May 1812 - Where taken: off Bordeaux - Date received: 31 Dec 1812 - From what ship: HM Ship-of-the-Line Northumberland - Born: Isle of France - Age: 19 - Discharged on 19 Feb 1813 and sent to Chatham on HM Frigate Ulysses.

Duvall, N. D. - Seaman - Number: 1091 - Prize Name: Hindostan - Ship type: MV - How taken: HM Brig Zenobia - When taken: 25 Jun 1813 - Where taken: off Lisbon - Date received: 1 Oct 1813 - From what ship: HM Ship-of-the-Line Barham - Born: Maryland - Age: 23 - Discharged on 17 Oct 1813 and sent to Chatham on HM

Store Ship Weymouth (see Prisoner Number 1066).

Duxey, Peter - Cook - Number: 453 - Prize Name: Sword Fish - Ship type: P - How taken: HM Ship-of-the-Line Elephant - When taken: 28 Dec 1812 - Where taken: at sea - Date received: 14 Jan 1813 - From what ship: HMS Elephant - Born: Marblehead - Age: 44 - Discharged on 11 Mar 1813 and sent to Chatham on HM Store Ship Abundance.

Dyer, Ezekiel - Seaman - Number: 158 - Prize Name: Diamond - Ship type: MV - How taken: Detained at Bermuda - When taken: 17 Apr 1812 - Where taken: Bermuda - Date received: 29 Oct 1812 - From what ship: HM Ship-of-the-Line Ardent - Born: Cape Elizabeth, MA - Age: 43 - Discharged on 19 Feb 1813 and sent to Chatham on HM Store Ship Dromedary.

Dyson, Henry - Midshipman - Number: 1201 - Prize Name: Fly, prize of US Frigate President - Ship type: MV - How taken: HM Transport Regulus & HM Frigate Melpomene - When taken: 11 Sep 1813 - Where taken: at sea - Date received: 13 Nov 1813 - From what ship: HM Transport Regulus - Born: Beverly, MA - Age: 25 - Discharged on 21 Dec 1814 and sent to Reading on parole.

Earl, Maris - Seaman - Number: 525 - Prize Name: Expectation - Ship type: MV - How taken: HMS Butain - When taken: 17 Dec 1812 - Where taken: at sea - Date received: 25 Jan 1813 - From what ship: HM Ship-of-the-Line Queen - Born: New York - Age: 27 - Discharged on 11 Mar 1813 and sent to Chatham on HM Store Ship Abundance.

Eastlake, James - Seaman - Number: 991 - Prize Name: Jane, prize of the Privateer Snap Dragon - Ship type: MV - How taken: HM Frigate Crescent & HM Ship of-the-Line Bellerophon - When taken: 28 Jun 1813 - Where taken: at sea - Date received: 9 Aug 1813 - From what ship: HM Sloop Hazard - Born: North Carolina - Age: 21 - Discharged on 13 Aug 1813 and sent to Chatham on HM Brig Cadmus.

Eaton, James - Seaman - Number: 846 - How taken: Gave himself up from HM Ship-of-the-Line Malta - Date received: 15 Jun 1813 - From what ship: HM Sloop Helena - Born: Philadelphia - Age: 26 - Discharged on 2 Jul 1813 and sent to Chatham on HM Frigate Tribune.

Eaton, John - Seaman - Number: 551 - Prize Name: Rossie - Ship type: MV - How taken: HM Frigate Dryand - When taken: 7 Jan 1813 - Where taken: at sea - Date received: 25 Jan 1813 - From what ship: HM Ship-of-the-Line Queen - Born: Cohasset, MA - Age: 21 - Discharged on 11 Mar 1813 and sent to Chatham on HM Store Ship Abundance.

Edwards, Isaac - Seaman - Number: 801 - How taken: Gave himself up from HM Ship-of-the-Line Scepter - Date received: 21 Apr 1813 - From what ship: HM Guardship Royal William - Born: Gorham, MA - Age: 34 - Discharged on 27 Apr 1813 and sent to Chatham on HM Sloop-of-War Bonne Citoyenne.

Edwards, John - Seaman - Number: 776 - How taken: Gave himself up from HM Frigate Brune - Date received: 1 Apr 1813 - From what ship: HM Ship-of-the-Line Blake - Born: New York - Age: 34 - Race: Black - Discharged on 3 Apr 1813 and sent to Chatham on HM Transport Chatham.

Eldridge, Samuel - Seaman - Number: 89 - Prize Name: HM Frigate Janus - Ship type: MW - How taken: Detained by Court of Admiralty - When taken: 31 Jul 1812 - Where taken: Portsmouth harbor - Date received: 16 Oct 1812 San Antonio - From what ship: HM Frigate Janus - Born: Lyman, MA - Age: 22 - Discharged on 19 Feb 1813 and sent to Chatham on HM Frigate Ulysses.

Elfe, James - Boy - Number: 1069 - Prize Name: Hindostan - Ship type: MV - How taken: HM Brig Zenobia - When taken: 25 Jun 1813 - Where taken: off Lisbon - Date received: 19 Sep 1813 - From what ship: HM Brig Imogen - Born: Charlestown - Age: 12 - Discharged on 29 Sep 1813 and sent to Chatham on HM Transport Chatham (see Prisoner Number 1094).

Elfe, James - Boy - Number: 1094 - Prize Name: Hindostan - Ship type: MV - How taken: HM Brig Zenobia - When taken: 25 Jun 1813 - Where taken: off Lisbon - Date received: 1 Oct 1813 - From what ship: HM Ship-of-the-Line Barham - Born: Charleston - Age: 15 - Discharged on 17 Oct 1813 and sent to Chatham on HM Store Ship Weymouth (see Prisoner Number 1069).

Ellingwood, William H. - Marine - Number: 1319 - Prize Name: Growler - Ship type: P - How taken: HM Brig Electra - When taken: 7 Jul 1813 - Where taken: off St. Johns - Date received: 24 Dec 1813 - From what ship: HM Schooner Adonis - Born: Beverly - Age: 28 - Discharged on 26 Dec 1813 and sent to Chatham on

HMS Frigate Nemesis.

Ellis, John - Seaman - Number: 7 - Prize Name: USRM Cutter James Madison - Ship type: MW - How taken: HM Frigate Barbadoes - When taken: 22 Aug 1812 - Where taken: at sea - Date received: 12 Oct 1812 San Antonio - From what ship: HM Ship-of-the-Line Polyphemus - Born: Copstown, MD - Age: 23 - Discharged on 19 Feb 1813 and sent to Chatham on HM Frigate Ulysses.

Ellis, John - Seaman - Number: 350 - Prize Name: Experiment - Ship type: MV - How taken: HM Brig Rover - When taken: 10 Nov 1812 - Where taken: off Bordeaux - Date received: 31 Dec 1812 - From what ship: HM Ship-of-the-Line Northumberland - Born: New York - Age: 21 - Discharged on 4 Mar 1813 and sent to Chatham on HM Ship-of-the-Line Queen.

Ellis, William - Seaman - Number: 550 - Prize Name: Rossie - Ship type: MV - How taken: HM Frigate Dryand - When taken: 7 Jan 1813 - Where taken: at sea - Date received: 25 Jan 1813 - From what ship: HM Ship-of-the-Line Queen - Born: Baltimore - Age: 26 - Discharged on 11 Mar 1813 and sent to Chatham on HM Store Ship Abundance.

Ellwell, Jonathan - Seaman - Number: 459 - Prize Name: Sword Fish - Ship type: P - How taken: HM Ship-of-the-Line Elephant - When taken: 28 Dec 1812 - Where taken: at sea - Date received: 14 Jan 1813 - From what ship: HMS Elephant - Born: St. George - Age: 28 - Discharged on 11 Mar 1813 and sent to Chatham on HM Store Ship Abundance.

Elwell, Benjamin (1) - Mate - Number: 1197 - Prize Name: Fire Fly of Gloucester - Ship type: MV - How taken: HM Frigate Revolutionnaire - When taken: 19 Oct 1813 - Where taken: at sea - Date received: 9 Nov 1813 - From what ship: HMS Revolutionaire - Born: Boston - Age: 25 - Discharged on 26 Dec 1813 and sent to Chatham on HM Ship of-the-Line Diomede.

Elwell, Benjamin (2) - Master - Number: 1186 - Prize Name: Fire Fly of Gloucester - Ship type: MV - How taken: HM Frigate Revolutionnaire - When taken: 19 Oct 1813 - Where taken: at sea - Date received: 9 Nov 1813 - From what ship: HMS Revolutionaire - Born: Boston - Age: 35 - Discharged on 16 Nov 1814 and sent to Reading on parole.

Emery, Adrien D. - Marine - Number: 1473 - Prize Name: Bunker Hill - Ship type: P - How taken: HM Frigate Pomone & HM Frigate Cydnus - When taken: 4 Mar 1814 - Where taken: French coast - Date received: 11 Apr 1814 - From what ship: HMS Ship-on-the-Line San Domaso - Born: Melun, France - Age: 17 - Discharged on 28 Apr 1814 and sent to Chatham on HM Store Ship Weymouth.

Emerson, David - Marine - Number: 1220 - Prize Name: Growler - Ship type: P - How taken: HM Brig Electra - When taken: 7 Jul 1813 - Where taken: at sea - Date received: 16 Nov 1813 - From what ship: HM Sloop Talbot - Born: Newbury - Age: 22 - Discharged on 26 Dec 1813 and sent to Chatham on HM Ship of-the-Line Diomede.

Esperaza, Jacob - Seaman - Number: 532 - Prize Name: Expectation - Ship type: MV - How taken: HMS Butain - When taken: 17 Dec 1812 - Where taken: at sea - Date received: 25 Jan 1813 - From what ship: HM Ship-of-the-Line Queen - Born: Virginia - Age: 34 - Discharged on 11 Mar 1813 and sent to Chatham on HM Store Ship Abundance.

Estery, William - Seaman - Number: 840 - How taken: Gave himself up from HMS Horatio - Date received: 11 Jun 1813 - From what ship: HMS Horatio - Born: Morristown, NJ - Age: 22 - Discharged on 2 Jul 1813 and sent to Chatham on HM Frigate Tribune.

Euston, Ephraim - Seaman - Number: 1219 - Prize Name: Growler - Ship type: P - How taken: HM Brig Electra - When taken: 7 Jul 1813 - Where taken: at sea - Date received: 16 Nov 1813 - From what ship: HM Sloop Talbot - Born: Marblehead - Age: 20 - Discharged on 26 Dec 1813 and sent to Chatham on HM Ship of-the-Line Diomede.

Evans, John - Seaman - Number: 290 - Prize Name: Thomas Willson - Ship type: MV - How taken: Taken up on shore - When taken: 18 Oct 1812 - Where taken: Liverpool - Date received: 31 Dec 1812 - From what ship: HM Ship-of-the-Line Northumberland - Born: Norfolk - Age: 20 - Discharged on 19 Feb 1813 and sent to Chatham on HM Frigate Ulysses.

Evans, John - Captain - Number: 502 - Prize Name: Sword Fish - Ship type: P - How taken: HM Ship-of-the-Line

Elephant - When taken: 28 Dec 1812 - Where taken: at sea - Date received: 15 Jan 1813 - From what ship: HMS Elephant - Born: Gloucester - Age: 29 - Discharged on 11 Mar 1813 and sent to Chatham on HM Store Ship Abundance.

Evans, Thomas - Seaman - Number: 418 - Prize Name: Rising Sun - Ship type: MV - How taken: HMS Defense - When taken: 6 Dec 1812 - Where taken: at sea - Date received: 10 Jan 1813 - From what ship: HM Guardship Royal William - Born: Rhode Island - Age: 32 - Discharged on 6 Mar 1813 and sent to Chatham on HMS Frigate Alexandria.

Even, Peter - Sailmaker - Number: 6 - Prize Name: USRM Cutter James Madison - Ship type: MW - How taken: HM Frigate Barbadoes - When taken: 22 Aug 1812 - Where taken: at sea - Date received: 12 Oct 1812 San Antonio - From what ship: HM Ship-of-the-Line Polyphemus - Born: Nantes, France - Age: 45 - Discharged on 19 Feb 1813 and sent to Chatham on HM Frigate Ulysses.

Ewell, Edward - Seaman - Number: 1442 - Prize Name: HMS Devon Transport No. 15, prize of Privateer Bunker Hill - Ship type: MV - How taken: HM Brig Fly - When taken: 21 Jan 1814 - Where taken: at sea - Date received: 1 Mar 1814 - From what ship: HMS Helicone - Born: Norfolk - Age: 21 - Discharged on 28 Apr 1814 and sent to Chatham on HM Brig Cordelia.

Farman, William - Carpenter - Number: 1307 - Prize Name: Growler - Ship type: P - How taken: HM Brig Electra - When taken: 7 Jul 1813 - Where taken: off St. Johns - Date received: 22 Dec 1813 - From what ship: HM Frigate Hyperion - Born: Eaton, NH - Age: 27 - Discharged on 26 Dec 1813 and sent to Chatham on HMS Frigate Nemesis.

Farrel, John - Seaman - Number: 328 - Prize Name: Independence - Ship type: MV - How taken: HM Frigate Medusa - When taken: 9 Nov 1812 - Where taken: off St. Sebastian - Date received: 31 Dec 1812 - From what ship: HM Ship-of-the-Line Northumberland - Born: New Jersey - Age: 24 - Discharged on 4 Mar 1813 and sent to Chatham on HM Ship-of-the-Line Queen.

Farris, Jacob - Seaman - Number: 592 - How taken: Gave himself up from HM Ship-of-the-Line Mars - Date received: 31 Jan 1813 - From what ship: HMS Mars - Born: New York - Age: 32 - Discharged on 11 Mar 1813 and sent to Chatham on HM Store Ship Abundance.

Fate, Thomas - Seaman - Number: 345 - Prize Name: Experiment - Ship type: MV - How taken: HM Brig Rover - When taken: 10 Nov 1812 - Where taken: off Bordeaux - Date received: 31 Dec 1812 - From what ship: HM Ship-of-the-Line Northumberland - Born: Maryland - Age: 34 - Discharged on 4 Mar 1813 and sent to Chatham on HM Ship-of-the-Line Queen.

Ferguson, John T. - Seaman - Number: 518 - How taken: Gave himself up from HM Ship-of-the-Line Tigre - Date received: 23 Jan 1813 - From what ship: HMS Tigre - Born: Wiscasset, MA - Age: 27 - Discharged on 11 Mar 1813 and sent to Chatham on HM Store Ship Abundance.

Ferlecque, Augustine - Seaman - Number: 1472 - Prize Name: Bunker Hill - Ship type: P - How taken: HM Frigate Pomone & HM Frigate Cydnus - When taken: 4 Mar 1814 - Where taken: French coast - Date received: 11 Apr 1814 - From what ship: HMS Ship-on-the-Line San Domaso - Born: Brest, France - Age: 27 - Discharged on 28 Apr 1814 and sent to Chatham on HM Store Ship Weymouth.

Fernandes, Anthony - Seaman - Number: 465 - Prize Name: Sword Fish - Ship type: P - How taken: HM Ship-of-the-Line Elephant - When taken: 28 Dec 1812 - Where taken: at sea - Date received: 14 Jan 1813 - From what ship: HMS Elephant - Born: Corunna, Spain - Age: 24 - Discharged on 11 Mar 1813 and sent to Chatham on HM Store Ship Abundance.

Ferriers, George - Seaman - Number: 654 - How taken: Sent into custody from Hyde Rendezvous - Date received: 4 Feb 1813 - From what ship: Hyde Rendezvous - Born: Ipswich, MA - Age: 26 - Discharged on 11 Mar 1813 and sent to Chatham on HM Store Ship Abundance.

Ferris, James - Seaman - Number: 1229 - How taken: Gave himself up from HM Ship-of-the-Line Invincible - Date received: 24 Nov 1813 - From what ship: HM Transport Leopard - Born: Cambridge - Age: 26 - Discharged on 26 Dec 1813 and sent to Chatham on HM Ship of-the-Line Diomede.

Fields, Alexander - Seaman - Number: 947 - How taken: Gave himself up from HM Frigate Unicorn - Date received: 8 Jun 1813 - From what ship: HMS Eldegon - Born: Charlestown - Age: 23 - Discharged on 7 Aug

1813 and sent to Chatham on HM Brig Rinaldo.

Fisher, Archibald - Seaman - Number: 247 - Prize Name: Antelope - Ship type: P - How taken: HM Brig Zephyr - When taken: 10 Dec 1812 - Where taken: at sea - Date received: 27 Dec 1812 - From what ship: HMS Zephyr - Born: Renfewshire, Scotland - Age: 26 - Released on 3 Jan 1813.

Fiske, Lebairs - Seaman - Number: 1372 - Prize Name: Brillliant, prize to Privateer Prince Neuchatel - Ship type: MV - How taken: Caught on the Alderney Island - When taken: 26 Jan 1814 - Where taken: Alderney - Date received: 7 Feb 1814 - From what ship: Mary from Guernsey - Born: Massachusetts - Age: 27 - Discharged on 13 Feb 1814 and sent to Chatham on HM Transport Malabar No. 352.

Fitch, William - Seaman - Number: 768 - Prize Name: Pallas - Ship type: MV - How taken: HM Brig Rebuff - When taken: 23 Jan 1813 - Where taken: Cadiz - Date received: 1 Apr 1813 - From what ship: HM Ship-of-the-Line Blake - Born: New York - Age: 21 - Discharged on 3 Apr 1813 and sent to Chatham on HM Transport Chatham.

Fleming, Alexander - Seaman - Number: 1146 - Prize Name: Maydock - Ship type: MV - How taken: HM Brig Rebuff - When taken: 16 Jun 1813 - Where taken: St. Mary's - Date received: 6 Oct 1813 - From what ship: HM Sloop Kingfisher - Born: Massachusetts - Age: 26 - Discharged on 17 Oct 1813 and sent to Chatham on HM Transport Malabar No. 352.

Flinn, Pearce - Seaman - Number: 1494 - Prize Name: Traveler, prize of the Privateer Surprise - Ship type: MV - How taken: HM Schooner Canso - When taken: 14 May 1814 - Where taken: at sea - Date received: 1 Jun 1814 - From what ship: HMS Canso - Born: Charlestown - Age: 22 - Discharged on 2 Jun 1814 and sent to Plymouth on HMS Growler.

Flood, John - Able Seaman - Number: 797 - How taken: Gave himself up from HM Ship-of-the-Line Sterling Castle - Date received: 18 Apr 1813 - From what ship: HM Guardship Royal William - Born: Portland - Age: 22 - Discharged on 27 Apr 1813 and sent to Chatham on HM Sloop-of-War Bonne Citoyenne.

Florence, Charles - Gunner - Number: 1305 - Prize Name: Growler - Ship type: P - How taken: HM Brig Electra - When taken: 7 Jul 1813 - Where taken: off St. Johns - Date received: 22 Dec 1813 - From what ship: HM Frigate Hyperion - Born: Marblehead - Age: 55 - Discharged on 26 Dec 1813 and sent to Chatham on HMS Frigate Nemesis.

Flower, Artemas - Seaman - Number: 357 - Prize Name: Argus - Ship type: MV - How taken: Fancy, cutter - When taken: 19 Dec 1812 - Where taken: Bay of Biscay - Date received: 31 Dec 1812 - From what ship: HM Ship-of-the-Line Northumberland - Born: Connecticut - Age: 35 - Discharged on 4 Mar 1813 and sent to Chatham on HM Ship-of-the-Line Queen.

Floyd, James - Seaman - Number: 319 - Prize Name: Taken on shore - How taken: HM Battery Princess - When taken: 27 Oct 1812 - Where taken: Liverpool - Date received: 31 Dec 1812 - From what ship: HM Ship-of-the-Line Northumberland - Born: New York - Age: 28 - Race: Black - Discharged on 4 Mar 1813 and sent to Chatham on HM Ship-of-the-Line Queen.

Foler, Frederic - Seaman - Number: 1102 - How taken: Gave himself up from HM Ship-of-the-Line Swiftsure - Date received: 5 Oct 1813 - From what ship: HM Ship-of-the-Line Achille - Born: Baltimore - Age: 27 - Discharged on 17 Oct 1813 and sent to Chatham on HM Store Ship Weymouth.

Folga, Noah - Seaman - Number: 1007 - Prize Name: Fame - Ship type: MV - How taken: HM Ship of-the-Line Cressy - When taken: 20 Jul 1813 - Where taken: at sea - Date received: 18 Aug 1813 - From what ship: HMS Cressy - Born: Nantucket - Age: 18 - Released on 12 Sep 1813 and sent to London.

Follingsby, William - Seaman - Number: 935 - Prize Name: Tender of the True Blooded Yankee - Ship type: P - How taken: HM Ship-of-the-Line Fame - When taken: 24 Jun 1813 - Where taken: at sea - Date received: 1 Jul 1813 - From what ship: HM Brig Hope - Born: Newburyport - Age: 29 - Discharged on 2 Jul 1813 and sent to Chatham on HM Brig Scorpion.

Fontain, Isaac - Seaman - Number: 326 - Prize Name: Independence - Ship type: MV - How taken: HM Frigate Medusa - When taken: 9 Nov 1812 - Where taken: off St. Sebastian - Date received: 31 Dec 1812 - From what ship: HM Ship-of-the-Line Northumberland - Born: New York - Age: 25 - Discharged on 4 Mar 1813 and sent to Chatham on HM Ship-of-the-Line Queen.

Ford, M. Benjamin - Seaman - Number: 556 - Prize Name: Rossie - Ship type: MV - How taken: HM Frigate Dryand - When taken: 7 Jan 1813 - Where taken: at sea - Date received: 25 Jan 1813 - From what ship: HM Ship-of-the-Line Queen - Born: Charlestown - Age: 20 - Discharged on 11 Mar 1813 and sent to Chatham on HM Store Ship Abundance.

Forest, James - Seaman - Number: 845 - How taken: Gave himself up from HM Ship-of-the-Line Malta - Date received: 15 Jun 1813 - From what ship: HM Sloop Helena - Born: Philadelphia - Age: 40 - Discharged on 2 Jul 1813 and sent to Chatham on HM Frigate Tribune.

Foster, George - Seaman - Number: 1315 - Prize Name: Growler - Ship type: P - How taken: HM Brig Electra - When taken: 7 Jul 1813 - Where taken: off St. Johns - Date received: 22 Dec 1813 - From what ship: HM Frigate Hyperion - Born: Marblehead - Age: 42 - Discharged on 26 Dec 1813 and sent to Chatham on HMS Frigate Nemesis.

Foster, Thomas - Seaman - Number: 1048 - How taken: Gave himself up from HM Ship-of-the-Line Scipion - Date received: 14 Sep 1813 - From what ship: HM Brig Savage - Born: Plymouth, MA - Age: 28 - Discharged on 29 Sep 1813 and sent to Chatham on HM Ship-of-the-Line Barham.

Francis, Frederick - Seaman - Number: 462 - Prize Name: Sword Fish - Ship type: P - How taken: HM Ship-of-the-Line Elephant - When taken: 28 Dec 1812 - Where taken: at sea - Date received: 14 Jan 1813 - From what ship: HMS Elephant - Born: Salem - Age: 19 - Race: Black - Discharged on 11 Mar 1813 and sent to Chatham on HM Store Ship Abundance.

Francis, John - Seaman - Number: 816 - How taken: Gave himself up from HM Service - Date received: 10 May 1813 - From what ship: HMS Puifrant - Born: Baltimore - Age: 38 - Race: Mulatto - Discharged on 17 May 1813 and sent to Chatham on HMS Impeleux.

Francis, John - Seaman - Number: 1231 - How taken: Gave himself up from HM Sloop-of-War Bonne Citoyenne - Date received: 25 Nov 1813 - From what ship: HMS Bonne Citeyenne - Born: Nantucket - Age: 22 - Race: Black - Discharged on 26 Dec 1813 and sent to Chatham on HM Ship of-the-Line Diomede.

Francis, Prince - Seaman - Number: 651 - How taken: Gave himself up from HM Sloop Albacore - Date received: 3 Feb 1813 - From what ship: HMS Albacore - Born: Connecticut - Age: 32 - Race: Black - Discharged on 11 Mar 1813 and sent to Chatham on HM Store Ship Abundance.

Francoise, James - Seaman - Number: 333 - Prize Name: Independence - Ship type: MV - How taken: HM Frigate Medusa - When taken: 9 Nov 1812 - Where taken: off St. Sebastian - Date received: 31 Dec 1812 - From what ship: HM Ship-of-the-Line Northumberland - Born: New Orleans - Age: 16 - Race: Colored - Discharged on 4 Mar 1813 and sent to Chatham on HM Ship-of-the-Line Queen.

Frazier, John - Seaman - Number: 854 - How taken: Gave himself up from HM Frigate Leonidas - Date received: 22 Jun 1813 - From what ship: HM Ship-of-the-Line Vigo - Born: New York - Age: 29 - Discharged on 2 Jul 1813 and sent to Chatham on HM Frigate Tribune.

Frazier, William - Seaman - Number: 1166 - Prize Name: Russian merchant vessel - How taken: Taken out of the HM Ship-of-the-Line Neptune - When taken: 28 Sep 1813 - Where taken: Cork - Date received: 12 Oct 1813 - From what ship: HM Brig Hope - Born: Pennsylvania - Age: 31 - Discharged on 17 Oct 1813 and sent to Chatham on HM Transport Malabar No. 352.

Frederick, John (1) - Seaman - Number: 1251 - Prize Name: Dart - Ship type: P - How taken: HM Frigate Niger & HMS Fortunee - Where taken: at sea - Date received: 19 Dec 1813 - From what ship: HMS Fortunee - Born: New Orleans - Age: 32 - Discharged on 26 Dec 1813 and sent to Chatham on HM Ship of-the-Line Diomede.

Frederick, John (2) - Seaman - Number: 769 - Prize Name: Miser Merchant Ship - How taken: Taken from the HM Transport Mariner No. 146 - Date received: 1 Apr 1813 - From what ship: HM Ship-of-the-Line Blake - Born: New Orleans - Age: 20 - Race: Colored - Discharged on 3 Apr 1813 and sent to Chatham on HM Transport Chatham.

Freeman, Alkine - Seaman - Number: 309 - Prize Name: Catherine - Ship type: MV - How taken: HM Frigate Leonidas - When taken: 31 Dec 1812 - Where taken: off Ireland - Date received: 31 Dec 1812 - From what ship: HM Ship-of-the-Line Northumberland - Born: Boston - Age: 17 - Discharged on 4 Mar 1813 and sent to Chatham on HM Ship-of-the-Line Queen.

Frobes, Robert - Seaman - Number: 968 - How taken: Gave himself up from HM Ship-of-the-Line Leviathan - Date received: 31 Jul 1813 - From what ship: HMS Leviathan - Born: New Jersey - Age: 32 - Discharged on 7 Aug 1813 and sent to Chatham on HM Brig Rinaldo.

Fron, Frederick - Seaman - Number: 390 - Prize Name: Empress - Ship type: MV - How taken: HM Brig Rover - When taken: 30 Nov 1812 - Where taken: at sea - Date received: 10 Jan 1813 - From what ship: HM Guardship Royal William - Born: Bremen, Germany - Age: 25 - Discharged on 4 Mar 1813 and sent to Chatham on HM Ship-of-the-Line Queen.

Fry, Thomas - Seaman - Number: 1127 - How taken: Gave himself up from HM Ship-of-the-Line Achille - Date received: 5 Oct 1813 - From what ship: HM Ship-of-the-Line Achille - Born: Newport, RI - Age: 36 - Discharged on 17 Oct 1813 and sent to Chatham on HM Transport Malabar No. 352.

Fuller, John - Seaman - Number: 924 - Prize Name: Tender of the True Blooded Yankee - Ship type: P - How taken: HM Ship-of-the-Line Fame - When taken: 24 Jun 1813 - Where taken: at sea - Date received: 1 Jul 1813 - From what ship: HM Brig Hope - Born: Salem - Age: 27 - Discharged on 2 Jul 1813 and sent to Chatham on HM Brig Scorpion.

Fuster, Peter - Seaman - Number: 278 - Prize Name: King of Rome - Ship type: MV - How taken: HM Brig Wolverine - When taken: 23 Dec 1812 - Where taken: at sea - Date received: 30 Dec 1812 - From what ship: HM Brig Zephyr - Born: New Holland - Age: 20 - Discharged on 19 Feb 1813 and sent to Chatham on HM Store Ship Dromedary.

Fyans, Joseph - Seaman - Number: 928 - Prize Name: Tender of the True Blooded Yankee - Ship type: P - How taken: HM Ship-of-the-Line Fame - When taken: 24 Jun 1813 - Where taken: at sea - Date received: 1 Jul 1813 - From what ship: HM Brig Hope - Born: New York - Age: 29 - Race: Mulatto - Discharged on 2 Jul 1813 and sent to Chatham on HM Brig Scorpion.

Gage, Zachariah - Seaman - Number: 82 - Prize Name: HM Ship-of-the-Line Ganges - Ship type: MW - How taken: Detained by Court of Admiralty - When taken: 31 Jul 1812 - Where taken: Portsmouth harbor - Date received: 16 Oct 1812 San Antonio - From what ship: HM Ship-of-the-Line Ganges - Born: Beverly, MA - Age: 20 - Discharged on 19 Feb 1813 and sent to Chatham on HM Frigate Ulysses.

Gale, Oliver - Seaman - Number: 43 - Prize Name: USRM Cutter James Madison - Ship type: MW - How taken: HM Frigate Barbadoes - When taken: 22 Aug 1812 - Where taken: at sea - Date received: 12 Oct 1812 San Antonio - From what ship: HM Ship-of-the-Line Polyphemus - Born: New York - Age: 26 - Race: Colored - Discharged on 19 Feb 1813 and sent to Chatham on HM Frigate Ulysses.

Gall, William - Seaman - Number: 203 - Prize Name: Rising States - Ship type: MV - How taken: HMS Fortunee - When taken: 28 Aug 1812 - Where taken: at sea - Date received: 25 Nov 1812 - From what ship: HM Guardship Royal William - Born: Long Island - Age: 35 - Race: Black - Discharged on 19 Feb 1813 and sent to Chatham on HM Store Ship Dromedary.

Gammell, Samuel - Seaman - Number: 657 - How taken: Gave himself up from HM Guardship Royal William - Date received: 6 Feb 1813 - From what ship: HMS Royal William - Born: Boston - Age: 37 - Discharged on 11 Mar 1813 and sent to Chatham on HM Store Ship Abundance.

Gard, Gelab - Seaman - Number: 21 - Prize Name: USRM Cutter James Madison - Ship type: MW - How taken: HM Frigate Barbadoes - When taken: 22 Aug 1812 - Where taken: at sea - Date received: 12 Oct 1812 San Antonio - From what ship: HM Ship-of-the-Line Polyphemus - Born: Groton - Age: 20 - Discharged on 19 Feb 1813 and sent to Chatham on HM Frigate Ulysses.

Gardiner, Amboy - Seaman - Number: 577 - Prize Name: Industry - Ship type: MV - How taken: HM Frigate Dryand - When taken: 7 Jan 1813 - Where taken: at sea - Date received: 25 Jan 1813 - From what ship: HM Ship-of-the-Line Queen - Born: Middleton, NJ - Age: 29 - Race: Black - Discharged on 28 Mar 1813 and sent to Chatham on HMS Scraphid.

Gardner, George - Seaman - Number: 1128 - How taken: Gave himself up from HM Ship-of-the-Line Achille - Date received: 5 Oct 1813 - From what ship: HM Ship-of-the-Line Achille - Born: New York - Age: 21 - Race: Black - Discharged on 17 Oct 1813 and sent to Chatham on HM Transport Malabar No. 352.

Gardner, James - Seaman - Number: 1086 - How taken: Gave himself up from HM Ship-of-the-Line Hibernia - Date received: 1 Oct 1813 - From what ship: HM Ship-of-the-Line Barham - Born: Hartford - Age: 31 - Discharged on 17 Oct 1813 and sent to Chatham on HM Store Ship Weymouth.

Gardner, James - Seaman - Number: 1060 - How taken: Gave himself up from HM Ship-of-the-Line Hibernia - Date received: 19 Sep 1813 - From what ship: HM Brig Imogen - Born: Hartford, CT - Age: 31 - Discharged on 29 Sep 1813 and sent to Chatham on HM Transport Chatham.

Gardner, Jerry - Seaman - Number: 1443 - How taken: Gave himself up from HM Ship-of-the-Line Salvador del Mundo - Date received: 1 Mar 1814 - From what ship: HMS Helicone - Born: Rhode Island - Age: 27 - Race: Black - Discharged on 28 Apr 1814 and sent to Chatham on HM Brig Cordelia.

Garney, Thomas - Prize Master - Number: 442 - Prize Name: Sword Fish - Ship type: P - How taken: HM Ship-of-the-Line Elephant - When taken: 28 Dec 1812 - Where taken: at sea - Date received: 14 Jan 1813 - From what ship: HMS Elephant - Born: Marblehead - Age: 29 - Discharged on 6 Mar 1813 and sent to Chatham on HMS Frigate Alexandria.

Garrett, Simon T. - Master's Mate - Number: 1301 - Prize Name: Growler - Ship type: P - How taken: HM Brig Electra - When taken: 7 Jul 1813 - Where taken: off St. Johns - Date received: 22 Dec 1813 - From what ship: HM Frigate Hyperion - Born: Petersburg, VA - Age: 21 - Discharged on 26 Dec 1813 and sent to Chatham on HMS Frigate Nemesis.

Garrison, John - Seaman - Number: 330 - Prize Name: Independence - Ship type: MV - How taken: HM Frigate Medusa - When taken: 9 Nov 1812 - Where taken: off St. Sebastian - Date received: 31 Dec 1812 - From what ship: HM Ship-of-the-Line Northumberland - Born: New York - Age: 22 - Discharged on 4 Mar 1813 and sent to Chatham on HM Ship-of-the-Line Queen.

Gatchell, John G. - Prize Master - Number: 1217 - Prize Name: Growler - Ship type: P - How taken: HM Brig Electra - When taken: 7 Jul 1813 - Where taken: at sea - Date received: 16 Nov 1813 - From what ship: HM Sloop Talbot - Born: Marblehead - Age: 26 - Discharged on 26 Dec 1813 and sent to Chatham on HM Ship of-the-Line Diomede.

Gavot, Henry - Marine - Number: 1467 - Prize Name: Bunker Hill - Ship type: P - How taken: HM Frigate Pomone & HM Frigate Cydnus - When taken: 4 Mar 1814 - Where taken: French coast - Date received: 11 Apr 1814 - From what ship: HMS Ship-on-the-Line San Domaso - Born: Isle de Basse, France - Age: 28 - Discharged on 28 Apr 1814 and sent to Chatham on HM Store Ship Weymouth.

Gebers, Henry - Seaman - Number: 38 - Prize Name: USRM Cutter James Madison - Ship type: MW - How taken: HM Frigate Barbadoes - When taken: 22 Aug 1812 - Where taken: at sea - Date received: 12 Oct 1812 San Antonio - From what ship: HM Ship-of-the-Line Polyphemus - Born: Swinemunde, Germany - Age: 31 - Discharged on 19 Feb 1813 and sent to Chatham on HM Frigate Ulysses.

Geely, Joseph - Seaman - Number: 69 - Prize Name: Diana, prize of Privateer Decatur - Ship type: MV - How taken: HM Ship-of-the-Line Polyphemus - When taken: 14 Sep 1812 - Where taken: at sea - Date received: 12 Oct 1812 San Antonio - From what ship: HM Ship-of-the-Line Polyphemus - Born: Mount Desert Island, MA - Age: 20 - Discharged on 19 Feb 1813 and sent to Chatham on HM Frigate Ulysses.

George, Isaac - Seaman - Number: 521 - Prize Name: Columbia - Ship type: MV - How taken: HMS Butain - When taken: 17 Dec 1812 - Where taken: at sea - Date received: 25 Jan 1813 - From what ship: HM Ship-of-the-Line Queen - Born: New York - Age: 31 - Discharged on 11 Mar 1813 and sent to Chatham on HM Store Ship Abundance.

George, Peter - Seaman - Number: 137 - Prize Name: Gossypium - Ship type: MV - How taken: HM Sloop Goree - When taken: 15 Aug 1812 - Where taken: off Bermuda - Date received: 29 Oct 1812 - From what ship: HM Ship-of-the-Line Ardent - Born: Charleston, SC - Age: 32 - Discharged on 19 Feb 1813 and sent to Chatham on HM Store Ship Dromedary.

George, Thomas - Seaman - Number: 32 - Prize Name: USRM Cutter James Madison - Ship type: MW - How taken: HM Frigate Barbadoes - When taken: 22 Aug 1812 - Where taken: at sea - Date received: 12 Oct 1812 San Antonio - From what ship: HM Ship-of-the-Line Polyphemus - Born: Norfolk - Age: 23 - Discharged on 6 Mar 1813 and sent to Chatham on HM Ship-of-the-Line Cornwall.

George, William Main - Seaman - Number: 751 - How taken: Gave himself up from HM Ship-of-the-Line Colossus

- Date received: 26 Mar 1813 - From what ship: HMS Colossus - Born: Watertown, MA - Age: 23 - Discharged on 28 Mar 1813 and sent to Chatham on HM Store Ship Seaphis.

George, William U. - Seaman - Number: 689 - Prize Name: Rachael - Ship type: MV - How taken: HM Schooner Herring - When taken: 8 Feb 1813 - Where taken: at sea - Date received: 20 Feb 1813 - From what ship: HMS Herring - Born: Marblehead - Age: 20 - Discharged on 6 Mar 1813 and sent to Chatham on HM Ship-of-the-Line Cornwall.

Gibbons, Andrew - Seaman - Number: 359 - Prize Name: Argus - Ship type: MV - How taken: Fancy, cutter - When taken: 19 Dec 1812 - Where taken: Bay of Biscay - Date received: 31 Dec 1812 - From what ship: HM Ship-of-the-Line Northumberland - Born: New York - Age: 22 - Discharged on 4 Mar 1813 and sent to Chatham on HM Ship-of-the-Line Queen.

Gibbs, Daniel - Seaman - Number: 894 - Prize Name: Weasel - Ship type: MV - How taken: Foxhound, privateer - When taken: 25 May 1813 - Where taken: Bay of Biscay - Date received: 24 Jun 1813 - From what ship: HM Frigate Unicorn - Born: Newport - Age: 19 - Discharged on 2 Jul 1813 and sent to Chatham on HM Frigate Tribune.

Gibson, William - Seaman - Number: 144 - Prize Name: William - Ship type: MV - How taken: HM Brig Recruit - When taken: 29 Aug 1812 - Where taken: at sea - Date received: 29 Oct 1812 - From what ship: HM Ship-of-the-Line Ardent - Born: Williamstown, DE - Age: 21 - Race: Black - Discharged on 19 Feb 1813 and sent to Chatham on HM Store Ship Dromedary.

Gifford, Barry - Seaman - Number: 303 - Prize Name: Catherine - Ship type: MV - How taken: HM Frigate Leonidas - When taken: 31 Dec 1812 - Where taken: off Ireland - Date received: 31 Dec 1812 - From what ship: HM Ship-of-the-Line Northumberland - Born: Westport - Age: 22 - Discharged on 4 Mar 1813 and sent to Chatham on HM Ship-of-the-Line Queen.

Gifford, Francis - Seaman - Number: 242 - Prize Name: Antelope - Ship type: P - How taken: HM Brig Zephyr - When taken: 10 Dec 1812 - Where taken: at sea - Date received: 27 Dec 1812 - From what ship: HMS Zephyr - Born: Monmouth, NJ - Age: 26 - Discharged on 19 Feb 1813 and sent to Chatham on HM Store Ship Dromedary.

Gilbert, Thomas - Seaman - Number: 620 - How taken: Gave himself up from HM Guardship Royal William - Date received: 3 Feb 1813 - From what ship: HMS Royal William - Born: New York - Age: 27 - Discharged on 11 Mar 1813 and sent to Chatham on HM Store Ship Abundance.

Giles, John - Seaman - Number: 232 - Prize Name: Antelope - Ship type: P - How taken: HM Brig Zephyr - When taken: 10 Dec 1812 - Where taken: at sea - Date received: 27 Dec 1812 - From what ship: HMS Zephyr - Born: New York - Age: 48 - Discharged on 19 Feb 1813 and sent to Chatham on HM Store Ship Dromedary.

Gilpin, John - Seaman - Number: 780 - How taken: Gave himself up from HM Frigate Franchise - Date received: 1 Apr 1813 - From what ship: HM Ship-of-the-Line Blake - Born: Philadelphia - Age: 28 - Race: Mulatto - Discharged on 3 Apr 1813 and sent to Chatham on HM Transport Chatham.

Glower, Samuel - Seaman - Number: 1103 - How taken: Gave himself up from HM Ship-of-the-Line Swiftsure - Date received: 5 Oct 1813 - From what ship: HM Ship-of-the-Line Achille - Born: North Carolina - Age: 21 - Discharged on 17 Oct 1813 and sent to Chatham on HM Store Ship Weymouth.

Godsoe, William - Seaman - Number: 216 - Prize Name: Preseverence - Ship type: MV - How taken: HM Sloop Atalante - When taken: 31 Jul 1812 - Where taken: at sea - Date received: 23 Dec 1812 - From what ship: HM Guardship Royal William - Born: Titrey, NH - Age: 43 - Discharged on 19 Feb 1813 and sent to Chatham on HM Store Ship Dromedary.

Goodwin, John - Captain - Number: 75 - Prize Name: HMS Belleville - Ship type: MW - How taken: Detained by Court of Admiralty - When taken: 31 Jul 1812 - Where taken: Portsmouth harbor - Date received: 16 Oct 1812 San Antonio - From what ship: Belleville - Born: Portland, MA - Age: 50 - Discharged on 26 Oct 1813 and sent to Odiham on parole.

Goodwin, Jonas B. - Seaman - Number: 683 - Prize Name: Benjamin - Ship type: MV - How taken: HM Frigate Medusa - When taken: 31 Dec 1812 - Where taken: at sea - Date received: 14 Feb 1813 - From what ship: HM Transport Maister No. 84 - Born: Marblehead - Age: 17 - Discharged on 6 Mar 1813 and sent to

Chatham on HM Ship-of-the-Line Cornwall.

Goold, John - Seaman - Number: 739 - Prize Name: Dart - Ship type: MV - How taken: HM Brig Doterel - When taken: 5 Mar 1813 - Where taken: at sea - Date received: 21 Mar 1813 - From what ship: HMS Dotteril - Born: Kittery, MA - Age: 25 - Discharged on 28 Mar 1813 and sent to Chatham on HM Store Ship Seaphis.

Gotier, Charles - Seaman - Number: 1375 - Prize Name: Pilate - Ship type: P - How taken: Victoria, privateer of Guernsey - When taken: 28 Jan 1814 - Where taken: off Bordeaux - Date received: 7 Feb 1814 - From what ship: Mary from Guernsey - Born: Salem - Age: 23 - Discharged on 28 Apr 1814 and sent to Chatham on HM Store Ship Weymouth.

Gourley, William - Seaman - Number: 966 - How taken: Gave himself up from HM Ship-of-the-Line Leviathan - Date received: 31 Jul 1813 - From what ship: HMS Leviathan - Born: Philadelphia - Age: 26 - Discharged on 7 Aug 1813 and sent to Chatham on HM Brig Rinaldo.

Grant, Christian - Seaman - Number: 475 - Prize Name: Sword Fish - Ship type: P - How taken: HM Ship-of-the-Line Elephant - When taken: 28 Dec 1812 - Where taken: at sea - Date received: 14 Jan 1813 - From what ship: HMS Elephant - Born: Marblehead - Age: 22 - Discharged on 11 Mar 1813 and sent to Chatham on HM Store Ship Abundance.

Gravelee, Joseph - Seaman - Number: 1434 - Prize Name: HMS Devon Transport No. 15, prize of Privateer Bunker Hill - Ship type: MV - How taken: HM Brig Fly - When taken: 21 Jan 1814 - Where taken: at sea - Date received: 1 Mar 1814 - From what ship: HMS Helicone - Born: Lorient - Age: 71 - Discharged on 28 Apr 1814 and sent to Chatham on HM Brig Cordelia.

Gray, Thomas - Seaman - Number: 790 - How taken: Gave himself up from HM Brig Ringdove - Date received: 4 Apr 1813 - From what ship: HMS Ringdove - Born: New York - Age: 30 - Discharged on 27 Apr 1813 and sent to Chatham on HM Sloop-of-War Bonne Citoyenne.

Green John - Seaman - Number: 310 - Prize Name: Wasp - Ship type: MV - How taken: Earl Spencer, cutter - When taken: 4 Aug 1812 - Where taken: off Cape Clear - Date received: 31 Dec 1812 - From what ship: HM Ship-of-the-Line Northumberland - Born: Albany - Age: 23 - Race: Black - Discharged on 4 Mar 1813 and sent to Chatham on HM Ship-of-the-Line Queen.

Green, Beckwith - Boatswain - Number: 1260 - Prize Name: Dart - Ship type: P - How taken: HM Frigate Niger & HMS Fortunee - Where taken: at sea - Date received: 19 Dec 1813 - From what ship: HMS Fortunee - Born: Alexandria, VA - Age: 30 - Discharged on 26 Dec 1813 and sent to Chatham on HM Ship of-the-Line Diomede.

Green, George - Seaman - Number: 1118 - How taken: Gave himself up from HM Ship-of-the-Line America - Date received: 5 Oct 1813 - From what ship: HM Ship-of-the-Line Achille - Born: Baltimore - Age: 44 - Race: Black - Discharged on 17 Oct 1813 and sent to Chatham on HM Store Ship Weymouth.

Green, Henry - Seaman - Number: 612 - Prize Name: Sword Fish - Ship type: P - How taken: HM Ship-of-the-Line Elephant - When taken: 20 Dec 1812 - Where taken: at sea - Date received: 1 Feb 1813 - From what ship: HM Frigate Hermes - Born: Baltimore - Age: 27 - Race: Black - Discharged on 11 Mar 1813 and sent to Chatham on HM Store Ship Abundance.

Green, Samuel - Seaman - Number: 358 - Prize Name: Argus - Ship type: MV - How taken: Fancy, cutter - When taken: 19 Dec 1812 - Where taken: Bay of Biscay - Date received: 31 Dec 1812 - From what ship: HM Ship-of-the-Line Northumberland - Born: Massachusetts - Age: 29 - Discharged on 4 Mar 1813 and sent to Chatham on HM Ship-of-the-Line Queen.

Green, William - Quartermaster - Number: 1363 - Prize Name: Elbridge Gerry - Ship type: P - How taken: HM Frigate Crescent - When taken: 16 Sep 1813 - Where taken: at sea - Date received: 1 Feb 1814 - From what ship: HM Frigate Sybille - Born: Baltimore - Age: 36 - Discharged on 13 Feb 1814 and sent to Chatham on HM Transport Malabar No. 352.

Greenfield, William - Seaman - Number: 230 - Prize Name: Antelope - Ship type: P - How taken: HM Brig Zephyr - When taken: 10 Dec 1812 - Where taken: at sea - Date received: 27 Dec 1812 - From what ship: HMS Zephyr - Born: Charlestown - Age: 40 - Discharged on 19 Feb 1813 and sent to Chatham on HM Store Ship Dromedary.

Gregory, George - Seaman - Number: 1413 - Prize Name: Squirrel - Ship type: MV - How taken: HM Frigate Belle Poule - When taken: 14 Dec 1813 - Where taken: at sea - Date received: 1 Mar 1814 - From what ship: HMS Helicone - Born: Maryland - Age: 23 - Discharged on 28 Apr 1814 and sent to Chatham on HM Sloop Favorite.

Grey, Charles - Seaman - Number: 384 - How taken: Gave himself up from HM Ship-of-the-Line Salvador del Mundo - Date received: 10 Jan 1813 - From what ship: HM Guardship Royal William - Born: Prince George, MD - Age: 38 - Race: Colored - Discharged on 4 Mar 1813 and sent to Chatham on HM Ship-of-the-Line Queen.

Griffin, James - Seaman - Number: 473 - Prize Name: Sword Fish - Ship type: P - How taken: HM Ship-of-the-Line Elephant - When taken: 28 Dec 1812 - Where taken: at sea - Date received: 14 Jan 1813 - From what ship: HMS Elephant - Born: Maryland - Age: 20 - Discharged on 11 Mar 1813 and sent to Chatham on HM Store Ship Abundance.

Griffin, William - Seaman - Number: 1294 - Prize Name: Mary, prize to the True Blooded Yankee - Ship type: MV - How taken: HM Ship of-the-Line Bellerophon - When taken: 16 Dec 1813 - Where taken: off Land's End - Date received: 22 Dec 1813 - From what ship: HMS Bellerophon - Born: Philadelphia - Age: 45 - Discharged on 26 Dec 1813 and sent to Chatham on HMS Frigate Nemesis.

Griswold, Josiah - 3rd Lieutenant - Number: 1001 - Prize Name: Blockade - Ship type: P - How taken: HM Brig Charybdis - When taken: 31 Oct 1813 - Where taken: at sea - Date received: 18 Aug 1813 - From what ship: HM Ship of-the-Line Cressy - Born: Connecticut - Age: 24 - Discharged on 21 Sep 1813 and sent to Chatham on HM Ship-of-the-Line Queen.

Grose, Daniel - Seaman - Number: 427 - Prize Name: Brunswick - Ship type: MV - How taken: HM Frigate Iris - When taken: 16 Dec 1812 - Where taken: at sea - Date received: 10 Jan 1813 - From what ship: HM Guardship Royal William - Born: New York - Age: 38 - Discharged on 6 Mar 1813 and sent to Chatham on HMS Frigate Alexandria.

Grosette, John M. - Seaman - Number: 1437 - Prize Name: HMS Devon Transport No. 15, prize of Privateer Bunker Hill - Ship type: MV - How taken: HM Brig Fly - When taken: 21 Jan 1814 - Where taken: at sea - Date received: 1 Mar 1814 - From what ship: HMS Helicone - Born: Perouse, France - Age: 15 - Discharged on 28 Apr 1814 and sent to Chatham on HM Brig Cordelia.

Grush, Nathaniel - Seaman - Number: 1320 - Prize Name: Growler - Ship type: P - How taken: HM Brig Electra - When taken: 7 Jul 1813 - Where taken: off St. Johns - Date received: 24 Dec 1813 - From what ship: HM Schooner Adonis - Born: Marblehead - Age: 17 - Discharged on 26 Dec 1813 and sent to Chatham on HMS Frigate Nemesis.

Gudlers, George - Seaman - Number: 601 - Prize Name: Sword Fish - Ship type: P - How taken: HM Ship-of-the-Line Elephant - When taken: 20 Dec 1812 - Where taken: at sea - Date received: 1 Feb 1813 - From what ship: HM Frigate Hermes - Born: Marblehead - Age: 24 - Discharged on 11 Mar 1813 and sent to Chatham on HM Store Ship Abundance.

Guier, Andrew - Seaman - Number: 964 - How taken: Gave himself up from HM Ship-of-the-Line Leviathan - Date received: 31 Jul 1813 - From what ship: HMS Leviathan - Born: Pennsylvania - Age: 42 - Discharged on 7 Aug 1813 and sent to Chatham on HM Brig Rinaldo.

Guillider, William - Seaman - Number: 280 - How taken: Gave himself up from HM Ship-of-the-Line Vigo - When taken: 30 Dec 1812 - Date received: 30 Dec 1812 - From what ship: HM Brig Zephyr - Born: Boston - Age: 40 - Discharged on 19 Feb 1813 and sent to Chatham on HM Store Ship Dromedary (see Prisoner Number 585).

Guillider, William - Seaman - Number: 585 - How taken: Gave himself up from HM Ship-of-the-Line Vigo - Date received: 30 Jan 1813 - From what ship: HMS Vigo - Born: Boston - Age: 40 - Re-entered by mistake (see Prisoner Number 280).

Gunnell, William - Sailmaker's mate - Number: 380 - How taken: Gave himself up from HM Transport Romulus - Date received: 4 Jan 1813 - From what ship: HMS Romulus - Born: New York - Age: 45 - Discharged on 4 Mar 1813 and sent to Chatham on HM Ship-of-the-Line Queen.

Gyer, Henry - Seaman - Number: 1326 - How taken: Gave himself up from HM Ship-of-the-Line Invincible - Date received: 26 Dec 1813 - From what ship: HM Transport Sir John B. Warren No. 183 - Born: Boston - Age: 29 - Discharged on 13 Feb 1814 and sent to Chatham on HM Transport Malabar No. 352.

Hackett, Theophilus - Seaman - Number: 53 - Prize Name: Fame, prize of Privateer Decatur - Ship type: MV - How taken: HM Ship-of-the-Line Polyphemus - When taken: 13 Sep 1812 - Where taken: at sea - Date received: 12 Oct 1812 San Antonio - From what ship: HM Ship-of-the-Line Polyphemus - Born: Newburyport - Age: 19 - Discharged on 19 Feb 1813 and sent to Chatham on HM Frigate Ulysses.

Hadley, George - Seaman - Number: 1073 - Prize Name: Falcon, prize of the US Frigate President - Ship type: MV - How taken: Spanish army - When taken: 2 Jul 1813 - Where taken: Passage Harbor - Date received: 1 Oct 1813 - From what ship: HM Ship-of-the-Line Barham - Born: Newtown - Age: 32 - Discharged on 17 Oct 1813 and sent to Chatham on HM Store Ship Weymouth (see Prisoner Number 1039).

Hadley, George - Seaman - Number: 1039 - Prize Name: Falcon, prize of the US Frigate President - Ship type: MV - How taken: Spanish forces - When taken: 2 Jul 1813 - Where taken: Passage Harbor - Date received: 9 Sep 1813 - From what ship: HMS Ship-of-the-Line Kron Princessen - Born: Newtown - Age: 32 - Discharged on 29 Sep 1813 and sent to Chatham on HM Ship-of-the-Line Barham (see Prisoner Number 1073).

Halden, Lewis - Seaman - Number: 378 - How taken: Gave himself up from HM Sloop Comet - When taken: 25 Nov 1812 - Date received: 4 Jan 1813 - From what ship: HMS Muros - Born: Norfolk - Age: 22 - Race: Black - Discharged on 4 Mar 1813 and sent to Chatham on HM Ship-of-the-Line Queen.

Haley, Thomas - 1st Mate - Number: 404 - Prize Name: Hope - Ship type: MV - How taken: HM Sloop Pheasant - When taken: 13 Dec 1812 - Where taken: at sea - Date received: 10 Jan 1813 - From what ship: HM Guardship Royal William - Born: Princess Anne's County - Age: 28 - Discharged on 6 Mar 1813 and sent to Chatham on HMS Frigate Alexandria.

Hall, Thomas - Seaman - Number: 552 - Prize Name: Rossie - Ship type: MV - How taken: HM Frigate Dryand - When taken: 7 Jan 1813 - Where taken: at sea - Date received: 25 Jan 1813 - From what ship: HM Ship-of-the-Line Queen - Born: Philadelphia - Age: 23 - Discharged on 11 Mar 1813 and sent to Chatham on HM Store Ship Abundance.

Hall, Thomas - Prize Master - Number: 1490 - Prize Name: Traveler, prize of the Privateer Surprise - Ship type: MV - How taken: HM Schooner Canso - When taken: 14 May 1814 - Where taken: at sea - Date received: 1 Jun 1814 - From what ship: HMS Canso - Born: Maryland - Age: 23 - Discharged on 30 Jun 1814 and sent to Plymouth on HM Brig Steady.

Hall, William - Seaman - Number: 784 - How taken: Gave himself up from HM Frigate Franchise - Date received: 1 Apr 1813 - From what ship: HM Ship-of-the-Line Blake - Born: Charlestown - Age: 21 - Discharged on 3 Apr 1813 and sent to Chatham on HM Transport Chatham.

Halmore, Henry Michael - Seaman - Number: 537 - Prize Name: Expectation - Ship type: MV - How taken: HMS Butain - When taken: 17 Dec 1812 - Where taken: at sea - Date received: 25 Jan 1813 - From what ship: HM Ship-of-the-Line Queen - Born: New York - Age: 42 - Died on 27 Mar 1813.

Hamson, Henry - Quartermaster - Number: 483 - Prize Name: Sword Fish - Ship type: P - How taken: HM Ship-of-the-Line Elephant - When taken: 28 Dec 1812 - Where taken: at sea - Date received: 14 Jan 1813 - From what ship: HMS Elephant - Born: Marblehead - Age: 31 - Discharged on 11 Mar 1813 and sent to Chatham on HM Store Ship Abundance.

Hanson, William - Seaman - Number: 176 - Prize Name: Baltimore - Ship type: P - How taken: HM Transport Diadem - When taken: 7 Oct 1812 - Where taken: S. Andera - Date received: 3 Nov 1812 San Antonio - From what ship: HMS Diadem - Born: Stockholm, Sweden - Age: 28 - Discharged on 19 Feb 1813 and sent to Chatham on HM Store Ship Dromedary.

Harder, John - Boy - Number: 1496 - Prize Name: Traveler, prize of the Privateer Surprise - Ship type: MV - How taken: HM Schooner Canso - When taken: 14 May 1814 - Where taken: at sea - Date received: 1 Jun 1814 - From what ship: HMS Canso - Born: Maryland - Age: 17 - Discharged on 2 Jun 1814 and sent to Plymouth on HMS Growler.

Hardiman, John - Seaman - Number: 934 - Prize Name: Tender of the True Blooded Yankee - Ship type: P - How taken: HM Ship-of-the-Line Fame - When taken: 24 Jun 1813 - Where taken: at sea - Date received: 1 Jul 1813 - From what ship: HM Brig Hope - Born: Georgetown - Age: 36 - Discharged on 2 Jul 1813 and sent to Chatham on HM Brig Scorpion.

Harding, J. Christian - Seaman - Number: 1254 - Prize Name: Dart - Ship type: P - How taken: HM Frigate Niger & HMS Fortunee - Where taken: at sea - Date received: 19 Dec 1813 - From what ship: HMS Fortunee - Born: Prussia - Age: 25 - Discharged on 26 Dec 1813 and sent to Chatham on HM Ship of-the-Line Diomede.

Harding, Joseph - Seaman - Number: 12 - Prize Name: USRM Cutter James Madison - Ship type: MW - How taken: HM Frigate Barbadoes - When taken: 22 Aug 1812 - Where taken: at sea - Date received: 12 Oct 1812 San Antonio - From what ship: HM Ship-of-the-Line Polyphemus - Born: Savannah, GA - Age: 35 - Discharged on 19 Feb 1813 and sent to Chatham on HM Frigate Ulysses.

Harding, William - Seaman - Number: 1406 - Prize Name: Pilot - Ship type: P - How taken: Victoria, privateer of Guernsey - When taken: 28 Jan 1814 - Where taken: off Bordeaux - Date received: 16 Feb 1814 - From what ship: HM Transport Malabar No. 352 - Born: South Carolina - Age: 23 - Race: Black - Discharged on 28 Apr 1814 and sent to Chatham on HM Store Ship Weymouth.

Harding, William - Seaman - Number: 1383 - Prize Name: Pilate - Ship type: P - How taken: Victoria, privateer of Guernsey - When taken: 28 Jan 1814 - Where taken: off Bordeaux - Date received: 7 Feb 1814 - From what ship: Mary from Guernsey - Born: South Carolina - Age: 23 - Race: Black - Discharged on 13 Feb 1814 and sent to Chatham on HM Transport Malabar No. 352.

Hardwood, William - Seaman - Number: 1147 - Prize Name: Maydock - Ship type: MV - How taken: HM Brig Rebuff - When taken: 16 Jun 1813 - Where taken: St. Mary's - Date received: 6 Oct 1813 - From what ship: HM Sloop Kingfisher - Born: Maryland - Age: 31 - Discharged on 17 Oct 1813 and sent to Chatham on HM Transport Malabar No. 352.

Hardy, John - Steward - Number: 539 - Prize Name: Expectation - Ship type: MV - How taken: HMS Butain - When taken: 17 Dec 1812 - Where taken: at sea - Date received: 25 Jan 1813 - From what ship: HM Ship-of-the-Line Queen - Born: Philadelphia - Age: 27 - Discharged on 11 Mar 1813 and sent to Chatham on HM Store Ship Abundance.

Harlow, Sylvanus - Seaman - Number: 83 - Prize Name: HM Ship-of-the-Line Ganges - Ship type: MW - How taken: Detained by Court of Admiralty - When taken: 31 Jul 1812 - Where taken: Portsmouth harbor - Date received: 16 Oct 1812 San Antonio - From what ship: HM Ship-of-the-Line Ganges - Born: Plymouth - Age: 32 - Discharged on 19 Feb 1813 and sent to Chatham on HM Frigate Ulysses.

Harman, Isaac - Quartermaster - Number: 1209 - Prize Name: Elbridge Gerry - Ship type: P - How taken: HM Frigate Crescent & HM Ship of-the-Line Bellerophon - When taken: 16 Sep 1813 - Where taken: at sea - Date received: 16 Nov 1813 - From what ship: HM Sloop Talbot - Born: Buckstown, MA - Age: 24 - Discharged on 26 Dec 1813 and sent to Chatham on HM Ship of-the-Line Diomede.

Harris, Abraham Harris - Seaman - Number: 49 - Prize Name: Fame, prize of Privateer Decatur - Ship type: MV - How taken: HM Ship-of-the-Line Polyphemus - When taken: 13 Sep 1812 - Where taken: at sea - Date received: 12 Oct 1812 San Antonio - From what ship: HM Ship-of-the-Line Polyphemus - Born: Ipswich - Age: 24 - Discharged on 19 Feb 1813 and sent to Chatham on HM Frigate Ulysses.

Harris, David - Seaman - Number: 60 - Prize Name: Diana, prize of Privateer Decatur - Ship type: MV - How taken: HM Ship-of-the-Line Polyphemus - When taken: 14 Sep 1812 - Where taken: at sea - Date received: 12 Oct 1812 San Antonio - From what ship: HM Ship-of-the-Line Polyphemus - Born: Ipswich - Age: 20 - Discharged on 19 Feb 1813 and sent to Chatham on HM Frigate Ulysses.

Harris, Ebenezer - Seaman - Number: 1427 - Prize Name: Minerva - Ship type: MV - How taken: HM Ship-of-the-Line Conquestador - When taken: 19 Jan 1814 - Where taken: Bay of Biscay - Date received: 1 Mar 1814 - From what ship: HMS Helicone - Born: North Yarmouth, MA - Age: 25 - Discharged on 28 Apr 1814 and sent to Chatham on HM Sloop Favorite.

Harris, George - Seaman - Number: 335 - Prize Name: Independence - Ship type: MV - How taken: HM Frigate Medusa - When taken: 9 Nov 1812 - Where taken: off St. Sebastian - Date received: 31 Dec 1812 - From what ship: HM Ship-of-the-Line Northumberland - Born: Baltimore - Age: 32 - Race: Black - Died on 6 Mar 1813.

Harris, James - Seaman - Number: 353 - Prize Name: Experiment - Ship type: MV - How taken: HM Brig Rover - When taken: 10 Nov 1812 - Where taken: off Bordeaux - Date received: 31 Dec 1812 - From what ship: HM Ship-of-the-Line Northumberland - Born: Maryland - Age: 26 - Discharged on 4 Mar 1813 and sent to Chatham on HM Ship-of-the-Line Queen.

Harris, John - Seaman - Number: 1445 - How taken: Gave himself up from Royal E. Middlesex - Where taken: Belfast - Date received: 1 Mar 1814 - From what ship: HMS Helicone - Born: Virginia - Age: 26 - Race: Mulatto - Discharged on 28 Apr 1814 and sent to Chatham on HM Brig Cordelia.

Harris, Simon - Seaman - Number: 1420 - Prize Name: Zephyr, prize of Privateer Rattlesnake - Ship type: MV - How taken: HM Frigate Surveillante - When taken: 6 Jan 1814 - Where taken: Bay of Biscay - Date received: 1 Mar 1814 - From what ship: HMS Helicone - Born: Virginia - Age: 40 - Race: Black - Discharged on 28 Apr 1814 and sent to Chatham on HM Sloop Favorite.

Harris, William - Seaman - Number: 844 - How taken: Gave himself up from HM Ship-of-the-Line Malta - Date received: 15 Jun 1813 - From what ship: HM Sloop Helena - Born: New York - Age: 37 - Discharged on 2 Jul 1813 and sent to Chatham on HM Frigate Tribune.

Harris, William - Seaman - Number: 36 - Prize Name: USRM Cutter James Madison - Ship type: MW - How taken: HM Frigate Barbadoes - When taken: 22 Aug 1812 - Where taken: at sea - Date received: 12 Oct 1812 San Antonio - From what ship: HM Ship-of-the-Line Polyphemus - Born: Portland - Age: 35 - Discharged on 28 Mar 1813 and sent to Chatham on HM Store Ship Seraphis.

Harrison, James - Seaman - Number: 811 - How taken: Gave himself up from HM Ship-of-the-Line Sterling Castle - Date received: 21 Apr 1813 - From what ship: HM Guardship Royal William - Born: Lancaster - Age: 21 - Race: Black - Discharged on 27 Apr 1813 and sent to Chatham on HM Sloop-of-War Bonne Citoyenne.

Hart, William - Seaman - Number: 1222 - Prize Name: Growler - Ship type: P - How taken: HM Brig Electra - When taken: 7 Jul 1813 - Where taken: at sea - Date received: 16 Nov 1813 - From what ship: HM Sloop Talbot - Born: Massachusetts - Age: 22 - Discharged on 26 Dec 1813 and sent to Chatham on HM Ship of-the-Line Diomede.

Hartford, James - Seaman - Number: 422 - How taken: Taken out of the MV Martin - When taken: 6 Dec 1812 - Where taken: at Cork - Date received: 10 Jan 1813 - From what ship: HM Guardship Royal William - Born: New Market, NH - Age: 29 - Discharged on 6 Mar 1813 and sent to Chatham on HMS Frigate Alexandria.

Harvey, Anthony - Cook - Number: 1321 - Prize Name: Growler - Ship type: P - How taken: HM Brig Electra - When taken: 7 Jul 1813 - Where taken: off St. Johns - Date received: 24 Dec 1813 - From what ship: HM Schooner Adonis - Born: Baltimore - Age: 28 - Race: Black - Discharged on 26 Dec 1813 and sent to Chatham on HMS Frigate Nemesis.

Harvey, Joseph - Seaman - Number: 1424 - Prize Name: Hannah - Ship type: MV - How taken: HM Ship-of-the-Line Conquestador - When taken: 15 Jan 1814 - Where taken: at sea - Date received: 1 Mar 1814 - From what ship: HMS Helicone - Born: Beverly - Age: 33 - Discharged on 28 Apr 1814 and sent to Chatham on HM Sloop Favorite.

Harvey, Peter - Seaman - Number: 1111 - How taken: Gave himself up from HM Ship-of-the-Line America - Date received: 5 Oct 1813 - From what ship: HM Ship-of-the-Line Achille - Born: Philadelphia - Age: 29 - Race: Black - Discharged on 17 Oct 1813 and sent to Chatham on HM Store Ship Weymouth.

Harvey, Peter - Seaman - Number: 1269 - Prize Name: US Schooner Growler - Ship type: MW - How taken: Sir James Yeo's Squadron - When taken: 11 Aug 1813 - Where taken: Lake Ontario - Date received: 22 Dec 1813 - From what ship: HMS Elalion - Born: Portland, MA - Age: 25 - Discharged on 26 Dec 1813 and sent to Chatham on HM Ship of-the-Line Diomede.

Hastings, Johnson - Seaman - Number: 122 - Prize Name: Hannibal - Ship type: P - How taken: MV Patent - When taken: 24 Sep 1812 - Where taken: off Bermuda - Date received: 28 Oct 1812 - From what ship: MV Patent - Born: Boston - Age: 22 - Discharged on 19 Feb 1813 and sent to Chatham on HM Store Ship Dromedary.

Hathaway, William N. - Boy - Number: 315 - Prize Name: Perseverance - Ship type: MV - How taken: HM Frigate Sybille - When taken: 12 Aug 1812 - Where taken: off Cape Clear - Date received: 31 Dec 1812 - From what ship: HM Ship-of-the-Line Northumberland - Born: New York - Age: 14 - Discharged on 4 Mar 1813 and sent to Chatham on HM Ship-of-the-Line Queen.

Hatton, Peter - Seaman - Number: 1202 - Prize Name: Fly, prize of US Frigate President - Ship type: MV - How taken: HM Transport Regulus & HM Frigate Melpomene - When taken: 11 Sep 1813 - Where taken: at sea - Date received: 13 Nov 1813 - From what ship: HM Transport Regulus - Born: New Hampshire - Age: 40 - Discharged on 26 Dec 1813 and sent to Chatham on HM Ship of-the-Line Diomede.

Haven, Thomas - Supercargo - Number: 734 - Prize Name: Dart - Ship type: MV - How taken: HM Brig Doterel - When taken: 5 Mar 1813 - Where taken: at sea - Date received: 21 Mar 1813 - From what ship: HMS Dotteril - Born: Portsmouth, NH - Age: 30 - Discharged on 28 Mar 1813 and sent to Chatham on HM Store Ship Seaphis.

Hawley, Frederick - Seaman - Number: 643 - How taken: Gave himself up from HM Guardship Royal William - Date received: 3 Feb 1813 - From what ship: HMS Royal William - Born: Wilmington - Age: 22 - Discharged on 11 Mar 1813 and sent to Chatham on HM Store Ship Abundance.

Haywood, John - Seaman - Number: 135 - Prize Name: Gossypium - Ship type: MV - How taken: HM Sloop Goree - When taken: 15 Aug 1812 - Where taken: off Bermuda - Date received: 29 Oct 1812 - From what ship: HM Ship-of-the-Line Ardent - Born: New York - Age: 21 - Discharged on 19 Feb 1813 and sent to Chatham on HM Store Ship Dromedary.

Hazard, Thomas - Seaman - Number: 314 - Prize Name: Warren - Ship type: MV - How taken: HM Frigate Sybille and HMS Fortunee - When taken: 5 Sep 1812 - Where taken: at sea - Date received: 31 Dec 1812 - From what ship: HM Ship-of-the-Line Northumberland - Born: South Kingston - Age: 23 - Race: Black - Discharged on 4 Mar 1813 and sent to Chatham on HM Ship-of-the-Line Queen.

Head, James - 1st Lieutenant - Number: 1204 - Prize Name: Elbridge Gerry - Ship type: P - How taken: HM Frigate Crescent & HM Ship of-the-Line Bellerophon - When taken: 16 Sep 1813 - Where taken: at sea - Date received: 16 Nov 1813 - From what ship: HM Sloop Talbot - Born: Haverhill, MA - Age: 28 - Discharged on 26 Dec 1813 and sent to Chatham on HM Ship of-the-Line Diomede.

Heady, Linsay - Seaman - Number: 1046 - How taken: Gave himself up from HM Ship-of-the-Line Union - Date received: 14 Sep 1813 - From what ship: HM Brig Savage - Born: New Jersey - Age: 38 - Discharged on 29 Sep 1813 and sent to Chatham on HM Ship-of-the-Line Barham.

Heater, William - Seaman - Number: 1199 - How taken: Gave himself up from HM Schooner Charlotte - Date received: 9 Nov 1813 - From what ship: HM Store Ship Seraphis - Born: Hampshire - Age: 26 - Discharged on 26 Dec 1813 and sent to Chatham on HM Ship of-the-Line Diomede.

Heaton, Henry - Seaman - Number: 1110 - How taken: Gave himself up from HM Ship-of-the-Line America - Date received: 5 Oct 1813 - From what ship: HM Ship-of-the-Line Achille - Born: Lancaster - Age: 33 - Discharged on 17 Oct 1813 and sent to Chatham on HM Store Ship Weymouth.

Hecox, George - Seaman - Number: 66 - Prize Name: Diana, prize of Privateer Decatur - Ship type: MV - How taken: HM Ship-of-the-Line Polyphemus - When taken: 14 Sep 1812 - Where taken: at sea - Date received: 12 Oct 1812 San Antonio - From what ship: HM Ship-of-the-Line Polyphemus - Born: New Haven - Age: 28 - Discharged on 19 Feb 1813 and sent to Chatham on HM Frigate Ulysses.

Hedley, John - Seaman - Number: 659 - How taken: Gave himself up from HM Guardship Royal William - Date received: 6 Feb 1813 - From what ship: HMS Royal William - Born: New York - Age: 29 - Discharged on 6 Mar 1813 and sent to Chatham on HM Ship-of-the-Line Cornwall.

Helman, John - Seaman - Number: 13 - Prize Name: USRM Cutter James Madison - Ship type: MW - How taken: HM Frigate Barbadoes - When taken: 22 Aug 1812 - Where taken: at sea - Date received: 12 Oct 1812 San Antonio - From what ship: HM Ship-of-the-Line Polyphemus - Born: Eastport, MA - Age: 18 - Discharged on 19 Feb 1813 and sent to Chatham on HM Frigate Ulysses.

Hemonder, Peter - Seaman - Number: 1462 - Prize Name: Bunker Hill - Ship type: P - How taken: HM Frigate Pomone & HM Frigate Cydnus - When taken: 4 Mar 1814 - Where taken: French coast - Date received: 11 Apr 1814 - From what ship: HMS Ship-on-the-Line San Domaso - Born: Visby, Sweden - Age: 20 - Discharged on 28 Apr 1814 and sent to Chatham on HM Store Ship Weymouth.

Henderson, Benjamin - Seaman - Number: 96 - Prize Name: HMS Eos - Ship type: MW - How taken: Detained by

Court of Admiralty - When taken: 31 Jul 1812 - Where taken: Portsmouth harbor - Date received: 16 Oct 1812 San Antonio - From what ship: Eos - Born: Newburyport - Age: 26 - Discharged on 19 Feb 1813 and sent to Chatham on HM Frigate Ulysses.

Henricks, Jeremiah - Seaman - Number: 31 - Prize Name: USRM Cutter James Madison - Ship type: MW - How taken: HM Frigate Barbadoes - When taken: 22 Aug 1812 - Where taken: at sea - Date received: 12 Oct 1812 San Antonio - From what ship: HM Ship-of-the-Line Polyphemus - Born: Baltimore - Age: 16 - Discharged on 19 Feb 1813 and sent to Chatham on HM Frigate Ulysses.

Henry, Henry - Seaman - Number: 1038 - Prize Name: Falcon, prize of the US Frigate President - Ship type: MV - How taken: Spanish forces - When taken: 2 Jul 1813 - Where taken: Passage Harbor - Date received: 9 Sep 1813 - From what ship: HMS Ship-of-the-Line Kron Princessen - Born: Bingham, MA - Age: 26 - Discharged on 29 Sep 1813 and sent to Chatham on HM Ship-of-the-Line Barham (see Prisoner Number 1072).

Henry, Henry - Seaman - Number: 1072 - Prize Name: Falcon, prize of the US Frigate President - Ship type: MV - How taken: Spanish army - When taken: 2 Jul 1813 - Where taken: Passage Harbor - Date received: 1 Oct 1813 - From what ship: HM Ship-of-the-Line Barham - Born: Bingham, MA - Age: 25 - Discharged on 17 Oct 1813 and sent to Chatham on HM Store Ship Weymouth (see Prisoner Number 1038).

Henton, John - Seaman - Number: 812 - How taken: Gave himself up from HM Ship-of-the-Line Tigre - Date received: 24 Apr 1813 - From what ship: HM Fire Ship Spitfire - Born: North Carolina - Age: 22 - Discharged on 27 Apr 1813 and sent to Chatham on HM Sloop-of-War Bonne Citoyenne.

Herle, Hiram - 2nd in command - Number: 916 - Prize Name: Tender of the True Blooded Yankee - Ship type: P - How taken: HM Ship-of-the-Line Fame - When taken: 24 Jun 1813 - Where taken: at sea - Date received: 1 Jul 1813 - From what ship: HM Brig Hope - Born: Berwick, MA - Age: 29 - Discharged on 7 Aug 1813 and sent to Chatham on HM Brig Rinaldo.

Heyden, William - Seaman - Number: 750 - How taken: Gave himself up from HM Ship of-the-Line Bellerophon - Date received: 25 Mar 1813 - From what ship: HMS Bellerophon - Born: Boston - Age: 32 - Discharged on 28 Mar 1813 and sent to Chatham on HM Store Ship Seaphis.

Heywood, John - Seaman - Number: 800 - How taken: Gave himself up from HM Ship-of-the-Line Scepter - Date received: 21 Apr 1813 - From what ship: HM Guardship Royal William - Born: Baltimore - Age: 25 - Discharged on 27 Apr 1813 and sent to Chatham on HM Sloop-of-War Bonne Citoyenne.

Higgins, William - Seaman - Number: 297 - Prize Name: Charles - Ship type: MV - How taken: Taken up on shore - When taken: 18 Oct 1812 - Where taken: Liverpool - Date received: 31 Dec 1812 - From what ship: HM Ship-of-the-Line Northumberland - Born: Virginia - Age: 24 - Race: Black - Discharged on 4 Mar 1813 and sent to Chatham on HM Ship-of-the-Line Queen.

Hill, Daniel - Seaman - Number: 1430 - Prize Name: Minerva - Ship type: MV - How taken: HM Ship-of-the-Line Conquestador - When taken: 19 Jan 1814 - Where taken: Bay of Biscay - Date received: 1 Mar 1814 - From what ship: HMS Helicone - Born: Saco - Age: 22 - Discharged on 28 Apr 1814 and sent to Chatham on HM Sloop Favorite.

Hill, Ephraim - Seaman - Number: 874 - Prize Name: Tiger - Ship type: MV - How taken: HM Brig Scylla - When taken: 22 Mar 1813 - Where taken: Bay of Biscay - Date received: 24 Jun 1813 - From what ship: HM Frigate Unicorn - Born: Hartford - Age: 24 - Discharged on 2 Jul 1813 and sent to Chatham on HM Frigate Tribune.

Hill, George - Seaman - Number: 261 - Prize Name: King of Rome - Ship type: P - How taken: HM Brig Wolverine - When taken: 13 Dec 1812 - Where taken: at sea - Date received: 27 Dec 1812 - From what ship: HMS Wolverine - Born: New York - Age: 16 - Discharged on 19 Feb 1813 and sent to Chatham on HM Store Ship Dromedary.

Hill, James - Seaman - Number: 1332 - How taken: Gave himself up from HM Ship-of-the-Line Invincible - Date received: 27 Dec 1813 - From what ship: HMS Frigate Nemesis - Born: Boston - Age: 31 - Race: Mulatto - Discharged on 27 Dec 1813 and sent to Chatham on HMS Frigate Nemesis.

Hill, Jeremiah - Seaman - Number: 1344 - Prize Name: Watson, prize of the True Blooded Yankee - Ship type: MV

- How taken: Change, privateer of Jersey - When taken: 15 Dec 1813 - Where taken: at sea - Date received: 4 Jan 1814 - From what ship: Earl S. Vincent Packet - Born: Baltimore - Age: 27 - Discharged on 5 Jan 1814 and sent to Chatham on HM Ship-of-the-Line Poictiers.

Hill, John - Seaman - Number: 1245 - Prize Name: British South Sea Whaler - How taken: HM Ship-of-the-Line Illustrious - When taken: 22 Oct 1813 - Where taken: at sea - Date received: 26 Nov 1813 - From what ship: HMS Illustrious - Born: Salem - Age: 26 - Discharged on 26 Dec 1813 and sent to Chatham on HM Ship of-the-Line Diomede.

Hill, Josiah - Seaman - Number: 866 - Prize Name: Tiger - Ship type: MV - How taken: HM Brig Scylla - When taken: 22 Mar 1813 - Where taken: Bay of Biscay - Date received: 24 Jun 1813 - From what ship: HM Frigate Unicorn - Born: New Orleans - Age: 20 - Race: Black - Discharged on 2 Jul 1813 and sent to Chatham on HM Frigate Tribune.

Hill, Pompey - Seaman - Number: 558 - Prize Name: Rossie - Ship type: MV - How taken: HM Frigate Dryand - When taken: 7 Jan 1813 - Where taken: at sea - Date received: 25 Jan 1813 - From what ship: HM Ship-of-the-Line Queen - Born: Maryland - Age: 34 - Race: Black - Discharged on 11 Mar 1813 and sent to Chatham on HM Store Ship Abundance.

Hill, William - Seaman - Number: 545 - Prize Name: Rossie - Ship type: MV - How taken: HM Frigate Dryand - When taken: 7 Jan 1813 - Where taken: at sea - Date received: 25 Jan 1813 - From what ship: HM Ship-of-the-Line Queen - Born: Philadelphia - Age: 25 - Discharged on 11 Mar 1813 and sent to Chatham on HM Store Ship Abundance.

Hitchcock, Elior - Seaman - Number: 761 - How taken: Gave himself up from HM Ship-of-the-Line Blake - Date received: 1 Apr 1813 - From what ship: HMS Blake - Born: Newark - Age: 46 - Race: Black - Discharged on 3 Apr 1813 and sent to Chatham on HM Transport Chatham.

Hitchi, John - Boy - Number: 411 - Prize Name: Otter - Ship type: MV - How taken: HM Ship-Sloop Jalouse - When taken: 1 Dec 1812 - Where taken: at sea - Date received: 10 Jan 1813 - From what ship: HM Guardship Royal William - Born: Africa - Age: 15 - Race: Mulatto - Discharged on 6 Mar 1813 and sent to Chatham on HMS Frigate Alexandria.

Hobart, George - Seaman - Number: 830 - How taken: Gave himself up from HM Frigate North Star - Date received: 26 May 1813 - From what ship: HMS North Star - Born: Hingham, MA - Age: 19 - Discharged on 10 Jun 1813 and sent to Chatham on HM Frigate Arethusa.

Hobdyke, John - Seaman - Number: 566 - Prize Name: Rossie - Ship type: MV - How taken: HM Frigate Dryand - When taken: 7 Jan 1813 - Where taken: at sea - Date received: 25 Jan 1813 - From what ship: HM Ship-of-the-Line Queen - Born: Portsmouth - Age: 16 - Discharged on 11 Mar 1813 and sent to Chatham on HM Store Ship Abundance.

Hogan, William - Seaman - Number: 656 - How taken: Gave himself up from HM Guardship Royal William - Date received: 6 Feb 1813 - From what ship: HMS Royal William - Born: Portland - Age: 43 - Discharged on 11 Mar 1813 and sent to Chatham on HM Store Ship Abundance.

Holland, James - Seaman - Number: 1486 - Prize Name: Indian Lass, prize of Privateer Grand Turk - Ship type: MV - How taken: HM Transport Akbar - When taken: 20 Apr 1814 - Where taken: at sea - Date received: 28 May 1814 - From what ship: HMS Akbar - Born: Cape Ann - Age: 27 - Discharged on 2 Jun 1814 and sent to Plymouth on HMS Growler.

Holstein, Richard - Seaman - Number: 1232 - Prize Name: British South Sea Whaler - How taken: HM Ship-of-the-Line Illustrious - When taken: 5 Aug 1813 - Where taken: St. Helena - Date received: 26 Nov 1813 - From what ship: HMS Illustrious - Born: Virginia - Age: 31 - Discharged on 26 Dec 1813 and sent to Chatham on HM Ship of-the-Line Diomede.

Holt, Simeon - Seaman - Number: 102 - Prize Name: HMS Eos - Ship type: MW - How taken: Detained by Court of Admiralty - When taken: 31 Jul 1812 - Where taken: Portsmouth harbor - Date received: 16 Oct 1812 San Antonio - From what ship: Eos - Born: Boston - Age: 17 - Discharged on 19 Feb 1813 and sent to Chatham on HM Frigate Ulysses.

Homan, John - Seaman - Number: 687 - Prize Name: Rachael - Ship type: MV - How taken: HM Schooner Herring

- When taken: 8 Feb 1813 - Where taken: at sea - Date received: 20 Feb 1813 - From what ship: HMS Herring - Born: Marblehead - Age: 27 - Discharged on 6 Mar 1813 and sent to Chatham on HM Ship-of-the-Line Cornwall.

Homan, Jonas - Seaman - Number: 688 - Prize Name: Rachael - Ship type: MV - How taken: HM Schooner Herring - When taken: 8 Feb 1813 - Where taken: at sea - Date received: 20 Feb 1813 - From what ship: HMS Herring - Born: Marblehead - Age: 19 - Discharged on 6 Mar 1813 and sent to Chatham on HM Ship-of-the-Line Cornwall.

Homan, Joseph - Seaman - Number: 58 - Prize Name: Diana, prize of Privateer Decatur - Ship type: MV - How taken: HM Ship-of-the-Line Polyphemus - When taken: 14 Sep 1812 - Where taken: at sea - Date received: 12 Oct 1812 San Antonio - From what ship: HM Ship-of-the-Line Polyphemus - Born: Marblehead - Age: 24 - Discharged on 19 Feb 1813 and sent to Chatham on HM Frigate Ulysses.

Hook, Aaron - Seaman - Number: 413 - Prize Name: Otter - Ship type: MV - How taken: HM Ship-Sloop Jalouse - When taken: 1 Dec 1812 - Where taken: at sea - Date received: 10 Jan 1813 - From what ship: HM Guardship Royal William - Born: Chichester, NH - Age: 20 - Discharged on 6 Mar 1813 and sent to Chatham on HMS Frigate Alexandria.

Hooper, Joseph A. - Gunner's Mate - Number: 1306 - Prize Name: Growler - Ship type: P - How taken: HM Brig Electra - When taken: 7 Jul 1813 - Where taken: off St. Johns - Date received: 22 Dec 1813 - From what ship: HM Frigate Hyperion - Born: Marblehead - Age: 23 - Discharged on 26 Dec 1813 and sent to Chatham on HMS Frigate Nemesis.

Hooseman, John - Seaman - Number: 624 - How taken: Gave himself up from HM Guardship Royal William - Date received: 3 Feb 1813 - From what ship: HMS Royal William - Born: Maryland - Age: 22 - Discharged on 11 Mar 1813 and sent to Chatham on HM Store Ship Abundance.

Horbert, Christopher - Carpenter - Number: 1346 - How taken: Gave himself up from HMS Service - Date received: 5 Jan 1814 - From what ship: HM Ship-of-the-Line Prince - Born: Virginia - Age: 41 - Discharged on 5 Jan 1814 and sent to Chatham on HM Ship-of-the-Line Poictiers.

Horner, John - Seaman - Number: 1040 - Prize Name: Falcon, prize of the US Frigate President - Ship type: MV - How taken: Spanish forces - When taken: 2 Jul 1813 - Where taken: Passage Harbor - Date received: 9 Sep 1813 - From what ship: HMS Ship-of-the-Line Kron Princessen - Born: Boston - Age: 27 - Discharged on 29 Sep 1813 and sent to Chatham on HM Ship-of-the-Line Barham (see Prisoner Number 1074).

Horner, John - Seaman - Number: 1074 - Prize Name: Falcon, prize of the US Frigate President - Ship type: MV - How taken: Spanish army - When taken: 2 Jul 1813 - Where taken: Passage Harbor - Date received: 1 Oct 1813 - From what ship: HM Ship-of-the-Line Barham - Born: Boston - Age: 27 - Discharged on 17 Oct 1813 and sent to Chatham on HM Store Ship Weymouth (see Prisoner Number 1040).

Hoskins, John - Seaman - Number: 1170 - How taken: Gave himself up from HM Hospital Ship Trent - Date received: 12 Oct 1813 - From what ship: HM Brig Hope - Born: Bedford, MA - Age: 20 - Discharged on 17 Oct 1813 and sent to Chatham on HM Transport Malabar No. 352.

Howard, Henry - Seaman - Number: 570 - Prize Name: Rossie - Ship type: MV - How taken: HM Frigate Dryand - When taken: 7 Jan 1813 - Where taken: at sea - Date received: 25 Jan 1813 - From what ship: HM Ship-of-the-Line Queen - Born: Philadelphia - Age: 29 - Discharged on 11 Mar 1813 and sent to Chatham on HM Store Ship Abundance.

Howateer, Henry - Seaman - Number: 936 - Prize Name: Tender of the True Blooded Yankee - Ship type: P - How taken: HM Ship-of-the-Line Fame - When taken: 24 Jun 1813 - Where taken: at sea - Date received: 1 Jul 1813 - From what ship: HM Brig Hope - Born: Wappen Creek, NY - Age: 24 - Race: Black - Discharged on 2 Jul 1813 and sent to Chatham on HM Brig Scorpion.

Howell, John - Seaman - Number: 802 - How taken: Gave himself up from HM Ship-of-the-Line Scepter - Date received: 21 Apr 1813 - From what ship: HM Guardship Royal William - Born: Philadelphia - Age: 24 - Discharged on 27 Apr 1813 and sent to Chatham on HM Sloop-of-War Bonne Citoyenne.

Howell, William - Seaman - Number: 1376 - Prize Name: Pilate - Ship type: P - How taken: Victoria, privateer of Guernsey - When taken: 28 Jan 1814 - Where taken: off Bordeaux - Date received: 7 Feb 1814 - From what ship: Mary from Guernsey - Born: New York - Age: 23 - Discharged on 13 Feb 1814 and sent to Chatham on HM Transport Malabar No. 352.

Howland, William - Seaman - Number: 362 - Prize Name: Three Brothers - Ship type: MV - How taken: HM Brig Bermuda - When taken: 9 Dec 1812 - Where taken: off St. Valery - Date received: 2 Jan 1813 - From what ship: HM Prison Ship Assistance - Born: Greenfield - Age: 24 - Discharged on 4 Mar 1813 and sent to Chatham on HM Ship-of-the-Line Queen.

Howlen, Samuel - Seaman - Number: 415 - Prize Name: Otter - Ship type: MV - How taken: HM Ship-Sloop Jalouse - When taken: 1 Dec 1812 - Where taken: at sea - Date received: 10 Jan 1813 - From what ship: HM Guardship Royal William - Born: Plymouth, MA - Age: 25 - Discharged on 6 Mar 1813 and sent to Chatham on HMS Frigate Alexandria.

Hoyt, Ichabod - Seaman - Number: 107 - Prize Name: Nancy - Ship type: MV - How taken: HM Brig Parthian - When taken: 1 Aug 1812 - Where taken: off the Needles - Date received: 16 Oct 1812 San Antonio - From what ship: HM Brig Nancy - Born: Amesbury, MA - Age: 24 - Discharged on 19 Feb 1813 and sent to Chatham on HM Frigate Ulysses.

Hoyt, James - Seaman - Number: 1482 - How taken: Gave himself up from HMS Nerias - Date received: 28 May 1814 - From what ship: HM Transport Akba - Born: Newark - Age: 46 - Discharged on 2 Jun 1814 and sent to Plymouth on HMS Growler.

Hubbard, Alfred - 2nd Mate - Number: 878 - Prize Name: Prompt - Ship type: MV - How taken: Chance, privateer - When taken: 28 Mar 1813 - Where taken: Bay of Biscay - Date received: 24 Jun 1813 - From what ship: HM Frigate Unicorn - Born: New Haven - Age: 28 - Discharged on 2 Jul 1813 and sent to Chatham on HM Frigate Tribune.

Hubbard, William - Seaman - Number: 1099 - How taken: Gave himself up from HM Ship-of-the-Line Union - Date received: 5 Oct 1813 - From what ship: HM Ship-of-the-Line Achille - Born: Connecticut - Age: 24 - Discharged on 17 Oct 1813 and sent to Chatham on HM Store Ship Weymouth.

Hubbart, Joseph - Seaman - Number: 1108 - How taken: Gave himself up from HM Ship-of-the-Line Swiftsure - Date received: 5 Oct 1813 - From what ship: HM Ship-of-the-Line Achille - Born: Boston - Age: 37 - Discharged on 17 Oct 1813 and sent to Chatham on HM Store Ship Weymouth.

Hubbell, James - Seaman - Number: 1441 - Prize Name: HMS Devon Transport No. 15, prize of Privateer Bunker Hill - Ship type: MV - How taken: HM Brig Fly - When taken: 21 Jan 1814 - Where taken: at sea - Date received: 1 Mar 1814 - From what ship: HMS Helicone - Born: Fairfield - Age: 29 - Discharged on 28 Apr 1814 and sent to Chatham on HM Brig Cordelia.

Hubi, Pierre M. - Boy - Number: 1470 - Prize Name: Bunker Hill - Ship type: P - How taken: HM Frigate Pomone & HM Frigate Cydnus - When taken: 4 Mar 1814 - Where taken: French coast - Date received: 11 Apr 1814 - From what ship: HMS Ship-on-the-Line San Domaso - Born: Lorient - Age: 11 - Discharged on 28 Apr 1814 and sent to Chatham on HM Store Ship Weymouth.

Huff, Charles - Seaman - Number: 608 - Prize Name: Sword Fish - Ship type: P - How taken: HM Ship-of-the-Line Elephant - When taken: 20 Dec 1812 - Where taken: at sea - Date received: 1 Feb 1813 - From what ship: HM Frigate Hermes - Born: Kennebunk - Age: 20 - Discharged on 28 Mar 1813 and sent to Chatham on HMS Scraphid.

Hughes, John - Seaman - Number: 834 - How taken: Gave himself up from HM Ship-of-the-Line Boyne - Date received: 5 Jun 1813 - From what ship: HM Guardship Royal William - Born: Baltimore - Age: 24 - Discharged on 10 Jun 1813 and sent to Chatham on HM Frigate Arethusa.

Hughes, Peter - Seaman - Number: 20 - Prize Name: USRM Cutter James Madison - Ship type: MW - How taken: HM Frigate Barbadoes - When taken: 22 Aug 1812 - Where taken: at sea - Date received: 12 Oct 1812 San Antonio - From what ship: HM Ship-of-the-Line Polyphemus - Born: South Plain, NJ - Age: 18 - Discharged on 3 Apr 1813 and sent to Chatham on HM Transport Chatham.

Hull, Edward - Seaman - Number: 895 - Prize Name: Weasel - Ship type: MV - How taken: Foxhound, privateer - When taken: 25 May 1813 - Where taken: Bay of Biscay - Date received: 24 Jun 1813 - From what ship: HM Frigate Unicorn - Born: Newport - Age: 19 - Discharged on 2 Jul 1813 and sent to Chatham on HM Frigate

Tribune.

Hunt, Dudley - Seaman - Number: 136 - Prize Name: Gossypium - Ship type: MV - How taken: HM Sloop Goree - When taken: 15 Aug 1812 - Where taken: off Bermuda - Date received: 29 Oct 1812 - From what ship: HM Ship-of-the-Line Ardent - Born: Providence, RI - Age: 25 - Discharged on 19 Feb 1813 and sent to Chatham on HM Store Ship Dromedary.

Hunt, Samuel - Seaman - Number: 1341 - Prize Name: Volunteer - Ship type: MV - How taken: Victoria, privateer of Guernsey - When taken: 26 Dec 1813 - Where taken: at sea - Date received: 4 Jan 1814 - From what ship: Earl S. Vincent Packet - Born: New York - Age: 29 - Discharged on 13 Feb 1814 and sent to Chatham on HM Transport Malabar No. 352.

Hurd, Abel - Seaman - Number: 1169 - How taken: Gave himself up from HM Hospital Ship Trent - Date received: 12 Oct 1813 - From what ship: HM Brig Hope - Born: Boston - Age: 35 - Discharged on 17 Oct 1813 and sent to Chatham on HM Transport Malabar No. 352.

Hurd, William - Seaman - Number: 248 - Prize Name: Antelope - Ship type: P - How taken: HM Brig Zephyr - When taken: 10 Dec 1812 - Where taken: at sea - Date received: 27 Dec 1812 - From what ship: HMS Zephyr - Born: Whitham, England - Age: 23 - Discharged on 31 Dec 1812 and sent to Chatham on HM Guardship Royal Williams.

Hurtt, Samuel - Seaman - Number: 564 - Prize Name: Rossie - Ship type: MV - How taken: HM Frigate Dryand - When taken: 7 Jan 1813 - Where taken: at sea - Date received: 25 Jan 1813 - From what ship: HM Ship-of-the-Line Queen - Born: Harford - Age: 24 - Discharged on 11 Mar 1813 and sent to Chatham on HM Store Ship Abundance.

Huse, Ebenezer - Seaman - Number: 998 - Prize Name: Kitty, prize of US Frigate President - Ship type: MV - How taken: Dart, privateer of Guernsey - When taken: 20 Jun 1813 - Where taken: at sea - Date received: 18 Aug 1813 - From what ship: HMS Dexterous - Born: Cape Ann, MA - Age: 24 - Discharged on 21 Sep 1813 and sent to Chatham on HM Ship-of-the-Line Queen.

Hussy, Edward - Cooper - Number: 1008 - Prize Name: Fame - Ship type: MV - How taken: HM Ship of-the-Line Cressy - When taken: 20 Jul 1813 - Where taken: at sea - Date received: 18 Aug 1813 - From what ship: HMS Cressy - Born: Nantucket - Age: 19 - Discharged on 21 Sep 1813 and sent to Chatham on HM Ship-of-the-Line Queen.

Hutchens, Townsend - Seaman - Number: 747 - How taken: Gave himself up from HM Ship of-the-Line Bellerophon - Date received: 25 Mar 1813 - From what ship: HMS Bellerophon - Born: Long Island - Age: 52 - Discharged on 28 Mar 1813 and sent to Chatham on HM Store Ship Seaphis.

Hutchings, Joseph - Boy - Number: 84 - Prize Name: HM Ship-of-the-Line Ganges - Ship type: MW - How taken: Detained by Court of Admiralty - When taken: 31 Jul 1812 - Where taken: Portsmouth harbor - Date received: 16 Oct 1812 San Antonio - From what ship: HM Ship-of-the-Line Ganges - Born: Wiscasset - Age: 14 - Discharged on 6 Mar 1813 and sent to Chatham on HM Ship-of-the-Line Cornwall.

Hutchings, William - Prize Master - Number: 1210 - Prize Name: Elbridge Gerry - Ship type: P - How taken: HM Frigate Crescent & HM Ship-of-the-Line Bellerophon - When taken: 16 Sep 1813 - Where taken: at sea - Date received: 16 Nov 1813 - From what ship: HM Sloop Talbot - Born: Machias, MA - Age: 23 - Discharged on 26 Dec 1813 and sent to Chatham on HM Ship of-the-Line Diomede.

Hutchins, William - Seaman - Number: 10 - Prize Name: USRM Cutter James Madison - Ship type: MW - How taken: HM Frigate Barbadoes - When taken: 22 Aug 1812 - Where taken: at sea - Date received: 12 Oct 1812 San Antonio - From what ship: HM Ship-of-the-Line Polyphemus - Born: Rocketts, VA - Age: 29 - Discharged on 19 Feb 1813 and sent to Chatham on HM Frigate Ulysses.

Hyatt, William - Seaman - Number: 266 - Prize Name: King of Rome - Ship type: P - How taken: HM Brig Wolverine - When taken: 13 Dec 1812 - Where taken: at sea - Date received: 27 Dec 1812 - From what ship: HMS Wolverine - Born: New York - Age: 28 - Discharged on 19 Feb 1813 and sent to Chatham on HM Store Ship Dromedary.

Inberg, Gabriel - Seaman - Number: 264 - Prize Name: King of Rome - Ship type: P - How taken: HM Brig Wolverine - When taken: 13 Dec 1812 - Where taken: at sea - Date received: 27 Dec 1812 - From what ship:

HMS Wolverine - Born: Obo, Finland - Age: 27 - Discharged on 19 Feb 1813 and sent to Chatham on HM Store Ship Dromedary.

Ingalls, Samuel - Carpenter - Number: 447 - Prize Name: Sword Fish - Ship type: P - How taken: HM Ship-of-the-Line Elephant - When taken: 28 Dec 1812 - Where taken: at sea - Date received: 14 Jan 1813 - From what ship: HMS Elephant - Born: Marblehead - Age: 24 - Discharged on 6 Mar 1813 and sent to Chatham on HMS Frigate Alexandria.

Ingesoll, Abraham - Seaman - Number: 921 - Prize Name: Tender of the True Blooded Yankee - Ship type: P - How taken: HM Ship-of-the-Line Fame - When taken: 24 Jun 1813 - Where taken: at sea - Date received: 1 Jul 1813 - From what ship: HM Brig Hope - Born: Boston - Age: 33 - Discharged on 2 Jul 1813 and sent to Chatham on HM Brig Scorpion.

Inghram, John - Seaman - Number: 822 - Prize Name: Ajax, prize to the Privateer Governor Tomkins - Ship type: MV - How taken: HM Frigate Revolutionnaire - When taken: 10 Apr 1813 - Where taken: at sea - Date received: 13 May 1813 - From what ship: HMS Revolutionaire - Born: New York - Age: 20 - Discharged on 17 May 1813 and sent to Chatham on HMS Impeleux.

Ingraham, Peter - Seaman - Number: 535 - Prize Name: Expectation - Ship type: MV - How taken: HMS Butain - When taken: 17 Dec 1812 - Where taken: at sea - Date received: 25 Jan 1813 - From what ship: HM Ship-of-the-Line Queen - Born: Lancaster, PA - Age: 33 - Discharged on 11 Mar 1813 and sent to Chatham on HM Store Ship Abundance.

Innes, John - Boy - Number: 488 - Prize Name: Sword Fish - Ship type: P - How taken: HM Ship-of-the-Line Elephant - When taken: 28 Dec 1812 - Where taken: at sea - Date received: 14 Jan 1813 - From what ship: HMS Elephant - Born: Boston - Age: 12 - Discharged on 11 Mar 1813 and sent to Chatham on HM Store Ship Abundance.

Isdale, James - Seaman - Number: 823 - Prize Name: Ajax, prize to the Privateer Governor Tomkins - Ship type: MV - How taken: HM Frigate Revolutionnaire - When taken: 10 Apr 1813 - Where taken: at sea - Date received: 13 May 1813 - From what ship: HMS Revolutionaire - Born: Philadelphia - Age: 25 - Discharged on 17 May 1813 and sent to Chatham on HMS Impeleux.

Jackson, Allison - Seaman - Number: 807 - How taken: Gave himself up from HM Frigate Hotspur - Date received: 21 Apr 1813 - From what ship: HM Guardship Royal William - Born: Charles City - Age: 26 - Race: Colored - Discharged on 27 Apr 1813 and sent to Chatham on HM Sloop-of-War Bonne Citoyenne.

Jackson, John - Seaman - Number: 98 - Prize Name: HMS Eos - Ship type: MW - How taken: Detained by Court of Admiralty - When taken: 31 Jul 1812 - Where taken: Portsmouth harbor - Date received: 16 Oct 1812 San Antonio - From what ship: Eos - Born: New York - Age: 29 - Race: Black - Discharged on 19 Feb 1813 and sent to Chatham on HM Frigate Ulysses.

Jackson, Lederick - Seaman - Number: 1393 - Prize Name: Pilate - Ship type: P - How taken: Victoria, privateer of Guernsey - When taken: 28 Jan 1814 - Where taken: off Bordeaux - Date received: 7 Feb 1814 - From what ship: Mary from Guernsey - Born: Maryland - Age: 22 - Race: Black - Discharged on 13 Feb 1814 and sent to Chatham on HM Transport Malabar No. 352.

Jackson, William - Ordinary Seaman - Number: 798 - How taken: Gave himself up from HM Ship-of-the-Line Sterling Castle - Date received: 18 Apr 1813 - From what ship: HM Guardship Royal William - Born: New Town, Long Island - Age: 38 - Discharged on 27 Apr 1813 and sent to Chatham on HM Sloop-of-War Bonne Citoyenne.

Jackson, William - Seaman - Number: 1234 - Prize Name: British South Sea Whaler - How taken: HM Ship-of-the-Line Illustrious - When taken: 5 Aug 1813 - Where taken: St. Helena - Date received: 26 Nov 1813 - From what ship: HMS Illustrious - Born: Long Island - Age: 30 - Race: Black - Discharged on 26 Dec 1813 and sent to Chatham on HM Ship of-the-Line Diomede.

Jacobson, Jacob - Seaman - Number: 364 - Prize Name: Three Brothers - Ship type: MV - How taken: HM Brig Bermuda - When taken: 9 Dec 1812 - Where taken: off St. Valery - Date received: 2 Jan 1813 - From what ship: HM Prison Ship Assistance - Born: Achim, Prussia - Age: 20 - Discharged on 4 Mar 1813 and sent to Chatham on HM Ship-of-the-Line Queen.

James, John - Seaman - Number: 1351 - How taken: Gave himself up from HMS Muros - Date received: 26 Jan 1814 - From what ship: HMS Muros - Born: Philadelphia - Age: 26 - Race: Mulatto - Discharged on 13 Feb 1814 and sent to Chatham on HM Transport Malabar No. 352.

James, John - Seaman - Number: 1227 - How taken: Gave himself up from HM Brig Port Mahon - Date received: 23 Nov 1813 - From what ship: HMS Port Mahon - Born: Pennsylvania - Age: 29 - Discharged on 26 Dec 1813 and sent to Chatham on HM Ship of-the-Line Diomede.

James, John - Seaman - Number: 4 - Prize Name: USRM Cutter James Madison - Ship type: MW - How taken: HM Frigate Barbadoes - When taken: 22 Aug 1812 - Where taken: at sea - Date received: 12 Oct 1812 San Antonio - From what ship: HM Ship-of-the-Line Polyphemus - Born: Hackettstown, NJ - Age: 25 - Discharged on 19 Feb 1813 and sent to Chatham on HM Frigate Ulysses.

James, John - Seaman - Number: 1018 - How taken: Gave himself up from HM Ship-of-the-Line Prince of Wales - Date received: 7 Sep 1813 - From what ship: HM Frigate Unicorn - Born: Carolina - Age: 26 - Race: Black - Discharged on 21 Sep 1813 and sent to Chatham on HM Ship-of-the-Line Queen.

James, Peter - Seaman - Number: 324 - Prize Name: Independence - Ship type: MV - How taken: HM Frigate Medusa - When taken: 9 Nov 1812 - Where taken: off St. Sebastian - Date received: 31 Dec 1812 - From what ship: HM Ship-of-the-Line Northumberland - Born: Boston - Age: 20 - Discharged on 4 Mar 1813 and sent to Chatham on HM Ship-of-the-Line Queen.

Jameson, George - Seaman - Number: 398 - Prize Name: Empress - Ship type: MV - How taken: HM Brig Rover - When taken: 30 Nov 1812 - Where taken: at sea - Date received: 10 Jan 1813 - From what ship: HM Guardship Royal William - Born: Charlestown - Age: 40 - Race: Colored - Discharged on 6 Mar 1813 and sent to Chatham on HMS Frigate Alexandria.

Jamison, George - Seaman - Number: 1081 - How taken: Gave himself up from HM Ship-of-the-Line Hibernia - Date received: 1 Oct 1813 - From what ship: HM Ship-of-the-Line Barham - Born: Philadelphia - Age: 53 - Race: Black - Discharged on 17 Oct 1813 and sent to Chatham on HM Store Ship Weymouth.

Jamison, George - Seaman - Number: 1055 - How taken: Gave himself up from HM Ship-of-the-Line Hibernia - Date received: 19 Sep 1813 - From what ship: HM Brig Imogen - Born: Philadelphia - Age: 53 - Race: Black - Discharged on 29 Sep 1813 and sent to Chatham on HM Transport Chatham.

Jane, Joseph - Seaman - Number: 312 - Prize Name: Warren - Ship type: MV - How taken: HM Frigate Sybille and HMS Fortunee - When taken: 5 Sep 1812 - Where taken: at sea - Date received: 31 Dec 1812 - From what ship: HM Ship-of-the-Line Northumberland - Born: Providence - Age: 20 - Discharged on 4 Mar 1813 and sent to Chatham on HM Ship-of-the-Line Queen.

Jardine, Samuel - Seaman - Number: 1458 - How taken: Gave himself up from HM Transport Ceylon - Date received: 10 Apr 1814 - From what ship: HMS Primer - Born: Massachusetts - Age: 23 - Discharged on 28 Apr 1814 and sent to Chatham on HM Store Ship Weymouth.

Jeffers, Henry - Seaman - Number: 1200 - Prize Name: Spanish merchant vessel, prize of Privateer Le Lion - Ship type: MV - How taken: HM Frigate Revolutionnaire - When taken: 2 Nov 1813 - Where taken: at sea - Date received: 9 Nov 1813 - From what ship: HMS Revolutionaire - Born: Delaware - Age: 23 - Discharged on 26 Dec 1813 and sent to Chatham on HM Ship of-the-Line Diomede.

Jefferys, Philip - Seaman - Number: 132 - How taken: Gave himself up from HM Ship-of-the-Line Ruby - When taken: 30 Aug 1812 - Date received: 29 Oct 1812 - From what ship: HM Ship-of-the-Line Ardent - Born: Camptown, Philadelphia - Age: 32 - Discharged on 19 Feb 1813 and sent to Chatham on HM Store Ship Dromedary.

Jeremy, Stephen - Seaman - Number: 472 - Prize Name: Sword Fish - Ship type: P - How taken: HM Ship-of-the-Line Elephant - When taken: 28 Dec 1812 - Where taken: at sea - Date received: 14 Jan 1813 - From what ship: HMS Elephant - Born: Baltimore - Age: 27 - Race: Colored - Discharged on 11 Mar 1813 and sent to Chatham on HM Store Ship Abundance.

Jerry, Daniel - Seaman - Number: 412 - Prize Name: Otter - Ship type: MV - How taken: HM Ship-Sloop Jalouse - When taken: 1 Dec 1812 - Where taken: at sea - Date received: 10 Jan 1813 - From what ship: HM Guardship Royal William - Born: Connecticut - Age: 20 - Discharged on 6 Mar 1813 and sent to Chatham on

HMS Frigate Alexandria.

Jewett, Theodore - Captain - Number: 731 - Prize Name: Dart - Ship type: MV - How taken: HM Brig Doterel - When taken: 5 Mar 1813 - Where taken: at sea - Date received: 21 Mar 1813 - From what ship: HMS Dotteril - Born: New Hampshire - Age: 26 - Discharged on 25 Mar 1814 and sent to Reading on parole.

John, Richard J. - Seaman - Number: 534 - Prize Name: Expectation - Ship type: MV - How taken: HMS Butain - When taken: 17 Dec 1812 - Where taken: at sea - Date received: 25 Jan 1813 - From what ship: HM Ship-of-the-Line Queen - Born: Norfolk - Age: 20 - Discharged on 11 Mar 1813 and sent to Chatham on HM Store Ship Abundance.

Johnson 2nd, John - Seaman - Number: 672 - How taken: Gave himself up from HM Frigate Ulysses - Date received: 10 Feb 1813 - From what ship: HM Brig Electra - Born: Boston - Age: 30 - Discharged on 6 Mar 1813 and sent to Chatham on HM Ship-of-the-Line Cornwall.

Johnson, Andre - Seaman - Number: 173 - Prize Name: Baltimore - Ship type: P - How taken: HM Transport Diadem - When taken: 7 Oct 1812 - Where taken: S. Andera - Date received: 3 Nov 1812 San Antonio - From what ship: HMS Diadem - Born: Carlscrona, Sweden - Age: 30 - Discharged on 19 Feb 1813 and sent to Chatham on HM Store Ship Dromedary.

Johnson, Andrew - Seaman - Number: 27 - Prize Name: USRM Cutter James Madison - Ship type: MW - How taken: HM Frigate Barbadoes - When taken: 22 Aug 1812 - Where taken: at sea - Date received: 12 Oct 1812 San Antonio - From what ship: HM Ship-of-the-Line Polyphemus - Born: Carlscrona, Sweden - Age: 22 - Discharged on 19 Feb 1813 and sent to Chatham on HM Frigate Ulysses.

Johnson, Andrew - Boy - Number: 479 - Prize Name: Sword Fish - Ship type: P - How taken: HM Ship-of-the-Line Elephant - When taken: 28 Dec 1812 - Where taken: at sea - Date received: 14 Jan 1813 - From what ship: HMS Elephant - Born: Norfolk - Age: 17 - Discharged on 11 Mar 1813 and sent to Chatham on HM Store Ship Abundance.

Johnson, David - Seaman - Number: 402 - Prize Name: Empress - Ship type: MV - How taken: HM Brig Rover - When taken: 30 Nov 1812 - Where taken: at sea - Date received: 10 Jan 1813 - From what ship: HM Guardship Royal William - Born: Wilmington - Age: 22 - Discharged on 6 Mar 1813 and sent to Chatham on HMS Frigate Alexandria.

Johnson, Easton - Seaman - Number: 1235 - How taken: Gave himself up from HM Ship-of-the-Line Illustrious - Date received: 26 Nov 1813 - From what ship: HMS Illustrious - Born: Boston - Age: 24 - Discharged on 26 Dec 1813 and sent to Chatham on HM Ship of-the-Line Diomede.

Johnson, Edward - Seaman - Number: 773 - How taken: Gave himself up from HM Frigate Brune - Date received: 1 Apr 1813 - From what ship: HM Ship-of-the-Line Blake - Born: Kensington, CT - Age: 26 - Discharged on 3 Apr 1813 and sent to Chatham on HM Transport Chatham.

Johnson, Frederick - Seaman - Number: 635 - How taken: Gave himself up from HM Guardship Royal William - Date received: 3 Feb 1813 - From what ship: HMS Royal William - Born: Connecticut - Age: 51 - Discharged on 11 Mar 1813 and sent to Chatham on HM Store Ship Abundance.

Johnson, Henry - Seaman - Number: 294 - Prize Name: Hannah - Ship type: MV - How taken: Taken up on shore - When taken: 18 Oct 1812 - Where taken: Liverpool - Date received: 31 Dec 1812 - From what ship: HM Ship-of-the-Line Northumberland - Born: Philadelphia - Age: 34 - Race: Black - Discharged on 4 Mar 1813 and sent to Chatham on HM Ship-of-the-Line Queen.

Johnson, Henry - Seaman - Number: 1164 - Prize Name: Russian merchant vessel - How taken: Taken out of the HM Ship-of-the-Line Neptune - When taken: 28 Sep 1813 - Where taken: Cork - Date received: 12 Oct 1813 - From what ship: HM Brig Hope - Born: Danvers - Age: 20 - Discharged on 17 Oct 1813 and sent to Chatham on HM Transport Malabar No. 352.

Johnson, John - Seaman - Number: 1230 - How taken: Gave himself up from HM Ship-of-the-Line Invincible - Date received: 24 Nov 1813 - From what ship: HM Transport Leopard - Born: Newtown, MA - Age: 21 - Discharged on 26 Dec 1813 and sent to Chatham on HM Ship of-the-Line Diomede.

Johnson, John - Seaman - Number: 1252 - Prize Name: Dart - Ship type: P - How taken: HM Frigate Niger & HMS Fortunee - Where taken: at sea - Date received: 19 Dec 1813 - From what ship: HMS Fortunee - Born: New

York - Age: 25 - Discharged on 26 Dec 1813 and sent to Chatham on HM Ship of-the-Line Diomede.

Johnson, Oliver - Seaman - Number: 513 - How taken: Gave himself up from HMS Renealous - Date received: 22 Jan 1813 - From what ship: HMS Renelous - Born: Connecticut - Age: 28 - Discharged on 11 Mar 1813 and sent to Chatham on HM Store Ship Abundance.

Johnson, Robert - Seaman - Number: 1244 - Prize Name: British South Sea Whaler - How taken: HM Ship-of-the-Line Illustrious - When taken: 22 Oct 1813 - Where taken: at sea - Date received: 26 Nov 1813 - From what ship: HMS Illustrious - Born: Baltimore - Age: 24 - Discharged on 26 Dec 1813 and sent to Chatham on HM Ship of-the-Line Diomede.

Johnson, Robert - Seaman - Number: 340 - Prize Name: Ceres - Ship type: MV - How taken: HM Battery Princess - When taken: 39 Aug 1812 - Where taken: Liverpool - Date received: 31 Dec 1812 - From what ship: HM Ship-of-the-Line Northumberland - Born: New York - Age: 23 - Race: Black - Discharged on 4 Mar 1813 and sent to Chatham on HM Ship-of-the-Line Queen.

Johnson, Samuel - Seaman - Number: 583 - How taken: Gave himself up from HM Ship-of-the-Line Vigo - Date received: 30 Jan 1813 - From what ship: HMS Vigo - Born: Providence - Age: 59 - Re-entered by mistake (see Prisoner Number 279).

Johnson, Samuel - Seaman - Number: 279 - How taken: Gave himself up from HM Ship-of-the-Line Vigo - When taken: 30 Dec 1812 - Date received: 30 Dec 1812 - From what ship: HM Brig Zephyr - Born: Providence - Age: 59 - Discharged on 19 Feb 1813 and sent to Chatham on HM Store Ship Dromedary (see Prisoner Number 583).

Johnson, Samuel B. - Seaman - Number: 1447 - How taken: Gave himself up from HMS Eridmus - Date received: 1 Mar 1814 - From what ship: HMS Helicone - Born: Salem - Age: 39 - Discharged on 28 Apr 1814 and sent to Chatham on HM Brig Cordelia.

Johnson, William - Seaman - Number: 669 - How taken: Gave himself up from HM Brig Electra - Date received: 10 Feb 1813 - From what ship: HMS Electra - Born: New York - Age: 19 - Discharged on 6 Mar 1813 and sent to Chatham on HM Ship-of-the-Line Cornwall.

Johnson, William - Seaman - Number: 618 - How taken: Gave himself up from HM Guardship Royal William - Date received: 3 Feb 1813 - From what ship: HMS Royal William - Born: New York - Age: 34 - Discharged on 11 Mar 1813 and sent to Chatham on HM Store Ship Abundance.

Johnston, Richard - Seaman - Number: 1015 - Prize Name: Fame - Ship type: MV - How taken: HM Ship of-the-Line Cressy - When taken: 20 Jul 1813 - Where taken: at sea - Date received: 18 Aug 1813 - From what ship: HMS Cressy - Born: New York - Age: 42 - Race: Mulatto - Discharged on 21 Sep 1813 and sent to Chatham on HM Ship-of-the-Line Queen.

Johnston, Thomas - Seaman - Number: 848 - How taken: Gave himself up from HM Ship-of-the-Line Malta - Date received: 15 Jun 1813 - From what ship: HM Sloop Helena - Born: Baltimore - Age: 27 - Discharged on 2 Jul 1813 and sent to Chatham on HM Frigate Tribune.

Jones, Anthony - Seaman - Number: 1175 - How taken: Gave himself up from HM Frigate Astrea - Date received: 16 Oct 1813 - From what ship: HMS Astrea - Born: New Orleans - Age: 32 - Discharged on 17 Oct 1813 and sent to Chatham on HM Transport Malabar No. 352.

Jones, Cabal - 2nd Mate - Number: 543 - Prize Name: Leader - Ship type: MV - How taken: HMS Butain - When taken: 17 Dec 1812 - Where taken: at sea - Date received: 25 Jan 1813 - From what ship: HM Ship-of-the-Line Queen - Born: Kent - Age: 29 - Discharged on 11 Mar 1813 and sent to Chatham on HM Store Ship Abundance.

Jones, James - Passenger - Number: 875 - Prize Name: Tiger - Ship type: MV - How taken: HM Brig Scylla - When taken: 22 Mar 1813 - Where taken: Bay of Biscay - Date received: 24 Jun 1813 - From what ship: HM Frigate Unicorn - Born: Connecticut - Age: 35 - Discharged on 2 Jul 1813 and sent to Chatham on HM Frigate Tribune.

Jones, Theodore - Seaman - Number: 1355 - How taken: Gave himself up from HM Ship-of-the-Line Bulwark - Date received: 28 Jan 1814 - From what ship: HMS Bulmark - Born: Maryland - Age: 26 - Discharged on 13 Feb 1814 and sent to Chatham on HM Transport Malabar No. 352.

Jones, Thomas - Seaman - Number: 1335 - How taken: Gave himself up from HM Ship-of-the-Line Invincible - Date received: 27 Dec 1813 - From what ship: HMS Frigate Nemesis - Born: Baltimore - Age: 25 - Discharged on 27 Dec 1813 and sent to Chatham on HMS Frigate Nemesis.

Jones, Thomas - Cook - Number: 1281 - Prize Name: Growler - Ship type: P - How taken: HM Brig Electra - When taken: 7 Jul 1813 - Where taken: off St. Johns - Date received: 22 Dec 1813 - From what ship: HM Ship of-the-Line Bellerophon - Born: Baltimore - Age: 38 - Race: Black - Discharged on 26 Dec 1813 and sent to Chatham on HMS Frigate Nemesis.

Jones, William - Seaman - Number: 234 - Prize Name: Antelope - Ship type: P - How taken: HM Brig Zephyr - When taken: 10 Dec 1812 - Where taken: at sea - Date received: 27 Dec 1812 - From what ship: HMS Zephyr - Born: New York - Age: 31 - Discharged on 19 Feb 1813 and sent to Chatham on HM Store Ship Dromedary.

Jordon, Artemas - Seaman - Number: 1033 - How taken: Gave himself up from HM Battery Gorgon - Date received: 7 Sep 1813 - From what ship: HM Frigate Unicorn - Born: Plymouth, MA - Age: 28 - Discharged on 21 Sep 1813 and sent to Chatham on HM Ship-of-the-Line Queen.

Joseph, Michael - Cook - Number: 361 - Prize Name: Argus - Ship type: MV - How taken: Fancy, cutter - When taken: 19 Dec 1812 - Where taken: Bay of Biscay - Date received: 31 Dec 1812 - From what ship: HM Ship-of-the-Line Northumberland - Born: New York - Age: 24 - Discharged on 4 Mar 1813 and sent to Chatham on HM Ship-of-the-Line Queen.

Joseph, Michael - Boy - Number: 1283 - Prize Name: Growler - Ship type: P - How taken: HM Brig Electra - When taken: 7 Jul 1813 - Where taken: off St. Johns - Date received: 22 Dec 1813 - From what ship: HM Ship of-the-Line Bellerophon - Born: Marblehead - Age: 14 - Discharged on 26 Dec 1813 and sent to Chatham on HMS Frigate Nemesis.

Jourdan, John - Seaman - Number: 1274 - Prize Name: Pomona, prize of Privateer Prince Neuchatel - Ship type: MV - How taken: HM Frigate Ethalion - When taken: 14 Dec 1813 - Where taken: at sea - Date received: 22 Dec 1813 - From what ship: HMS Ethalion - Born: New Orleans - Age: 24 - Discharged on 26 Dec 1813 and sent to Chatham on HM Ship of-the-Line Diomede.

Kanady, James - Able Seaman - Number: 715 - How taken: Gave himself up from HM Frigate Hamadryad - Date received: 27 Feb 1813 - From what ship: HMS Hamadryad - Born: Baltimore - Age: 20 - Discharged on 6 Mar 1813 and sent to Chatham on HM Ship-of-the-Line Cornwall.

Keen, Joseph - Seaman - Number: 1419 - Prize Name: Zephyr, prize of Privateer Rattlesnake - Ship type: MV - How taken: HM Frigate Surveillante - When taken: 6 Jan 1814 - Where taken: Bay of Biscay - Date received: 1 Mar 1814 - From what ship: HMS Helicone - Born: Pennsylvania - Age: 26 - Discharged on 28 Apr 1814 and sent to Chatham on HM Sloop Favorite.

Kemp, James - Seaman - Number: 853 - How taken: Gave himself up from HM Frigate Leonidas - Date received: 22 Jun 1813 - From what ship: HM Ship-of-the-Line Vigo - Born: New York - Age: 27 - Race: Mulatto - Discharged on 2 Jul 1813 and sent to Chatham on HM Frigate Tribune.

Kennedy, Dennis - Seaman - Number: 1342 - Prize Name: Volunteer - Ship type: MV - How taken: Victoria, privateer of Guernsey - When taken: 26 Dec 1813 - Where taken: at sea - Date received: 4 Jan 1814 - From what ship: Earl S. Vincent Packet - Born: South Carolina - Age: 31 - Discharged on 5 Jan 1814 and sent to Chatham on HM Ship-of-the-Line Poictiers.

Kennedy, Henry - 2nd Mate - Number: 95 - Prize Name: HMS Eos - Ship type: MW - How taken: Detained by Court of Admiralty - When taken: 31 Jul 1812 - Where taken: Portsmouth harbor - Date received: 16 Oct 1812 San Antonio - From what ship: Eos - Born: Boston - Age: 27 - Discharged on 19 Feb 1813 and sent to Chatham on HM Frigate Ulysses.

Kenner, John Downing - Seaman - Number: 145 - Prize Name: William - Ship type: MV - How taken: HM Brig Recruit - When taken: 29 Aug 1812 - Where taken: at sea - Date received: 29 Oct 1812 - From what ship: HM Ship-of-the-Line Ardent - Born: Northumberland, VA - Age: 24 - Discharged on 11 Mar 1813 and sent to Chatham on HM Store Ship Abundance.

Kenny, George - Boy - Number: 489 - Prize Name: Sword Fish - Ship type: P - How taken: HM Ship-of-the-Line

Elephant - When taken: 28 Dec 1812 - Where taken: at sea - Date received: 14 Jan 1813 - From what ship: HMS Elephant - Born: Salem - Age: 14 - Discharged on 11 Mar 1813 and sent to Chatham on HM Store Ship Abundance.

Kerban, Thomas - Seaman - Number: 338 - How taken: Impressed at Belfast - When taken: 15 Sep 1812 - Date received: 31 Dec 1812 - From what ship: HM Ship-of-the-Line Northumberland - Born: New Orleans - Age: 29 - Discharged on 4 Mar 1813 and sent to Chatham on HM Ship-of-the-Line Queen.

Kerhon, Abraham - Seaman - Number: 864 - Prize Name: Tiger - Ship type: MV - How taken: HM Brig Scylla - When taken: 22 Mar 1813 - Where taken: Bay of Biscay - Date received: 24 Jun 1813 - From what ship: HM Frigate Unicorn - Born: Long Island - Age: 32 - Discharged on 2 Jul 1813 and sent to Chatham on HM Frigate Tribune.

Kerhow, Samuel - Seaman - Number: 603 - Prize Name: Sword Fish - Ship type: P - How taken: HM Ship-of-the-Line Elephant - When taken: 20 Dec 1812 - Where taken: at sea - Date received: 1 Feb 1813 - From what ship: HM Frigate Hermes - Born: Salem - Age: 44 - Discharged on 11 Mar 1813 and sent to Chatham on HM Store Ship Abundance.

Keys, Zenas - Seaman - Number: 1223 - Prize Name: Growler - Ship type: P - How taken: HM Brig Electra - When taken: 7 Jul 1813 - Where taken: at sea - Date received: 16 Nov 1813 - From what ship: HM Sloop Talbot - Born: Massachusetts - Age: 22 - Discharged on 26 Dec 1813 and sent to Chatham on HM Ship of-the-Line Diomede.

Kile, George - Seaman - Number: 471 - Prize Name: Sword Fish - Ship type: P - How taken: HM Ship-of-the-Line Elephant - When taken: 28 Dec 1812 - Where taken: at sea - Date received: 14 Jan 1813 - From what ship: HMS Elephant - Born: Philadelphia - Age: 23 - Discharged on 11 Mar 1813 and sent to Chatham on HM Store Ship Abundance.

King, John - Seaman - Number: 899 - Prize Name: Weasel - Ship type: MV - How taken: Foxhound, privateer - When taken: 25 May 1813 - Where taken: Bay of Biscay - Date received: 24 Jun 1813 - From what ship: HM Frigate Unicorn - Born: New York - Age: 20 - Discharged on 2 Jul 1813 and sent to Chatham on HM Frigate Tribune.

King, Peter - Seaman - Number: 1373 - Prize Name: Brilliant, prize to Privateer Prince Neuchatel - Ship type: MV - How taken: Caught on the Alderney Island, England - When taken: 26 Jan 1814 - Where taken: Alderney - Date received: 7 Feb 1814 - From what ship: Mary from Guernsey - Born: Boston - Age: 40 - Discharged on 13 Feb 1814 and sent to Chatham on HM Transport Malabar No. 352.

Kingbutton, John - Seaman - Number: 1239 - Prize Name: British South Sea Whaler - How taken: HM Ship-of-the-Line Illustrious - When taken: 22 Oct 1813 - Where taken: at sea - Date received: 26 Nov 1813 - From what ship: HMS Illustrious - Born: Province Town - Age: 26 - Discharged on 26 Dec 1813 and sent to Chatham on HM Ship of-the-Line Diomede.

Kinnard, Charles - Carpenter - Number: 1257 - Prize Name: Dart - Ship type: P - How taken: HM Frigate Niger & HMS Fortunee - Where taken: at sea - Date received: 19 Dec 1813 - From what ship: HMS Fortunee - Born: New Orleans - Age: 27 - Discharged on 26 Dec 1813 and sent to Chatham on HM Ship-of-the-Line Diomede.

Kirk, Thomas - Seaman - Number: 251 - Prize Name: King of Rome - Ship type: P - How taken: HM Brig Wolverine - When taken: 13 Dec 1812 - Where taken: at sea - Date received: 27 Dec 1812 - From what ship: HMS Wolverine - Born: New York - Age: 36 - Discharged on 19 Feb 1813 and sent to Chatham on HM Store Ship Dromedary.

Knapp, Walker - Seaman - Number: 284 - Prize Name: Rhode & Betsey - Ship type: MV - How taken: HM Sloop Talbot - When taken: 12 Aug 1812 - Where taken: off Cape Clear - Date received: 31 Dec 1812 - From what ship: HM Ship-of-the-Line Northumberland - Born: Stanford - Age: 21 - Discharged on 19 Feb 1813 and sent to Chatham on HM Store Ship Dromedary.

Knight, Ira - Seaman - Number: 215 - How taken: Gave himself up from HM Ship-of-the-Line Victory - Date received: 23 Dec 1812 - From what ship: HM Guardship Royal William - Born: Portland - Age: 26 - Discharged on 19 Feb 1813 and sent to Chatham on HM Store Ship Dromedary.

Knox, John - Seaman - Number: 1484 - How taken: Gave himself up from HMS Nerias - Date received: 28 May

1814 - From what ship: HM Transport Akba - Born: New York - Age: 47 - Discharged on 2 Jun 1814 and sent to Plymouth on HMS Growler.

Kraft, Michael - Seaman - Number: 1221 - Prize Name: Growler - Ship type: P - How taken: HM Brig Electra - When taken: 7 Jul 1813 - Where taken: at sea - Date received: 16 Nov 1813 - From what ship: HM Sloop Talbot - Born: Philadelphia - Age: 20 - Discharged on 26 Dec 1813 and sent to Chatham on HM Ship of-the-Line Diomede.

La Roche, John B. - Seaman - Number: 1275 - Prize Name: Pomona, prize of Privateer Prince Neuchatel - Ship type: MV - How taken: HM Frigate Ethalion - When taken: 14 Dec 1813 - Where taken: at sea - Date received: 22 Dec 1813 - From what ship: HMS Ethalion - Born: New Orleans - Age: 24 - Race: Black - Discharged on 26 Dec 1813 and sent to Chatham on HM Ship of-the-Line Diomede.

Labbas, John - Seaman - Number: 576 - Prize Name: Industry - Ship type: MV - How taken: HM Frigate Dryand - When taken: 7 Jan 1813 - Where taken: at sea - Date received: 25 Jan 1813 - From what ship: HM Ship-of-the-Line Queen - Born: New Orleans - Age: 25 - Discharged on 11 Mar 1813 and sent to Chatham on HM Store Ship Abundance.

Lake, Daniel - Seaman - Number: 1504 - How taken: Gave himself up from HM Frigate Amphion - Date received: 27 Jun 1814 - From what ship: HMS Amphion - Born: Staten Island - Age: 35 - Discharged on 30 Jun 1814 and sent to Plymouth on HM Brig Steady.

Lake, Noah - Seaman - Number: 713 - How taken: Taken up at the Gosport Rendezvous - Date received: 24 Feb 1813 - From what ship: Gosport Rendezvous - Born: Taunton, MA - Age: 26 - Discharged on 6 Mar 1813 and sent to Chatham on HM Ship-of-the-Line Cornwall.

Lakeman, Samuel - Seaman - Number: 61 - Prize Name: Diana, prize of Privateer Decatur - Ship type: MV - How taken: HM Ship-of-the-Line Polyphemus - When taken: 14 Sep 1812 - Where taken: at sea - Date received: 12 Oct 1812 San Antonio - From what ship: HM Ship-of-the-Line Polyphemus - Born: Ipswich - Age: 24 - Discharged on 19 Feb 1813 and sent to Chatham on HM Frigate Ulysses.

Lamb, Jack - Cook - Number: 1092 - Prize Name: Hindostan - Ship type: MV - How taken: HM Brig Zenobia - When taken: 25 Jun 1813 - Where taken: off Lisbon - Date received: 1 Oct 1813 - From what ship: HM Ship-of-the-Line Barham - Born: Africa - Age: 20 - Race: Black - Discharged on 17 Oct 1813 and sent to Chatham on HM Store Ship Weymouth (see Prisoner Number 1067).

Lamb, Jack - Cook - Number: 1067 - Prize Name: Hindostan - Ship type: MV - How taken: HM Brig Zenobia - When taken: 25 Jun 1813 - Where taken: off Lisbon - Date received: 19 Sep 1813 - From what ship: HM Brig Imogen - Born: Africa - Age: 20 - Race: Black - Discharged on 29 Sep 1813 and sent to Chatham on HM Transport Chatham (see Prisoner Number 1092).

Lambert, John - Seaman - Number: 463 - Prize Name: Sword Fish - Ship type: P - How taken: HM Ship-of-the-Line Elephant - When taken: 28 Dec 1812 - Where taken: at sea - Date received: 14 Jan 1813 - From what ship: HMS Elephant - Born: Woolwich, MA - Age: 22 - Discharged on 11 Mar 1813 and sent to Chatham on HM Store Ship Abundance.

Lambleson, Edward - Seaman - Number: 170 - Prize Name: Baltimore - Ship type: P - How taken: HM Transport Diadem - When taken: 7 Oct 1812 - Where taken: S. Andera - Date received: 3 Nov 1812 San Antonio - From what ship: HMS Diadem - Born: Philadelphia - Age: 25 - Discharged on 19 Feb 1813 and sent to Chatham on HM Store Ship Dromedary.

Lamboard, Thomas - Seaman - Number: 1017 - How taken: Gave himself up from Royal Naval Hospital Haslar - Date received: 24 Aug 1813 - From what ship: Royal Naval Hospital Haslar - Born: Weymouth, MA - Age: 39 - Discharged on 21 Sep 1813 and sent to Chatham on HM Ship-of-the-Line Queen.

Lamon, James - Seaman - Number: 568 - Prize Name: Rossie - Ship type: MV - How taken: HM Frigate Dryand - When taken: 7 Jan 1813 - Where taken: at sea - Date received: 25 Jan 1813 - From what ship: HM Ship-of-the-Line Queen - Born: Wilmington - Age: 36 - Race: Black - Discharged on 11 Mar 1813 and sent to Chatham on HM Store Ship Abundance.

Lane, James - Prize Master - Number: 1272 - Prize Name: Pomona, prize of Privateer Prince Neuchatel - Ship type: MV - How taken: HM Frigate Ethalion - When taken: 14 Dec 1813 - Where taken: at sea - Date received: 22

Dec 1813 - From what ship: HMS Ethalion - Born: Massachusetts - Age: 32 - Discharged on 26 Dec 1813 and sent to Chatham on HM Ship of-the-Line Diomede.

Lane, William - Seaman - Number: 1364 - How taken: Gave himself up from HM Sloop Comet - Date received: 1 Feb 1814 - From what ship: HM Frigate Sybille - Born: New York - Age: 32 - Discharged on 13 Feb 1814 and sent to Chatham on HM Transport Malabar No. 352.

Lapham, Cushion - Prize Master - Number: 717 - Prize Name: Quebec, prize of the Privateer Paul Jones - Ship type: MV - How taken: HM Brig Dewent - When taken: 29 Jan 1813 - Where taken: at sea - Date received: 28 Feb 1813 - From what ship: HMS Derwent - Age: 32 - Discharged on 6 Mar 1813 and sent to Chatham on HM Ship-of-the-Line Cornwall.

Lassier, Florence - Seaman - Number: 542 - Prize Name: Leader - Ship type: MV - How taken: HMS Butain - When taken: 17 Dec 1812 - Where taken: at sea - Date received: 25 Jan 1813 - From what ship: HM Ship-of-the-Line Queen - Born: Massachusetts - Age: 20 - Discharged on 11 Mar 1813 and sent to Chatham on HM Store Ship Abundance.

Latish, Joseph - Boy - Number: 288 - Prize Name: Purse - Ship type: MV - How taken: HM Frigate Armide - When taken: 29 May 1812 - Where taken: off Bordeaux - Date received: 31 Dec 1812 - From what ship: HM Ship-of-the-Line Northumberland - Born: Philadelphia - Age: 10 - Discharged on 19 Feb 1813 and sent to Chatham on HM Frigate Ulysses.

Lavan, Thomas - Seaman - Number: 1334 - How taken: Gave himself up from HM Ship-of-the-Line Invincible - Date received: 27 Dec 1813 - From what ship: HMS Frigate Nemesis - Born: Coxsackie, NY - Age: 24 - Race: Black - Discharged on 27 Dec 1813 and sent to Chatham on HMS Frigate Nemesis.

Lawrence, Peter - Seaman - Number: 460 - Prize Name: Sword Fish - Ship type: P - How taken: HM Ship-of-the-Line Elephant - When taken: 28 Dec 1812 - Where taken: at sea - Date received: 14 Jan 1813 - From what ship: HMS Elephant - Born: Petersburg - Age: 21 - Race: Black - Discharged on 11 Mar 1813 and sent to Chatham on HM Store Ship Abundance.

Lawson, James - Seaman - Number: 922 - Prize Name: Tender of the True Blooded Yankee - Ship type: P - How taken: HM Ship-of-the-Line Fame - When taken: 24 Jun 1813 - Where taken: at sea - Date received: 1 Jul 1813 - From what ship: HM Brig Hope - Born: New York - Age: 48 - Discharged on 2 Jul 1813 and sent to Chatham on HM Brig Scorpion.

Lawson, Laurence - Seaman - Number: 940 - Prize Name: Tender of the True Blooded Yankee - Ship type: P - How taken: HM Ship-of-the-Line Fame - When taken: 24 Jun 1813 - Where taken: at sea - Date received: 1 Jul 1813 - From what ship: HM Brig Hope - Born: Old York - Age: 26 - Discharged on 2 Jul 1813 and sent to Chatham on HM Brig Scorpion.

Lawson, Mathew - Seaman - Number: 224 - Prize Name: Antelope - Ship type: P - How taken: HM Brig Zephyr - When taken: 10 Dec 1812 - Where taken: at sea - Date received: 27 Dec 1812 - From what ship: HMS Zephyr - Born: Baltimore - Age: 31 - Discharged on 19 Feb 1813 and sent to Chatham on HM Store Ship Dromedary.

Le Goff, Herve - Boy - Number: 1465 - Prize Name: Bunker Hill - Ship type: P - How taken: HM Frigate Pomone & HM Frigate Cydnus - When taken: 4 Mar 1814 - Where taken: French coast - Date received: 11 Apr 1814 - From what ship: HMS Ship-on-the-Line San Domaso - Born: Brest, France - Age: 10 - Discharged on 28 Apr 1814 and sent to Chatham on HM Store Ship Weymouth.

Le Petit, John Baptiste - Marine - Number: 1466 - Prize Name: Bunker Hill - Ship type: P - How taken: HM Frigate Pomone & HM Frigate Cydnus - When taken: 4 Mar 1814 - Where taken: French coast - Date received: 11 Apr 1814 - From what ship: HMS Ship-on-the-Line San Domaso - Born: Caen, France - Age: 18 - Discharged on 28 Apr 1814 and sent to Chatham on HM Store Ship Weymouth.

Le Saut, Jacques - Marine - Number: 1477 - Prize Name: Bunker Hill - Ship type: P - How taken: HM Frigate Pomone & HM Frigate Cydnus - When taken: 4 Mar 1814 - Where taken: French coast - Date received: 11 Apr 1814 - From what ship: HMS Ship-on-the-Line San Domaso - Born: St. Pollion, France - Age: 22 - Discharged on 28 Apr 1814 and sent to Chatham on HM Store Ship Weymouth.

Lear, Alexander - Seaman - Number: 456 - Prize Name: Sword Fish - Ship type: P - How taken: HM Ship-of-the-

Line Elephant - When taken: 28 Dec 1812 - Where taken: at sea - Date received: 14 Jan 1813 - From what ship: HMS Elephant - Born: Portsmouth - Age: 47 - Discharged on 11 Mar 1813 and sent to Chatham on HM Store Ship Abundance.

Lebon, Philip - Seaman - Number: 259 - Prize Name: King of Rome - Ship type: P - How taken: HM Brig Wolverine - When taken: 13 Dec 1812 - Where taken: at sea - Date received: 27 Dec 1812 - From what ship: HMS Wolverine - Born: New Orleans - Age: 25 - Discharged on 19 Feb 1813 and sent to Chatham on HM Store Ship Dromedary.

Lebour, Francois - Seaman - Number: 1463 - Prize Name: Bunker Hill - Ship type: P - How taken: HM Frigate Pomone & HM Frigate Cydnus - When taken: 4 Mar 1814 - Where taken: French coast - Date received: 11 Apr 1814 - From what ship: HMS Ship-on-the-Line San Domaso - Born: Brest, France - Age: 29 - Discharged on 28 Apr 1814 and sent to Chatham on HM Store Ship Weymouth.

Lee, Edward - Seaman - Number: 799 - How taken: Gave himself up from HM Ship-of-the-Line Scepter - Date received: 21 Apr 1813 - From what ship: HM Guardship Royal William - Born: Dorset County, MD - Age: 25 - Discharged on 27 Apr 1813 and sent to Chatham on HM Sloop-of-War Bonne Citoyenne.

Lee, John - Seaman - Number: 1179 - How taken: Gave himself up from HM Frigate Spartan - Date received: 30 Oct 1813 - From what ship: HMS Spartan - Born: New Orleans - Age: 40 - Race: Mulatto - Discharged on 26 Dec 1813 and sent to Chatham on HM Ship of-the-Line Diomede.

Lee, Nathaniel - Boy - Number: 994 - Prize Name: Growler - Ship type: P - How taken: HM Brig Electra - When taken: 7 Jul 1813 - Where taken: at sea - Date received: 9 Aug 1813 - From what ship: HM Sloop Hazard - Born: Marblehead - Age: 12 - Discharged on 13 Aug 1813 and sent to Chatham on HM Brig Cadmus.

Lee, Richard - Seaman - Number: 474 - Prize Name: Sword Fish - Ship type: P - How taken: HM Ship-of-the-Line Elephant - When taken: 28 Dec 1812 - Where taken: at sea - Date received: 14 Jan 1813 - From what ship: HMS Elephant - Born: Marblehead - Age: 51 - Discharged on 11 Mar 1813 and sent to Chatham on HM Store Ship Abundance.

Lee, Samuel - Seaman - Number: 559 - Prize Name: Rossie - Ship type: MV - How taken: HM Frigate Dryand - When taken: 7 Jan 1813 - Where taken: at sea - Date received: 25 Jan 1813 - From what ship: HM Ship-of-the-Line Queen - Born: Maryland - Age: 25 - Race: Black - Discharged on 11 Mar 1813 and sent to Chatham on HM Store Ship Abundance.

Legere, Joseph - Seaman - Number: 267 - Prize Name: King of Rome - Ship type: P - How taken: HM Brig Wolverine - When taken: 13 Dec 1812 - Where taken: at sea - Date received: 27 Dec 1812 - From what ship: HMS Wolverine - Born: Tohe, Spain - Age: 34 - Discharged on 19 Feb 1813 and sent to Chatham on HM Store Ship Dromedary.

Leighton, Otis - Seaman - Number: 134 - How taken: Gave himself up from HM Ship-of-the-Line Ruby - When taken: 30 Aug 1812 - Date received: 29 Oct 1812 - From what ship: HM Ship-of-the-Line Ardent - Born: Columbia, MA - Age: 19 - Discharged on 19 Feb 1813 and sent to Chatham on HM Store Ship Dromedary.

Lemmon, Henry - Seaman - Number: 893 - Prize Name: Weasel - Ship type: MV - How taken: Foxhound, privateer - When taken: 25 May 1813 - Where taken: Bay of Biscay - Date received: 24 Jun 1813 - From what ship: HM Frigate Unicorn - Born: Savannah - Age: 22 - Discharged on 2 Jul 1813 and sent to Chatham on HM Frigate Tribune.

Lemon, Nicholas, C. - 2nd Lieutenant - Number: 1002 - Prize Name: John of Salem - Ship type: P - How taken: HM Brig Peruvian - When taken: 6 Feb 1813 - Where taken: at sea - Date received: 18 Aug 1813 - From what ship: HM Ship of-the-Line Cressy - Born: Marblehead - Age: 33 - Discharged on 21 Sep 1813 and sent to Chatham on HM Ship-of-the-Line Queen.

Lenderson, Henry - Carpenter - Number: 321 - Prize Name: Taken on shore - How taken: HM Battery Princess - When taken: 5 Nov 1812 - Where taken: Liverpool - Date received: 31 Dec 1812 - From what ship: HM Ship-of-the-Line Northumberland - Born: New York - Age: 30 - Race: Black - Discharged on 4 Mar 1813 and sent to Chatham on HM Ship-of-the-Line Queen.

Leonard, Robert - Seaman - Number: 1121 - Prize Name: Sampson - Ship type: MV - How taken: HM Brig Rebuff - When taken: 12 May 1813 - Where taken: off Cape St. Vincent - Date received: 5 Oct 1813 - From what ship: HM Ship-of-the-Line Achille - Born: New York - Age: 29 - Discharged on 17 Oct 1813 and sent to Chatham on HM Transport Malabar No. 352.

Lerocque, Olivier (alias Peter Rock) - Seaman - Number: 1476 - Prize Name: Bunker Hill - Ship type: P - How taken: HM Frigate Pomone & HM Frigate Cydnus - When taken: 4 Mar 1814 - Where taken: French coast - Date received: 11 Apr 1814 - From what ship: HMS Ship-on-the-Line San Domaso - Born: New York - Age: 32 - Discharged on 28 Apr 1814 and sent to Chatham on HM Store Ship Weymouth.

Lescombe, John - Seaman - Number: 374 - Prize Name: Mariner - Ship type: MV - How taken: HM Brig Lyra - When taken: 15 Dec 1812 - Where taken: off Bilboa, Spain - Date received: 3 Jan 1813 - From what ship: HM Frigate Fox - Born: Portsmouth - Age: 20 - Discharged on 4 Mar 1813 and sent to Chatham on HM Ship-of-the-Line Queen.

Lessingwell, Benajah - Captain - Number: 70 - Prize Name: HM Frigate Leonidas - Ship type: MW - How taken: Detained by Court of Admiralty - When taken: 31 Jul 1812 - Where taken: Portsmouth harbor - Date received: 16 Oct 1812 San Antonio - From what ship: HM Frigate Leonidas - Born: Norwich, MA - Age: 47 - Discharged on 26 Oct 1813 and sent to Odiham on parole.

Lewis, John - Seaman - Number: 1505 - How taken: Gave himself up from HM Frigate Amphion - Date received: 27 Jun 1814 - From what ship: HMS Amphion - Born: Pennsylvania - Age: 21 - Race: Black - Discharged on 30 Jun 1814 and sent to Plymouth on HM Brig Steady.

Lewis, John - Seaman - Number: 743 - Prize Name: Dart - Ship type: MV - How taken: HM Brig Doterel - When taken: 5 Mar 1813 - Where taken: at sea - Date received: 21 Mar 1813 - From what ship: HMS Dotteril - Born: Natchez, MS - Age: 27 - Race: Black - Discharged on 28 Mar 1813 and sent to Chatham on HM Store Ship Seaphis.

Lewis, John - Seaman - Number: 329 - Prize Name: Independence - Ship type: MV - How taken: HM Frigate Medusa - When taken: 9 Nov 1812 - Where taken: off St. Sebastian - Date received: 31 Dec 1812 - From what ship: HM Ship-of-the-Line Northumberland - Born: Maryland - Age: 25 - Race: Black - Discharged on 4 Mar 1813 and sent to Chatham on HM Ship-of-the-Line Queen.

Lewis, John - Seaman - Number: 260 - Prize Name: King of Rome - Ship type: P - How taken: HM Brig Wolverine - When taken: 13 Dec 1812 - Where taken: at sea - Date received: 27 Dec 1812 - From what ship: HMS Wolverine - Born: New Orleans - Age: 34 - Discharged on 19 Feb 1813 and sent to Chatham on HM Store Ship Dromedary.

Lewis, Peter - Seaman - Number: 1295 - Prize Name: Mary, prize to the True Blooded Yankee - Ship type: MV - How taken: HM Ship of-the-Line Bellerophon - When taken: 16 Dec 1813 - Where taken: off Land's End - Date received: 22 Dec 1813 - From what ship: HMS Bellerophon - Born: Charleston - Age: 34 - Discharged on 26 Dec 1813 and sent to Chatham on HMS Frigate Nemesis.

Liddle, John - Seaman - Number: 236 - Prize Name: Antelope - Ship type: P - How taken: HM Brig Zephyr - When taken: 10 Dec 1812 - Where taken: at sea - Date received: 27 Dec 1812 - From what ship: HMS Zephyr - Born: Dorchester, MA - Age: 17 - Discharged on 19 Feb 1813 and sent to Chatham on HM Store Ship Dromedary.

Liddle, Morris - Seaman - Number: 666 - How taken: Gave himself up from HM Frigate Ulysses - Date received: 7 Feb 1813 - From what ship: HMS Ulysses - Born: Maryland - Age: 26 - Discharged on 6 Mar 1813 and sent to Chatham on HM Ship-of-the-Line Cornwall.

Liemo, Frederick - Seaman - Number: 1475 - Prize Name: Bunker Hill - Ship type: P - How taken: HM Frigate Pomone & HM Frigate Cydnus - When taken: 4 Mar 1814 - Where taken: French coast - Date received: 11 Apr 1814 - From what ship: HMS Ship-on-the-Line San Domaso - Born: Stralsund, Germany - Age: 28 - Discharged on 28 Apr 1814 and sent to Chatham on HM Store Ship Weymouth.

Lind, Andrew - Seaman - Number: 393 - Prize Name: Empress - Ship type: MV - How taken: HM Brig Rover - When taken: 30 Nov 1812 - Where taken: at sea - Date received: 10 Jan 1813 - From what ship: HM Guardship Royal William - Born: Nuremberg, Germany - Age: 49 - Discharged on 4 Mar 1813 and sent to Chatham on HM Ship-of-the-Line Queen.

Lindholm, Nicholas - Seaman - Number: 178 - Prize Name: Baltimore - Ship type: P - How taken: HM Transport

Diadem - When taken: 7 Oct 1812 - Where taken: S. Andera - Date received: 3 Nov 1812 San Antonio - From what ship: HMS Diadem - Born: Carlscrona, Sweden - Age: 33 - Discharged on 19 Feb 1813 and sent to Chatham on HM Store Ship Dromedary.

Lindsay, Nathaniel - Captain - Number: 993 - Prize Name: Growler - Ship type: P - How taken: HM Brig Electra - When taken: 7 Jul 1813 - Where taken: at sea - Date received: 9 Aug 1813 - From what ship: HM Sloop Hazard - Born: Salem - Age: 42 - Discharged on 13 Aug 1813 and sent to Chatham on HM Brig Cadmus.

Lint, Joseph - Seaman - Number: 724 - How taken: Gave himself up from HM Frigate Niobe - Date received: 13 Mar 1813 - From what ship: HMS Niobe - Born: Salem - Age: 39 - Discharged on 28 Mar 1813 and sent to Chatham on HM Store Ship Seaphis.

Lippen, Stephen - Seaman - Number: 255 - Prize Name: King of Rome - Ship type: P - How taken: HM Brig Wolverine - When taken: 13 Dec 1812 - Where taken: at sea - Date received: 27 Dec 1812 - From what ship: HMS Wolverine - Born: New Orleans - Age: 29 - Discharged on 19 Feb 1813 and sent to Chatham on HM Store Ship Dromedary.

Lister, Louis - Seaman - Number: 663 - How taken: Gave himself up from HM Frigate Ulysses - Date received: 7 Feb 1813 - From what ship: HMS Ulysses - Born: Virginia - Age: 24 - Discharged on 6 Mar 1813 and sent to Chatham on HM Ship-of-the-Line Cornwall.

Livingston, Henry - Seaman - Number: 1382 - Prize Name: Pilate - Ship type: P - How taken: Victoria, privateer of Guernsey - When taken: 28 Jan 1814 - Where taken: off Bordeaux - Date received: 7 Feb 1814 - From what ship: Mary from Guernsey - Born: New York - Age: 25 - Race: Black - Discharged on 13 Feb 1814 and sent to Chatham on HM Transport Malabar No. 352.

Lock, Nathaniel - Seaman - Number: 156 - Prize Name: Diamond - Ship type: MV - How taken: Detained at Bermuda - When taken: 17 Apr 1812 - Where taken: Bermuda - Date received: 29 Oct 1812 - From what ship: HM Ship-of-the-Line Ardent - Born: Yalmouth, MA - Age: 24 - Discharged on 19 Feb 1813 and sent to Chatham on HM Store Ship Dromedary.

Lockerby, William - Chief Mate - Number: 756 - Prize Name: Pallas - Ship type: MV - How taken: HM Brig Rebuff - When taken: 23 Jan 1813 - Where taken: Cadiz - Date received: 1 Apr 1813 - From what ship: HM Ship-of-the-Line Blake - Born: New York - Age: 29 - Discharged on 3 Apr 1813 and sent to Chatham on HM Transport Chatham.

Lockett, Thomas R. - Seaman - Number: 578 - Prize Name: Industry - Ship type: MV - How taken: HM Frigate Dryand - When taken: 7 Jan 1813 - Where taken: at sea - Date received: 25 Jan 1813 - From what ship: HM Ship-of-the-Line Queen - Born: Virginia - Age: 19 - Race: Black - Discharged on 11 Mar 1813 and sent to Chatham on HM Store Ship Abundance.

Long, Ebenezer - Seaman - Number: 109 - Prize Name: Nancy - Ship type: MV - How taken: HM Brig Parthian - When taken: 1 Aug 1812 - Where taken: off the Needles - Date received: 16 Oct 1812 San Antonio - From what ship: HM Brig Nancy - Born: Amesbury, MA - Age: 24 - Discharged on 8 Jan 1813 and sent to Odiham on parole.

Long, James - Seaman - Number: 1497 - Prize Name: Traveler, prize of the Privateer Surprise - Ship type: MV - How taken: HM Schooner Canso - When taken: 14 May 1814 - Where taken: at sea - Date received: 1 Jun 1814 - From what ship: HMS Canso - Born: Baltimore - Age: 36 - Discharged on 2 Jun 1814 and sent to Plymouth on HMS Growler.

Longwell, Amos - Seaman - Number: 554 - Prize Name: Rossie - Ship type: MV - How taken: HM Frigate Dryand - When taken: 7 Jan 1813 - Where taken: at sea - Date received: 25 Jan 1813 - From what ship: HM Ship-of-the-Line Queen - Born: Maryland - Age: 24 - Discharged on 11 Mar 1813 and sent to Chatham on HM Store Ship Abundance.

Lopaus, William - Seaman - Number: 881 - Prize Name: Prompt - Ship type: MV - How taken: Chance, privateer - When taken: 28 Mar 1813 - Where taken: Bay of Biscay - Date received: 24 Jun 1813 - From what ship: HM Frigate Unicorn - Born: Boston - Age: 27 - Discharged on 2 Jul 1813 and sent to Chatham on HM Frigate Tribune.

Lothrop, James - Seaman - Number: 655 - How taken: Gave himself up from HM Guardship Royal William - Date received: 6 Feb 1813 - From what ship: HMS Royal William - Born: New York - Age: 30 - Discharged on 11 Mar 1813 and sent to Chatham on HM Store Ship Abundance.

Lowdie, Samuel - Seaman - Number: 913 - How taken: Gave himself up from HM Frigate Hyperion - Date received: 1 Jul 1813 - From what ship: HM Frigate Tribune - Born: New York - Age: 25 - Race: Mulatto - Discharged on 2 Jul 1813 and sent to Chatham on HM Brig Scorpion.

Lowe, Thomas - Seaman - Number: 1031 - How taken: Gave himself up from HM Battery Gorgon - Date received: 7 Sep 1813 - From what ship: HM Frigate Unicorn - Born: Massachusetts - Age: 23 - Discharged on 21 Sep 1813 and sent to Chatham on HM Ship-of-the-Line Queen.

Lucas, Benjamin - Seaman - Number: 179 - Prize Name: Baltimore - Ship type: P - How taken: HM Transport Diadem - When taken: 7 Oct 1812 - Where taken: S. Andera - Date received: 3 Nov 1812 San Antonio - From what ship: HMS Diadem - Born: Baltimore - Age: 21 - Discharged on 19 Feb 1813 and sent to Chatham on HM Store Ship Dromedary.

Lucas, Francois Rene - Marine - Number: 1468 - Prize Name: Bunker Hill - Ship type: P - How taken: HM Frigate Pomone & HM Frigate Cydnus - When taken: 4 Mar 1814 - Where taken: French coast - Date received: 11 Apr 1814 - From what ship: HMS Ship-on-the-Line San Domaso - Born: Brest, France - Age: 36 - Discharged on 28 Apr 1814 and sent to Chatham on HM Store Ship Weymouth.

Lucas, Martin - Seaman - Number: 1100 - How taken: Gave himself up from HM Ship-of-the-Line Swiftsure - Date received: 5 Oct 1813 - From what ship: HM Ship-of-the-Line Achille - Born: New York - Age: 50 - Race: Black - Discharged on 17 Oct 1813 and sent to Chatham on HM Store Ship Weymouth.

Ludlow, John - Seaman - Number: 281 - How taken: Gave himself up from HM Ship-of-the-Line Vigo - When taken: 30 Dec 1812 - Date received: 30 Dec 1812 - From what ship: HM Brig Zephyr - Born: New Bedford - Age: 36 - Race: Black - Discharged on 19 Feb 1813 and sent to Chatham on HM Store Ship Dromedary (see Prisoner Number 584).

Ludlow, Ruben - Seaman - Number: 867 - Prize Name: Tiger - Ship type: MV - How taken: HM Brig Scylla - When taken: 22 Mar 1813 - Where taken: Bay of Biscay - Date received: 24 Jun 1813 - From what ship: HM Frigate Unicorn - Born: Philadelphia - Age: 33 - Discharged on 2 Jul 1813 and sent to Chatham on HM Frigate Tribune.

Ludlow, William - Seaman - Number: 584 - How taken: Gave himself up from HM Ship-of-the-Line Vigo - Date received: 30 Jan 1813 - From what ship: HMS Vigo - Born: New Bedford - Age: 36 - Race: Black - Re-entered by mistake (see Prisoner Number 281).

Lumburger, Jacob - Prize Master - Number: 917 - Prize Name: Tender of the True Blooded Yankee - Ship type: P - How taken: HM Ship-of-the-Line Fame - When taken: 24 Jun 1813 - Where taken: at sea - Date received: 1 Jul 1813 - From what ship: HM Brig Hope - Born: Pennsylvania - Age: 28 - Discharged on 7 Aug 1813 and sent to Chatham on HM Brig Rinaldo.

Lupy, Marcus - Seaman - Number: 1276 - Prize Name: Pomona, prize of Privateer Prince Neuchatel - Ship type: MV - How taken: HM Frigate Ethalion - When taken: 14 Dec 1813 - Where taken: at sea - Date received: 22 Dec 1813 - From what ship: HMS Ethalion - Born: Isle de France (Mauritius) - Age: 20 - Discharged on 26 Dec 1813 and sent to Chatham on HM Ship of-the-Line Diomede.

Lynch, Thomas - Seaman - Number: 1153 - How taken: Gave himself up from HM Frigate Orpheus - Date received: 7 Oct 1813 - From what ship: HM Frigate Spartan - Born: Maryland - Age: 38 - Discharged on 17 Oct 1813 and sent to Chatham on HM Transport Malabar No. 352.

Lynch, William - Seaman - Number: 351 - Prize Name: Experiment - Ship type: MV - How taken: HM Brig Rover - When taken: 10 Nov 1812 - Where taken: off Bordeaux - Date received: 31 Dec 1812 - From what ship: HM Ship-of-the-Line Northumberland - Born: Maryland - Age: 21 - Discharged on 4 Mar 1813 and sent to Chatham on HM Ship-of-the-Line Queen.

Macey, George - Master - Number: 368 - Prize Name: Mariner - Ship type: MV - How taken: HM Brig Lyra - When taken: 15 Dec 1812 - Where taken: off Bilboa, Spain - Date received: 3 Jan 1813 - From what ship: HM Frigate Fox - Born: Nantucket - Age: 42 - Discharged on 11 Feb 1813 and sent to Odiham on parole.

Macrombie, Elijah - Seaman - Number: 204 - Prize Name: Perseverance - Ship type: MV - How taken: HM Sloop

Atalante - When taken: 31 Jul 1812 - Where taken: at sea - Date received: 25 Nov 1812 - From what ship: HM Guardship Royal William - Born: Taunton, MA - Age: 25 - Discharged on 19 Feb 1813 and sent to Chatham on HM Store Ship Dromedary.

Magrath, James - Seaman - Number: 212 - How taken: Gave himself up from HM Prison Ship Minerve - Date received: 14 Dec 1812 - From what ship: HM Guardship Royal William - Born: New York - Age: 30 - Discharged on 19 Feb 1813 and sent to Chatham on HM Store Ship Dromedary.

Mains, John - Seaman - Number: 1446 - How taken: Gave himself up from HM Schooner Whiting - Date received: 1 Mar 1814 - From what ship: HMS Helicone - Born: Shrewsbury, MA - Age: 39 - Discharged on 28 Apr 1814 and sent to Chatham on HM Brig Cordelia.

Malcomb, Alexander - Seaman - Number: 1225 - Prize Name: Growler - Ship type: P - How taken: HM Brig Electra - When taken: 7 Jul 1813 - Where taken: at sea - Date received: 16 Nov 1813 - From what ship: HM Sloop Talbot - Born: Marblehead - Age: 22 - Discharged on 26 Dec 1813 and sent to Chatham on HM Ship of-the-Line Diomede.

Males, Joseph - Seaman - Number: 634 - How taken: Gave himself up from HM Guardship Royal William - Date received: 3 Feb 1813 - From what ship: HMS Royal William - Born: Virginia - Age: 29 - Discharged on 11 Mar 1813 and sent to Chatham on HM Store Ship Abundance.

Mallan, James - Seaman - Number: 772 - How taken: Gave himself up from HM Frigate Brune - Date received: 1 Apr 1813 - From what ship: HM Ship-of-the-Line Blake - Born: New Jersey - Age: 37 - Discharged on 3 Apr 1813 and sent to Chatham on HM Transport Chatham.

Mallet, William - Seaman - Number: 1278 - Prize Name: US Schooner Growler - Ship type: MW - How taken: Sir James Yeo's Squadron - When taken: 11 Aug 1813 - Where taken: Lake Ontario - Date received: 22 Dec 1813 - From what ship: HM Frigate Ethalion - Born: New York - Age: 23 - Discharged on 26 Dec 1813 and sent to Chatham on HM Ship of-the-Line Diomede.

Manley, David - Seaman - Number: 1405 - Prize Name: Pilot - Ship type: P - How taken: Victoria, privateer of Guernsey - When taken: 28 Jan 1814 - Where taken: off Bordeaux - Date received: 16 Feb 1814 - From what ship: HM Transport Malabar No. 352 - Born: Portsmouth, VA - Age: 30 - Race: Mulatto - Discharged on 28 Apr 1814 and sent to Chatham on HM Store Ship Weymouth.

Manley, Rudolph - Seaman - Number: 1123 - Prize Name: Sampson - Ship type: MV - How taken: HM Brig Rebuff - When taken: 12 May 1813 - Where taken: off Cape St. Vincent - Date received: 5 Oct 1813 - From what ship: HM Ship-of-the-Line Achille - Born: Maryland - Age: 26 - Discharged on 17 Oct 1813 and sent to Chatham on HM Transport Malabar No. 352.

Manly, David - Seaman - Number: 1377 - Prize Name: Pilate - Ship type: P - How taken: Victoria, privateer of Guernsey - When taken: 28 Jan 1814 - Where taken: off Bordeaux - Date received: 7 Feb 1814 - From what ship: Mary from Guernsey - Born: Portsmouth, VA - Age: 30 - Race: Mulatto - Discharged on 13 Feb 1814 and sent to Chatham on HM Transport Malabar No. 352.

Manning, Burrel - Boy - Number: 1282 - Prize Name: Growler - Ship type: P - How taken: HM Brig Electra - When taken: 7 Jul 1813 - Where taken: off St. Johns - Date received: 22 Dec 1813 - From what ship: HM Ship of-the-Line Bellerophon - Born: Salem - Age: 11 - Discharged on 26 Dec 1813 and sent to Chatham on HMS Frigate Nemesis.

Manning, Enoch - Marine Officer & Captain's Clerk - Number: 439 - Prize Name: Sword Fish - Ship type: P - How taken: HM Ship-of-the-Line Elephant - When taken: 28 Dec 1812 - Where taken: at sea - Date received: 14 Jan 1813 - From what ship: HMS Elephant - Born: Amherst - Age: 28 - Discharged on 6 Mar 1813 and sent to Chatham on HMS Frigate Alexandria.

Manning, Thomas - Seaman - Number: 73 - Prize Name: HM Frigate Leonidas - Ship type: MW - How taken: Detained by Court of Admiralty - When taken: 31 Jul 1812 - Where taken: Portsmouth harbor - Date received: 16 Oct 1812 San Antonio - From what ship: HM Frigate Leonidas - Born: Salem - Age: 23 - Discharged on 19 Feb 1813 and sent to Chatham on HM Frigate Ulysses.

Manuel, John - Seaman - Number: 332 - Prize Name: Independence - Ship type: MV - How taken: HM Frigate Medusa - When taken: 9 Nov 1812 - Where taken: off St. Sebastian - Date received: 31 Dec 1812 - From what ship: HM Ship-of-the-Line Northumberland - Born: New Orleans - Age: 37 - Race: Black - Discharged on 4 Mar 1813 and sent to Chatham on HM Ship-of-the-Line Queen.

Manuel, Joseph - Seaman - Number: 313 - Prize Name: Warren - Ship type: MV - How taken: HM Frigate Sybille and HMS Fortunee - When taken: 5 Sep 1812 - Where taken: at sea - Date received: 31 Dec 1812 - From what ship: HM Ship-of-the-Line Northumberland - Born: Oporto, Portugal - Age: 24 - Discharged on 4 Mar 1813 and sent to Chatham on HM Ship-of-the-Line Queen.

March, Joseph (alias Merron) - Marine - Number: 484 - Prize Name: Sword Fish - Ship type: P - How taken: HM Ship-of-the-Line Elephant - When taken: 28 Dec 1812 - Where taken: at sea - Date received: 14 Jan 1813 - From what ship: HMS Elephant - Born: Brookfield - Age: 19 - Discharged on 11 Mar 1813 and sent to Chatham on HM Store Ship Abundance.

Marest, Charles - Seaman - Number: 1471 - Prize Name: Bunker Hill - Ship type: P - How taken: HM Frigate Pomone & HM Frigate Cydnus - When taken: 4 Mar 1814 - Where taken: French coast - Date received: 11 Apr 1814 - From what ship: HMS Ship-on-the-Line San Domaso - Born: New Orleans - Age: 30 - Discharged on 26 Apr 1814 to Le Simon, a French luger.

Maris, Yeace - Boy - Number: 944 - Prize Name: Tender of the True Blooded Yankee - Ship type: P - How taken: HM Ship-of-the-Line Fame - When taken: 24 Jun 1813 - Where taken: at sea - Date received: 1 Jul 1813 - From what ship: HM Brig Hope - Born: New Orleans - Age: 12 - Discharged on 2 Jul 1813 and sent to Chatham on HM Brig Scorpion.

Marks, Peter - Seaman - Number: 516 - How taken: Gave himself up from HM Ship-of-the-Line Tigre - Date received: 23 Jan 1813 - From what ship: HMS Tigre - Born: New Orleans - Age: 31 - Discharged on 11 Mar 1813 and sent to Chatham on HM Store Ship Abundance.

Marlborough, Francis - Seaman - Number: 1338 - How taken: Gave himself up from HMS Dannemark - Date received: 4 Jan 1814 - From what ship: HMS Dannemark - Born: Harford, PA - Age: 47 - Race: Black - Discharged on 5 Jan 1814 and sent to Chatham on HM Ship-of-the-Line Poictiers.

Marlow, Owen - Seaman - Number: 1343 - Prize Name: Volunteer - Ship type: MV - How taken: Victoria, privateer of Guernsey - When taken: 26 Dec 1813 - Where taken: at sea - Date received: 4 Jan 1814 - From what ship: Earl S. Vincent Packet - Born: Massachusetts - Age: 22 - Discharged on 5 Jan 1814 and sent to Chatham on HM Ship-of-the-Line Poictiers.

Mars, George - Seaman - Number: 865 - Prize Name: Tiger - Ship type: MV - How taken: HM Brig Scylla - When taken: 22 Mar 1813 - Where taken: Bay of Biscay - Date received: 24 Jun 1813 - From what ship: HM Frigate Unicorn - Born: Massachusetts - Age: 39 - Discharged on 2 Jul 1813 and sent to Chatham on HM Frigate Tribune.

Marshall, Francis - Seaman - Number: 665 - How taken: Gave himself up from HM Frigate Ulysses - Date received: 7 Feb 1813 - From what ship: HMS Ulysses - Born: Portland - Age: 28 - Discharged on 6 Mar 1813 and sent to Chatham on HM Ship-of-the-Line Cornwall.

Martel, Stephen - Supercargo - Number: 519 - Prize Name: Columbia - Ship type: MV - How taken: HMS Butain - When taken: 17 Dec 1812 - Where taken: at sea - Date received: 25 Jan 1813 - From what ship: HM Ship-of-the-Line Queen - Born: St. Domingo (Haiti) - Age: 32 - Discharged on 29 Jan 1813 and sent to Odiham on parole.

Martin, Henry - Seaman - Number: 729 - How taken: Gave himself up from HM Ship-of-the-Line Christian VII - Date received: 19 Mar 1813 - From what ship: HMS Christian VII - Born: Albany - Age: 28 - Discharged on 28 Mar 1813 and sent to Chatham on HM Store Ship Seaphis.

Martin, John J. - Seaman - Number: 649 - How taken: Gave himself up from HM Guardship Royal William - Date received: 3 Feb 1813 - From what ship: HMS Royal William - Born: New York - Age: 30 - Discharged on 11 Mar 1813 and sent to Chatham on HM Store Ship Abundance.

Martin, Jonathan - Seaman - Number: 28 - Prize Name: USRM Cutter James Madison - Ship type: MW - How taken: HM Frigate Barbadoes - When taken: 22 Aug 1812 - Where taken: at sea - Date received: 12 Oct 1812 San Antonio - From what ship: HM Ship-of-the-Line Polyphemus - Born: Baltimore - Age: 37 - Discharged on 19 Feb 1813 and sent to Chatham on HM Frigate Ulysses.

Mash, Hercules - Seaman - Number: 1010 - Prize Name: Fame - Ship type: MV - How taken: HM Ship of-the-Line Cressy - When taken: 20 Jul 1813 - Where taken: at sea - Date received: 18 Aug 1813 - From what ship: HMS Cressy - Born: Rhode Island - Age: 19 - Discharged on 21 Sep 1813 and sent to Chatham on HM Ship-of-the-Line Queen.

Mason, John - Seaman - Number: 675 - How taken: Gave himself up from HM Sloop Ariel - Date received: 11 Feb 1813 - From what ship: HMS Ariel - Born: New York - Age: 42 - Discharged on 6 Mar 1813 and sent to Chatham on HM Ship-of-the-Line Cornwall.

Mason, Joseph J. - Sailing Master - Number: 1003 - Prize Name: John of Salem - Ship type: P - How taken: HM Brig Peruvian - When taken: 6 Feb 1813 - Where taken: at sea - Date received: 18 Aug 1813 - From what ship: HM Ship of-the-Line Cressy - Born: Marblehead - Age: 26 - Discharged on 21 Sep 1813 and sent to Chatham on HM Ship-of-the-Line Queen.

Matheuron, Andrew - Seaman - Number: 238 - Prize Name: Antelope - Ship type: P - How taken: HM Brig Zephyr - When taken: 10 Dec 1812 - Where taken: at sea - Date received: 27 Dec 1812 - From what ship: HMS Zephyr - Born: New York - Age: 26 - Discharged on 19 Feb 1813 and sent to Chatham on HM Store Ship Dromedary.

Mathews, John - Seaman - Number: 1029 - How taken: Gave himself up from HMS Underunter - Date received: 7 Sep 1813 - From what ship: HM Frigate Unicorn - Born: Delaware - Age: 27 - Discharged on 21 Sep 1813 and sent to Chatham on HM Ship-of-the-Line Queen.

Mathews, Lewis - Seaman - Number: 925 - Prize Name: Tender of the True Blooded Yankee - Ship type: P - How taken: HM Ship-of-the-Line Fame - When taken: 24 Jun 1813 - Where taken: at sea - Date received: 1 Jul 1813 - From what ship: HM Brig Hope - Born: Dover, DE - Age: 35 - Race: Black - Discharged on 2 Jul 1813 and sent to Chatham on HM Brig Scorpion.

McAlpin, Cornelius - Seaman - Number: 1172 - How taken: Gave himself up from HM Brig Hope - Date received: 12 Oct 1813 - From what ship: HM Brig Hope - Born: Philadelphia - Age: 28 - Discharged on 17 Oct 1813 and sent to Chatham on HM Transport Malabar No. 352.

McCumber, Job - Seaman - Number: 1154 - How taken: Gave himself up from HM Frigate Orpheus - Date received: 7 Oct 1813 - From what ship: HM Frigate Spartan - Born: Dartmouth - Age: 27 - Discharged on 17 Oct 1813 and sent to Chatham on HM Transport Malabar No. 352.

McDonald, John (alias John Wheeler) - Seaman - Number: 616 - How taken: Gave himself up from HM Guardship Royal William - Date received: 3 Feb 1813 - From what ship: HMS Royal William - Born: New York - Age: 44 - Discharged on 11 Mar 1813 and sent to Chatham on HM Store Ship Abundance.

McGee, Robert - Seaman - Number: 951 - How taken: Gave himself up from HM Ship-of-the-Line Swiftsure - Date received: 28 Jul 1813 - From what ship: HM Sloop Volentaire - Born: Pennsylvania - Age: 35 - Discharged on 7 Aug 1813 and sent to Chatham on HM Brig Rinaldo.

McGreen, John - Seaman - Number: 1506 - How taken: Gave himself up from HM Ship-of-the-Line Rodney - Date received: 30 Jun 1814 - From what ship: HMS Rodney - Born: Hudson, NY - Age: 24 - Discharged on 30 Jun 1814 and sent to Plymouth on HM Brig Steady.

McInley, James - Seaman - Number: 1340 - How taken: Gave himself up from HMS Dannemark - Date received: 4 Jan 1814 - From what ship: HMS Dannemark - Born: New York - Age: 33 - Discharged on 5 Jan 1814 and sent to Chatham on HM Ship-of-the-Line Poictiers.

McIntire, Alexander - Seaman - Number: 159 - Prize Name: HMS Leonidas - Ship type: MV - How taken: Detained from HM Frigate Leonidas - When taken: 31 Jul 1812 - Where taken: Portsmouth harbor - Date received: 30 Nov 1812 - From what ship: Leonidas - Born: New York City - Age: 21 - Discharged on 19 Feb 1813 and sent to Chatham on HM Store Ship Dromedary.

McIntyre, William - Seaman - Number: 992 - Prize Name: Jane, prize of the Privateer Snap Dragon - Ship type: MV - How taken: HM Frigate Crescent & HM Ship of-the-Line Bellerophon - When taken: 28 Jun 1813 - Where taken: at sea - Date received: 9 Aug 1813 - From what ship: HM Sloop Hazard - Born: Antrim, Ireland - Age: 55 - Discharged on 13 Aug 1813 and sent to Chatham on HM Brig Cadmus.

McIver, John - Seaman - Number: 979 - How taken: Gave himself up from HM Ship-of-the-Line Kent - Date received: 31 Jul 1813 - From what ship: HM Ship-of-the-Line Leviathan - Born: Plymouth, MA - Age: 29 - Discharged on 13 Aug 1813 and sent to Chatham on HM Brig Cadmus.

McKenzie, John - Seaman - Number: 311 - Prize Name: Wasp - Ship type: MV - How taken: Earl Spencer, cutter - When taken: 4 Aug 1812 - Where taken: off Cape Clear - Date received: 31 Dec 1812 - From what ship: HM Ship-of-the-Line Northumberland - Born: Massachusetts - Age: 25 - Race: Black - Discharged on 4 Mar 1813 and sent to Chatham on HM Ship-of-the-Line Queen.

McKenzie, William - Seaman - Number: 1143 - Prize Name: Hepsey - Ship type: MV - How taken: HM Brig Zenobia - When taken: 22 Jun 1813 - Where taken: Lisbon - Date received: 6 Oct 1813 - From what ship: HM Sloop Kingfisher - Born: New York - Age: 23 - Discharged on 17 Oct 1813 and sent to Chatham on HM Transport Malabar No. 352.

McMichael, James - Seaman - Number: 706 - Prize Name: Tom Thumb - Ship type: MV - How taken: Lion, Privateer - When taken: 15 Feb 1813 - Where taken: at sea - Date received: 24 Feb 1813 - From what ship: HM Brig Escort - Born: New York - Age: 19 - Race: Colored - Discharged on 6 Mar 1813 and sent to Chatham on HM Ship-of-the-Line Cornwall.

McNeal, Alexander - Steward - Number: 244 - Prize Name: Antelope - Ship type: P - How taken: HM Brig Zephyr - When taken: 10 Dec 1812 - Where taken: at sea - Date received: 27 Dec 1812 - From what ship: HMS Zephyr - Born: Chester, PA - Age: 34 - Race: Colored - Discharged on 19 Feb 1813 and sent to Chatham on HM Store Ship Dromedary.

McPinnis, Barney - Seaman - Number: 1132 - How taken: Gave himself up from HM Frigate Cerberus - Date received: 6 Oct 1813 - From what ship: HM Sloop Kingfisher - Born: Pennsylvania - Age: 23 - Discharged on 17 Oct 1813 and sent to Chatham on HM Transport Malabar No. 352.

McWaren, Nathaniel - Seaman - Number: 851 - How taken: Gave himself up from HM Frigate Leonidas - Date received: 22 Jun 1813 - From what ship: HM Ship-of-the-Line Vigo - Born: Durham, MA - Age: 33 - Discharged on 2 Jul 1813 and sent to Chatham on HM Frigate Tribune.

Meath, Solomon - Seaman - Number: 1228 - How taken: Gave himself up from HM Ship-of-the-Line Invincible - Date received: 24 Nov 1813 - From what ship: HM Transport Leopard - Born: Maryland - Age: 24 - Race: Black - Discharged on 26 Dec 1813 and sent to Chatham on HM Ship of-the-Line Diomede.

Meirell, John - Seaman - Number: 1479 - Prize Name: Colombes - Ship type: MV - How taken: Sir John, privateer of Halifax - When taken: March 1814 - Where taken: at sea - Date received: 29 Apr 1814 - From what ship: HMS Primer - Born: North Yarmouth, MA - Age: 33 - Discharged on 2 Jun 1814 and sent to Plymouth on HMS Growler.

Melvin, John - Seaman - Number: 1185 - How taken: Gave himself up from HMS Minstrel - Date received: 9 Nov 1813 - From what ship: HMS Minstral - Born: Boston - Age: 22 - Discharged on 26 Dec 1813 and sent to Chatham on HM Ship of-the-Line Diomede.

Merkell, John - Seaman - Number: 809 - How taken: Gave himself up from HMS Pigne - Date received: 21 Apr 1813 - From what ship: HM Guardship Royal William - Born: Boston - Age: 23 - Discharged on 27 Apr 1813 and sent to Chatham on HM Sloop-of-War Bonne Citoyenne.

Merle, John - Seaman - Number: 728 - How taken: Gave himself up from HM Ship-of-the-Line Christian VII - Date received: 19 Mar 1813 - From what ship: HMS Christian VII - Born: New York - Age: 24 - Discharged on 28 Mar 1813 and sent to Chatham on HM Store Ship Serapis.

Merpaux, Brian - Seaman - Number: 187 - Prize Name: Baltimore - Ship type: P - How taken: HM Transport Diadem - When taken: 7 Oct 1812 - Where taken: S. Andera - Date received: 10 Nov 1812 - From what ship: HMS Diadem - Born: Baltimore - Age: 23 - Discharged on 19 Feb 1813 and sent to Chatham on HM Store Ship Dromedary.

Merrel, Enoch - Seaman - Number: 1426 - Prize Name: Minerva - Ship type: MV - How taken: HM Ship-of-the-Line Conquestador - When taken: 19 Jan 1814 - Where taken: Bay of Biscay - Date received: 1 Mar 1814 - From what ship: HMS Helicone - Born: Falmouth - Age: 19 - Discharged on 28 Apr 1814 and sent to Chatham on HM Sloop Favorite.

Merriday, John - Seaman - Number: 480 - Prize Name: Sword Fish - Ship type: P - How taken: HM Ship-of-the-

- Line Elephant - When taken: 28 Dec 1812 - Where taken: at sea - Date received: 14 Jan 1813 - From what ship: HMS Elephant - Born: Kent Island - Age: 30 - Discharged on 11 Mar 1813 and sent to Chatham on HM Store Ship Abundance.
- Metcalf, William - Seaman - Number: 175 - Prize Name: Baltimore - Ship type: P - How taken: HM Transport Diadem - When taken: 7 Oct 1812 - Where taken: S. Andera - Date received: 3 Nov 1812 San Antonio - From what ship: HMS Diadem - Born: Sag Harbor, NY - Age: 21 - Discharged on 19 Feb 1813 and sent to Chatham on HM Store Ship Dromedary.
- Meyer, John - Seaman - Number: 172 - Prize Name: Baltimore - Ship type: P - How taken: HM Transport Diadem - When taken: 7 Oct 1812 - Where taken: S. Andera - Date received: 3 Nov 1812 San Antonio - From what ship: HMS Diadem - Born: Bremen, Prussia - Age: 24 - Discharged on 19 Feb 1813 and sent to Chatham on HM Store Ship Dromedary.
- Meyer, Peter - Seaman - Number: 166 - Prize Name: Baltimore - Ship type: P - How taken: HM Transport Diadem - When taken: 7 Oct 1812 - Where taken: S. Andera - Date received: 3 Nov 1812 San Antonio - From what ship: HMS Diadem - Born: Baton Rouge - Age: 21 - Discharged on 19 Feb 1813 and sent to Chatham on HM Store Ship Dromedary.
- Meyers, James - Seaman - Number: 1120 - How taken: Gave himself up from HM Frigate Ganymede - Date received: 5 Oct 1813 - From what ship: HM Ship-of-the-Line Achille - Born: Philadelphia - Age: 24 - Discharged on 17 Oct 1813 and sent to Chatham on HM Transport Malabar No. 352.
- Michael, Peter - Seaman - Number: 405 - Prize Name: Hope - Ship type: MV - How taken: HM Sloop Pheasant - When taken: 13 Dec 1812 - Where taken: at sea - Date received: 10 Jan 1813 - From what ship: HM Guardship Royal William - Age: 25 - Discharged on 6 Mar 1813 and sent to Chatham on HMS Frigate Alexandria.
- Middleton, John - Seaman - Number: 1353 - How taken: Gave himself up from HMS Muros & HMS Rosamond - Date received: 28 Jan 1814 - From what ship: HM Ship-of-the-Line Prince - Born: Maryland - Age: 24 - Race: Mulatto - Discharged on 13 Feb 1814 and sent to Chatham on HM Transport Malabar No. 352.
- Middleton, Reuben - Seaman - Number: 454 - Prize Name: Sword Fish - Ship type: P - How taken: HM Ship-of-the-Line Elephant - When taken: 28 Dec 1812 - Where taken: at sea - Date received: 14 Jan 1813 - From what ship: HMS Elephant - Born: Salem - Age: 22 - Discharged on 11 Mar 1813 and sent to Chatham on HM Store Ship Abundance.
- Mids, Michael - Seaman - Number: 1390 - Prize Name: Pilate - Ship type: P - How taken: Victoria, privateer of Guernsey - When taken: 28 Jan 1814 - Where taken: off Bordeaux - Date received: 7 Feb 1814 - From what ship: Mary from Guernsey - Born: Baltimore - Age: 21 - Discharged on 13 Feb 1814 and sent to Chatham on HM Transport Malabar No. 352.
- Miller, George - Carpenter - Number: 692 - Prize Name: Calcutta - Ship type: East Indian Ship - How taken: Two Brothers, privateer of Guernsey - When taken: 23 Nov 1812 - Where taken: at sea - Date received: 24 Feb 1813 - From what ship: HM Brig Escort - Born: Seopus, NY - Age: 24 - Discharged on 6 Mar 1813 and sent to Chatham on HMS Frigate Alexandria.
- Miller, James - Seaman - Number: 1259 - Prize Name: Dart - Ship type: P - How taken: HM Frigate Niger & HMS Fortunee - Where taken: at sea - Date received: 19 Dec 1813 - From what ship: HMS Fortunee - Born: Charleston - Age: 27 - Discharged on 26 Dec 1813 and sent to Chatham on HM Ship of-the-Line Diomede.
- Miller, John - Seaman - Number: 939 - Prize Name: Tender of the True Blooded Yankee - Ship type: P - How taken: HM Ship-of-the-Line Fame - When taken: 24 Jun 1813 - Where taken: at sea - Date received: 1 Jul 1813 - From what ship: HM Brig Hope - Born: Troy, NY - Age: 28 - Discharged on 2 Jul 1813 and sent to Chatham on HM Brig Scorpion.
- Miller, John Jacob - Seaman - Number: 180 - Prize Name: Baltimore - Ship type: P - How taken: HM Transport Diadem - When taken: 7 Oct 1812 - Where taken: S. Andera - Date received: 3 Nov 1812 San Antonio - From what ship: HMS Diadem - Born: Philadelphia - Age: 29 - Discharged on 19 Feb 1813 and sent to Chatham on HM Store Ship Dromedary.
- Millet, Joseph - Seaman - Number: 1191 - Prize Name: Fire Fly of Gloucester - Ship type: MV - How taken: HM

Frigate Revolutionnaire - When taken: 19 Oct 1813 - Where taken: at sea - Date received: 9 Nov 1813 - From what ship: HMS Revolutionaire - Born: Gloucester - Age: 39 - Discharged on 26 Dec 1813 and sent to Chatham on HM Ship of-the-Line Diomede.

Mills, Henry - Seaman - Number: 466 - Prize Name: Sword Fish - Ship type: P - How taken: HM Ship-of-the-Line Elephant - When taken: 28 Dec 1812 - Where taken: at sea - Date received: 14 Jan 1813 - From what ship: HMS Elephant - Born: Kittery, MA - Age: 40 - Race: Black - Discharged on 11 Mar 1813 and sent to Chatham on HM Store Ship Abundance.

Mills, John - Seaman - Number: 1253 - Prize Name: Dart - Ship type: P - How taken: HM Frigate Niger & HMS Fortunee - Where taken: at sea - Date received: 19 Dec 1813 - From what ship: HMS Fortunee - Born: Whitehall, NY - Age: 18 - Discharged on 26 Dec 1813 and sent to Chatham on HM Ship of-the-Line Diomede.

Mills, John - Seaman - Number: 342 - How taken: Gave himself up from HM Frigate Belle Poule - Date received: 31 Dec 1812 - From what ship: HM Ship-of-the-Line Northumberland - Born: Portsmouth - Age: 21 - Discharged on 4 Mar 1813 and sent to Chatham on HM Ship-of-the-Line Queen.

Milson, William - Seaman - Number: 989 - Prize Name: Jane, prize of the Privateer Snap Dragon - Ship type: MV - How taken: HM Frigate Crescent & HM Ship of-the-Line Bellerophon - When taken: 28 Jun 1813 - Where taken: at sea - Date received: 9 Aug 1813 - From what ship: HM Sloop Hazard - Born: Philadelphia - Age: 31 - Discharged on 13 Aug 1813 and sent to Chatham on HM Brig Cadmus.

Miner, Benjamin F. - Seaman - Number: 694 - Prize Name: Calcutta - Ship type: East Indian Ship - How taken: Two Brothers, privateer of Guernsey - When taken: 23 Nov 1812 - Where taken: at sea - Date received: 24 Feb 1813 - From what ship: HM Brig Escort - Born: Northfield, MA - Age: 22 - Discharged on 6 Mar 1813 and sent to Chatham on HMS Frigate Alexandria.

Mingalls, Robert - Seaman - Number: 1503 - How taken: Gave himself up from HM Frigate Amphion - Date received: 27 Jun 1814 - From what ship: HMS Amphion - Born: Weymouth, MA - Age: 25 - Race: Mulatto - Discharged on 30 Jun 1814 and sent to Plymouth on HM Brig Steady.

Miramon, Roch - Passenger & Merchant - Number: 1266 - Prize Name: Dart - Ship type: P - How taken: HM Frigate Niger & HMS Fortunee - Where taken: at sea - Date received: 19 Dec 1813 - From what ship: HMS Fortunee - Born: New Orleans - Age: 45 - Discharged on 26 Dec 1813 and sent to Chatham on HM Ship of-the-Line Diomede.

Mirrel, Samuel B. - Surgeon - Number: 1292 - Prize Name: Growler - Ship type: P - How taken: HM Brig Electra - When taken: 7 Jul 1813 - Where taken: off St. Johns - Date received: 22 Dec 1813 - From what ship: HM Ship of-the-Line Bellerophon - Born: Buxton, MA - Age: 24 - Discharged on 26 Dec 1813 and sent to Chatham on HMS Frigate Nemesis.

Mitchel, John - Seaman - Number: 162 - Prize Name: Baltimore - Ship type: P - How taken: HM Transport Diadem - When taken: 7 Oct 1812 - Where taken: S. Andera - Date received: 3 Nov 1812 San Antonio - From what ship: HMS Diadem - Born: Baltimore - Age: 23 - Discharged on 19 Feb 1813 and sent to Chatham on HM Store Ship Dromedary.

Mitchell, Francis - Seaman - Number: 548 - Prize Name: Rossie - Ship type: MV - How taken: HM Frigate Dryand - When taken: 7 Jan 1813 - Where taken: at sea - Date received: 25 Jan 1813 - From what ship: HM Ship-of-the-Line Queen - Born: New Orleans - Age: 40 - Discharged on 11 Mar 1813 and sent to Chatham on HM Store Ship Abundance.

Mitchell, Thomas - Seaman - Number: 641 - How taken: Gave himself up from HM Guardship Royal William - Date received: 3 Feb 1813 - From what ship: HMS Royal William - Born: Marblehead - Age: 34 - Discharged on 11 Mar 1813 and sent to Chatham on HM Store Ship Abundance.

Modre, John - Seaman - Number: 1417 - Prize Name: Zephyr, prize of Privateer Rattlesnake - Ship type: MV - How taken: HM Frigate Surveillante - When taken: 6 Jan 1814 - Where taken: Bay of Biscay - Date received: 1 Mar 1814 - From what ship: HMS Helicone - Born: Maderia - Age: 26 - Discharged on 28 Apr 1814 and sent to Chatham on HM Sloop Favorite.

Molley, Peter - Seaman - Number: 1349 - How taken: Gave himself up from HMS Muros - Date received: 26 Jan

1814 - From what ship: HMS Muros - Born: New York - Age: 44 - Discharged on 13 Feb 1814 and sent to Chatham on HM Transport Malabar No. 352.

Monion, Jean - Seaman - Number: 1165 - Prize Name: Russian merchant vessel - How taken: Taken out of the HM Ship-of-the-Line Neptune - When taken: 28 Sep 1813 - Where taken: Cork - Date received: 12 Oct 1813 - From what ship: HM Brig Hope - Born: New Orleans - Age: 33 - Discharged on 17 Oct 1813 and sent to Chatham on HM Transport Malabar No. 352.

Moore, Benjamin - Seaman - Number: 705 - Prize Name: Tom Thumb - Ship type: MV - How taken: Lion, Privateer - When taken: 15 Feb 1813 - Where taken: at sea - Date received: 24 Feb 1813 - From what ship: HM Brig Escort - Born: Brattleboro - Age: 30 - Discharged on 6 Mar 1813 and sent to Chatham on HM Ship-of-the-Line Cornwall.

Moore, Daniel - Seaman - Number: 110 - Prize Name: Nancy - Ship type: MV - How taken: HM Brig Parthian - When taken: 1 Aug 1812 - Where taken: off the Needles - Date received: 16 Oct 1812 San Antonio - From what ship: HM Brig Nancy - Born: York - Age: 21 - Discharged on 19 Feb 1813 and sent to Chatham on HM Frigate Ulysses.

Moore, Jacob - Seaman - Number: 389 - Prize Name: Empress - Ship type: MV - How taken: HM Brig Rover - When taken: 30 Nov 1812 - Where taken: at sea - Date received: 10 Jan 1813 - From what ship: HM Guardship Royal William - Born: New York - Age: 21 - Discharged on 4 Mar 1813 and sent to Chatham on HM Ship-of-the-Line Queen.

Moore, James - Seaman - Number: 1095 - How taken: Gave himself up from HM Brig Rapid - Date received: 5 Oct 1813 - From what ship: HMS Rapid - Born: New York - Age: 32 - Race: Mulatto - Discharged on 17 Oct 1813 and sent to Chatham on HM Store Ship Weymouth.

Moore, John - Seaman - Number: 929 - Prize Name: Tender of the True Blooded Yankee - Ship type: P - How taken: HM Ship-of-the-Line Fame - When taken: 24 Jun 1813 - Where taken: at sea - Date received: 1 Jul 1813 - From what ship: HM Brig Hope - Born: Norwich, CT - Age: 26 - Discharged on 2 Jul 1813 and sent to Chatham on HM Brig Scorpion.

Moore, Michael - Seaman - Number: 399 - Prize Name: Empress - Ship type: MV - How taken: HM Brig Rover - When taken: 30 Nov 1812 - Where taken: at sea - Date received: 10 Jan 1813 - From what ship: HM Guardship Royal William - Born: New York - Age: 23 - Discharged on 6 Mar 1813 and sent to Chatham on HMS Frigate Alexandria.

Moore, Thomas - Passenger & Merchant - Number: 207 - Prize Name: Susanna - Ship type: MV - How taken: HM Sloop Hazard - When taken: 13 Sep 1812 - Where taken: at sea - Date received: 3 Dec 1812 - From what ship: HM Schooner Antelope - Born: Charleston, SC - Age: 30 - Discharged on 10 Jan 1813 and sent to Odiham on parole.

Morell, John - Seaman - Number: 777 - How taken: Gave himself up from HM Frigate Mermaid - Date received: 1 Apr 1813 - From what ship: HM Ship-of-the-Line Blake - Born: Havia - Age: 31 - Discharged on 3 Apr 1813 and sent to Chatham on HM Transport Chatham.

Morrel, Jacob - Seaman - Number: 1401 - Prize Name: Harriet, prize of Privateer Fox - Ship type: MV - How taken: HM Transport Dover - When taken: 20 Jun 1813 - Where taken: Grand Banks - Date received: 16 Feb 1814 - From what ship: HM Transport Malabar No. 352 - Born: Massachusetts - Age: 22 - Discharged on 27 Jul 1814 and sent to the Royal Naval Hospital Haslar at Gosport.

Morris, George - Cook - Number: 711 - Prize Name: Tom Thumb - Ship type: MV - How taken: Lion, Privateer - When taken: 15 Feb 1813 - Where taken: at sea - Date received: 24 Feb 1813 - From what ship: HM Brig Escort - Born: Worcester, MA - Age: 17 - Race: Colored - Discharged on 6 Mar 1813 and sent to Chatham on HM Ship-of-the-Line Cornwall.

Morris, James - Steward - Number: 891 - Prize Name: Tigre - Ship type: MV - How taken: HM Brig Scylla - When taken: 22 Mar 1813 - Where taken: Bay of Biscay - Date received: 24 Jun 1813 - From what ship: HM Frigate Unicorn - Born: New York - Age: 29 - Discharged on 2 Jul 1813 and sent to Chatham on HM Frigate Tribune.

Morris, Louis - Seaman - Number: 727 - How taken: Gave himself up from HM Ship-of-the-Line Christian VII -

Date received: 19 Mar 1813 - From what ship: HMS Christian VII - Born: New Haven, CT - Age: 23 - Discharged on 28 Mar 1813 and sent to Chatham on HM Store Ship Seaphis.

Morrison, James - 2nd Lieutenant - Number: 438 - Prize Name: Sword Fish - Ship type: P - How taken: HM Ship-of-the-Line Elephant - When taken: 28 Dec 1812 - Where taken: at sea - Date received: 14 Jan 1813 - From what ship: HMS Elephant - Born: Salem - Age: 30 - Discharged on 6 Mar 1813 and sent to Chatham on HMS Frigate Alexandria.

Morrison, John - Seaman - Number: 779 - How taken: Gave himself up from HM Frigate Mermaid - Date received: 1 Apr 1813 - From what ship: HM Ship-of-the-Line Blake - Born: Philadelphia - Age: 22 - Discharged on 3 Apr 1813 and sent to Chatham on HM Transport Chatham.

Morrison, William - Boy - Number: 971 - How taken: Gave himself up from HM Ship-of-the-Line Leviathan - Date received: 31 Jul 1813 - From what ship: HMS Leviathan - Born: New York - Age: 17 - Discharged on 7 Aug 1813 and sent to Chatham on HM Brig Rinaldo.

Morslender, Ruben - Seaman - Number: 862 - Prize Name: Tiger - Ship type: MV - How taken: HM Brig Scylla - When taken: 22 Mar 1813 - Where taken: Bay of Biscay - Date received: 24 Jun 1813 - From what ship: HM Frigate Unicorn - Born: Nantucket - Age: 22 - Discharged on 2 Jul 1813 and sent to Chatham on HM Frigate Tribune.

Moulden, William - Seaman - Number: 766 - How taken: Gave himself up from HM Ship-of-the-Line Blake - Date received: 1 Apr 1813 - From what ship: HMS Blake - Born: Andover - Age: 41 - Discharged on 3 Apr 1813 and sent to Chatham on HM Transport Chatham.

Mountain, Emanuel - Seaman - Number: 533 - Prize Name: Expectation - Ship type: MV - How taken: HMS Butain - When taken: 17 Dec 1812 - Where taken: at sea - Date received: 25 Jan 1813 - From what ship: HM Ship-of-the-Line Queen - Born: Massachusetts - Age: 23 - Discharged on 11 Mar 1813 and sent to Chatham on HM Store Ship Abundance.

Mukelroey, Samuel - Seaman - Number: 836 - How taken: Gave himself up from HM Frigate Menelaus - Date received: 6 Jun 1813 - From what ship: HM Guardship Royal William - Born: Philadelphia - Age: 40 - Discharged on 10 Jun 1813 and sent to Chatham on HM Frigate Arethusa.

Muller, William - Seaman - Number: 887 - How taken: Gave himself up from HMS Servius - Date received: 24 Jun 1813 - From what ship: HM Frigate Unicorn - Born: Boston - Age: 22 - Discharged on 2 Jul 1813 and sent to Chatham on HM Frigate Tribune.

Mumery, James - Seaman - Number: 33 - Prize Name: USRM Cutter James Madison - Ship type: MW - How taken: HM Frigate Barbadoes - When taken: 22 Aug 1812 - Where taken: at sea - Date received: 12 Oct 1812 San Antonio - From what ship: HM Ship-of-the-Line Polyphemus - Born: New York - Age: 33 - Discharged on 19 Feb 1813 and sent to Chatham on HM Frigate Ulysses.

Muncy, Daniel - Seaman - Number: 678 - Prize Name: Hope - Ship type: MV - How taken: HM Schooner Bramble - When taken: 2 Dec 1812 - Where taken: at sea - Date received: 14 Feb 1813 - From what ship: HM Transport Maister No. 84 - Born: Cumberland, NJ - Age: 23 - Discharged on 6 Mar 1813 and sent to Chatham on HM Ship-of-the-Line Cornwall.

Munro, John - Seaman - Number: 648 - How taken: Gave himself up from HM Guardship Royal William - Date received: 3 Feb 1813 - From what ship: HMS Royal William - Born: New York - Age: 31 - Discharged on 11 Mar 1813 and sent to Chatham on HM Store Ship Abundance.

Murray, Charles - Passenger - Number: 1264 - Prize Name: Dart - Ship type: P - How taken: HM Frigate Niger & HMS Fortunee - Where taken: at sea - Date received: 19 Dec 1813 - From what ship: HMS Fortunee - Born: Philadelphia - Age: 45 - Race: Black - Discharged on 26 Dec 1813 and sent to Chatham on HM Ship of-the-Line Diomede.

Murray, David - Seaman - Number: 1397 - Prize Name: Vivid - Ship type: MV - How taken: HM Frigate Nymphe - When taken: 20 Apr 1813 - Where taken: off Boston - Date received: 16 Feb 1814 - From what ship: HM Transport Malabar No. 352 - Born: Boston - Age: 20 - Discharged on 28 Apr 1814 and sent to Chatham on HM Store Ship Weymouth.

Murray, John - Seaman - Number: 341 - Prize Name: Experiment - Ship type: MV - How taken: HM Transport

Deptford - When taken: 2 Nov 1812 - Where taken: Dublin - Date received: 31 Dec 1812 - From what ship: HM Ship-of-the-Line Northumberland - Born: New Castle, DE - Age: 22 - Discharged on 4 Mar 1813 and sent to Chatham on HM Ship-of-the-Line Queen.

Murray, Nathaniel - Seaman - Number: 202 - Prize Name: Rising States - Ship type: MV - How taken: HMS Fortunee - When taken: 28 Aug 1812 - Where taken: at sea - Date received: 25 Nov 1812 - From what ship: HM Guardship Royal William - Born: Long Island - Age: 27 - Race: Mulatto - Discharged on 19 Feb 1813 and sent to Chatham on HM Store Ship Dromedary.

Myers, Jacob - Seaman - Number: 257 - Prize Name: King of Rome - Ship type: P - How taken: HM Brig Wolverine - When taken: 13 Dec 1812 - Where taken: at sea - Date received: 27 Dec 1812 - From what ship: HMS Wolverine - Born: Philadelphia - Age: 24 - Discharged on 19 Feb 1813 and sent to Chatham on HM Store Ship Dromedary.

Myrick, William - Seaman - Number: 371 - Prize Name: Mariner - Ship type: MV - How taken: HM Brig Lyra - When taken: 15 Dec 1812 - Where taken: off Bilboa, Spain - Date received: 3 Jan 1813 - From what ship: HM Frigate Fox - Born: Nantucket - Age: 23 - Discharged on 4 Mar 1813 and sent to Chatham on HM Ship-of-the-Line Queen.

Nald, John - Seaman - Number: 381 - How taken: Gave himself up from HM Frigate Pomone - Date received: 9 Jan 1813 - From what ship: HMS Pomone - Born: New York - Age: 20 - Discharged on 4 Mar 1813 and sent to Chatham on HM Ship-of-the-Line Queen.

Neal, John - Seaman - Number: 1366 - How taken: Gave himself up from HM Ship-of-the-Line Saturn - Date received: 3 Feb 1814 - From what ship: HM Ship-of-the-Line Prince - Born: Gloucester, NJ - Age: 30 - Discharged on 13 Feb 1814 and sent to Chatham on HM Transport Malabar No. 352.

Necylnenee, Peter - Seaman - Number: 976 - How taken: Gave himself up from HM Ship-of-the-Line Caledonia - Date received: 31 Jul 1813 - From what ship: HMS Leviathan - Born: New York - Age: 55 - Race: Black - Discharged on 13 Aug 1813 and sent to Chatham on HM Brig Cadmus.

Nelson, Samuel A. - Seaman - Number: 91 - Prize Name: HM Frigate Janus - Ship type: MW - How taken: Detained by Court of Admiralty - When taken: 31 Jul 1812 - Where taken: Portsmouth harbor - Date received: 16 Oct 1812 San Antonio - From what ship: HM Frigate Janus - Born: Portsmouth, NH - Age: 32 - Discharged on 19 Feb 1813 and sent to Chatham on HM Frigate Ulysses.

Newby, John - Seaman - Number: 56 - Prize Name: Fame, prize of Privateer Decatur - Ship type: MV - How taken: HM Ship-of-the-Line Polyphemus - When taken: 13 Sep 1812 - Where taken: at sea - Date received: 12 Oct 1812 San Antonio - From what ship: HM Ship-of-the-Line Polyphemus - Born: Isle of Wight, England - Age: 27 - Discharged on 19 Feb 1813 and sent to Chatham on HM Frigate Ulysses.

Newell, Paul - Seaman - Number: 1174 - How taken: Gave himself up from HM Frigate Astrea - Date received: 16 Oct 1813 - From what ship: HMS Astrea - Born: Marblehead - Age: 22 - Discharged on 17 Oct 1813 and sent to Chatham on HM Transport Malabar No. 352.

Nicholas, James - Seaman - Number: 1224 - Prize Name: Growler - Ship type: P - How taken: HM Brig Electra - When taken: 7 Jul 1813 - Where taken: at sea - Date received: 16 Nov 1813 - From what ship: HM Sloop Talbot - Born: Marblehead - Age: 21 - Discharged on 26 Dec 1813 and sent to Chatham on HM Ship of-the-Line Diomede.

Nichols, John - Seaman - Number: 220 - How taken: Gave himself up from HM Ship-of-the-Line Aboukir - When taken: 29 Oct 1812 - Date received: 26 Dec 1812 - From what ship: HMS Abonkir - Born: Durham - Age: 22 - Discharged on 19 Feb 1813 and sent to Chatham on HM Store Ship Dromedary.

Nichols, Samuel - Captain - Number: 113 - Prize Name: HMS Eos - Ship type: MV - How taken: Detained by Court of Admiralty - When taken: 31 Aug 1812 - Where taken: Portsmouth harbor - Date received: 20 Oct 1812 - From what ship: Eos - Born: Newburyport - Age: 28 - Discharged on 26 Oct 1813 and sent to Odiham on parole.

Nichols, Thomas - Seaman - Number: 1006 - Prize Name: Fame - Ship type: MV - How taken: HM Ship of-the-Line Cressy - When taken: 20 Jul 1813 - Where taken: at sea - Date received: 18 Aug 1813 - From what ship: HMS Cressy - Born: Rhode Island - Age: 22 - Race: Black - Discharged on 21 Sep 1813 and sent to Chatham on HM Ship-of-the-Line Queen.

Nichols, William - Captain - Number: 909 - Prize Name: Decatur - Ship type: P - How taken: HM Frigate Surprise - When taken: 16 Jan 1813 - Where taken: at sea - Date received: 1 Jul 1813 - From what ship: HM Frigate Tribune - Born: Newburyport - Age: 31 - Discharged on 2 Jul 1813 and sent to Chatham on HM Brig Scorpion.

Nicholson, Charles - Seaman - Number: 955 - How taken: Gave himself up from HM Ship-of-the-Line Swiftsure - Date received: 28 Jul 1813 - From what ship: HM Sloop Volentaire - Born: Baltimore - Age: 25 - Race: Black - Discharged on 7 Aug 1813 and sent to Chatham on HM Brig Rinaldo.

Nicholson, Jonas - Seaman - Number: 1289 - Prize Name: Growler - Ship type: P - How taken: HM Brig Electra - When taken: 7 Jul 1813 - Where taken: off St. Johns - Date received: 22 Dec 1813 - From what ship: HM Ship of-the-Line Bellerophon - Born: Marblehead - Age: 23 - Discharged on 26 Dec 1813 and sent to Chatham on HMS Frigate Nemesis.

Nickel, Hugh - Prize Master - Number: 987 - Prize Name: Jane, prize of the Privateer Snap Dragon - Ship type: MV - How taken: HM Frigate Crescent & HM Ship of-the-Line Bellerophon - When taken: 28 Jun 1813 - Where taken: at sea - Date received: 9 Aug 1813 - From what ship: HM Sloop Hazard - Born: North Carolina - Age: 28 - Discharged on 13 Aug 1813 and sent to Chatham on HM Brig Cadmus.

Nicolas, John - Seaman - Number: 872 - Prize Name: Tiger - Ship type: MV - How taken: HM Brig Scylla - When taken: 22 Mar 1813 - Where taken: Bay of Biscay - Date received: 24 Jun 1813 - From what ship: HM Frigate Unicorn - Born: New York - Age: 18 - Discharged on 2 Jul 1813 and sent to Chatham on HM Frigate Tribune.

Nillim, George - Seaman - Number: 211 - How taken: Gave himself up from HM Sloop Cherub - Date received: 11 Dec 1812 - From what ship: HMS Cherub - Born: Philadelphia - Age: 25 - Discharged on 19 Feb 1813 and sent to Chatham on HM Store Ship Dromedary.

Noble, Charles - Seaman - Number: 1023 - How taken: Gave himself up from HM Ship-of-the-Line Scipion - Date received: 7 Sep 1813 - From what ship: HM Frigate Unicorn - Born: Cape Ann - Age: 22 - Discharged on 21 Sep 1813 and sent to Chatham on HM Ship-of-the-Line Queen.

Noonan, William - Seaman - Number: 602 - Prize Name: Sword Fish - Ship type: P - How taken: HM Ship-of-the-Line Elephant - When taken: 20 Dec 1812 - Where taken: at sea - Date received: 1 Feb 1813 - From what ship: HM Frigate Hermes - Born: Boston - Age: 15 - Discharged on 11 Mar 1813 and sent to Chatham on HM Store Ship Abundance.

Norton, David - Prize Master - Number: 1360 - Prize Name: Elbridge Gerry - Ship type: P - How taken: HM Frigate Crescent - When taken: 16 Sep 1813 - Where taken: at sea - Date received: 1 Feb 1814 - From what ship: HM Frigate Sybille - Born: Massachusetts - Age: 24 - Discharged on 13 Feb 1814 and sent to Chatham on HM Transport Malabar No. 352.

Nowell, Stephen C. - Seaman - Number: 1145 - Prize Name: Hepsey - Ship type: MV - How taken: HM Brig Zenobia - When taken: 22 Jun 1813 - Where taken: Lisbon - Date received: 6 Oct 1813 - From what ship: HM Sloop Kingfisher - Born: Newburyport - Age: 20 - Discharged on 17 Oct 1813 and sent to Chatham on HM Transport Malabar No. 352.

Nowland, Andrew (1) - Seaman - Number: 477 - Prize Name: Sword Fish - Ship type: P - How taken: HM Ship-of-the-Line Elephant - When taken: 28 Dec 1812 - Where taken: at sea - Date received: 14 Jan 1813 - From what ship: HMS Elephant - Born: Marblehead - Age: 44 - Discharged on 11 Mar 1813 and sent to Chatham on HM Store Ship Abundance.

Nowland, Andrew (2) - Seaman - Number: 501 - Prize Name: Sword Fish - Ship type: P - How taken: HM Ship-of-the-Line Elephant - When taken: 28 Dec 1812 - Where taken: at sea - Date received: 14 Jan 1813 - From what ship: HMS Elephant - Born: Marblehead - Age: 15 - Discharged on 11 Mar 1813 and sent to Chatham on HM Store Ship Abundance.

Nunns, William - Seaman - Number: 579 - Prize Name: Industry - Ship type: MV - How taken: HM Frigate Dryand - When taken: 7 Jan 1813 - Where taken: at sea - Date received: 25 Jan 1813 - From what ship: HM Ship-of-the-Line Queen - Born: Philadelphia - Age: 34 - Discharged on 11 Mar 1813 and sent to Chatham on HM

Store Ship Abundance.

Nuting, Charles - Seaman - Number: 42 - Prize Name: USRM Cutter James Madison - Ship type: MW - How taken: HM Frigate Barbadoes - When taken: 22 Aug 1812 - Where taken: at sea - Date received: 12 Oct 1812 San Antonio - From what ship: HM Ship-of-the-Line Polyphemus - Born: Gloucester - Age: 29 - Discharged on 19 Feb 1813 and sent to Chatham on HM Frigate Ulysses.

Nutrash, Ezekiel (Metrash) - Seaman - Number: 143 - Prize Name: William - Ship type: MV - How taken: HM Brig Recruit - When taken: 29 Aug 1812 - Where taken: at sea - Date received: 29 Oct 1812 - From what ship: HM Ship-of-the-Line Ardent - Born: Norwalk, CT - Age: 19 - Race: Colored - Discharged on 19 Feb 1813 and sent to Chatham on HM Store Ship Dromedary.

Nutt, Adam - Seaman - Number: 184 - How taken: Sent into custody by order of the commander in chief - Date received: 4 Nov 1812 - From what ship: HM Guardship Royal William - Born: Charlestown, MA - Age: 35 - Discharged on 10 Nov 1812 to the Ann of Arundel.

Oaks, George - Seaman - Number: 62 - Prize Name: Diana, prize of Privateer Decatur - Ship type: MV - How taken: HM Ship-of-the-Line Polyphemus - When taken: 14 Sep 1812 - Where taken: at sea - Date received: 12 Oct 1812 San Antonio - From what ship: HM Ship-of-the-Line Polyphemus - Born: Marblehead - Age: 18 - Discharged on 19 Feb 1813 and sent to Chatham on HM Frigate Ulysses.

Oberville, Michael - Seaman - Number: 561 - Prize Name: Rossie - Ship type: MV - How taken: HM Frigate Dryand - When taken: 7 Jan 1813 - Where taken: at sea - Date received: 25 Jan 1813 - From what ship: HM Ship-of-the-Line Queen - Born: New Orleans - Age: 26 - Discharged on 11 Mar 1813 and sent to Chatham on HM Store Ship Abundance.

Odion, John B. H. - Seaman - Number: 1218 - Prize Name: Growler - Ship type: P - How taken: HM Brig Electra - When taken: 7 Jul 1813 - Where taken: at sea - Date received: 16 Nov 1813 - From what ship: HM Sloop Talbot - Born: Dover, NH - Age: 21 - Discharged on 26 Dec 1813 and sent to Chatham on HM Ship of-the-Line Diomede.

Oilson, Andrew - Seaman - Number: 208 - How taken: Gave himself up from HM Schooner Antelope - Date received: 3 Dec 1812 - From what ship: HMS Antelope - Born: Postcrown, Norway - Age: 24 - Discharged on 19 Feb 1813 and sent to Chatham on HM Store Ship Dromedary.

Orn, James - Captain - Number: 85 - Prize Name: HM Frigate Janus - Ship type: MW - How taken: Detained by Court of Admiralty - When taken: 31 Jul 1812 - Where taken: Portsmouth harbor - Date received: 16 Oct 1812 San Antonio - From what ship: HM Frigate Janus - Born: Portsmouth, NH - Age: 50 - Discharged on 26 Oct 1813 and sent to Odiham on parole.

Orn, W. B. - Captain - Number: 719 - How taken: Gave himself up from HMS Portsmouth - Date received: 3 Mar 1813 - From what ship: HMS Portsmouth - Born: Marblehead - Age: 28 - Discharged on 11 Mar 1813 and sent to Chatham on HM Store Ship Abundance.

Orne, Josiah - Prize Master - Number: 1299 - Prize Name: Growler - Ship type: P - How taken: HM Brig Electra - When taken: 7 Jul 1813 - Where taken: off St. Johns - Date received: 22 Dec 1813 - From what ship: HM Frigate Hyperion - Born: Salem - Age: 27 - Discharged on 26 Dec 1813 and sent to Chatham on HMS Frigate Nemesis.

Orr, Levi - Seaman - Number: 127 - How taken: Gave himself up from HM Ship-of-the-Line Ruby - When taken: 30 Aug 1812 - Date received: 29 Oct 1812 - From what ship: HM Ship-of-the-Line Ardent - Born: New York - Age: 45 - Discharged on 19 Feb 1813 and sent to Chatham on HM Store Ship Dromedary.

Osborne, Thomas - Seaman - Number: 8 - Prize Name: USRM Cutter James Madison - Ship type: MW - How taken: HM Frigate Barbadoes - When taken: 22 Aug 1812 - Where taken: at sea - Date received: 12 Oct 1812 San Antonio - From what ship: HM Ship-of-the-Line Polyphemus - Born: Kentucky - Age: 26 - Discharged on 19 Feb 1813 and sent to Chatham on HM Frigate Ulysses.

Osbourne, Lewis - Seaman - Number: 1049 - How taken: Gave himself up from HM Ship-of-the-Line Scipion - Date received: 14 Sep 1813 - From what ship: HM Brig Savage - Born: East Hampton, NY - Age: 30 - Discharged on 29 Sep 1813 and sent to Chatham on HM Ship-of-the-Line Barham.

Osburne, Peter - Seaman - Number: 293 - Prize Name: Rising Sun - Ship type: MV - How taken: Taken up on shore

- When taken: 18 Oct 1812 - Where taken: Liverpool - Date received: 31 Dec 1812 - From what ship: HM Ship-of-the-Line Northumberland - Born: Long Island - Age: 23 - Race: Black - Discharged on 4 Mar 1813 and sent to Chatham on HM Ship-of-the-Line Queen.

Osgood, David - Seaman - Number: 661 - How taken: Sent into custom from the Cowes Rendezvous - Date received: 6 Feb 1813 - From what ship: Cowes Rendezvous - Born: Baltimore - Age: 24 - Discharged on 6 Mar 1813 and sent to Chatham on HM Ship-of-the-Line Cornwall.

Osmond, David - Seaman - Number: 1012 - Prize Name: Fame - Ship type: MV - How taken: HM Ship of-the-Line Cressy - When taken: 20 Jul 1813 - Where taken: at sea - Date received: 18 Aug 1813 - From what ship: HMS Cressy - Born: Connecticut - Age: 20 - Discharged on 21 Sep 1813 and sent to Chatham on HM Ship-of-the-Line Queen.

Owen, Burden - Seaman - Number: 1024 - How taken: Gave himself up from HM Ship-of-the-Line Ocean - Date received: 7 Sep 1813 - From what ship: HM Frigate Unicorn - Born: New York - Age: 47 - Discharged on 21 Sep 1813 and sent to Chatham on HM Ship-of-the-Line Queen.

Packard, William - Seaman - Number: 343 - How taken: Gave himself up from HM Frigate Belle Poule - Date received: 31 Dec 1812 - From what ship: HM Ship-of-the-Line Northumberland - Born: Bridgewater - Age: 23 - Discharged on 4 Mar 1813 and sent to Chatham on HM Ship-of-the-Line Queen.

Page, John - Seaman - Number: 199 - Prize Name: Rising States - Ship type: MV - How taken: HMS Fortunee - When taken: 28 Aug 1812 - Where taken: at sea - Date received: 25 Nov 1812 - From what ship: HM Guardship Royal William - Born: New York - Age: 21 - Discharged on 19 Feb 1813 and sent to Chatham on HM Store Ship Dromedary.

Pain, Clement - Clerk - Number: 1205 - Prize Name: Elbridge Gerry - Ship type: P - How taken: HM Frigate Crescent & HM Ship of-the-Line Bellerophon - When taken: 16 Sep 1813 - Where taken: at sea - Date received: 16 Nov 1813 - From what ship: HM Sloop Talbot - Born: Kennebunk, MA - Age: 20 - Discharged on 26 Dec 1813 and sent to Chatham on HM Ship of-the-Line Diomede.

Pain, James - Seaman - Number: 886 - How taken: Gave himself up from HMS Servius - Date received: 24 Jun 1813 - From what ship: HM Frigate Unicorn - Born: Block Island - Age: 32 - Discharged on 2 Jul 1813 and sent to Chatham on HM Frigate Tribune.

Paine, Joshua - Seaman - Number: 1 - Prize Name: Preseverence - Ship type: MV - How taken: HM Sloop Atalante - When taken: 31 Jul 1812 - Where taken: at sea - Date received: 11 Oct 1812 San Antonio - From what ship: Devon Militia - Born: Bath, MA - Age: 35 - Discharged on 19 Feb 1813 and sent to Chatham on HM Frigate Ulysses.

Palm, William - Seaman - Number: 37 - Prize Name: USRM Cutter James Madison - Ship type: MW - How taken: HM Frigate Barbadoes - When taken: 22 Aug 1812 - Where taken: at sea - Date received: 12 Oct 1812 San Antonio - From what ship: HM Ship-of-the-Line Polyphemus - Born: Philadelphia - Age: 28 - Discharged on 19 Feb 1813 and sent to Chatham on HM Frigate Ulysses.

Palmer, Peter - Seaman - Number: 708 - Prize Name: Tom Thumb - Ship type: MV - How taken: Lion, Privateer - When taken: 15 Feb 1813 - Where taken: at sea - Date received: 24 Feb 1813 - From what ship: HM Brig Escort - Born: Branford - Age: 22 - Discharged on 6 Mar 1813 and sent to Chatham on HM Ship-of-the-Line Cornwall.

Palmer, William - Seaman - Number: 839 - How taken: Gave himself up from HMS Horatio - Date received: 11 Jun 1813 - From what ship: HMS Horatio - Born: Portsmouth, NH - Age: 21 - Discharged on 2 Jul 1813 and sent to Chatham on HM Frigate Tribune.

Parditt, Charles - Seaman - Number: 190 - How taken: Gave himself up from HM Ship-of-the-Line Ocean - Date received: 21 Nov 1812 - From what ship: HM Ship-of-the-Line Ville de Paris - Born: New Orleans - Age: 28 - Discharged on 19 Feb 1813 and sent to Chatham on HM Store Ship Dromedary.

Pardoe, John - Seaman - Number: 320 - Prize Name: Taken on shore - How taken: HM Battery Princess - When taken: 5 Nov 1812 - Where taken: Liverpool - Date received: 31 Dec 1812 - From what ship: HM Ship-of-the-Line Northumberland - Born: Bridgeport - Age: 23 - Discharged on 4 Mar 1813 and sent to Chatham on HM Ship-of-the-Line Queen.

Parish, Samuel - Seaman - Number: 116 - How taken: Taken out of the HM Transport Simpson - When taken: 28 Oct 1812 - Where taken: Portsmouth harbor - Date received: 28 Oct 1812 - From what ship: Gosport Rendezvous - Born: Little York - Age: 27 - Discharged on 19 Feb 1813 and sent to Chatham on HM Store Ship Dromedary.

Parker, George - Seaman - Number: 837 - How taken: Gave himself up from HM Frigate Menelaus - Date received: 6 Jun 1813 - From what ship: HM Guardship Royal William - Born: Massachusetts - Age: 26 - Discharged on 10 Jun 1813 and sent to Chatham on HM Frigate Arethusa.

Parse, William - Landsman - Number: 716 - How taken: Gave himself up from HMS Muros - Date received: 27 Feb 1813 - From what ship: HMS Muros - Born: Providence - Age: 18 - Discharged on 6 Mar 1813 and sent to Chatham on HM Ship-of-the-Line Cornwall.

Parsons, Andrew - Seaman - Number: 495 - Prize Name: Sword Fish - Ship type: P - How taken: HM Ship-of-the-Line Elephant - When taken: 28 Dec 1812 - Where taken: at sea - Date received: 14 Jan 1813 - From what ship: HMS Elephant - Born: Salem - Age: 24 - Discharged on 11 Mar 1813 and sent to Chatham on HM Store Ship Abundance.

Parsons, John - Armourer - Number: 1208 - Prize Name: Elbridge Gerry - Ship type: P - How taken: HM Frigate Crescent & HM Ship of-the-Line Bellerophon - When taken: 16 Sep 1813 - Where taken: at sea - Date received: 16 Nov 1813 - From what ship: HM Sloop Talbot - Born: Newburyport, MA - Age: 25 - Discharged on 26 Dec 1813 and sent to Chatham on HM Ship of-the-Line Diomede.

Parsons, Joseph - 1st Mate - Number: 540 - Prize Name: Leader - Ship type: MV - How taken: HMS Butain - When taken: 17 Dec 1812 - Where taken: at sea - Date received: 25 Jan 1813 - From what ship: HM Ship-of-the-Line Queen - Born: Salem, MA - Age: 24 - Discharged on 22 Feb 1813 and sent to Ashburton on parole.

Parsons, Joseph - Seaman - Number: 680 - Prize Name: Hope - Ship type: MV - How taken: HM Schooner Bramble - When taken: 2 Dec 1812 - Where taken: at sea - Date received: 14 Feb 1813 - From what ship: HM Transport Maister No. 84 - Born: Sussex, DE - Age: 21 - Discharged on 6 Mar 1813 and sent to Chatham on HM Ship-of-the-Line Cornwall.

Parsons, Rufus - Seaman - Number: 736 - Prize Name: Dart - Ship type: MV - How taken: HM Brig Doterel - When taken: 5 Mar 1813 - Where taken: at sea - Date received: 21 Mar 1813 - From what ship: HMS Dotteril - Born: York, MA - Age: 22 - Discharged on 28 Mar 1813 and sent to Chatham on HM Store Ship Seaphis.

Parsons, Thomas - Seaman - Number: 499 - Prize Name: Sword Fish - Ship type: P - How taken: HM Ship-of-the-Line Elephant - When taken: 28 Dec 1812 - Where taken: at sea - Date received: 14 Jan 1813 - From what ship: HMS Elephant - Born: Old York - Age: 51 - Discharged on 6 Mar 1813 and sent to Chatham on HM Ship-of-the-Line Cornwall.

Patten, Joseph - Seaman - Number: 735 - Prize Name: Dart - Ship type: MV - How taken: HM Brig Doterel - When taken: 5 Mar 1813 - Where taken: at sea - Date received: 21 Mar 1813 - From what ship: HMS Dotteril - Born: Durham, NH - Age: 23 - Discharged on 28 Mar 1813 and sent to Chatham on HM Store Ship Seaphis.

Patterson, John - Seaman - Number: 723 - How taken: Gave himself up from HM Frigate Niobe - Date received: 13 Mar 1813 - From what ship: HMS Niobe - Born: New York - Age: 26 - Discharged on 28 Mar 1813 and sent to Chatham on HM Store Ship Seaphis.

Patterson, Peter - Seaman - Number: 617 - How taken: Gave himself up from HM Guardship Royal William - Date received: 3 Feb 1813 - From what ship: HMS Royal William - Born: New York - Age: 24 - Discharged on 11 Mar 1813 and sent to Chatham on HM Store Ship Abundance.

Patterson, Samuel - Captain - Number: 78 - Prize Name: HM Ship-of-the-Line Ganges - Ship type: MW - How taken: Detained by Court of Admiralty - When taken: 31 Jul 1812 - Where taken: Portsmouth harbor - Date received: 16 Oct 1812 San Antonio - From what ship: HM Ship-of-the-Line Ganges - Born: Dresden - Age: 45 - Discharged on 26 Oct 1813 and sent to Odiham on parole.

Patterson, William - Seaman - Number: 1182 - How taken: Gave himself up from HM Brig Racehorse - Date received: 5 Nov 1813 - From what ship: HMS Racehorse - Born: Pennsylvania - Age: 26 - Discharged on 26 Dec 1813 and sent to Chatham on HM Ship of-the-Line Diomede.

Pattingale, Enoch - Seaman - Number: 301 - Prize Name: Phillipsburgh - Ship type: MV - How taken: Taken up on shore - When taken: 9 Nov 1812 - Where taken: Liverpool - Date received: 31 Dec 1812 - From what ship: HM Ship-of-the-Line Northumberland - Born: Boston - Age: 24 - Discharged on 4 Mar 1813 and sent to Chatham on HM Ship-of-the-Line Queen.

Paul, Jacob - Seaman - Number: 740 - Prize Name: Dart - Ship type: MV - How taken: HM Brig Doterel - When taken: 5 Mar 1813 - Where taken: at sea - Date received: 21 Mar 1813 - From what ship: HMS Dotteril - Born: Elliot - Age: 21 - Discharged on 28 Mar 1813 and sent to Chatham on HM Store Ship Seaphis.

Paulfrey, Richard - Seaman - Number: 604 - Prize Name: Sword Fish - Ship type: P - How taken: HM Ship-of-the-Line Elephant - When taken: 20 Dec 1812 - Where taken: at sea - Date received: 1 Feb 1813 - From what ship: HM Frigate Hermes - Born: Salem - Age: 12 - Discharged on 11 Mar 1813 and sent to Chatham on HM Store Ship Abundance.

Pault, Beloner - Seaman - Number: 44 - Prize Name: USRM Cutter James Madison - Ship type: MW - How taken: HM Frigate Barbadoes - When taken: 22 Aug 1812 - Where taken: at sea - Date received: 12 Oct 1812 San Antonio - From what ship: HM Ship-of-the-Line Polyphemus - Born: Savannah, GA - Age: 15 - Race: Colored - Discharged on 19 Feb 1813 and sent to Chatham on HM Frigate Ulysses.

Payne, Ransom - Seaman - Number: 754 - How taken: Gave himself up from HM Ship-of-the-Line Sterling Castle - Date received: 28 Mar 1813 - From what ship: HMS Sterling Castle - Born: Huntington, NY - Age: 21 - Discharged on 28 Mar 1813 and sent to Chatham on HM Store Ship Seaphis.

Peadon, William - Seaman - Number: 1180 - How taken: Gave himself up from HM Transport Dictator - Date received: 5 Nov 1813 - From what ship: HMS Dictator - Born: Philadelphia - Age: 34 - Discharged on 26 Dec 1813 and sent to Chatham on HM Ship of-the-Line Diomede.

Peake, John W. - Seaman - Number: 726 - How taken: Gave himself up from HM Ship-of-the-Line Christian VII - Date received: 19 Mar 1813 - From what ship: HMS Christian VII - Born: Albany, NY - Age: 26 - Discharged on 28 Mar 1813 and sent to Chatham on HM Store Ship Seaphis.

Peal, Andrea - Seaman - Number: 1500 - How taken: Gave himself up from HM Brig Urgent - Date received: 16 Jun 1814 - From what ship: HMS Urgent - Born: Marblehead - Age: 22 - Discharged on 30 Jun 1814 and sent to Plymouth on HM Brig Steady.

Pearce, Edward - Seaman - Number: 317 - How taken: Gave himself up from HM Frigate Circe - When taken: 31 Dec 1812 - Date received: 31 Dec 1812 - From what ship: HM Ship-of-the-Line Northumberland - Born: Baltimore - Age: 26 - Discharged on 4 Mar 1813 and sent to Chatham on HM Ship-of-the-Line Queen.

Pearce, Emanuel - Seaman - Number: 563 - Prize Name: Rossie - Ship type: MV - How taken: HM Frigate Dryand - When taken: 7 Jan 1813 - Where taken: at sea - Date received: 25 Jan 1813 - From what ship: HM Ship-of-the-Line Queen - Born: New Orleans - Age: 20 - Discharged on 11 Mar 1813 and sent to Chatham on HM Store Ship Abundance.

Pearce, Thomas - Seaman - Number: 833 - How taken: Gave himself up from HM Frigate Amelia - Date received: 5 Jun 1813 - From what ship: HM Guardship Royal William - Born: Boston - Age: 30 - Discharged on 10 Jun 1813 and sent to Chatham on HM Frigate Arethusa.

Pearson, Samuel - Seaman - Number: 283 - Prize Name: Charles - Ship type: MV - How taken: HMS Intelligent - When taken: 1 Aug 1812 - Where taken: Channel - Date received: 31 Dec 1812 - From what ship: HM Ship-of-the-Line Northumberland - Born: Gloucester - Age: 22 - Discharged on 19 Feb 1813 and sent to Chatham on HM Store Ship Dromedary.

Pearson, Samuel - Seaman - Number: 1188 - Prize Name: Fire Fly of Gloucester - Ship type: MV - How taken: HM Frigate Revolutionnaire - When taken: 19 Oct 1813 - Where taken: at sea - Date received: 9 Nov 1813 - From what ship: HMS Revolutionaire - Born: Gloucester - Age: 24 - Discharged on 26 Dec 1813 and sent to Chatham on HM Ship of-the-Line Diomede.

Pearson, Thomas - 1st Mate - Number: 690 - Prize Name: Calcutta - Ship type: East Indian Ship - How taken: Two Brothers, privateer of Guernsey - When taken: 23 Nov 1812 - Where taken: at sea - Date received: 24 Feb 1813 - From what ship: HM Brig Escort - Born: Boston - Age: 33 - Discharged on 6 Mar 1813 and sent to Chatham on HM Ship-of-the-Line Cornwall.

Peckham, Hazard - Seaman - Number: 932 - Prize Name: Tender of the True Blooded Yankee - Ship type: P - How

84 Portsmouth Depot

taken: HM Ship-of-the-Line Fame - When taken: 24 Jun 1813 - Where taken: at sea - Date received: 1 Jul 1813 - From what ship: HM Brig Hope - Born: Boston - Age: 22 - Discharged on 2 Jul 1813 and sent to Chatham on HM Brig Scorpion.

Peckham, Isaac - Seaman - Number: 1136 - Prize Name: Maydock - Ship type: MV - How taken: HM Brig Rebuff - When taken: 16 Jun 1813 - Where taken: St. Mary's - Date received: 6 Oct 1813 - From what ship: HM Sloop Kingfisher - Born: Dartmouth - Age: 23 - Discharged on 17 Oct 1813 and sent to Chatham on HM Transport Malabar No. 352.

Pedrick, Joseph - Seaman - Number: 124 - Prize Name: Nancy - Ship type: MV - How taken: HM Brig Parthian - When taken: 1 Aug 1812 - Where taken: off the Needles - Date received: 29 Oct 1812 - From what ship: HM Brig Nancy - Born: Marblehead - Age: 27 - Discharged on 19 Feb 1813 and sent to Chatham on HM Store Ship Dromedary.

Pegale, Amos - Seaman - Number: 16 - Prize Name: USRM Cutter James Madison - Ship type: MW - How taken: HM Frigate Barbadoes - When taken: 22 Aug 1812 - Where taken: at sea - Date received: 12 Oct 1812 San Antonio - From what ship: HM Ship-of-the-Line Polyphemus - Born: Gilmanton, NH - Age: 24 - Discharged on 19 Feb 1813 and sent to Chatham on HM Frigate Ulysses.

Pendleton, Asa - Seaman - Number: 219 - How taken: Gave himself up from HM Ship-of-the-Line Aboukir - When taken: 29 Oct 1812 - Date received: 26 Dec 1812 - From what ship: HMS Abonkir - Born: Marlborough, MA - Age: 24 - Discharged on 19 Feb 1813 and sent to Chatham on HM Store Ship Dromedary.

Penfield, John - Seaman - Number: 1365 - How taken: Gave himself up from HM Brig Swinger - Date received: 2 Feb 1814 - From what ship: HMS Swinger - Born: Baltimore - Age: 26 - Discharged on 13 Feb 1814 and sent to Chatham on HM Transport Malabar No. 352.

Penn, John - Seaman - Number: 1130 - How taken: Gave himself up from HM Ship-of-the-Line Achille - Date received: 5 Oct 1813 - From what ship: HM Ship-of-the-Line Achille - Born: Long Island - Age: 26 - Race: Black - Discharged on 17 Oct 1813 and sent to Chatham on HM Transport Malabar No. 352.

Penny, James - Seaman - Number: 990 - Prize Name: Jane, prize of the Privateer Snap Dragon - Ship type: MV - How taken: HM Frigate Crescent & HM Ship of-the-Line Bellerophon - When taken: 28 Jun 1813 - Where taken: at sea - Date received: 9 Aug 1813 - From what ship: HM Sloop Hazard - Born: Newburgh - Age: 21 - Discharged on 13 Aug 1813 and sent to Chatham on HM Brig Cadmus.

Perkins, Henry - Seaman - Number: 433 - How taken: Gave himself up from HM Ship of-the-Line Cressy - Date received: 11 Jan 1813 - From what ship: HMS Cressy - Born: Boston - Age: 25 - Discharged on 6 Mar 1813 and sent to Chatham on HMS Frigate Alexandria.

Perkins, William - Seaman - Number: 810 - How taken: Gave himself up from HM Ship-of-the-Line Pembroke - Date received: 21 Apr 1813 - From what ship: HM Guardship Royal William - Born: New Hampshire - Age: 23 - Discharged on 27 Apr 1813 and sent to Chatham on HM Sloop-of-War Bonne Citoyenne.

Perott, John Francis - Seaman - Number: 1433 - Prize Name: HMS Devon Transport No. 15, prize of Privateer Bunker Hill - Ship type: MV - How taken: HM Brig Fly - When taken: 21 Jan 1814 - Where taken: at sea - Date received: 1 Mar 1814 - From what ship: HMS Helicone - Born: Lemevin, France - Age: 69 - Discharged on 28 Apr 1814 and sent to Chatham on HM Sloop Favorite.

Perry, Samuel - Seaman - Number: 1115 - How taken: Gave himself up from HM Ship-of-the-Line America - Date received: 5 Oct 1813 - From what ship: HM Ship-of-the-Line Achille - Born: Salem - Age: 25 - Race: Mulatto - Discharged on 17 Oct 1813 and sent to Chatham on HM Store Ship Weymouth.

Perry, William - Seaman - Number: 1168 - How taken: Gave himself up from HM Hospital Ship Trent - Date received: 12 Oct 1813 - From what ship: HM Brig Hope - Born: Massachusetts - Age: 31 - Discharged on 17 Oct 1813 and sent to Chatham on HM Transport Malabar No. 352.

Peter, Thomas - Seaman - Number: 1097 - How taken: Gave himself up from HM Ship-of-the-Line Berwick - Date received: 5 Oct 1813 - From what ship: HM Ship-of-the-Line Achille - Born: Baltimore - Age: 39 - Race: Black - Discharged on 17 Oct 1813 and sent to Chatham on HM Store Ship Weymouth.

Peters, John - Seaman - Number: 142 - Prize Name: William - Ship type: MV - How taken: HM Brig Recruit - When taken: 29 Aug 1812 - Where taken: at sea - Date received: 29 Oct 1812 - From what ship: HM Ship-of-the-Line Ardent - Born: Philadelphia - Age: 24 - Race: Colored - Discharged on 19 Feb 1813 and sent to Chatham on HM Store Ship Dromedary.

Peters, William - Seaman - Number: 768 - Prize Name: Miser Merchant Ship - How taken: Taken from the HM Transport Mariner No. 146 - Date received: 1 Apr 1813 - From what ship: HM Ship-of-the-Line Blake - Born: New Orleans - Age: 27 - Race: Colored - Discharged on 3 Apr 1813 and sent to Chatham on HM Transport Chatham.

Peterson, Peter - Seaman - Number: 115 - How taken: Sent into custody by order of the commander in chief - Date received: 22 Oct 1812 - From what ship: HM Guardship Royal William - Born: Copenhagan - Age: 35 - Discharged on 19 Feb 1813 and sent to Chatham on HM Frigate Ulysses.

Petingale, John - Seaman - Number: 24 - Prize Name: USRM Cutter James Madison - Ship type: MW - How taken: HM Frigate Barbadoes - When taken: 22 Aug 1812 - Where taken: at sea - Date received: 12 Oct 1812 San Antonio - From what ship: HM Ship-of-the-Line Polyphemus - Born: Haverhill - Age: 45 - Discharged on 19 Feb 1813 and sent to Chatham on HM Frigate Ulysses.

Petterson, Andrew - Seaman - Number: 1400 - Prize Name: open boat - How taken: Nautilus - When taken: 10 Jun 1813 - Where taken: Chesapeake - Date received: 16 Feb 1814 - From what ship: HM Transport Malabar No. 352 - Born: Gothenburg, Sweden - Age: 70 - Discharged on 28 Apr 1814 and sent to Chatham on HM Store Ship Weymouth.

Phellibrown, William - Seaman - Number: 434 - How taken: Gave himself up from HM Ship of-the-Line Cressy - Date received: 11 Jan 1813 - From what ship: HMS Cressy - Born: Boston - Age: 26 - Discharged on 6 Mar 1813 and sent to Chatham on HMS Frigate Alexandria.

Philbrook, Bartholomew - Seaman - Number: 674 - How taken: Gave himself up from HM Brig Forester - Date received: 10 Feb 1813 - From what ship: HMS Forster - Born: New York - Age: 40 - Discharged on 6 Mar 1813 and sent to Chatham on HM Ship-of-the-Line Cornwall.

Phillips, Benjamin - Carpenter - Number: 1148 - How taken: Gave himself up from HM Frigate Castor - Date received: 6 Oct 1813 - From what ship: HM Bomb Vessel Thunder - Born: Charleston - Age: 29 - Discharged on 17 Oct 1813 and sent to Chatham on HM Transport Malabar No. 352.

Phillips, William - Seaman - Number: 737 - Prize Name: Dart - Ship type: MV - How taken: HM Brig Doterel - When taken: 5 Mar 1813 - Where taken: at sea - Date received: 21 Mar 1813 - From what ship: HMS Dotteril - Born: York, MA - Age: 29 - Discharged on 28 Mar 1813 and sent to Chatham on HM Store Ship Seaphis.

Pickett, Richard - Prize Master - Number: 57 - Prize Name: Diana, prize of Privateer Decatur - Ship type: MV - How taken: HM Ship-of-the-Line Polyphemus - When taken: 14 Sep 1812 - Where taken: at sea - Date received: 12 Oct 1812 San Antonio - From what ship: HM Ship-of-the-Line Polyphemus - Born: Marblehead - Age: 24 - Discharged on 19 Feb 1813 and sent to Chatham on HM Frigate Ulysses.

Pincham, Stephen B. - Mate - Number: 369 - Prize Name: Mariner - Ship type: MV - How taken: HM Brig Lyra - When taken: 15 Dec 1812 - Where taken: off Bilboa, Spain - Date received: 3 Jan 1813 - From what ship: HM Frigate Fox - Born: Nantucket - Age: 23 - Discharged on 11 Feb 1813 and sent to Odiham on parole.

Pinkham, Allen - Seaman - Number: 785 - How taken: Gave himself up from HM Frigate Franchise - Date received: 1 Apr 1813 - From what ship: HM Ship-of-the-Line Blake - Born: Bristol - Age: 25 - Discharged on 3 Apr 1813 and sent to Chatham on HM Transport Chatham.

Pinkham, David - 2nd Mate - Number: 1238 - Prize Name: British South Sea Whaler - How taken: HM Ship-of-the-Line Illustrious - When taken: 22 Oct 1813 - Where taken: at sea - Date received: 26 Nov 1813 - From what ship: HMS Illustrious - Born: Nantucket - Age: 30 - Discharged on 26 Dec 1813 and sent to Chatham on HM Ship of-the-Line Diomede.

Pitman, Benjamin - Seaman - Number: 1312 - Prize Name: Growler - Ship type: P - How taken: HM Brig Electra - When taken: 7 Jul 1813 - Where taken: off St. Johns - Date received: 22 Dec 1813 - From what ship: HM Frigate Hyperion - Born: Marblehead - Age: 21 - Discharged on 26 Dec 1813 and sent to Chatham on HMS Frigate Nemesis.

Pitt, William - Seaman - Number: 1331 - How taken: Gave himself up from HM Ship-of-the-Line Invincible - Date received: 27 Dec 1813 - From what ship: HMS Frigate Nemesis - Born: Salem - Age: 26 - Race: Mulatto -

Discharged on 27 Dec 1813 and sent to Chatham on HMS Frigate Nemesis.

Pitterson, John - Seaman - Number: 25 - Prize Name: USRM Cutter James Madison - Ship type: MW - How taken: HM Frigate Barbadoes - When taken: 22 Aug 1812 - Where taken: at sea - Date received: 12 Oct 1812 San Antonio - From what ship: HM Ship-of-the-Line Polyphemus - Born: Sweden - Age: 24 - Discharged on 19 Feb 1813 and sent to Chatham on HM Frigate Ulysses.

Pitts, Charles - Seaman - Number: 1135 - Prize Name: Maydock - Ship type: MV - How taken: HM Brig Rebuff - When taken: 16 Jun 1813 - Where taken: St. Mary's - Date received: 6 Oct 1813 - From what ship: HM Sloop Kingfisher - Born: Bedford - Age: 20 - Discharged on 17 Oct 1813 and sent to Chatham on HM Transport Malabar No. 352.

Plasted, William - 1st Mate - Number: 86 - Prize Name: HM Frigate Janus - Ship type: MW - How taken: Detained by Court of Admiralty - When taken: 31 Jul 1812 - Where taken: Portsmouth harbor - Date received: 16 Oct 1812 San Antonio - From what ship: HM Frigate Janus - Born: Portsmouth, NH - Age: 21 - Discharged on 26 Oct 1813 and sent to Odiham on parole.

Platt, Daniel - Seaman - Number: 1386 - Prize Name: Pilate - Ship type: P - How taken: Victoria, privateer of Guernsey - When taken: 28 Jan 1814 - Where taken: off Bordeaux - Date received: 7 Feb 1814 - From what ship: Mary from Guernsey - Born: Long Island - Age: 21 - Race: Black - Discharged on 13 Feb 1814 and sent to Chatham on HM Transport Malabar No. 352.

Platt, John Henry - Seaman - Number: 256 - Prize Name: King of Rome - Ship type: P - How taken: HM Brig Wolverine - When taken: 13 Dec 1812 - Where taken: at sea - Date received: 27 Dec 1812 - From what ship: HMS Wolverine - Born: Boxford, MA - Age: 25 - Discharged on 19 Feb 1813 and sent to Chatham on HM Store Ship Dromedary.

Plumber, William Reed - Seaman - Number: 1416 - Prize Name: Zephyr, prize of Privateer Rattlesnake - Ship type: MV - How taken: HM Frigate Surveillante - When taken: 6 Jan 1814 - Where taken: Bay of Biscay - Date received: 1 Mar 1814 - From what ship: HMS Helicone - Born: Connecticut - Age: 32 - Discharged on 28 Apr 1814 and sent to Chatham on HM Sloop Favorite.

Plur, Henry - Soldier - Number: 1328 - Date received: 27 Dec 1813 - From what ship: HMS Frigate Nemesis - Died on 27 Dec 1813.

Polles, Edward - Seaman - Number: 1262 - Prize Name: Dart - Ship type: P - How taken: HM Frigate Niger & HMS Fortunee - Where taken: at sea - Date received: 19 Dec 1813 - From what ship: HMS Fortunee - Born: Baltimore - Age: 22 - Discharged on 26 Dec 1813 and sent to Chatham on HM Ship of-the-Line Diomede.

Poole, John - Seaman - Number: 615 - How taken: Gave himself up from HM Guardship Royal William - Date received: 3 Feb 1813 - From what ship: HMS Royal William - Born: Baltimore - Age: 27 - Race: Black - Discharged on 11 Mar 1813 and sent to Chatham on HM Store Ship Abundance.

Poole, Richard - Seaman - Number: 820 - Prize Name: Ajax, prize to the Privateer Governor Tomkins - Ship type: MV - How taken: HM Frigate Revolutionnaire - When taken: 10 Apr 1813 - Where taken: at sea - Date received: 13 May 1813 - From what ship: HMS Revolutionaire - Born: Bristol, MA - Age: 23 - Discharged on 17 May 1813 and sent to Chatham on HMS Impeleux.

Pope, William - Seaman - Number: 782 - How taken: Gave himself up from HM Frigate Franchise - Date received: 1 Apr 1813 - From what ship: HM Ship-of-the-Line Blake - Born: Blemham, NY - Age: 30 - Discharged on 3 Apr 1813 and sent to Chatham on HM Transport Chatham.

Port, John - Seaman - Number: 1448 - Prize Name: Harvest, prize of Privateer Bunker Hill - Ship type: MV - How taken: HM Brig Orestes - When taken: 21 Jan 1814 - Where taken: Bay of Biscay - Date received: 1 Mar 1814 - From what ship: HMS Helicone - Born: Rhode Island - Age: 21 - Race: Black - Discharged on 28 Apr 1814 and sent to Chatham on HM Brig Cordelia.

Porter, Charel - Seaman - Number: 1241 - Prize Name: British South Sea Whaler - How taken: HM Ship-of-the-Line Illustrious - When taken: 22 Oct 1813 - Where taken: at sea - Date received: 26 Nov 1813 - From what ship: HMS Illustrious - Born: Massachusetts - Age: 28 - Discharged on 26 Dec 1813 and sent to Chatham on HM Ship of-the-Line Diomede.

Porter, Nathaniel - Seaman - Number: 243 - Prize Name: Antelope - Ship type: P - How taken: HM Brig Zephyr -

When taken: 10 Dec 1812 - Where taken: at sea - Date received: 27 Dec 1812 - From what ship: HMS Zephyr - Born: Middlesex, MA - Age: 32 - Discharged on 19 Feb 1813 and sent to Chatham on HM Store Ship Dromedary.

Porter, Samuel - Seaman - Number: 967 - How taken: Gave himself up from HM Ship-of-the-Line Leviathan - Date received: 31 Jul 1813 - From what ship: HMS Leviathan - Born: Boston - Age: 23 - Discharged on 7 Aug 1813 and sent to Chatham on HM Brig Rinaldo.

Posey, Valentine - Passenger - Number: 824 - Prize Name: Messenger - Ship type: MV - How taken: HM Frigate Iris - When taken: 10 Mar 1813 - Where taken: at sea - Date received: 13 May 1813 - From what ship: HM Frigate Medusa - Born: Baltimore - Age: 24 - Discharged on 17 May 1813 and sent to Chatham on HMS Impeleux.

Potter, Jacob - Seaman - Number: 808 - How taken: Gave himself up from HM Schooner Antelope - Date received: 21 Apr 1813 - From what ship: HM Guardship Royal William - Born: Lewistown, DE - Age: 30 - Discharged on 27 Apr 1813 and sent to Chatham on HM Sloop-of-War Bonne Citoyenne.

Potter, John (1) - Seaman - Number: 1052 - How taken: Gave himself up from HM Ship-of-the-Line Pompee - Date received: 14 Sep 1813 - From what ship: HM Brig Savage - Born: New York - Age: 27 - Discharged on 29 Sep 1813 and sent to Chatham on HM Transport Chatham.

Potter, John (2) - Seaman - Number: 1078 - How taken: Gave himself up from HM Ship-of-the-Line Pompee - Date received: 1 Oct 1813 - From what ship: HM Ship-of-the-Line Barham - Born: New York - Age: 27 - Discharged on 17 Oct 1813 and sent to Chatham on HM Store Ship Weymouth.

Powell, Elijah - Seaman - Number: 572 - Prize Name: Rossie - Ship type: MV - How taken: HM Frigate Dryand - When taken: 7 Jan 1813 - Where taken: at sea - Date received: 25 Jan 1813 - From what ship: HM Ship-of-the-Line Queen - Born: Harford, MD - Age: 34 - Discharged on 11 Mar 1813 and sent to Chatham on HM Store Ship Abundance.

Powell, Joseph - Seaman - Number: 1035 - How taken: Gave himself up from HM Ship-of-the-Line Berwick - Date received: 7 Sep 1813 - From what ship: HM Frigate Unicorn - Born: Philadelphia - Age: 32 - Race: Black - Discharged on 21 Sep 1813 and sent to Chatham on HM Ship-of-the-Line Queen.

Powell, Joseph - Seaman - Number: 1226 - Prize Name: Falcon, prize of the US Frigate President - Ship type: MV - How taken: Spanish forces - When taken: 2 Jul 1813 - Where taken: Passage Harbor - Date received: 21 Nov 1813 - From what ship: Fortan - Born: Baltimore - Age: 32 - Race: Black - Discharged on 26 Dec 1813 and sent to Chatham on HM Ship of-the-Line Diomede.

Powell, Richard - Seaman - Number: 229 - Prize Name: Antelope - Ship type: P - How taken: HM Brig Zephyr - When taken: 10 Dec 1812 - Where taken: at sea - Date received: 27 Dec 1812 - From what ship: HMS Zephyr - Born: New York - Age: 37 - Discharged on 19 Feb 1813 and sent to Chatham on HM Store Ship Dromedary.

Powers, William - Seaman - Number: 149 - Prize Name: William - Ship type: MV - How taken: HM Brig Recruit - When taken: 29 Aug 1812 - Where taken: at sea - Date received: 29 Oct 1812 - From what ship: HM Ship-of-the-Line Ardent - Born: Georgetown, MD - Age: 18 - Discharged on 19 Feb 1813 and sent to Chatham on HM Store Ship Dromedary.

Pratt, Asa - Seaman - Number: 108 - Prize Name: Nancy - Ship type: MV - How taken: HM Brig Parthian - When taken: 1 Aug 1812 - Where taken: off the Needles - Date received: 16 Oct 1812 San Antonio - From what ship: HM Brig Nancy - Born: Weymouth, MA - Age: 18 - Discharged on 19 Feb 1813 and sent to Chatham on HM Frigate Ulysses.

Prendewell, James - Seaman - Number: 168 - Prize Name: Baltimore - Ship type: P - How taken: HM Transport Diadem - When taken: 7 Oct 1812 - Where taken: S. Andera - Date received: 3 Nov 1812 San Antonio - From what ship: HMS Diadem - Born: Baltimore - Age: 20 - Discharged on 19 Feb 1813 and sent to Chatham on HM Store Ship Dromedary.

Prentiss, Christian - Prize Master - Number: 443 - Prize Name: Sword Fish - Ship type: P - How taken: HM Ship-of-the-Line Elephant - When taken: 28 Dec 1812 - Where taken: at sea - Date received: 14 Jan 1813 - From what ship: HMS Elephant - Born: Marblehead - Age: 28 - Discharged on 6 Mar 1813 and sent to Chatham on

HMS Frigate Alexandria.

Preston, William - Seaman - Number: 104 - Prize Name: HM Brig Richmond - Ship type: MV - How taken: Detained by Court of Admiralty - When taken: 31 Jul 1812 - Where taken: Portsmouth harbor - Date received: 16 Oct 1812 San Antonio - From what ship: HM Brig Richmond - Born: Philadelphia - Age: 21 - Race: Black - Discharged on 19 Feb 1813 and sent to Chatham on HM Frigate Ulysses.

Price, Carlton - Seaman - Number: 1173 - How taken: Gave himself up from HM Frigate Laurel - Date received: 15 Oct 1813 - From what ship: HMS Laurel - Born: Concord - Age: 21 - Discharged on 17 Oct 1813 and sent to Chatham on HM Transport Malabar No. 352.

Price, John - Seaman - Number: 642 - How taken: Gave himself up from HM Guardship Royal William - Date received: 3 Feb 1813 - From what ship: HMS Royal William - Born: Wilmington - Age: 23 - Discharged on 11 Mar 1813 and sent to Chatham on HM Store Ship Abundance.

Primas, James - Seaman - Number: 1233 - Prize Name: British South Sea Whaler - How taken: HM Ship-of-the-Line Illustrious - When taken: 5 Aug 1813 - Where taken: St. Helena - Date received: 26 Nov 1813 - From what ship: HMS Illustrious - Born: Long Island - Age: 33 - Race: Black - Discharged on 26 Dec 1813 and sent to Chatham on HM Ship of-the-Line Diomede.

Prince, William - Seaman - Number: 210 - How taken: Gave himself up from HM Sloop Cherub - Date received: 11 Dec 1812 - From what ship: HMS Cherub - Born: York - Age: 24 - Discharged on 19 Feb 1813 and sent to Chatham on HM Store Ship Dromedary.

Pritchard, Israel - Seaman - Number: 1421 - Prize Name: Hannah - Ship type: MV - How taken: HM Ship-of-the-Line Conquestador - When taken: 15 Jan 1814 - Where taken: at sea - Date received: 1 Mar 1814 - From what ship: HMS Helicone - Born: Marblehead - Age: 22 - Discharged on 28 Apr 1814 and sent to Chatham on HM Sloop Favorite.

Procter, Edward - 1st Mate - Number: 117 - Prize Name: Hannibal - Ship type: P - How taken: MV Patent - When taken: 24 Sep 1812 - Where taken: off Bermuda - Date received: 28 Oct 1812 - From what ship: MV Patent - Born: Boston - Age: 27 - Discharged on 11 Nov 1812 and sent to Odiham on parole.

Putnam, Allen - Mate & Passenger - Number: 1163 - Prize Name: Russian merchant vessel - How taken: Taken out of the HM Ship-of-the-Line Neptune - When taken: 28 Sep 1813 - Where taken: Cork - Date received: 12 Oct 1813 - From what ship: HM Brig Hope - Born: Danvers - Age: 20 - Discharged on 17 Oct 1813 and sent to Chatham on HM Transport Malabar No. 352.

Quackenbush, William - Seaman - Number: 863 - Prize Name: Tiger - Ship type: MV - How taken: HM Brig Scylla - When taken: 22 Mar 1813 - Where taken: Bay of Biscay - Date received: 24 Jun 1813 - From what ship: HM Frigate Unicorn - Born: New York - Age: 33 - Discharged on 2 Jul 1813 and sent to Chatham on HM Frigate Tribune.

Quarterman, William - Seaman - Number: 1053 - How taken: Gave himself up from HM Ship-of-the-Line Ocean - Date received: 14 Sep 1813 - From what ship: HM Brig Savage - Born: Charlestown, NC - Age: 23 - Discharged on 29 Sep 1813 and sent to Chatham on HM Transport Chatham.

Quarterman, William - Seaman - Number: 1079 - How taken: Gave himself up from HM Ship-of-the-Line Ocean - Date received: 1 Oct 1813 - From what ship: HM Ship-of-the-Line Barham - Born: South Carolina - Age: 23 - Discharged on 17 Oct 1813 and sent to Chatham on HM Store Ship Weymouth.

Quasir, Zeph. - Seaman - Number: 45 - Prize Name: USRM Cutter James Madison - Ship type: MW - How taken: HM Frigate Barbadoes - When taken: 22 Aug 1812 - Where taken: at sea - Date received: 12 Oct 1812 San Antonio - From what ship: HM Ship-of-the-Line Polyphemus - Born: Savannah, GA - Age: 20 - Race: Colored - Discharged on 19 Feb 1813 and sent to Chatham on HM Frigate Ulysses.

Rainars, Nicholas - Seaman - Number: 64 - Prize Name: Diana, prize of Privateer Decatur - Ship type: MV - How taken: HM Ship-of-the-Line Polyphemus - When taken: 14 Sep 1812 - Where taken: at sea - Date received: 12 Oct 1812 San Antonio - From what ship: HM Ship-of-the-Line Polyphemus - Born: Holland - Age: 18 - Discharged on 19 Feb 1813 and sent to Chatham on HM Frigate Ulysses.

Randolf, Exum - Seaman - Number: 125 - Prize Name: Nancy - Ship type: MV - How taken: HM Brig Parthian - When taken: 1 Aug 1812 - Where taken: off the Needles - Date received: 29 Oct 1812 - From what ship: HM

Brig Nancy - Born: Nansemond, VA - Age: 26 - Race: Black - Discharged on 2 May 1813 and sent to Chatham on HM Sloop-of-War Bonne Citoyenne.

Rankins, William - Caulker - Number: 1149 - How taken: Gave himself up from HM Frigate Castor - Date received: 6 Oct 1813 - From what ship: HM Bomb Vessel Thunder - Born: Delaware - Age: 32 - Discharged on 17 Oct 1813 and sent to Chatham on HM Transport Malabar No. 352.

Ranlot, John - Seaman - Number: 1155 - How taken: Gave himself up from HM Frigate Orpheus - Date received: 7 Oct 1813 - From what ship: HM Frigate Spartan - Born: Newport - Age: 27 - Discharged on 17 Oct 1813 and sent to Chatham on HM Transport Malabar No. 352.

Raymond, Caleb - Seaman - Number: 1064 - Prize Name: Hindostan - Ship type: MV - How taken: HM Brig Zenobia - When taken: 25 Jun 1813 - Where taken: off Lisbon - Date received: 19 Sep 1813 - From what ship: HM Brig Imogen - Born: Portsmouth, NH - Age: 33 - Discharged on 29 Sep 1813 and sent to Chatham on HM Transport Chatham (see Prisoner Number 1089).

Raymond, Caleb - Seaman - Number: 1089 - Prize Name: Hindostan - Ship type: MV - How taken: HM Brig Zenobia - When taken: 25 Jun 1813 - Where taken: off Lisbon - Date received: 1 Oct 1813 - From what ship: HM Ship-of-the-Line Barham - Born: Portsmouth, NH - Age: 33 - Discharged on 17 Oct 1813 and sent to Chatham on HM Store Ship Weymouth (see Prisoner Number 1064).

Raymond, George - Quartermaster - Number: 382 - How taken: Gave himself up from HM Schooner Arrow - Date received: 10 Jan 1813 - From what ship: HM Guardship Royal William - Born: Newburgh, NY - Age: 26 - Discharged on 4 Mar 1813 and sent to Chatham on HM Ship-of-the-Line Queen.

Read, William - Seaman - Number: 1339 - How taken: Gave himself up from HMS Dannemark - Date received: 4 Jan 1814 - From what ship: HMS Dannemark - Born: Philadelphia - Age: 44 - Race: Black - Discharged on 5 Jan 1814 and sent to Chatham on HM Ship-of-the-Line Poictiers.

Record, Frederick - Seaman - Number: 222 - Prize Name: Antelope - Ship type: P - How taken: HM Brig Zephyr - When taken: 10 Dec 1812 - Where taken: at sea - Date received: 27 Dec 1812 - From what ship: HMS Zephyr - Born: Rhyne, Germany - Age: 38 - Discharged on 19 Feb 1813 and sent to Chatham on HM Store Ship Dromedary.

Rectout, John J. - Seaman - Number: 948 - How taken: Gave himself up from HM Frigate Unicorn - Date received: 8 Jun 1813 - From what ship: HMS Eldegon - Born: Baltimore - Age: 28 - Discharged on 7 Aug 1813 and sent to Chatham on HM Brig Rinaldo.

Redman, David - Seaman - Number: 1152 - How taken: Gave himself up from HM Ship-of-the-Line Scepter - Date received: 7 Oct 1813 - From what ship: HM Frigate Spartan - Born: Maryland - Age: 21 - Discharged on 17 Oct 1813 and sent to Chatham on HM Transport Malabar No. 352.

Reed, H. W. - Prize Master - Number: 446 - Prize Name: Sword Fish - Ship type: P - How taken: HM Ship-of-the-Line Elephant - When taken: 28 Dec 1812 - Where taken: at sea - Date received: 14 Jan 1813 - From what ship: HMS Elephant - Born: Salem - Age: 31 - Discharged on 6 Mar 1813 and sent to Chatham on HMS Frigate Alexandria.

Reed, James - Seaman - Number: 835 - How taken: Gave himself up from HM Frigate Arethusa - Date received: 5 Jun 1813 - From what ship: HM Guardship Royal William - Born: New York - Age: 48 - Discharged on 10 Jun 1813 and sent to Chatham on HM Frigate Arethusa.

Reed, John - Boatswain - Number: 912 - Prize Name: Benjamin Franklin - Ship type: P - How taken: Row boat out of Martinique - When taken: 11 Oct 1812 - Date received: 1 Jul 1813 - From what ship: HM Frigate Tribune - Born: New Castle, DE - Age: 25 - Discharged on 2 Jul 1813 and sent to Chatham on HM Brig Scorpion.

Reed, John - Seaman - Number: 52 - Prize Name: Fame, prize of Privateer Decatur - Ship type: MV - How taken: HM Ship-of-the-Line Polyphemus - When taken: 13 Sep 1812 - Where taken: at sea - Date received: 12 Oct 1812 San Antonio - From what ship: HM Ship-of-the-Line Polyphemus - Born: Marblehead - Age: 19 - Discharged on 19 Feb 1813 and sent to Chatham on HM Frigate Ulysses.

Reed, Joseph - Seaman - Number: 984 - Prize Name: Jane, prize of the Privateer Snap Dragon - Ship type: MV - How taken: HM Frigate Crescent & HM Ship of-the-Line Bellerophon - When taken: 28 Jun 1813 - Where taken: at sea - Date received: 9 Aug 1813 - From what ship: HM Sloop Hazard - Born: Plymouth - Age: 27 -

Discharged on 13 Aug 1813 and sent to Chatham on HM Brig Cadmus.

Reid, John - Seaman - Number: 1036 - How taken: Gave himself up from HM Schooner Charlotte - Date received: 7 Sep 1813 - From what ship: HM Frigate Unicorn - Born: Philadelphia - Age: 24 - Race: Black - Discharged on 29 Sep 1813 and sent to Chatham on HM Ship-of-the-Line Barham.

Reid, John - Seaman - Number: 1037 - How taken: Gave himself up from HM Frigate Undaunted - Date received: 7 Sep 1813 - From what ship: HM Frigate Unicorn - Born: Virginia - Age: 49 - Discharged on 29 Sep 1813 and sent to Chatham on HM Ship-of-the-Line Barham.

Reid, William - Seaman - Number: 1181 - How taken: Gave himself up from HM Brig Racehorse - Date received: 5 Nov 1813 - From what ship: HMS Racehorse - Born: Portsmouth, NH - Age: 25 - Discharged on 26 Dec 1813 and sent to Chatham on HM Ship of-the-Line Diomede.

Rennell, States William - Seaman - Number: 668 - How taken: Gave himself up from HMS Freya - Date received: 9 Feb 1813 - From what ship: HMS Freya - Born: New York - Age: 22 - Discharged on 6 Mar 1813 and sent to Chatham on HM Ship-of-the-Line Cornwall.

Reynolds, Caleb - Supercargo - Number: 118 - Prize Name: Hannibal - Ship type: P - How taken: MV Patent - When taken: 24 Sep 1812 - Where taken: off Bermuda - Date received: 28 Oct 1812 - From what ship: MV Patent - Born: Boston - Age: 38 - Discharged on 11 Nov 1812 and sent to Odiham on parole.

Richards, Edward - Seaman - Number: 849 - How taken: Gave himself up from HM Bomb Vessel Strombolo - Date received: 15 Jun 1813 - From what ship: HM Sloop Helena - Born: Portland, MA - Age: 46 - Discharged on 2 Jul 1813 and sent to Chatham on HM Frigate Tribune.

Richards, George - Seaman - Number: 200 - Prize Name: Rising States - Ship type: MV - How taken: HMS Fortunee - When taken: 28 Aug 1812 - Where taken: at sea - Date received: 25 Nov 1812 - From what ship: HM Guardship Royal William - Born: New York - Age: 27 - Race: Mulatto - Discharged on 19 Feb 1813 and sent to Chatham on HM Store Ship Dromedary.

Richards, John - Seaman - Number: 933 - Prize Name: Tender of the True Blooded Yankee - Ship type: P - How taken: HM Ship-of-the-Line Fame - When taken: 24 Jun 1813 - Where taken: at sea - Date received: 1 Jul 1813 - From what ship: HM Brig Hope - Born: Charles City - Age: 28 - Discharged on 2 Jul 1813 and sent to Chatham on HM Brig Scorpion.

Richardson, John - Seaman - Number: 960 - How taken: Gave himself up from HM Ship-of-the-Line Leviathan - Date received: 31 Jul 1813 - From what ship: HMS Leviathan - Born: Jersey - Age: 42 - Race: Black - Discharged on 7 Aug 1813 and sent to Chatham on HM Brig Rinaldo.

Richardson, John - Seaman - Number: 1508 - How taken: Gave himself up from HM Ship-of-the-Line Rodney - Date received: 30 Jun 1814 - From what ship: HMS Rodney - Born: New York - Age: 23 - Race: Black - Discharged on 30 Jun 1814 and sent to Plymouth on HM Brig Steady.

Richardson, Perry - Seaman - Number: 610 - Prize Name: Sword Fish - Ship type: P - How taken: HM Ship-of-the-Line Elephant - When taken: 20 Dec 1812 - Where taken: at sea - Date received: 1 Feb 1813 - From what ship: HM Frigate Hermes - Born: Maryland - Age: 21 - Discharged on 11 Mar 1813 and sent to Chatham on HM Store Ship Abundance.

Richardson, Robert - Seaman - Number: 1105 - How taken: Gave himself up from HM Ship-of-the-Line Swiftsure - Date received: 5 Oct 1813 - From what ship: HM Ship-of-the-Line Achille - Born: Philadelphia - Age: 43 - Race: Mulatto - Discharged on 17 Oct 1813 and sent to Chatham on HM Store Ship Weymouth.

Richardson, Samuel - Seaman - Number: 676 - How taken: Gave himself up from HMS Dannemark - Date received: 12 Feb 1813 - From what ship: HMS Dannemark - Born: Boston - Age: 30 - Discharged on 6 Mar 1813 and sent to Chatham on HM Ship-of-the-Line Cornwall.

Ricker, Samuel - Seaman - Number: 99 - Prize Name: HMS Eos - Ship type: MW - How taken: Detained by Court of Admiralty - When taken: 31 Jul 1812 - Where taken: Portsmouth harbor - Date received: 16 Oct 1812 San Antonio - From what ship: Eos - Born: Wells County, NY - Age: 24 - Discharged on 19 Feb 1813 and sent to Chatham on HM Frigate Ulysses.

Riley, Jonathan - Seaman - Number: 209 - Prize Name: Felix - Ship type: MV - How taken: HM Frigate Gladiator -

When taken: 5 Dec 1812 - Where taken: Portsmouth harbor - Date received: 5 Dec 1812 - From what ship: HMS Gladiator - Born: York - Age: 33 - Discharged on 19 Feb 1813 and sent to Chatham on HM Store Ship Dromedary.

Riley, William - Seaman - Number: 316 - How taken: Gave himself up from HM Frigate Circe - When taken: 31 Dec 1812 - Date received: 31 Dec 1812 - From what ship: HM Ship-of-the-Line Northumberland - Born: New Jersey - Age: 22 - Discharged on 4 Mar 1813 and sent to Chatham on HM Ship-of-the-Line Queen.

Rippaviere, John - Seaman - Number: 363 - Prize Name: Three Brothers - Ship type: MV - How taken: HM Brig Bermuda - When taken: 9 Dec 1812 - Where taken: off St. Valery - Date received: 2 Jan 1813 - From what ship: HM Prison Ship Assistance - Born: Basel, Switzerland - Age: 38 - Discharged on 4 Mar 1813 and sent to Chatham on HM Ship-of-the-Line Queen.

Roberton, William - Seaman - Number: 1240 - Prize Name: British South Sea Whaler - How taken: HM Ship-of-the-Line Illustrious - When taken: 22 Oct 1813 - Where taken: at sea - Date received: 26 Nov 1813 - From what ship: HMS Illustrious - Born: Philadelphia - Age: 26 - Discharged on 26 Dec 1813 and sent to Chatham on HM Ship of-the-Line Diomede.

Roberts, George - Seaman - Number: 464 - Prize Name: Sword Fish - Ship type: P - How taken: HM Ship-of-the-Line Elephant - When taken: 28 Dec 1812 - Where taken: at sea - Date received: 14 Jan 1813 - From what ship: HMS Elephant - Born: Marblehead - Age: 24 - Discharged on 11 Mar 1813 and sent to Chatham on HM Store Ship Abundance.

Roberts, James - Seaman - Number: 767 - How taken: Gave himself up from HM Ship-of-the-Line Blake - Date received: 1 Apr 1813 - From what ship: HMS Blake - Born: Philadelphia - Age: 31 - Race: Black - Discharged on 3 Apr 1813 and sent to Chatham on HM Transport Chatham.

Roberts, Josiah - Seaman - Number: 400 - Prize Name: Empress - Ship type: MV - How taken: HM Brig Rover - When taken: 30 Nov 1812 - Where taken: at sea - Date received: 10 Jan 1813 - From what ship: HM Guardship Royal William - Born: New Jersey - Age: 22 - Discharged on 6 Mar 1813 and sent to Chatham on HMS Frigate Alexandria.

Roberts, Robert - Seaman - Number: 510 - How taken: Gave himself up from HM Brig Zephyr - Date received: 20 Jan 1813 - From what ship: HMS Zepher - Born: New York - Age: 27 - Discharged on 11 Mar 1813 and sent to Chatham on HM Store Ship Abundance.

Robin, Thomas - Seaman - Number: 852 - How taken: Gave himself up from HM Frigate Leonidas - Date received: 22 Jun 1813 - From what ship: HM Ship-of-the-Line Vigo - Born: Plymouth - Age: 28 - Discharged on 2 Jul 1813 and sent to Chatham on HM Frigate Tribune.

Robinson, Benjamin - Seaman - Number: 646 - How taken: Gave himself up from HM Guardship Royal William - Date received: 3 Feb 1813 - From what ship: HMS Royal William - Born: Boston - Age: 31 - Discharged on 11 Mar 1813 and sent to Chatham on HM Store Ship Abundance.

Robinson, Charles - Seaman - Number: 192 - Prize Name: Felix - Ship type: MV - How taken: HM Frigate Indefatigable - When taken: 13 Nov 1812 - Where taken: Portsmouth harbor - Date received: 22 Nov 1812 - From what ship: HM Frigate Gladiator - Born: Nantucket - Age: 31 - Discharged on 19 Feb 1813 and sent to Chatham on HM Store Ship Dromedary.

Robinson, Edward - Seaman - Number: 195 - How taken: Sent into custody by order of the commander in chief - Date received: 22 Nov 1812 - From what ship: HM Guardship Royal William - Born: Talbot, MD - Age: 24 - Discharged on 19 Feb 1813 and sent to Chatham on HM Store Ship Dromedary.

Robinson, Edward - Seaman - Number: 580 - Prize Name: Industry - Ship type: MV - How taken: HM Frigate Dryand - When taken: 7 Jan 1813 - Where taken: at sea - Date received: 25 Jan 1813 - From what ship: HM Ship-of-the-Line Queen - Born: Boston - Age: 27 - Discharged on 11 Mar 1813 and sent to Chatham on HM Store Ship Abundance.

Robinson, John - Seaman - Number: 1113 - How taken: Gave himself up from HM Ship-of-the-Line America - Date received: 5 Oct 1813 - From what ship: HM Ship-of-the-Line Achille - Born: Massachusetts - Age: 26 - Discharged on 17 Oct 1813 and sent to Chatham on HM Store Ship Weymouth.

Robson, Robert - Seaman - Number: 223 - Prize Name: Antelope - Ship type: P - How taken: HM Brig Zephyr -

When taken: 10 Dec 1812 - Where taken: at sea - Date received: 27 Dec 1812 - From what ship: HMS Zephyr - Born: Salem, MA - Age: 32 - Discharged on 19 Feb 1813 and sent to Chatham on HM Store Ship Dromedary.

Roderick, Frank - Seaman - Number: 914 - Prize Name: Decatur - Ship type: P - How taken: HM Frigate Surprise - When taken: 16 Jan 1813 - Where taken: at sea - Date received: 1 Jul 1813 - From what ship: HM Frigate Tribune - Born: Newport - Age: 26 - Discharged on 2 Jul 1813 and sent to Chatham on HM Brig Scorpion.

Roger, Christopher - Seaman - Number: 1464 - Prize Name: Bunker Hill - Ship type: P - How taken: HM Frigate Pomone & HM Frigate Cydnus - When taken: 4 Mar 1814 - Where taken: French coast - Date received: 11 Apr 1814 - From what ship: HMS Ship-on-the-Line San Domaso - Born: Brest, France - Age: 46 - Discharged on 28 Apr 1814 and sent to Chatham on HM Store Ship Weymouth.

Rogers, Abithan - Chief Mate - Number: 270 - Prize Name: Antelope - Ship type: P - How taken: HM Brig Zephyr - When taken: 10 Dec 1812 - Where taken: at sea - Date received: 29 Dec 1812 - From what ship: HMS Zephyr - Born: Massachusetts - Age: 35 - Discharged on 31 Dec 1812 and sent to Odiham on parole.

Rogers, Abraham - Seaman - Number: 1250 - Prize Name: Dart - Ship type: P - How taken: HM Frigate Niger & HMS Fortunee - Where taken: at sea - Date received: 19 Dec 1813 - From what ship: HMS Fortunee - Born: Delaware - Age: 21 - Discharged on 26 Dec 1813 and sent to Chatham on HM Ship of-the-Line Diomede.

Rogers, Epinetus - Seaman - Number: 986 - Prize Name: Jane, prize of the Privateer Snap Dragon - Ship type: MV - How taken: HM Frigate Crescent & HM Ship of-the-Line Bellerophon - When taken: 28 Jun 1813 - Where taken: at sea - Date received: 9 Aug 1813 - From what ship: HM Sloop Hazard - Born: Long Island - Age: 22 - Discharged on 13 Aug 1813 and sent to Chatham on HM Brig Cadmus.

Rogers, Francis - Seaman - Number: 937 - Prize Name: Tender of the True Blooded Yankee - Ship type: P - How taken: HM Ship-of-the-Line Fame - When taken: 24 Jun 1813 - Where taken: at sea - Date received: 1 Jul 1813 - From what ship: HM Brig Hope - Born: Philadelphia - Age: 33 - Discharged on 2 Jul 1813 and sent to Chatham on HM Brig Scorpion.

Rogers, James - Seaman - Number: 611 - Prize Name: Sword Fish - Ship type: P - How taken: HM Ship-of-the-Line Elephant - When taken: 20 Dec 1812 - Where taken: at sea - Date received: 1 Feb 1813 - From what ship: HM Frigate Hermes - Born: Newport - Age: 29 - Race: Black - Discharged on 11 Mar 1813 and sent to Chatham on HM Store Ship Abundance.

Rogers, Samuel - Seaman - Number: 999 - Prize Name: Kitty, prize of US Frigate President - Ship type: MV - How taken: Dart, privateer of Guernsey - When taken: 20 Jun 1813 - Where taken: at sea - Date received: 18 Aug 1813 - From what ship: HMS Dexterous - Born: Boston - Age: 18 - Discharged on 21 Sep 1813 and sent to Chatham on HM Ship-of-the-Line Queen.

Rogers, William - Seaman - Number: 169 - Prize Name: Baltimore - Ship type: P - How taken: HM Transport Diadem - When taken: 7 Oct 1812 - Where taken: S. Andera - Date received: 3 Nov 1812 San Antonio - From what ship: HMS Diadem - Born: Wilmington - Age: 21 - Discharged on 19 Feb 1813 and sent to Chatham on HM Store Ship Dromedary.

Rollo, William - Seaman - Number: 746 - How taken: Gave himself up from HM Guardship Royal William - Date received: 11 Mar 1813 - From what ship: HMS Royal William - Born: Gloucester - Age: 33 - Discharged on 28 Mar 1813 and sent to Chatham on HM Store Ship Seaphis.

Ron, Richard - Seaman - Number: 827 - How taken: Gave himself up from HM Frigate North Star - Date received: 26 May 1813 - From what ship: HMS North Star - Born: Philadelphia - Age: 40 - Discharged on 10 Jun 1813 and sent to Chatham on HM Frigate Arethusa.

Roper, John - Seaman - Number: 469 - Prize Name: Sword Fish - Ship type: P - How taken: HM Ship-of-the-Line Elephant - When taken: 28 Dec 1812 - Where taken: at sea - Date received: 14 Jan 1813 - From what ship: HMS Elephant - Born: Gloucester - Age: 17 - Discharged on 11 Mar 1813 and sent to Chatham on HM Store Ship Abundance.

Rosignol, James - 1st Mate - Number: 703 - Prize Name: Tom Thumb - Ship type: MV - How taken: Lion, Privateer - When taken: 15 Feb 1813 - Where taken: at sea - Date received: 24 Feb 1813 - From what ship: HM Brig Escort - Born: Boston - Age: 23 - Discharged on 6 Mar 1813 and sent to Chatham on HM Ship-of-the-Line

Cornwall.

Ross, John - Seaman - Number: 1150 - How taken: Gave himself up from HM Ship-of-the-Line Majestic - Date received: 7 Oct 1813 - From what ship: HM Frigate Spartan - Born: New York - Age: 51 - Discharged on 17 Oct 1813 and sent to Chatham on HM Transport Malabar No. 352.

Rotan, John - Seaman - Number: 1336 - Prize Name: Calmar - Ship type: MV - How taken: Friends, privateer from Antigua - When taken: 1 Mar 1813 - Where taken: off St. Bartholomew - Date received: 3 Jan 1814 - From what ship: HM Ship-of-the-Line Prince - Born: Maryland - Age: 26 - Discharged on 5 Jan 1814 and sent to Chatham on HM Ship-of-the-Line Poictiers.

Roundey, Jonathan - Seaman - Number: 395 - Prize Name: Empress - Ship type: MV - How taken: HM Brig Rover - When taken: 30 Nov 1812 - Where taken: at sea - Date received: 10 Jan 1813 - From what ship: HM Guardship Royal William - Born: Lynd, MA - Age: 35 - Discharged on 6 Mar 1813 and sent to Chatham on HMS Frigate Alexandria.

Roundy, Jeremiah - Boy - Number: 1310 - Prize Name: Growler - Ship type: P - How taken: HM Brig Electra - When taken: 7 Jul 1813 - Where taken: off St. Johns - Date received: 22 Dec 1813 - From what ship: HM Frigate Hyperion - Born: Marblehead - Age: 17 - Discharged on 26 Dec 1813 and sent to Chatham on HMS Frigate Nemesis.

Roundy, Thomas - Boatswain - Number: 1303 - Prize Name: Growler - Ship type: P - How taken: HM Brig Electra - When taken: 7 Jul 1813 - Where taken: off St. Johns - Date received: 22 Dec 1813 - From what ship: HM Frigate Hyperion - Born: Marblehead - Age: 26 - Discharged on 26 Dec 1813 and sent to Chatham on HMS Frigate Nemesis.

Row, Simon - Seaman - Number: 841 - How taken: Gave himself up from HM Ship-of-the-Line Malta - Date received: 15 Jun 1813 - From what ship: HM Sloop Helena - Born: Seabrook, NH - Age: 25 - Discharged on 2 Jul 1813 and sent to Chatham on HM Frigate Tribune.

Rowe, John - Seaman - Number: 386 - How taken: Gave himself up from HM Ship-of-the-Line Salvador del Mundo - Date received: 10 Jan 1813 - From what ship: HM Guardship Royal William - Born: Cape Ann, MA - Age: 22 - Discharged on 4 Mar 1813 and sent to Chatham on HM Ship-of-the-Line Queen.

Rowe, William - Seaman - Number: 1187 - Prize Name: Fire Fly of Gloucester - Ship type: MV - How taken: HM Frigate Revolutionnaire - When taken: 19 Oct 1813 - Where taken: at sea - Date received: 9 Nov 1813 - From what ship: HMS Revolutionaire - Born: Boston - Age: 27 - Discharged on 26 Dec 1813 and sent to Chatham on HM Ship of-the-Line Diomede.

Roweth, William - Seaman - Number: 1184 - How taken: Gave himself up from HM Brig Racehorse - Date received: 5 Nov 1813 - From what ship: HMS Racehorse - Born: Burlington, NJ - Age: 37 - Discharged on 26 Dec 1813 and sent to Chatham on HM Ship of-the-Line Diomede.

Russel, Joseph (alias Wood) - Seaman - Number: 791 - How taken: Gave himself up from HM Ship-of-the-Line Sterling Castle - Date received: 7 Apr 1813 - From what ship: HMS Sterling Castle - Born: Philadelphia - Age: 28 - Discharged on 27 Apr 1813 and sent to Chatham on HM Sloop-of-War Bonne Citoyenne.

Russel, William - Seaman - Number: 375 - Prize Name: Casta - Ship type: MV - How taken: HM Schooner Antelope - When taken: 31 Jul 1812 - Where taken: at sea - Date received: 4 Jan 1813 - From what ship: HMS Muros - Born: New York - Age: 21 - Discharged on 4 Mar 1813 and sent to Chatham on HM Ship-of-the-Line Queen.

Russell, William - Seaman - Number: 1287 - Prize Name: Growler - Ship type: P - How taken: HM Brig Electra - When taken: 7 Jul 1813 - Where taken: off St. Johns - Date received: 22 Dec 1813 - From what ship: HM Ship of-the-Line Bellerophon - Born: Marblehead - Age: 19 - Discharged on 26 Dec 1813 and sent to Chatham on HMS Frigate Nemesis.

Rust, John - Steward - Number: 1309 - Prize Name: Growler - Ship type: P - How taken: HM Brig Electra - When taken: 7 Jul 1813 - Where taken: off St. Johns - Date received: 22 Dec 1813 - From what ship: HM Frigate Hyperion - Born: Bristol - Age: 33 - Discharged on 26 Dec 1813 and sent to Chatham on HMS Frigate Nemesis.

Rust, John - Mate - Number: 1454 - Prize Name: Soley - Ship type: MV - How taken: HM Brig Derment - When taken: 21 Jan 1814 - Where taken: at sea - Date received: 9 Apr 1814 - From what ship: HM Ship-of-the-Line Leyden - Born: Salem - Age: 27 - Discharged on 28 Apr 1814 and sent to Chatham on HM Store Ship Weymouth.

Rust, John - Seaman - Number: 154 - Prize Name: Lydia - Ship type: MV - How taken: HM Frigate Orpheus - When taken: 3 Sep 1812 - Where taken: at sea - Date received: 29 Oct 1812 - From what ship: HM Ship-of-the-Line Ardent - Born: Baltimore - Age: 29 - Discharged on 19 Feb 1813 and sent to Chatham on HM Store Ship Dromedary.

Rust, John - 1st Lieutenant - Number: 1297 - Prize Name: Growler - Ship type: P - How taken: HM Brig Electra - When taken: 7 Jul 1813 - Where taken: off St. Johns - Date received: 22 Dec 1813 - From what ship: HM Frigate Hyperion - Born: Salem - Age: 51 - Discharged on 26 Dec 1813 and sent to Chatham on HMS Frigate Nemesis.

Sabrian, James - Seaman - Number: 397 - Prize Name: Empress - Ship type: MV - How taken: HM Brig Rover - When taken: 30 Nov 1812 - Where taken: at sea - Date received: 10 Jan 1813 - From what ship: HM Guardship Royal William - Born: New Haven - Age: 30 - Discharged on 6 Mar 1813 and sent to Chatham on HMS Frigate Alexandria.

Salkins, Nathaniel - Seaman - Number: 59 - Prize Name: Diana, prize of Privateer Decatur - Ship type: MV - How taken: HM Ship-of-the-Line Polyphemus - When taken: 14 Sep 1812 - Where taken: at sea - Date received: 12 Oct 1812 San Antonio - From what ship: HM Ship-of-the-Line Polyphemus - Born: Marblehead - Age: 20 - Discharged on 19 Feb 1813 and sent to Chatham on HM Frigate Ulysses.

Salyear, John - Seaman - Number: 263 - Prize Name: King of Rome - Ship type: P - How taken: HM Brig Wolverine - When taken: 13 Dec 1812 - Where taken: at sea - Date received: 27 Dec 1812 - From what ship: HMS Wolverine - Born: North Carolina - Age: 26 - Discharged on 19 Feb 1813 and sent to Chatham on HM Store Ship Dromedary.

Sampson, Jacob - Seaman - Number: 873 - Prize Name: Tiger - Ship type: MV - How taken: HM Brig Scylla - When taken: 22 Mar 1813 - Where taken: Bay of Biscay - Date received: 24 Jun 1813 - From what ship: HM Frigate Unicorn - Born: New York - Age: 24 - Discharged on 2 Jul 1813 and sent to Chatham on HM Frigate Tribune.

Sandbach, Richard - Seaman - Number: 497 - Prize Name: Sword Fish - Ship type: P - How taken: HM Ship-of-the-Line Elephant - When taken: 28 Dec 1812 - Where taken: at sea - Date received: 14 Jan 1813 - From what ship: HMS Elephant - Born: Maryland - Age: 26 - Discharged on 11 Mar 1813 and sent to Chatham on HM Store Ship Abundance.

Sanderson, John - Seaman - Number: 401 - Prize Name: Empress - Ship type: MV - How taken: HM Brig Rover - When taken: 30 Nov 1812 - Where taken: at sea - Date received: 10 Jan 1813 - From what ship: HM Guardship Royal William - Born: Lienbach, Austria - Age: 54 - Race: Colored - Discharged on 6 Mar 1813 and sent to Chatham on HMS Frigate Alexandria.

Sands, Thomas - Seaman - Number: 679 - Prize Name: Hope - Ship type: MV - How taken: HM Schooner Bramble - When taken: 2 Dec 1812 - Where taken: at sea - Date received: 14 Feb 1813 - From what ship: HM Transport Maister No. 84 - Born: Gloucester - Age: 21 - Discharged on 6 Mar 1813 and sent to Chatham on HM Ship-of-the-Line Cornwall.

Saunders, James - Mate - Number: 988 - Prize Name: Jane, prize of the Privateer Snap Dragon - Ship type: MV - How taken: HM Frigate Crescent & HM Ship of-the-Line Bellerophon - When taken: 28 Jun 1813 - Where taken: at sea - Date received: 9 Aug 1813 - From what ship: HM Sloop Hazard - Born: North Carolina - Age: 23 - Discharged on 13 Aug 1813 and sent to Chatham on HM Brig Cadmus.

Saunders, Thomas - Seaman - Number: 470 - Prize Name: Sword Fish - Ship type: P - How taken: HM Ship-of-the-Line Elephant - When taken: 28 Dec 1812 - Where taken: at sea - Date received: 14 Jan 1813 - From what ship: HMS Elephant - Born: Boston - Age: 29 - Discharged on 11 Mar 1813 and sent to Chatham on HM Store Ship Abundance.

Saunders, Thomas - Seaman - Number: 590 - How taken: Gave himself up from HM Ship-of-the-Line Mars - Date received: 31 Jan 1813 - From what ship: HMS Mars - Born: Norfolk - Age: 22 - Discharged on 11 Mar 1813 and sent to Chatham on HM Store Ship Abundance.

Saunders, Thomas - Seaman - Number: 394 - Prize Name: Empress - Ship type: MV - How taken: HM Brig Rover - When taken: 30 Nov 1812 - Where taken: at sea - Date received: 10 Jan 1813 - From what ship: HM Guardship Royal William - Born: Baileyfield, Germany - Age: 30 - Discharged on 4 Mar 1813 and sent to Chatham on HM Ship-of-the-Line Queen.

Saunderson, William - Seaman - Number: 645 - How taken: Gave himself up from HM Guardship Royal William - Date received: 3 Feb 1813 - From what ship: HMS Royal William - Born: Baltimore - Age: 25 - Discharged on 11 Mar 1813 and sent to Chatham on HM Store Ship Abundance.

Sawyers, Jonathan - Gunner - Number: 1206 - Prize Name: Elbridge Gerry - Ship type: P - How taken: HM Frigate Crescent & HM Ship of-the-Line Bellerophon - When taken: 16 Sep 1813 - Where taken: at sea - Date received: 16 Nov 1813 - From what ship: HM Sloop Talbot - Born: Cape Elizabeth, MA - Age: 28 - Discharged on 26 Dec 1813 and sent to Chatham on HM Ship of-the-Line Diomede.

Scaff, Nicholas - Seaman - Number: 245 - Prize Name: Antelope - Ship type: P - How taken: HM Brig Zephyr - When taken: 10 Dec 1812 - Where taken: at sea - Date received: 27 Dec 1812 - From what ship: HMS Zephyr - Born: Richmond, VA - Age: 24 - Discharged on 19 Feb 1813 and sent to Chatham on HM Store Ship Dromedary.

Scanel, Cornele - Seaman - Number: 295 - Prize Name: John - Ship type: MV - How taken: Taken up on shore - When taken: 18 Oct 1812 - Where taken: Liverpool - Date received: 31 Dec 1812 - From what ship: HM Ship-of-the-Line Northumberland - Born: Darby, PA - Age: 27 - Discharged on 4 Mar 1813 and sent to Chatham on HM Ship-of-the-Line Queen.

Schafft, Carl Hendrick - Marine Captain - Number: 1461 - Prize Name: Bunker Hill - Ship type: P - How taken: HM Frigate Pomone & HM Frigate Cydnus - When taken: 4 Mar 1814 - Where taken: French coast - Date received: 11 Apr 1814 - From what ship: HMS Ship-on-the-Line San Domaso - Born: Berlin - Age: 34 - Discharged on 11 Apr 1814 and sent to Reading on parole.

Schiffky, Jacobus Orgen - Marine - Number: 1474 - Prize Name: Bunker Hill - Ship type: P - How taken: HM Frigate Pomone & HM Frigate Cydnus - When taken: 4 Mar 1814 - Where taken: French coast - Date received: 11 Apr 1814 - From what ship: HMS Ship-on-the-Line San Domaso - Born: Danzig, Prussia - Age: 42 - Discharged on 28 Apr 1814 and sent to Chatham on HM Store Ship Weymouth.

Scofield, Wells - Carpenter - Number: 704 - Prize Name: Tom Thumb - Ship type: MV - How taken: Lion, Privateer - When taken: 15 Feb 1813 - Where taken: at sea - Date received: 24 Feb 1813 - From what ship: HM Brig Escort - Born: East Haddam, MA - Age: 23 - Discharged on 6 Mar 1813 and sent to Chatham on HM Ship-of-the-Line Cornwall.

Scott, Henry - Seaman - Number: 1403 - Prize Name: Volante - Ship type: P - How taken: HM Brig Curley - When taken: 26 Mar 1813 - Where taken: at sea - Date received: 16 Feb 1814 - From what ship: HM Transport Malabar No. 352 - Born: Boston - Age: 43 - Discharged on 28 Apr 1814 and sent to Chatham on HM Store Ship Weymouth.

Scott, James - Steward - Number: 289 - Prize Name: Elizabeth - Ship type: MV - How taken: Taken up on shore - When taken: 18 Oct 1812 - Where taken: Liverpool - Date received: 31 Dec 1812 - From what ship: HM Ship-of-the-Line Northumberland - Born: Boston - Age: 27 - Discharged on 19 Feb 1813 and sent to Chatham on HM Frigate Ulysses.

Scribner, William - Seaman - Number: 637 - How taken: Gave himself up from HM Guardship Royal William - Date received: 3 Feb 1813 - From what ship: HMS Royal William - Born: New Haven - Age: 38 - Discharged on 11 Mar 1813 and sent to Chatham on HM Store Ship Abundance.

Seely, James - Seaman - Number: 119 - Prize Name: Hannibal - Ship type: P - How taken: MV Patent - When taken: 24 Sep 1812 - Where taken: off Bermuda - Date received: 28 Oct 1812 - From what ship: MV Patent - Born: Pittstown, NY - Age: 26 - Discharged on 19 Feb 1813 and sent to Chatham on HM Store Ship Dromedary.

Selman, Francis, G. - 2nd Lieutenant - Number: 1215 - Prize Name: Growler - Ship type: P - How taken: HM Brig Electra - When taken: 7 Jul 1813 - Where taken: at sea - Date received: 16 Nov 1813 - From what ship: HM Sloop Talbot - Born: Marblehead - Age: 31 - Discharged on 26 Dec 1813 and sent to Chatham on HM Ship of-the-Line Diomede.

Selman, John - Seaman - Number: 1422 - Prize Name: Hannah - Ship type: MV - How taken: HM Ship-of-the-Line Conquestador - When taken: 15 Jan 1814 - Where taken: at sea - Date received: 1 Mar 1814 - From what ship: HMS Helicone - Born: Marblehead - Age: 19 - Discharged on 28 Apr 1814 and sent to Chatham on HM Sloop Favorite.

Senholm, Jacob - Seaman - Number: 22 - Prize Name: USRM Cutter James Madison - Ship type: MW - How taken: HM Frigate Barbadoes - When taken: 22 Aug 1812 - Where taken: at sea - Date received: 12 Oct 1812 San Antonio - From what ship: HM Ship-of-the-Line Polyphemus - Born: Neland, Finland - Age: 33 - Discharged on 19 Feb 1813 and sent to Chatham on HM Frigate Ulysses.

Setchell, Samuel - Master's Mate - Number: 451 - Prize Name: Sword Fish - Ship type: P - How taken: HM Ship-of-the-Line Elephant - When taken: 28 Dec 1812 - Where taken: at sea - Date received: 14 Jan 1813 - From what ship: HMS Elephant - Born: Gloucester - Age: 26 - Discharged on 11 Mar 1813 and sent to Chatham on HM Store Ship Abundance.

Severence, George - Seaman - Number: 681 - Prize Name: Benjamin - Ship type: MV - How taken: HM Frigate Medusa - When taken: 31 Dec 1812 - Where taken: at sea - Date received: 14 Feb 1813 - From what ship: HM Transport Maister No. 84 - Born: Chester, NH - Age: 28 - Discharged on 6 Mar 1813 and sent to Chatham on HM Ship-of-the-Line Cornwall.

Shaw, Henry - Cook - Number: 1198 - Prize Name: Fire Fly of Gloucester - Ship type: MV - How taken: HM Frigate Revolutionnaire - When taken: 19 Oct 1813 - Where taken: at sea - Date received: 9 Nov 1813 - From what ship: HMS Revolutionaire - Born: Boston - Age: 23 - Race: Black - Discharged on 26 Dec 1813 and sent to Chatham on HM Ship of-the-Line Diomede.

Shaw, Samuel - Prize Master - Number: 1317 - Prize Name: Elbridge Gerry - Ship type: P - How taken: HM Frigate Crescent - When taken: 16 Sep 1813 - Where taken: at sea - Date received: 22 Dec 1813 - From what ship: HM Frigate Hyperion - Born: Portland, MA - Age: 48 - Discharged on 26 Dec 1813 and sent to Chatham on HMS Frigate Nemesis.

Shed, William - Seaman - Number: 606 - Prize Name: Sword Fish - Ship type: P - How taken: HM Ship-of-the-Line Elephant - When taken: 20 Dec 1812 - Where taken: at sea - Date received: 1 Feb 1813 - From what ship: HM Frigate Hermes - Born: Salem - Age: 20 - Discharged on 11 Mar 1813 and sent to Chatham on HM Store Ship Abundance.

Shepherd, Daniel - Seaman - Number: 410 - Prize Name: Otter - Ship type: MV - How taken: HM Ship-Sloop Jalouse - When taken: 1 Dec 1812 - Where taken: at sea - Date received: 10 Jan 1813 - From what ship: HM Guardship Royal William - Born: Boston - Age: 24 - Discharged on 6 Mar 1813 and sent to Chatham on HMS Frigate Alexandria.

Sheppard, Joseph - Seaman - Number: 599 - Prize Name: Sword Fish - Ship type: P - How taken: HM Ship-of-the-Line Elephant - When taken: 20 Dec 1812 - Where taken: at sea - Date received: 1 Feb 1813 - From what ship: HM Frigate Hermes - Born: Dartmouth, MA - Age: 35 - Discharged on 11 Mar 1813 and sent to Chatham on HM Store Ship Abundance.

Sheridan, Henry - Seaman - Number: 1096 - How taken: Gave himself up from HM Ship-of-the-Line Scipion - Date received: 5 Oct 1813 - From what ship: HM Ship-of-the-Line Achille - Born: New York - Age: 22 - Race: Black - Discharged on 17 Oct 1813 and sent to Chatham on HM Store Ship Weymouth.

Sheriff, Benjamin P. - Seaman - Number: 1071 - How taken: Gave himself up from HM Ship-of-the-Line Implacable - Date received: 30 Sep 1813 - From what ship: HM Frigate Andromeda - Born: Exeter - Age: 22 - Discharged on 17 Oct 1813 and sent to Chatham on HM Store Ship Weymouth.

Shilling, Naurish - Seaman - Number: 1246 - How taken: Gave himself up from HM Brig Echo - Date received: 28 Nov 1813 - From what ship: HMS Echo - Born: Stonington - Age: 24 - Discharged on 26 Dec 1813 and sent to Chatham on HM Ship of-the-Line Diomede.

Shipley, Charles - Seaman - Number: 667 - How taken: Gave himself up from HM Frigate Gladiator - Date received: 7 Feb 1813 - From what ship: HMS Gladiator - Born: New York - Age: 27 - Discharged on 6 Mar 1813 and sent to Chatham on HM Ship-of-the-Line Cornwall.

Shirly, Phares - Captain - Number: 685 - Prize Name: Rachael - Ship type: MV - How taken: HM Schooner Herring

- When taken: 8 Feb 1813 - Where taken: at sea - Date received: 20 Feb 1813 - From what ship: HMS Herring - Born: Marblehead - Age: 29 - Discharged on 11 Mar 1813 and sent to Chatham on HM Store Ship Abundance.

Shoe, Barnard - Sailmaker - Number: 1451 - Prize Name: Lord Ponsonbe, prize of the Privateer Diomede - Ship type: MV - How taken: HM Brig Sappho - When taken: 27 Feb 1814 - Where taken: at sea - Date received: 31 May 1814 - From what ship: HM Ship-of-the-Line Valiant - Born: Amsterdam, Holland - Age: 53 - Discharged on 28 Apr 1814 and sent to Chatham on HM Store Ship Weymouth.

Sholes, Giles - Seaman - Number: 253 - Prize Name: King of Rome - Ship type: P - How taken: HM Brig Wolverine - When taken: 13 Dec 1812 - Where taken: at sea - Date received: 27 Dec 1812 - From what ship: HMS Wolverine - Born: Nantucket - Age: 22 - Discharged on 19 Feb 1813 and sent to Chatham on HM Store Ship Dromedary.

Shot, John - Boy - Number: 482 - Prize Name: Sword Fish - Ship type: P - How taken: HM Ship-of-the-Line Elephant - When taken: 28 Dec 1812 - Where taken: at sea - Date received: 14 Jan 1813 - From what ship: HMS Elephant - Born: Salem - Age: 13 - Discharged on 11 Mar 1813 and sent to Chatham on HM Store Ship Abundance.

Sibert, Frederick - Seaman - Number: 697 - Prize Name: Calcutta - Ship type: East Indian Ship - How taken: Two Brothers, privateer of Guernsey - When taken: 23 Nov 1812 - Where taken: at sea - Date received: 24 Feb 1813 - From what ship: HM Brig Escort - Born: Philadelphia - Age: 22 - Discharged on 6 Mar 1813 and sent to Chatham on HMS Frigate Alexandria.

Sidebottom, John - Seaman - Number: 614 - How taken: Gave himself up from HM Guardship Royal William - Date received: 3 Feb 1813 - From what ship: HMS Royal William - Born: Virginia - Age: 25 - Discharged on 11 Mar 1813 and sent to Chatham on HM Store Ship Abundance.

Sillock, Amos - Seaman - Number: 888 - How taken: Gave himself up from HMS Servius - Date received: 24 Jun 1813 - From what ship: HM Frigate Unicorn - Born: Sheffield, MA - Age: 30 - Discharged on 2 Jul 1813 and sent to Chatham on HM Frigate Tribune.

Silsby, Nathaniel - Seaman - Number: 597 - How taken: Gave himself up from HMS Dapper - Date received: 31 Jan 1813 - From what ship: HMS Dapper - Born: Newbury - Age: 18 - Discharged on 11 Mar 1813 and sent to Chatham on HM Store Ship Abundance.

Simmons, Daniel - Seaman - Number: 644 - How taken: Gave himself up from HM Guardship Royal William - Date received: 3 Feb 1813 - From what ship: HMS Royal William - Born: Pennsylvania - Age: 49 - Race: Black - Discharged on 11 Mar 1813 and sent to Chatham on HM Store Ship Abundance.

Simmons, John - Seaman - Number: 1492 - Prize Name: Traveler, prize of the Privateer Surprise - Ship type: MV - How taken: HM Schooner Canso - When taken: 14 May 1814 - Where taken: at sea - Date received: 1 Jun 1814 - From what ship: HMS Canso - Born: Staten Island - Age: 18 - Discharged on 2 Jun 1814 and sent to Plymouth on HMS Growler.

Simms, Clement - Seaman - Number: 778 - How taken: Gave himself up from HM Frigate Mermaid - Date received: 1 Apr 1813 - From what ship: HM Ship-of-the-Line Blake - Born: Baltimore - Age: 30 - Race: Black - Discharged on 3 Apr 1813 and sent to Chatham on HM Transport Chatham.

Simonds, Henry - Seaman - Number: 1388 - Prize Name: Pilate - Ship type: P - How taken: Victoria, privateer of Guernsey - When taken: 28 Jan 1814 - Where taken: off Bordeaux - Date received: 7 Feb 1814 - From what ship: Mary from Guernsey - Born: Staten Island - Age: 23 - Race: Black - Discharged on 13 Feb 1814 and sent to Chatham on HM Transport Malabar No. 352.

Simonds, Joseph - Seaman - Number: 547 - Prize Name: Rossie - Ship type: MV - How taken: HM Frigate Dryand - When taken: 7 Jan 1813 - Where taken: at sea - Date received: 25 Jan 1813 - From what ship: HM Ship-of-the-Line Queen - Born: Alexandria, VA - Age: 21 - Discharged on 11 Mar 1813 and sent to Chatham on HM Store Ship Abundance.

Simpson, James - Seaman - Number: 536 - Prize Name: Expectation - Ship type: MV - How taken: HMS Butain - When taken: 17 Dec 1812 - Where taken: at sea - Date received: 25 Jan 1813 - From what ship: HM Ship-of-the-Line Queen - Age: 36 - Discharged on 11 Mar 1813 and sent to Chatham on HM Store Ship Abundance.

Simpson, John - Seaman - Number: 982 - How taken: Gave himself up from HM Brig Swallow - Date received: 31 Jul 1813 - From what ship: HM Ship-of-the-Line Leviathan - Born: New York - Age: 33 - Discharged on 13 Aug 1813 and sent to Chatham on HM Brig Cadmus.

Siters, John - Seaman - Number: 969 - How taken: Gave himself up from HM Ship-of-the-Line Leviathan - Date received: 31 Jul 1813 - From what ship: HMS Leviathan - Born: Pennsylvania - Age: 29 - Discharged on 7 Aug 1813 and sent to Chatham on HM Brig Rinaldo.

Skinner, Ebenezer - 1st Mate - Number: 1237 - Prize Name: British South Sea Whaler - How taken: HM Ship-of-the-Line Illustrious - When taken: 22 Oct 1813 - Where taken: at sea - Date received: 26 Nov 1813 - From what ship: HMS Illustrious - Born: Nantucket - Age: 33 - Discharged on 26 Dec 1813 and sent to Chatham on HM Ship of-the-Line Diomede.

Small, George D. - Seaman - Number: 871 - Prize Name: Tiger - Ship type: MV - How taken: HM Brig Scylla - When taken: 22 Mar 1813 - Where taken: Bay of Biscay - Date received: 24 Jun 1813 - From what ship: HM Frigate Unicorn - Born: New York - Age: 24 - Discharged on 2 Jul 1813 and sent to Chatham on HM Frigate Tribune.

Small, Thomas - Seaman - Number: 468 - Prize Name: Sword Fish - Ship type: P - How taken: HM Ship-of-the-Line Elephant - When taken: 28 Dec 1812 - Where taken: at sea - Date received: 14 Jan 1813 - From what ship: HMS Elephant - Born: Portsmouth - Age: 16 - Discharged on 11 Mar 1813 and sent to Chatham on HM Store Ship Abundance.

Smith, Benjamin - Seaman - Number: 1288 - Prize Name: Growler - Ship type: P - How taken: HM Brig Electra - When taken: 7 Jul 1813 - Where taken: off St. Johns - Date received: 22 Dec 1813 - From what ship: HM Ship of-the-Line Bellerophon - Born: Salem - Age: 19 - Discharged on 26 Dec 1813 and sent to Chatham on HMS Frigate Nemesis.

Smith, Caesar - Seaman - Number: 636 - How taken: Gave himself up from HM Guardship Royal William - Date received: 3 Feb 1813 - From what ship: HMS Royal William - Born: Long Island - Age: 32 - Discharged on 11 Mar 1813 and sent to Chatham on HM Store Ship Abundance.

Smith, Henry - Seaman - Number: 1106 - How taken: Gave himself up from HM Ship-of-the-Line Swiftsure - Date received: 5 Oct 1813 - From what ship: HM Ship-of-the-Line Achille - Born: Massachusetts - Age: 22 - Discharged on 17 Oct 1813 and sent to Chatham on HM Store Ship Weymouth.

Smith, Henry - Seaman - Number: 693 - Prize Name: Calcutta - Ship type: East Indian Ship - How taken: Two Brothers, privateer of Guernsey - When taken: 23 Nov 1812 - Where taken: at sea - Date received: 24 Feb 1813 - From what ship: HM Brig Escort - Born: South Carolina - Age: 25 - Discharged on 6 Mar 1813 and sent to Chatham on HMS Frigate Alexandria.

Smith, Henry - Seaman - Number: 46 - Prize Name: USRM Cutter James Madison - Ship type: MW - How taken: HM Frigate Barbadoes - When taken: 22 Aug 1812 - Where taken: at sea - Date received: 12 Oct 1812 San Antonio - From what ship: HM Ship-of-the-Line Polyphemus - Born: Berkshire, MA - Age: 26 - Discharged on 19 Feb 1813 and sent to Chatham on HM Frigate Ulysses.

Smith, J. W. - Seaman - Number: 1380 - Prize Name: Pilate - Ship type: P - How taken: Victoria, privateer of Guernsey - When taken: 28 Jan 1814 - Where taken: off Bordeaux - Date received: 7 Feb 1814 - From what ship: Mary from Guernsey - Born: New York - Age: 23 - Race: Black - Discharged on 13 Feb 1814 and sent to Chatham on HM Transport Malabar No. 352.

Smith, Jacob - Seaman - Number: 344 - Prize Name: Experiment - Ship type: MV - How taken: HM Brig Rover - When taken: 10 Nov 1812 - Where taken: off Bordeaux - Date received: 31 Dec 1812 - From what ship: HM Ship-of-the-Line Northumberland - Born: Prussia - Age: 36 - Discharged on 4 Mar 1813 and sent to Chatham on HM Ship-of-the-Line Queen.

Smith, Jeremiah - Prize Master - Number: 1298 - Prize Name: Growler - Ship type: P - How taken: HM Brig Electra - When taken: 7 Jul 1813 - Where taken: off St. Johns - Date received: 22 Dec 1813 - From what ship: HM Frigate Hyperion - Born: Marblehead - Age: 35 - Discharged on 26 Dec 1813 and sent to Chatham on HMS Frigate Nemesis.

Smith, John - Seaman - Number: 626 - How taken: Gave himself up from HM Guardship Royal William - Date received: 3 Feb 1813 - From what ship: HMS Royal William - Born: Philadelphia - Age: 29 - Race: Black - Discharged on 11 Mar 1813 and sent to Chatham on HM Store Ship Abundance.

Smith, John - Seaman - Number: 1236 - How taken: Gave himself up from HM Ship-of-the-Line Illustrious - Date received: 26 Nov 1813 - From what ship: HMS Illustrious - Born: Delaware - Age: 36 - Discharged on 26 Dec 1813 and sent to Chatham on HM Ship of-the-Line Diomede.

Smith, John - Seaman - Number: 1285 - Prize Name: Growler - Ship type: P - How taken: HM Brig Electra - When taken: 7 Jul 1813 - Where taken: off St. Johns - Date received: 22 Dec 1813 - From what ship: HM Ship of-the-Line Bellerophon - Born: Marblehead - Age: 25 - Discharged on 26 Dec 1813 and sent to Chatham on HMS Frigate Nemesis.

Smith, John - Seaman - Number: 1267 - Prize Name: US Schooner Julia - Ship type: MW - How taken: Sir James Yeo's Squadron - When taken: 11 Aug 1813 - Where taken: Lake Ontario - Date received: 22 Dec 1813 - From what ship: HMS Elalion - Born: New York - Age: 21 - Discharged on 26 Dec 1813 and sent to Chatham on HM Ship of-the-Line Diomede.

Smith, John - Seaman - Number: 1085 - How taken: Gave himself up from HM Ship-of-the-Line Hibernia - Date received: 1 Oct 1813 - From what ship: HM Ship-of-the-Line Barham - Born: Boston - Age: 43 - Discharged on 17 Oct 1813 and sent to Chatham on HM Store Ship Weymouth.

Smith, John - Seaman - Number: 1059 - How taken: Gave himself up from HM Ship-of-the-Line Hibernia - Date received: 19 Sep 1813 - From what ship: HM Brig Imogen - Born: Boston - Age: 43 - Discharged on 29 Sep 1813 and sent to Chatham on HM Transport Chatham.

Smith, John - Seaman - Number: 1313 - Prize Name: Growler - Ship type: P - How taken: HM Brig Electra - When taken: 7 Jul 1813 - Where taken: off St. Johns - Date received: 22 Dec 1813 - From what ship: HM Frigate Hyperion - Born: Marblehead - Age: 27 - Discharged on 26 Dec 1813 and sent to Chatham on HMS Frigate Nemesis.

Smith, Richard - Seaman - Number: 1412 - Prize Name: General Kemp, prize of Privateer Grand Turk - Ship type: P - How taken: HM Brig Foxhound - When taken: 18 Dec 1813 - Where taken: at sea - Date received: 1 Mar 1814 - From what ship: HMS Helicone - Born: Salem - Age: 24 - Discharged on 28 Apr 1814 and sent to Chatham on HM Sloop Favorite.

Smith, Thomas - Seaman - Number: 1459 - How taken: Gave himself up from HMS Rota - Date received: 10 Apr 1814 - From what ship: HMS Primer - Born: Virginia - Age: 26 - Race: Mulatto - Discharged on 28 Apr 1814 and sent to Chatham on HM Store Ship Weymouth.

Smith, Thomas - Seaman - Number: 765 - How taken: Gave himself up from HM Ship-of-the-Line Blake - Date received: 1 Apr 1813 - From what ship: HMS Blake - Born: New York - Age: 28 - Discharged on 3 Apr 1813 and sent to Chatham on HM Transport Chatham.

Smith, Thomas - Seaman - Number: 805 - How taken: Gave himself up from HM Ship-of-the-Line Plantagenet - Date received: 21 Apr 1813 - From what ship: HM Guardship Royal William - Born: Dutchess County - Age: 18 - Discharged on 27 Apr 1813 and sent to Chatham on HM Sloop-of-War Bonne Citoyenne.

Smith, Thomas - Seaman - Number: 1263 - Prize Name: Dart - Ship type: P - How taken: HM Frigate Niger & HMS Fortunee - Where taken: at sea - Date received: 19 Dec 1813 - From what ship: HMS Fortunee - Born: Massachusetts - Age: 25 - Discharged on 26 Dec 1813 and sent to Chatham on HM Ship of-the-Line Diomede.

Smith, Thomas R. - Seaman - Number: 147 - Prize Name: William - Ship type: MV - How taken: HM Brig Recruit - When taken: 29 Aug 1812 - Where taken: at sea - Date received: 29 Oct 1812 - From what ship: HM Ship-of-the-Line Ardent - Born: Altona - Age: 25 - Discharged on 19 Feb 1813 and sent to Chatham on HM Store Ship Dromedary.

Smith, Thomas R. - Seaman - Number: 419 - Prize Name: Rising Sun - Ship type: MV - How taken: HMS Defense - When taken: 6 Dec 1812 - Where taken: at sea - Date received: 10 Jan 1813 - From what ship: HM Guardship Royal William - Born: Charlestown - Age: 22 - Discharged on 6 Mar 1813 and sent to Chatham on HMS Frigate Alexandria.

Smith, William - Seaman - Number: 391 - Prize Name: Empress - Ship type: MV - How taken: HM Brig Rover -

When taken: 30 Nov 1812 - Where taken: at sea - Date received: 10 Jan 1813 - From what ship: HM Guardship Royal William - Born: New York - Age: 22 - Discharged on 4 Mar 1813 and sent to Chatham on HM Ship-of-the-Line Queen.

Smith, William - Seaman - Number: 138 - Prize Name: Gossypium - Ship type: MV - How taken: HM Sloop Goree - When taken: 15 Aug 1812 - Where taken: off Bermuda - Date received: 29 Oct 1812 - From what ship: HM Ship-of-the-Line Ardent - Born: Columbia, NY - Age: 21 - Discharged on 19 Feb 1813 and sent to Chatham on HM Store Ship Dromedary.

Smith, William B. - Cook - Number: 1457 - Prize Name: Soley - Ship type: MV - How taken: HM Brig Derment - When taken: 21 Jan 1814 - Where taken: at sea - Date received: 9 Apr 1814 - From what ship: HM Ship-of-the-Line Leyden - Born: Salem - Age: 17 - Discharged on 28 Apr 1814 and sent to Chatham on HM Store Ship Weymouth.

Smith, William Pitt - Seaman - Number: 183 - How taken: Sent into custody by order of the commander in chief - Date received: 4 Nov 1812 - From what ship: HM Guardship Royal William - Born: New York - Age: 22 - Discharged on 19 Feb 1813 and sent to Chatham on HM Store Ship Dromedary.

Snider, Lewis - 2nd Mate - Number: 423 - Prize Name: Brunswick - Ship type: MV - How taken: HM Frigate Iris - When taken: 16 Dec 1812 - Where taken: at sea - Date received: 10 Jan 1813 - From what ship: HM Guardship Royal William - Born: New Orleans - Age: 26 - Discharged on 6 Mar 1813 and sent to Chatham on HMS Frigate Alexandria.

Somes, Stephen - Seaman - Number: 1192 - Prize Name: Fire Fly of Gloucester - Ship type: MV - How taken: HM Frigate Revolutionnaire - When taken: 19 Oct 1813 - Where taken: at sea - Date received: 9 Nov 1813 - From what ship: HMS Revolutionaire - Born: Gloucester - Age: 18 - Discharged on 26 Dec 1813 and sent to Chatham on HM Ship of-the-Line Diomede.

Southard, Samuel W. - Seaman - Number: 541 - Prize Name: Leader - Ship type: MV - How taken: HMS Butain - When taken: 17 Dec 1812 - Where taken: at sea - Date received: 25 Jan 1813 - From what ship: HM Ship-of-the-Line Queen - Born: Stratford, CT - Age: 25 - Discharged on 11 Mar 1813 and sent to Chatham on HM Store Ship Abundance.

Southwick, Israel - Seaman - Number: 954 - How taken: Gave himself up from HM Ship-of-the-Line Swiftsure - Date received: 28 Jul 1813 - From what ship: HM Sloop Volentaire - Born: Boston - Age: 22 - Discharged on 7 Aug 1813 and sent to Chatham on HM Brig Rinaldo.

Sparrow, John - Seaman - Number: 730 - How taken: Gave himself up from HM Ship-of-the-Line Christian VII - Date received: 19 Mar 1813 - From what ship: HMS Christian VII - Born: Norfolk - Age: 22 - Race: Colored - Discharged on 28 Mar 1813 and sent to Chatham on HM Store Ship Seaphis.

Spencer, John - Seaman - Number: 814 - How taken: Taken out of the Gosport Rendezvous - Date received: 24 Apr 1813 - From what ship: Gosport Rendezvous - Born: Exeter, NH - Age: 26 - Released on 27 Apr 1813 to the Transport Simpson.

Spencer, Leonard - Seaman - Number: 858 - Prize Name: Tiger - Ship type: MV - How taken: HM Brig Scylla - When taken: 22 Mar 1813 - Where taken: Bay of Biscay - Date received: 24 Jun 1813 - From what ship: HM Frigate Unicorn - Born: East Harford, CT - Age: 32 - Discharged on 2 Jul 1813 and sent to Chatham on HM Frigate Tribune.

Spinney, Nathaniel - Seaman - Number: 93 - Prize Name: HM Frigate Janus - Ship type: MW - How taken: Detained by Court of Admiralty - When taken: 31 Jul 1812 - Where taken: Portsmouth harbor - Date received: 16 Oct 1812 San Antonio - From what ship: HM Frigate Janus - Born: Kennebunkport, MA - Age: 17 - Discharged on 19 Feb 1813 and sent to Chatham on HM Frigate Ulysses.

Spratt, Thomas - Seaman - Number: 660 - How taken: Gave himself up from HMS Ettiation - Date received: 6 Feb 1813 - From what ship: HMS Ettiation - Born: Virginia - Age: 32 - Discharged on 6 Mar 1813 and sent to Chatham on HM Ship-of-the-Line Cornwall.

Spurling, William - Seaman - Number: 65 - Prize Name: Diana, prize of Privateer Decatur - Ship type: MV - How taken: HM Ship-of-the-Line Polyphemus - When taken: 14 Sep 1812 - Where taken: at sea - Date received: 12 Oct 1812 San Antonio - From what ship: HM Ship-of-the-Line Polyphemus - Born: Mount Desert Inland,

MA - Age: 19 - Discharged on 19 Feb 1813 and sent to Chatham on HM Frigate Ulysses.

Spurr, Elijah - Seaman - Number: 1410 - Prize Name: General Kemp, prize of Privateer Grand Turk - Ship type: P - How taken: HM Brig Foxhound - When taken: 18 Dec 1813 - Where taken: at sea - Date received: 1 Mar 1814 - From what ship: HMS Helicone - Born: Boston - Age: 18 - Discharged on 28 Apr 1814 and sent to Chatham on HM Sloop Favorite.

Stacey, William - Seaman - Number: 55 - Prize Name: Fame, prize of Privateer Decatur - Ship type: MV - How taken: HM Ship-of-the-Line Polyphemus - When taken: 13 Sep 1812 - Where taken: at sea - Date received: 12 Oct 1812 San Antonio - From what ship: HM Ship-of-the-Line Polyphemus - Born: Marblehead - Age: 22 - Discharged on 19 Feb 1813 and sent to Chatham on HM Frigate Ulysses.

Stacy, Perry - Seaman - Number: 760 - How taken: Gave himself up from HM Ship-of-the-Line Blake - Date received: 1 Apr 1813 - From what ship: HMS Blake - Born: Baltimore - Age: 28 - Race: Colored - Discharged on 3 Apr 1813 and sent to Chatham on HM Transport Chatham.

Stafford, John - Apprentice - Number: 1392 - Prize Name: Pilate - Ship type: P - How taken: Victoria, privateer of Guernsey - When taken: 28 Jan 1814 - Where taken: off Bordeaux - Date received: 7 Feb 1814 - From what ship: Mary from Guernsey - Born: Virginia - Age: 30 - Race: Black - Discharged on 13 Feb 1814 and sent to Chatham on HM Transport Malabar No. 352.

Stage, William - Seaman - Number: 1087 - Prize Name: Hindostan - Ship type: MV - How taken: HM Brig Zenobia - When taken: 25 Jun 1813 - Where taken: off Lisbon - Date received: 1 Oct 1813 - From what ship: HM Ship-of-the-Line Barham - Born: Charlestown - Age: 26 - Discharged on 17 Oct 1813 and sent to Chatham on HM Store Ship Weymouth (see Prisoner Number 1062).

Stage, William - Seaman - Number: 1062 - Prize Name: Hindostan - Ship type: MV - How taken: HM Brig Zenobia - When taken: 25 Jun 1813 - Where taken: off Lisbon - Date received: 19 Sep 1813 - From what ship: HM Brig Imogen - Born: Charleston, SC - Age: 26 - Discharged on 29 Sep 1813 and sent to Chatham on HM Transport Chatham (see Prisoner Number 1087).

Staggs, Henry - Seaman - Number: 514 - How taken: Gave himself up from HMS Renealous - Date received: 22 Jan 1813 - From what ship: HMS Renelous - Born: Harford - Age: 32 - Discharged on 11 Mar 1813 and sent to Chatham on HM Store Ship Abundance.

Stanford, James - Seaman - Number: 1034 - How taken: Gave himself up from HM Ship-of-the-Line Berwick - Date received: 7 Sep 1813 - From what ship: HM Frigate Unicorn - Born: Philadelphia - Age: 31 - Race: Mulatto - Discharged on 21 Sep 1813 and sent to Chatham on HM Ship-of-the-Line Queen.

Stanton, George A. - Seaman - Number: 695 - Prize Name: Calcutta - Ship type: East Indian Ship - How taken: Two Brothers, privateer of Guernsey - When taken: 23 Nov 1812 - Where taken: at sea - Date received: 24 Feb 1813 - From what ship: HM Brig Escort - Born: Westbury, NY - Age: 20 - Discharged on 6 Mar 1813 and sent to Chatham on HMS Frigate Alexandria.

Stanton, James - Seaman - Number: 1131 - How taken: Gave himself up from HM Ship-of-the-Line Achille - Date received: 5 Oct 1813 - From what ship: HM Ship-of-the-Line Achille - Born: Baltimore - Age: 24 - Discharged on 17 Oct 1813 and sent to Chatham on HM Transport Malabar No. 352.

Stanwood, Timothy - Seaman - Number: 217 - How taken: Gave himself up from HM Ship-of-the-Line Aboukir - When taken: 29 Oct 1812 - Date received: 26 Dec 1812 - From what ship: HMS Abonkir - Born: Newburyport - Age: 23 - Discharged on 19 Feb 1813 and sent to Chatham on HM Store Ship Dromedary.

Staples, James - Seaman - Number: 1243 - Prize Name: British South Sea Whaler - How taken: HM Ship-of-the-Line Illustrious - When taken: 22 Oct 1813 - Where taken: at sea - Date received: 26 Nov 1813 - From what ship: HMS Illustrious - Born: Boston - Age: 21 - Discharged on 26 Dec 1813 and sent to Chatham on HM Ship of-the-Line Diomede.

Stegman, Christian - Seaman - Number: 1068 - Prize Name: Hindostan - Ship type: MV - How taken: HM Brig Zenobia - When taken: 25 Jun 1813 - Where taken: off Lisbon - Date received: 19 Sep 1813 - From what ship: HM Brig Imogen - Born: Stockholm - Age: 40 - Discharged on 29 Sep 1813 and sent to Chatham on HM Transport Chatham (see Prisoner Number 1093).

Stegman, Christian - Seaman - Number: 1093 - Prize Name: Hindostan - Ship type: MV - How taken: HM Brig

Zenobia - When taken: 25 Jun 1813 - Where taken: off Lisbon - Date received: 1 Oct 1813 - From what ship: HM Ship-of-the-Line Barham - Born: Stockholm - Age: 40 - Discharged on 17 Oct 1813 and sent to Chatham on HM Store Ship Weymouth (see Prisoner Number 1068).

Stenchcombe, George - Seaman - Number: 825 - Prize Name: Price - Ship type: P - How taken: HM Frigate Iris - When taken: 13 Apr 1813 - Where taken: at sea - Date received: 13 May 1813 - From what ship: HM Frigate Revolutionnaire - Born: Maryland - Age: 24 - Discharged on 17 May 1813 and sent to Chatham on HMS Impeleux.

Stephens, David - Seaman - Number: 487 - Prize Name: Sword Fish - Ship type: P - How taken: HM Ship-of-the-Line Elephant - When taken: 28 Dec 1812 - Where taken: at sea - Date received: 14 Jan 1813 - From what ship: HMS Elephant - Born: Gloucester - Age: 49 - Discharged on 11 Mar 1813 and sent to Chatham on HM Store Ship Abundance.

Stephens, Michael - Seaman - Number: 233 - Prize Name: Antelope - Ship type: P - How taken: HM Brig Zephyr - When taken: 10 Dec 1812 - Where taken: at sea - Date received: 27 Dec 1812 - From what ship: HMS Zephyr - Born: Prussia - Age: 30 - Discharged on 19 Feb 1813 and sent to Chatham on HM Store Ship Dromedary.

Stephens, Thomas - Seaman - Number: 126 - Prize Name: Nancy - Ship type: MV - How taken: HM Brig Parthian - When taken: 1 Aug 1812 - Where taken: off the Needles - Date received: 29 Oct 1812 - From what ship: HM Brig Nancy - Born: Marblehead - Age: 26 - Discharged on 19 Feb 1813 and sent to Chatham on HM Store Ship Dromedary.

Stephens, Trey - Seaman - Number: 605 - Prize Name: Sword Fish - Ship type: P - How taken: HM Ship-of-the-Line Elephant - When taken: 20 Dec 1812 - Where taken: at sea - Date received: 1 Feb 1813 - From what ship: HM Frigate Hermes - Born: Massachusetts - Age: 15 - Race: Black - Discharged on 11 Mar 1813 and sent to Chatham on HM Store Ship Abundance.

Stephenson, George - Prize Master - Number: 819 - Prize Name: Ajax, prize to the Privateer Governor Tomkins - Ship type: MV - How taken: HM Frigate Revolutionnaire - When taken: 10 Apr 1813 - Where taken: at sea - Date received: 13 May 1813 - From what ship: HMS Revolutionaire - Born: New York - Age: 34 - Discharged on 17 May 1813 and sent to Chatham on HMS Impeleux.

Sterns, Henry - Seaman - Number: 696 - Prize Name: Calcutta - Ship type: East Indian Ship - How taken: Two Brothers, privateer of Guernsey - When taken: 23 Nov 1812 - Where taken: at sea - Date received: 24 Feb 1813 - From what ship: HM Brig Escort - Born: Boston - Age: 19 - Discharged on 6 Mar 1813 and sent to Chatham on HMS Frigate Alexandria.

Sterns, Joseph - Seaman - Number: 1399 - Prize Name: Elbridge Gerry - Ship type: P - How taken: HM Frigate Crescent - When taken: 13 Nov 1813 - Where taken: off St. Johns - Date received: 16 Feb 1814 - From what ship: HM Transport Malabar No. 352 - Born: Portland - Age: 24 - Discharged on 28 Apr 1814 and sent to Chatham on HM Store Ship Weymouth.

Stevenson, Thomas - Seaman - Number: 164 - Prize Name: Baltimore - Ship type: P - How taken: HM Transport Diadem - When taken: 7 Oct 1812 - Where taken: S. Andera - Date received: 3 Nov 1812 San Antonio - From what ship: HMS Diadem - Born: Havre de Grace, MD - Age: 19 - Discharged on 19 Feb 1813 and sent to Chatham on HM Store Ship Dromedary.

Stevenson, Thaddeus - Seaman - Number: 565 - Prize Name: Rossie - Ship type: MV - How taken: HM Frigate Dryand - When taken: 7 Jan 1813 - Where taken: at sea - Date received: 25 Jan 1813 - From what ship: HM Ship-of-the-Line Queen - Born: Baltimore - Age: 30 - Discharged on 11 Mar 1813 and sent to Chatham on HM Store Ship Abundance.

Steward, Alexander - Seaman - Number: 370 - Prize Name: Mariner - Ship type: MV - How taken: HM Brig Lyra - When taken: 15 Dec 1812 - Where taken: off Bilboa, Spain - Date received: 3 Jan 1813 - From what ship: HM Frigate Fox - Born: Lisbon, MA - Age: 28 - Discharged on 4 Mar 1813 and sent to Chatham on HM Ship-of-the-Line Queen.

Steward, John - Seaman - Number: 973 - How taken: Gave himself up from HM Ship-of-the-Line Caledonia - Date received: 31 Jul 1813 - From what ship: HMS Leviathan - Born: Philadelphia - Age: 35 - Discharged on 13 Aug 1813 and sent to Chatham on HM Brig Cadmus.

Steward, John - Seaman - Number: 842 - How taken: Gave himself up from HM Ship-of-the-Line Malta - Date received: 15 Jun 1813 - From what ship: HM Sloop Helena - Born: Norfolk, VA - Age: 26 - Discharged on 2 Jul 1813 and sent to Chatham on HM Frigate Tribune.

Stone, Henry - Seaman - Number: 1030 - How taken: Gave himself up from HM Battery Gorgon - Date received: 7 Sep 1813 - From what ship: HM Frigate Unicorn - Born: Connecticut - Age: 26 - Discharged on 21 Sep 1813 and sent to Chatham on HM Ship-of-the-Line Queen.

Stone, John - Seaman - Number: 39 - Prize Name: USRM Cutter James Madison - Ship type: MW - How taken: HM Frigate Barbadoes - When taken: 22 Aug 1812 - Where taken: at sea - Date received: 12 Oct 1812 San Antonio - From what ship: HM Ship-of-the-Line Polyphemus - Born: Levone, Italy - Age: 22 - Discharged on 19 Feb 1813 and sent to Chatham on HM Frigate Ulysses.

Stone, Samuel - Seaman - Number: 1489 - Prize Name: Indian Lass, prize of Privateer Grand Turk - Ship type: MV - How taken: HM Transport Akbar - When taken: 20 Apr 1814 - Where taken: at sea - Date received: 28 May 1814 - From what ship: HMS Akbar - Born: Massachusetts - Age: 19 - Discharged on 2 Jun 1814 and sent to Plymouth on HMS Growler.

Stoss, Samuel - Seaman - Number: 111 - Prize Name: HM Frigate Leonidas - Ship type: MV - How taken: Detained by Court of Admiralty - When taken: 31 Jul 1812 - Where taken: Portsmouth harbor - Date received: 17 Oct 1812 San Antonio - From what ship: W. Lindegreon, deputy marshal - Born: New York - Age: 24 - Race: Colored - Discharged on 19 Feb 1813 and sent to Chatham on HM Frigate Ulysses.

Strong, William - Seaman - Number: 457 - Prize Name: Sword Fish - Ship type: P - How taken: HM Ship-of-the-Line Elephant - When taken: 28 Dec 1812 - Where taken: at sea - Date received: 14 Jan 1813 - From what ship: HMS Elephant - Born: Marblehead - Age: 22 - Discharged on 11 Mar 1813 and sent to Chatham on HM Store Ship Abundance.

Sutton, John - Seaman - Number: 861 - Prize Name: Tiger - Ship type: MV - How taken: HM Brig Scylla - When taken: 22 Mar 1813 - Where taken: Bay of Biscay - Date received: 24 Jun 1813 - From what ship: HM Frigate Unicorn - Born: Nantucket - Age: 26 - Discharged on 2 Jul 1813 and sent to Chatham on HM Frigate Tribune.

Sutton, John - Seaman - Number: 1325 - How taken: Gave himself up from HMS Scopard - Date received: 25 Dec 1813 - From what ship: HMS Scopard - Born: Washington - Age: 39 - Discharged on 26 Dec 1813 and sent to Chatham on HMS Frigate Nemesis.

Sutton, Prince - Seaman - Number: 749 - How taken: Gave himself up from HM Ship of-the-Line Bellerophon - Date received: 25 Mar 1813 - From what ship: HMS Bellerophon - Born: Rhode Island - Age: 15 - Race: Mulatto - Discharged on 28 Mar 1813 and sent to Chatham on HM Store Ship Seaphis.

Swain, James - Seaman - Number: 1005 - Prize Name: Fame - Ship type: MV - How taken: HM Ship of-the-Line Cressy - When taken: 20 Jul 1813 - Where taken: at sea - Date received: 18 Aug 1813 - From what ship: HMS Cressy - Born: Nantucket - Age: 19 - Discharged on 21 Sep 1813 and sent to Chatham on HM Ship-of-the-Line Queen.

Swain, Thomas - Prize Master - Number: 575 - Prize Name: Industry - Ship type: MV - How taken: HM Frigate Dryand - When taken: 7 Jan 1813 - Where taken: at sea - Date received: 25 Jan 1813 - From what ship: HM Ship-of-the-Line Queen - Born: Newburyport - Age: 29 - Discharged on 11 Mar 1813 and sent to Chatham on HM Store Ship Abundance.

Swainton, John - Prize Master - Number: 1449 - Prize Name: Endeavour, prized to the Privateer Globe - Ship type: MV - How taken: HM Brig Fantome - When taken: 29 May 1813 - Where taken: at sea - Date received: 4 Mar 1814 - From what ship: HMS Prense - Born: Kilkenny, Ireland - Age: 41 - Discharged on 27 Jul 1814 and sent to the Royal Naval Hospital Haslar at Gosport.

Swanton, John - Seaman - Number: 300 - Prize Name: Phillipsburgh - Ship type: MV - How taken: Taken up on shore - When taken: 9 Nov 1812 - Where taken: Liverpool - Date received: 31 Dec 1812 - From what ship: HM Ship-of-the-Line Northumberland - Born: Pennsylvania - Age: 24 - Discharged on 4 Mar 1813 and sent to Chatham on HM Ship-of-the-Line Queen.

Swett, Moses - Seaman - Number: 157 - Prize Name: Diamond - Ship type: MV - How taken: Detained at Bermuda

- When taken: 17 Apr 1812 - Where taken: Bermuda - Date received: 29 Oct 1812 - From what ship: HM Ship-of-the-Line Ardent - Born: Yalmouth, MA - Age: 21 - Discharged on 19 Feb 1813 and sent to Chatham on HM Store Ship Dromedary.

Symes, John - Seaman - Number: 1507 - How taken: Gave himself up from HM Ship-of-the-Line Rodney - Date received: 30 Jun 1814 - From what ship: HMS Rodney - Born: Virginia - Age: 36 - Discharged on 30 Jun 1814 and sent to Plymouth on HM Brig Steady.

Syway, Peter - Seaman - Number: 671 - How taken: Gave himself up from HM Frigate Ulysses - Date received: 10 Feb 1813 - From what ship: HM Brig Electra - Born: New Jersey - Age: 26 - Discharged on 6 Mar 1813 and sent to Chatham on HM Ship-of-the-Line Cornwall.

Tafe, Henry - Seaman - Number: 702 - Prize Name: Calcutta - Ship type: East Indian Ship - How taken: Two Brothers, privateer of Guernsey - When taken: 23 Nov 1812 - Where taken: at sea - Date received: 24 Feb 1813 - From what ship: HM Brig Escort - Born: Long Island - Age: 38 - Race: Colored - Discharged on 6 Mar 1813 and sent to Chatham on HM Ship-of-the-Line Cornwall.

Tanner, John - Seaman - Number: 194 - Prize Name: Felix - Ship type: MV - How taken: HM Frigate Indefatigable - When taken: 13 Nov 1812 - Where taken: Portsmouth harbor - Date received: 22 Nov 1812 - From what ship: HM Frigate Gladiator - Born: New York - Age: 22 - Discharged on 19 Feb 1813 and sent to Chatham on HM Store Ship Dromedary.

Tar, Caleb - Seaman - Number: 1189 - Prize Name: Fire Fly of Gloucester - Ship type: MV - How taken: HM Frigate Revolutionnaire - When taken: 19 Oct 1813 - Where taken: at sea - Date received: 9 Nov 1813 - From what ship: HMS Revolutionaire - Born: Gloucester - Age: 29 - Discharged on 26 Dec 1813 and sent to Chatham on HM Ship of-the-Line Diomede.

Tardy, Anthony - Chief Mate - Number: 1256 - Prize Name: Dart - Ship type: P - How taken: HM Frigate Niger & HMS Fortunee - Where taken: at sea - Date received: 19 Dec 1813 - From what ship: HMS Fortunee - Born: New York - Age: 22 - Discharged on 26 Dec 1813 and sent to Chatham on HM Ship of-the-Line Diomede.

Tardy, Edward - Seaman - Number: 1255 - Prize Name: Dart - Ship type: P - How taken: HM Frigate Niger & HMS Fortunee - Where taken: at sea - Date received: 19 Dec 1813 - From what ship: HMS Fortunee - Born: New York - Age: 16 - Discharged on 26 Dec 1813 and sent to Chatham on HM Ship of-the-Line Diomede.

Tarlton, Thomas P. - Seaman - Number: 742 - Prize Name: Dart - Ship type: MV - How taken: HM Brig Doterel - When taken: 5 Mar 1813 - Where taken: at sea - Date received: 21 Mar 1813 - From what ship: HMS Dotteril - Born: Greenland, NH - Age: 21 - Discharged on 28 Mar 1813 and sent to Chatham on HM Store Ship Seaphis.

Taylor, George - Seaman - Number: 1394 - Prize Name: Pilate - Ship type: P - How taken: Victoria, privateer of Guernsey - When taken: 28 Jan 1814 - Where taken: off Bordeaux - Date received: 7 Feb 1814 - From what ship: Mary from Guernsey - Born: Rhode Island - Age: 26 - Race: Mulatto - Discharged on 13 Feb 1814 and sent to Chatham on HM Transport Malabar No. 352.

Taylor, James - Seaman - Number: 889 - How taken: Gave himself up from HMS Servius - Date received: 24 Jun 1813 - From what ship: HM Frigate Unicorn - Born: Philadelphia - Age: 27 - Discharged on 2 Jul 1813 and sent to Chatham on HM Frigate Tribune.

Taylor, Joseph - Seaman - Number: 981 - How taken: Gave himself up from HM Ship-of-the-Line Fame - Date received: 31 Jul 1813 - From what ship: HM Ship-of-the-Line Leviathan - Born: Philadelphia - Age: 24 - Discharged on 13 Aug 1813 and sent to Chatham on HM Brig Cadmus.

Taylor, Peter - Seaman - Number: 927 - Prize Name: Tender of the True Blooded Yankee - Ship type: P - How taken: HM Ship-of-the-Line Fame - When taken: 24 Jun 1813 - Where taken: at sea - Date received: 1 Jul 1813 - From what ship: HM Brig Hope - Born: New York - Age: 22 - Discharged on 2 Jul 1813 and sent to Chatham on HM Brig Scorpion.

Taylor, William - Seaman - Number: 682 - Prize Name: Benjamin - Ship type: MV - How taken: HM Frigate Medusa - When taken: 31 Dec 1812 - Where taken: at sea - Date received: 14 Feb 1813 - From what ship: HM Transport Maister No. 84 - Born: Billerica, MA - Age: 21 - Discharged on 6 Mar 1813 and sent to Chatham on HM Ship-of-the-Line Cornwall.

Tewell, Samuel - Seaman - Number: 352 - Prize Name: Experiment - Ship type: MV - How taken: HM Brig Rover - When taken: 10 Nov 1812 - Where taken: off Bordeaux - Date received: 31 Dec 1812 - From what ship: HM Ship-of-the-Line Northumberland - Born: Maryland - Age: 20 - Discharged on 4 Mar 1813 and sent to Chatham on HM Ship-of-the-Line Queen.

Thaley, Abraham - Seaman - Number: 1080 - How taken: Gave himself up from HM Ship-of-the-Line Hibernia - Date received: 1 Oct 1813 - From what ship: HM Ship-of-the-Line Barham - Born: New York - Age: 32 - Race: Black - Discharged on 17 Oct 1813 and sent to Chatham on HM Store Ship Weymouth.

Thaley, Abraham - Seaman - Number: 1054 - How taken: Gave himself up from HM Ship-of-the-Line Hibernia - Date received: 19 Sep 1813 - From what ship: HM Brig Imogen - Born: New York - Age: 32 - Race: Black - Discharged on 29 Sep 1813 and sent to Chatham on HM Transport Chatham.

Thayer, James - Seaman - Number: 1032 - How taken: Gave himself up from HM Battery Gorgon - Date received: 7 Sep 1813 - From what ship: HM Frigate Unicorn - Born: Massachusetts - Age: 23 - Discharged on 21 Sep 1813 and sent to Chatham on HM Ship-of-the-Line Queen.

Thayer, Laban - Prize Master - Number: 1359 - Prize Name: Elbridge Gerry - Ship type: P - How taken: HM Frigate Crescent - When taken: 16 Sep 1813 - Where taken: at sea - Date received: 1 Feb 1814 - From what ship: HM Frigate Sybille - Born: Taunton, MA - Age: 30 - Discharged on 13 Feb 1814 and sent to Chatham on HM Transport Malabar No. 352.

Thomas, Charles - Seaman - Number: 781 - How taken: Gave himself up from HM Frigate Franchise - Date received: 1 Apr 1813 - From what ship: HM Ship-of-the-Line Blake - Born: Boston - Age: 24 - Race: Mulatto - Discharged on 3 Apr 1813 and sent to Chatham on HM Transport Chatham.

Thomas, Francis - Seaman - Number: 748 - How taken: Gave himself up from HM Ship of-the-Line Bellerophon - Date received: 25 Mar 1813 - From what ship: HMS Bellerophon - Born: Salem - Age: 32 - Race: Black - Discharged on 28 Mar 1813 and sent to Chatham on HM Store Ship Seaphis.

Thomas, James - Seaman - Number: 1374 - Prize Name: Brilliant, prize to Privateer Prince Neuchatel - Ship type: MV - How taken: Caught on the Alderney Island - When taken: 26 Jan 1814 - Where taken: Alderney - Date received: 7 Feb 1814 - From what ship: Mary from Guernsey - Born: New Haven, CT - Age: 21 - Race: Mulatto - Discharged on 13 Feb 1814 and sent to Chatham on HM Transport Malabar No. 352.

Thomas, John - Boatswain's mate - Number: 383 - How taken: Gave himself up from HM Schooner Arrow - Date received: 10 Jan 1813 - From what ship: HM Guardship Royal William - Born: North Carolina - Age: 40 - Race: Black - Discharged on 4 Mar 1813 and sent to Chatham on HM Ship-of-the-Line Queen.

Thomas, John - Steward - Number: 1387 - Prize Name: Pilate - Ship type: P - How taken: Victoria, privateer of Guernsey - When taken: 28 Jan 1814 - Where taken: off Bordeaux - Date received: 7 Feb 1814 - From what ship: Mary from Guernsey - Born: Maryland - Age: 29 - Race: Mulatto - Discharged on 13 Feb 1814 and sent to Chatham on HM Transport Malabar No. 352.

Thomas, John - Seaman - Number: 1396 - Prize Name: Pilate - Ship type: P - How taken: Victoria, privateer of Guernsey - When taken: 28 Jan 1814 - Where taken: off Bordeaux - Date received: 7 Feb 1814 - From what ship: Mary from Guernsey - Born: Long Island - Age: 22 - Race: Mulatto - Discharged on 3 Mar 1814 and sent to Chatham on HM Sloop Favorite.

Thomas, John - Cook - Number: 538 - Prize Name: Expectation - Ship type: MV - How taken: HMS Butain - When taken: 17 Dec 1812 - Where taken: at sea - Date received: 25 Jan 1813 - From what ship: HM Ship-of-the-Line Queen - Born: Boston - Age: 26 - Race: Black - Discharged on 11 Mar 1813 and sent to Chatham on HM Store Ship Abundance.

Thomas, Moses - Seaman - Number: 1101 - How taken: Gave himself up from HM Ship-of-the-Line Swiftsure - Date received: 5 Oct 1813 - From what ship: HM Ship-of-the-Line Achille - Born: Norfolk, VA - Age: 21 - Race: Black.

Thomas, William - Seaman - Number: 978 - How taken: Gave himself up from HM Ship-of-the-Line Malta - Date received: 31 Jul 1813 - From what ship: HM Ship-of-the-Line Leviathan - Born: North Carolina - Age: 26 - Discharged on 13 Aug 1813 and sent to Chatham on HM Brig Cadmus.

Thompson, George - Seaman - Number: 1058 - How taken: Gave himself up from HM Ship-of-the-Line Hibernia -

Date received: 19 Sep 1813 - From what ship: HM Brig Imogen - Born: New York - Age: 27 - Discharged on 29 Sep 1813 and sent to Chatham on HM Transport Chatham.

Thompson, George - Seaman - Number: 1084 - How taken: Gave himself up from HM Ship-of-the-Line Hibernia - Date received: 1 Oct 1813 - From what ship: HM Ship-of-the-Line Barham - Born: New York - Age: 27 - Discharged on 17 Oct 1813 and sent to Chatham on HM Store Ship Weymouth.

Thompson, James - Seaman - Number: 1324 - How taken: Gave himself up from HMS Scopard - Date received: 25 Dec 1813 - From what ship: HMS Scopard - Born: Boston - Age: 34 - Discharged on 26 Dec 1813 and sent to Chatham on HMS Frigate Nemesis.

Thompson, John - Seaman - Number: 549 - Prize Name: Rossie - Ship type: MV - How taken: HM Frigate Dryand - When taken: 7 Jan 1813 - Where taken: at sea - Date received: 25 Jan 1813 - From what ship: HM Ship-of-the-Line Queen - Born: Baltimore - Age: 16 - Discharged on 11 Mar 1813 and sent to Chatham on HM Store Ship Abundance.

Thompson, John - Seaman - Number: 1493 - Prize Name: Traveler, prize of the Privateer Surprise - Ship type: MV - How taken: HM Schooner Canso - When taken: 14 May 1814 - Where taken: at sea - Date received: 1 Jun 1814 - From what ship: HMS Canso - Born: Delaware - Age: 45 - Discharged on 2 Jun 1814 and sent to Plymouth on HMS Growler.

Thompson, John - Seaman - Number: 376 - Prize Name: Enterprize - Ship type: MV - How taken: HM Sloop Hazard - When taken: 30 Sep 1812 - Where taken: at sea - Date received: 4 Jan 1813 - From what ship: HMS Muros - Born: Long Island - Age: 22 - Discharged on 4 Mar 1813 and sent to Chatham on HM Ship-of-the-Line Queen.

Thompson, Joseph - Seaman - Number: 515 - How taken: Gave himself up from HMS Renealous - Date received: 22 Jan 1813 - From what ship: HMS Renelous - Born: Meriden, CT - Age: 28 - Discharged on 11 Mar 1813 and sent to Chatham on HM Store Ship Abundance.

Thompson, Laurence - Seaman - Number: 1478 - Prize Name: Bunker Hill - Ship type: P - How taken: HM Frigate Pomone & HM Frigate Cydnus - When taken: 4 Mar 1814 - Where taken: French coast - Date received: 11 Apr 1814 - From what ship: HMS Ship-on-the-Line San Domaso - Born: Alderlla, Sweden - Age: 25 - Discharged on 28 Apr 1814 and sent to Chatham on HM Store Ship Weymouth.

Thompson, Nathaniel - Seaman - Number: 880 - Prize Name: Prompt - Ship type: MV - How taken: Chance, privateer - When taken: 28 Mar 1813 - Where taken: Bay of Biscay - Date received: 24 Jun 1813 - From what ship: HM Frigate Unicorn - Born: Virginia - Age: 31 - Discharged on 2 Jul 1813 and sent to Chatham on HM Frigate Tribune.

Thompson, William - Seaman - Number: 786 - How taken: Gave himself up from HM Frigate Franchise - Date received: 1 Apr 1813 - From what ship: HM Ship-of-the-Line Blake - Born: Copenhagen, Denmark - Age: 29 - Discharged on 3 Apr 1813 and sent to Chatham on HM Transport Chatham.

Thompson, James - Seaman - Number: 956 - How taken: Gave himself up from HM Ship-of-the-Line Swiftsure - Date received: 28 Jul 1813 - From what ship: HM Sloop Volentaire - Born: Hudson, NY - Age: 32 - Discharged on 7 Aug 1813 and sent to Chatham on HM Brig Rinaldo.

Thorning, Thomas - Seaman - Number: 1279 - Prize Name: US Schooner Growler - Ship type: MW - How taken: Sir James Yeo's Squadron - When taken: 11 Aug 1813 - Where taken: Lake Ontario - Date received: 22 Dec 1813 - From what ship: HM Frigate Ethalion - Born: New York - Age: 19 - Discharged on 26 Dec 1813 and sent to Chatham on HM Ship of-the-Line Diomede.

Thornton, David - Seaman - Number: 1124 - Prize Name: Sampson - Ship type: MV - How taken: HM Brig Rebuff - When taken: 12 May 1813 - Where taken: off Cape St. Vincent - Date received: 5 Oct 1813 - From what ship: HM Ship-of-the-Line Achille - Born: Virginia - Age: 24 - Discharged on 17 Oct 1813 and sent to Chatham on HM Transport Malabar No. 352.

Thuel, Briste - Seaman - Number: 1011 - Prize Name: Fame - Ship type: MV - How taken: HM Ship of-the-Line Cressy - When taken: 20 Jul 1813 - Where taken: at sea - Date received: 18 Aug 1813 - From what ship: HMS Cressy - Born: Nantucket - Age: 38 - Race: Black - Discharged on 21 Sep 1813 and sent to Chatham on HM Ship-of-the-Line Queen.

Tiffs, Joseph - Seaman - Number: 903 - Prize Name: Weasel - Ship type: MV - How taken: Foxhound, privateer - When taken: 25 May 1813 - Where taken: Bay of Biscay - Date received: 24 Jun 1813 - From what ship: HM Frigate Unicorn - Born: Gloucester - Age: 29 - Discharged on 2 Jul 1813 and sent to Chatham on HM Frigate Tribune.

Tillman, John - Seaman - Number: 1409 - Prize Name: Agnes, prize of the Privateer Ramble - Ship type: MV - How taken: Jane, privateer of London - When taken: 20 Nov 1813 - Where taken: Bay of Biscay - Date received: 1 Mar 1814 - From what ship: HMS Helicone - Born: Boston - Age: 17 - Discharged on 28 Apr 1814 and sent to Chatham on HM Sloop Favorite.

Tink, Henry - Seaman - Number: 720 - How taken: Gave himself up from HM Ship-of-the-Line Pembroke - Date received: 10 Mar 1813 - From what ship: HMS Guardship Royal William - Born: Salem - Age: 23 - Discharged on 11 Mar 1813 and sent to Chatham on HM Store Ship Abundance.

Tinkham, Seth - 2nd Mate - Number: 80 - Prize Name: HM Ship-of-the-Line Ganges - Ship type: MW - How taken: Detained by Court of Admiralty - When taken: 31 Jul 1812 - Where taken: Portsmouth harbor - Date received: 16 Oct 1812 San Antonio - From what ship: HM Ship-of-the-Line Ganges - Born: Wiscasset - Age: 23 - Discharged on 19 Feb 1813 and sent to Chatham on HM Frigate Ulysses.

Tipp, Nicholas - Seaman - Number: 1261 - Prize Name: Dart - Ship type: P - How taken: HM Frigate Niger & HMS Fortunee - Where taken: at sea - Date received: 19 Dec 1813 - From what ship: HMS Fortunee - Born: New Orleans - Age: 19 - Discharged on 26 Dec 1813 and sent to Chatham on HM Ship of-the-Line Diomede.

Tishure, Samuel - Master's Mate - Number: 1302 - Prize Name: Growler - Ship type: P - How taken: HM Brig Electra - When taken: 7 Jul 1813 - Where taken: off St. Johns - Date received: 22 Dec 1813 - From what ship: HM Frigate Hyperion - Born: Marblehead - Age: 26 - Discharged on 26 Dec 1813 and sent to Chatham on HMS Frigate Nemesis.

Titcomb, John H. - 1st Mate - Number: 94 - Prize Name: HMS Eos - Ship type: MW - How taken: Detained by Court of Admiralty - When taken: 31 Jul 1812 - Where taken: Portsmouth harbor - Date received: 16 Oct 1812 San Antonio - From what ship: Eos - Born: Newburyport - Age: 24 - Discharged on 26 Oct 1813 and sent to Odiham on parole.

Tolele, Garret - Seaman - Number: 1112 - How taken: Gave himself up from HM Ship-of-the-Line America - Date received: 5 Oct 1813 - From what ship: HM Ship-of-the-Line Achille - Born: Virginia - Age: 42 - Discharged on 17 Oct 1813 and sent to Chatham on HM Store Ship Weymouth.

Tolson, Jeremy - Seaman - Number: 339 - Prize Name: Elk - Ship type: MV - How taken: Rose, tender - When taken: 27 Sep 1812 - Where taken: Greenoch - Date received: 31 Dec 1812 - From what ship: HM Ship-of-the-Line Northumberland - Born: Richmond - Age: 22 - Race: Black - Discharged on 4 Mar 1813 and sent to Chatham on HM Ship-of-the-Line Queen.

Tombinson, George William - Marine - Number: 1158 - How taken: Gave himself up from HM Ship-of-the-Line Plantagenet - Date received: 9 Oct 1813 - From what ship: Portsmouth Barracks - Born: New York - Age: 25 - Discharged on 17 Oct 1813 and sent to Chatham on HM Transport Malabar No. 352.

Touche, Pierre - Surgeon Major - Number: 1460 - Prize Name: Bunker Hill - Ship type: P - How taken: HM Frigate Pomone & HM Frigate Cydnus - When taken: 4 Mar 1814 - Where taken: French coast - Date received: 11 Apr 1814 - From what ship: HMS Ship-on-the-Line San Domaso - Born: Marseille, France - Age: 30 - Discharged on 11 Apr 1814 and sent to Reading on parole.

Townsend, Solomon - Seaman - Number: 529 - Prize Name: Expectation - Ship type: MV - How taken: HMS Butain - When taken: 17 Dec 1812 - Where taken: at sea - Date received: 25 Jan 1813 - From what ship: HM Ship-of-the-Line Queen - Born: New Haven - Age: 28 - Discharged on 11 Mar 1813 and sent to Chatham on HM Store Ship Abundance.

Trask, William - Seaman - Number: 774 - How taken: Gave himself up from HM Frigate Brune - Date received: 1 Apr 1813 - From what ship: HM Ship-of-the-Line Blake - Born: Boston - Age: 25 - Discharged on 3 Apr 1813 and sent to Chatham on HM Transport Chatham.

Treadwell, Alpheus - Seaman - Number: 139 - Prize Name: Gossypium - Ship type: MV - How taken: HM Sloop Goree - When taken: 15 Aug 1812 - Where taken: off Bermuda - Date received: 29 Oct 1812 - From what ship: HM Ship-of-the-Line Ardent - Born: Bridgeport, CT - Age: 27 - Discharged on 19 Feb 1813 and sent to Chatham on HM Store Ship Dromedary.

Tristram, Joseph - Seaman - Number: 47 - Prize Name: USRM Cutter James Madison - Ship type: MW - How taken: HM Frigate Barbadoes - When taken: 22 Aug 1812 - Where taken: at sea - Date received: 12 Oct 1812 San Antonio - From what ship: HM Ship-of-the-Line Polyphemus - Born: Warrington - Age: 25 - Discharged on 19 Feb 1813 and sent to Chatham on HM Frigate Ulysses.

Trought, Joseph - Seaman - Number: 277 - Prize Name: King of Rome - Ship type: MV - How taken: HM Brig Wolverine - When taken: 23 Dec 1812 - Where taken: at sea - Date received: 30 Dec 1812 - From what ship: HM Brig Zephyr - Born: Breton, NJ - Age: 22 - Discharged on 19 Feb 1813 and sent to Chatham on HM Store Ship Dromedary.

Truman, John - Marine Sergeant - Number: 1213 - Prize Name: Elbridge Gerry - Ship type: P - How taken: HM Frigate Crescent - When taken: 16 Sep 1813 - Where taken: at sea - Date received: 16 Nov 1813 - From what ship: HM Sloop Talbot - Born: Cape Elizabeth - Age: 23 - Discharged on 26 Dec 1813 and sent to Chatham on HM Ship of-the-Line Diomede.

Tucker, Andrew - Prize Master - Number: 1311 - Prize Name: Growler - Ship type: P - How taken: HM Brig Electra - When taken: 7 Jul 1813 - Where taken: off St. Johns - Date received: 22 Dec 1813 - From what ship: HM Frigate Hyperion - Born: Marblehead - Age: 27 - Discharged on 26 Dec 1813 and sent to Chatham on HMS Frigate Nemesis.

Tucker, Nathaniel - Seaman - Number: 1125 - Prize Name: Sampson - Ship type: MV - How taken: HM Brig Rebuff - When taken: 12 May 1813 - Where taken: off Cape St. Vincent - Date received: 5 Oct 1813 - From what ship: HM Ship-of-the-Line Achille - Born: New Hampshire - Age: 20 - Discharged on 17 Oct 1813 and sent to Chatham on HM Transport Malabar No. 352.

Tucker, Nathaniel - Seaman - Number: 1318 - Prize Name: Growler - Ship type: P - How taken: HM Brig Electra - When taken: 7 Jul 1813 - Where taken: off St. Johns - Date received: 24 Dec 1813 - From what ship: HM Schooner Adonis - Born: Marblehead - Age: 22 - Discharged on 26 Dec 1813 and sent to Chatham on HMS Frigate Nemesis.

Tucker, Samuel - 1st Mate - Number: 712 - Prize Name: Endeavour - Ship type: MV - How taken: Lion, Privateer - When taken: 27 Sep 1812 - Where taken: at sea - Date received: 24 Feb 1813 - From what ship: HM Brig Escort - Born: Marblehead - Age: 21 - Discharged on 6 Mar 1813 and sent to Chatham on HM Ship-of-the-Line Cornwall.

Tufts, Eleazar - Seaman - Number: 5 - Prize Name: USRM Cutter James Madison - Ship type: MW - How taken: HM Frigate Barbadoes - When taken: 22 Aug 1812 - Where taken: at sea - Date received: 12 Oct 1812 San Antonio - From what ship: HM Ship-of-the-Line Polyphemus - Born: Medford - Age: 24 - Discharged on 19 Feb 1813 and sent to Chatham on HM Frigate Ulysses.

Tull, John - Seaman - Number: 177 - Prize Name: Baltimore - Ship type: P - How taken: HM Transport Diadem - When taken: 7 Oct 1812 - Where taken: S. Andera - Date received: 3 Nov 1812 San Antonio - From what ship: HMS Diadem - Born: St. Michaels, MD - Age: 27 - Discharged on 19 Feb 1813 and sent to Chatham on HM Store Ship Dromedary.

Tullock, William - 1st Mate - Number: 732 - Prize Name: Dart - Ship type: MV - How taken: HM Brig Doterel - When taken: 5 Mar 1813 - Where taken: at sea - Date received: 21 Mar 1813 - From what ship: HMS Dotteril - Born: Gloucester - Age: 31 - Discharged on 28 Mar 1813 and sent to Chatham on HM Store Ship Seaphis.

Turnbull, James - Seaman - Number: 512 - How taken: Gave himself up from HMS Renealous - Date received: 22 Jan 1813 - From what ship: HMS Renelous - Born: Charlestown - Age: 33 - Discharged on 11 Mar 1813 and sent to Chatham on HM Store Ship Abundance.

Turner, John - Seaman - Number: 41 - Prize Name: USRM Cutter James Madison - Ship type: MW - How taken: HM Frigate Barbadoes - When taken: 22 Aug 1812 - Where taken: at sea - Date received: 12 Oct 1812 San Antonio - From what ship: HM Ship-of-the-Line Polyphemus - Born: Randolph, MA - Age: 23 - Discharged on 19 Feb 1813 and sent to Chatham on HM Frigate Ulysses.

Turner, Samuel - Master - Number: 286 - Prize Name: Purse - Ship type: MV - How taken: HM Frigate Armide -

When taken: 29 May 1812 - Where taken: off Bordeaux - Date received: 31 Dec 1812 - From what ship: HM Ship-of-the-Line Northumberland - Born: New York - Age: 24 - Discharged on 19 Feb 1813 and sent to Chatham on HM Frigate Ulysses.

Turner, Samuel - Master - Number: 1203 - Prize Name: Elbridge Gerry - Ship type: P - How taken: HM Frigate Crescent & HM Ship of-the-Line Bellerophon - When taken: 16 Sep 1813 - Where taken: at sea - Date received: 16 Nov 1813 - From what ship: HM Sloop Talbot - Born: New York - Age: 26 - Discharged on 26 Dec 1813 and sent to Chatham on HM Ship of-the-Line Diomede.

Turner, Samuel - Seaman - Number: 598 - How taken: Sent into custody from Hyde Rendezvous - Date received: 1 Feb 1813 - From what ship: Hyde Rendezvous - Born: New York - Age: 20 - Discharged on 11 Mar 1813 and sent to Chatham on HM Store Ship Abundance.

Tuttle, Joseph - Seaman - Number: 1438 - Prize Name: HMS Devon Transport No. 15, prize of Privateer Bunker Hill - Ship type: MV - How taken: HM Brig Fly - When taken: 21 Jan 1814 - Where taken: at sea - Date received: 1 Mar 1814 - From what ship: HMS Helicone - Born: Freeport, MA - Age: 27 - Discharged on 28 Apr 1814 and sent to Chatham on HM Brig Cordelia.

Tyler, Lewis - Seaman - Number: 908 - How taken: Gave himself up from HM Ship-of-the-Line Puissant - Date received: 28 Jun 1813 - From what ship: HMS Puissant - Born: Bedford, NY - Age: 23 - Discharged on 2 Jul 1813 and sent to Chatham on HM Frigate Tribune.

Underwood, John Francis - Seaman - Number: 305 - Prize Name: Catherine - Ship type: MV - How taken: HM Frigate Leonidas - When taken: 31 Dec 1812 - Where taken: off Ireland - Date received: 31 Dec 1812 - From what ship: HM Ship-of-the-Line Northumberland - Born: New York - Age: 21 - Discharged on 4 Mar 1813 and sent to Chatham on HM Ship-of-the-Line Queen.

Unknown American - Number: 1327 - How taken: Received dead for interment - Date received: 26 Dec 1813 - From what ship: HM Transport Sir John B. Warren No. 183 - Died on 26 Dec 1813.

Urey, Peter - Seaman - Number: 589 - How taken: Gave himself up from HM Ship-of-the-Line Mars - Date received: 31 Jan 1813 - From what ship: HMS Mars - Born: New York - Age: 22 - Discharged on 11 Mar 1813 and sent to Chatham on HM Store Ship Abundance.

Valentine, Andrew - Seaman - Number: 51 - Prize Name: Fame, prize of Privateer Decatur - Ship type: MV - How taken: HM Ship-of-the-Line Polyphemus - When taken: 13 Sep 1812 - Where taken: at sea - Date received: 12 Oct 1812 San Antonio - From what ship: HM Ship-of-the-Line Polyphemus - Born: Marblehead - Age: 26 - Discharged on 19 Feb 1813 and sent to Chatham on HM Frigate Ulysses.

Valentine, John - Seaman - Number: 1119 - How taken: Gave himself up from HM Ship-of-the-Line America - Date received: 5 Oct 1813 - From what ship: HM Ship-of-the-Line Achille - Born: Boston - Age: 37 - Race: Black - Discharged on 17 Oct 1813 and sent to Chatham on HM Store Ship Weymouth.

Van Donveer, Peter - Seaman - Number: 331 - Prize Name: Independence - Ship type: MV - How taken: HM Frigate Medusa - When taken: 9 Nov 1812 - Where taken: off St. Sebastian - Date received: 31 Dec 1812 - From what ship: HM Ship-of-the-Line Northumberland - Born: New Jersey - Age: 24 - Discharged on 4 Mar 1813 and sent to Chatham on HM Ship-of-the-Line Queen.

Vangostet, Cato - Seaman - Number: 903 - Prize Name: Weasel - Ship type: MV - How taken: Foxhound, privateer - When taken: 25 May 1813 - Where taken: Bay of Biscay - Date received: 24 Jun 1813 - From what ship: HM Frigate Unicorn - Born: New Jersey - Age: 22 - Race: Black - Discharged on 2 Jul 1813 and sent to Chatham on HM Frigate Tribune.

Veazey, Edward - Master - Number: 185 - Prize Name: Baltimore - Ship type: P - How taken: HM Transport Diadem - When taken: 7 Oct 1812 - Where taken: S. Andera - Date received: 10 Nov 1812 - From what ship: HMS Diadem - Born: Cecil, MA - Age: 28 - Discharged on 11 Nov 1812 and sent to Odiham on parole.

Veney, George - Seaman - Number: 725 - Prize Name: Tom Thumb - Ship type: MV - How taken: Lion, Privateer - When taken: 15 Feb 1813 - Where taken: at sea - Date received: 19 Mar 1813 - From what ship: Gosport Rendezvous - Born: Philadelphia - Age: 22 - Race: Mulatto - Discharged on 28 Mar 1813 and sent to Chatham on HM Store Ship Seaphis.

Villodas, Matias - Seaman - Number: 265 - Prize Name: King of Rome - Ship type: P - How taken: HM Brig

Wolverine - When taken: 13 Dec 1812 - Where taken: at sea - Date received: 27 Dec 1812 - From what ship: HMS Wolverine - Born: Havana, Cuba - Age: 25 - Race: Black - Discharged on 19 Feb 1813 and sent to Chatham on HM Store Ship Dromedary.

Vincent, Henry - Seaman - Number: 1134 - Prize Name: Sampson - Ship type: MV - How taken: HM Brig Rebuff - When taken: 12 May 1813 - Where taken: off Cape St. Vincent - Date received: 6 Oct 1813 - From what ship: HM Sloop Kingfisher - Born: Massachusetts - Age: 23 - Discharged on 17 Oct 1813 and sent to Chatham on HM Transport Malabar No. 352.

Vincent, Stephen Stiles - Seaman - Number: 1381 - Prize Name: Pilate - Ship type: P - How taken: Victoria, privateer of Guernsey - When taken: 28 Jan 1814 - Where taken: off Bordeaux - Date received: 7 Feb 1814 - From what ship: Mary from Guernsey - Born: New Jersey - Age: 20 - Race: Black - Discharged on 13 Feb 1814 and sent to Chatham on HM Transport Malabar No. 352.

Vine, William - Seaman - Number: 396 - Prize Name: Empress - Ship type: MV - How taken: HM Brig Rover - When taken: 30 Nov 1812 - Where taken: at sea - Date received: 10 Jan 1813 - From what ship: HM Guardship Royal William - Born: South Carolina - Age: 21 - Discharged on 6 Mar 1813 and sent to Chatham on HMS Frigate Alexandria.

Voight, Henry - Seaman - Number: 952 - How taken: Gave himself up from HM Ship-of-the-Line Swiftsure - Date received: 28 Jul 1813 - From what ship: HM Sloop Volentaire - Born: Pennsylvania - Age: 31 - Discharged on 7 Aug 1813 and sent to Chatham on HM Brig Rinaldo.

Voohis, James - Seaman - Number: 896 - Prize Name: Weasel - Ship type: MV - How taken: Foxhound, privateer - When taken: 25 May 1813 - Where taken: Bay of Biscay - Date received: 24 Jun 1813 - From what ship: HM Frigate Unicorn - Born: New Jersey - Age: 20 - Discharged on 2 Jul 1813 and sent to Chatham on HM Frigate Tribune.

Vorge, James - Seaman - Number: 567 - Prize Name: Rossie - Ship type: MV - How taken: HM Frigate Dryand - When taken: 7 Jan 1813 - Where taken: at sea - Date received: 25 Jan 1813 - From what ship: HM Ship-of-the-Line Queen - Born: Harford - Age: 24 - Discharged on 11 Mar 1813 and sent to Chatham on HM Store Ship Abundance.

Wade, Otis - Seaman - Number: 414 - Prize Name: Otter - Ship type: MV - How taken: HM Ship-Sloop Jalouse - When taken: 1 Dec 1812 - Where taken: at sea - Date received: 10 Jan 1813 - From what ship: HM Guardship Royal William - Born: Scituate, MA - Age: 27 - Discharged on 6 Mar 1813 and sent to Chatham on HMS Frigate Alexandria.

Wadsworth, Daniel - Passenger - Number: 1345 - Prize Name: Volunteer - Ship type: MV - How taken: Victoria, privateer of Guernsey - When taken: 26 Dec 1813 - Where taken: at sea - Date received: 4 Jan 1814 - From what ship: Earl S. Vincent Packet - Born: Connecticut - Age: 22 - Discharged on 5 Jan 1814 and sent to Chatham on HM Ship-of-the-Line Poictiers.

Wadsworth, Thomas - Seaman - Number: 1501 - How taken: Gave himself up at the gate - Date received: 20 Jun 1814 - From what ship: HMS Pulsta - Born: Salem - Age: 65 - Discharged on 30 Jun 1814 and sent to Plymouth on HM Brig Steady.

Walden, James - Seaman - Number: 962 - How taken: Gave himself up from HM Ship-of-the-Line Leviathan - Date received: 31 Jul 1813 - From what ship: HMS Leviathan - Born: New London - Age: 32 - Discharged on 7 Aug 1813 and sent to Chatham on HM Brig Rinaldo.

Walker, Benjamin - Seaman - Number: 1157 - How taken: Gave himself up from HM Store Ship Woolwich - Date received: 7 Oct 1813 - From what ship: HM Frigate Spartan - Born: Maryland - Age: 27 - Race: Mulatto - Discharged on 17 Oct 1813 and sent to Chatham on HM Transport Malabar No. 352.

Walker, James - Seaman - Number: 285 - Prize Name: Friendship - Ship type: MV - How taken: Rosamond - When taken: 12 Aug 1812 - Where taken: Halifax - Date received: 31 Dec 1812 - From what ship: HM Ship-of-the-Line Northumberland - Born: Boston - Age: 33 - Race: Black - Discharged on 19 Feb 1813 and sent to Chatham on HM Store Ship Dromedary.

Walker, Seth - Prize Master - Number: 1415 - Prize Name: Zephyr, prize of Privateer Rattlesnake - Ship type: MV - How taken: HM Frigate Surveillante - When taken: 6 Jan 1814 - Where taken: Bay of Biscay - Date received:

1 Mar 1814 - From what ship: HMS Helicone - Born: Portsmouth - Age: 35 - Discharged on 28 Apr 1814 and sent to Chatham on HM Sloop Favorite.

Walker, William - Seaman - Number: 1160 - How taken: Gave himself up from HM Ship-Sloop Jalouse - Date received: 9 Oct 1813 - From what ship: HM Sloop Stork - Born: New Hampshire - Age: 36 - Race: Black - Discharged on 17 Oct 1813 and sent to Chatham on HM Transport Malabar No. 352.

Wallace, William - Seaman - Number: 426 - Prize Name: Brunswick - Ship type: MV - How taken: HM Frigate Iris - When taken: 16 Dec 1812 - Where taken: at sea - Date received: 10 Jan 1813 - From what ship: HM Guardship Royal William - Born: New Jersey - Age: 32 - Discharged on 6 Mar 1813 and sent to Chatham on HMS Frigate Alexandria.

Walter, George - Seaman - Number: 160 - Prize Name: Baltimore - Ship type: P - How taken: HM Transport Diadem - When taken: 7 Oct 1812 - Where taken: S. Andera - Date received: 3 Nov 1812 San Antonio - From what ship: HMS Diadem - Born: River Neek, MD - Age: 24 - Discharged on 19 Feb 1813 and sent to Chatham on HM Store Ship Dromedary.

Ward, James - Seaman - Number: 90 - Prize Name: HM Frigate Janus - Ship type: MW - How taken: Detained by Court of Admiralty - When taken: 31 Jul 1812 - Where taken: Portsmouth harbor - Date received: 16 Oct 1812 San Antonio - From what ship: HM Frigate Janus - Born: New Market, NH - Age: 24 - Discharged on 19 Feb 1813 and sent to Chatham on HM Frigate Ulysses.

Ward, Thomas - Prize Master - Number: 1271 - Prize Name: Pomona, prize of Privateer Prince Neuchatel - Ship type: MV - How taken: HM Frigate Ethalion - When taken: 14 Dec 1813 - Where taken: at sea - Date received: 22 Dec 1813 - From what ship: HMS Ethalion - Born: Baltimore - Age: 39 - Discharged on 26 Dec 1813 and sent to Chatham on HM Ship of-the-Line Diomede.

Warner, John - Seaman - Number: 1142 - Prize Name: Hepsey - Ship type: MV - How taken: HM Brig Zenobia - When taken: 22 Jun 1813 - Where taken: Lisbon - Date received: 6 Oct 1813 - From what ship: HM Sloop Kingfisher - Born: Gothenburg, Sweden - Age: 29 - Discharged on 17 Oct 1813 and sent to Chatham on HM Transport Malabar No. 352.

Waterman, John - 2nd Mate - Number: 890 - Prize Name: Tigre - Ship type: MV - How taken: HM Brig Scylla - When taken: 22 Mar 1813 - Where taken: Bay of Biscay - Date received: 24 Jun 1813 - From what ship: HM Frigate Unicorn - Born: Nantucket - Age: 21 - Discharged on 2 Jul 1813 and sent to Chatham on HM Frigate Tribune.

Waterman, William - Seaman - Number: 227 - Prize Name: Antelope - Ship type: P - How taken: HM Brig Zephyr - When taken: 10 Dec 1812 - Where taken: at sea - Date received: 27 Dec 1812 - From what ship: HMS Zephyr - Born: Nantucket - Age: 17 - Discharged on 19 Feb 1813 and sent to Chatham on HM Store Ship Dromedary.

Watkins, Frederick - Seaman - Number: 298 - Prize Name: Washington - Ship type: MV - How taken: Taken up on shore - When taken: 18 Oct 1812 - Where taken: Liverpool - Date received: 31 Dec 1812 - From what ship: HM Ship-of-the-Line Northumberland - Born: New York - Age: 22 - Discharged on 4 Mar 1813 and sent to Chatham on HM Ship-of-the-Line Queen.

Watkins, George - Seaman - Number: 769 - How taken: Gave himself up from HM Ship-of-the-Line Blake - Date received: 1 Apr 1813 - From what ship: HM Ship-of-the-Line Blake - Born: Newport, RI - Age: 43 - Discharged on 3 Apr 1813 and sent to Chatham on HM Transport Chatham.

Watson, David - Seaman - Number: 1270 - Prize Name: US Schooner Growler - Ship type: MW - How taken: Sir James Yeo's Squadron - When taken: 11 Aug 1813 - Where taken: Lake Ontario - Date received: 22 Dec 1813 - From what ship: HMS Elalion - Born: New York - Age: 22 - Discharged on 26 Dec 1813 and sent to Chatham on HM Ship of-the-Line Diomede.

Watson, James - Seaman - Number: 997 - Prize Name: Kitty, prize of US Frigate President - Ship type: MV - How taken: Dart, privateer of Guernsey - When taken: 20 Jun 1813 - Where taken: at sea - Date received: 18 Aug 1813 - From what ship: HMS Dexterous - Born: Boston - Age: 18 - Discharged on 21 Sep 1813 and sent to Chatham on HM Ship-of-the-Line Queen.

Watson, William - Seaman - Number: 1428 - Prize Name: Minerva - Ship type: MV - How taken: HM Ship-of-the-

Line Conquestador - When taken: 19 Jan 1814 - Where taken: Bay of Biscay - Date received: 1 Mar 1814 - From what ship: HMS Helicone - Born: Scarborough - Age: 20 - Discharged on 28 Apr 1814 and sent to Chatham on HM Sloop Favorite.

Watson, Daniel - Seaman - Number: 1104 - How taken: Gave himself up from HM Ship-of-the-Line Swiftsure - Date received: 5 Oct 1813 - From what ship: HM Ship-of-the-Line Achille - Born: Rhode Island - Age: 24 - Race: Mulatto - Discharged on 17 Oct 1813 and sent to Chatham on HM Store Ship Weymouth.

Webb, Nathan - Quarter Gunner - Number: 1212 - Prize Name: Elbridge Gerry - Ship type: P - How taken: HM Frigate Crescent - When taken: 16 Sep 1813 - Where taken: at sea - Date received: 16 Nov 1813 - From what ship: HM Sloop Talbot - Born: Danvers, MA - Age: 24 - Discharged on 26 Dec 1813 and sent to Chatham on HM Ship of-the-Line Diomede.

Webb, Stephen - Seaman - Number: 165 - Prize Name: Baltimore - Ship type: P - How taken: HM Transport Diadem - When taken: 7 Oct 1812 - Where taken: S. Andera - Date received: 3 Nov 1812 San Antonio - From what ship: HMS Diadem - Born: Baltimore - Age: 31 - Discharged on 19 Feb 1813 and sent to Chatham on HM Store Ship Dromedary.

Webster, William - Seaman - Number: 961 - How taken: Gave himself up from HM Ship-of-the-Line Leviathan - Date received: 31 Jul 1813 - From what ship: HMS Leviathan - Born: New York - Age: 28 - Discharged on 7 Aug 1813 and sent to Chatham on HM Brig Rinaldo.

Wedgewood, James - Seaman - Number: 741 - Prize Name: Dart - Ship type: MV - How taken: HM Brig Doterel - When taken: 5 Mar 1813 - Where taken: at sea - Date received: 21 Mar 1813 - From what ship: HMS Dotteril - Born: Massachusetts - Age: 29 - Discharged on 28 Mar 1813 and sent to Chatham on HM Store Ship Seaphis.

Weed, Ebenezer - Seaman - Number: 254 - Prize Name: King of Rome - Ship type: P - How taken: HM Brig Wolverine - When taken: 13 Dec 1812 - Where taken: at sea - Date received: 27 Dec 1812 - From what ship: HMS Wolverine - Born: Stanford - Age: 22 - Died on 11 Feb 1813.

Weeden, Richard - Cook - Number: 1014 - Prize Name: Fame - Ship type: MV - How taken: HM Ship of-the-Line Cressy - When taken: 20 Jul 1813 - Where taken: at sea - Date received: 18 Aug 1813 - From what ship: HMS Cressy - Born: Rhode Island - Age: 30 - Discharged on 21 Sep 1813 and sent to Chatham on HM Ship-of-the-Line Queen.

Weeks, George - Seaman - Number: 258 - Prize Name: King of Rome - Ship type: P - How taken: HM Brig Wolverine - When taken: 13 Dec 1812 - Where taken: at sea - Date received: 27 Dec 1812 - From what ship: HMS Wolverine - Born: New York - Age: 16 - Discharged on 19 Feb 1813 and sent to Chatham on HM Store Ship Dromedary.

Weilright, Joseph - Seaman - Number: 67 - Prize Name: Diana, prize of Privateer Decatur - Ship type: MV - How taken: HM Ship-of-the-Line Polyphemus - When taken: 14 Sep 1812 - Where taken: at sea - Date received: 12 Oct 1812 San Antonio - From what ship: HM Ship-of-the-Line Polyphemus - Born: Boston - Age: 20 - Discharged on 19 Feb 1813 and sent to Chatham on HM Frigate Ulysses.

Welch, John - Seaman - Number: 855 - How taken: Gave himself up from HM Frigate Leonidas - Date received: 22 Jun 1813 - From what ship: HM Ship-of-the-Line Vigo - Born: Virginia - Age: 28 - Discharged on 2 Jul 1813 and sent to Chatham on HM Frigate Tribune.

Welch, William - Seaman - Number: 201 - Prize Name: Rising States - Ship type: MV - How taken: HMS Fortunee - When taken: 28 Aug 1812 - Where taken: at sea - Date received: 25 Nov 1812 - From what ship: HM Guardship Royal William - Born: New York - Age: 25 - Discharged on 19 Feb 1813 and sent to Chatham on HM Store Ship Dromedary.

Wells, Moses - Boy - Number: 486 - Prize Name: Sword Fish - Ship type: P - How taken: HM Ship-of-the-Line Elephant - When taken: 28 Dec 1812 - Where taken: at sea - Date received: 14 Jan 1813 - From what ship: HMS Elephant - Born: Newburyport - Age: 15 - Discharged on 11 Mar 1813 and sent to Chatham on HM Store Ship Abundance.

Wells, Thomas - Cook - Number: 100 - Prize Name: HMS Eos - Ship type: MW - How taken: Detained by Court of Admiralty - When taken: 31 Jul 1812 - Where taken: Portsmouth harbor - Date received: 16 Oct 1812 San

Antonio - From what ship: Eos - Born: New York - Age: 39 - Race: Black - Discharged on 19 Feb 1813 and sent to Chatham on HM Frigate Ulysses.

West, George - Seaman - Number: 843 - How taken: Gave himself up from HM Ship-of-the-Line Malta - Date received: 15 Jun 1813 - From what ship: HM Sloop Helena - Born: Baltimore - Age: 24 - Discharged on 2 Jul 1813 and sent to Chatham on HM Frigate Tribune.

West, Henry - Prize Master - Number: 911 - Prize Name: Blockage - Ship type: P - How taken: HM Brig Charybdis - When taken: 30 Oct 1812 - Where taken: at sea - Date received: 1 Jul 1813 - From what ship: HM Frigate Tribune - Born: Rhode Island - Age: 27 - Discharged on 2 Jul 1813 and sent to Chatham on HM Brig Scorpion.

West, John - Seaman - Number: 296 - Prize Name: Martin - Ship type: MV - How taken: Taken up on shore - When taken: 18 Oct 1812 - Where taken: Liverpool - Date received: 31 Dec 1812 - From what ship: HM Ship-of-the-Line Northumberland - Born: Orleans - Age: 20 - Discharged on 4 Mar 1813 and sent to Chatham on HM Ship-of-the-Line Queen.

Weton, William (alias Andrew Quicker) - Seaman - Number: 792 - How taken: Gave himself up from HM Ship-of-the-Line Ajax - Date received: 13 Apr 1813 - From what ship: HMS Ajax - Born: New York - Age: 21 - Discharged on 27 Apr 1813 and sent to Chatham on HM Sloop-of-War Bonne Citoyenne.

Whitchouse, Lewis - Marine - Number: 492 - Prize Name: Sword Fish - Ship type: P - How taken: HM Ship-of-the-Line Elephant - When taken: 28 Dec 1812 - Where taken: at sea - Date received: 14 Jan 1813 - From what ship: HMS Elephant - Born: Brookfield - Age: 19 - Discharged on 11 Mar 1813 and sent to Chatham on HM Store Ship Abundance.

White, Aldin - Seaman - Number: 304 - Prize Name: Catherine - Ship type: MV - How taken: HM Frigate Leonidas - When taken: 31 Dec 1812 - Where taken: off Ireland - Date received: 31 Dec 1812 - From what ship: HM Ship-of-the-Line Northumberland - Born: New Bedford - Age: 20 - Discharged on 4 Mar 1813 and sent to Chatham on HM Ship-of-the-Line Queen.

White, Benjamin - Prize Master - Number: 445 - Prize Name: Sword Fish - Ship type: P - How taken: HM Ship-of-the-Line Elephant - When taken: 28 Dec 1812 - Where taken: at sea - Date received: 14 Jan 1813 - From what ship: HMS Elephant - Born: Hampshire, England - Age: 27 - Discharged on 6 Mar 1813 and sent to Chatham on HMS Frigate Alexandria.

White, Charles - Seaman - Number: 965 - How taken: Gave himself up from HM Ship-of-the-Line Leviathan - Date received: 31 Jul 1813 - From what ship: HMS Leviathan - Born: New York - Age: 38 - Race: Black - Discharged on 7 Aug 1813 and sent to Chatham on HM Brig Rinaldo.

White, John - Prize Master - Number: 918 - Prize Name: Tender of the True Blooded Yankee - Ship type: P - How taken: HM Ship-of-the-Line Fame - When taken: 24 Jun 1813 - Where taken: at sea - Date received: 1 Jul 1813 - From what ship: HM Brig Hope - Born: Portsmouth, NH - Age: 29 - Discharged on 2 Jul 1813 and sent to Chatham on HM Brig Scorpion.

White, John W. - Prize Master - Number: 444 - Prize Name: Sword Fish - Ship type: P - How taken: HM Ship-of-the-Line Elephant - When taken: 28 Dec 1812 - Where taken: at sea - Date received: 14 Jan 1813 - From what ship: HMS Elephant - Born: Marblehead - Age: 23 - Discharged on 6 Mar 1813 and sent to Chatham on HMS Frigate Alexandria.

White, John W. - Seaman - Number: 594 - How taken: Gave himself up from HM Ship-of-the-Line Mars - Date received: 31 Jan 1813 - From what ship: HMS Mars - Born: Petersburg - Age: 23 - Race: Black - Discharged on 11 Mar 1813 and sent to Chatham on HM Store Ship Abundance.

White, John W. - Seaman - Number: 87 - Prize Name: HM Frigate Janus - Ship type: MW - How taken: Detained by Court of Admiralty - When taken: 31 Jul 1812 - Where taken: Portsmouth harbor - Date received: 16 Oct 1812 San Antonio - From what ship: HM Frigate Janus - Born: Providence, RI - Age: 29 - Discharged on 19 Feb 1813 and sent to Chatham on HM Frigate Ulysses.

White, Philip - Prize Master - Number: 1485 - Prize Name: Indian Lass, prize of Privateer Grand Turk - Ship type: MV - How taken: HM Transport Akbar - When taken: 20 Apr 1814 - Where taken: at sea - Date received: 28 May 1814 - From what ship: HMS Akbar - Born: Marblehead - Age: 30 - Discharged on 2 Jun 1814 and sent to Plymouth on HMS Growler.

White, Thomas - Seaman - Number: 239 - Prize Name: Antelope - Ship type: P - How taken: HM Brig Zephyr - When taken: 10 Dec 1812 - Where taken: at sea - Date received: 27 Dec 1812 - From what ship: HMS Zephyr - Born: Peashore, NJ - Age: 20 - Discharged on 10 Jun 1813 and sent to Chatham on HM Frigate Arethusa.

White, William - Seaman - Number: 950 - Prize Name: Fame, West Indianman - How taken: Impressed at London - When taken: 4 Jul 1812 - Date received: 19 Jun 1813 - From what ship: HM Prison Ship Victorious - Born: Philadelphia - Age: 29 - Discharged on 7 Aug 1813 and sent to Chatham on HM Brig Rinaldo.

Whithmore, William - Seaman - Number: 407 - How taken: Taken up at Dublin - When taken: 12 Nov 1812 - Date received: 10 Jan 1813 - From what ship: HM Guardship Royal William - Born: Bath, MA - Age: 25 - Discharged on 6 Mar 1813 and sent to Chatham on HMS Frigate Alexandria.

Whittlebank, Edward - Seaman - Number: 114 - How taken: Sent into custody by order of the commander in chief - Date received: 22 Oct 1812 - From what ship: HM Guardship Royal William - Born: Portsmouth, NH - Age: 21 - Discharged on 19 Feb 1813 and sent to Chatham on HM Frigate Ulysses.

Wickham, Ezekiel - Seaman - Number: 983 - How taken: Gave himself up from HM Ship-of-the-Line Goliath - Date received: 8 Aug 1813 - From what ship: HM Ship-of-the-Line Medway - Born: Connecticut - Age: 25 - Discharged on 13 Aug 1813 and sent to Chatham on HM Brig Cadmus.

Wickham, Thaddeus - Seaman - Number: 771 - How taken: Gave himself up from HM Frigate Brune - Date received: 1 Apr 1813 - From what ship: HM Ship-of-the-Line Blake - Born: Bridgewater - Age: 28 - Race: Colored - Discharged on 3 Apr 1813 and sent to Chatham on HM Transport Chatham.

Wicks, Littleton - Seaman - Number: 291 - Prize Name: Hannah - Ship type: MV - How taken: Taken up on shore - When taken: 18 Oct 1812 - Where taken: Liverpool - Date received: 31 Dec 1812 - From what ship: HM Ship-of-the-Line Northumberland - Born: Virginia - Age: 27 - Race: Black - Discharged on 4 Mar 1813 and sent to Chatham on HM Ship-of-the-Line Queen.

Wickwall, Joseph (alias Wickwire) - Seaman - Number: 432 - How taken: Gave himself up from HM Ship of-the-Line Cressy - Date received: 11 Jan 1813 - From what ship: HMS Cressy - Born: Bennington, VT - Age: 23 – Discharged on 6 Mar 1813 and sent to Chatham on HMS Frigate Alexandria.

Widger, Joseph - Seaman - Number: 1286 - Prize Name: Growler - Ship type: P - How taken: HM Brig Electra - When taken: 7 Jul 1813 - Where taken: off St. Johns - Date received: 22 Dec 1813 - From what ship: HM Ship of-the-Line Bellerophon - Born: Marblehead - Age: 21 - Discharged on 26 Dec 1813 and sent to Chatham on HMS Frigate Nemesis.

Weir, Frederick - 2nd Mate - Number: 76 - Prize Name: HMS Belleville - Ship type: MW - How taken: Detained by Court of Admiralty - When taken: 31 Jul 1812 - Where taken: Portsmouth harbor - Date received: 16 Oct 1812 San Antonio - From what ship: Belleville - Born: Oldenburg, Germany - Age: 27 - Discharged on 19 Feb 1813 and sent to Chatham on HM Frigate Ulysses.

Wiley, David - Seaman - Number: 789 - How taken: Gave himself up from HM Frigate Unicorn - Date received: 3 Apr 1813 - From what ship: HM Ship-of-the-Line Boyne - Born: Wellfleet, MA - Age: 37 - Discharged on 27 Apr 1813 and sent to Chatham on HM Sloop-of-War Bonne Citoyenne.

Wilky, Timothy - Seaman - Number: 1137 - Prize Name: Maydock - Ship type: MV - How taken: HM Brig Rebuff - When taken: 16 Jun 1813 - Where taken: St. Mary's - Date received: 6 Oct 1813 - From what ship: HM Sloop Kingfisher - Born: Dartmouth - Age: 18 - Discharged on 17 Oct 1813 and sent to Chatham on HM Transport Malabar No. 352.

Williams, George - Seaman - Number: 306 - Prize Name: Catherine - Ship type: MV - How taken: HM Frigate Leonidas - When taken: 31 Dec 1812 - Where taken: off Ireland - Date received: 31 Dec 1812 - From what ship: HM Ship-of-the-Line Northumberland - Born: Queen Ann County - Age: 23 - Race: Black - Discharged on 4 Mar 1813 and sent to Chatham on HM Ship-of-the-Line Queen.

Williams, George - Seaman - Number: 307 - Prize Name: Catherine - Ship type: MV - How taken: HM Frigate Leonidas - When taken: 31 Dec 1812 - Where taken: off Ireland - Date received: 31 Dec 1812 - From what ship: HM Ship-of-the-Line Northumberland - Born: Baltimore - Age: 26 - Race: Black - Discharged on 4

Mar 1813 and sent to Chatham on HM Ship-of-the-Line Queen.

Williams, John - Seaman - Number: 930 - Prize Name: Tender of the True Blooded Yankee - Ship type: P - How taken: HM Ship-of-the-Line Fame - When taken: 24 Jun 1813 - Where taken: at sea - Date received: 1 Jul 1813 - From what ship: HM Brig Hope - Born: Virginia - Age: 27 - Discharged on 2 Jul 1813 and sent to Chatham on HM Brig Scorpion.

Williams, John - Seaman - Number: 941 - Prize Name: Tender of the True Blooded Yankee - Ship type: P - How taken: HM Ship-of-the-Line Fame - When taken: 24 Jun 1813 - Where taken: at sea - Date received: 1 Jul 1813 - From what ship: HM Brig Hope - Born: Staten Island - Age: 42 - Race: Mulatto - Discharged on 2 Jul 1813 and sent to Chatham on HM Brig Scorpion.

Williams, Alexander - Seaman - Number: 299 - Prize Name: Industry - Ship type: MV - How taken: Taken up on shore - When taken: 18 Oct 1812 - Where taken: Liverpool - Date received: 31 Dec 1812 - From what ship: HM Ship-of-the-Line Northumberland - Born: Long Island - Age: 21 - Race: Black - Discharged on 4 Mar 1813 and sent to Chatham on HM Ship-of-the-Line Queen.

Williams, Benjamin - Seaman - Number: 560 - Prize Name: Rossie - Ship type: MV - How taken: HM Frigate Dryand - When taken: 7 Jan 1813 - Where taken: at sea - Date received: 25 Jan 1813 - From what ship: HM Ship-of-the-Line Queen - Born: Baltimore - Age: 14 - Discharged on 11 Mar 1813 and sent to Chatham on HM Store Ship Abundance.

Williams, Charles - Seaman - Number: 1407 - Prize Name: Pilot - Ship type: P - How taken: Victoria, privateer of Guernsey - When taken: 28 Jan 1814 - Where taken: off Bordeaux - Date received: 16 Feb 1814 - From what ship: HM Transport Malabar No. 352 - Born: New London - Age: 22 - Race: Black - Discharged on 28 Apr 1814 and sent to Chatham on HM Store Ship Weymouth.

Williams, Charles - Seaman - Number: 1381 - Prize Name: Pilate - Ship type: P - How taken: Victoria, privateer of Guernsey - When taken: 28 Jan 1814 - Where taken: off Bordeaux - Date received: 7 Feb 1814 - From what ship: Mary from Guernsey - Born: New London - Age: 22 - Race: Black - Discharged on 13 Feb 1814 and sent to Chatham on HM Transport Malabar No. 352.

Williams, Charles - Seaman - Number: 241 - Prize Name: Antelope - Ship type: P - How taken: HM Brig Zephyr - When taken: 10 Dec 1812 - Where taken: at sea - Date received: 27 Dec 1812 - From what ship: HMS Zephyr - Born: Bremen, Germany - Age: 28 - Discharged on 19 Feb 1813 and sent to Chatham on HM Store Ship Dromedary.

Williams, Darius - Seaman - Number: 128 - How taken: Gave himself up from HM Ship-of-the-Line Ruby - When taken: 30 Aug 1812 - Date received: 29 Oct 1812 - From what ship: HM Ship-of-the-Line Ardent - Born: Seabrook, NH - Age: 27 - Race: Colored - Discharged on 19 Feb 1813 and sent to Chatham on HM Store Ship Dromedary.

Williams, David - Seaman - Number: 206 - Prize Name: Caster - Ship type: MV - How taken: HM Schooner Antelope - When taken: 30 Jul 1812 - Where taken: at sea - Date received: 3 Dec 1812 - From what ship: HMS Antelope - Born: Winchester, PA - Age: 23 - Discharged on 19 Feb 1813 and sent to Chatham on HM Store Ship Dromedary.

Williams, Gaspar - Seaman - Number: 2 - Prize Name: USRM Cutter James Madison - Ship type: MW - How taken: HM Frigate Barbadoes - When taken: 22 Aug 1812 - Where taken: at sea - Date received: 12 Oct 1812 San Antonio - From what ship: HM Ship-of-the-Line Polyphemus - Born: Dunkirk, France - Age: 42 - Discharged on 19 Feb 1813 and sent to Chatham on HM Frigate Ulysses.

Williams, George - Seaman - Number: 633 - How taken: Gave himself up from HM Guardship Royal William - Date received: 3 Feb 1813 - From what ship: HMS Royal William - Born: New York - Age: 32 - Discharged on 11 Mar 1813 and sent to Chatham on HM Store Ship Abundance.

Williams, George - Seaman - Number: 972 - How taken: Gave himself up from HM Ship-of-the-Line Caledonia - Date received: 31 Jul 1813 - From what ship: HMS Leviathan - Born: Bedford, NY - Age: 39 - Race: Black - Discharged on 13 Aug 1813 and sent to Chatham on HM Brig Cadmus.

Williams, Henry - 2nd Mate - Number: 249 - Prize Name: King of Rome - Ship type: P - How taken: HM Brig Wolverine - When taken: 13 Dec 1812 - Where taken: at sea - Date received: 27 Dec 1812 - From what ship:

HMS Wolverine - Born: Seabrook, KY - Age: 24 - Discharged on 19 Feb 1813 and sent to Chatham on HM Store Ship Dromedary.

Williams, James - Seaman - Number: 793 - How taken: Gave himself up from HM Frigate Loire - Date received: 14 Apr 1813 - From what ship: HMS Loire - Born: Taunton, MA - Age: 26 - Discharged on 27 Apr 1813 and sent to Chatham on HM Sloop-of-War Bonne Citoyenne.

Williams, John - Seaman - Number: 1019 - How taken: Gave himself up from HM Ship-of-the-Line Prince of Wales - Date received: 7 Sep 1813 - From what ship: HM Frigate Unicorn - Born: New Jersey - Age: 26 - Discharged on 21 Sep 1813 and sent to Chatham on HM Ship-of-the-Line Queen.

Williams, John - Seaman - Number: 498 - Prize Name: Sword Fish - Ship type: P - How taken: HM Ship-of-the-Line Elephant - When taken: 28 Dec 1812 - Where taken: at sea - Date received: 14 Jan 1813 - From what ship: HMS Elephant - Born: Portland - Age: 31 - Discharged on 11 Mar 1813 and sent to Chatham on HM Store Ship Abundance.

Williams, Joseph - Seaman - Number: 639 - How taken: Gave himself up from HM Guardship Royal William - Date received: 3 Feb 1813 - From what ship: HMS Royal William - Born: Philadelphia - Age: 29 - Race: Black - Discharged on 11 Mar 1813 and sent to Chatham on HM Store Ship Abundance.

Williams, Josiah - Seaman - Number: 377 - How taken: Gave himself up from HM Sloop Comet - When taken: 25 Nov 1812 - Date received: 4 Jan 1813 - From what ship: HMS Muros - Born: Boston - Age: 36 - Race: Black - Discharged on 4 Mar 1813 and sent to Chatham on HM Ship-of-the-Line Queen.

Williams, Robert - Seaman - Number: 1044 - How taken: Gave himself up from HM Ship-of-the-Line Scipion - Date received: 14 Sep 1813 - From what ship: HM Brig Savage - Born: New York - Age: 24 - Race: Black - Discharged on 29 Sep 1813 and sent to Chatham on HM Ship-of-the-Line Barham.

Williams, Robert - Seaman - Number: 1050 - How taken: Gave himself up from HM Ship-of-the-Line Union - Date received: 14 Sep 1813 - From what ship: HM Brig Savage - Born: New York - Age: 23 - Discharged on 29 Sep 1813 and sent to Chatham on HM Ship-of-the-Line Barham.

Williams, Stephen - Seaman - Number: 1013 - Prize Name: Fame - Ship type: MV - How taken: HM Ship of-the-Line Cressy - When taken: 20 Jul 1813 - Where taken: at sea - Date received: 18 Aug 1813 - From what ship: HMS Cressy - Born: Albany - Age: 27 - Race: Black - Discharged on 21 Sep 1813 and sent to Chatham on HM Ship-of-the-Line Queen.

Williams, Thomas - Seaman - Number: 1140 - Prize Name: Hepsey - Ship type: MV - How taken: HM Brig Zenobia - When taken: 22 Jun 1813 - Where taken: Lisbon - Date received: 6 Oct 1813 - From what ship: HM Sloop Kingfisher - Born: Baltimore - Age: 40 - Discharged on 17 Oct 1813 and sent to Chatham on HM Transport Malabar No. 352.

Williams, Thomas - Seaman - Number: 949 - How taken: Gave himself up from HM Frigate Unicorn - Date received: 8 Jun 1813 - From what ship: HMS Eldegon - Born: Connecticut - Age: 27 - Discharged on 7 Aug 1813 and sent to Chatham on HM Brig Rinaldo.

Williams, Thomas - Seaman - Number: 970 - How taken: Gave himself up from HM Ship-of-the-Line Leviathan - Date received: 31 Jul 1813 - From what ship: HMS Leviathan - Born: Maryland - Age: 27 - Race: Black - Discharged on 7 Aug 1813 and sent to Chatham on HM Brig Rinaldo.

Williams, William - Boy - Number: 1194 - Prize Name: Fire Fly of Gloucester - Ship type: MV - How taken: HM Frigate Revolutionnaire - When taken: 19 Oct 1813 - Where taken: at sea - Date received: 9 Nov 1813 - From what ship: HMS Revolutionaire - Born: Gloucester - Age: 14 - Discharged on 26 Dec 1813 and sent to Chatham on HM Ship of-the-Line Diomede.

Williamson, Charles - Seaman - Number: 347 - Prize Name: Experiment - Ship type: MV - How taken: HM Brig Rover - When taken: 10 Nov 1812 - Where taken: off Bordeaux - Date received: 31 Dec 1812 - From what ship: HM Ship-of-the-Line Northumberland - Born: Maryland - Age: 27 - Discharged on 4 Mar 1813 and sent to Chatham on HM Ship-of-the-Line Queen.

Williamson, David - Seaman - Number: 1418 - Prize Name: Zephyr, prize of Privateer Rattlesnake - Ship type: MV - How taken: HM Frigate Surveillante - When taken: 6 Jan 1814 - Where taken: Bay of Biscay - Date received: 1 Mar 1814 - From what ship: HMS Helicone - Born: Philadelphia - Age: 25 - Discharged on 28

Apr 1814 and sent to Chatham on HM Sloop Favorite.

Williamson, George J. - Seaman - Number: 582 - How taken: Sent into custody from Farham Rendezvous - Date received: 26 Jan 1813 - From what ship: Farham Rendezvous - Born: Philadelphia - Age: 24 - Discharged on 11 Mar 1813 and sent to Chatham on HM Store Ship Abundance.

Williamson, John - Seaman - Number: 673 - How taken: Gave himself up from HM Frigate Ulysses - Date received: 10 Feb 1813 - From what ship: HM Brig Electra - Born: Boston - Age: 34 - Discharged on 6 Mar 1813 and sent to Chatham on HM Ship-of-the-Line Cornwall.

Williamson, John - Seaman - Number: 1258 - Prize Name: Dart - Ship type: P - How taken: HM Frigate Niger & HMS Fortunee - Where taken: at sea - Date received: 19 Dec 1813 - From what ship: HMS Fortunee - Born: Boston - Age: 37 - Discharged on 26 Dec 1813 and sent to Chatham on HM Ship of-the-Line Diomede.

Williamson, William - Seaman - Number: 1455 - Prize Name: Soley - Ship type: MV - How taken: HM Brig Derment - When taken: 21 Jan 1814 - Where taken: at sea - Date received: 9 Apr 1814 - From what ship: HM Ship-of-the-Line Leyden - Born: Salem - Age: 39 - Discharged on 28 Apr 1814 and sent to Chatham on HM Store Ship Weymouth.

Williams, Moses - Seaman - Number: 1453 - Prize Name: Lord Ponsonbe, prize of the Privateer Diomede - Ship type: MV - How taken: HM Brig Sappho - When taken: 27 Feb 1814 - Where taken: at sea - Date received: 31 May 1814 - From what ship: HM Ship-of-the-Line Valiant - Born: Connecticut - Age: 21 - Race: Mulatto - Discharged on 28 Apr 1814 and sent to Chatham on HM Store Ship Weymouth.

Willingsworth, Jeffery - Seaman - Number: 349 - Prize Name: Experiment - Ship type: MV - How taken: HM Brig Rover - When taken: 10 Nov 1812 - Where taken: off Bordeaux - Date received: 31 Dec 1812 - From what ship: HM Ship-of-the-Line Northumberland - Born: Lancaster - Age: 48 - Race: Mulatto - Discharged on 4 Mar 1813 and sent to Chatham on HM Ship-of-the-Line Queen.

Wilmer, Isaac - Seaman - Number: 167 - Prize Name: Baltimore - Ship type: P - How taken: HM Transport Diadem - When taken: 7 Oct 1812 - Where taken: S. Andera - Date received: 3 Nov 1812 San Antonio - From what ship: HMS Diadem - Born: Rock Hall, MD - Age: 27 - Discharged on 19 Feb 1813 and sent to Chatham on HM Store Ship Dromedary.

Wilson, Charles - Seaman - Number: 975 - How taken: Gave himself up from HM Ship-of-the-Line Caledonia - Date received: 31 Jul 1813 - From what ship: HMS Leviathan - Born: Rhode Island - Age: 46 - Race: Mulatto - Discharged on 13 Aug 1813 and sent to Chatham on HM Brig Cadmus.

Wilson, Daniel - Seaman - Number: 745 - How taken: Gave himself up from HM Guardship Royal William - Date received: 21 Mar 1813 - From what ship: HMS Royal William - Born: Boston - Age: 29 - Discharged on 28 Mar 1813 and sent to Chatham on HM Store Ship Seaphis.

Wilson, David (alias John Perry) - Seaman - Number: 826 - How taken: Gave himself up from HM Ship-of-the-Line Tigre - Date received: 19 May 1813 - From what ship: HMS Tigre - Born: North Yarmouth, MA - Age: 28 - Discharged on 10 Jun 1813 and sent to Chatham on HM Frigate Arethusa.

Wilson, Francis - Seaman - Number: 1358 - How taken: Gave himself up from HM Transport Dover - Date received: 29 Jan 1814 - From what ship: HMS Dover - Born: New York - Age: 31 - Discharged on 13 Feb 1814 and sent to Chatham on HM Transport Malabar No. 352.

Wilson, John - Seaman - Number: 1495 - Prize Name: Traveler, prize of the Privateer Surprise - Ship type: MV - How taken: HM Schooner Canso - When taken: 14 May 1814 - Where taken: at sea - Date received: 1 Jun 1814 - From what ship: HMS Canso - Born: Baltimore - Age: 23 - Discharged on 2 Jun 1814 and sent to Plymouth on HMS Growler.

Wilson, John - Seaman - Number: 699 - Prize Name: Calcutta - Ship type: East Indian Ship - How taken: Two Brothers, privateer of Guernsey - When taken: 23 Nov 1812 - Where taken: at sea - Date received: 24 Feb 1813 - From what ship: HM Brig Escort - Born: Stralsund, Sweden - Age: 21 - Discharged on 6 Mar 1813 and sent to Chatham on HMS Frigate Alexandria.

Wilson, Nathaniel - Passenger - Number: 977 - Ship type: MV - How taken: HM Sloop Volentaire - When taken: Unknown - Where taken: at sea - Date received: 31 Jul 1813 - From what ship: HM Ship-of-the-Line Leviathan - Born: Warren, MA - Age: 24 - Discharged on 13 Aug 1813 and sent to Chatham on HM Brig

Cadmus.

Wilson, Peter - Seaman - Number: 327 - Prize Name: Independence - Ship type: MV - How taken: HM Frigate Medusa - When taken: 9 Nov 1812 - Where taken: off St. Sebastian - Date received: 31 Dec 1812 - From what ship: HM Ship-of-the-Line Northumberland - Born: New York - Age: 42 - Race: Colored - Discharged on 4 Mar 1813 and sent to Chatham on HM Ship-of-the-Line Queen.

Wilson, Robert - Seaman - Number: 1117 - How taken: Gave himself up from HM Ship-of-the-Line America - Date received: 5 Oct 1813 - From what ship: HM Ship-of-the-Line Achille - Born: Connecticut - Age: 45 - Discharged on 17 Oct 1813 and sent to Chatham on HM Store Ship Weymouth.

Wilson, Robert G. - Passenger - Number: 1371 - Prize Name: Atlante - Ship type: MV - How taken: HM Ship-of-the-Line Swiftsure - Where taken: off Corsica - Date received: 4 Feb 1814 - From what ship: HM Frigate Bombay - Born: New York - Age: 25 - Discharged on 13 Feb 1814 and sent to Chatham on HM Transport Malabar No. 352.

Wilson, Thomas - Seaman - Number: 907 - How taken: Gave himself up from HMS Service - Date received: 24 Jun 1813 - From what ship: HM Frigate Unicorn - Born: Alexandria - Age: 34 - Discharged on 2 Jul 1813 and sent to Chatham on HM Frigate Tribune.

Wilson, William - Seaman - Number: 325 - Prize Name: Independence - Ship type: MV - How taken: HM Frigate Medusa - When taken: 9 Nov 1812 - Where taken: off St. Sebastian - Date received: 31 Dec 1812 - From what ship: HM Ship-of-the-Line Northumberland - Born: Richmond - Age: 21 - Discharged on 4 Mar 1813 and sent to Chatham on HM Ship-of-the-Line Queen.

Wilson, William - Seaman - Number: 30 - Prize Name: USRM Cutter James Madison - Ship type: MW - How taken: HM Frigate Barbadoes - When taken: 22 Aug 1812 - Where taken: at sea - Date received: 12 Oct 1812 San Antonio - From what ship: HM Ship-of-the-Line Polyphemus - Born: Providence - Age: 30 - Discharged on 19 Feb 1813 and sent to Chatham on HM Frigate Ulysses.

Wilson, William - Seaman - Number: 1350 - How taken: Gave himself up from HMS Muros - Date received: 26 Jan 1814 - From what ship: HMS Muros - Born: Boston - Age: 32 - Discharged on 13 Feb 1814 and sent to Chatham on HM Transport Malabar No. 352.

Wilson, William - Seaman - Number: 764 - How taken: Gave himself up from HM Ship-of-the-Line Blake - Date received: 1 Apr 1813 - From what ship: HMS Blake - Born: Ackton, England - Age: 28 - Discharged on 3 Apr 1813 and sent to Chatham on HM Transport Chatham.

Winberg, John - Seaman - Number: 81 - Prize Name: HM Ship-of-the-Line Ganges - Ship type: MW - How taken: Detained by Court of Admiralty - When taken: 31 Jul 1812 - Where taken: Portsmouth harbor - Date received: 16 Oct 1812 San Antonio - From what ship: HM Ship-of-the-Line Ganges - Born: Edenton, NC - Age: 32 - Discharged on 19 Feb 1813 and sent to Chatham on HM Frigate Ulysses.

Winchester, Richard - Seaman - Number: 1193 - Prize Name: Fire Fly of Gloucester - Ship type: MV - How taken: HM Frigate Revolutionnaire - When taken: 19 Oct 1813 - Where taken: at sea - Date received: 9 Nov 1813 - From what ship: HMS Revolutionaire - Born: Salem - Age: 22 - Discharged on 26 Dec 1813 and sent to Chatham on HM Ship of-the-Line Diomede.

Windford, Charles - Seaman - Number: 753 - How taken: Gave himself up from HM Ship-of-the-Line Sterling Castle - Date received: 28 Mar 1813 - From what ship: HMS Sterling Castle - Born: New York - Age: 31 - Race: Colored - Discharged on 28 Mar 1813 and sent to Chatham on HM Store Ship Seaphis.

Wingate, David - Seaman - Number: 1027 - How taken: Gave himself up from HM Battery Gorgon - Date received: 7 Sep 1813 - From what ship: HM Frigate Unicorn - Born: New Hampshire - Age: 23 - Discharged on 21 Sep 1813 and sent to Chatham on HM Ship-of-the-Line Queen.

Winslow, William - Carpenter's Mate - Number: 454 - Prize Name: Sword Fish - Ship type: P - How taken: HM Ship-of-the-Line Elephant - When taken: 28 Dec 1812 - Where taken: at sea - Date received: 14 Jan 1813 - From what ship: HMS Elephant - Born: Salem - Age: 26 - Discharged on 11 Mar 1813 and sent to Chatham on HM Store Ship Abundance.

Wise, John - Seaman - Number: 1070 - How taken: Gave himself up from HM Ship-of-the-Line Implacable - Date received: 30 Sep 1813 - From what ship: HM Frigate Andromeda - Born: New York - Age: 26 - Race:

Mulatto - Discharged on 17 Oct 1813 and sent to Chatham on HM Store Ship Weymouth.

Wise, John - Seaman - Number: 174 - Prize Name: Baltimore - Ship type: P - How taken: HM Transport Diadem - When taken: 7 Oct 1812 - Where taken: S. Andera - Date received: 3 Nov 1812 San Antonio - From what ship: HMS Diadem - Born: Altona - Age: 35 - Discharged on 19 Feb 1813 and sent to Chatham on HM Store Ship Dromedary.

Witherell, Charles - Seaman - Number: 1414 - Prize Name: Amity, prize of the Privateer Prince Neuchatel - Ship type: MV - How taken: HM Brig Achates - When taken: 22 Dec 1813 - Where taken: Bay of Biscay - Date received: 1 Mar 1814 - From what ship: HMS Helicone - Born: Massachusetts - Age: 28 - Discharged on 28 Apr 1814 and sent to Chatham on HM Sloop Favorite.

Withers, Edward - Seaman - Number: 26 - Prize Name: USRM Cutter James Madison - Ship type: MW - How taken: HM Frigate Barbadoes - When taken: 22 Aug 1812 - Where taken: at sea - Date received: 12 Oct 1812 San Antonio - From what ship: HM Ship-of-the-Line Polyphemus - Born: Berke, GA - Age: 23 - Discharged on 6 Mar 1813 and sent to Chatham on HM Ship-of-the-Line Cornwall.

Withiem, Burrel - Boatswain's Mate - Number: 1304 - Prize Name: Growler - Ship type: P - How taken: HM Brig Electra - When taken: 7 Jul 1813 - Where taken: off St. Johns - Date received: 22 Dec 1813 - From what ship: HM Frigate Hyperion - Born: Marblehead - Age: 23 - Discharged on 26 Dec 1813 and sent to Chatham on HMS Frigate Nemesis.

Witlock, Sidney B. - 2nd Mate - Number: 403 - Prize Name: Empress - Ship type: MV - How taken: HM Brig Rover - When taken: 30 Nov 1812 - Where taken: at sea - Date received: 10 Jan 1813 - From what ship: HM Guardship Royal William - Born: New York - Age: 19 - Discharged on 6 Mar 1813 and sent to Chatham on HM Ship-of-the-Line Cornwall.

Wolfe, Andre - Seaman - Number: 591 - How taken: Gave himself up from HM Ship-of-the-Line Mars - Date received: 31 Jan 1813 - From what ship: HMS Mars - Born: Virginia or Baltimore - Age: 28 - Discharged on 11 Mar 1813 and sent to Chatham on HM Store Ship Abundance.

Wood, George - Steward - Number: 450 - Prize Name: Sword Fish - Ship type: P - How taken: HM Ship-of-the-Line Elephant - When taken: 28 Dec 1812 - Where taken: at sea - Date received: 14 Jan 1813 - From what ship: HMS Elephant - Age: 23 - Discharged on 11 Mar 1813 and sent to Chatham on HM Store Ship Abundance.

Wood, Thomas - Cook - Number: 74 - Prize Name: HM Frigate Leonidas - Ship type: MW - How taken: Detained by Court of Admiralty - When taken: 31 Jul 1812 - Where taken: Portsmouth harbor - Date received: 16 Oct 1812 San Antonio - From what ship: HM Frigate Leonidas - Born: Newcastle, England - Age: 55 - Released on 25 Oct 1812 for being a British subject.

Woodard, Elijah - Seaman - Number: 356 - Prize Name: Argus - Ship type: MV - How taken: Fancy, cutter - When taken: 19 Dec 1812 - Where taken: Bay of Biscay - Date received: 31 Dec 1812 - From what ship: HM Ship-of-the-Line Northumberland - Born: Massachusetts - Age: 24 - Discharged on 4 Mar 1813 and sent to Chatham on HM Ship-of-the-Line Queen.

Woods, Charles - Seaman - Number: 500 - Prize Name: Sword Fish - Ship type: P - How taken: HM Ship-of-the-Line Elephant - When taken: 28 Dec 1812 - Where taken: at sea - Date received: 14 Jan 1813 - From what ship: HMS Elephant - Born: Gloucester - Age: 44 - Discharged on 11 Mar 1813 and sent to Chatham on HM Store Ship Abundance.

Woods, William - Seaman - Number: 481 - Prize Name: Sword Fish - Ship type: P - How taken: HM Ship-of-the-Line Elephant - When taken: 28 Dec 1812 - Where taken: at sea - Date received: 14 Jan 1813 - From what ship: HMS Elephant - Born: New York - Age: 26 - Discharged on 11 Mar 1813 and sent to Chatham on HM Store Ship Abundance.

Woods, William - Seaman - Number: 1028 - How taken: Gave himself up from HM Ship-of-the-Line Ocean - Date received: 7 Sep 1813 - From what ship: HM Frigate Unicorn - Born: Philadelphia - Age: 22 - Discharged on 21 Sep 1813 and sent to Chatham on HM Ship-of-the-Line Queen.

Works, Alfred - Seaman - Number: 1487 - Prize Name: Indian Lass, prize of Privateer Grand Turk - Ship type: MV - How taken: HM Transport Akbar - When taken: 20 Apr 1814 - Where taken: at sea - Date received: 28 May 1814 - From what ship: HMS Akbar - Born: Connecticut - Age: 21 - Discharged on 2 Jun 1814 and sent to

Plymouth on HMS Growler.

Wright, Edward - Seaman - Number: 1126 - How taken: Gave himself up from HM Ship-of-the-Line Achille - Date received: 5 Oct 1813 - From what ship: HM Ship-of-the-Line Achille - Born: New Jersey - Age: 25 - Race: Black - Discharged on 17 Oct 1813 and sent to Chatham on HM Transport Malabar No. 352.

Wright, John - Seaman - Number: 509 - How taken: Gave himself up from HM Frigate Stag - Date received: 20 Jan 1813 - From what ship: HMS Stag - Born: Stafford, VA - Age: 32 - Race: Colored - Discharged on 11 Mar 1813 and sent to Chatham on HM Store Ship Abundance.

Wright, Samuel - Seaman - Number: 379 - How taken: Gave himself up from HM Sloop Comet - When taken: 25 Nov 1812 - Date received: 4 Jan 1813 - From what ship: HMS Muros - Born: Rhode Island - Age: 23 - Race: Black - Discharged on 4 Mar 1813 and sent to Chatham on HM Ship-of-the-Line Queen.

Wright, Thomas - Supercargo - Number: 522 - Prize Name: Expectation - Ship type: MV - How taken: HMS Butain - When taken: 17 Dec 1812 - Where taken: at sea - Date received: 25 Jan 1813 - From what ship: HM Ship-of-the-Line Queen - Born: Philadelphia - Age: 27 - Discharged on 29 Jan 1813 and sent to Odiham on parole.

Wyatt, Joseph - Seaman - Number: 54 - Prize Name: Fame, prize of Privateer Decatur - Ship type: MV - How taken: HM Ship-of-the-Line Polyphemus - When taken: 13 Sep 1812 - Where taken: at sea - Date received: 12 Oct 1812 San Antonio - From what ship: HM Ship-of-the-Line Polyphemus - Born: Ipswich - Age: 18 - Discharged on 19 Feb 1813 and sent to Chatham on HM Frigate Ulysses.

Yale, Nathaniel - Cook - Number: 406 - Prize Name: Hope - Ship type: MV - How taken: HMS Pleasant - When taken: 13 Dec 1812 - Where taken: at sea - Date received: 10 Jan 1813 - From what ship: HM Guardship Royal William - Born: Prince George County - Age: 27 - Discharged on 6 Mar 1813 and sent to Chatham on HM Ship-of-the-Line Cornwall.

Yatton, James - Seaman - Number: 1133 - How taken: Gave himself up from HM Frigate Cerberus - Date received: 6 Oct 1813 - From what ship: HM Sloop Kingfisher - Born: New Hampshire - Age: 30 - Discharged on 17 Oct 1813 and sent to Chatham on HM Transport Malabar No. 352.

York, Nathaniel - Seaman - Number: 496 - Prize Name: Sword Fish - Ship type: P - How taken: HM Ship-of-the-Line Elephant - When taken: 28 Dec 1812 - Where taken: at sea - Date received: 14 Jan 1813 - From what ship: HMS Elephant - Born: Exeter, NH - Age: 50 - Discharged on 11 Mar 1813 and sent to Chatham on HM Store Ship Abundance.

Young, Eben. R. - Seaman - Number: 193 - Prize Name: Felix - Ship type: MV - How taken: HM Frigate Indefatigable - When taken: 13 Nov 1812 - Where taken: Portsmouth harbor - Date received: 22 Nov 1812 - From what ship: HM Frigate Gladiator - Born: Nantucket - Age: 32 - Discharged on 19 Feb 1813 and sent to Chatham on HM Store Ship Dromedary.

Young, Moses - Seaman - Number: 131 - How taken: Gave himself up from HM Ship-of-the-Line Ruby - When taken: 30 Aug 1812 - Date received: 29 Oct 1812 - From what ship: HM Ship-of-the-Line Ardent - Born: Chatham, MA - Age: 23 - Discharged on 19 Feb 1813 and sent to Chatham on HM Store Ship Dromedary.

Young, William - Seaman - Number: 420 - Prize Name: Rising Sun - Ship type: MV - How taken: HMS Defense - When taken: 6 Dec 1812 - Where taken: at sea - Date received: 10 Jan 1813 - From what ship: HM Guardship Royal William - Born: Richmond - Age: 23 - Discharged on 6 Mar 1813 and sent to Chatham on HMS Frigate Alexandria.

Younger, Lewis - Seaman - Number: 1051 - How taken: Gave himself up from HM Ship-of-the-Line Pompee - Date received: 14 Sep 1813 - From what ship: HM Brig Savage - Born: Gloucester - Age: 27 - Discharged on 29 Sep 1813 and sent to Chatham on HM Transport Chatham.

Younger, Lewis - Seaman - Number: 1077 - How taken: Gave himself up from HM Ship-of-the-Line Pompee - Date received: 1 Oct 1813 - From what ship: HM Ship-of-the-Line Barham - Born: Massachusetts - Age: 27 - Discharged on 17 Oct 1813 and sent to Chatham on HM Store Ship Weymouth.

Numeric listing by prisoner number

1	Paine, Joshua		48	Dorr, Edward
2	Williams, Gaspar		49	Harris, Abraham Harris
3	Bearbere, John		50	Cruff, William
4	James, John		51	Valentine, Andrew
5	Tufts, Elazar		52	Reed, John
6	Even, Peter		53	Hackett, Theophilus
7	Ellis, John		54	Wyatt, Joseph
8	Osborne, Thomas		55	Stacey, William
9	Daymen, Celeb		56	Newby, John
10	Hutchins, William		57	Pickett, Richard
11	Clements, Henry		58	Homan, Joseph
12	Harding, Joseph		59	Salkins, Nathaniel
13	Helmen, John		60	Harris, David
14	Drinkwater, Andrew		61	Lakeman, Samuel
15	Blankinship, Charles		62	Oaks, George
16	Pegale, Amos		63	Antonie, John
17	Alley, Jacob		64	Rainars, Nicholas
18	Anderson, Andrew		65	Spurling, William
19	Anderson, Oliver		66	Hecox, George
20	Hughes, Peter		67	Weilright, Joseph
21	Gard, Gelab		68	Dominico, Joseph
22	Senholm, Jacob		69	Geely, Joseph
23	Davis, Nathan		70	Lessingwell, Benajah
24	Petingale, John		71	Coffin, Daniel G.
25	Petterson, John		72	Christy, William
26	Withers, Edward		73	Manning, Thomas
27	Johnson, Andrew		74	Wood, Thomas
28	Martin, Jonathan		75	Goodwin, John
29	Baker, Henry		76	Weir, Frederick
30	Wilson, William		77	Dennis, Thomas
31	Henricks, Jeremiah		78	Patterson, Samuel
32	George, Thomas		79	Baxter, John
33	Mumery, James		80	Tinkham, Seth
34	Chase, Samuel		81	Winberg, John
35	Coleman, Daniel		82	Gage, Zachariah
36	Harris, William		83	Harlow, Sylvanus
37	Palm, William		84	Hutchings, Joseph
38	Gebers, Henry		85	Orn, James
39	Stone, John		86	Plasted, William
40	Carebo, Henry		87	White, John W.
41	Turner, John		88	Boston, Robert
42	Nuting, Charles		89	Eldridge, Samuel
43	Gale, Oliver		90	Ward, James
44	Pault, Beloner		91	Nelson, Samuel A.
45	Quasir, Zeph.		92	De Soder, Bastian
46	Smith, Henry		93	Spinney, Nathaniel
47	Tristram, Joseph		94	Titcomb, John H.

95	Kennedy, Henry	144	Gibson, William
96	Henderson, Benjamin	145	Kenner, John Downing
97	Chase, Eliphalet	146	Chidsey, Abraham
98	Jackson, John	147	Smith, Thomas R.
99	Ricker, Samuel	148	Cooper, James
100	Wells, Thomas	149	Powers, William
101	Berry, John	150	Barry, John
102	Holt, Simeon	151	Dennis, Thomas
103	Anderson, John	152	Clark, Jean
104	Preston, William	153	Clark, Aaron
105	Clarke, Alexander	154	Rust, John
106	Bachelor, Benjamin	155	Davis, Michael
107	Hoyt, Ichabod	156	Lock, Nathaniel
108	Pratt, Asa	157	Swett, Moses
109	Long, Ebenezer	158	Dyer, Ezekiel
110	Moore, Daniel	159	McIntire, Alexander
111	Stoss, Samuel	160	Walter, George
112	Coggins, George	161	Anthony, Luke
113	Nichols, Samuel	162	Mitchel, John
114	Whittlebank, Edward	163	Allen, Barnes
115	Peterson, Peter	164	Stevenson, Thomas
116	Parish, Samuel	165	Webb, Stephen
117	Procter, Edward	166	Meyer, Peter
118	Reynolds, Caleb	167	Wilmer, Isaac
119	Seely, James	168	Prendewell, James
120	Barton, Elijah	169	Rogers, William
121	Clerk, William	170	Lambleson, Edward
122	Hastings, Johnson	171	Chattles, John
123	Chaple, Samuel	172	Meyer, John
124	Pedrick, Joseph	173	Johnson, Andre
125	Randolf, Exum	174	Wise, John
126	Stephens, Thomas	175	Metcalf, William
127	Orr, Levi	176	Hanson, William
128	Williams, Darius	177	Tull, John
129	Cummings, Edward	178	Lindholm, Nicholas
130	Congdon, Henry	179	Lucas, Benjamin
131	Young, Moses	180	Miller, John Jacob
132	Jeffreys, Philip	181	Cunningham, John
133	Dowling, Peter	182	Coates, S. Murray
134	Leighton, Otis	183	Smith, William Pitt
135	Haywood, John	184	Nutt, Adam
136	Hunt, Dudley	185	Veazey, Edward
137	George, Peter	186	Coleman, Christian
138	Smith, William	187	Merpaux, Brian
139	Treadwell, Alpheus	188	Andrey, Alexander
140	Arve, Joseph	189	Chastante, John Baptist
141	Brooks, Edward	190	Parditt, Charles
142	Peters, John	191	Dobbs, Jeremiah
143	Nutrash, Ezekiel	192	Robinson, Charles

193	Young, Eben. R.		242	Gifford, Francis
194	Tanner, John		243	Porter, Nathaniel
195	Robinson, Edward		244	McNeal, Alexander
196	Barnett, John		245	Scaff, Nicholas
197	Clark, John D.		246	Beckner, Henry
198	Ball, John		247	Fisher, Archibald
199	Page, John		248	Hurd, William
200	Richards, George		249	Williams, Henry
201	Welch, William		250	Allen, Peter
202	Murray, Nathaniel		251	Kirk, Thomas
203	Gall, William		252	Dennis, John
204	Macrombie, Elijah		253	Sholes, Giles
205	Armstrong, Thomas		254	Weed, Ebenezer
206	Williams, David		255	Lippen, Stephen
207	Moore, Thomas		256	Platt, John Henry
208	Oilson, Andrew		257	Myers, Jacob
209	Riley, Jonathan		258	Weeks, George
210	Prince, William		259	Lebon, Philip
211	Nillim, George		260	Lewis, John
212	Magrath, James		261	Hill, George
213	Boyd, John		262	Burke, James
214	Armstrong, Elijah		263	Salyear, John
215	Knight, Ira		264	Inberg, Gabriel
216	Godsoe, William		265	Villodas, Matias
217	Stanwood, Timothy		266	Hyatt, William
218	Davis, Daniel		267	Legere, Joseph
219	Pendleton, Asa		268	Bessey, Jonas
220	Nichols, John		269	Conklin, Enoch
221	Davis, John		270	Rogers, Abithan
222	Record, Frederick		271	Bowie, Henry
223	Robson, Robert		272	Brewster, Sturges
224	Lawson, Mathew		273	Cocks, Isaac
225	Branham, Stephen		274	Distouet, John
226	Coullay, Andrew		275	Coffin, Edward
227	Waterman, William		276	Clark, George
228	Cornelius, John		277	Trought, Joseph
229	Powell, Richard		278	Fuster, Peter
230	Greenfield, William		279	Johnson, Samuel
231	Andson, John		280	Guillider, William
232	Giles, John		281	Ludlow, John
233	Stephens, Michael		282	Bramblecome, David
234	Jones, William		283	Pearson, Samuel
235	Cowen, William		284	Knapp, Walker
236	Liddle, John		285	Walker, James
237	Cross, John		286	Turner, Samuel
238	Matheuron, Andrew		287	Dussing, Caesar
239	White, Thomas		288	Latish, Joseph
240	Delancey, William		289	Scott, James
241	Williams, Charles		290	Evans, John

291	Wicks, Littleton	340	Johnson, Robert
292	Beckett, William	341	Murray, John
293	Osburne, Peter	342	Mills, John
294	Johnson, Henry	343	Packard, William
295	Scanel, Cornele	344	Smith, Jacob
296	West, John	345	Fate, Thomas
297	Higgins, William	346	Anthony, John
298	Watkins, Frederick	347	Williamson, Charles
299	Williams, Alexander	348	Benner, Lewis
300	Swanton, John	349	Willingsworth, Jeffery
301	Pattingale, Enoch	350	Ellis, John
302	Brightman, Joseph	351	Lynch, William
303	Gifford, Barry	352	Tewell, Samuel
304	White, Aldin	353	Harris, James
305	Underwood, John Francis	354	Dunn, Hezekiah
306	Williams, George (1)	355	Drybourgh, James
307	Williams, George (2)	356	Woodard, Elijah
308	Allen, Elihu	357	Flower, Artemas
309	Freeman, Alkine	358	Green, Samuel
310	Green John	359	Gibbons, Andrew
311	McKenzie, John	360	Arthur, Alexander
312	Jane, Joseph	361	Joseph, Michael
313	Manuel, Joseph	362	Howland, William
314	Hazard, Thomas	363	Rippaviere, John
315	Hathaway, William N.	364	Jacobson, Jacob
316	Riley, William	365	Andermach, John
317	Pearce, Edward	366	Caroline, Tobias
318	Cunningham, John	367	Coleman, Jonathan
319	Floyd, James	368	Macey, George
320	Pardoe, John	369	Pincham, Stephen B.
321	Lenderson, Henry	370	Steward, Alexander
322	Conway, Samuel	371	Myrick, William
323	Beachman, George	372	Allen, William
324	James, Peter	373	DeBuck, Cornelius
325	Wilson, William	374	Lescombe, John
326	Fontain, Isaac	375	Russel, William
327	Wilson, Peter	376	Thompson, John
328	Farrel, John	377	Williams, Josiah
329	Lewis, John	378	Halden, Lewis
330	Garrison, John	379	Wright, Samuel
331	Van Donveer, Peter	380	Gunnell, William
332	Manuel, John	381	Nald, John
333	Francoise, James	382	Raymond, George
334	Davis, John	383	Thomas, John
335	Harris, George	384	Grey, Charles
336	Brown, John	385	Bocalt, John
337	Carr, Richard	386	Rowe, John
338	Kerban, Thomas	387	Chute, Davis
339	Tolson, Jeremy	388	Burns, George

389	Moore, Jacob		438	Morrison, James
390	Fron, Frederick		439	Manning, Enoch
391	Smith, William		440	Anderton, Samuel
392	Chandler, Henry		441	Bridges, Philip
393	Lind, Andrew		442	Garney, Thomas
394	Saunders, Thomas		443	Prentess, Christian
395	Roundey, Jonathan		444	White, John W.
396	Vine, William		445	White, Benjamin
397	Sabrian, James		446	Reed, H. W.
398	Jameson, George		447	Ingalls, Samuel
399	Moore, Michael		448	Cloutman, George
400	Roberts, Josiah		449	Allen, Henry
401	Sanderson, John		450	Wood, George
402	Johnson, David		451	Setchell, Samuel
403	Witlock, Sidney B.		452	Doevall, Francis
404	Haley, Thomas		453	Duxey, Peter
405	Michael, Peter		454	Middleton, Reuben
406	Yale, Nathaniel		454	Winslow, William
407	Whithmore, William		456	Lear, Alexander
408	Coleman, John		457	Strong, William
409	Brown, John		458	Booder, Jacob
410	Shepherd, Daniel		459	Ellwell, Jonathan
411	Hitchi, John		460	Lawrence, Peter
412	Jerry, Daniel		461	Black, John
413	Hook, Aaron		462	Francis, Frederick
414	Wade, Otis		463	Lambert, John
415	Howlen, Samuel		464	Roberts, George
416	Benster, John		465	Fernandes, Anthony
417	Carr, Samuel		466	Mills, Henry
418	Evans, Thomas		467	Cox, Daniel
419	Smith, Thomas R.		468	Small, Thomas
420	Young, William		469	Roper, John
421	Dawson, John		470	Saunders, Thomas
422	Hartford, James		471	Kile, George
423	Snider, Lewis		472	Jeremy, Stephen
424	Chambers, Charles		473	Griffin, James
425	Black, William		474	Lee, Richard
426	Wallace, William		475	Grant, Christian
427	Grose, Daniel		476	Anderton, Thomas
428	Baptiste, John		477	Nowland, Andrew
429	Douglas, Thomas		478	Brimmer, John
430	Castor, Charles		479	Johnson, Andrew
431	Cobb, Samuel		480	Merriday, John
432	Wickwall, Joseph		481	Woods, William
433	Perkins, Henry		482	Shot, John
434	Phellibrown, William		483	Hamson, Henry
435	Butler, George		484	March, Joseph
436	Drew, William		485	Bessom, Nicholas
437	Cloutman, Robert		486	Wells, Moses

487	Stephens, David	536	Simpson, James
488	Innes, John	537	Halmore, Henry Michael
489	Kenny, George	538	Thomas, John
490	Asten, John	539	Hardy, John
491	Dalliber, James	540	Parsons, Joseph
492	Whitchouse, Lewis	541	Southard, Samuel W.
493	Dudley, Ephraim	542	Lassier, Florence
494	Carrel, Michael	543	Jones, Cabal
495	Parsons, Andrew	544	Brady, Jason
496	York, Nathaniel	545	Hill, William
497	Sandbach, Richard	546	Barber, John
498	Williams, John	547	Simonds, Joseph
499	Parsons, Thomas	548	Mitchell, Francis
500	Woods, Charles	549	Thompson, John
501	Nowland, Andrew	550	Ellis, William
502	Evans, John	551	Eaton, John
503	Bartlett, George B.	552	Hall, Thomas
504	Bagley, Moses	553	Boyd, John
505	Anderson, Joseph	554	Longwell, Amos
506	Corban, Daniel	555	Copasses, Matthew
507	Conner, Jesse	556	Ford, M. Benjamin
508	Buddington, Asa	557	Berry, Joseph
509	Wright, John	558	Hill, Pompey
510	Roberts, Robert	559	Lee, Samuel
511	Branton, James	560	Williams, Benjamin
512	Turnbull, James	561	Oberville, Michael
513	Johnson, Oliver	562	Combs, Thomas
514	Staggs, Henry	563	Pearce, Emanuel
515	Thompson, Joseph	564	Hurtt, Samuel
516	Marks, Peter	565	Stevenson, Thaddeus
517	Clarke, Arnold	566	Hobdyke, John
518	Ferguson, John T.	567	Vorge, James
519	Martel, Stephen	568	Lamon, James
520	Berry, Joseph	569	Bayman, James
521	George, Isaac	570	Howard, Henry
522	Wright, Thomas	571	Douglas, Charles
523	Anderson, Thomas	572	Powell, Elijah
524	Baker, John	573	Chambers, Joseph
525	Earl, Maris	574	Duhard, Thomas
526	Beazley, Edward	575	Swain, Thomas
527	Benjamin, James	576	Labbas, John
528	Bitters, John	577	Gardiner, Amboy
529	Townsend, Solomon	578	Lockett, Thomas R.
530	Colwell, John	579	Nunns, William
531	Beans, Samuel	580	Robinson, Edward
532	Esperaza, Jacob	581	Carmon, James
533	Mountain, Emanuel	582	Williamson, George J.
534	John, Richard J.	583	Johnson, Samuel
535	Ingraham, Peter	584	Ludlow, William

585	Guillider, William		634	Males, Joseph
586	Dunslan, John		635	Johnson, Frederick
587	Comtis, Thomas		636	Smith, Caesar
588	Dildure, Samuel		637	Scribner, William
589	Urey, Peter		638	Dairs, William
590	Saunders, Thomas		639	Williams, Joseph
591	Wolfe, Andre		640	Beck, William
592	Farris, Jacob		641	Mitchell, Thomas
593	Conaway, Samuel		642	Price, John
594	White, John W.		643	Hawley, Frederick
595	Bean, Amos		644	Simmons, Daniel
596	Alexander, Robert		645	Saunderson, William
597	Silsby, Nathaniel		646	Robinson, Benjamin
598	Turner, Samuel		647	Davies, George
599	Sheppard, Joseph		648	Munro, John
600	Blake, Charles		649	Martin, John J.
601	Gudlers, George		650	Best, John
602	Noonan, William		651	Francis, Prince
603	Kerhow, Samuel		652	Barrett, James
604	Paulfrey, Richard		653	Burnham, David
605	Stephens, Trey		654	Ferriers, George
606	Shed, William		655	Lothrop, James
607	Bistie, Asaph		656	Hogan, William
608	Huff, Charles		657	Gammell, Samuel
609	Bray, Zachariah		658	Carney, William
610	Richardson, Perry		659	Hedley, John
611	Rogers, James		660	Spratt, Thomas
612	Green, Henry		661	Osgood, David
613	Deistel, John		662	Church, Richard
614	Sidebottom, John		663	Lister, Louis
615	Poole, John		664	Brown, William
616	McDonald, John		665	Marshall, Francis
617	Patterson, Peter		666	Liddle, Morris
618	Johnson, William		667	Shipley, Charles
619	Benjamin, Joseph		668	Rennell, States William
620	Gilbert, Thomas		669	Johnson, William
621	Babb, Benjamin		670	Conway, Andrew
622	Church, Benjamin		671	Syway, Peter
623	Covelle, Ephraim		672	Johnson 2nd, John
624	Hooseman, John		673	Williamson, John
625	Brainard, Richard		674	Philbrook, Bartholomew
626	Smith, John		675	Mason, John
627	Attwood, Edward		676	Richardson, Samuel
628	Brenton, York		677	Burnham, John
629	Albet, John		678	Muncy, Daniel
630	Bark, David		679	Sands, Thomas
631	Booth, Thomas		680	Parsons, Joseph
632	Denham, William		681	Severence, George
633	Williams, George		682	Taylor, William

683	Goodwin, Jonas B.		732	Tullock, William
684	Doliber, Joseph		733	Delenne, John
685	Shirly, Phares		734	Haven, Thomas
686	Broden, Norman		735	Patten, Joseph
687	Homan, John		736	Parsons, Rufus
688	Homan, Jonas		737	Phillips, William
689	George, William U.		738	Clarke, Samuel
690	Pearson, Thomas		739	Goold, John
691	Cole, Hutchinson A.		740	Paul, Jacob
692	Miller, George		741	Wedgewood, James
693	Smith, Henry		742	Tarlton, Thomas P.
694	Miner, Benjamin F.		743	Lewis, John
695	Stanton, George A.		744	Deselva, Manuel
696	Sterns, Henry		745	Wilson, Daniel
697	Sibert, Frederick		746	Rollo, William
698	Borwer, Frederick		747	Hutchens, Townsend
699	Wilson, John		748	Thomas, Francis
700	Anderson, Aaron		749	Sutton, Prince
701	Caban, Samuel		750	Heyden, William
702	Tafe, Henry		751	George, William Main
703	Rosignol, James		752	David, Daniel
704	Scofield, Wells		753	Windford, Charles
705	Moore, Benjamin		754	Payne, Ransom
706	McMichael, James		755	Bennymans, John
707	Blazon, Stephen		756	Lockerby, William
708	Palmer, Peter		757	Benjamin, Polasskie
709	Arnold, William		760	Stacy, Perry
710	Cooper, Alfred		761	Hitchcock, Elior
711	Morris, George		762	Albro, George
712	Tucker, Samuel		763	Burton, William
713	Lake, Noah		764	Wilson, William
714	Caine, Enoch		765	Smith, Thomas
715	Kanady, James		766	Moulden, William
716	Parse, William		767	Roberts, James
717	Lapham, Cushion		768	Fitch, William
718	Dennison, Lawson		768	Peters, William
719	Orn, W. B.		769	Fredrick, John
720	Tink, Henry		769	Watkins, George
721	Coon, John		770	Campbell, John
722	Deventer, William		771	Wickhm, Thaddeus
723	Patterson, John		772	Mallan, James
724	Lint, Joseph		773	Johnson, Edward
725	Veney, George		774	Trask, William
726	Peake, John W.		775	Clifford, States Laurence
727	Morris, Louis		776	Edwards, John
728	Merle, John		777	Morell, John
729	Martin, Henry		778	Simms, Clement
730	Sparrow, John		779	Morrison, John
731	Jewett, Theodore		780	Gilpin, John

781	Thomas, Charles		830	Hobart, George
782	Pope, William		831	Bensin, Leven
783	Brown, Elisha		832	Berry, John
784	Hall, William		833	Pearce, Thomas
785	Pinkham, Allen		834	Hughes, John
786	Thompson, William		835	Reed, James
787	Chipp, Charles		836	Mukelroey, Samuel
788	Busson, John		837	Parker, George
789	Wiley, David		838	Dews, William
790	Gray, Thomas		839	Palmer, William
791	Russel, Joseph		840	Estery, William
792	Weton, William		841	Row, Simon
793	Williams, James		842	Steward, John
794	Corvet, Isaac		843	West, George
795	Banta, John		844	Harris, William
796	Davis, James		845	Forest, James
797	Flood, John		846	Eaton, James
798	Jackson, William		847	Benn, William
799	Lee, Edward		848	Johnston, Thomas
800	Heywood, John		849	Richards, Edward
801	Edwards, Isaac		850	Avery, Charles
802	Howell, John		851	McWaren, Nathaniel
803	Clay, John		852	Robin, Thomas
804	Butler, Thomas		853	Kemp, James
805	Smith, Thomas		854	Frazier, John
806	Bumpus, Asa		855	Welch, John
807	Jackson, Allison		856	Cody, James
808	Potter, Jacob		857	Anderson, James
809	Merkell, John		858	Spencer, Leonard
810	Perkins, William		859	Calder, John H.
811	Harrison, James		860	Churchill, Timothy
812	Henton, John		861	Sutton, John
813	Barrett, George		862	Morslender, Ruben
814	Spencer, John		863	Quackenbush, William
815	Bryant, Moses		864	Kerhon, Abraham
816	Francis, John		865	Mars, George
817	Cool, John		866	Hill, Josiah
818	Davis, Francis		867	Ludlow, Ruben
819	Stephenson, George		868	Byer, Peter
820	Poole, Richard		869	Cadwell, Samuel
821	Anderson, Henry		870	Bartholf, Nicholas
822	Inghram, John		871	Small, George D.
823	Isdale, James		872	Nicolas, John
824	Posey, Valentine		873	Sampson, Jacob
825	Stenchcombe, George		874	Hill, Ephraim
826	Wilson, David		875	Jones, James
827	Ron, Richard		876	Donaldson, Josiah
828	Clark, William		877	Bishop, Edward
829	Benson, Jonas		878	Hubbard, Alfred

879	Cole, William		928	Fyans, Joseph
880	Thompson, Nathaniel		929	Moore, John
881	Lopaus, William		930	Williams, John (1)
882	Bartis, John		931	Allen, William
883	Chase, Nathaniel		932	Peckham, Hazard
884	Atwood, Thomas		933	Richards, John
885	Beecher, William Palmer		934	Hardiman, John
886	Pain, James		935	Follingsby, William
887	Muller, William		936	Howateer, Henry
888	Sillock, Amos		937	Rogers, Francis
889	Taylor, James		938	Brown, Seth
890	Waterman, John		939	Miller, John
891	Morris, James		940	Lawson, Laurence
892	Allen, John		941	Williams, John (2)
893	Lemmon, Henry		942	Cole, William
894	Gibbs, Daniel		943	Baurs, Francis
895	Hull, Edward		944	Maris, Yeace
896	Voohis, James		945	Carter, Thomas
897	Ashfield, Henry		946	Dunn, James
898	Cappel, John		947	Fields, Alexander
899	King, John		948	Rectout, John J.
900	Blackman, Moses		949	Williams, Thomas
901	Dunn, David		950	White, William
902	Bailey, John		951	McGee, Robert
903	Tiffs, Joseph		952	Voight, Henry
903	Vangostet, Cato		953	Armstrong, Thomas
905	Brill, John		954	Southwick, Israel
906	Corta, John		955	Nicholson, Charles
907	Wilson, Thomas		956	Thompson, James
908	Tyler, Lewis		957	Codding, Caleb
909	Nichols, William		958	Brown, Joseph
910	Cole, Stephen		959	Brooks, John
911	West, Henry		960	Richardson, John
912	Reed, John		961	Webster, William
913	Lowdie, Samuel		962	Walden, James
914	Roderick, Frank		963	Brown, Mark
915	Clark, Abraham D.		964	Guier, Andrew
916	Herle, Hiram		965	White, Charles
917	Lumburger, Jacob		966	Gourley, William
918	White, John		967	Porter, Samuel
919	Botrell, John		968	Frobes, Robert
920	Dennis, Thomas		969	Siters, John
921	Ingesoll, Abraham		970	Williams, Thomas
922	Lawson, James		971	Morrison, William
923	Briggs, Bolon		972	Williams, George
924	Fuller, John		973	Steward, John
925	Mathews, Lewis		974	Brown, James
926	Christie, John		975	Wilson, Charles
927	Taylor, Peter		976	Necylnenee, Peter

977	Wilson, Nathaniel		1026	Campbell, Nicholas
978	Thomas, William		1027	Wingate, David
979	McIver, John		1028	Woods, William
980	Campbell, James		1029	Mathews, John
981	Taylor, Joseph		1030	Stone, Henry
982	Simpson, John		1031	Lowe, Thomas
983	Wickham, Ezekiel		1032	Thayer, James
984	Reed, Joseph		1033	Jordon, Artemas
985	Bowker, Nicholas		1034	Stanford, James
986	Rogers, Epinetus		1035	Powell, Joseph
987	Nickel, Hugh		1036	Reid, John (1)
988	Saunders, James		1037	Reid, John (2)
989	Milson, William		1038	Henry, Henry
990	Penny, James		1039	Hadley, George
991	Eastlake, James		1040	Horner, John
992	McIntyre, William		1041	Branch, Anthony
993	Lindsay, Nathaniel		1042	Clawson, John
994	Lee, Nathaniel		1043	Butts, Joseph W.
995	Davis, George		1044	Williams, Robert
996	Alfos, Robert		1045	Brown, Isaac
997	Watson, James		1046	Heady, Linsay
998	Huse, Ebenezer		1047	Brown, George
999	Rogers, Samuel		1048	Foster, Thomas
1000	Chase, Nathaniel		1049	Osbourne, Lewis
1001	Griswold, Josiah		1050	Williams, Robert
1002	Lemon, Nicholas. C.		1051	Younger, Lewis
1003	Mason, Joseph J.		1052	Potter, John
1004	Dunham, Daniel		1053	Quarterman, William
1005	Swain, James		1054	Thaley, Abraham
1006	Nichols, Thomas		1055	Jamison, George
1007	Folga, Noah		1056	Duncan, Edward
1008	Hussy, Edward		1057	Baker, Robert
1009	Bunker, Thomas		1058	Thompson, George
1010	Mash, Hercules		1059	Smith, John
1011	Thuel, Briste		1060	Gardner, James
1012	Osmond, David		1061	Burke, Charles
1013	Williams, Stephen		1062	Stage, William
1014	Weeden, Richard		1063	Boyd, Stephen
1015	Johnston, Richard		1064	Raymond, Caleb
1016	Clark, John		1065	Davidson, John
1017	Lamboard, Thomas		1066	Dunvall, N. D.
1018	James, John		1067	Lamb, Jack
1019	Williams, John		1068	Stegman, Christian
1020	Cock, Isaac		1069	Elfe, James
1021	Dunham, John		1070	Wise, John
1022	Caldwell, Abraham		1071	Sheriff, Benjamin P.
1023	Noble, Charles		1072	Henry, Henry
1024	Owen, Burden		1073	Hadley, George
1025	Boyd, John		1074	Horner, John

1075	Branch, Anthony		1124	Thornton, David
1076	Clawson, John		1125	Tucker, Nathaniel
1077	Younger, Lewis		1126	Wright, Edward
1078	Potter, John		1127	Fry, Thomas
1079	Quarterman, William		1128	Gardner, George
1080	Thaley, Abraham		1129	Copland, Thomas
1081	Jamison, George		1130	Penn, John
1082	Duncan, Edward		1131	Stanton, James
1083	Baker, Robert		1132	McPinnis, Barney
1084	Thompson, George		1133	Yatton, James
1085	Smith, John		1134	Vincent, Henry
1086	Gardner, James		1135	Pitts, Charles
1087	Stage, William		1136	Peckham, Isaac
1088	Boyd, Stephen		1137	Wilky, Timothy
1089	Raymond, Caleb		1138	Barber, Major
1090	Davidson, John		1139	Boyd, Andrew
1091	Duvall, N. D.		1140	Williams, Thomas
1092	Lamb, Jack		1141	Bakeman, Ely
1093	Stegman, Christian		1142	Warner, John
1094	Elfe, James		1143	McKenzie, William
1095	Moore, James		1144	Bissel, Samuel W.
1096	Sheridan, Henry		1145	Nowell, Stephen C.
1097	Peter, Thomas		1146	Fleming, Alexander
1098	Adzard, Thomas		1147	Hardwood, William
1099	Hubbard, William		1148	Phillips, Benjamin
1100	Lucas, Martin		1149	Rankins, William
1101	Thomas, Moses		1150	Ross, John
1102	Foler, Frederic		1151	Cottril, Henry
1103	Glower, Samuel		1152	Redman, David
1104	Watson, Daniel		1153	Lynch, Thomas
1105	Richardson, Robert		1154	McCumber, Job
1106	Smith, Henry		1155	Ranlot, John
1107	Bates, Joseph		1156	Brown, Thomas
1108	Hubbart, Joseph		1157	Walker, Benjamin
1109	Davis, Osborn		1158	Tombinson, George William
1110	Heaton, Henry		1159	Barry, Peter
1111	Harvey, Peter		1160	Walker, William
1112	Tolele, Garret		1161	Caesar, James
1113	Robinson, John		1162	Buffington, James
1114	Andrews (1), John		1163	Putnam, Allen
1115	Perry, Samuel		1164	Johnson, Henry
1116	Andrews (2), John		1165	Monion, Jean
1117	Wilson, Robert		1166	Frazier, William
1118	Green, George		1167	Brown, Francis
1119	Valentine, John		1168	Perry, William
1120	Meyers, James		1169	Hurd, Abel
1121	Leonard, Robert		1170	Hoskins, John
1122	Coffin, James		1171	Darrow, Aaron
1123	Manley, Rudolph		1172	McAlpin, Cornelius

1173	Price, Carlton	1222	Hart, William
1174	Newell, Paul	1223	Keys, Zenas
1175	Jones, Anthony	1224	Nicholas, James
1176	Anderson, John	1225	Malcomb, Alexander
1177	Cooper, Thomas	1226	Powell, Joseph
1178	de Peyster, Arent S.	1227	James, John
1179	Lee, John	1228	Meath, Solomon
1180	Peadon, William	1229	Ferris, James
1181	Reid, William	1230	Johnson, John
1182	Patterson, William	1231	Francis, John
1183	Chase, Oliver	1232	Holstein, Richard
1184	Roweth, William	1233	Primas, James
1185	Melvin, John	1234	Jackson, William
1186	Elwell, Benjamin	1235	Johnson, Easton
1187	Rowe, William	1236	Smith, John
1188	Pearson, Samuel	1237	Skinner, Ebenezer
1189	Tar, Caleb	1238	Pinkham, David
1190	Allen, David	1239	Kingbutton, John
1191	Millet, Joseph	1240	Roberton, William
1192	Somes, Stephen	1241	Porter, Charel
1193	Winchester, Richard	1242	Clabby, Martin John
1194	Williams, William	1243	Staples, James
1195	Day, John	1244	Johnson, Robert
1196	Dempsey, Daniel	1245	Hill, John
1197	Elwell, Benjamin (2)	1246	Shilling, Naurish
1198	Shaw, Henry	1247	Davis, Nicolas
1199	Heater, William	1248	Day, Thomas
1200	Jeffers, Henry	1249	Collins, George
1201	Dyson, Henry	1250	Rogers, Abraham
1202	Hatton, Peter	1251	Frederick, John
1203	Turner, Samuel	1252	Johnson, John
1204	Head, James	1253	Mills, John
1205	Pain, Clement	1254	Harding, J. Christian
1206	Sawyers, Jonathan	1255	Tardy, Edward
1207	Cook, Silvanus	1256	Tardy, Anthony
1208	Parsons, John	1257	Kinnard, Charles
1209	Harman, Isaac	1258	Williamson, John
1210	Hutchings, William	1259	Miller, James
1211	Brown, John	1260	Green, Beckwith
1212	Webb, Nathan	1261	Tipp, Nicholas
1213	Truman, John	1262	Polles, Edward
1214	Davis, John	1263	Smith, Thomas
1215	Selman, Francis, G.	1264	Murray, Charles
1216	Brown, Joseph	1265	Camsure, Dominick
1217	Gatchell, John G.	1266	Miramon, Roch
1218	Odion, John B. H.	1267	Smith, John
1219	Euston, Ephraim	1268	Clawson, Henry
1220	Emmerson, David	1269	Harvey, Peter
1221	Kraft, Michael	1270	Watson, David

1271	Ward, Thomas		1320	Grush, Nathaniel
1272	Lane, James		1321	Harvey, Anthony
1273	Baron, Peter		1322	Davy, William
1274	Jourdan, John		1323	Beckwith, James
1275	La Roche, John B.		1324	Thompson, James
1276	Lupy, Marcus		1325	Sutton, John
1277	Buel, Jeremiah		1326	Gyer, Henry
1278	Mallet, William		1327	Unknown American
1279	Thorning, Thomas		1328	Plur, Henry
1280	Bartlett, Robert		1329	Coffin, Joseph
1281	Jones, Thomas		1330	Brown, Sawyer
1282	Manning, Burrel		1331	Pitt, William
1283	Joseph, Michael		1332	Hill, James
1284	Bowden, William		1333	Conon, John
1285	Smith, John		1334	Lavan, Thomas
1286	Widger, Joseph		1335	Jones, Thomas
1287	Russell, William		1336	Rotan, John
1288	Smith, Benjamin		1337	Angel, Silvester
1289	Nicholson, Jonas		1338	Marlborough, Francis
1290	Deering, William F,		1339	Read, William
1291	Crocker, Silvanus		1340	McInley, James
1292	Mirrel, Samuel B.		1341	Hunt, Samuel
1293	Aldridge, Richard		1342	Kennedy, Dennis
1294	Griffin, William		1343	Marlow, Owen
1295	Lewis, Peter		1344	Hill, Jeremiah
1296	Benjamin, Everard		1345	Wadsworth, Daniel
1297	Rust, John		1346	Horbert, Christopher
1298	Smith, Jeremiah		1347	Cooper, Thomas
1299	Orne, Josiah		1348	Caleb, Lewis
1300	Bowden, Benjamin		1349	Molley, Peter
1301	Garrett, Simon T.		1350	Wilson, William
1302	Tishure, Samuel		1351	James, John
1303	Roundy, Thomas		1352	Curtis, Enoch
1304	Withiem, Burrel		1353	Middleton, John
1305	Florence, Charles		1354	Cannon, Thomas
1306	Hooper, Joseph A.		1355	Jones, Theodore
1307	Farman, William		1356	Burke, John
1308	Deverence, Benjamin		1357	Butler, Thomas
1309	Rust, John		1358	Wilson, Francis
1310	Roundy, Jeremiah		1359	Thayer, Laban
1311	Tucker, Andrew		1360	Norton, David
1312	Pitman, Benjamin		1361	Dean, Jeremiah B.
1313	Smith, John		1362	Barnes, William Smith
1314	Coombs, Michael		1363	Green, William
1315	Foster, George		1364	Lane, William
1316	Bradford, George		1365	Penfield, John
1317	Shaw, Samuel		1366	Neal, John
1318	Tucker, Nathaniel		1367	Boyd, Jesse
1319	Ellingwood, William H.		1368	Dixon, Peter

1369	Dibble, Zachariah	1418	Williamson, David
1370	Crow, John	1419	Keen, Joseph
1371	Wilson, Robert G.	1420	Harris, Simon
1372	Fiske, Lebairs	1421	Pritchard, Israel
1373	King, Peter	1422	Selman, John
1374	Thomas, James	1423	Bird, David
1375	Gotier, Charles	1424	Harvey, Joseph
1376	Howel, William	1425	Carter, Henry
1377	Manly, David	1426	Merrel, Enoch
1378	Downs, William	1427	Harris, Ebenezer
1379	Downs, John	1428	Watson, William
1380	Smith, J. W.	1429	Conner, Michael
1381	Vincent, Stephen Stiles	1430	Hill, Daniel
1381	Williams, Charles	1431	Campbell, William
1382	Livingston, Henry	1432	Debarize, Francis John
1383	Harding, William	1433	Perott, John Francis
1384	Anderson, John	1434	Gravelee, Joseph
1385	Coffin, Edward	1435	Chauvel, Thomas
1386	Platt, Daniel	1436	Demerie, Ephraim
1387	Thomas, John	1437	Grosette, John M.
1388	Simonds, Henry	1438	Tuttle, Joseph
1390	Mids, Michael	1439	Carter, Enoch
1391	Demalo, Francis	1440	Bloomdose, John
1392	Staford, John	1441	Hubbell, James
1393	Jackson, Lederick	1442	Ewell, Edward
1394	Taylor, George	1443	Gardner, Jerry
1395	Brickum, James	1444	Conklin, Smith
1396	Thomas, John	1445	Harris, John
1397	Murray, David	1446	Mains, John
1398	Bartlett, John	1447	Johnson, Samuel B.
1399	Sterns, Joseph	1448	Port, John
1400	Petterson, Andrew	1449	Swainton, John
1401	Morrel, Jacob	1450	Arnold, Benjamin
1402	Baisley, Abraham	1451	Shoe, Barnard
1403	Scott, Henry	1452	Doosenberry, Richard
1404	Bassett, William	1453	Williams, Moses
1405	Manley, David	1454	Rust, John
1406	Harding, William	1455	Williamson, William
1407	Williams, Charles	1456	Boston, John
1408	Calleb, Lewis	1457	Smith, William B.
1409	Tillman, John	1458	Jardine, Samuel
1410	Spurr, Elijah	1459	Smith, Thomas
1411	Diemar, John	1460	Touche, Pierre
1412	Smith, Richard	1461	Schafft, Carl Hendrick
1413	Gregory, George	1462	Hemonder, Peter
1414	Witherell, Charles	1463	Lebour, Francois
1415	Walker, Seth	1464	Roger, Christopher
1416	Plumber, William Reed	1465	Le Goff, Herve
1417	Modre, John	1466	Le Petit, John Baptiste

Portsmouth Depot

1467	Gavot, Henry		1489	Stone, Samuel
1468	Lucas, Francois Rene		1490	Hall, Thomas
1469	Boite, Julius Pierre		1491	Church, William
1470	Hubi, Pierre M.		1492	Simmons, John
1471	Marest, Charles		1493	Thompson, John
1472	Ferlecque, Augustine		1494	Flinn, Pearce
1473	Emery, Adrien D.		1495	Wilson, John
1474	Schiffky, Jacobus Orgen		1496	Harder, John
1475	Liemo, Frederick		1497	Long, James
1476	Lerocque, Olivier		1498	Brown, William
1477	Le Saut, Jacques		1499	Dunning, William
1478	Thompson, Laurence		1500	Peal, Andrea
1479	Meirell, John		1501	Wadsworth, Thomas
1480	Charles, Philip		1502	Davenport, Russel
1481	Barford, James		1503	Mingalls, Robert
1482	Hoyt, James		1504	Lake, Daniel
1483	Chaon, Daniel		1505	Lewis, John
1484	Knox, John		1506	McGreen, John
1485	White, Philip		1507	Symes, John
1486	Holland, James		1508	Richardson, John
1487	Works, Alfred		1509	Crawford, George
1488	Basset, Gorum			

Crew listing

Unknown ship

Adzard, Thomas
Albet, John
Albro, George
Alexander, Robert
Alfos, Robert
Anderson, James
Anderson, John
Anderson, Joseph
Andrews, John (1)
Andrews, John (2)
Angel, Silvester
Armstrong, Elijah
Armstrong, Thomas
Attwood, Edward
Avery, Charles
Babb, Benjamin
Baker, Robert
Ball, John
Banta, John
Barford, James
Bark, David
Barnett, John
Barrett, George
Barrett, James
Barry, Peter
Bates, Joseph
Bean, Amos
Beck, William
Beckwith, James
Benjamin, Joseph
Benn, William
Bennymans, John
Bensin, Leven
Benson, Jonas
Berry, John
Best, John
Bocalt, John
Booth, Thomas
Boyd, Jesse
Boyd, John
Brainard, Richard
Branch, Anthony
Branton, James
Brenton, York
Brightman, Joseph
Brooks, John
Brown, Elisha

Unknown ship

Brown, George
Brown, Isaac
Brown, James
Brown, John
Brown, Joseph
Brown, Mark
Brown, Sawyer
Brown, Thomas
Brown, William
Bryant, Moses
Buddington, Asa
Bumpus, Asa
Burke, Charles
Burke, John
Burnham, David
Burnham, John
Burton, William
Butler, George
Butler, Thomas
Butts, Joseph W.
Caine, Enoch
Caldwell, Abraham
Caleb, Lewis (1)
Caleb, Lewis (2)
Campbell, James
Campbell, Nicholas
Cannon, Thomas
Carmon, James
Carney, William
Caroline, Tobias
Caesar, James
Chaon, Daniel
Charles, Philip
Chase, Oliver
Church, Benjamin
Church, Richard
Chute, Davis
Clark, John D.
Clark, William
Clarke, Arnold
Clawson, John
Clay, John
Clifford, States Laurence
Cock, Isaac
Codding, Caleb
Cody, James
Coffin, Joseph

138 Portsmouth Depot

Unknown ship

- Coleman, John
- Coleman, Jonathan
- Collins, George
- Comtis, Thomas
- Congdon, Henry
- Conklin, Smith
- Conaway, Samuel
- Conner, Jesse
- Conon, John
- Conway, Andrew
- Coon, John
- Cooper, Thomas
- Copland, Thomas
- Corban, Daniel
- Corvet, Isaac
- Cottril, Henry
- Covelle, Ephraim
- Crawford, George
- Crow, John
- Cummings, Edward
- Curtis, Enoch
- Dairs, William
- Darrow, Aaron
- Davenport, Russel
- David, Daniel
- Davies, George
- Davis, Daniel
- Davis, George
- Davis, John
- Davis, Nicolas
- Davis, Osborn
- Davy, William
- Dawson, John
- Day, Thomas
- Denham, William
- Dennison, Lawson
- Deventer, William
- Dews, William
- Dibble, Zachariah
- Dildure, Samuel
- Dixon, Peter
- Dowling, Peter
- Drew, William
- Duncan, Edward
- Dunham, John
- Dunn, James
- Dunning, William
- Dunslan, John
- Eaton, James

Unknown ship

- Edwards, Isaac
- Edwards, John
- Estery, William
- Farris, Jacob
- Ferguson, John T.
- Ferriers, George
- Ferris, James
- Fields, Alexander
- Flood, John
- Foler, Frederic
- Forest, James
- Foster, Thomas
- Francis, John
- Francis, Prince
- Frazier, John
- Frobes, Robert
- Fry, Thomas
- Gammell, Samuel
- Gardner, George
- Gardner, James
- Gardner, Jerry
- George, William Main
- Gilbert, Thomas
- Gilpin, John
- Glower, Samuel
- Gourley, William
- Gray, Thomas
- Green, George
- Grey, Charles
- Guier, Andrew
- Guillider, William
- Gunnell, William
- Gyer, Henry
- Halden, Lewis
- Hall, William
- Harris, John
- Harris, William
- Harrison, James
- Hartford, James
- Harvey, Peter
- Hawley, Frederick
- Heady, Linsay
- Heater, William
- Heaton, Henry
- Hedley, John
- Henton, John
- Heyden, William
- Heywood, John
- Hill, James

Unknown ship		Unknown ship	
	Hitchcock, Elior		Lister, Louis
	Hobart, George		Lothrop, James
	Hogan, William		Lowdie, Samuel
	Hooseman, John		Lowe, Thomas
	Horbert, Christopher		Lucas, Martin
	Hoskins, John		Ludlow, John
	Howell, John		Ludlow, William
	Hoyt, James		Lynch, Thomas
	Hubbard, William		Magrath, James
	Hubbart, Joseph		Mains, John
	Hughes, John		Males, Joseph
	Hurd, Abel		Mallan, James
	Hutchens, Townsend		Marks, Peter
	Jackson, Allison		Marlborough, Francis
	Jackson, William		Marshal, Francis
	James, John		Martin, Henry
	Jamison, George		Martin, John J.
	Jardine, Samuel		Mason, John
	Jefferys, Philip		Mathews, John
	Johnson 2nd, John		McAlpin, Cornelius
	Johnson, Easton		McCumber, Job
	Johnson, Edward		McDonald, John
	Johnson, Frederick		McGee, Robert
	Johnson, John		McGreen, John
	Johnson, Oliver		McInley, James
	Johnson, Samuel		McIver, John
	Johnson, Samuel B.		McPinnis, Barney
	Johnson, William		McWaren, Nathaniel
	Johnston, Thomas		Meath, Solomon
	Jones, Anthony		Melvin, John
	Jones, Theodore		Merkell, John
	Jones, Thomas		Merle, John
	Jordon, Artemas		Meyers, James
	Kanady, James		Middleton, John
	Kemp, James		Mills, John
	Kerban, Thomas		Mingalls, Robert
	Knight, Ira		Mitchell, Thomas
	Knox, John		Molley, Peter
	Lake, Daniel		Moore, James
	Lake, Noah		Morell, John
	Lamboard, Thomas		Morris, Louis
	Lane, William		Morrison, John
	Lavan, Thomas		Morrison, William
	Lee, Edward		Moulden, William
	Lee, John		Mukelroey, Samuel
	Leighton, Otis		Muller, William
	Lewis, John		Munro, John
	Liddle, Morris		Nald, John
	Lint, Joseph		Neal, John

140 Portsmouth Depot

Unknown ship

- Necylnenee, Peter
- Newell, Paul
- Nichols, John
- Nicholson, Charles
- Nillim, George
- Noble, Charles
- Nutt, Adam
- Oilson, Andrew
- Orn, W. B.
- Orr, Levi
- Osbourne, Lewis
- Osgood, David
- Owen, Burden
- Packard, William
- Pain, James
- Palmer, William
- Parditt, Charles
- Parish, Samuel
- Parker, George
- Parse, William
- Patterson, John
- Patterson, Peter
- Patterson, William
- Payne, Ransom
- Peadon, William
- Peake, John W.
- Peal, Andrea
- Pearce, Edward
- Pearce, Thomas
- Pendleton, Asa
- Penfield, John
- Penn, John
- Perkins, Henry
- Perkins, William
- Perry, Samuel
- Perry, William
- Peter, Thomas
- Peterson, Peter
- Phellibrown, William
- Philbrook, Bartholomew
- Phillips, Benjamin
- Pinkham, Allen
- Pitt, William
- Plur, Henry
- Poole, John
- Pope, William
- Porter, Samuel
- Potter, Jacob
- Potter, John

Unknown ship

- Powell, Joseph
- Price, Carlton
- Price, John
- Prince, William
- Quarterman, William
- Rankins, William
- Ranlot, John
- Raymond, George
- Read, William
- Rectout, John J.
- Reid, John (1)
- Redman, David
- Reed, James
- Reid, John (2)
- Reid, William
- Rennell, States William
- Richards, Edward
- Richardson, John
- Richardson, Robert
- Richardson, Samuel
- Riley, William
- Roberts, James
- Roberts, Robert
- Robin, Thomas
- Robinson, Benjamin
- Robinson, Edward
- Robinson, John
- Rollo, William
- Ron, Richard
- Ross, John
- Row, Simon
- Rowe, John
- Roweth, William
- Russel, Joseph
- Saunders, Thomas
- Saunderson, William
- Scribner, William
- Sheridan, Henry
- Sheriff, Benjamin P.
- Shilling, Naurish
- Shipley, Charles
- Sidebottom, John
- Sillock, Amos
- Silsby, Nathaniel
- Simmons, Daniel
- Simms, Clement
- Simpson, John
- Siters, John
- Smith, Caesar

Unknown ship	Smith, Henry	Unknown ship	Watkins, George
	Smith, John		Watson, Daniel
	Smith, Thomas		Webster, William
	Smith, William Pitt		Welch, John
	Southwick, Israel		West, George
	Sparrow, John		Weton, William
	Spencer, John		White, Charles
	Spratt, Thomas		White, John W.
	Stacy, Perry		Whithmore, William
	Staggs, Henry		Whittlebank, Edward
	Stanford, James		Wickham, Ezekiel
	Stanton, James		Wickhm, Thaddeus
	Stanwood, Timothy		Wickwall, Joseph
	Steward, John		Wiley, David
	Stone, Henry		Williams, Darius
	Sutton, John		Williams, George
	Sutton, Prince		Williams, James
	Symes, John		Williams, John
	Syway, Peter		Williams, Joseph
	Taylor, James		Williams, Josiah
	Taylor, Joseph		Williams, Robert
	Thaley, Abraham		Williams, Thomas
	Thayer, James		Williamson, George J.
	Thomas, Charles		Williamson, John
	Thomas, Francis		Wilson, Charles
	Thomas, John		Wilson, Daniel
	Thomas, Moses		Wilson, David
	Thomas, William		Wilson, Francis
	Thompson, George		Wilson, Nathaniel
	Thompson, James		Wilson, Robert
	Thompson, Joseph		Wilson, Thomas
	Thompson, William		Wilson, William
	Thompson, James		Windford, Charles
	Tink, Henry		Wingate, David
	Tolele, Garret		Wise, John
	Tombinson, George William		Wolfe, Andre
			Woods, William
	Trask, William		Wright, Edward
	Turnbull, James		Wright, John
	Turner, Samuel		Wright, Samuel
	Tyler, Lewis		Yatton, James
	Unknown American		Young, Moses
	Urey, Peter		Younger, Lewis
	Valentine, John		
	Voight, Henry	Agnes	Tillman, John
	Wadsworth, Thomas		
	Walden, James	Ajax	Anderson, Henry
	Walker, Benjamin		Cool, John
	Walker, William		Davis, Francis

Ajax	Inghram, John	Baltimore	Allen, Barnes
	Isdale, James		Andrey, Alexander
	Poole, Richard		Anthony, Luke
	Stephenson, George		Chastante, John Baptist
			Chattles, John
Amity	Witherell, Charles		Coates, S. Murray
			Coleman, Christian
Antelope	Andson, John		Cunningham, John
	Beckner, Henry		Hanson, William
	Bowie, Henry		Johnson, Andre
	Branham, Stephen		Lambleson, Edward
	Brewster, Sturges		Lindholm, Nicholas
	Cocks, Isaac		Lucas, Benjamin
	Conklin, Enoch		Merpaux, Brian
	Cornelius, John		Metcalf, William
	Coullay, Andrew		Meyer, John
	Cowen, William		Meyer, Peter
	Cross, John		Miller, John Jacob
	Delancey, William		Mitchel, John
	Fisher, Archibald		Prendewell, James
	Gifford, Francis		Rogers, William
	Giles, John		Stevenson, Thomas
	Greenfield, William		Tull, John
	Hurd, William		Veazey, Edward
	Jones, William		Walter, George
	Lawson, Mathew		Webb, Stephen
	Liddle, John		Wilmer, Isaac
	Matheuron, Andrew		Wise, John
	McNeal, Alexander		
	Porter, Nathaniel	Benjamin	Goodwin, Jonas B.
	Powell, Richard		Severence, George
	Record, Frederick		Taylor, William
	Robson, Robert		
	Rogers, Abithan	Benjamin Franklin	Reed, John
	Scaff, Nicholas		
	Stephens, Michael	Blockade	Griswold, Josiah
	Waterman, William		West, Henry
	White, Thomas		
	Williams, Charles	Brilliant	Fiske, Lebairs
			King, Peter
Argus	Arthur, Alexander		Thomas, James
	Drybourgh, James		
	Flower, Artemas	British South	Clabby, Martin John
	Gibbons, Andrew	Sea Whaler	Hill, John
	Green, Samuel		Holstein, Richard
	Joseph, Michael		Jackson, William
	Woodard, Elijah		Johnson, Robert
Atlante	Wilson, Robert G.		Kingbutton, John
			Pinkham, David

Ship	Name
British South Sea Whaler	Porter, Charel
	Primas, James
	Roberton, William
	Skinner, Eben.ezer
	Staples, James
Brunswick	Baptiste, John
	Black, William
	Chambers, Charles
	Grose, Daniel
	Snider, Lewis
	Wallace, William
Bunker Hill	Boite, Julius Pierre
	Emery, Adrien D.
	Ferlecque, Augustine
	Gavot, Henry
	Hemonder, Peter
	Hubi, Pierre M.
	Le Goff, Herve
	Le Petit, John Baptiste
	Le Saut, Jacques
	Lebour, Francois
	Lerocque, Olivier
	Liemo, Frederick
	Lucas, Francois Rene
	Marest, Charles
	Roger, Christopher
	Schafft, Carl Hendrick
	Schiffky, Jacobus Orgen
	Thompson, Laurence
	Touche, Pierre
Calcutta	Anderson, Aaron
	Borwer, Frederick
	Caban, Samuel
	Cole, Hutchinson A.
	Miller, George
	Miner, Benjamin F.
	Pearson, Thomas
	Sibert, Frederick
	Smith, Henry
Calcutta	Stanton, George A.
	Sterns, Henry
	Tafe, Henry
	Wilson, John
Calmar	Rotan, John
Casta	Russel, William
Caster	Williams, David
Catherine	Allen, Elihu
	Freeman, Alkine
	Gifford, Barry
	Underwood, John Francis
	White, Aldin
	Williams, George (1)
	Williams, George (2)
Ceres	Johnson, Robert
Charles	Higgins, William
	Pearson, Samuel
Colombes	Meirell, John
Columbia	Berry, Joseph
	Castor, Charles
	Douglas, Thomas
	George, Isaac
	Martel, Stephen
Cornelia	Bramblecome, David
Dart	Camsure, Dominick
	Clarke, Samuel
	Delenne, John
	Deselva, Manuel
	Frederick, John
	Goold, John
	Green, Beckwith
	Harding, J. Christian
	Haven, Thomas
	Jewett, Theodore
	Johnson, John
	Kinnard, Charles
	Lewis, John
	Miller, James
Dart	Mills, John
	Miramon, Roch
	Murray, Charles
	Parsons, Rufus
	Patten, Joseph
	Paul, Jacob
	Phillips, William
	Polles, Edward
	Rogers, Abraham
	Smith, Thomas

Dart	Tardy, Anthony	Elbridge Gerry	Shaw, Samuel
	Tardy, Edward		Sterns, Joseph
	Tarlton, Thomas P.		Thayer, Laban
	Tipp, Nicholas		Truman, John
	Tullock, William		Turner, Samuel
	Wedgewood, James		Webb, Nathan
	Williamson, John		
		Elizabeth	Scott, James
Decatur	Nichols, William		
	Roderick, Frank	Elizabeth, tender	Davis, James
Diamond	Dyer, Ezekiel	Elk	Tolson, Jeremy
	Lock, Nathaniel		
	Swett, Moses	Empress	Burns, George
			Chandler, Henry
Diana	Antonie, John		Fron, Frederick
	Dominico, Joseph		Jameson, George
	Geely, Joseph		Johnson, David
	Harris, David		Lind, Andrew
	Hecox, George		Moore, Jacob
	Homan, Joseph		Moore, Michael
	Lakeman, Samuel		Roberts, Josiah
	Oaks, George		Roundey, Jonathan
	Pickett, Richard		Sabrian, James
	Rainars, Nicholas		Sanderson, John
	Salkins, Nathaniel		Saunders, Thomas
	Spurling, William		Smith, William
	Weilright, Joseph		Vine, William
			Witlock, Sidney B.
Dick	Bishop, Edward		
	Busson, John	Endeavour	Tucker, Samuel
	Chipp, Charles		Swainton, John
	Donaldson, Josiah		
		Enterprize	Thompson, John
Elbridge Gerry	Barnes, William Smith		
	Bartlett, John	Expectation	Anderson, Thomas
	Bradford, George		Baker, John
	Brown, John		Beans, Samuel
	Cook, Silvanus		Beazley, Edward
	Davis, John		Benjamin, James
	Dean, Jeremiah B.		Bitters, John
	Green, William		Colwell, John
	Harman, Isaac		Earl, Maris
	Head, James		Esperaza, Jacob
	Hutchings, William		Halmore, Henry Michael
	Norton, David		Hardy, John
	Pain, Clement		Ingraham, Peter
	Parsons, John		John, Richard J.
	Sawyers, Jonathan		Mountain, Emanuel

Expectation	Simpson, James	Felix	Dobbs, Jeremiah
	Thomas, John		Riley, Jonathan
	Townsend, Solomon		Robinson, Charles
	Wright, Thomas		Tanner, John
			Young, Eben. R.
Experiment	Anthony, John		
	Benner, Lewis	Fire Fly of Gloucester	Allen, David
	Cobb, Samuel		Day, John
	Dunn, Hezekiah		Dempsey, Daniel
	Ellis, John		Elwell, Benjamin (1)
	Fate, Thomas		Elwell, Benjamin (2)
	Harris, James		Millet, Joseph
	Lynch, William		Pearson, Samuel
	Murray, John		Rowe, William
	Smith, Jacob		Shaw, Henry
	Tewell, Samuel		Somes, Stephen
	Williamson, Charles		Tar, Caleb
	Willingsworth, Jeffery		Williams, William
			Winchester, Richard
Falcon	Hadley, George		
	Henry, Henry	Fly	Dyson, Henry
	Horner, John		Hatton, Peter
	Powell, Joseph		
		Friendship	Walker, James
Fame	Bunker, Thomas		
	Clark, John	General Kemp	Diemar, John
	Dunham, Daniel		Smith, Richard
	Folga, Noah		Spurr, Elijah
Fame	Hussy, Edward		
	Johnston, Richard	Gleamer	Corta, John
	Mash, Hercules		
	Nichols, Thomas	Gossypium	Arve, Joseph
	Osmond, David		Brooks, Edward
	Swain, James		George, Peter
	Thuel, Briste		Haywood, John
	Weeden, Richard		Hunt, Dudley
	Williams, Stephen		Smith, William
	Cruff, William		Treadwell, Alpheus
	Dorr, Edward		
	Hackett, Theophilus	Growler	Bartlett, Robert
	Harris, Abraham Harris		Bowden, Benjamin
	Newby, John		Bowden, William
	Reed, John		Brown, Joseph
	Stacey, William		Coombs, Michael
	Valentine, Andrew		Crocker, Silvanus
	Wyatt, Joseph		Deering, William F,
			Deverence, Benjamin
Fame, West Indianman	White, William		Ellingwood, William H.
			Emmerson, David

Growler	Euston, Ephraim	Hannibal	Reynolds, Caleb
	Farman, William		Seely, James
	Florence, Charles		
	Foster, George	Harriet	Morrel, Jacob
	Garrett, Simon T.		
	Gatchell, John G.	Harvest	Carter, Henry
	Grush, Nathaniel		Port, John
	Hart, William		
	Harvey, Anthony	Hepsey	Bakeman, Ely
	Hooper, Joseph A.		Bissel, Samuel W.
	Jones, Thomas		Boyd, Andrew
	Joseph, Michael		McKenzie, William
	Keys, Zenas		Nowell, Stephen C.
	Kraft, Michael		Warner, John
	Lee, Nathaniel		Williams, Thomas
	Lindsay, Nathaniel	Hibernia	Beckett, William
	Malcomb, Alexander		
	Manning, Burrel	Hindostan	Boyd, Stephen
	Mirrel, Samuel B.		Davidson, John
	Nicholas, James		Dunvall, N. D. (1)
	Nicholson, Jonas		Duvall, N. D. (2)
	Odion, John B. H.		Elfe, James
	Orne, Josiah		Lamb, Jack
	Pitman, Benjamin		Raymond, Caleb
	Roundy, Jeremiah		Stage, William
	Roundy, Thomas		Stegman, Christian
	Russell, William		
	Rust, John	HM Brig Nancy	Coggins, George
	Selman, Francis, G.		
	Smith, Benjamin	HM Brig Richmond	Anderson, John
	Smith, Jeremiah		Clarke, Alexander
	Smith, John		Preston, William
	Tishure, Samuel		
	Tucker, Andrew	HM Frigate Janus	Boston, Robert
	Tucker, Nathaniel		De Soder, Bastian
	Widger, Joseph		Eldridge, Samuel
	Withiem, Burrel		Nelson, Samuel A.
			Orn, James
Hannah	Bird, David		Plasted, William
	Harvey, Joseph		Spinney, Nathaniel
	Johnson, Henry		Ward, James
	Pritchard, Israel		White, John W.
	Selman, John		
	Wicks, Littleton	HM Frigate Leonidas	Christy, William
			Coffin, Daniel G.
Hannibal	Barton, Elijah		Lessingwell, Benajah
	Clerk, William		Manning, Thomas
	Hastings, Johnson		Stoss, Samuel
	Procter, Edward		Wood, Thomas

HM Ship-of-the-Line Ganges	Baxter, John Gage, Zachariah Harlow, Sylvanus Hutchings, Joseph McIntire, Alexander Patterson, Samuel Tinkham, Seth Winberg, John	Independence	Harris, George James, Peter Lewis, John Manuel, John Van Donveer, Peter Wilson, Peter Wilson, William
HMS Belleville HMS Belleville	Dennis, Thomas Goodwin, John Weir, Frederick	Indian Lass	Basset, Gorum Holland, James Stone, Samuel White, Philip Works, Alfred
HMS Devon Transport No. 15	Bloomdose, John Carter, Enoch Chauvel, Thomas Debarize, Francis John Demerie, Ephraim Ewell, Edward Gravelee, Joseph Grosette, John M. Hubbell, James Perott, John Francis Tuttle, Joseph	Industry	Gardiner, Amboy Labbas, John Lockett, Thomas R. Nunns, William Robinson, Edward Swain, Thomas Williams, Alexander
		Jane	Bowker, Nicholas Eastlake, James McIntyre, William
HMS Eos	Berry, John Chase, Eliphalet Henderson, Benjamin Holt, Simeon Jackson, John Kennedy, Henry Nichols, Samuel Ricker, Samuel Titcomb, John H. Wells, Thomas		Milson, William Nickel, Hugh Penny, James Reed, Joseph Rogers, Epinetus Saunders, James
		John John of Salem	Scanel, Cornele Lemon, Nicholas, C. Mason, Joseph J.
Hope	Haley, Thomas Michael, Peter Muncy, Daniel Parsons, Joseph Sands, Thomas Yale, Nathaniel	King of Rome	Allen, Peter Bessey, Jonas Burke, James Clark, George Coffin, Edward Dennis, John
Independence	Beachman, George Davis, John Farrel, John Fontain, Isaac Francoise, James Garrison, John		Distouet, John Fuster, Peter Hill, George Hyatt, William Inberg, Gabriel Kirk, Thomas

King of Rome	Lebon, Philip	Maydock	Fleming, Alexander
	Legere, Joseph		Hardwood, William
	Lewis, John		Peckham, Isaac
	Lippen, Stephen		Pitts, Charles
	Myers, Jacob		Wilky, Timothy
	Platt, John Henry		
	Salyear, John	Messenger	Posey, Valentine
	Sholes, Giles		
	Trought, Joseph	Minerva	Campbell, William
	Villodas, Matias		Conner, Michael
	Weed, Ebenezer		Harris, Ebenezer
	Weeks, George		Hill, Daniel
	Williams, Henry		Merrel, Enoch
			Watson, William
Kitty	Chase, Nathaniel		
	Huse, Ebenezer	Miser	Campbell, John
	Rogers, Samuel		Fredrick, John
	Watson, James		Peters, William
Leader	Jones, Cabal	Monticello	de Peyster, Arent S.
	Lassier, Florence		
	Parsons, Joseph	Nancy	Bachelor, Benjamin
	Southard, Samuel W.		Chaple, Samuel
			Hoyt, Ichabod
Lord Ponsonbe	Arnold, Benjamin		Long, Ebenezer
	Doosenberry, Richard		Moore, Daniel
	Shoe, Barnard		Pedrick, Joseph
	Williams, Moses		Pratt, Asa
			Randolf, Exum
Lydia	Clark, Aaron		Stephens, Thomas
	Davis, Michael		
	Rust, John	on shore	Carr, Richard
Mariner	Allen, William	open boat	Petterson, Andrew
	DeBuck, Cornelius		
	Lescombe, John	Otter	Benster, John
	Macey, George		Brown, John
	Myrick, William		Carr, Samuel
	Pincham, Stephen B.		Hitchi, John
	Steward, Alexander		Hook, Aaron
			Howlen, Samuel
Martin	West, John		Jerry, Daniel
			Shepherd, Daniel
Mary	Aldridge, Richard		Wade, Otis
	Benjamin, Everard		
	Griffin, William	Pallas	Benjamin, Polasskie
	Lewis, Peter		Fitch, William
			Lockerby, William
Maydock	Barber, Major		

Perseverance	Armstrong, Thomas	Prompt	Cole, William
	Hataway, William N.		Hubbard, Alfred
	Macrombie, Elijah		Lopaus, William
			Thompson, Nathaniel
Phillipsburgh	Pattingale, Enoch		
	Swanton, John	Purse	Dussing, Caesar
			Latish, Joseph
Pilate	Anderson, John		Turner, Samuel
	Brickum, James		
	Coffin, Edward	Quebec	Lapham, Cushion
	Demalo, Francis		
	Downs, John	Rachael	Broden, Norman
	Downs, William		Doliber, Joseph
	Gotier, Charles		George, William U.
	Harding, William		Homan, John
	Howel, William		Homan, Jonas
	Jackson, Lederick		Shirly, Phares
	Livingston, Henry		
	Manly, David	Rhode & Betsey	Knapp, Walker
	Mids, Michael		
	Platt, Daniel	Rising States	Gall, William
	Simonds, Henry		Murray, Nathaniel
	Smith, J. W.		Page, John
	Staford, John		Richards, George
	Taylor, George		Welch, William
	Thomas, John		
	Vincent, Stephen Stiles	Rising Sun	Evans, Thomas
	Williams, Charles		Osburne, Peter
			Smith, Thomas R.
Pilot	Harding, William		Young, William
	Manley, David		
	Williams, Charles	Rossie	Barber, John
			Bayman, James
Pomona	Baron, Peter		Berry, Joseph
	Jourdan, John		Boyd, John
	La Roche, John B.		Brady, Jason
	Lane, James		Chambers, Joseph
	Lupy, Marcus	Rossie	Combs, Thomas
	Ward, Thomas		Copasses, Matthew
			Douglas, Charles
Preseverence	Godsoe, William		Duhard, Thomas
Price	Paine, Joshua		Eaton, John
	Stenchcombe, George		Ellis, William
			Ford, M. Benjamin
Prompt	Allen, John		Hall, Thomas
	Atwood, Thomas		Hill, Pompey
	Bartis, John		Hill, William
	Beecher, William Palmer		Hobdyke, John
	Chase, Nathaniel		Howard, Henry

Rossie	Hurtt, Samuel	Sword Fish	Booder, Jacob
	Lamon, James		Bray, Zachariah
	Lee, Samuel		Bridges, Philip
	Longwell, Amos		Brimmer, John
	Mitchell, Francis		Carrel, Michael
	Oberville, Michael		Cloutman, George
	Pearce, Emanuel		Cloutman, Robert
	Powell, Elijah		Cox, Daniel
	Simonds, Joseph		Dalliber, James
	Stevenson, Thaddeus		Deistel, John
	Thompson, John		Doevall, Francis
	Vorge, James		Dudley, Ephraim
	Williams, Benjamin		Duxey, Peter
			Ellwell, Jonathan
Russian MV	Brown, Francis		Evans, John
	Buffington, James		Fernandes, Anthony
	Frazier, William		Francis, Frederick
	Johnson, Henry		Garney, Thomas
	Monion, Jean		Grant, Christian
	Putnam, Allen		Green, Henry
			Griffin, James
Sampson	Coffin, James		Gudlers, George
	Leonard, Robert		Hamson, Henry
	Manley, Rudolph		Huff, Charles
	Thornton, David		Ingalls, Samuel
	Tucker, Nathaniel		Innes, John
	Vincent, Henry		Jeremy, Stephen
			Johnson, Andrew
Soley	Boston, John		Kenny, George
	Rust, John		Kerhow, Samuel
	Smith, William B.		Kile, George
	Williamson, William		Lambert, John
			Lawrence, Peter
Spanish MV	Jeffers, Henry		Lear, Alexander
			Lee, Richard
Squirrel	Gregory, George		Manning, Enoch
			March, Joseph
Susanna	Moore, Thomas		Merriday, John
			Middleton, Reuben
Sword Fish	Allen, Henry		Mills, Henry
	Anderton, Thomas		Morrison, James
	Anderton, Samuel		Noonan, William
	Asten, John		Nowland, Andrew
	Bagley, Moses		Parsons, Andrew
	Bartlett, George B.		Parsons, Thomas
	Bessom, Nicholas		Paulfrey, Richard
	Bistie, Asaph		Prentess, Christian
	Black, John		Reed, H. W.
	Blake, Charles		Richardson, Perry

Portsmouth Depot 151

Sword Fish	Roberts, George	Tender of the True	Lumburger, Jacob
	Rogers, James	Blooded Yankee	Maris, Yeace
	Roper, John		Mathews, Lewis
	Sandbach, Richard		Miller, John
	Saunders, Thomas		Moore, John
	Setchell, Samuel		Peckham, Hazard
	Shed, William		Richards, John
	Sheppard, Joseph		Rogers, Francis
	Shot, John		Taylor, Peter
	Small, Thomas		White, John
	Stephens, David		Williams, John (1)
	Stephens, Trey		Williams, John (2)
	Strong, William	Thomas Willson	Evans, John
	Wells, Moses		
	Whitchouse, Lewis	Three Brothers	Andermach, John
	White, Benjamin		Howland, William
	White, John W.		Jacobson, Jacob
	Williams, John		Rippaviere, John
	Winslow, William		
	Wood, George	Tiger	Bartholf, Nicholas
	Woods, Charles		Byer, Peter
	Woods, William		Cadwell, Samuel
	York, Nathaniel		Calder, John H.
			Churchill, Timothy
taken on shore	Conway, Samuel		Hill, Ephraim
	Cunningham, John		Hill, Josiah
	Floyd, James		Jones, James
	Lenderson, Henry		Kerhon, Abraham
	Pardoe, John		Ludlow, Ruben
			Mars, George
Tender of the True	Allen, William		Morslender, Ruben
Blooded Yankee	Baurs, Francis		Nicolas, John
	Botrell, John		Quackenbush, William
	Briggs, Bolon		Sampson, Jacob
	Brown, Seth		Small, George D.
	Carter, Thomas		Spencer, Leonard
	Christie, John		Sutton, John
	Clark, Abraham D.		
	Cole, William	Tigre	Morris, James
	Dennis, Thomas		Waterman, John
	Follingsby, William		
	Fuller, John	Tom Thumb	Arnold, William
	Fyans, Joseph		Blazon, Stephen
	Hardiman, John		Cooper, Alfred
	Herle, Hiram		McMichael, James
	Howateer, Henry		Moore, Benjamin
	Ingesoll, Abraham		Morris, George
	Lawson, James		Palmer, Peter
	Lawson, Laurence		Rosignol, James

Tom Thumb	Scofield, Wells	USRM Cutter James Madison	Hutchins, William
	Veney, George		James, John
			Johnson, Andrew
Traveler	Church, William		Martin, Jonathan
	Flinn, Pearce		Mumery, James
	Hall, Thomas		Nuting, Charles
	Harder, John		Osborne, Thomas
	Long, James		Palm, William
	Simmons, John		Pault, Beloner
	Thompson, John		Pegale, Amos
	Wilson, John		Petingale, John
			Petterson, John
Treaser	Bassett, William		Quasir, Zeph.
			Senholm, Jacob
Union	Cooper, Thomas		Smith, Henry
			Stone, John
US Schooner Growler	Buel, Jeremiah		Tristram, Joseph
	Harvey, Peter		Tufts, Eleazar
	Mallet, William		Turner, John
	Thorning, Thomas		Williams, Gaspar
	Watson, David		Wilson, William
			Withers, Edward
US Schooner Julia	Clawson, Henry	Vivid	Murray, David
	Smith, John		
		Volante	Scott, Henry
USRM Cutter James Madison	Alley, Jacob		
	Anderson, Andrew	Volunteer	Hunt, Samuel
	Anderson, Oliver		Kennedy, Dennis
	Baker, Henry		Marlow, Owen
	Bearbere, John		Wadsworth, Daniel
	Blankinship, Charles		
	Carebo, Henry	Warren	Hazard, Thomas
	Chase, Samuel		Jane, Joseph
	Clements, Henry		Manuel, Joseph
	Coleman, Daniel		
	Davis, Nathan	Washington	Watkins, Frederick
	Daymen, Celeb		
	Drinkwater, Andrew	Wasp	Green John
	Ellis, John		McKenzie, John
	Even, Peter		
	Gale, Oliver	Watson	Hill, Jeremiah
	Gard, Gelab		
	Gebers, Henry	Weasel	Ashfield, Henry
	George, Thomas		Bailey, John
	Harding, Joseph		Blackman, Moses
	Harris, William		Brill, John
	Helmen, John		Cappel, John
	Henricks, Jeremiah		Dunn, David
	Hughes, Peter		Gibbs, Daniel

Weasel	Hull, Edward	William	Peters, John
	King, John		Powers, William
	Lemmon, Henry		Smith, Thomas R.
	Tiffs, Joseph		
	Vangostet, Cato	William Rathbourne	Cole, Stephen
	Voohis, James		
		Yorktown	Baisley, Abraham
William	Barry, John		
	Chidsey, Abraham	Zephyr	Harris, Simon
	Clark, Jean		Keen, Joseph
	Cooper, James		Modre, John
	Dennis, Thomas		Plumber, William Reed
	Gibson, William		Walker, Seth
	Kenner, John Downing		Williamson, David
	Nutrash, Ezekiel		

Stapleton Depot

Alberson, John N. - Seaman - Number: 292 - Prize name: Messenger - Ship type: MV - How taken: HM Frigate Iris - When taken: 10 Mar 1813 - Where taken: off Cape Ortegal (Spain) - Date received: 11 Jul 1813 - From what ship: Plymouth - Born: Groton - Age: 27 - Discharged on 13 Jun 1814 and sent to Dartmoor.

Allen, John - Seaman - Number: 50 - Prize name: Paul Jones - Ship type: P - How taken: HM Frigate Leonidas - When taken: 23 May 1813 - Where taken: off Cape Clear (Ireland) - Date received: 8 Jul 1813 - From what ship: Plymouth - Born: Seabrook, MA - Age: 37 - Discharged on 13 Jun 1814 and sent to Dartmoor.

Alman, John - Seaman - Number: 401 - Prize name: Paul Jones - Ship type: P - How taken: HM Frigate Leonidas - When taken: 23 May 1813 - Where taken: off Cape Clear (Ireland) - Date received: 11 Jul 1813 - From what ship: Plymouth - Born: Baltimore - Age: 25 - Race: Colored - Discharged on 16 Jun 1814 and sent to Dartmoor.

Amerson, Charles - Seaman - Number: 228 - Prize name: Essex - Ship type: MV - How taken: HM Frigate Pyramus - When taken: 2 Apr 1813 - Where taken: Bay of Biscay - Date received: 11 Jul 1813 - From what ship: Plymouth - Born: Massachusetts - Age: 18 - Discharged on 16 Jun 1814 and sent to Dartmoor.

Anderson, Daniel - Seaman - Number: 164 - Prize name: Leo - Ship type: P - How taken: HM Frigate Magiciene - When taken: 4 Jun 1813 - Where taken: Bay of Biscay - Date received: 8 Jul 1813 - From what ship: Plymouth - Born: Massachusetts - Age: 22 - Discharged on 13 Jun 1814 and sent to Dartmoor.

Anderson, David - Seaman - Number: 273 - Prize name: Caroline - Ship type: MV - How taken: HM Frigate Medusa - When taken: 12 Apr 1813 - Where taken: Bay of Biscay - Date received: 11 Jul 1813 - From what ship: Plymouth - Born: Maryland - Age: 30 - Race: Negro - Discharged on 16 Jun 1814 and sent to Dartmoor.

Anderson, James - Seaman - Number: 34 - Prize name: Paul Jones - Ship type: P - How taken: HM Frigate Leonidas - When taken: 23 May 1813 - Where taken: off Cape Clear (Ireland) - Date received: 8 Jul 1813 - From what ship: Plymouth - Born: Maryland - Age: 26 - Race: Negro - Discharged on 13 Jun 1814 and sent to Dartmoor.

Andress, Daniel - Seaman - Number: 347 - Prize name: Fox - Ship type: P - How taken: HM Sloop Pheasant - When taken: 23 Apr 1813 - Where taken: Bay of Biscay - Date received: 11 Jul 1813 - From what ship: Plymouth - Born: Philadelphia - Age: 25 - Discharged on 16 Jun 1814 and sent to Dartmoor.

Anthony, Stephen - Seaman - Number: 123 - Prize name: Courier - Ship type: P - How taken: HM Brig Rover - When taken: 14 Mar 1813 - Where taken: Bay of Biscay - Date received: 8 Jul 1813 - From what ship: Plymouth - Born: Maryland - Age: 28 - Race: Colored - Discharged on 13 Jun 1814 and sent to Dartmoor.

Armstrong, James - Seaman - Number: 179 - How taken: Impressed at Liverpool - When taken: 19 Mar 1813 - Date received: 8 Jul 1813 - From what ship: Plymouth - Born: Alexandria, VA - Age: 26 - Discharged on 13 Jun 1814 and sent to Dartmoor.

Armstrong, William - Seaman - Number: 204 - Prize name: Governor Gerry - Ship type: MV - How taken: HM Brig Royalist - When taken: 1 Jan 1813 - Where taken: Bay of Biscay - Date received: 8 Jul 1813 - From what ship: Plymouth - Born: Philadelphia - Age: 36 - Race: Negro - Discharged on 13 Jun 1814 and sent to Dartmoor.

Askwick, William Victor - Sailmaker - Number: 67 - Prize name: Paul Jones - Ship type: P - How taken: HM Frigate Leonidas - When taken: 23 May 1813 - Where taken: off Cape Clear (Ireland) - Date received: 8 Jul 1813 - From what ship: Plymouth - Born: Hudson, NY - Age: 25 - Discharged on 13 Jun 1814 and sent to Dartmoor.

Atkins, Joseph - Seaman - Number: 84 - Prize name: Courier - Ship type: P - How taken: HM Brig Rover - When taken: 14 Mar 1813 - Where taken: Bay of Biscay - Date received: 8 Jul 1813 - From what ship: Plymouth - Born: Massachusetts - Age: 21 - Discharged on 13 Jun 1814 and sent to Dartmoor.

Avis, James - Seaman - Number: 256 - Prize name: Zebra - Ship type: P - How taken: HM Frigate Pyramus - When taken: 20 Apr 1813 - Where taken: Bay of Biscay - Date received: 11 Jul 1813 - From what ship: Plymouth -

Born: New York - Age: 19 - Discharged on 16 Jun 1814 and sent to Dartmoor.

Baker, Stephen - Seaman - Number: 13 - Prize name: Anne - How taken: Impressed - When taken: 7 Jul 1813 - Date received: 7 Jul 1813 - From what ship: Bristol - Born: Providence, RI - Age: 23 - Discharged on 13 Jun 1814 and sent to Dartmoor.

Baldwin, John - Seaman - Number: 341 - Prize name: Fox - Ship type: P - How taken: HM Sloop Pheasant - When taken: 23 Apr 1813 - Where taken: Bay of Biscay - Date received: 11 Jul 1813 - From what ship: Plymouth - Born: Boston - Age: 23 - Discharged on 16 Jun 1814 and sent to Dartmoor.

Barasau, John - Seaman - Number: 128 - Prize name: Miranda - Ship type: Prize of Paul Jones - How taken: HM Frigate Unicorn - When taken: 21 May 1813 - Where taken: Bay of Biscay - Date received: 8 Jul 1813 - From what ship: Plymouth - Born: Rochelle, France - Age: 22 - Discharged on 13 Jun 1814 and sent to Dartmoor.

Barber, William - Seaman - Number: 108 - Prize name: Zebra - Ship type: P - How taken: HM Frigate Pyramus - When taken: 20 Apr 1813 - Where taken: Bay of Biscay - Date received: 8 Jul 1813 - From what ship: Plymouth - Born: Newport - Age: 40 - Race: Negro - Discharged on 13 Jun 1814 and sent to Dartmoor.

Bariston, Peter - Seaman - Number: 278 - Prize name: Caroline - Ship type: MV - How taken: HM Frigate Medusa - When taken: 12 Apr 1813 - Where taken: Bay of Biscay - Date received: 11 Jul 1813 - From what ship: Plymouth - Born: Philadelphia - Age: 32 - Discharged on 16 Jun 1814 and sent to Dartmoor.

Barker, Robert - Seaman - Number: 268 - Prize name: Zebra - Ship type: P - How taken: HM Frigate Pyramus - When taken: 20 Apr 1813 - Where taken: Bay of Biscay - Date received: 11 Jul 1813 - From what ship: Plymouth - Born: New York - Age: 18 - Discharged on 16 Jun 1814 and sent to Dartmoor.

Barnes, Nathaniel - Seaman - Number: 69 - Prize name: Paul Jones - Ship type: P - How taken: HM Frigate Leonidas - When taken: 23 May 1813 - Where taken: off Cape Clear (Ireland) - Date received: 8 Jul 1813 - From what ship: Plymouth - Born: New York - Age: 35 - Discharged on 13 Jun 1814 and sent to Dartmoor.

Bartlett, Caleb - Seaman - Number: 155 - Prize name: Leo - Ship type: P - How taken: HM Frigate Magiciene - When taken: 4 Jun 1813 - Where taken: Bay of Biscay - Date received: 8 Jul 1813 - From what ship: Plymouth - Born: Plymouth, MA - Age: 24 - Discharged on 13 Jun 1814 and sent to Dartmoor.

Beard, Francis - Seaman - Number: 346 - Prize name: Fox - Ship type: P - How taken: HM Sloop Pheasant - When taken: 23 Apr 1813 - Where taken: Bay of Biscay - Date received: 11 Jul 1813 - From what ship: Plymouth - Born: Saint Domingue (Haiti) - Age: 31 - Discharged on 16 Jun 1814 and sent to Dartmoor.

Beck, Stewart - Seaman - Number: 391 - Prize name: Henry Clements - Ship type: MV - How taken: HM Brig Orestes - When taken: 13 Apr 1813 - Where taken: Bay of Biscay - Date received: 11 Jul 1813 - From what ship: Plymouth - Born: Maryland - Age: 18 - Discharged on 16 Jun 1814 and sent to Dartmoor.

Bernard, John - Seaman - Number: 57 - Prize name: Paul Jones - Ship type: P - How taken: HM Frigate Leonidas - When taken: 23 May 1813 - Where taken: off Cape Clear (Ireland) - Date received: 8 Jul 1813 - From what ship: Plymouth - Born: New Orleans - Age: 35 - Discharged on 13 Jun 1814 and sent to Dartmoor.

Berryman, John - Seaman - Number: 122 - Prize name: Courier - Ship type: P - How taken: HM Brig Rover - When taken: 14 Mar 1813 - Where taken: Bay of Biscay - Date received: 8 Jul 1813 - From what ship: Plymouth - Born: Maryland - Age: 25 - Race: Colored - Discharged on 13 Jun 1814 and sent to Dartmoor.

Best, Robert - Seaman - Number: 173 - Prize name: Tickler - Ship type: P - How taken: HM Frigate Magiciene - When taken: 5 Jun 1813 - Where taken: Bay of Biscay - Date received: 8 Jul 1813 - From what ship: Plymouth - Born: New Jersey - Age: 22 - Discharged on 13 Jun 1814 and sent to Dartmoor.

Bickwith, Benjamin (see prisoner number 419) - Seaman - Number: 371 - Prize name: Tom - Ship type: P - How taken: HM Frigate Magiciene - When taken: 27 Apr 1813 - Where taken: Bay of Biscay - Date received: 11 Jul 1813 - From what ship: Plymouth - Born: Pennsylvania - Age: 25 - Escaped in Feb 1814 and recaptured.

Bickwith, Benjamin - Seaman - Number: 419 - Prize name: Tom - Ship type: P - Date received: 9 Nov 1813 - From what ship: Naval Rendezvous Bristol - Born: Pennsylvania - Age: 25 - Discharged on 16 Jun 1814 and sent to Dartmoor.

Biddlefield, James - Seaman - Number: 42 - Prize name: Paul Jones - Ship type: P - How taken: HM Frigate

Leonidas - When taken: 23 May 1813 - Where taken: off Cape Clear (Ireland) - Date received: 8 Jul 1813 - From what ship: Plymouth - Born: Wells, MA - Age: 28 - Discharged on 13 Jun 1814 and sent to Dartmoor.

Biss, Daniel W. - Seaman - Number: 90 - Prize name: Courier - Ship type: P - How taken: HM Brig Rover - When taken: 14 Mar 1813 - Where taken: Bay of Biscay - Date received: 8 Jul 1813 - From what ship: Plymouth - Born: Massachusetts - Age: 25 - Discharged on 13 Jun 1814 and sent to Dartmoor.

Blanchet, Simon - Seaman - Number: 311 - Prize name: Price - Ship type: MV - How taken: HM Frigate Pyramus - When taken: 13 Apr 1813 - Where taken: Bay of Biscay - Date received: 11 Jul 1813 - From what ship: Plymouth - Born: Charlestown - Age: 21 - Discharged on 16 Jun 1814 and sent to Dartmoor.

Blodget, Caleb - Seaman - Number: 231 - Prize name: Essex - Ship type: MV - How taken: HM Frigate Pyramus - When taken: 2 Apr 1813 - Where taken: Bay of Biscay - Date received: 11 Jul 1813 - From what ship: Plymouth - Born: New Hampshire - Age: 23 - Discharged on 16 Jun 1814 and sent to Dartmoor.

Boriesa, John - Seaman - Number: 116 - Prize name: Good Friends - Ship type: MV - How taken: HM Frigate Andromache - When taken: 2 Apr 1813 - Where taken: Bay of Biscay - Date received: 8 Jul 1813 - From what ship: Plymouth - Born: Maryland - Age: 23 - Race: Negro - Discharged on 13 Jun 1814 and sent to Dartmoor.

Bosset, David - Seaman - Number: 199 - Prize name: Governor Gerry - Ship type: MV - How taken: HM Brig Royalist - When taken: 1 Jan 1813 - Where taken: Bay of Biscay - Date received: 8 Jul 1813 - From what ship: Plymouth - Born: Baltimore - Age: 43 - Race: Negro - Discharged on 13 Jun 1814 and sent to Dartmoor.

Bourton, George - Seaman - Number: 12 - Prize name: King David - How taken: Impressed at Bristol - When taken: 30 Jun 1813 - Date received: 30 Jun 1813 - From what ship: Bristol - Born: Massachusetts - Age: 23 - Discharged on 13 Jun 1814 and sent to Dartmoor.

Bowen, John - Seaman - Number: 190 - Prize name: Revenge - Ship type: P - How taken: HM Frigate Belle Poule - When taken: 10 May 1813 - Where taken: Bay of Biscay - Date received: 8 Jul 1813 - From what ship: Plymouth - Born: Charleston - Age: 24 - Discharged on 11 Dec 1813 and sent to the Regulatory Office Bristol for naval service.

Bower, Joseph - Seaman - Number: 102 - Prize name: Courier - Ship type: P - How taken: HM Brig Rover - When taken: 14 Mar 1813 - Where taken: Bay of Biscay - Date received: 8 Jul 1813 - From what ship: Plymouth - Born: Maryland - Age: 28 - Discharged on 13 Jun 1814 and sent to Dartmoor.

Bradford, Charles - Seaman - Number: 220 - Prize name: Napoleon - Ship type: MV - How taken: HM Frigate Belle Poule - When taken: 3 Apr 1813 - Where taken: Bay of Biscay - Date received: 11 Jul 1813 - From what ship: Plymouth - Born: Massachusetts - Age: 19 - Discharged on 13 Jun 1814 and sent to Dartmoor.

Brandage, John - Seaman - Number: 170 - Prize name: Tickler - Ship type: P - How taken: HM Frigate Pyramus - When taken: 5 Jun 1813 - Where taken: Bay of Biscay - Date received: 8 Jul 1813 - From what ship: Plymouth - Born: Greece - Age: 22 - Discharged on 1 Feb 1814 and sent to the Naval Rendezvous Bristol.

Brant, Thomas - Seaman - Number: 261 - Prize name: Zebra - Ship type: P - How taken: HM Frigate Pyramus - When taken: 20 Apr 1813 - Where taken: Bay of Biscay - Date received: 11 Jul 1813 - From what ship: Plymouth - Born: New York - Age: 19 - Discharged on 16 Jun 1814 and sent to Dartmoor.

Bright, George - Seaman - Number: 357 - Prize name: Fox - Ship type: P - How taken: HM Sloop Pheasant - When taken: 24 Apr 1813 - Where taken: Bay of Biscay - Date received: 11 Jul 1813 - From what ship: Plymouth - Born: New Jersey - Age: 22 - Discharged on 16 Jun 1814 and sent to Dartmoor.

Broadwater, Samuel - Seaman - Number: 287 - Prize name: Messenger - Ship type: MV - How taken: HM Frigate Iris - When taken: 10 Mar 1813 - Where taken: off Cape Ortegal (Spain) - Date received: 11 Jul 1813 - From what ship: Plymouth - Born: Maryland - Age: 21 - Discharged on 16 Jun 1814 and sent to Dartmoor.

Brown, Benjamin - Seaman - Number: 189 - Prize name: Revenge - Ship type: P - How taken: HM Frigate Belle Poule - When taken: 10 May 1813 - Where taken: Bay of Biscay - Date received: 8 Jul 1813 - From what ship: Plymouth - Born: Westborough - Age: 21 - Discharged on 13 Jun 1814 and sent to Dartmoor.

Brown, Charles - Seaman - Number: 47 - Prize name: Paul Jones - Ship type: P - How taken: HM Frigate Leonidas -

160 Stapleton Depot

When taken: 23 May 1813 - Where taken: off Cape Clear (Ireland) - Date received: 8 Jul 1813 - From what ship: Plymouth - Born: Richmond, VA - Age: 23 - Race: Negro - Discharged on 13 Jun 1814 and sent to Dartmoor.

Brown, John - Seaman - Number: 310 - Prize name: Price - Ship type: MV - How taken: HM Frigate Iris - When taken: 13 Apr 1813 - Where taken: Bay of Biscay - Date received: 11 Jul 1813 - From what ship: Plymouth - Born: New Jersey - Age: 23 - Discharged on 16 Jun 1814 and sent to Dartmoor.

Brown, John William - Seaman - Number: 365 - Prize name: Tom - Ship type: P - How taken: HM Frigate Surveillante - When taken: 27 Apr 1813 - Where taken: Bay of Biscay - Date received: 11 Jul 1813 - From what ship: Plymouth - Born: Albany - Age: 27 - Discharged on 16 Jun 1814 and sent to Dartmoor.

Brown, Samuel - Seaman - Number: 229 - Prize name: Essex - Ship type: MV - How taken: HM Frigate Pyramus - When taken: 2 Apr 1813 - Where taken: Bay of Biscay - Date received: 11 Jul 1813 - From what ship: Plymouth - Born: New Hampshire - Age: 19 - Discharged on 16 Jun 1814 and sent to Dartmoor.

Brown, William - Seaman - Number: 214 - Prize name: Hebe - Ship type: MV - How taken: HM Frigate Stag - When taken: 18 Apr 1813 - Where taken: Bay of Biscay - Date received: 11 Jul 1813 - From what ship: Plymouth - Born: Copenhagen - Age: 27 - Discharged on 5 Feb 1814, released, a Danish citizen.

Brown, William - Cook - Number: 363 - Prize name: Tom - Ship type: P - How taken: HM Frigate Surveillante - When taken: 27 Apr 1813 - Where taken: Bay of Biscay - Date received: 11 Jul 1813 - From what ship: Plymouth - Born: New York - Age: 33 - Race: Negro - Discharged on 16 Jun 1814 and sent to Dartmoor.

Bryant, Stephen - Seaman - Number: 9 - How taken: Impressed at Bristol - When taken: 28 Jun 1813 - Date received: 20 Jun 1813 - From what ship: Bristol - Born: South Carolina - Age: 22 - Discharged on 13 Jun 1814 and sent to Dartmoor.

Bullman, John - Seaman - Number: 376 - Prize name: Tom - Ship type: P - How taken: HM Frigate Surveillante - When taken: 27 Apr 1813 - Where taken: Bay of Biscay - Date received: 11 Jul 1813 - From what ship: Plymouth - Born: Maryland - Age: 38 - Discharged on 16 Jun 1814 and sent to Dartmoor.

Burit, Benjamin - Seaman - Number: 192 - Prize name: Revenge - Ship type: P - How taken: HM Frigate Belle Poule - When taken: 10 May 1813 - Where taken: Bay of Biscay - Date received: 8 Jul 1813 - From what ship: Plymouth - Born: New Haven - Age: 34 - Discharged on 13 Jun 1814 and sent to Dartmoor.

Burnett, Charles - Seaman - Number: 298 - Prize name: Price - Ship type: MV - How taken: HM Frigate Iris - When taken: 13 Apr 1813 - Where taken: Bay of Biscay - Date received: 11 Jul 1813 - From what ship: Plymouth - Born: New York - Age: 24 - Discharged on 16 Jun 1814 and sent to Dartmoor.

Burnham, Enoch - Seaman - Number: 244 - Prize name: Essex - Ship type: MV - How taken: HM Frigate Pyramus - When taken: 2 Apr 1813 - Where taken: Bay of Biscay - Date received: 11 Jul 1813 - From what ship: Plymouth - Born: Boston - Age: 22 - Discharged on 16 Jun 1814 and sent to Dartmoor.

Burns, Charles - Seaman - Number: 280 - Prize name: Caroline - Ship type: MV - How taken: HM Frigate Medusa - When taken: 12 Apr 1813 - Where taken: Bay of Biscay - Date received: 11 Jul 1813 - From what ship: Plymouth - Born: Salem - Age: 21 - Race: Negro - Discharged on 16 Jun 1814 and sent to Dartmoor.

Burstead, John - Seaman - Number: 55 - Prize name: Paul Jones - Ship type: P - How taken: HM Frigate Leonidas - When taken: 23 May 1813 - Where taken: off Cape Clear (Ireland) - Date received: 8 Jul 1813 - From what ship: Plymouth - Born: New York - Age: 30 - Discharged on 13 Jun 1814 and sent to Dartmoor.

Butler, George - Seaman - Number: 133 - Prize name: Orders in Council - Ship type: P - How taken: Rebecca - When taken: 1 Jun 1813 - Where taken: Bay of Biscay - Date received: 8 Jul 1813 - From what ship: Plymouth - Born: Massachusetts - Age: 28 - Discharged on 13 Jun 1814 and sent to Dartmoor.

Butman, Charles P. - Seaman - Number: 177 - Prize name: Tickler - Ship type: P - How taken: HM Frigate Magiciene - When taken: 5 Jun 1813 - Where taken: Bay of Biscay - Date received: 8 Jul 1813 - From what ship: Plymouth - Born: Massachusetts - Age: 24 - Discharged on 13 Jun 1814 and sent to Dartmoor.

Byard, Joseph - Seaman - Number: 18 - Prize name: Paul Jones - Ship type: P - How taken: HM Frigate Leonidas - When taken: 23 May 1813 - Where taken: off Cape Clear (Ireland) - Date received: 8 Jul 1813 - From what ship: Plymouth - Born: France - Age: 28 - Discharged on 13 Jun 1814 and sent to Dartmoor.

Calhoun, Richard - Seaman - Number: 345 - Prize name: Fox - Ship type: P - How taken: HM Sloop Pheasant - When taken: 23 Apr 1813 - Where taken: Bay of Biscay - Date received: 11 Jul 1813 - From what ship: Plymouth - Born: New York - Age: 19 - Discharged on 16 Jun 1814 and sent to Dartmoor.

Cambon, Joseph - Seaman - Number: 344 - Prize name: Fox - Ship type: P - How taken: HM Sloop Pheasant - When taken: 23 Apr 1813 - Where taken: Bay of Biscay - Date received: 11 Jul 1813 - From what ship: Plymouth - Born: Spain - Age: 30 - Discharged on 16 Jun 1814 and sent to Dartmoor.

Campbell, Reynold - Seaman - Number: 350 - Prize name: Shadow - Ship type: P - How taken: HM Brig Reindeer - When taken: 6 Apr 1813 - Where taken: Bay of Biscay - Date received: 11 Jul 1813 - From what ship: Plymouth - Born: Philadelphia - Age: 25 - Discharged on 16 Jun 1814 and sent to Dartmoor.

Cantrill, Norville (see prisoner number 412) - Armorer - Number: 362 - Prize name: Tom - Ship type: P - How taken: HM Frigate Surveillante - When taken: 27 Apr 1813 - Where taken: Bay of Biscay - Date received: 11 Jul 1813 - From what ship: Plymouth - Born: New Orleans - Age: 22 - Escaped on 2 Sep 1813 from the black hole.

Cantrill, Norville - Armorer - Number: 412 - Prize name: Tom - Ship type: P - How taken: HM Frigate Surveillante - When taken: 27 Apr 1813 - Where taken: Bay of Biscay - Date received: 4 Sep 1813 - From what ship: Naval Rendezvous Bristol - Born: New Orleans - Age: 22 - Escaped on 14 Sep 1814.

Carter, Daniel - Seaman - Number: 106 - Prize name: Zebra - Ship type: P - How taken: HM Frigate Pyramus - When taken: 20 Apr 1813 - Where taken: Bay of Biscay - Date received: 8 Jul 1813 - From what ship: Plymouth - Born: Virginia - Age: 26 - Discharged on 13 Jun 1814 and sent to Dartmoor.

Carter, Edward - Seaman - Number: 105 - Prize name: Zebra - Ship type: P - How taken: HM Frigate Pyramus - When taken: 20 Apr 1813 - Where taken: Bay of Biscay - Date received: 8 Jul 1813 - From what ship: Plymouth - Born: Norfolk - Age: 28 - Discharged on 16 Jun 1814 and sent to Dartmoor.

Cary, John - Seaman - Number: 165 - Prize name: Leo - Ship type: P - How taken: HM Frigate Magiciene - When taken: 4 Jun 1813 - Where taken: Bay of Biscay - Date received: 8 Jul 1813 - From what ship: Plymouth - Born: Brunswick - Age: 24 - Discharged on 13 Jun 1814 and sent to Dartmoor.

Cato, John - Seaman - Number: 35 - Prize name: Paul Jones - Ship type: P - How taken: HM Frigate Leonidas - When taken: 23 May 1813 - Where taken: off Cape Clear (Ireland) - Date received: 8 Jul 1813 - From what ship: Plymouth - Born: New London - Age: 35 - Race: Negro - Discharged on 13 Jun 1814 and sent to Dartmoor.

Chandler, Simon - Seaman - Number: 234 - Prize name: Essex - Ship type: MV - How taken: HM Frigate Pyramus - When taken: 2 Apr 1813 - Where taken: Bay of Biscay - Date received: 11 Jul 1813 - From what ship: Plymouth - Born: Massachusetts - Age: 19 - Discharged on 16 Jun 1814 and sent to Dartmoor.

Chiseldino, John - Seaman - Number: 217 - Prize name: Hebe - Ship type: MV - How taken: HM Frigate Stag - When taken: 18 Apr 1813 - Where taken: Bay of Biscay - Date received: 11 Jul 1813 - From what ship: Plymouth - Born: Newbury - Age: 20 - Discharged on 13 Jun 1814 and sent to Dartmoor.

Christie, James - Seaman - Number: 169 - Prize name: Tickler - Ship type: P - How taken: HM Frigate Magiciene - When taken: 5 Jun 1813 - Where taken: Bay of Biscay - Date received: 8 Jul 1813 - From what ship: Plymouth - Born: New York - Age: 23 - Discharged on 13 Jun 1814 and sent to Dartmoor.

Clepp, Abraham - Seaman - Number: 227 - Prize name: Napoleon - Ship type: MV - How taken: HM Frigate Belle Poule - When taken: 3 Apr 1813 - Where taken: Bay of Biscay - Date received: 11 Jul 1813 - From what ship: Plymouth - Born: Massachusetts - Age: 22 - Discharged on 13 Jun 1814 and sent to Dartmoor.

Clothey, Thomas - Seaman - Number: 295 - Prize name: Essex - Ship type: MV - How taken: HM Frigate Pyramus - When taken: 6 Apr 1813 - Where taken: Bay of Biscay - Date received: 11 Jul 1813 - From what ship: Plymouth - Born: Marblehead - Age: 19 - Discharged on 16 Jun 1814 and sent to Dartmoor.

Cockburn, Abel - Seaman - Number: 14 - Prize name: Anne - How taken: Impressed - When taken: 7 Jul 1813 - Date received: 7 Jul 1813 - From what ship: Bristol - Born: Connecticut - Age: 24 - Discharged on 13 Jun 1814 and sent to Dartmoor.

Codman, Richard - Seaman - Number: 156 - Prize name: Leo - Ship type: P - How taken: HM Frigate Magiciene -

When taken: 4 Jun 1813 - Where taken: Bay of Biscay - Date received: 8 Jul 1813 - From what ship: Plymouth - Born: Portland - Age: 20 - Discharged on 13 Jun 1814 and sent to Dartmoor.

Coleman, David - Seaman - Number: 64 - Prize name: Paul Jones - Ship type: P - How taken: HM Frigate Leonidas - When taken: 23 May 1813 - Where taken: off Cape Clear (Ireland) - Date received: 8 Jul 1813 - From what ship: Plymouth - Born: New York - Age: 15 - Discharged on 13 Jun 1814 and sent to Dartmoor.

Colton, Walter - Lieutenant Marines - Number: 68 - Prize name: Paul Jones - Ship type: P - How taken: HM Frigate Leonidas - When taken: 23 May 1813 - Where taken: off Cape Clear (Ireland) - Date received: 8 Jul 1813 - From what ship: Plymouth - Born: Springfield, MA - Age: 30 - Discharged on 13 Jun 1814 and sent to Dartmoor.

Cook, Charles Howe - Seaman - Number: 49 - Prize name: Paul Jones - Ship type: P - How taken: HM Frigate Leonidas - When taken: 23 May 1813 - Where taken: off Cape Clear (Ireland) - Date received: 8 Jul 1813 - From what ship: Plymouth - Born: South Carolina - Age: 26 - Race: Colored - Discharged on 13 Jun 1814 and sent to Dartmoor.

Cooke, William - Seaman - Number: 44 - Prize name: Paul Jones - Ship type: P - How taken: HM Frigate Leonidas - When taken: 23 May 1813 - Where taken: off Cape Clear (Ireland) - Date received: 8 Jul 1813 - From what ship: Plymouth - Born: New York - Age: 19 - Discharged on 13 Jun 1814 and sent to Dartmoor.

Cooper, Andrew A. - Seaman - Number: 37 - Prize name: Paul Jones - Ship type: P - How taken: HM Frigate Leonidas - When taken: 23 May 1813 - Where taken: off Cape Clear (Ireland) - Date received: 8 Jul 1813 - From what ship: Plymouth - Born: Albany - Age: 28 - Discharged on 13 Jun 1814 and sent to Dartmoor.

Cooper, Charles - Seaman - Number: 81 - Prize name: Grand Napoleon - How taken: HM Brig Goldfinch - When taken: 17 Apr 1813 - Where taken: Bay of Biscay - Date received: 8 Jul 1813 - From what ship: Plymouth - Born: New York - Age: 23 - Discharged on 1 Feb 1814 and sent to the Naval Rendezvous Bristol.

Cornwall, Arthur - Seaman - Number: 80 - Prize name: Grand Napoleon - How taken: HM Brig Goldfinch - When taken: 17 Apr 1813 - Where taken: Bay of Biscay - Date received: 8 Jul 1813 - From what ship: Plymouth - Born: Philadelphia - Age: 25 - Discharged on 13 Jun 1814 and sent to Dartmoor.

Cotton, Samuel - Seaman - Number: 10 - How taken: Taken from the MV Avon - When taken: 30 Jun 1813 - Date received: 30 Jun 1813 - From what ship: Bristol - Born: Massachusetts - Age: 25 - Race: Negro - Discharged on 13 Jun 1814 and sent to Dartmoor.

Cramstead, James - Seaman - Number: 38 - Prize name: Paul Jones - Ship type: P - How taken: HM Frigate Leonidas - When taken: 23 May 1813 - Where taken: off Cape Clear (Ireland) - Date received: 8 Jul 1813 - From what ship: Plymouth - Born: New York - Age: 32 - Discharged on 13 Jun 1814 and sent to Dartmoor.

Cross, Oliver - Seaman - Number: 144 - Prize name: Governor Gerry - Ship type: MV - How taken: HM Brig Royalist - When taken: 31 May 1813 - Where taken: Bay of Biscay - Date received: 8 Jul 1813 - From what ship: Plymouth - Born: New York - Age: 44 - Race: Negro - Discharged on 13 Jun 1814 and sent to Dartmoor.

Cudsworth, Henry - Seaman - Number: 141 - Prize name: Governor Gerry - Ship type: MV - How taken: HM Brig Royalist - When taken: 31 May 1813 - Where taken: Bay of Biscay - Date received: 8 Jul 1813 - From what ship: Plymouth - Born: Charleston - Age: 19 - Discharged on 13 Jun 1814 and sent to Dartmoor.

Cummins, James - Seaman - Number: 385 - Prize name: Tom - Ship type: P - How taken: HM Frigate Surveillante - When taken: 27 Apr 1813 - Where taken: Bay of Biscay - Date received: 11 Jul 1813 - From what ship: Plymouth - Born: Connecticut - Age: 22 - Discharged on 16 Jun 1814 and sent to Dartmoor.

Davis, James - Seaman - Number: 240 - Prize name: Essex - Ship type: MV - How taken: HM Frigate Pyramus - When taken: 2 Apr 1813 - Where taken: Bay of Biscay - Date received: 11 Jul 1813 - From what ship: Plymouth - Born: New Brunswick - Age: 26 - Discharged on 16 Jun 1814 and sent to Dartmoor.

Davis, John - Seaman - Number: 158 - Prize name: Leo - Ship type: P - How taken: HM Frigate Magiciene - When taken: 4 Jun 1813 - Where taken: Bay of Biscay - Date received: 8 Jul 1813 - From what ship: Plymouth - Born: Biddeford - Age: 29 - Discharged on 13 Jun 1814 and sent to Dartmoor.

Davis, John - Seaman - Number: 381 - Prize name: Tom - Ship type: P - How taken: HM Frigate Surveillante -

When taken: 27 Apr 1813 - Where taken: Bay of Biscay - Date received: 11 Jul 1813 - From what ship: Plymouth - Born: Massachusetts - Age: 24 - Discharged on 16 Jun 1814 and sent to Dartmoor.

Davis, John - Seaman - Number: 364 - Prize name: Tom - Ship type: P - How taken: HM Frigate Surveillante - When taken: 27 Apr 1813 - Where taken: Bay of Biscay - Date received: 11 Jul 1813 - From what ship: Plymouth - Born: New Orleans - Age: 18 - Discharged on 16 Jun 1814 and sent to Dartmoor.

Davis, William - Seaman - Number: 263 - Prize name: Zebra - Ship type: P - How taken: HM Frigate Pyramus - When taken: 20 Apr 1813 - Where taken: Bay of Biscay - Date received: 11 Jul 1813 - From what ship: Plymouth - Born: Charlestown - Age: 20 - Discharged on 16 Jun 1814 and sent to Dartmoor.

Dean, Jonas - Seaman - Number: 309 - Prize name: Price - Ship type: MV - How taken: HM Frigate Iris - When taken: 13 Apr 1813 - Where taken: Bay of Biscay - Date received: 11 Jul 1813 - From what ship: Plymouth - Born: Massachusetts - Age: 29 - Discharged on 16 Jun 1814 and sent to Dartmoor.

Dean, Nat Benjamin - Seaman - Number: 389 - Prize name: Tom - Ship type: P - How taken: HM Frigate Surveillante - When taken: 27 Apr 1813 - Where taken: Bay of Biscay - Date received: 11 Jul 1813 - From what ship: Plymouth - Born: New Hampshire - Age: 21 - Discharged on 16 Jun 1814 and sent to Dartmoor.

Dibble, Reuben - Seaman - Number: 51 - Prize name: Paul Jones - Ship type: P - How taken: HM Frigate Leonidas - When taken: 23 May 1813 - Where taken: off Cape Clear (Ireland) - Date received: 8 Jul 1813 - From what ship: Plymouth - Born: Hartford, CT - Age: 22 - Discharged on 13 Jun 1814 and sent to Dartmoor.

Dickenson, Chester - Seaman - Number: 92 - Prize name: Courier - Ship type: P - How taken: HM Brig Rover - When taken: 14 Mar 1813 - Where taken: Bay of Biscay - Date received: 8 Jul 1813 - From what ship: Plymouth - Born: Massachusetts - Age: 28 - Discharged on 16 Jun 1814 and sent to Dartmoor.

Dilno, Benjamin - Seaman - Number: 233 - Prize name: Essex - Ship type: MV - How taken: HM Frigate Pyramus - When taken: 2 Apr 1813 - Where taken: Bay of Biscay - Date received: 11 Jul 1813 - From what ship: Plymouth - Born: Massachusetts - Age: 19 - Discharged on 16 Jun 1814 and sent to Dartmoor.

Doliver, William - Seaman - Number: 325 - Prize name: Essex - Ship type: MV - How taken: HM Frigate Pyramus - When taken: 6 Apr 1813 - Where taken: Bay of Biscay - Date received: 11 Jul 1813 - From what ship: Plymouth - Born: Massachusetts - Age: 16 - Discharged on 16 Jun 1814 and sent to Dartmoor.

Doolittle, Henry - Seaman - Number: 384 - Prize name: Tom - Ship type: P - How taken: HM Frigate Surveillante - When taken: 27 Apr 1813 - Where taken: Bay of Biscay - Date received: 11 Jul 1813 - From what ship: Plymouth - Born: Connecticut - Age: 21 - Discharged on 16 Jun 1814 and sent to Dartmoor.

Dougall, Thomas - Seaman - Number: 172 - Prize name: Tickler - Ship type: P - How taken: HM Frigate Magiciene - When taken: 5 Jun 1813 - Where taken: Bay of Biscay - Date received: 8 Jul 1813 - From what ship: Plymouth - Born: Waterford, Ireland - Age: 50 - Discharged on 13 Jun 1814 and sent to Dartmoor.

Doughty, Jesse - Seaman - Number: 160 - Prize name: Leo - Ship type: P - How taken: HM Frigate Magiciene - When taken: 4 Jun 1813 - Where taken: Bay of Biscay - Date received: 8 Jul 1813 - From what ship: Plymouth - Born: Massachusetts - Age: 21 - Discharged on 13 Jun 1814 and sent to Dartmoor.

Doughty, Levi - Seaman - Number: 134 - Prize name: Orders in Council - Ship type: P - How taken: Rebecca - When taken: 1 Jun 1813 - Where taken: Bay of Biscay - Date received: 8 Jul 1813 - From what ship: Plymouth - Born: Brunswick - Age: 22 - Discharged on 13 Jun 1814 and sent to Dartmoor.

Dunn, John - Seaman - Number: 333 - Prize name: Fox - Ship type: P - How taken: HM Sloop Pheasant - When taken: 23 Apr 1813 - Where taken: Bay of Biscay - Date received: 11 Jul 1813 - From what ship: Plymouth - Born: Savannah - Age: 34 - Died on 8 Jun 1814 in hospital.

Durand, John - Seaman - Number: 104 - Prize name: Zebra - Ship type: P - How taken: HM Frigate Pyramus - When taken: 20 Apr 1813 - Where taken: Bay of Biscay - Date received: 8 Jul 1813 - From what ship: Plymouth - Born: New Orleans - Age: 22 - Race: Colored - Discharged on 13 Jun 1814 and sent to Dartmoor.

Edsom, John - Seaman - Number: 114 - Prize name: Zebra - Ship type: P - How taken: HM Frigate Pyramus - When taken: 20 Apr 1813 - Where taken: Bay of Biscay - Date received: 8 Jul 1813 - From what ship: Plymouth - Born: New Hampshire - Age: 28 - Discharged on 16 Jun 1814 and sent to Dartmoor.

Edwards, David - Seaman - Number: 271 - Prize name: Caroline - Ship type: MV - How taken: HM Frigate Medusa

- When taken: 12 Apr 1813 - Where taken: Bay of Biscay - Date received: 11 Jul 1813 - From what ship: Plymouth - Born: New York - Age: 28 - Race: Colored - Discharged on 16 Jun 1814 and sent to Dartmoor.

Edwards, John - Seaman - Number: 36 - Prize name: Paul Jones - Ship type: P - How taken: HM Frigate Leonidas - When taken: 23 May 1813 - Where taken: off Cape Clear (Ireland) - Date received: 8 Jul 1813 - From what ship: Plymouth - Born: Louisiana - Age: 26 - Discharged on 13 Jun 1814 and sent to Dartmoor.

Edwards, John - Carpenter - Number: 396 - Prize name: Paul Jones - Ship type: P - How taken: HM Frigate Leonidas - When taken: 23 May 1813 - Where taken: off Cape Clear (Ireland) - Date received: 11 Jul 1813 - From what ship: Plymouth - Born: New York - Age: 42 - Discharged on 16 Jun 1814 and sent to Dartmoor.

Elwell, Thomas - Seaman - Number: 209 - Prize name: Good Intents - Ship type: Prize - How taken: HM Frigate Pyramus - When taken: 26 Jan 1813 - Where taken: Coast of France - Date received: 11 Jul 1813 - From what ship: Plymouth - Born: Massachusetts - Age: 19 - Discharged on 20 Sep 1813 and sent to the Regulatory Office Bristol for naval service.

English, Edward - Seaman - Number: 147 - Prize name: Revenge - Ship type: P - How taken: HM Frigate Belle Poule - When taken: 10 May 1813 - Where taken: Coast of Spain - Date received: 8 Jul 1813 - From what ship: Plymouth - Born: New York - Age: 25 - Discharged on 13 Jun 1814 and sent to Dartmoor.

Evans, Moses - Seaman - Number: 277 - Prize name: Caroline - Ship type: MV - How taken: HM Frigate Medusa - When taken: 12 Apr 1813 - Where taken: Bay of Biscay - Date received: 11 Jul 1813 - From what ship: Plymouth - Born: Madison County - Age: 25 - Race: Negro - Discharged on 16 Jun 1814 and sent to Dartmoor.

Evelish, William - Seaman - Number: 149 - Prize name: Revenge - Ship type: P - How taken: HM Frigate Belle Poule - When taken: 10 May 1813 - Where taken: Coast of Spain - Date received: 8 Jul 1813 - From what ship: Plymouth - Born: Providence - Age: 17 - Discharged on 13 Jun 1814 and sent to Dartmoor.

Everill, Daniel - Seaman - Number: 221 - Prize name: Napoleon - Ship type: MV - How taken: HM Frigate Belle Poule - When taken: 3 Apr 1813 - Where taken: Bay of Biscay - Date received: 11 Jul 1813 - From what ship: Plymouth - Born: Connecticut - Age: 20 - Discharged on 13 Jun 1814 and sent to Dartmoor.

Faye, Salmon - Seaman - Number: 259 - Prize name: Zebra - Ship type: P - How taken: HM Frigate Pyramus - When taken: 20 Apr 1813 - Where taken: Bay of Biscay - Date received: 11 Jul 1813 - From what ship: Plymouth - Born: Massachusetts - Age: 29 - Discharged on 16 Jun 1814 and sent to Dartmoor.

Fieto, Francis - Seaman - Number: 318 - Prize name: Eliza - Ship type: MV - How taken: HM Frigate Surveillante - When taken: 22 Apr 1813 - Where taken: Bay of Biscay - Date received: 11 Jul 1813 - From what ship: Plymouth - Born: Marblehead - Age: 22 - Discharged on 16 Jun 1814 and sent to Dartmoor.

Fink, Johan - Seaman - Number: 399 - Prize name: Paul Jones - Ship type: P - How taken: HM Frigate Leonidas - When taken: 23 May 1813 - Where taken: off Cape Clear (Ireland) - Date received: 11 Jul 1813 - From what ship: Plymouth - Born: Germany - Age: 25 - Discharged on 16 Jun 1814 and sent to Dartmoor.

Fish, Joseph - Seaman - Number: 216 - Prize name: Hebe - Ship type: MV - How taken: HM Frigate Stag - When taken: 18 Apr 1813 - Where taken: Bay of Biscay - Date received: 11 Jul 1813 - From what ship: Plymouth - Born: Boston - Age: 22 - Race: Mulatto - Discharged on 13 Jun 1814 and sent to Dartmoor.

Fisher, Lewis - Seaman - Number: 207 - Prize name: Essex - Ship type: MV - How taken: HM Frigate Pyramus - When taken: 2 Apr 1813 - Where taken: Bay of Biscay - Date received: 11 Jul 1813 - From what ship: Plymouth - Born: Pennsylvania - Age: 25 - Race: Colored - Discharged on 13 Jun 1814 and sent to Dartmoor.

Fitts, Joseph - Seaman - Number: 274 - Prize name: Caroline - Ship type: MV - How taken: HM Frigate Medusa - When taken: 12 Apr 1813 - Where taken: Bay of Biscay - Date received: 11 Jul 1813 - From what ship: Plymouth - Born: Philadelphia - Age: 41 - Discharged on 16 Jun 1814 and sent to Dartmoor.

Fletcher, James - Seaman - Number: 356 - Prize name: Fox - Ship type: P - How taken: HM Sloop Pheasant - When taken: 24 Apr 1813 - Where taken: Bay of Biscay - Date received: 11 Jul 1813 - From what ship: Plymouth - Born: Massachusetts - Age: 21 - Discharged on 20 Sep 1813 and sent to the Regulatory Office Bristol for naval service.

Flinn, Abraham - Seaman - Number: 150 - Prize name: Revenge - Ship type: P - How taken: HM Frigate Belle Poule - When taken: 10 May 1813 - Where taken: Coast of Spain - Date received: 8 Jul 1813 - From what ship: Plymouth - Born: Boston - Age: 23 - Discharged on 13 Jun 1814 and sent to Dartmoor.

Ford, George - 2nd Mate - Number: 358 - Prize name: Tom - Ship type: P - How taken: HM Frigate Surveillante - When taken: 27 Apr 1813 - Where taken: Bay of Biscay - Date received: 11 Jul 1813 - From what ship: Plymouth - Born: Connecticut - Age: 28 - Discharged on 16 Jun 1814 and sent to Dartmoor.

Foss, Edward - Seaman - Number: 163 - Prize name: Leo - Ship type: P - How taken: HM Frigate Magiciene - When taken: 4 Jun 1813 - Where taken: Bay of Biscay - Date received: 8 Jul 1813 - From what ship: Plymouth - Born: Lymington - Age: 21 - Discharged on 13 Jun 1814 and sent to Dartmoor.

Foss, Joseph - Seaman - Number: 166 - Prize name: Leo - Ship type: P - How taken: HM Frigate Magiciene - When taken: 4 Jun 1813 - Where taken: Bay of Biscay - Date received: 8 Jul 1813 - From what ship: Plymouth - Born: Scarborough - Age: 22 - Discharged on 13 Jun 1814 and sent to Dartmoor.

Foster, John Thomas - 2nd Mate - Number: 167 - Prize name: Tickler - Ship type: P - How taken: HM Frigate Magiciene - When taken: 5 Jun 1813 - Where taken: Bay of Biscay - Date received: 8 Jul 1813 - From what ship: Plymouth - Born: Gloucester - Age: 23 - Discharged on 13 Jun 1814 and sent to Dartmoor.

Fraiser, John - Seaman - Number: 366 - Prize name: Tom - Ship type: P - How taken: HM Frigate Surveillante - When taken: 27 Apr 1813 - Where taken: Bay of Biscay - Date received: 11 Jul 1813 - From what ship: Plymouth - Born: Maryland - Age: 27 - Discharged on 16 Jun 1814 and sent to Dartmoor.

Francis, James - Seaman - Number: 307 - Prize name: Price - Ship type: MV - How taken: HM Frigate Iris - When taken: 13 Apr 1813 - Where taken: Bay of Biscay - Date received: 11 Jul 1813 - From what ship: Plymouth - Born: New York - Age: 18 - Discharged on 16 Jun 1814 and sent to Dartmoor.

Francis, John - Seaman - Number: 305 - Prize name: Price - Ship type: MV - How taken: HM Frigate Iris - When taken: 13 Apr 1813 - Where taken: Bay of Biscay - Date received: 11 Jul 1813 - From what ship: Plymouth - Born: Rhode Island - Age: 23 - Discharged on 16 Jun 1814 and sent to Dartmoor.

Francis, Joseph B. - 2nd Mate - Number: 210 - Prize name: Hebe - Ship type: MV - How taken: HM Frigate Stag - When taken: 18 Apr 1813 - Where taken: Bay of Biscay - Date received: 11 Jul 1813 - From what ship: Plymouth - Born: Providence - Age: 26 - Died on 21 May 1814 in hospital.

Freeman, John - Seaman - Number: 402 - Prize name: Paul Jones - Ship type: P - How taken: HM Frigate Leonidas - When taken: 23 May 1813 - Where taken: off Cape Clear (Ireland) - Date received: 11 Jul 1813 - From what ship: Plymouth - Born: Boston - Age: 32 - Race: Negro - Discharged on 16 Jun 1814 and sent to Dartmoor.

Friday, John - Steward - Number: 397 - Prize name: Paul Jones - Ship type: P - How taken: HM Frigate Leonidas - When taken: 23 May 1813 - Where taken: off Cape Clear (Ireland) - Date received: 11 Jul 1813 - From what ship: Plymouth - Born: New Orleans - Age: 21 - Race: Colored - Discharged on 16 Jun 1814 and sent to Dartmoor.

Gabriel, Joseph - Steward - Number: 195 - Prize name: Governor Gerry - Ship type: MV - How taken: HM Brig Royalist - When taken: 1 Jan 1813 - Where taken: Bay of Biscay - Date received: 8 Jul 1813 - From what ship: Plymouth - Born: New Orleans - Age: 30 - Race: Negro - Discharged on 13 Jun 1814 and sent to Dartmoor.

Gage, Isaac - Seaman - Number: 139 - Prize name: Governor Gerry - Ship type: MV - How taken: HM Brig Royalist - When taken: 31 May 1813 - Where taken: Bay of Biscay - Date received: 8 Jul 1813 - From what ship: Plymouth - Born: Baltimore - Age: 27 - Discharged on 13 Jun 1814 and sent to Dartmoor.

Gardner, Joseph - Seaman - Number: 194 - Prize name: Revenge - Ship type: P - How taken: HM Frigate Belle Poule - When taken: 10 May 1813 - Where taken: Bay of Biscay - Date received: 8 Jul 1813 - From what ship: Plymouth - Born: Boston - Age: 21 - Race: Negro - Discharged on 13 Jun 1814 and sent to Dartmoor.

Gee, Thomas - Seaman - Number: 405 - Prize name: Tom - Ship type: P - How taken: HM Frigate Surveillante - When taken: 27 Apr 1813 - Where taken: Bay of Biscay - Date received: 11 Jul 1813 - From what ship: Plymouth - Born: Virginia - Age: 29 - Discharged on 16 Jun 1814 and sent to Dartmoor.

Geyer, Joseph - Carpenter - Number: 183 - Prize name: Revenge - Ship type: P - How taken: HM Frigate Belle

Poule - When taken: 10 May 1813 - Where taken: Bay of Biscay - Date received: 8 Jul 1813 - From what ship: Plymouth - Born: Boston - Age: 28 - Discharged on 13 Jun 1814 and sent to Dartmoor.

Gibbs, Henry - Seaman - Number: 25 - Prize name: Paul Jones - Ship type: P - How taken: HM Frigate Leonidas - When taken: 23 May 1813 - Where taken: off Cape Clear (Ireland) - Date received: 8 Jul 1813 - From what ship: Plymouth - Born: Massachusetts - Age: 18 - Discharged on 13 Jun 1814 and sent to Dartmoor.

Godfrey, William - Seaman - Number: 20 - Prize name: Paul Jones - Ship type: P - How taken: HM Frigate Leonidas - When taken: 23 May 1813 - Where taken: off Cape Clear (Ireland) - Date received: 8 Jul 1813 - From what ship: Plymouth - Born: Providence, RI - Age: 19 - Race: Colored - Discharged on 13 Jun 1814 and sent to Dartmoor.

Goodwin, William - Seaman - Number: 132 - Prize name: Orders in Council - Ship type: P - How taken: Rebecca - When taken: 1 Jun 1813 - Where taken: Bay of Biscay - Date received: 8 Jul 1813 - From what ship: Plymouth - Born: New York - Age: 29 - Discharged on 13 Jun 1814 and sent to Dartmoor.

Gore, William (see prisoner number 421) - Seaman - Number: 162 - Prize name: Leo - Ship type: P - How taken: HM Frigate Magiciene - When taken: 4 Jun 1813 - Where taken: Bay of Biscay - Date received: 8 Jul 1813 - From what ship: Plymouth - Born: Waterford - Age: 20 - Escaped on 22 Apr 1814 and recaptured.

Gore, William - Seaman - Number: 421 - Prize name: Leo - Ship type: L - How taken: HM Frigate Magiciene - When taken: 2 Jun 1813 - Where taken: Bay of Biscay - Date received: 26 Apr 1813 - From what ship: Retaken at Bristol - Born: Waterford - Age: 20 - Discharged on 16 Jun 1814 and sent to Dartmoor.

Gray, Morehouse - Seaman - Number: 223 - Prize name: Napoleon - Ship type: MV - How taken: HM Frigate Belle Poule - When taken: 3 Apr 1813 - Where taken: Bay of Biscay - Date received: 11 Jul 1813 - From what ship: Plymouth - Born: Connecticut - Age: 25 - Discharged on 13 Jun 1814 and sent to Dartmoor.

Green, William - Seaman - Number: 48 - Prize name: Paul Jones - Ship type: P - How taken: HM Frigate Leonidas - When taken: 23 May 1813 - Where taken: off Cape Clear (Ireland) - Date received: 8 Jul 1813 - From what ship: Plymouth - Born: New Jersey - Age: 39 - Race: Negro - Discharged on 13 Jun 1814 and sent to Dartmoor.

Grosse, William - Boy - Number: 63 - Prize name: Paul Jones - Ship type: P - How taken: HM Frigate Leonidas - When taken: 23 May 1813 - Where taken: off Cape Clear (Ireland) - Date received: 8 Jul 1813 - From what ship: Plymouth - Born: New York - Age: 14 - Discharged on 13 Jun 1814 and sent to Dartmoor.

Guillard, Louis - Seaman - Number: 59 - Prize name: Paul Jones - Ship type: P - How taken: HM Frigate Leonidas - When taken: 23 May 1813 - Where taken: off Cape Clear (Ireland) - Date received: 8 Jul 1813 - From what ship: Plymouth - Born: New Orleans - Age: 21 - Discharged on 13 Jun 1814 and sent to Dartmoor.

Guillard, Peter - Seaman - Number: 54 - Prize name: Paul Jones - Ship type: P - How taken: HM Frigate Leonidas - When taken: 23 May 1813 - Where taken: off Cape Clear (Ireland) - Date received: 8 Jul 1813 - From what ship: Plymouth - Born: Nantz, France - Age: 20 - Discharged on 13 Jun 1814 and sent to Dartmoor.

Hacking, Robert - Seaman - Number: 176 - Prize name: Tickler - Ship type: P - How taken: HM Frigate Magiciene - When taken: 5 Jun 1813 - Where taken: Bay of Biscay - Date received: 8 Jul 1813 - From what ship: Plymouth - Born: Hudson, NY - Age: 33 - Discharged on 10 Sep 1813 and sent to the Regulatory Office Bristol for naval service.

Haight, John - Seaman - Number: 78 - Prize name: Grand Napoleon - How taken: HM Brig Goldfinch - When taken: 17 Apr 1813 - Where taken: Bay of Biscay - Date received: 8 Jul 1813 - From what ship: Plymouth - Born: New York - Age: 39 - Discharged on 11 Sep 1813 and sent to the Regulatory Office Bristol for naval service.

Hale, Shederick - Seaman - Number: 293 - Prize name: Messenger - Ship type: MV - How taken: HM Frigate Iris - When taken: 10 Mar 1813 - Where taken: off Cape Ortegal (Spain) - Date received: 11 Jul 1813 - From what ship: Plymouth - Born: Baltimore - Age: 42 - Discharged on 16 Jun 1814 and sent to Dartmoor.

Hamilton, Alexander Montgomery - Boy - Number: 61 - Prize name: Paul Jones - Ship type: P - How taken: HM Frigate Leonidas - When taken: 23 May 1813 - Where taken: off Cape Clear (Ireland) - Date received: 8 Jul 1813 - From what ship: Plymouth - Born: Boston - Age: 14 - Discharged on 13 Jun 1814 and sent to Dartmoor.

Hammond, Joseph - Seaman - Number: 319 - Prize name: Eliza - Ship type: MV - How taken: HM Frigate Surveillante - When taken: 22 Apr 1813 - Where taken: Bay of Biscay - Date received: 11 Jul 1813 - From what ship: Plymouth - Born: Marblehead - Age: 21 - Discharged on 16 Jun 1814 and sent to Dartmoor.

Hanford, William - Seaman - Number: 267 - Prize name: Zebra - Ship type: P - How taken: HM Frigate Pyramus - When taken: 20 Apr 1813 - Where taken: Bay of Biscay - Date received: 11 Jul 1813 - From what ship: Plymouth - Born: Connecticut - Age: 24 - Discharged on 16 Jun 1814 and sent to Dartmoor.

Hanson, Christopher - Seaman - Number: 213 - Prize name: Hebe - Ship type: MV - How taken: HM Frigate Stag - When taken: 18 Apr 1813 - Where taken: Bay of Biscay - Date received: 11 Jul 1813 - From what ship: Plymouth - Born: Copenhagen - Age: 32 - Discharged on 20 Jan 1814 and sent to the Naval Rendezvous Bristol.

Harrington, Simon - Seaman - Number: 250 - Prize name: Zebra - Ship type: P - How taken: HM Frigate Pyramus - When taken: 20 Apr 1813 - Where taken: Bay of Biscay - Date received: 11 Jul 1813 - From what ship: Plymouth - Born: Massachusetts - Age: 23 - Discharged on 16 Jun 1814 and sent to Dartmoor.

Harris, James - Seaman - Number: 197 - Prize name: Governor Gerry - Ship type: MV - How taken: HM Brig Royalist - When taken: 1 Jan 1813 - Where taken: Bay of Biscay - Date received: 8 Jul 1813 - From what ship: Plymouth - Born: New Orleans - Age: 19 - Race: Negro - Discharged on 13 Jun 1814 and sent to Dartmoor.

Harris, John - Seaman - Number: 3 - How taken: Gave himself up from HM Frigate Venus - When taken: 2 Jan 1813 - Date received: 2 Jan 1813 - From what ship: Bristol - Born: Abbott County - Age: 20 - Race: Negro - Discharged on 13 Jun 1814 and sent to Dartmoor.

Harris, John - Seaman - Number: 338 - Prize name: Fox - Ship type: P - How taken: HM Sloop Pheasant - When taken: 23 Apr 1813 - Where taken: Bay of Biscay - Date received: 11 Jul 1813 - From what ship: Plymouth - Born: Pennsylvania - Age: 26 - Race: Negro - Discharged on 16 Jun 1814 and sent to Dartmoor.

Harris, William Burr - 2nd Mate - Number: 329 - Prize name: Fox - Ship type: P - How taken: HM Sloop Pheasant - When taken: 23 Apr 1813 - Where taken: Bay of Biscay - Date received: 11 Jul 1813 - From what ship: Plymouth - Born: New Jersey - Age: 28 - Discharged on 16 Jun 1814 and sent to Dartmoor.

Hart, James - Seaman - Number: 85 - Prize name: Courier - Ship type: P - How taken: HM Brig Rover - When taken: 14 Mar 1813 - Where taken: Bay of Biscay - Date received: 8 Jul 1813 - From what ship: Plymouth - Born: New London - Age: 28 - Discharged on 13 Jun 1814 and sent to Dartmoor.

Haskell, Robert - Mate - Number: 135 - Prize name: Orders in Council - Ship type: P - How taken: Rebecca - When taken: 1 Jun 1813 - Where taken: Bay of Biscay - Date received: 8 Jul 1813 - From what ship: Plymouth - Born: Manchester, MA - Age: 30 - Discharged on 13 Jun 1814 and sent to Dartmoor.

Haye, Moses - Boy - Number: 314 - Prize name: Price - Ship type: MV - How taken: HM Frigate Iris - When taken: 13 Apr 1813 - Where taken: Bay of Biscay - Date received: 11 Jul 1813 - From what ship: Plymouth - Born: Savannah - Age: 16 - Discharged on 16 Jun 1814 and sent to Dartmoor.

Healy, John - Seaman - Number: 188 - Prize name: Revenge - Ship type: P - How taken: HM Frigate Belle Poule - When taken: 10 May 1813 - Where taken: Bay of Biscay - Date received: 8 Jul 1813 - From what ship: Plymouth - Born: Boston - Age: 20 - Discharged on 13 Jun 1814 and sent to Dartmoor.

Heard, Thomas - Seaman - Number: 387 - Prize name: Tom - Ship type: P - How taken: HM Frigate Surveillante - When taken: 27 Apr 1813 - Where taken: Bay of Biscay - Date received: 11 Jul 1813 - From what ship: Plymouth - Born: New Jersey - Age: 28 - Discharged on 16 Jun 1814 and sent to Dartmoor.

Heckman, Joseph - Seaman - Number: 303 - Prize name: Price - Ship type: MV - How taken: HM Frigate Iris - When taken: 13 Apr 1813 - Where taken: Bay of Biscay - Date received: 11 Jul 1813 - From what ship: Plymouth - Born: New Jersey - Age: 22 - Discharged on 16 Jun 1814 and sent to Dartmoor.

Hensell, John - Seaman - Number: 323 - Prize name: Shadow - Ship type: P - How taken: HM Brig Reindeer - When taken: 6 Apr 1813 - Where taken: Bay of Biscay - Date received: 11 Jul 1813 - From what ship: Plymouth - Born: Philadelphia - Age: 27 - Discharged on 16 Jun 1814 and sent to Dartmoor.

Herrendon, John - Chief Mate - Number: 415 - How taken: Taken off the Portuguese MV Senora del Manda - When taken: 9 Nov 1813 - Date received: 9 Nov 1813 - From what ship: Naval Rendezvous Bristol - Born: Maine - Age: 27 - Escaped on 18 May 1814.

Hill, John - Seaman - Number: 202 - Prize name: Governor Gerry - Ship type: MV - How taken: HM Brig Royalist - When taken: 1 Jan 1813 - Where taken: Bay of Biscay - Date received: 8 Jul 1813 - From what ship: Plymouth - Born: Philadelphia - Age: 21 - Race: Colored - Discharged on 16 Jun 1814 and sent to Dartmoor.

Hobson, Abraham - Seaman - Number: 226 - Prize name: Napoleon - Ship type: MV - How taken: HM Frigate Belle Poule - When taken: 3 Apr 1813 - Where taken: Bay of Biscay - Date received: 11 Jul 1813 - From what ship: Plymouth - Born: Connecticut - Age: 21 - Discharged on 13 Jun 1814 and sent to Dartmoor.

Holland, Richard - Seaman - Number: 153 - Prize name: Revenge - Ship type: P - How taken: HM Frigate Belle Poule - When taken: 10 May 1813 - Where taken: Coast of Spain - Date received: 8 Jul 1813 - From what ship: Plymouth - Born: Maryland - Age: 25 - Discharged on 13 Jun 1814 and sent to Dartmoor.

Hollinger, William - Boatswain - Number: 360 - Prize name: Tom - Ship type: P - How taken: HM Frigate Surveillante - When taken: 27 Apr 1813 - Where taken: Bay of Biscay - Date received: 11 Jul 1813 - From what ship: Plymouth - Born: Virginia - Age: 29 - Race: Black - Discharged on 16 Jun 1814 and sent to Dartmoor.

Hooper, Benjamin C. - Seaman - Number: 203 - Prize name: Governor Gerry - Ship type: MV - How taken: HM Brig Royalist - When taken: 1 Jan 1813 - Where taken: Bay of Biscay - Date received: 8 Jul 1813 - From what ship: Plymouth - Born: New York - Age: 23 - Discharged on 13 Jun 1814 and sent to Dartmoor.

Hopkins, Daniel - Seaman - Number: 101 - Prize name: Courier - Ship type: P - How taken: HM Brig Rover - When taken: 14 Mar 1813 - Where taken: Bay of Biscay - Date received: 8 Jul 1813 - From what ship: Plymouth - Born: Maryland - Age: 28 - Discharged on 13 Jun 1814 and sent to Dartmoor.

Hopkins, Elisha - Seaman - Number: 181 - Prize name: Omer - Ship type: MV - How taken: New Boston - When taken: 13 May 1813 - Where taken: Channel - Date received: 8 Jul 1813 - From what ship: Plymouth - Born: Massachusetts - Age: 18 - Discharged on 3 Sep 1813 and sent to the Naval Rendezvous Bristol.

Howard, William - Boatswain - Number: 330 - Prize name: Fox - Ship type: P - How taken: HM Sloop Pheasant - When taken: 23 Apr 1813 - Where taken: Bay of Biscay - Date received: 11 Jul 1813 - From what ship: Plymouth - Born: Baltimore - Age: 26 - Discharged on 25 Mar 1814 and sent to the Naval Rendezvous Bristol.

Hudson, Thomas - Boy - Number: 145 - Prize name: Revenge - Ship type: P - How taken: HM Frigate Belle Poule - When taken: 10 May 1813 - Where taken: Coast of Spain - Date received: 8 Jul 1813 - From what ship: Plymouth - Born: Richmond, VA - Age: 18 - Discharged on 13 Jun 1814 and sent to Dartmoor.

Hunter, William - Seaman - Number: 306 - Prize name: Price - Ship type: MV - How taken: HM Frigate Iris - When taken: 13 Apr 1813 - Where taken: Bay of Biscay - Date received: 11 Jul 1813 - From what ship: Plymouth - Born: New York - Age: 18 - Discharged on 16 Jun 1814 and sent to Dartmoor.

Hutchins, Henry - Seaman - Number: 71 - Prize name: Grand Napoleon - How taken: HM Brig Goldfinch - When taken: 17 Apr 1813 - Where taken: Bay of Biscay - Date received: 8 Jul 1813 - From what ship: Plymouth - Born: New York - Age: 21 - Discharged on 13 Jun 1814 and sent to Dartmoor.

Ingerson, Michael - Seaman - Number: 304 - Prize name: Price - Ship type: MV - How taken: HM Frigate Iris - When taken: 13 Apr 1813 - Where taken: Bay of Biscay - Date received: 11 Jul 1813 - From what ship: Plymouth - Born: New Jersey - Age: 21 - Discharged on 16 Jun 1814 and sent to Dartmoor.

Ingle, John - Seaman - Number: 288 - Prize name: Messenger - Ship type: MV - How taken: HM Frigate Iris - When taken: 10 Mar 1813 - Where taken: off Cape Ortegal (Spain) - Date received: 11 Jul 1813 - From what ship: Plymouth - Born: Baltimore - Age: 26 - Discharged on 16 Jun 1814 and sent to Dartmoor.

Inglis, David - Seaman - Number: 178 - How taken: Impressed from the English Merchantman Nile - When taken: 15 Mar 1813 - Date received: 8 Jul 1813 - From what ship: Plymouth - Born: Chester - Age: 30 - Discharged on 13 Jun 1814 and sent to Dartmoor.

Irvin, Arthur - Boy - Number: 62 - Prize name: Paul Jones - Ship type: P - How taken: HM Frigate Leonidas - When taken: 23 May 1813 - Where taken: off Cape Clear (Ireland) - Date received: 8 Jul 1813 - From what ship:

Plymouth - Born: Philadelphia - Age: 16 - Discharged on 13 Jun 1814 and sent to Dartmoor.

Jackson, Henry - 2nd Lieutenant - Number: 93 - Prize name: Paul Jones - Ship type: P - How taken: HM Frigate Leonidas - When taken: 23 May 1813 - Where taken: off Cape Clear (Ireland) - Date received: 8 Jul 1813 - From what ship: Plymouth - Born: Maryland - Age: 25 - Escaped on 2 Sep 1813.

Jackson, Joseph - Seaman - Number: 251 - Prize name: Zebra - Ship type: P - How taken: HM Frigate Pyramus - When taken: 20 Apr 1813 - Where taken: Bay of Biscay - Date received: 11 Jul 1813 - From what ship: Plymouth - Born: New Brunswick - Age: 25 - Discharged on 16 Jun 1814 and sent to Dartmoor.

Jacobs, Evan - Seaman - Number: 11 - Prize name: Chantitle - Date received: 30 Jun 1813 - From what ship: Bristol - Born: Newburyport, MA - Age: 25 - Discharged on 9 Aug 1813 and sent to the Naval Rendezvous Bristol.

James, Daniel - Seaman - Number: 340 - Prize name: Fox - Ship type: P - How taken: HM Sloop Pheasant - When taken: 23 Apr 1813 - Where taken: Bay of Biscay - Date received: 11 Jul 1813 - From what ship: Plymouth - Born: Boston - Age: 26 - Discharged on 16 Jun 1814 and sent to Dartmoor.

Jassieu, Louis - Seaman - Number: 33 - Prize name: Paul Jones - Ship type: P - How taken: HM Frigate Leonidas - When taken: 23 May 1813 - Where taken: off Cape Clear (Ireland) - Date received: 8 Jul 1813 - From what ship: Plymouth - Born: New Orleans - Age: 18 - Discharged on 13 Jun 1814 and sent to Dartmoor.

Jefferson, Edward - Seaman - Number: 414 - How taken: Apprehended at Bristol - When taken: 14 Sep 1813 - Date received: 14 Sep 1813 - From what ship: Naval Rendezvous Bristol - Born: Virginia - Age: 20 - Discharged on 16 Jun 1814 and sent to Dartmoor.

Jenkins, Nathaniel - Seaman - Number: 388 - Prize name: Tom - Ship type: P - How taken: HM Frigate Surveillante - When taken: 27 Apr 1813 - Where taken: Bay of Biscay - Date received: 11 Jul 1813 - From what ship: Plymouth - Born: Baltimore - Age: 19 - Race: Negro - Discharged on 16 Jun 1814 and sent to Dartmoor.

Johnson, James - Seaman - Number: 284 - Prize name: Messenger - Ship type: MV - How taken: HM Frigate Iris - When taken: 10 Mar 1813 - Where taken: off Cape Ortegal (Spain) - Date received: 11 Jul 1813 - From what ship: Plymouth - Born: Maryland - Age: 19 - Discharged on 16 Jun 1814 and sent to Dartmoor.

Johnson, Joseph Toker - Seaman - Number: 43 - Prize name: Paul Jones - Ship type: P - How taken: HM Frigate Leonidas - When taken: 23 May 1813 - Where taken: off Cape Clear (Ireland) - Date received: 8 Jul 1813 - From what ship: Plymouth - Born: Hartford, CT - Age: 19 - Discharged on 13 Jun 1814 and sent to Dartmoor.

Johnson, Lambert - Seaman - Number: 29 - Prize name: Paul Jones - Ship type: P - How taken: HM Frigate Leonidas - When taken: 23 May 1813 - Where taken: off Cape Clear (Ireland) - Date received: 8 Jul 1813 - From what ship: Plymouth - Born: Middleton, NY - Age: 23 - Discharged on 13 Jun 1814 and sent to Dartmoor.

Johnstone, Simon - Seaman - Number: 351 - Prize name: Shadow - Ship type: P - How taken: HM Brig Reindeer - When taken: 6 Apr 1813 - Where taken: Bay of Biscay - Date received: 11 Jul 1813 - From what ship: Plymouth - Born: Hamburg - Age: 33 - Discharged on 16 Jun 1814 and sent to Dartmoor.

Joles, Robert - Seaman - Number: 174 - Prize name: Tickler - Ship type: P - How taken: HM Frigate Magiciene - When taken: 5 Jun 1813 - Where taken: Bay of Biscay - Date received: 8 Jul 1813 - From what ship: Plymouth - Born: Rhode Island - Age: 37 - Discharged on 13 Jun 1814 and sent to Dartmoor.

Jones, John - Seaman - Number: 352 - Prize name: Shadow - Ship type: P - How taken: HM Brig Reindeer - When taken: 6 Apr 1813 - Where taken: Bay of Biscay - Date received: 11 Jul 1813 - From what ship: Plymouth - Born: Guadeloupe - Age: 20 - Race: Negro - Discharged on 16 Jun 1814 and sent to Dartmoor.

Jones, Thomas - Seaman - Number: 407 - How taken: Impressed at Liverpool - When taken: 12 May 1813 - Date received: 20 Jul 1813 - From what ship: Bridgewater - Born: Baltimore - Age: 22 - Discharged on 16 Jun 1814 and sent to Dartmoor.

Jones, Thomas - Seaman - Number: 205 - Prize name: Governor Gerry - Ship type: MV - How taken: HM Brig Royalist - When taken: 1 Jan 1813 - Where taken: Bay of Biscay - Date received: 8 Jul 1813 - From what ship: Plymouth - Born: New York - Age: 28 - Discharged on 13 Jun 1814 and sent to Dartmoor.

Joseph, Francis - Seaman - Number: 206 - Prize name: Paul Jones - Ship type: P - How taken: HM Frigate Leonidas

- When taken: 23 May 1813 - Where taken: off Cape Clear (Ireland) - Date received: 8 Jul 1813 - From what ship: Plymouth - Born: Lisbon, Portugal - Age: 23 - Discharged on 2 Sep 1813 and sent to the Portuguese Consul.

Judson, Obadiah - Seaman - Number: 6 - How taken: Gave himself up from HMS Harmony - When taken: 26 Mar 1813 - Date received: 26 Mar 1813 - From what ship: Bristol - Born: New Haven - Age: 40 - Race: Negro - Discharged on 13 Jun 1814 and sent to Dartmoor.

Keg, Philip - Seaman - Number: 409 - How taken: Impressed from MV Hopewell - When taken: 16 Aug 1813 - Date received: 16 Aug 1813 - From what ship: Naval Rendezvous Bristol - Born: Pennsylvania - Age: 36 - Discharged on 16 Jun 1814 and sent to Dartmoor.

Keller, John - Seaman - Number: 196 - Prize name: Governor Gerry - Ship type: MV - How taken: HM Brig Royalist - When taken: 1 Jan 1813 - Where taken: Bay of Biscay - Date received: 8 Jul 1813 - From what ship: Plymouth - Born: Boston - Age: 40 - Discharged on 13 Jun 1814 and sent to Dartmoor.

Kellinger, John - Seaman - Number: 186 - Prize name: Revenge - Ship type: P - How taken: HM Frigate Belle Poule - When taken: 10 May 1813 - Where taken: Bay of Biscay - Date received: 8 Jul 1813 - From what ship: Plymouth - Born: Maryland - Age: 32 - Race: Mulatto - Discharged on 13 Jun 1814 and sent to Dartmoor.

King, Joseph - Seaman - Number: 398 - Prize name: Paul Jones - Ship type: P - How taken: HM Frigate Leonidas - When taken: 23 May 1813 - Where taken: off Cape Clear (Ireland) - Date received: 11 Jul 1813 - From what ship: Plymouth - Born: Lisbon, Portugal - Age: 48 - Discharged on 2 Sep 1813 and sent to the Portuguese Consul.

Lacour, John Baptist - Seaman - Number: 403 - Prize name: Paul Jones - Ship type: P - How taken: HM Frigate Leonidas - When taken: 23 May 1813 - Where taken: off Cape Clear (Ireland) - Date received: 11 Jul 1813 - From what ship: Plymouth - Born: Naples - Age: 51 - Discharged on 16 Jun 1814 and sent to Dartmoor.

Laill, Joseph - Cook - Number: 222 - Prize name: Napoleon - Ship type: MV - How taken: HM Frigate Belle Poule - When taken: 3 Apr 1813 - Where taken: Bay of Biscay - Date received: 11 Jul 1813 - From what ship: Plymouth - Born: New York - Age: 19 - Race: Negro - Discharged on 9 Aug 1813 and sent to the Naval Rendezvous Bristol.

Lake, Charles - Seaman - Number: 417 - How taken: Apprehended at Bristol - When taken: 9 Nov 1813 - Date received: 9 Nov 1813 - From what ship: Naval Rendezvous Bristol - Born: Philadelphia - Age: 23 - Discharged on 16 Jun 1814 and sent to Dartmoor.

Lambert, Joseph - Seaman - Number: 281 - Prize name: Caroline - Ship type: MV - How taken: HM Frigate Medusa - When taken: 12 Apr 1813 - Where taken: Bay of Biscay - Date received: 11 Jul 1813 - From what ship: Plymouth - Born: New York - Age: 24 - Race: Negro - Discharged on 9 Aug 1813 and sent to the Naval Rendezvous Bristol.

Lamond, John - Seaman - Number: 146 - Prize name: Revenge - Ship type: P - How taken: HM Frigate Belle Poule - When taken: 10 May 1813 - Where taken: Coast of Spain - Date received: 8 Jul 1813 - From what ship: Plymouth - Born: Philadelphia - Age: 37 - Discharged on 13 Jun 1814 and sent to Dartmoor.

Lane, James - Seaman - Number: 72 - Prize name: Grand Napoleon - How taken: HM Brig Goldfinch - When taken: 17 Apr 1813 - Where taken: Bay of Biscay - Date received: 8 Jul 1813 - From what ship: Plymouth - Born: New York - Age: 24 - Discharged on 13 Jun 1814 and sent to Dartmoor.

Laurence, John - Seaman - Number: 258 - Prize name: Zebra - Ship type: P - How taken: HM Frigate Pyramus - When taken: 20 Apr 1813 - Where taken: Bay of Biscay - Date received: 11 Jul 1813 - From what ship: Plymouth - Born: Isle of France - Age: 26 - Race: Colored - Discharged on 16 Jun 1814 and sent to Dartmoor.

Layfield, Littleton - Seaman - Number: 368 - Prize name: Tom - Ship type: P - How taken: HM Frigate Surveillante - When taken: 27 Apr 1813 - Where taken: Bay of Biscay - Date received: 11 Jul 1813 - From what ship: Plymouth - Born: Maryland - Age: 20 - Discharged on 16 Jun 1814 and sent to Dartmoor.

Lerna, John - Boy - Number: 117 - Prize name: Good Friends - Ship type: MV - How taken: HM Frigate Andromache - When taken: 2 Apr 1813 - Where taken: Bay of Biscay - Date received: 8 Jul 1813 - From what ship: Plymouth - Born: Leghorn, Italy - Age: 18 - Race: Negro - Discharged on 13 Jun 1814 and sent to

Dartmoor.

Lewis, Robert - Seaman - Number: 367 - Prize name: Tom - Ship type: P - How taken: HM Frigate Surveillante - When taken: 27 Apr 1813 - Where taken: Bay of Biscay - Date received: 11 Jul 1813 - From what ship: Plymouth - Born: Rhode Island - Age: 23 - Discharged on 16 Jun 1814 and sent to Dartmoor.

Libley, Moses - Seaman - Number: 245 - Prize name: Essex - Ship type: MV - How taken: HM Frigate Pyramus - When taken: 2 Apr 1813 - Where taken: Bay of Biscay - Date received: 11 Jul 1813 - From what ship: Plymouth - Born: New Hampshire - Age: 28 - Discharged on 16 Jun 1814 and sent to Dartmoor.

Lilley, Simon - Seaman - Number: 327 - Prize name: Shadow - Ship type: P - How taken: HM Brig Reindeer - When taken: 6 Apr 1813 - Where taken: Bay of Biscay - Date received: 11 Jul 1813 - From what ship: Plymouth - Born: Massachusetts - Age: 19 - Discharged on 16 Jun 1814 and sent to Dartmoor.

Linsey, Alexander - Boy - Number: 201 - Prize name: Governor Gerry - Ship type: MV - How taken: HM Brig Royalist - When taken: 1 Jan 1813 - Where taken: Bay of Biscay - Date received: 8 Jul 1813 - From what ship: Plymouth - Born: Baltimore - Age: 16 - Discharged on 13 Jun 1814 and sent to Dartmoor.

Little, George - Sailmaker - Number: 66 - Prize name: Paul Jones - Ship type: P - How taken: HM Frigate Leonidas - When taken: 23 May 1813 - Where taken: off Cape Clear (Ireland) - Date received: 8 Jul 1813 - From what ship: Plymouth - Born: Roxbury, MA - Age: 25 - Discharged on 13 Jun 1814 and sent to Dartmoor.

Littlefield, Rufus - Seaman - Number: 129 - Prize name: Miranda - Ship type: Prize of Paul Jones - How taken: HM Frigate Unicorn - When taken: 21 May 1813 - Where taken: Bay of Biscay - Date received: 8 Jul 1813 - From what ship: Plymouth - Born: Massachusetts - Age: 17 - Discharged on 13 Jun 1814 and sent to Dartmoor.

Lockwood, Rufus - Clerk - Number: 394 - Prize name: Paul Jones - Ship type: P - How taken: HM Frigate Leonidas - When taken: 23 May 1813 - Where taken: off Cape Clear (Ireland) - Date received: 11 Jul 1813 - From what ship: Plymouth - Born: Connecticut - Age: 22 - Escaped on 14 Jun 1814.

Logan, William - Seaman - Number: 97 - Prize name: Courier - Ship type: P - How taken: HM Brig Rover - When taken: 14 Mar 1813 - Where taken: Bay of Biscay - Date received: 8 Jul 1813 - From what ship: Plymouth - Born: Baltimore - Age: 23 - Discharged on 13 Jun 1814 and sent to Dartmoor.

Lomeril, Robert - Seaman - Number: 238 - Prize name: Essex - Ship type: MV - How taken: HM Frigate Pyramus - When taken: 2 Apr 1813 - Where taken: Bay of Biscay - Date received: 11 Jul 1813 - From what ship: Plymouth - Born: Massachusetts - Age: 19 - Escaped on 15 Jun 1814.

Longford, Samuel - Seaman - Number: 317 - Prize name: Eliza - Ship type: MV - How taken: HM Frigate Surveillante - When taken: 22 Apr 1813 - Where taken: Bay of Biscay - Date received: 11 Jul 1813 - From what ship: Plymouth - Born: Maryland - Age: 23 - Discharged on 16 Jun 1814 and sent to Dartmoor.

Lothrop, James - Seaman - Number: 152 - Prize name: Revenge - Ship type: P - How taken: HM Frigate Belle Poule - When taken: 10 May 1813 - Where taken: Coast of Spain - Date received: 8 Jul 1813 - From what ship: Plymouth - Born: Boston - Age: 26 - Discharged on 13 Jun 1814 and sent to Dartmoor.

Louis, Nicholas - Seaman - Number: 21 - Prize name: Paul Jones - Ship type: P - How taken: HM Frigate Leonidas - When taken: 23 May 1813 - Where taken: off Cape Clear (Ireland) - Date received: 8 Jul 1813 - From what ship: Plymouth - Born: Portsmouth, NH - Age: 44 - Discharged on 13 Jun 1814 and sent to Dartmoor.

Lowe, John - Seaman - Number: 247 - Prize name: Essex - Ship type: MV - How taken: HM Frigate Pyramus - When taken: 2 Apr 1813 - Where taken: Bay of Biscay - Date received: 11 Jul 1813 - From what ship: Plymouth - Born: Baltimore - Age: 18 - Discharged on 16 Jun 1814 and sent to Dartmoor.

Ludson, Daniel - Seaman - Number: 119 - Prize name: Eliza - Ship type: MV - How taken: HM Frigate Surveillante - When taken: 27 Mar 1813 - Where taken: Bay of Biscay - Date received: 8 Jul 1813 - From what ship: Plymouth - Born: Rhode Island - Age: 28 - Discharged on 13 Jun 1814 and sent to Dartmoor.

Lyon, Charles - Seaman - Number: 257 - Prize name: Zebra - Ship type: P - How taken: HM Frigate Pyramus - When taken: 20 Apr 1813 - Where taken: Bay of Biscay - Date received: 11 Jul 1813 - From what ship: Plymouth - Born: New Jersey - Age: 21 - Discharged on 16 Jun 1814 and sent to Dartmoor.

Mack, Theoron - Seaman - Number: 348 - Prize name: Fox - Ship type: P - How taken: HM Sloop Pheasant - When taken: 23 Apr 1813 - Where taken: Bay of Biscay - Date received: 11 Jul 1813 - From what ship: Plymouth - Born: New York - Age: 24 - Escaped on 15 Jun 1814.

Maine, William - Seaman - Number: 208 - Prize name: Essex - Ship type: MV - How taken: HM Frigate Pyramus - When taken: 2 Apr 1813 - Where taken: Bay of Biscay - Date received: 11 Jul 1813 - From what ship: Plymouth - Born: Marblehead - Age: 20 - Discharged on 13 Jun 1814 and sent to Dartmoor.

Mansfield, James - Seaman - Number: 378 - Prize name: Tom - Ship type: P - How taken: HM Frigate Surveillante - When taken: 27 Apr 1813 - Where taken: Bay of Biscay - Date received: 11 Jul 1813 - From what ship: Plymouth - Born: Boston - Age: 20 - Discharged on 16 Jun 1814 and sent to Dartmoor.

Manson, Jeremiah - 2nd Mate - Number: 249 - Prize name: Zebra - Ship type: P - How taken: HM Frigate Pyramus - When taken: 20 Apr 1813 - Where taken: Bay of Biscay - Date received: 11 Jul 1813 - From what ship: Plymouth - Born: Philadelphia - Age: 25 - Discharged on 16 Jun 1814 and sent to Dartmoor.

Manson, Nathaniel - Seaman - Number: 157 - Prize name: Leo - Ship type: P - How taken: HM Frigate Magiciene - When taken: 4 Jun 1813 - Where taken: Bay of Biscay - Date received: 8 Jul 1813 - From what ship: Plymouth - Born: Lymington - Age: 22 - Discharged on 13 Jun 1814 and sent to Dartmoor.

Manson, William - Seaman - Number: 86 - Prize name: Courier - Ship type: P - How taken: HM Brig Rover - When taken: 14 Mar 1813 - Where taken: Bay of Biscay - Date received: 8 Jul 1813 - From what ship: Plymouth - Born: Massachusetts - Age: 25 - Discharged on 13 Jun 1814 and sent to Dartmoor.

Marshall, Alexander - Seaman - Number: 322 - Prize name: Shadow - Ship type: P - How taken: HM Brig Reindeer - When taken: 6 Apr 1813 - Where taken: Bay of Biscay - Date received: 11 Jul 1813 - From what ship: Plymouth - Born: Philadelphia - Age: 23 - Discharged on 16 Jun 1814 and sent to Dartmoor.

Martin, Anthony - Seaman - Number: 272 - Prize name: Caroline - Ship type: MV - How taken: HM Frigate Medusa - When taken: 12 Apr 1813 - Where taken: Bay of Biscay - Date received: 11 Jul 1813 - From what ship: Plymouth - Born: New Orleans - Age: 32 - Discharged on 16 Jun 1814 and sent to Dartmoor.

Martin, Henry - Seaman - Number: 115 - Prize name: Good Friends - Ship type: MV - How taken: HM Frigate Andromache - When taken: 2 Apr 1813 - Where taken: Bay of Biscay - Date received: 8 Jul 1813 - From what ship: Plymouth - Born: Prussia - Age: 25 - Discharged on 13 Jun 1814 and sent to Dartmoor.

Martin, Isaac - Boy - Number: 60 - Prize name: Paul Jones - Ship type: P - How taken: HM Frigate Leonidas - When taken: 23 May 1813 - Where taken: off Cape Clear (Ireland) - Date received: 8 Jul 1813 - From what ship: Plymouth - Born: Baltimore - Age: 16 - Discharged on 13 Jun 1814 and sent to Dartmoor.

Martin, John - Seaman - Number: 98 - Prize name: Paul Jones - Ship type: P - How taken: HM Frigate Leonidas - When taken: 23 May 1813 - Where taken: off Cape Clear (Ireland) - Date received: 8 Jul 1813 - From what ship: Plymouth - Born: Salem - Age: 37 - Discharged on 13 Jun 1814 and sent to Dartmoor.

Martin, John - Seaman - Number: 4 - How taken: Gave himself up from HM Frigate Venus - When taken: 2 Jan 1813 - Date received: 26 Mar 1813 - From what ship: Bristol - Born: Abbott County - Age: 31 - Race: Negro - Discharged on 13 Jun 1814 and sent to Dartmoor.

Martin, John B. - Seaman - Number: 369 - Prize name: Tom - Ship type: P - How taken: HM Frigate Surveillante - When taken: 27 Apr 1813 - Where taken: Bay of Biscay - Date received: 11 Jul 1813 - From what ship: Plymouth - Born: Boston - Age: 18 - Discharged on 1 Feb 1814 and sent to the Naval Rendezvous Bristol.

Martin, Manuel - Seaman - Number: 41 - Prize name: Paul Jones - Ship type: P - How taken: HM Frigate Leonidas - When taken: 23 May 1813 - Where taken: off Cape Clear (Ireland) - Date received: 8 Jul 1813 - From what ship: Plymouth - Born: New Orleans - Age: 17 - Discharged on 13 Jun 1814 and sent to Dartmoor.

Matthews, Richard - Seaman - Number: 248 - How taken: Impressed at Bristol - When taken: 1 May 1813 - Date received: 11 Jul 1813 - From what ship: Plymouth - Born: New Jersey - Age: 34 - Discharged on 16 Jun 1814 and sent to Dartmoor.

May, Walter - Seaman - Number: 299 - Prize name: Price - Ship type: MV - How taken: HM Frigate Iris - When taken: 13 Apr 1813 - Where taken: Bay of Biscay - Date received: 11 Jul 1813 - From what ship: Plymouth - Born: Norfolk - Age: 28 - Discharged on 16 Jun 1814 and sent to Dartmoor.

McCoy, James Abercromby - Seaman - Number: 343 - Prize name: Fox - Ship type: P - How taken: HM Sloop

Pheasant - When taken: 23 Apr 1813 - Where taken: Bay of Biscay - Date received: 11 Jul 1813 - From what ship: Plymouth - Born: Philadelphia - Age: 21 - Discharged on 16 Jun 1814 and sent to Dartmoor.

McIntire, Samuel - Seaman - Number: 372 - Prize name: Tom - Ship type: P - How taken: HM Frigate Surveillante - When taken: 27 Apr 1813 - Where taken: Bay of Biscay - Date received: 11 Jul 1813 - From what ship: Plymouth - Born: Massachusetts - Age: 23 - Discharged on 16 Jun 1814 and sent to Dartmoor.

McKenny, John - Seaman - Number: 148 - Prize name: Revenge - Ship type: P - How taken: HM Frigate Belle Poule - When taken: 10 May 1813 - Where taken: Coast of Spain - Date received: 8 Jul 1813 - From what ship: Plymouth - Born: Georgetown - Age: 35 - Discharged on 13 Jun 1814 and sent to Dartmoor.

McKinnon, Nathaniel - Seaman - Number: 171 - Prize name: Tickler - Ship type: P - How taken: HM Frigate Magiciene - When taken: 5 Jun 1813 - Where taken: Bay of Biscay - Date received: 8 Jul 1813 - From what ship: Plymouth - Born: Baltimore - Age: 22 - Race: Negro - Discharged on 13 Jun 1814 and sent to Dartmoor.

McMakin, John - Seaman - Number: 354 - Prize name: Shadow - Ship type: P - How taken: HM Brig Reindeer - When taken: 6 Apr 1813 - Where taken: Bay of Biscay - Date received: 11 Jul 1813 - From what ship: Plymouth - Born: Pennsylvania - Age: 22 - Discharged on 20 Sep 1813 and sent to the Regulatory Office Bristol for naval service.

Merritt, Jonathan - Seaman - Number: 191 - Prize name: Revenge - Ship type: P - How taken: HM Frigate Belle Poule - When taken: 10 May 1813 - Where taken: Bay of Biscay - Date received: 8 Jul 1813 - From what ship: Plymouth - Born: New York - Age: 19 - Discharged on 13 Jun 1814 and sent to Dartmoor.

Merritt, Robert - Seaman - Number: 138 - Prize name: Governor Gerry - Ship type: MV - How taken: HM Brig Royalist - When taken: 31 May 1813 - Where taken: Bay of Biscay - Date received: 8 Jul 1813 - From what ship: Plymouth - Born: New York - Age: 34 - Discharged on 13 Jun 1814 and sent to Dartmoor.

Merritt, Thomas - Seaman - Number: 265 - Prize name: Zebra - Ship type: P - How taken: HM Frigate Pyramus - When taken: 20 Apr 1813 - Where taken: Bay of Biscay - Date received: 11 Jul 1813 - From what ship: Plymouth - Born: Boston - Age: 19 - Discharged on 16 Jun 1814 and sent to Dartmoor.

Mettley, Thomas - Seaman - Number: 285 - Prize name: Messenger - Ship type: MV - How taken: HM Frigate Iris - When taken: 10 Mar 1813 - Where taken: off Cape Ortegal (Spain) - Date received: 11 Jul 1813 - From what ship: Plymouth - Born: Philadelphia - Age: 25 - Discharged on 16 Jun 1814 and sent to Dartmoor.

Mezick, Elihu - Seaman - Number: 187 - Prize name: Revenge - Ship type: P - How taken: HM Frigate Belle Poule - When taken: 10 May 1813 - Where taken: Bay of Biscay - Date received: 8 Jul 1813 - From what ship: Plymouth - Born: Maryland - Age: 38 - Race: Mulatto - Discharged on 13 Jun 1814 and sent to Dartmoor.

Michel, Jacob - Seaman - Number: 282 - Prize name: Caroline - Ship type: MV - How taken: HM Frigate Medusa - When taken: 12 Apr 1813 - Where taken: Bay of Biscay - Date received: 11 Jul 1813 - From what ship: Plymouth - Born: Baltimore - Age: 24 - Race: Black - Died on 25 May 1814 in hospital.

Miller, Charles - Seaman - Number: 111 - Prize name: Zebra - Ship type: P - How taken: HM Frigate Pyramus - When taken: 20 Apr 1813 - Where taken: Bay of Biscay - Date received: 8 Jul 1813 - From what ship: Plymouth - Born: Gothenburg, Sweden - Age: 28 - Discharged on 4 May 1814 and sent to the Swedish Consul.

Miller, Thomas - Seaman - Number: 404 - Prize name: Paul Jones - Ship type: P - How taken: HM Frigate Leonidas - When taken: 23 May 1813 - Where taken: off Cape Clear (Ireland) - Date received: 11 Jul 1813 - From what ship: Plymouth - Born: New York - Age: 19 - Race: Colored - Discharged on 16 Jun 1814 and sent to Dartmoor.

Mills, William - Seaman - Number: 253 - Prize name: Zebra - Ship type: P - How taken: HM Frigate Pyramus - When taken: 20 Apr 1813 - Where taken: Bay of Biscay - Date received: 11 Jul 1813 - From what ship: Plymouth - Born: New Jersey - Age: 21 - Discharged on 16 Jun 1814 and sent to Dartmoor.

Mills, William - Seaman - Number: 100 - Prize name: Courier - Ship type: P - How taken: HM Brig Rover - When taken: 14 Mar 1813 - Where taken: Bay of Biscay - Date received: 8 Jul 1813 - From what ship: Plymouth - Born: Maryland - Age: 30 - Discharged on 13 Jun 1814 and sent to Dartmoor.

Mingle, Thomas - Seaman - Number: 335 - Prize name: Fox - Ship type: P - How taken: HM Sloop Pheasant - When taken: 23 Apr 1813 - Where taken: Bay of Biscay - Date received: 11 Jul 1813 - From what ship: Plymouth - Born: Africa - Age: 54 - Race: Negro - Discharged on 16 Jun 1814 and sent to Dartmoor.

Mingle, William - Seaman - Number: 326 - Prize name: Shadow - Ship type: P - How taken: HM Brig Reindeer - When taken: 6 Apr 1813 - Where taken: Bay of Biscay - Date received: 11 Jul 1813 - From what ship: Plymouth - Born: Philadelphia - Age: 19 - Discharged on 20 Sep 1813 and sent to the Regulatory Office Bristol for naval service.

Mode, David - Cook - Number: 211 - Prize name: Hebe - Ship type: MV - How taken: HM Frigate Stag - When taken: 18 Apr 1813 - Where taken: Bay of Biscay - Date received: 11 Jul 1813 - From what ship: Plymouth - Born: Delaware - Age: 21 - Race: Mulatto - Discharged on 13 Jun 1814 and sent to Dartmoor.

Mooney, Peter - Seaman - Number: 58 - Prize name: Paul Jones - Ship type: P - How taken: HM Frigate Leonidas - When taken: 23 May 1813 - Where taken: off Cape Clear (Ireland) - Date received: 8 Jul 1813 - From what ship: Plymouth - Born: New Orleans - Age: 18 - Discharged on 13 Jun 1814 and sent to Dartmoor.

Moore, Francis - Seaman - Number: 130 - Prize name: Governor Gerry - Ship type: P - How taken: HM Brig Lyra - When taken: 29 May 1813 - Where taken: Coast of Spain - Date received: 8 Jul 1813 - From what ship: Plymouth - Born: Philadelphia - Age: 22 - Race: Negro - Discharged on 19 Aug 1813 and sent to the Regulatory Office Bristol for naval service.

Moore, Richard - Seaman - Number: 336 - Prize name: Fox - Ship type: P - How taken: HM Sloop Pheasant - When taken: 23 Apr 1813 - Where taken: Bay of Biscay - Date received: 11 Jul 1813 - From what ship: Plymouth - Born: Pennsylvania - Age: 35 - Race: Negro - Discharged on 16 Jun 1814 and sent to Dartmoor.

Morgan, Henry - 2nd Mate - Number: 219 - Prize name: Napoleon - Ship type: MV - How taken: HM Frigate Belle Poule - When taken: 3 Apr 1813 - Where taken: Bay of Biscay - Date received: 11 Jul 1813 - From what ship: Plymouth - Born: Albany - Age: 20 - Discharged on 13 Jun 1814 and sent to Dartmoor.

Morgan, John - Seaman - Number: 290 - Prize name: Messenger - Ship type: MV - How taken: HM Frigate Iris - When taken: 10 Mar 1813 - Where taken: off Cape Ortegal (Spain) - Date received: 11 Jul 1813 - From what ship: Plymouth - Born: North Carolina - Age: 21 - Discharged on 16 Jun 1814 and sent to Dartmoor.

Morie, Joseph - Seaman - Number: 200 - Prize name: Governor Gerry - Ship type: MV - How taken: HM Brig Royalist - When taken: 1 Jan 1813 - Where taken: Bay of Biscay - Date received: 8 Jul 1813 - From what ship: Plymouth - Born: Lisbon, Portugal - Age: 22 - Discharged on 2 Sep 1813 and sent to the Portuguese Consul.

Mortbelly, William - Seaman - Number: 260 - Prize name: Zebra - Ship type: P - How taken: HM Frigate Pyramus - When taken: 20 Apr 1813 - Where taken: Bay of Biscay - Date received: 11 Jul 1813 - From what ship: Plymouth - Born: Savannah - Age: 24 - Discharged on 16 Jun 1814 and sent to Dartmoor.

Morris, A. G. - Seaman - Number: 180 - How taken: Impressed at Liverpool - When taken: 19 Mar 1813 - Date received: 8 Jul 1813 - From what ship: Plymouth - Born: Newport, RI - Age: 25 - Discharged on 13 Jun 1814 and sent to Dartmoor.

Moss, Thomas - Seaman - Number: 242 - Prize name: Essex - Ship type: MV - How taken: HM Frigate Pyramus - When taken: 2 Apr 1813 - Where taken: Bay of Biscay - Date received: 11 Jul 1813 - From what ship: Plymouth - Born: Marblehead - Age: 44 - Race: Black - Discharged on 16 Jun 1814 and sent to Dartmoor.

Muller, Edward - Seaman - Number: 353 - Prize name: Shadow - Ship type: P - How taken: HM Brig Reindeer - When taken: 6 Apr 1813 - Where taken: Bay of Biscay - Date received: 11 Jul 1813 - From what ship: Plymouth - Born: Pennsylvania - Age: 39 - Discharged on 16 Jun 1814 and sent to Dartmoor.

Mullins, James - Seaman - Number: 94 - Prize name: Courier - Ship type: P - How taken: HM Brig Rover - When taken: 14 Mar 1813 - Where taken: Bay of Biscay - Date received: 8 Jul 1813 - From what ship: Plymouth - Born: North Carolina - Age: 40 - Discharged on 13 Jun 1814 and sent to Dartmoor.

Muly, Edward - Seaman - Number: 19 - Prize name: Paul Jones - Ship type: P - How taken: HM Frigate Leonidas - When taken: 23 May 1813 - Where taken: off Cape Clear (Ireland) - Date received: 8 Jul 1813 - From what ship: Plymouth - Born: L'Orient, France - Age: 23 - Discharged on 13 Jun 1814 and sent to Dartmoor.

Munroe, John - Seaman - Number: 175 - Prize name: Tickler - Ship type: P - How taken: HM Frigate Magiciene - When taken: 5 Jun 1813 - Where taken: Bay of Biscay - Date received: 8 Jul 1813 - From what ship: Plymouth - Born: New York - Age: 30 - Discharged on 13 Jun 1814 and sent to Dartmoor.

Murray, Jacob - Seaman - Number: 316 - Prize name: Eliza - Ship type: MV - How taken: HM Frigate Surveillante - When taken: 22 Apr 1813 - Where taken: Bay of Biscay - Date received: 11 Jul 1813 - From what ship: Plymouth - Born: South Carolina - Age: 25 - Race: Colored - Discharged on 16 Jun 1814 and sent to Dartmoor.

Murray, John - Seaman - Number: 294 - Prize name: Messenger - Ship type: MV - How taken: HM Frigate Iris - When taken: 10 Mar 1813 - Where taken: off Cape Ortegal (Spain) - Date received: 11 Jul 1813 - From what ship: Plymouth - Born: Long Island - Age: 35 - Race: Colored - Discharged on 12 Sep 1813 and sent to the Naval Rendezvous Bristol.

Murrel, Mark - Seaman - Number: 328 - Prize name: Shadow - Ship type: P - How taken: HM Brig Reindeer - When taken: 6 Apr 1813 - Where taken: Bay of Biscay - Date received: 11 Jul 1813 - From what ship: Plymouth - Born: Marblehead - Age: 28 - Discharged on 16 Jun 1814 and sent to Dartmoor.

Neal, Denis - Seaman - Number: 124 - Prize name: Courier - Ship type: P - How taken: HM Brig Rover - When taken: 14 Mar 1813 - Where taken: Bay of Biscay - Date received: 8 Jul 1813 - From what ship: Plymouth - Born: Maryland - Age: 25 - Discharged on 13 Jun 1814 and sent to Dartmoor.

Nelly, Richard John - Seaman - Number: 374 - Prize name: Tom - Ship type: P - How taken: HM Frigate Surveillante - When taken: 27 Apr 1813 - Where taken: Bay of Biscay - Date received: 11 Jul 1813 - From what ship: Plymouth - Born: Pennsylvania - Age: 33 - Discharged on 16 Jun 1814 and sent to Dartmoor.

Newell, Isaac - Seaman - Number: 31 - Prize name: Paul Jones - Ship type: P - How taken: HM Frigate Leonidas - When taken: 23 May 1813 - Where taken: off Cape Clear (Ireland) - Date received: 8 Jul 1813 - From what ship: Plymouth - Born: York, MA - Age: 30 - Discharged on 13 Jun 1814 and sent to Dartmoor.

Nicholas, Stephen alias Nicholson - Seaman - Number: 82 - Prize name: Grand Napoleon - How taken: HM Brig Goldfinch - When taken: 17 Apr 1813 - Where taken: Bay of Biscay - Date received: 8 Jul 1813 - From what ship: Plymouth - Born: Prussia - Age: 29 - Discharged on 28 Jan 1814 and sent to the Prussian Consul.

Nickerson, Joseph - Seaman - Number: 137 - Prize name: Orders in Council - Ship type: P - How taken: Rebecca - When taken: 1 Jun 1813 - Where taken: Bay of Biscay - Date received: 8 Jul 1813 - From what ship: Plymouth - Born: Boston - Age: 19 - Discharged on 13 Jun 1814 and sent to Dartmoor.

Norris, Robert - Seaman - Number: 334 - Prize name: Fox - Ship type: P - How taken: HM Sloop Pheasant - When taken: 23 Apr 1813 - Where taken: Bay of Biscay - Date received: 11 Jul 1813 - From what ship: Plymouth - Born: Philadelphia - Age: 28 - Race: Negro - Discharged on 9 Aug 1813 and sent to the Naval Rendezvous Bristol.

North, Thomas - Seaman - Number: 416 - How taken: Taken off the Portuguese MV Senora del Manda - When taken: 9 Nov 1813 - Date received: 9 Nov 1813 - From what ship: Naval Rendezvous Bristol - Born: Maryland - Age: 39 - Discharged on 16 Jun 1814 and sent to Dartmoor.

Ostand, Michael - Seaman - Number: 83 - Prize name: Grand Napoleon - How taken: HM Brig Goldfinch - When taken: 17 Apr 1813 - Where taken: Bay of Biscay - Date received: 8 Jul 1813 - From what ship: Plymouth - Born: Paris - Age: 32 - Discharged on 13 Jun 1814 and sent to Dartmoor.

Page, Thomas - Seaman - Number: 215 - Prize name: Hebe - Ship type: MV - How taken: HM Frigate Stag - When taken: 18 Apr 1813 - Where taken: Bay of Biscay - Date received: 11 Jul 1813 - From what ship: Plymouth - Born: Massachusetts - Age: 20 - Discharged on 13 Jun 1814 and sent to Dartmoor.

Pain, Francis - Seaman - Number: 408 - How taken: Impressed from MV Hopewell - Date received: 16 Aug 1813 - From what ship: Naval Rendezvous Bristol - Born: Marblehead - Age: 27 - Discharged on 16 Jun 1814 and sent to Dartmoor.

Parish, Samuel - Seaman - Number: 77 - Prize name: Grand Napoleon - How taken: HM Brig Goldfinch - When taken: 17 Apr 1813 - Where taken: Bay of Biscay - Date received: 8 Jul 1813 - From what ship: Plymouth - Born: Norfolk - Age: 31 - Discharged on 13 Jun 1814 and sent to Dartmoor.

Parker, John A. - Seaman - Number: 235 - Prize name: Essex - Ship type: MV - How taken: HM Frigate Pyramus - When taken: 2 Apr 1813 - Where taken: Bay of Biscay - Date received: 11 Jul 1813 - From what ship: Plymouth - Born: Boston - Age: 16 - Discharged on 16 Jun 1814 and sent to Dartmoor.

Parmele, Benjamin - Seaman - Number: 126 - Prize name: Miranda - Ship type: Prize of Paul Jones - How taken: HM Frigate Unicorn - When taken: 21 May 1813 - Where taken: Bay of Biscay - Date received: 8 Jul 1813 - From what ship: Plymouth - Born: Connecticut - Age: 29 - Discharged on 13 Jun 1814 and sent to Dartmoor.

Payer, Walter - Seaman - Number: 252 - Prize name: Zebra - Ship type: P - How taken: HM Frigate Pyramus - When taken: 20 Apr 1813 - Where taken: Bay of Biscay - Date received: 11 Jul 1813 - From what ship: Plymouth - Born: New Orleans - Age: 34 - Discharged on 16 Jun 1814 and sent to Dartmoor.

Payne, Joseph S. - 3rd Mate - Number: 393 - Prize name: Tom - Ship type: P - How taken: HM Frigate Surveillante - When taken: 27 Apr 1813 - Where taken: Bay of Biscay - Date received: 11 Jul 1813 - From what ship: Plymouth - Born: Charlestown - Age: 17 - Discharged on 16 Jun 1814 and sent to Dartmoor.

Peck, Thomas - Seaman - Number: 22 - Prize name: Paul Jones - Ship type: P - How taken: HM Frigate Leonidas - When taken: 23 May 1813 - Where taken: off Cape Clear (Ireland) - Date received: 8 Jul 1813 - From what ship: Plymouth - Born: New London - Age: 39 - Race: Negro - Discharged on 13 Jun 1814 and sent to Dartmoor.

Pelton, Alexander - Seaman - Number: 375 - Prize name: Tom - Ship type: P - How taken: HM Frigate Surveillante - When taken: 27 Apr 1813 - Where taken: Bay of Biscay - Date received: 11 Jul 1813 - From what ship: Plymouth - Born: Massachusetts - Age: 21 - Discharged on 16 Jun 1814 and sent to Dartmoor.

Penman, Richard - Seaman - Number: 383 - Prize name: Tom - Ship type: P - How taken: HM Frigate Surveillante - When taken: 27 Apr 1813 - Where taken: Bay of Biscay - Date received: 11 Jul 1813 - From what ship: Plymouth - Born: New York - Age: 23 - Discharged on 16 Jun 1814 and sent to Dartmoor.

Peregrine, Tagart - Seaman - Number: 283 - Prize name: Caroline - Ship type: MV - How taken: HM Frigate Medusa - When taken: 12 Apr 1813 - Where taken: Bay of Biscay - Date received: 11 Jul 1813 - From what ship: Plymouth - Born: Maryland - Age: 28 - Discharged on 16 Jun 1814 and sent to Dartmoor.

Perry, Charles - Seaman - Number: 332 - Prize name: Fox - Ship type: P - How taken: HM Sloop Pheasant - When taken: 23 Apr 1813 - Where taken: Bay of Biscay - Date received: 11 Jul 1813 - From what ship: Plymouth - Born: Norfolk - Age: 29 - Discharged on 16 Jun 1814 and sent to Dartmoor.

Peterson, Peter - Seaman - Number: 32 - Prize name: Paul Jones - Ship type: P - How taken: HM Frigate Leonidas - When taken: 23 May 1813 - Where taken: off Cape Clear (Ireland) - Date received: 8 Jul 1813 - From what ship: Plymouth - Born: Gothenburg, Sweden - Age: 32 - Discharged on 31 Oct 1813 and sent to the Swedish Consul.

Petty, William - Seaman - Number: 2 - Date received: 2 Dec 1812 - From what ship: Bristol - Born: Abbott County - Age: 21 - Discharged on 17 May 1813 and sent to Bristol.

Phillips, John - Seaman - Number: 321 - Prize name: Eliza - Ship type: MV - How taken: HM Frigate Surveillante - When taken: 22 Apr 1813 - Where taken: Bay of Biscay - Date received: 11 Jul 1813 - From what ship: Plymouth - Born: Pennsylvania - Age: 25 - Discharged on 16 Jun 1814 and sent to Dartmoor.

Pitts, William - Seaman - Number: 110 - Prize name: Zebra - Ship type: P - How taken: HM Frigate Pyramus - When taken: 20 Apr 1813 - Where taken: Bay of Biscay - Date received: 8 Jul 1813 - From what ship: Plymouth - Born: Massachusetts - Age: 29 - Discharged on 13 Jun 1814 and sent to Dartmoor.

Plumber, Joseph - Boatswain - Number: 269 - Prize name: Caroline - Ship type: MV - How taken: HM Frigate Medusa - When taken: 12 Apr 1813 - Where taken: Bay of Biscay - Date received: 11 Jul 1813 - From what ship: Plymouth - Born: Virginia - Age: 23 - Discharged on 16 Jun 1814 and sent to Dartmoor.

Poland, Joseph - Seaman - Number: 75 - Prize name: Grand Napoleon - How taken: HM Brig Goldfinch - When taken: 17 Apr 1813 - Where taken: Bay of Biscay - Date received: 8 Jul 1813 - From what ship: Plymouth - Born: Beverly, MA - Age: 22 - Discharged on 13 Jun 1814 and sent to Dartmoor.

Pomp, William - Seaman - Number: 266 - Prize name: Zebra - Ship type: P - How taken: HM Frigate Pyramus - When taken: 20 Apr 1813 - Where taken: Bay of Biscay - Date received: 11 Jul 1813 - From what ship:

Plymouth - Born: Long Island - Age: 20 - Race: Black - Discharged on 16 Jun 1814 and sent to Dartmoor.

Pote, Jeremiah - Seaman - Number: 74 - Prize name: Grand Napoleon - How taken: HM Brig Goldfinch - When taken: 17 Apr 1813 - Where taken: Bay of Biscay - Date received: 8 Jul 1813 - From what ship: Plymouth - Born: Massachusetts - Age: 18 - Discharged on 13 Jun 1814 and sent to Dartmoor.

Prett, Benjamin - Seaman - Number: 225 - Prize name: Napoleon - Ship type: MV - How taken: HM Frigate Belle Poule - When taken: 3 Apr 1813 - Where taken: Bay of Biscay - Date received: 11 Jul 1813 - From what ship: Plymouth - Born: Connecticut - Age: 24 - Discharged on 13 Jun 1814 and sent to Dartmoor.

Price, Jacob - Seaman - Number: 301 - Prize name: Price - Ship type: MV - How taken: HM Frigate Iris - When taken: 13 Apr 1813 - Where taken: Bay of Biscay - Date received: 11 Jul 1813 - From what ship: Plymouth - Born: Connecticut - Age: 23 - Discharged on 16 Jun 1814 and sent to Dartmoor.

Price, John - 2nd Mate - Number: 349 - Prize name: Shadow - Ship type: P - How taken: HM Brig Reindeer - When taken: 6 Apr 1813 - Where taken: Bay of Biscay - Date received: 11 Jul 1813 - From what ship: Plymouth - Born: Delaware - Age: 23 - Discharged on 16 Jun 1814 and sent to Dartmoor.

Price, Samuel - Seaman - Number: 151 - Prize name: Revenge - Ship type: P - How taken: HM Frigate Belle Poule - When taken: 10 May 1813 - Where taken: Coast of Spain - Date received: 8 Jul 1813 - From what ship: Plymouth - Born: Boston - Age: 21 - Discharged on 13 Jun 1814 and sent to Dartmoor.

Prince, George - Seaman - Number: 39 - Prize name: Paul Jones - Ship type: P - How taken: HM Frigate Leonidas - When taken: 23 May 1813 - Where taken: off Cape Clear (Ireland) - Date received: 8 Jul 1813 - From what ship: Plymouth - Born: Newbury, MA - Age: 33 - Discharged on 13 Jun 1814 and sent to Dartmoor.

Putman, Charles - Seaman - Number: 184 - Prize name: Revenge - Ship type: P - How taken: HM Frigate Belle Poule - When taken: 10 May 1813 - Where taken: Bay of Biscay - Date received: 8 Jul 1813 - From what ship: Plymouth - Born: Massachusetts - Age: 30 - Discharged on 13 Jun 1814 and sent to Dartmoor.

Redding, John - Seaman - Number: 76 - Prize name: Grand Napoleon - How taken: HM Brig Goldfinch - When taken: 17 Apr 1813 - Where taken: Bay of Biscay - Date received: 8 Jul 1813 - From what ship: Plymouth - Born: Falmouth, MA - Age: 23 - Discharged on 13 Jun 1814 and sent to Dartmoor.

Reynolds, James - Seaman - Number: 113 - Prize name: Zebra - Ship type: P - How taken: HM Frigate Pyramus - When taken: 20 Apr 1813 - Where taken: Bay of Biscay - Date received: 8 Jul 1813 - From what ship: Plymouth - Born: Virginia - Age: 28 - Discharged on 13 Jun 1814 and sent to Dartmoor.

Ricks, Thomas - Seaman - Number: 410 - How taken: Impressed at Frederick - When taken: 16 Aug 1813 - Date received: 16 Aug 1813 - From what ship: Naval Rendezvous Bristol - Born: New York - Age: 20 - Race: Negro - Discharged on 16 Jun 1814 and sent to Dartmoor.

Ripley, Eben - Seaman - Number: 232 - Prize name: Essex - Ship type: MV - How taken: HM Frigate Pyramus - When taken: 2 Apr 1813 - Where taken: Bay of Biscay - Date received: 11 Jul 1813 - From what ship: Plymouth - Born: Massachusetts - Age: 19 - Discharged on 16 Jun 1814 and sent to Dartmoor.

Risings, John - Seaman - Number: 53 - Prize name: Paul Jones - Ship type: P - How taken: HM Frigate Leonidas - When taken: 23 May 1813 - Where taken: off Cape Clear (Ireland) - Date received: 8 Jul 1813 - From what ship: Plymouth - Born: Albany - Age: 29 - Race: Colored - Discharged on 13 Jun 1814 and sent to Dartmoor.

Roberson, James - Seaman - Number: 300 - Prize name: Price - Ship type: MV - How taken: HM Frigate Iris - When taken: 13 Apr 1813 - Where taken: Bay of Biscay - Date received: 11 Jul 1813 - From what ship: Plymouth - Born: Massachusetts - Age: 21 - Discharged on 16 Jun 1814 and sent to Dartmoor.

Roberts, Roleman Fr. M. - Seaman - Number: 5 - How taken: HMS Harmony - Date received: 26 Mar 1813 - From what ship: Bristol - Born: Virginia - Age: 49 - Race: Negro - Discharged on 6 May 1813.

Robertson, Robert - Seaman - Number: 127 - Prize name: Miranda - Ship type: Prize of Paul Jones - How taken: HM Frigate Unicorn - When taken: 21 May 1813 - Where taken: Bay of Biscay - Date received: 8 Jul 1813 - From what ship: Plymouth - Born: South Carolina - Age: 23 - Discharged on 13 Jun 1814 and sent to Dartmoor.

Robinson, Elias - Seaman - Number: 136 - Prize name: Orders in Council - Ship type: P - How taken: Rebecca - When taken: 1 Jun 1813 - Where taken: Bay of Biscay - Date received: 8 Jul 1813 - From what ship:

Plymouth - Born: Boston - Age: 19 - Discharged on 13 Jun 1814 and sent to Dartmoor.

Robinson, John - Seaman - Number: 400 - Prize name: Paul Jones - Ship type: P - How taken: HM Frigate Leonidas - When taken: 23 May 1813 - Where taken: off Cape Clear (Ireland) - Date received: 11 Jul 1813 - From what ship: Plymouth - Born: Connecticut - Age: 57 - Discharged on 16 Jun 1814 and sent to Dartmoor.

Roff, Isaac - Seaman - Number: 112 - Prize name: Zebra - Ship type: P - How taken: HM Frigate Pyramus - When taken: 20 Apr 1813 - Where taken: Bay of Biscay - Date received: 8 Jul 1813 - From what ship: Plymouth - Born: New Jersey - Age: 22 - Discharged on 16 Jun 1814 and sent to Dartmoor.

Roles, John - Seaman - Number: 96 - Prize name: Courier - Ship type: P - How taken: HM Brig Rover - When taken: 14 Mar 1813 - Where taken: Bay of Biscay - Date received: 8 Jul 1813 - From what ship: Plymouth - Born: Maryland - Age: 23 - Discharged on 13 Jun 1814 and sent to Dartmoor.

Roley, John - Seaman - Number: 52 - Prize name: Paul Jones - Ship type: P - How taken: HM Frigate Leonidas - When taken: 23 May 1813 - Where taken: off Cape Clear (Ireland) - Date received: 8 Jul 1813 - From what ship: Plymouth - Born: France - Age: 38 - Discharged on 13 Jun 1814 and sent to Dartmoor.

Rowe, John - Seaman - Number: 382 - Prize name: Tom - Ship type: P - How taken: HM Frigate Surveillante - When taken: 27 Apr 1813 - Where taken: Bay of Biscay - Date received: 11 Jul 1813 - From what ship: Plymouth - Born: Connecticut - Age: 26 - Discharged on 16 Jun 1814 and sent to Dartmoor.

Rowle, Benjamin - Carpenter - Number: 331 - Prize name: Fox - Ship type: P - How taken: HM Sloop Pheasant - When taken: 23 Apr 1813 - Where taken: Bay of Biscay - Date received: 11 Jul 1813 - From what ship: Plymouth - Born: Philadelphia - Age: 48 - Discharged on 16 Jun 1814 and sent to Dartmoor.

Rowley, Henry - Carpenter - Number: 361 - Prize name: Tom - Ship type: P - How taken: HM Frigate Surveillante - When taken: 27 Apr 1813 - Where taken: Bay of Biscay - Date received: 11 Jul 1813 - From what ship: Plymouth - Born: Pennsylvania - Age: 36 - Race: Colored - Discharged on 16 Jun 1814 and sent to Dartmoor.

Ruffield, Samuel - Seaman - Number: 45 - Prize name: Paul Jones - Ship type: P - How taken: HM Frigate Leonidas - When taken: 23 May 1813 - Where taken: off Cape Clear (Ireland) - Date received: 8 Jul 1813 - From what ship: Plymouth - Born: Norwich, CT - Age: 20 - Discharged on 13 Jun 1814 and sent to Dartmoor.

Russell, George - Gunner - Number: 359 - Prize name: Tom - Ship type: P - How taken: HM Frigate Surveillante - When taken: 27 Apr 1813 - Where taken: Bay of Biscay - Date received: 11 Jul 1813 - From what ship: Plymouth - Born: New Jersey - Age: 22 - Discharged on 1 Feb 1814 and sent to the Naval Rendezvous Bristol.

Russell, Patton - Seaman - Number: 236 - Prize name: Essex - Ship type: MV - How taken: HM Frigate Pyramus - When taken: 2 Apr 1813 - Where taken: Bay of Biscay - Date received: 11 Jul 1813 - From what ship: Plymouth - Born: Cambridge - Age: 19 - Discharged on 16 Jun 1814 and sent to Dartmoor.

Sanford, William - Seaman - Number: 406 - Prize name: Paul Jones - Ship type: P - How taken: HM Frigate Leonidas - When taken: 23 May 1813 - Where taken: off Cape Clear (Ireland) - Date received: 11 Jul 1813 - From what ship: Plymouth - Born: New York - Age: 20 - Discharged on 16 Jun 1814 and sent to Dartmoor.

Sardy, Anthony - Seaman - Number: 26 - Prize name: Paul Jones - Ship type: P - How taken: HM Frigate Leonidas - When taken: 23 May 1813 - Where taken: off Cape Clear (Ireland) - Date received: 8 Jul 1813 - From what ship: Plymouth - Born: Palermo - Age: 32 - Discharged on 13 Jun 1814 and sent to Dartmoor.

Scott, John - Seaman - Number: 182 - How taken: Impressed at Liverpool - When taken: 1 May 1813 - Date received: 8 Jul 1813 - From what ship: Plymouth - Born: Rhode Island - Age: 48 - Discharged on 13 Jun 1814 and sent to Dartmoor.

Sellie, Thomas - Seaman - Number: 107 - Prize name: Zebra - Ship type: P - How taken: HM Frigate Pyramus - When taken: 20 Apr 1813 - Where taken: Bay of Biscay - Date received: 8 Jul 1813 - From what ship: Plymouth - Born: New York - Age: 33 - Race: Negro - Discharged on 13 Jun 1814 and sent to Dartmoor.

Sentille, Francis - Seaman - Number: 40 - Prize name: Paul Jones - Ship type: P - How taken: HM Frigate Leonidas - When taken: 23 May 1813 - Where taken: off Cape Clear (Ireland) - Date received: 8 Jul 1813 - From what ship: Plymouth - Born: Charleston - Age: 17 - Discharged on 13 Jun 1814 and sent to Dartmoor.

Shaw, Richard - Seaman - Number: 89 - Prize name: Courier - Ship type: P - How taken: HM Brig Rover - When taken: 14 Mar 1813 - Where taken: Bay of Biscay - Date received: 8 Jul 1813 - From what ship: Plymouth - Born: Maryland - Age: 26 - Discharged on 13 Jun 1814 and sent to Dartmoor.

Shiffers, Stuben - Seaman - Number: 380 - Prize name: Tom - Ship type: P - How taken: HM Frigate Surveillante - When taken: 27 Apr 1813 - Where taken: Bay of Biscay - Date received: 11 Jul 1813 - From what ship: Plymouth - Born: Connecticut - Age: 19 - Discharged on 16 Jun 1814 and sent to Dartmoor.

Shipp, Stephen - Seaman - Number: 262 - Prize name: Zebra - Ship type: P - How taken: HM Frigate Pyramus - When taken: 20 Apr 1813 - Where taken: Bay of Biscay - Date received: 11 Jul 1813 - From what ship: Plymouth - Born: Massachusetts - Age: 26 - Discharged on 16 Jun 1814 and sent to Dartmoor.

Shovel, John - Seaman - Number: 239 - Prize name: Essex - Ship type: MV - How taken: HM Frigate Pyramus - When taken: 2 Apr 1813 - Where taken: Bay of Biscay - Date received: 11 Jul 1813 - From what ship: Plymouth - Born: Boston - Age: 19 - Discharged on 16 Jun 1814 and sent to Dartmoor.

Simmons, Robert - Seaman - Number: 8 - How taken: Naval Rendezvous Bristol - When taken: 10 Jun 1813 - Date received: 10 Jun 1813 - From what ship: Bristol - Born: Charleston - Age: 35 - Race: Negro - Discharged on 16 Jun 1814 and sent to Dartmoor.

Simpson, Thomas - Seaman - Number: 291 - Prize name: Messenger - Ship type: MV - How taken: HM Frigate Iris - When taken: 10 Mar 1813 - Where taken: off Cape Ortegal (Spain) - Date received: 11 Jul 1813 - From what ship: Plymouth - Born: Maryland - Age: 36 - Discharged on 16 Jun 1814 and sent to Dartmoor.

Slocom, Abraham - Seaman - Number: 339 - Prize name: Fox - Ship type: P - How taken: HM Sloop Pheasant - When taken: 23 Apr 1813 - Where taken: Bay of Biscay - Date received: 11 Jul 1813 - From what ship: Plymouth - Born: New Orleans - Age: 21 - Discharged on 16 Jun 1814 and sent to Dartmoor.

Smith, Andrew - Seaman - Number: 373 - Prize name: Tom - Ship type: P - How taken: HM Frigate Surveillante - When taken: 27 Apr 1813 - Where taken: Bay of Biscay - Date received: 11 Jul 1813 - From what ship: Plymouth - Born: Maryland - Age: 23 - Discharged on 16 Jun 1814 and sent to Dartmoor.

Smith, Christian - Seaman - Number: 121 - Prize name: Eliza - Ship type: MV - How taken: HM Frigate Surveillante - When taken: 27 Mar 1813 - Where taken: Bay of Biscay - Date received: 8 Jul 1813 - From what ship: Plymouth - Born: New Jersey - Age: 26 - Discharged on 13 Jun 1814 and sent to Dartmoor.

Smith, James - Seaman - Number: 198 - Prize name: Governor Gerry - Ship type: MV - How taken: HM Brig Royalist - When taken: 1 Jan 1813 - Where taken: Bay of Biscay - Date received: 8 Jul 1813 - From what ship: Plymouth - Born: Boston - Age: 25 - Race: Negro - Discharged on 13 Jun 1814 and sent to Dartmoor.

Smith, John - Seaman - Number: 24 - Prize name: Paul Jones - Ship type: P - How taken: HM Frigate Leonidas - When taken: 23 May 1813 - Where taken: off Cape Clear (Ireland) - Date received: 8 Jul 1813 - From what ship: Plymouth - Born: Providence, RI - Age: 20 - Discharged on 13 Jun 1814 and sent to Dartmoor.

Smith, John - Seaman - Number: 28 - Prize name: Paul Jones - Ship type: P - How taken: HM Frigate Leonidas - When taken: 23 May 1813 - Where taken: off Cape Clear (Ireland) - Date received: 8 Jul 1813 - From what ship: Plymouth - Born: Wells, MA - Age: 23 - Discharged on 9 Aug 1813 and sent to the Naval Rendezvous Bristol.

Smith, John - Seaman - Number: 142 - Prize name: Governor Gerry - Ship type: MV - How taken: HM Brig Royalist - When taken: 31 May 1813 - Where taken: Bay of Biscay - Date received: 8 Jul 1813 - From what ship: Plymouth - Born: Virginia - Age: 27 - Discharged on 13 Jun 1814 and sent to Dartmoor.

Smith, Richard - Seaman - Number: 143 - Prize name: Governor Gerry - Ship type: MV - How taken: HM Brig Royalist - When taken: 31 May 1813 - Where taken: Bay of Biscay - Date received: 8 Jul 1813 - From what ship: Plymouth - Born: New York - Age: 29 - Discharged on 15 Jan 1814 and sent to the Regulatory Office Bristol for naval service.

Smith, Thomas (1) - Boatswain - Number: 395 - Prize name: Paul Jones - Ship type: P - How taken: HM Frigate Leonidas - When taken: 23 May 1813 - Where taken: off Cape Clear (Ireland) - Date received: 11 Jul 1813 - From what ship: Plymouth - Born: New York - Age: 29 - Discharged on 16 Jun 1814 and sent to Dartmoor.

Smith, Thomas (2) - Seaman - Number: 392 - Prize name: Henry Clements - Ship type: MV - How taken: HM Brig

Orestes - When taken: 13 Apr 1813 - Where taken: Bay of Biscay - Date received: 11 Jul 1813 - From what ship: Plymouth - Born: Massachusetts - Age: 17 - Discharged on 16 Jun 1814 and sent to Dartmoor.

Sparrow, James - Seaman - Number: 313 - Prize name: Price - Ship type: MV - How taken: HM Frigate Iris - When taken: 13 Apr 1813 - Where taken: Bay of Biscay - Date received: 11 Jul 1813 - From what ship: Plymouth - Born: Virginia - Age: 35 - Discharged on 16 Jun 1814 and sent to Dartmoor.

Stag, John Boulton - Seaman - Number: 264 - Prize name: Zebra - Ship type: P - How taken: HM Frigate Pyramus - When taken: 20 Apr 1813 - Where taken: Bay of Biscay - Date received: 11 Jul 1813 - From what ship: Plymouth - Born: New York - Age: 25 - Discharged on 16 Jun 1814 and sent to Dartmoor.

Staney, Edward - Seaman - Number: 420 - How taken: Taken off the Strange of Plymouth - Date received: 5 Mar 1813 - From what ship: Bristol - Born: Philadelphia - Age: 36 - Discharged on 16 Jun 1814 and sent to Dartmoor.

Stanson, William - Seaman - Number: 91 - Prize name: Courier - Ship type: P - How taken: HM Brig Rover - When taken: 14 Mar 1813 - Where taken: Bay of Biscay - Date received: 8 Jul 1813 - From what ship: Plymouth - Born: Massachusetts - Age: 16 - Discharged on 16 Jun 1814 and sent to Dartmoor.

Stardingbroke, Theop. - Seaman - Number: 254 - Prize name: Zebra - Ship type: P - How taken: HM Frigate Pyramus - When taken: 20 Apr 1813 - Where taken: Bay of Biscay - Date received: 11 Jul 1813 - From what ship: Plymouth - Born: New Jersey - Age: 22 - Discharged on 16 Jun 1814 and sent to Dartmoor.

Stephens, William - Boy - Number: 65 - Prize name: Paul Jones - Ship type: P - How taken: HM Frigate Leonidas - When taken: 23 May 1813 - Where taken: off Cape Clear (Ireland) - Date received: 8 Jul 1813 - From what ship: Plymouth - Born: New London, CT - Age: 14 - Discharged on 13 Jun 1814 and sent to Dartmoor.

Stewart, William - Seaman - Number: 16 - Prize name: Paul Jones - Ship type: P - How taken: HM Frigate Leonidas - When taken: 23 May 1813 - Where taken: off Cape Clear (Ireland) - Date received: 8 Jul 1813 - From what ship: Plymouth - Born: New York - Age: 19 - Race: Negro - Discharged on 13 Jun 1814 and sent to Dartmoor.

Stockman, William B. - Seaman - Number: 243 - Prize name: Essex - Ship type: MV - How taken: HM Frigate Pyramus - When taken: 2 Apr 1813 - Where taken: Bay of Biscay - Date received: 11 Jul 1813 - From what ship: Plymouth - Born: Massachusetts - Age: 29 - Discharged on 16 Jun 1814 and sent to Dartmoor.

Struby, John - Seaman - Number: 320 - Prize name: Eliza - Ship type: MV - How taken: HM Frigate Surveillante - When taken: 22 Apr 1813 - Where taken: Bay of Biscay - Date received: 11 Jul 1813 - From what ship: Plymouth - Born: Massachusetts - Age: 22 - Discharged on 16 Jun 1814 and sent to Dartmoor.

Stutchins, Edward - Seaman - Number: 87 - Prize name: Courier - Ship type: P - How taken: HM Brig Rover - When taken: 14 Mar 1813 - Where taken: Bay of Biscay - Date received: 8 Jul 1813 - From what ship: Plymouth - Born: Maryland - Age: 22 - Race: Negro - Discharged on 13 Jun 1814 and sent to Dartmoor.

Suff, Francis - Seaman - Number: 289 - Prize name: Messenger - Ship type: MV - How taken: HM Frigate Iris - When taken: 10 Mar 1813 - Where taken: off Cape Ortegal (Spain) - Date received: 11 Jul 1813 - From what ship: Plymouth - Born: New York - Age: 20 - Discharged on 16 Jun 1814 and sent to Dartmoor.

Swatt, David - Seaman - Number: 308 - Prize name: Price - Ship type: MV - How taken: HM Frigate Iris - When taken: 13 Apr 1813 - Where taken: Bay of Biscay - Date received: 11 Jul 1813 - From what ship: Plymouth - Born: New York - Age: 22 - Died on 29 Jan 1814 in hospital.

Taylor, Samuel E. - Seaman - Number: 379 - Prize name: Tom - Ship type: P - How taken: HM Frigate Surveillante - When taken: 27 Apr 1813 - Where taken: Bay of Biscay - Date received: 11 Jul 1813 - From what ship: Plymouth - Born: Charlestown - Age: 22 - Discharged on 16 Jun 1814 and sent to Dartmoor.

Taylor, Thomas - Seaman - Number: 312 - Prize name: Price - Ship type: MV - How taken: HM Frigate Iris - When taken: 13 Apr 1813 - Where taken: Bay of Biscay - Date received: 11 Jul 1813 - From what ship: Plymouth - Born: Wilmington - Age: 23 - Discharged on 20 Sep 1813 and sent to the Regulatory Office Bristol for naval service.

Thomas, Abraham - Seaman - Number: 46 - Prize name: Paul Jones - Ship type: P - How taken: HM Frigate Leonidas - When taken: 23 May 1813 - Where taken: off Cape Clear (Ireland) - Date received: 8 Jul 1813 -

From what ship: Plymouth - Born: New Haven, CT - Age: 32 - Race: Negro - Discharged on 16 Jun 1814 and sent to Dartmoor.

Thompson, Charles - Seaman - Number: 297 - Prize name: Price - Ship type: MV - How taken: HM Frigate Iris - When taken: 13 Apr 1813 - Where taken: Bay of Biscay - Date received: 11 Jul 1813 - From what ship: Plymouth - Born: New York - Age: 25 - Discharged on 16 Jun 1814 and sent to Dartmoor.

Thompson, Joseph - Seaman - Number: 73 - Prize name: Grand Napoleon - How taken: HM Brig Goldfinch - When taken: 17 Apr 1813 - Where taken: Bay of Biscay - Date received: 8 Jul 1813 - From what ship: Plymouth - Born: Falmouth, MA - Age: 22 - Discharged on 13 Jun 1814 and sent to Dartmoor.

Thompson, William - Seaman - Number: 212 - Prize name: Hebe - Ship type: MV - How taken: HM Frigate Stag - When taken: 18 Apr 1813 - Where taken: Bay of Biscay - Date received: 11 Jul 1813 - From what ship: Plymouth - Born: Pennsylvania - Age: 24 - Discharged on 13 Jun 1814 and sent to Dartmoor.

Treffry, James - Seaman - Number: 355 - Prize name: Essex - Ship type: MV - How taken: HM Frigate Pyramus - When taken: 6 Apr 1813 - Where taken: Bay of Biscay - Date received: 11 Jul 1813 - From what ship: Plymouth - Born: Marblehead - Age: 16 - Discharged on 16 Jun 1814 and sent to Dartmoor.

Trefry, Peter - Seaman - Number: 386 - Prize name: Essex - Ship type: MV - How taken: HM Frigate Pyramus - When taken: 6 Apr 1813 - Where taken: Bay of Biscay - Date received: 11 Jul 1813 - From what ship: Plymouth - Born: Marblehead - Age: 25 - Discharged on 16 Jun 1814 and sent to Dartmoor.

Trifle, Jasper - Seaman - Number: 377 - Prize name: Tom - Ship type: P - How taken: HM Frigate Surveillante - When taken: 27 Apr 1813 - Where taken: Bay of Biscay - Date received: 11 Jul 1813 - From what ship: Plymouth - Born: Massachusetts - Age: 21 - Discharged on 16 Jun 1814 and sent to Dartmoor.

Tucker, George C. - 2nd Mate - Number: 154 - Prize name: Leo - Ship type: P - How taken: HM Frigate Magiciene - When taken: 4 Jun 1813 - Where taken: Bay of Biscay - Date received: 8 Jul 1813 - From what ship: Plymouth - Born: Portland - Age: 24 - Discharged on 16 Jun 1814 and sent to Dartmoor.

Tuttle, French - Seaman - Number: 161 - Prize name: Leo - Ship type: P - How taken: HM Frigate Magiciene - When taken: 4 Jun 1813 - Where taken: Bay of Biscay - Date received: 8 Jul 1813 - From what ship: Plymouth - Born: Falmouth - Age: 26 - Discharged on 13 Jun 1814 and sent to Dartmoor.

Tyler, Over - Seaman - Number: 15 - Prize name: Laura - Date received: 7 Jul 1813 - From what ship: Bristol - Born: Virginia - Age: 34 - Discharged on 10 Sep 1813.

Veal, Peter - Seaman - Number: 224 - Prize name: Napoleon - Ship type: MV - How taken: HM Frigate Pyramus - When taken: 3 Apr 1813 - Where taken: Bay of Biscay - Date received: 11 Jul 1813 - From what ship: Plymouth - Born: Connecticut - Age: 24 - Discharged on 13 Jun 1814 and sent to Dartmoor.

Veitch, William - Seaman - Number: 23 - Prize name: Paul Jones - Ship type: P - How taken: HM Frigate Leonidas - When taken: 23 May 1813 - Where taken: off Cape Clear (Ireland) - Date received: 8 Jul 1813 - From what ship: Plymouth - Born: New York - Age: 19 - Discharged on 13 Jun 1814 and sent to Dartmoor.

Vogel, Herman - Seaman - Number: 118 - Prize name: Good Friends - Ship type: MV - How taken: HM Frigate Andromache - When taken: 2 Apr 1813 - Where taken: Bay of Biscay - Date received: 8 Jul 1813 - From what ship: Plymouth - Born: Amsterdam - Age: 18 - Discharged on 28 Nov 1813 and sent to the Naval Rendezvous Bristol.

Waldren, Hiram - Seaman - Number: 418 - How taken: Taken off the Portuguese MV Senora del Manda - When taken: 9 Nov 1813 - Date received: 9 Nov 1813 - From what ship: Naval Rendezvous Bristol - Born: New Hampshire - Age: 27 - Discharged on 16 Jun 1814 and sent to Dartmoor.

Walker, Armstrong - Seaman - Number: 88 - Prize name: Courier - Ship type: P - How taken: HM Brig Rover - When taken: 14 Mar 1813 - Where taken: Bay of Biscay - Date received: 8 Jul 1813 - From what ship: Plymouth - Born: Baltimore - Age: 16 - Discharged on 13 Jun 1814 and sent to Dartmoor.

Walker, Francis - Seaman - Number: 255 - Prize name: Zebra - Ship type: P - How taken: HM Frigate Pyramus - When taken: 20 Apr 1813 - Where taken: Bay of Biscay - Date received: 11 Jul 1813 - From what ship: Plymouth - Born: Baltimore - Age: 25 - Discharged on 16 Jun 1814 and sent to Dartmoor.

Walker, Richard - Seaman - Number: 411 - How taken: Impressed at Duchford - When taken: 16 Aug 1813 - Date received: 16 Aug 1813 - From what ship: Naval Rendezvous Bristol - Born: Philadelphia - Age: 27 - Race: Negro - Discharged on 16 Jun 1814 and sent to Dartmoor.

Walker, William - Seaman - Number: 1 - How taken: Naval Rendezvous Bristol - Date received: 2 Dec 1812 - From what ship: Bristol - Born: Dighton, MA - Age: 22 - Discharged on 17 May 1813 and sent to Bristol.

Warren, David - Seaman - Number: 56 - Prize name: Paul Jones - Ship type: P - How taken: HM Frigate Leonidas - When taken: 23 May 1813 - Where taken: off Cape Clear (Ireland) - Date received: 8 Jul 1813 - From what ship: Plymouth - Born: Worcester, MA - Age: 36 - Discharged on 13 Jun 1814 and sent to Dartmoor.

Waters, Abraham - Seaman - Number: 246 - Prize name: Essex - Ship type: MV - How taken: HM Frigate Pyramus - When taken: 2 Apr 1813 - Where taken: Bay of Biscay - Date received: 11 Jul 1813 - From what ship: Plymouth - Born: Boston - Age: 17 - Discharged on 16 Jun 1814 and sent to Dartmoor.

Watson, Isaac - Seaman - Number: 337 - Prize name: Fox - Ship type: P - How taken: HM Sloop Pheasant - When taken: 23 Apr 1813 - Where taken: Bay of Biscay - Date received: 11 Jul 1813 - From what ship: Plymouth - Born: Charleston - Age: 23 - Race: Colored - Died on 21 May 1814 in hospital.

Watson, James - Seaman - Number: 218 - Prize name: Hebe - Ship type: MV - How taken: HM Frigate Stag - When taken: 18 Apr 1813 - Where taken: Bay of Biscay - Date received: 11 Jul 1813 - From what ship: Plymouth - Born: New York - Age: 24 - Discharged on 13 Jun 1814 and sent to Dartmoor.

Webb, John - Seaman - Number: 168 - Prize name: Tickler - Ship type: P - How taken: HM Frigate Magiciene - When taken: 5 Jun 1813 - Where taken: Bay of Biscay - Date received: 8 Jul 1813 - From what ship: Plymouth - Born: Maine - Age: 24 - Discharged on 13 Jun 1814 and sent to Dartmoor.

Weedon, Anthony - Seaman - Number: 120 - Prize name: Eliza - Ship type: MV - How taken: HM Frigate Surveillante - When taken: 27 Mar 1813 - Where taken: Bay of Biscay - Date received: 8 Jul 1813 - From what ship: Plymouth - Born: Rhode Island - Age: 31 - Race: Mulatto - Discharged on 13 Jun 1814 and sent to Dartmoor.

Weeks, David - Seaman - Number: 109 - Prize name: Zebra - Ship type: P - How taken: HM Frigate Pyramus - When taken: 20 Apr 1813 - Where taken: Bay of Biscay - Date received: 8 Jul 1813 - From what ship: Plymouth - Born: New Jersey - Age: 21 - Discharged on 13 Jun 1814 and sent to Dartmoor.

Weeks, James - Seaman - Number: 7 - How taken: Naval Rendezvous Bristol - When taken: 14 May 1813 - Date received: 14 May 1813 - From what ship: Bristol - Born: Maryland - Age: 32 - Race: Negro - Discharged on 13 Jun 1814 and sent to Dartmoor.

Welch, Benjamin - Seaman - Number: 230 - Prize name: Essex - Ship type: MV - How taken: HM Frigate Pyramus - When taken: 2 Apr 1813 - Where taken: Bay of Biscay - Date received: 11 Jul 1813 - From what ship: Plymouth - Born: Massachusetts - Age: 22 - Discharged on 16 Jun 1814 and sent to Dartmoor.

West, Dennis - Seaman - Number: 279 - Prize name: Caroline - Ship type: MV - How taken: HM Frigate Medusa - When taken: 12 Apr 1813 - Where taken: Bay of Biscay - Date received: 11 Jul 1813 - From what ship: Plymouth - Born: Massachusetts - Age: 25 - Discharged on 16 Jun 1814 and sent to Dartmoor.

West, Simon - Seaman - Number: 131 - Prize name: Governor Gerry - Ship type: P - How taken: HM Brig Lyra - When taken: 29 May 1813 - Where taken: Coast of Spain - Date received: 8 Jul 1813 - From what ship: Plymouth - Born: Rhode Island - Age: 23 - Discharged on 13 Jun 1814 and sent to Dartmoor.

Wester, Andrew - Seaman - Number: 275 - Prize name: Caroline - Ship type: MV - How taken: HM Frigate Medusa - When taken: 12 Apr 1813 - Where taken: Bay of Biscay - Date received: 11 Jul 1813 - From what ship: Plymouth - Born: Stockholm, Sweden - Age: 27 - Discharged on 31 Oct 1813 and sent to the Swedish Consul.

Weston, David - Seaman - Number: 140 - Prize name: Governor Gerry - Ship type: MV - How taken: HM Brig Royalist - When taken: 31 May 1813 - Where taken: Bay of Biscay - Date received: 8 Jul 1813 - From what ship: Plymouth - Born: Baltimore - Age: 27 - Discharged on 16 Jun 1814 and sent to Dartmoor.

Wheeler, John W. - Seaman - Number: 193 - Prize name: Revenge - Ship type: P - How taken: HM Frigate Belle Poule - When taken: 10 May 1813 - Where taken: Bay of Biscay - Date received: 8 Jul 1813 - From what ship: Plymouth - Born: Connecticut - Age: 26 - Discharged on 13 Jun 1814 and sent to Dartmoor.

White, Charles - Seaman - Number: 103 - Prize name: Meteor - Ship type: MV - How taken: Briton - When taken: 12 Mar 1813 - Where taken: Bay of Biscay - Date received: 8 Jul 1813 - From what ship: Plymouth - Born: Virginia - Age: 20 - Discharged on 15 Jan 1814 and sent to the Regulatory Office Bristol for naval service.

White, David - Seaman - Number: 95 - Prize name: Courier - Ship type: P - How taken: HM Brig Rover - When taken: 14 Mar 1813 - Where taken: Bay of Biscay - Date received: 8 Jul 1813 - From what ship: Plymouth - Born: Baltimore - Age: 15 - Discharged on 13 Jun 1814 and sent to Dartmoor.

White, Henry - Seaman - Number: 241 - Prize name: Essex - Ship type: MV - How taken: HM Frigate Pyramus - When taken: 2 Apr 1813 - Where taken: Bay of Biscay - Date received: 11 Jul 1813 - From what ship: Plymouth - Born: Marblehead - Age: 24 - Discharged on 16 Jun 1814 and sent to Dartmoor.

White, Isaac - Seaman - Number: 70 - Prize name: Grand Napoleon - How taken: HM Brig Goldfinch - When taken: 17 Apr 1813 - Where taken: Bay of Biscay - Date received: 8 Jul 1813 - From what ship: Plymouth - Born: Groton, CT - Age: 19 - Discharged on 13 Jun 1814 and sent to Dartmoor.

White, John - Seaman - Number: 185 - Prize name: Revenge - Ship type: P - How taken: HM Frigate Belle Poule - When taken: 10 May 1813 - Where taken: Bay of Biscay - Date received: 8 Jul 1813 - From what ship: Plymouth - Born: Boston - Age: 24 - Discharged on 13 Jun 1814 and sent to Dartmoor.

Whiting, Samuel - Seaman - Number: 30 - Prize name: Paul Jones - Ship type: P - How taken: HM Frigate Leonidas - When taken: 23 May 1813 - Where taken: off Cape Clear (Ireland) - Date received: 8 Jul 1813 - From what ship: Plymouth - Born: Providence, RI - Age: 25 - Discharged on 13 Jun 1814 and sent to Dartmoor.

Wilcox, Lewis - Seaman - Number: 79 - Prize name: Grand Napoleon - How taken: HM Brig Goldfinch - When taken: 17 Apr 1813 - Where taken: Bay of Biscay - Date received: 8 Jul 1813 - From what ship: Plymouth - Born: Rhode Island - Age: 32 - Discharged on 13 Jun 1814 and sent to Dartmoor.

Wild, Thomas - Seaman - Number: 27 - Prize name: Paul Jones - Ship type: P - How taken: HM Frigate Leonidas - When taken: 23 May 1813 - Where taken: off Cape Clear (Ireland) - Date received: 8 Jul 1813 - From what ship: Plymouth - Born: New Castle, DE - Age: 27 - Discharged on 13 Jun 1814 and sent to Dartmoor.

Wilkins, William - Seaman - Number: 342 - Prize name: Fox - Ship type: P - How taken: HM Sloop Pheasant - When taken: 23 Apr 1813 - Where taken: Bay of Biscay - Date received: 11 Jul 1813 - From what ship: Plymouth - Born: New Jersey - Age: 22 - Discharged on 16 Jun 1814 and sent to Dartmoor.

Williams, Elisha - Seaman - Number: 324 - Prize name: Shadow - Ship type: P - How taken: HM Brig Reindeer - When taken: 6 Apr 1813 - Where taken: Bay of Biscay - Date received: 11 Jul 1813 - From what ship: Plymouth - Born: Delaware - Age: 34 - Race: Negro - Discharged on 16 Jun 1814 and sent to Dartmoor.

Williams, James - Seaman - Number: 276 - Prize name: Caroline - Ship type: MV - How taken: HM Frigate Medusa - When taken: 12 Apr 1813 - Where taken: Bay of Biscay - Date received: 11 Jul 1813 - From what ship: Plymouth - Born: Connecticut - Age: 24 - Discharged on 16 Jun 1814 and sent to Dartmoor.

Williams, John - Seaman - Number: 315 - Prize name: Eliza - Ship type: MV - How taken: HM Frigate Surveillante - When taken: 22 Apr 1813 - Where taken: Bay of Biscay - Date received: 11 Jul 1813 - From what ship: Plymouth - Born: Rhode Island - Age: 29 - Discharged on 16 Jun 1814 and sent to Dartmoor.

Williams, John - Seaman - Number: 390 - Prize name: Henry Clements - Ship type: MV - How taken: HM Brig Orestes - When taken: 13 Apr 1813 - Where taken: Bay of Biscay - Date received: 11 Jul 1813 - From what ship: Plymouth - Born: Newburyport - Age: 22 - Race: Negro - Discharged on 9 Aug 1813 and sent to the Naval Rendezvous Bristol.

Williams, Thomas - Seaman - Number: 237 - Prize name: Essex - Ship type: MV - How taken: HM Frigate Pyramus - When taken: 2 Apr 1813 - Where taken: Bay of Biscay - Date received: 11 Jul 1813 - From what ship: Plymouth - Born: New York - Age: 22 - Race: Colored - Discharged on 16 Jun 1814 and sent to Dartmoor.

Wills, John - Seaman - Number: 286 - Prize name: Messenger - Ship type: MV - How taken: HM Frigate Iris - When taken: 10 Mar 1813 - Where taken: off Cape Ortegal (Spain) - Date received: 11 Jul 1813 - From what ship: Plymouth - Born: Pennsylvania - Age: 47 - Discharged on 16 Jun 1814 and sent to Dartmoor.

Wilson, James - Seaman - Number: 17 - Prize name: Paul Jones - Ship type: P - How taken: HM Frigate Leonidas - When taken: 23 May 1813 - Where taken: off Cape Clear (Ireland) - Date received: 8 Jul 1813 - From what ship: Plymouth - Born: Philadelphia - Age: 30 - Race: Mulatto - Discharged on 13 Jun 1814 and sent to Dartmoor.

Wilson, John - Seaman - Number: 370 - Prize name: Tom - Ship type: P - How taken: HM Frigate Surveillante - When taken: 27 Apr 1813 - Where taken: Bay of Biscay - Date received: 11 Jul 1813 - From what ship: Plymouth - Born: New York - Age: 19 - Discharged on 16 Jun 1814 and sent to Dartmoor.

Winter, Andrew - Seaman - Number: 413 - How taken: Impressed at Bristol - When taken: 7 Sep 1813 - Date received: 7 Sep 1813 - From what ship: Naval Rendezvous Bristol - Born: New York - Age: 31 - Discharged on 16 Jun 1814 and sent to Dartmoor.

Wood, John - Seaman - Number: 99 - Prize name: Courier - Ship type: P - How taken: HM Brig Rover - When taken: 14 Mar 1813 - Where taken: Bay of Biscay - Date received: 8 Jul 1813 - From what ship: Plymouth - Born: Virginia - Age: 22 - Discharged on 13 Jun 1814 and sent to Dartmoor.

Wood, Sylvester - Seaman - Number: 159 - Prize name: Leo - Ship type: P - How taken: HM Frigate Magiciene - When taken: 4 Jun 1813 - Where taken: Bay of Biscay - Date received: 8 Jul 1813 - From what ship: Plymouth - Born: New York - Age: 23 - Discharged on 13 Jun 1814 and sent to Dartmoor.

Wright, George - Seaman - Number: 270 - Prize name: Caroline - Ship type: MV - How taken: HM Frigate Medusa - When taken: 12 Apr 1813 - Where taken: Bay of Biscay - Date received: 11 Jul 1813 - From what ship: Plymouth - Born: Delaware - Age: 29 - Race: Negro - Discharged on 16 Jun 1814 and sent to Dartmoor.

Wright, John - Seaman - Number: 296 - Prize name: Price - Ship type: MV - How taken: HM Frigate Iris - When taken: 13 Apr 1813 - Where taken: Bay of Biscay - Date received: 11 Jul 1813 - From what ship: Plymouth - Born: New York - Age: 21 - Discharged on 16 Jun 1814 and sent to Dartmoor.

Yard, William - Seaman - Number: 125 - Prize name: Miranda - Ship type: Prize of Paul Jones - How taken: HM Frigate Unicorn - When taken: 21 May 1813 - Where taken: Bay of Biscay - Date received: 8 Jul 1813 - From what ship: Plymouth - Born: Trenton, NJ - Age: 26 - Discharged on 13 Jun 1814 and sent to Dartmoor.

Young, William - Seaman - Number: 302 - Prize name: Price - Ship type: MV - How taken: HM Frigate Iris - When taken: 13 Apr 1813 - Where taken: Bay of Biscay - Date received: 11 Jul 1813 - From what ship: Plymouth - Born: New York - Age: 21 - Discharged on 16 Jun 1814 and sent to Dartmoor.

Numeric listing by prisoner number

1. Walker, William
2. Petty, William
3. Harris, John
4. Martin, John
5. Roberts, Roleman Fr. M.
6. Judson, Obadiah
7. Weeks, James
8. Simmons, Robert
9. Bryant, Stephen
10. Cotton, Samuel
11. Jacobs, Evan
12. Bourton, George
13. Baker, Stephen
14. Cockburn, Abel
15. Tyler, Over
16. Stewart, William
17. Wilson, James
18. Byard, Joseph
19. Muly, Edward
20. Godfrey, William
21. Louis, Nicholas
22. Peck, Thomas
23. Veitch, William
24. Smith, John
25. Gibbs, Henry
26. Sardy, Anthony
27. Wild, Thomas
28. Smith, John
29. Johnson, Lambert
30. Whiting, Samuel
31. Newell, Isaac
32. Peterson, Peter
33. Jassieu, Louis
34. Anderson, James
35. Cato, John
36. Edwards, John
37. Cooper, Andrew A.
38. Cramstead, James
39. Prince, George
40. Sentille, Francis
41. Martin, Manuel
42. Biddlefield, James
43. Johnson, Joseph Toker
44. Cooke, William
45. Ruffield, Samuel
46. Thomas, Abraham
47. Brown, Charles
48. Green, William
49. Cook, Charles Howe
50. Allen, John
51. Dibble, Reuben
52. Roley, John
53. Risings, John
54. Guillard, Peter
55. Burstead, John
56. Warren, David
57. Bernard, John
58. Mooney, Peter
59. Guillard, Louis
60. Martin, Isaac
61. Hamilton, Alexander Montgomery
62. Irvin, Arthur
63. Grosse, William
64. Colman, David
65. Stephens, William
66. Little, George
67. Askwick, William Victor
68. Colton, Walter
69. Barnes, Nathaniel
70. White, Isaac
71. Hutchins, Henry
72. Lane, James
73. Thompson, Joseph
74. Pote, Jeremiah
75. Poland, Joseph
76. Redding, John
77. Parish, Samuel
78. Haight, John
79. Wilcox, Lewis
80. Cornwall, Arthur
81. Cooper, Charles
82. Nicholas, Stephen
83. Ostand, Michael
84. Atkins, Joseph
85. Hart, James
86. Manson, William
87. Stutchins, Edward
88. Walker, Armstrong
89. Shaw, Richard
90. Biss, Daniel W.
91. Stanson, William
92. Dickenson, Chester
93. Jackson, Henry
94. Mullins, James

#	Name	#	Name
95	White, David	144	Cross, Oliver
96	Roles, John	145	Hudson, Thomas
97	Logan, William	146	Lamond, John
98	Martin, John	147	English, Edward
99	Wood, John	148	McKenny, John
100	Mills, William	149	Evelish, William
101	Hopkins, Daniel	150	Flinn, Abraham
102	Bower, Joseph	151	Price, Samuel
103	White, Charles	152	Lothrop, James
104	Durand, John	153	Holland, Richard
105	Carter, Edward	154	Tucker, George C.
106	Carter, Daniel	155	Bartlett, Caleb
107	Sellie, Thomas	156	Codman, Richard
108	Barber, William	157	Manson, Nathaniel
109	Weeks, David	158	Davis, John
110	Pitts, William	159	Wood, Sylvester
111	Miller, Charles	160	Doughty, Jesse
112	Roff, Isaac	161	Tuttle, French
113	Reynolds, James	162	Gore, William
114	Edsom, John	163	Foss, Edward
115	Martin, Henry	164	Anderson, Daniel
116	Boriesa, John	165	Cary, John
117	Lerna, John	166	Foss, Joseph
118	Vogel, Herman	167	Foster, John Thomas
119	Ludson, Daniel	168	Webb, John
120	Weedon, Anthony	169	Christie, James
121	Smith, Christian	170	Brandage, John
122	Berryman, John	171	McKinnon, Nathaniel
123	Anthony, Stephen	172	Dougall, Thomas
124	Neal, Denis	173	Best, Robert
125	Yard, William	174	Joles, Robert
126	Parmele, Benjamin	175	Munroe, John
127	Robertson, Robert	176	Hacking, Robert
128	Barasau, John	177	Butman, Charles P.
129	Littlefield, Rufus	178	Inglis, David
130	Moore, Francis	179	Armstrong, James
131	West, Simon	180	Morris, A. G.
132	Goodwin, William	181	Hopkins, Elisha
133	Butler, George	182	Scott, John
134	Doughty, Levi	183	Geyer, Joseph
135	Haskell, Robert	184	Putman, Charles
136	Robinson, Elias	185	White, John
137	Nickerson, Joseph	186	Kellinger, John
138	Merritt, Robert	187	Mezick, Elihu
139	Gage, Isaac	188	Healy, John
140	Weston, David	189	Brown, Benjamin
141	Cudsworth, Henry	190	Bowen, John
142	Smith, John	191	Merritt, Jonathan
143	Smith, Richard	192	Burit, Benjamin

193	Wheeler, John W.	242	Moss, Thomas
194	Gardner, Joseph	243	Stockman, William B.
195	Gabriel, Joseph	244	Burnham, Enoch
196	Keller, John	245	Libley, Moses
197	Harris, James	246	Waters, Abraham
198	Smith, James	247	Lowe, John
199	Bosset, David	248	Matthews, Richard
200	Morie, Joseph	249	Manson, Jeremiah
201	Linsey, Alexander	250	Harrington, Simon
202	Hill, John	251	Jackson, Joseph
203	Hooper, Benjamin C.	252	Payer, Walter
204	Armstrong, William	253	Mills, William
205	Jones, Thomas	254	Stardingbroke, Theop.
206	Joseph, Francis	255	Walker, Francis
207	Fisher, Lewis	256	Avis, James
208	Maine, William	257	Lyon, Charles
209	Elwel, Thomas	258	Laurence, John
210	Francis, Joseph B.	259	Faye, Salmon
211	Mode, David	260	Mortbelly, William
212	Thompson, William	261	Brant, Thomas
213	Hanson, Christopher	262	Shipp, Stephen
214	Brown, William	263	Davis, William
215	Page, Thomas	264	Stag, John Boulton
216	Fish, Joseph	265	Merrit, Thomas
217	Chiseldino, John	266	Pomp, William
218	Watson, James	267	Hanford, William
219	Morgan, Henry	268	Barker, Robert
220	Bradford, Charles	269	Plumber, Joseph
221	Everill, Daniel	270	Wright, George
222	Laill, Joseph	271	Edwards, David
223	Gray, Morehouse	272	Martin, Anthony
224	Veal, Peter	273	Anderson, David
225	Prett, Benjamin	274	Fitts, Joseph
226	Hobson, Abraham	275	Wester, Andrew
227	Clepp, Abraham	276	Williams, James
228	Amerson, Charles	277	Evans, Moses
229	Brown, Samuel	278	Bariston, Peter
230	Welch, Benjamin	279	West, Dennis
231	Blodget, Caleb	280	Burns, Charles
232	Ripley, Eben.	281	Lambert, Joseph
233	Dilno, Benjamin	282	Michel, Jacob
234	Chandler, Simon	283	Peregrine, Taggart
235	Parker, John A.	284	Johnson, James
236	Russell, Patton	285	Mettley, Thomas
237	Williams, Thomas	286	Wills, John
238	Lomeril, Robert	287	Broadwater, Samuel
239	Shovel, John	288	Ingle, John
240	Davis, James	289	Suff, Francis
241	White, Henry	290	Morgan, John

Stapleton Depot

291	Simpson, Thomas		340	James, Daniel
292	Alberson, John N.		341	Baldwin, John
293	Hale, Shederick		342	Wilkins, William
294	Murray, John		343	McCoy, James Abercromby
295	Clothey, Thomas		344	Cambon, Joseph
296	Wright, John		345	Calhoun, Richard
297	Thompson, Charles		346	Beard, Francis
298	Burnett, Charles		347	Andress, Daniel
299	May, Walter		348	Mack, Theoron
300	Roberson, James		349	Price, John
301	Price, Jacob		350	Campbell, Reynold
302	Young, William		351	Johnstone, Simon
303	Heckman, Joseph		352	Jones, John
304	Ingerson, Michael		353	Muller, Edward
305	Francis, John		354	McMakin, John
306	Hunter, William		355	Treffry, James
307	Francis, James		356	Fletcher, James
308	Swatt, David		357	Bright, George
309	Dean, Jonas		358	Ford, George
310	Brown, John		359	Russell, George
311	Blanchet, Simon		360	Hollinger, William
312	Taylor, Thomas		361	Rowley, Henry
313	Sparrow, James		362	Cantrill, Norville
314	Haye, Moses		363	Brown, William
315	Williams, John		364	Davis, John
316	Murray, Jacob		365	Brown, John William
317	Longford, Samuel		366	Fraiser, John
318	Fieto, Francis		367	Lewis, Robert
319	Hammond, Joseph		368	Layfield, Littleton
320	Struby, John		369	Martin, John B.
321	Phillips, John		370	Wilson, John
322	Marshall, Alexander		371	Bickwith, Benjamin
323	Hensell, John		372	McIntire, Samuel
324	Williams, Elisha		373	Smith, Andrew
325	Doliver, William		374	Nelly, Richard John
326	Mingle, William		375	Pelton, Alexander
327	Lilley, Simon		376	Bullman, John
328	Murrel, Mark		377	Trifle, Jasper
329	Harris, William Burr		378	Mansfield, James
330	Howard, William		379	Taylor, Samuel E.
331	Rowle, Benjamin		380	Shiffers, Stuben
332	Perry, Charles		381	Davis, John
333	Dunn, John		382	Rowe, John
334	Norris, Robert		383	Penman, Richard
335	Mingle, Thomas		384	Doolittle, Henry
336	Moore, Richard		385	Cummins, James
337	Watson, Isaac		386	Trefry, Peter
338	Harris, John		387	Heard, Thomas
339	Slocom, Abraham		388	Jenkins, Nathaniel

389 Dean, Nat Benjamin
390 Williams, John
391 Beck, Stewart
392 Smith, Thomas
393 Payne, Joseph S.
394 Lockwood, Rufus
395 Smith, Thomas
396 Edwards, John
397 Friday, John
398 King, Joseph
399 Fink, Johan
400 Robinson, John
401 Alman, John
402 Freeman, John
403 Lacour, John Baptist
404 Miller, Thomas
405 Gee, Thomas
406 Sanford, William

407 Jones, Thomas
408 Pain, Francis
409 Keg, Philip
410 Ricks, Thomas
411 Walker, Richard
412 Cantrill, Norville
413 Winter, Andrew
414 Jefferson, Edward
415 Herrendon, John
416 North, Thomas
417 Lake, Charles
418 Waldren, Hiram
419 Bickwith, Benjamin
420 Staney, Edward
421 Gore, William
422 Not used
423 Not used

Crew listing

Ship	Crew	Ship	Crew
Unknown ship	Armstrong, James	Chantitle	Jacobs, Evan
	Bryant, Stephen		
	Cotton, Samuel	Courier	Anthony, Stephen
	Harris, John		Atkins, Joseph
	Herrendon, John		Berryman, John
	Inglis, David		Biss, Daniel W.
	Jefferson, Edward		Bower, Joseph
	Jones, Thomas		Dickenson, Chester
	Judson, Obadiah		Hart, James
	Keg, Philip		Hopkins, Daniel
	Lake, Charles		Logan, William
	Martin, John		Manson, William
	Matthews, Richard	Courier	Mills, William
	Morris, A. G.		Mullins, James
	North, Thomas		Neal, Denis
	Pain, Francis		Roles, John
	Petty, William		Shaw, Richard
	Ricks, Thomas		Stanson, William
	Roberts, Roleman Fr. M.		Stutchins, Edward
	Scott, John		Walker, Armstrong
	Simmons, Robert		White, David
	Staney, Edward		Wood, John
	Waldren, Hiram		
	Walker, Richard	Eliza	Fieto, Francis
	Walker, William		Hammond, Joseph
	Weeks, James		Longford, Samuel
	Winter, Andrew		Ludson, Daniel
			Murray, Jacob
Anne	Baker, Stephen		Phillips, John
	Cockburn, Abel		Smith, Christian
			Struby, John
Caroline	Anderson, David		Weedon, Anthony
	Bariston, Peter		Williams, John
	Burns, Charles		
	Edwards, David	Essex	Amerson, Charles
	Evans, Moses		Blodget, Caleb
	Fitts, Joseph		Brown, Samuel
	Lambert, Joseph		Burnham, Enoch
	Martin, Anthony		Chandler, Simon
	Michel, Jacob	Essex	Clothey, Thomas
	Peregrine, Tagart		Davis, James
	Plumber, Joseph		Dilno, Benjamin
	West, Dennis		Doliver, William
Caroline	Wester, Andrew		Fisher, Lewis
	Williams, James		Libley, Moses
	Wright, George		Lomeril, Robert
			Lowe, John

Essex	Maine, William	Governor Gerry	Gage, Isaac
	Moss, Thomas		Harris, James
	Parker, John A.		Hill, John
	Ripley, Eben		Hooper, Benjamin C.
	Russell, Patton		Jones, Thomas
	Shovel, John		Keller, John
	Stockman, William B.		Linsey, Alexander
	Treffry, James		Merritt, Robert
	Trefry, Peter		Moore, Francis
	Waters, Abraham		Morie, Joseph
	Welch, Benjamin		Smith, James
	White, Henry		Smith, John
	Williams, Thomas		Smith, Richard
			West, Simon
Fox	Andress, Daniel		Weston, David
	Baldwin, John		
	Beard, Francis	Grand Napoleon	Cooper, Charles
	Bright, George		Cornwall, Arthur
	Calhoun, Richard		Haight, John
	Cambon, Joseph		Hutchins, Henry
	Dunn, John		Lane, James
	Fletcher, James		Nicholas, Stephen
	Harris, John		Ostand, Michael
	Harris, William Burr		Parish, Samuel
	Howard, William		Poland, Joseph
	James, Daniel		Pote, Jeremiah
	Mack, Theoron		Redding, John
	McCoy, James Abercromby		Thompson, Joseph
	Mingle, Thomas		White, Isaac
	Moore, Richard		Wilcox, Lewis
	Norris, Robert		
	Perry, Charles	Hebe	Brown, William
	Rowle, Benjamin		Chiseldino, John
	Slocom, Abraham		Fish, Joseph
	Watson, Isaac		Francis, Joseph B.
	Wilkins, William		Hanson, Christopher
			Mode, David
Good Friends	Boriesa, John		Page, Thomas
	Lerna, John		Thompson, William
	Martin, Henry		Watson, James
	Vogel, Herman		
		Henry Clements	Beck, Stewart
Good Intents	Elwel, Thomas		Smith, Thomas
			Williams, John
Governor Gerry	Armstrong, William		
	Bosset, David	King David	Bourton, George
	Cross, Oliver		
	Cudsworth, Henry	Laura	Tyler, Over
	Gabriel, Joseph		

Leo	Anderson, Daniel	Orders in	Haskell, Robert
	Bartlett, Caleb	Council	Nickerson, Joseph
	Cary, John		Robinson, Elias
	Codman, Richard		
	Davis, John	Paul Jones	Allen, John
	Doughty, Jesse		Alman, John
	Foss, Edward		Anderson, James
	Foss, Joseph		Askwick, William Victor
	Gore, William		Barnes, Nathaniel
	Manson, Nathaniel		Bernard, John
	Tucker, George C.		Biddlefield, James
	Tuttle, French		Brown, Charles
	Wood, Sylvester		Burstead, John
			Byard, Joseph
Messenger	Alberson, John N.		Cato, John
	Broadwater, Samuel		Colman, David
	Hale, Shederick		Colton, Walter
	Ingle, John		Cook, Charles Howe
	Johnson, James		Cooke, William
	Mettley, Thomas		Cooper, Andrew A.
	Morgan, John		Cramstead, James
	Murray, John		Dibble, Reuben
	Simpson, Thomas		Edwards, John
	Suff, Francis		Fink, Johan
	Wills, John		Freeman, John
			Friday, John
Meteor	White, Charles		Gibbs, Henry
			Godfrey, William
Miranda	Barasau, John		Green, William
	Littlefield, Rufus		Grosse, William
	Parmele, Benjamin		Guillard, Louis
	Robertson, Robert		Guillard, Peter
	Yard, William		Hamilton, Alexander Montgomery
			Irvin, Arthur
Napoleon	Bradford, Charles		Jackson, Henry
	Clepp, Abraham		Jassieu, Louis
	Everill, Daniel		Johnson, Joseph Toker
	Gray, Morehouse		Johnson, Lambert
	Hobson, Abraham		Joseph, Francis
	Laill, Joseph		King, Joseph
	Morgan, Henry		Lacour, John Baptist
	Prett, Benjamin		Little, George
	Veal, Peter		Lockwood, Rufus
			Louis, Nicholas
Omer	Hopkins, Elisha		Martin, Isaac
			Martin, John
Orders in	Butler, George		Martin, Manuel
Council	Doughty, Levi		Miller, Thomas
	Goodwin, William		Mooney, Peter

Paul Jones	Muly, Edward	Revenge	Gardner, Joseph
	Newell, Isaac		Geyer, Joseph
	Peck, Thomas		Healy, John
	Peterson, Peter		Holland, Richard
	Prince, George		Hudson, Thomas
	Risings, John		Kellinger, John
	Robinson, John		Lamond, John
	Roley, John		Lothrop, James
	Ruffield, Samuel		McKenny, John
	Sanford, William		Merritt, Jonathan
	Sardy, Anthony		Mezick, Elihu
	Sentille, Francis		Price, Samuel
	Smith, John		Putman, Charles
	Smith, Thomas		Wheeler, John W.
	Stephens, William		White, John
	Stewart, William		
	Thomas, Abraham	Shadow	Campbell, Reynold
	Veitch, William		Hensell, John
	Warren, David		Johnstone, Simon
	Whiting, Samuel		Jones, John
	Wild, Thomas		Lilley, Simon
	Wilson, James		Marshall, Alexander
			McMakin, John
Price	Blanchet, Simon		Mingle, William
	Brown, John		Muller, Edward
	Burnett, Charles		Murrel, Mark
	Dean, Jonas		Price, John
	Francis, James		Williams, Elisha
	Francis, John		
	Haye, Moses	Tickler	Best, Robert
	Heckman, Joseph		Brandage, John
	Hunter, William		Butman, Charles P.
	Ingerson, Michael		Christie, James
	May, Walter		Dougall, Thomas
	Price, Jacob		Foster, John Thomas
	Roberson, James		Hacking, Robert
	Sparrow, James		Joles, Robert
	Swatt, David		McKinnon, Nathaniel
	Taylor, Thomas		Munroe, John
	Thompson, Charles		Webb, John
	Wright, John		
	Young, William	Tom	Bickwith, Benjamin
			Brown, John William
Revenge	Bowen, John		Brown, William
	Brown, Benjamin		Bullman, John
	Burit, Benjamin		Cantrill, Norville
	English, Edward		Cummins, James
	Evelish, William		Davis, John
	Flinn, Abraham		Dean, Nat Benjamin

Stapleton Depot

Tom	Doolittle, Henry	Zebra	Brant, Thomas
	Ford, George		Carter, Daniel
	Fraiser, John		Carter, Edward
	Gee, Thomas		Davis, William
	Heard, Thomas		Durand, John
	Hollinger, William		Edsom, John
	Jenkins, Nathaniel		Faye, Salmon
	Layfield, Littleton		Hanford, William
	Lewis, Robert		Harrington, Simon
	Mansfield, James		Jackson, Joseph
	Martin, John B.		Laurence, John
	McIntire, Samuel		Lyon, Charles
	Nelly, Richard John		Manson, Jeremiah
	Payne, Joseph S.		Merrit, Thomas
	Pelton, Alexander		Miller, Charles
	Penman, Richard		Mills, William
	Rowe, John		Mortbelly, William
	Rowley, Henry		Payer, Walter
	Russell, George		Pitts, William
	Shiffers, Stuben		Pomp, William
	Smith, Andrew		Reynolds, James
	Taylor, Samuel E.		Roff, Isaac
	Trifle, Jasper		Sellie, Thomas
	Wilson, John		Shipp, Stephen
			Stag, John Boulton
Zebra	Avis, James		Stardingbroke, Theop.
	Barber, William		Walker, Francis
	Barker, Robert		Weeks, David

Gibraltar

Adams, Thomas - Seaman - Number: 648 - How taken: HM Battery Gorgon - Date taken: 28 May 1813 - Where taken: Mahon (Island of Minorca) - Date received: 1 Jul 1813 - From what ship: HMT Royal Boston No. 344 - Discharged on 12 Jul 1813 - How discharged: HM Sloop Bacchus.

Adams, Thomas - Number: 704 - How taken: Taken off the HM Frigate Ganymede - Discharged on 24 Jul 1813 - How discharged: HM Store Ship Tortoise.

Affan, John - Seaman - Number: 9 - Prize name: Margaret - Ship type: MV - How taken: HM Ship-of-the-Line San Juan - Date taken: 10 Aug 1812 - Where taken: Gibraltar Bay - Date received: 12 Aug 1812 - From what ship: Margaret - Discharged on 15 Jan 1813 - How discharged: HM Brig Derwent.

Alexander, George - Seaman - Number: 568 - Date received: 1 Jul 1813 - From what ship: HMT Royal Boston No. 344 - Discharged on 28 Jun 1813 - How discharged: HMT Minstraele.

Alford, Edward - 2nd Mate - Number: 333 - Prize name: John L. Kees - Ship type: MV - How taken: HM Brig Basilisk - Date taken: 6 Jan 1813 - Where taken: near Cadiz - Date received: 27 Jan 1813; Returned to ship on 29 Jan 1813 - From what ship: HM Brig Basilisk - Discharged on 14 Apr 1813 - How discharged: Being a licensed vessel.

Allen, Henry - Clerk - Number: 781 - Prize name: Leo - Ship type: P - How taken: HM Ship-of-the-Line Grampus - Date taken: 2 Dec 1814 - Where taken: off Lisbon - Date received: 9 Dec 1814 - From what ship: HM Frigate Granicus - Discharged on 15 Dec 1814 - How discharged: HMS Eurasso.

Allen, William - Seaman - Number: 575 - Where taken: Mahon (Island of Minorca) - Date received: 1 Jul 1813 - From what ship: HMT Royal Boston No. 344 - Discharged on 12 Jul 1813 - How discharged: HM Sloop Bacchus.

Allen, William - Seaman - Number: 34 - Prize name: Allegany - Ship type: MV - How taken: HM Ship-of-the-Line San Juan - Date taken: 10 Aug 1812 - Where taken: Gibraltar Bay - Date received: 12 Aug 1812 - From what ship: Allegany - Discharged on 15 Jan 1813 - How discharged: HM Brig Derwent.

Amens, John - 2nd Mate - Number: 290 - Prize name: George & Albert - Ship type: MV - How taken: HMS Myrtle - Date taken: 5 Jan 1813 - Where taken: off Cape St. Mary (Portugal) - Date received: 10 Jan 1813 - From what ship: HMS Myrtle - Discharged on 14 Apr 1813 - How discharged: Being a licensed vessel.

Anbeck, John A. - Seaman - Number: 219 - Prize name: Topaz - Ship type: MV - How taken: HM Ship-of-the-Line Grampus - Date taken: 19 Oct 1812 - Where taken: On passage to Cadiz - Date received: 21 Nov 1812 - From what ship: HM Ship-of-the-Line Grampus - Discharged on 14 Dec 1812 - How discharged: Being a licensed vessel.

Anderson, Peter - Seaman - Number: 293 - Prize name: George & Albert - Ship type: MV - How taken: HMS Myrtle - Date taken: 5 Jan 1813 - Where taken: off Cape St. Mary (Portugal) - Date received: 10 Jan 1813 - From what ship: HMS Myrtle - Discharged on 14 Apr 1813 - How discharged: Being a licensed vessel.

Andrews, George - Seaman - Number: 545 - Prize name: Isabella - Ship type: MV - How taken: HM Brig Zenoha - Date taken: 27 Jun 1813 - Where taken: off Cape St. Mary (Portugal) - Date received: 1 Jul 1813 - From what ship: HM Brig Protection - Discharged on 4 Sep 1813 - How discharged: HM Brig Teazer.

Andrews, John - Seaman - Number: 256 - Prize name: Apollo - Ship type: MV - How taken: HM Ship-of-the-Line Grampus - Date taken: 29 Oct 1812 - Where taken: On passage to Cadiz - Date received: 21 Nov 1812 - From what ship: HM Ship-of-the-Line Grampus - Discharged on 14 Dec 1812 - How discharged: Being a licensed vessel.

Andrews, John (1) - Seaman - Number: 719 - Discharged on Aug 1813 - How discharged: HM Ship-of-the-Line Achille.

Andrews, John (2) - Seaman - Number: 721 - Discharged on Aug 1813 - How discharged: HM Ship-of-the-Line Achille.

Appleton, William - Master - Number: 15 - Prize name: Horace - Ship type: MV - How taken: HM Ship-of-the-Line

San Juan - Date taken: 10 Aug 1812 - Where taken: Gibraltar Bay - Date received: 12 Aug 1812 - From what ship: Horace - Discharged on 29 Aug 1812 - How discharged: Being a licensed vessel.

Archibald, Robert - Master - Number: 405 - Prize name: Veroni - Ship type: MV - How taken: HM Sloop Comet - Date taken: 14 Jan 1813 - Where taken: near Cadiz - Date received: 13 Feb 1813 - From what ship: Veroni Prize - Discharged on 14 Apr 1813 - How discharged: Being a licensed vessel.

Armshell, John - Seaman - Number: 241 - Prize name: Conde Mary - Ship type: MV - How taken: HM Ship-of-the-Line Grampus - Date taken: 24 Oct 1812 - Where taken: On passage to Cadiz - Date received: 21 Nov 1812 - From what ship: HM Ship-of-the-Line Grampus - Discharged on 31 Dec 1812 - How discharged: Being a licensed vessel.

Arnold, Alfred - Seaman - Number: 480 - Discharged on 22 Mar 1813 - How discharged: Being a licensed vessel.

Aroid, Aaron - Seaman - Number: 178 - Prize name: Sally - Ship type: MV - How taken: Not mentioned - Date taken: 22 Aug 1812 - Discharged on 30 Sep 1812 - How discharged: Either a Moor or a Spaniard.

Arthurs, Williams - Seaman - Number: 411 - Prize name: Thomas Wilson - Ship type: MV - How taken: HM Sloop Comet - Date taken: 14 Jan 1813 - Where taken: near Cadiz - Date received: 18 Feb 1813 - From what ship: HM Brig Charger - Discharged on 10 Apr 1813 - How discharged: Being a licensed vessel.

Ash, Luke - Seaman - Number: 259 - Prize name: Lydia - Ship type: MV - How taken: HM Ship-of-the-Line Grampus - Date taken: 2 Nov 1812 - Where taken: On passage to Cadiz - Date received: 21 Nov 1812 - From what ship: HM Ship-of-the-Line Grampus - Discharged on 14 Dec 1812 - How discharged: Being a licensed vessel.

Ashbourne, Luke - Seaman - Number: 258 - Prize name: Lydia - Ship type: MV - How taken: HM Ship-of-the-Line Grampus - Date taken: 2 Nov 1812 - Where taken: On passage to Cadiz - Date received: 21 Nov 1812 - From what ship: HM Ship-of-the-Line Grampus - Discharged on 14 Dec 1812 - How discharged: Being a licensed vessel.

Ashwood, Ralph - Seaman - Number: 235 - Prize name: Julian Mary - Ship type: MV - How taken: HM Ship-of-the-Line Grampus - Date taken: 21 Oct 1812 - Where taken: On passage to Cadiz - Date received: 21 Nov 1812 - From what ship: HM Ship-of-the-Line Grampus - Discharged on 14 Dec 1812 - How discharged: Being a licensed vessel.

Atkens, Uriah - Seaman - Number: 48 - Prize name: Tiger - Ship type: MV - How taken: HM Ship-of-the-Line San Juan - Date taken: 10 Aug 1812 - Where taken: Gibraltar Bay - Date received: 12 Aug 1812 - From what ship: Tiger - Discharged on 15 Jan 1813 - How discharged: HM Frigate Andromeda.

Augustus, Benjamin - Seaman - Number: 615 - How taken: HM Ship-of-the-Line Royal George - Date taken: 28 May 1813 - Where taken: Mahon (Island of Minorca) - Date received: 1 Jul 1813 - From what ship: HMT Royal Boston No. 344 - Discharged on 3 Jul 1813 - How discharged: HM Frigate Thames.

Austin, James - Seaman - Number: 629 - How taken: HM Ship-of-the-Line Prince of Wales - Date taken: 28 May 1813 - Where taken: Mahon (Island of Minorca) - Date received: 1 Jul 1813 - From what ship: HMT Royal Boston No. 344 - Discharged on 3 Jul 1813 - How discharged: HM Frigate Thames.

Avery, Charles - Seaman - Number: 501 - How taken: Gave himself up from HM Ship-of-the-Line Malta - Date taken: 2 Jan 1813 - Where taken: Gibraltar - Date received: 9 Apr 1813 - From what ship: HM Bomb Vessel Strombolo - Discharged on 23 Apr 1813 - How discharged: HM Sloop Helena.

Babcock, John - Seaman - Number: 338 - Prize name: Essex - Ship type: MV - How taken: HM Gunboat No. 22 - Date taken: 12 Jan 1813 - Where taken: near Cadiz - Date received: 19 Jan 1813 - From what ship: HM Gunboat No. 22 - Discharged on 16 Apr 1813 - How discharged: Being a licensed vessel.

Bailey, William - Number: 633 - Discharged on 28 Jun 1813 - How discharged: HMT Minstraele.

Bain, Daniel - Seaman - Number: 222 - Prize name: Topaz - Ship type: MV - How taken: HM Ship-of-the-Line Grampus - Date taken: 19 Oct 1812 - Where taken: On passage to Cadiz - Date received: 21 Nov 1812 - From what ship: HM Ship-of-the-Line Grampus - Discharged on 14 Dec 1812 - How discharged: Being a licensed vessel.

Baker, Daniel - Seaman - Number: 628 - How taken: HM Ship-of-the-Line Prince of Wales - Date taken: 28 May

1813 - Where taken: Mahon (Island of Minorca) - Date received: 1 Jul 1813 - From what ship: HMT Royal Boston No. 344 - Discharged on 3 Jul 1813 - How discharged: HM Frigate Thames.

Barber, John - Seaman - Number: 537 - How taken: Taken off the Spanish MV Maydock - Discharged on 8 Aug 1813 - How discharged: HM Sloop Kingfisher.

Barclay, D. William - Seaman - Number: 729 - Prize name: Engenia - Ship type: MV - How taken: HM Brig Papillion - Date taken: 17 Jul 1813 - Where taken: near Cadiz - Date received: 10 Aug 1813 - From what ship: HM Brig Papillion - Discharged on 7 Oct 1813 - How discharged: Eugenia.

Bartlett, John (see prisoner number 107) - Master - Number: 43 - Prize name: Tiger - Ship type: MV - How taken: HM Ship-of-the-Line San Juan - Date taken: 10 Aug 1812 - Where taken: Gibraltar Bay - Date received: 12 Aug 1812 - From what ship: Tiger - Discharged on 15 Jan 1813 - How discharged: HM Frigate Andromeda.

Bartlett, John - Master - Number: 107 - Prize name: Tiger - Ship type: MV - How taken: HM Ship-of-the-Line San Juan - Date taken: 10 Aug 1812 - Where taken: Gibraltar Bay - Date received: 2 Sep 1813 - From what ship: HM Ship-of-the-Line Tremendous.

Bartoll, Samuel - Seaman - Number: 761 - Prize name: Adeline - Ship type: LM - How taken: HM Frigate Magiciene - Date taken: 14 Mar 1814 - Where taken: at sea - Date received: 14 Apr 1814 - From what ship: HM Frigate Magiciene - Discharged on 22 Apr 1814 - How discharged: HM Store Ship Tortoise.

Barton, Matthew - Seaman - Number: 61 - How taken: Gave himself up from HM Brig Sabine - Date received: 15 Aug 1812 - From what ship: HM Brig Sabine - Discharged on 5 Sep 1812 - How discharged: Returned to HM Brig Sabine.

Batchelor, Nathaniel (see prisoner number 111) - Master - Number: 52 - Prize name: Phoenix - Ship type: MV - How taken: HM Ship-of-the-Line San Juan - Date taken: 10 Aug 1812 - Where taken: Gibraltar Bay - Date received: 12 Aug 1812 - From what ship: Tiger - Discharged on 22 Jan 1813 - How discharged: HM Sloop Comet.

Batchelor, Nathaniel - Seaman - Number: 111 - Prize name: Phoenix - Ship type: MV - How taken: HM Ship-of-the-Line San Juan - Date taken: 10 Aug 1812 - Where taken: Gibraltar Bay - Date received: 2 Sep 1813 - From what ship: HM Ship-of-the-Line Tremendous.

Bateman, Ely - Seaman - Number: 553 - Prize name: Hepsey - Ship type: MV - Discharged on 8 Aug 1813 - How discharged: HM Sloop Kingfisher.

Bates, Joseph - Seaman - Number: 712 - Discharged on Aug 1813 - How discharged: HM Ship-of-the-Line Achille.

Beard, Richard - Captain - Number: 786 - Prize name: Sine Qua Non - Ship type: P - How taken: HMS Eske - Date taken: 20 Feb 1815 - Where taken: off Madeira - Date received: 14 Mar 1815 - From what ship: HMS Eske - Discharged on 14 Mar 1815 - How discharged: HMT Ann No. 124 for England.

Beates, John - Seaman - Number: 700 - Prize name: La Guera - Ship type: MV - How taken: Sophia, Letter of Marque - Date taken: 25 Jun 1813 - Where taken: near Lisbon - Date received: 2 Jul 1813 - From what ship: HM Brig Protector.

Begnall, Charles - Seaman - Number: 273 - Prize name: Topaz - Ship type: MV - How taken: HM Ship-of-the-Line Grampus - Date taken: 19 Oct 1812 - Date received: 23 Nov 1812 - From what ship: Topaz - Discharged on 14 Dec 1812 - How discharged: Being a licensed vessel.

Bell, Peter (1) - Master - Number: 266 - Prize name: Apollo - Ship type: MV - How taken: HM Ship-of-the-Line Grampus - Date taken: 29 Oct 1812 - Where taken: On passage to Cadiz - Date received: 22 Nov 1812 - From what ship: Apollo - Discharged on 1 Dec 1812.

Bell, Peter (2) - Seaman - Number: 267 - Prize name: Apollo - Ship type: MV - How taken: HM Ship-of-the-Line Grampus - Date taken: 29 Oct 1812 - Where taken: On passage to Cadiz - Date received: 22 Nov 1812 - From what ship: Apollo - Discharged on 14 Dec 1812 - How discharged: Being a licensed vessel.

Bellar, John - Mate - Number: 185 - Prize name: Draper - Ship type: MV - How taken: HM Brig Fearly - Date taken: 18 Sep 1812 - Where taken: near Cadiz - Date received: 27 Sep 1812 - From what ship: HM Brig Fearless - Discharged on 22 Jan 1813 - How discharged: HM Sloop Comet.

Benjamin, Vallasky - Seaman - Number: 392 - Prize name: Pallas - Ship type: MV - How taken: HMS Rebuff - Date taken: 24 Dec 1812 - Where taken: near Cadiz - Date received: 9 Feb 1813 - From what ship: Pallas Prize - Discharged on 6 Mar 1813 - How discharged: HM Ship-of-the-Line Blake.

Benn, William - Seaman - Number: 498 - How taken: Gave himself up from HM Ship-of-the-Line Malta - Date taken: 2 Jan 1813 - Where taken: Gibraltar - Date received: 9 Apr 1813 - From what ship: HM Bomb Vessel Strombolo - Discharged on 23 Apr 1813 - How discharged: HM Sloop Helena.

Bennett, Thomas - Seaman - Number: 272 - Prize name: Topaz - Ship type: MV - How taken: HM Ship-of-the-Line Grampus - Date taken: 19 Oct 1812 - Date received: 23 Nov 1812 - From what ship: Topaz - Discharged on 14 Dec 1812 - How discharged: Being a licensed vessel.

Bennett, William - Seaman - Number: 236 - Prize name: Julian Mary - Ship type: MV - How taken: HM Ship-of-the-Line Grampus - Date taken: 21 Oct 1812 - Where taken: On passage to Cadiz - Date received: 21 Nov 1812 - From what ship: HM Ship-of-the-Line Grampus - Discharged on 14 Dec 1812 - How discharged: Being a licensed vessel.

Bentley, Samuel (see prisoner number 146) - Number: 137 - Prize name: Commerce - Ship type: MV - How taken: HM Brig Rebuff - Date taken: 28 Aug 1812 - Where taken: near Cadiz - Date received: Returned to ship on 16 Sep 1812.

Bentley, Samuel - Seaman - Number: 146 - Prize name: Commerce - Ship type: MV - How taken: HM Brig Desperate - Date taken: 22 Aug 1812 - Where taken: near Cadiz - Discharged on 28 Jan 1813 - How discharged: Being a licensed vessel.

Berroy, John - Seaman - Number: 299 - Prize name: George & Albert - Ship type: MV - How taken: HMS Myrtle - Date taken: 5 Jan 1813 - Where taken: off Cape St. Mary (Portugal) - Date received: 10 Jan 1813 - From what ship: HMS Myrtle - Discharged on 14 Apr 1813 - How discharged: Being a licensed vessel.

Bert, R. - Seaman - Number: 209 - Prize name: Meser - Ship type: MV - How taken: Not mentioned - Where taken: Unknown - Discharged on 13 Nov 1813 - How discharged: Being a licensed vessel.

Bhovey, Josiah - Seaman - Number: 83 - Prize name: Taken in an open boat formerly belonging to American ship Fame which was captured by the French - How taken: HM Brig Desperate - Date taken: 22 Aug 1812 - Where taken: near Cadiz - Date received: 31 Aug 1813 - From what ship: HM Frigate Argo.

Biera, Manuel - Seaman - Number: 246 - Prize name: Conde Mary - Ship type: MV - How taken: HM Ship-of-the-Line Grampus - Date taken: 24 Oct 1812 - Where taken: On passage to Cadiz - Date received: 21 Nov 1812 - From what ship: HM Ship-of-the-Line Grampus - Discharged on 31 Dec 1812 - How discharged: Being a licensed vessel.

Bird, James - Seaman - Number: 510 - How taken: Gave himself up from HM Ship-of-the-Line Fame and HM Brig Philomel - Date taken: 2 Jan 1813 - Where taken: Gibraltar - Date received: 20 May 1813 - From what ship: HMS Ephegema - Discharged on 22 May 1813 - How discharged: HM Brig Zephyr.

Birket, James - Mate - Number: 262 - Prize name: Lydia - Ship type: MV - How taken: HM Ship-of-the-Line Grampus - Date taken: 2 Nov 1812 - Where taken: On passage to Cadiz - Date received: 22 Nov 1812 - From what ship: Lydia - Discharged on 14 Dec 1812 - How discharged: Being a licensed vessel.

Bissell, Samuel F. - Seaman - Number: 691 - Prize name: Hepsey - Ship type: MV - Discharged on 8 Aug 1813 - How discharged: HM Sloop Kingfisher.

Blackloch, John - Seaman - Number: 531 - Prize name: Spanish MV - How taken: HM Brig Papillion - Date taken: Jun 1813 - Where taken: near Cadiz - Date received: 1 Aug 1813 - From what ship: Majesty's Naval Hospital.

Blake, William - Seaman - Number: 675 - How taken: HM Ship-of-the-Line Repulse - Date taken: 28 May 1813 - Where taken: Mahon (Island of Minorca) - Date received: 1 Jul 1813 - Discharged on 3 Jul 1813 - How discharged: HM Frigate Thames.

Blanchard, Calvin - Seaman - Number: 51 - Prize name: Tiger - Ship type: MV - How taken: HM Ship-of-the-Line San Juan - Date taken: 10 Aug 1812 - Where taken: Gibraltar Bay - Date received: 12 Aug 1812 - From what ship: Tiger - Discharged on 15 Jan 1813 - How discharged: HM Frigate Andromeda.

Bond, Samuel - Number: 659 - How taken: HM Ship-of-the-Line Ocean - Date taken: 28 May 1813 - Where taken: Mahon (Island of Minorca) - Discharged on 28 Jun 1813 - How discharged: HMT Minstraele.

Booth, John - Seaman - Number: 374 - Prize name: George - Ship type: MV - How taken: HM Brig Columbine - Date taken: 13 Jan 1813 - Where taken: off Lisbon - Date received: 22 Jan 1813 - From what ship: HM Sloop Comet - Discharged on 15 Apr 1813 - How discharged: Being a licensed vessel.

Bordley, George - Seaman - Number: 670 - Discharged on 28 Jun 1813 - How discharged: HMT Minstraele.

Borne, John - Seaman - Number: 30 - Prize name: Allegany - Ship type: MV - How taken: HM Ship-of-the-Line San Juan - Date taken: 10 Aug 1812 - Where taken: Gibraltar Bay - Date received: 12 Aug 1812 - From what ship: Allegany - Discharged on 15 Jan 1813 - How discharged: HM Brig Derwent.

Boswell, James - Seaman - Number: 639 - How taken: Taken off the HM Battery Gorgon - Date received: 1 Jul 1813 - From what ship: HMT Royal Boston No. 344 - Discharged on 28 Jun 1813 - How discharged: HMT Minstraele.

Boyd, Andrew - Seaman - Number: 550 - Prize name: Hepsey - Ship type: MV - Discharged on 8 Aug 1813 - How discharged: HM Sloop Kingfisher.

Boyd, John - Seaman - Number: 590 - Where taken: Mahon (Island of Minorca) - Date received: 1 Jul 1813 - From what ship: HMT Royal Boston No. 344 - Discharged on 21 Jul 1813 - How discharged: HM Brig Savage.

Boyd, Stephen - Seaman - Number: 556 - Date received: 8 Aug 1813 - From what ship: Hepsey Prize - Discharged on 22 Aug 1813 - How discharged: HM Brig Imogen.

Brazier, William - Seaman - Number: 117 - Prize name: John - Ship type: MV - How taken: HM Sloop Blossom - Date taken: 10 Aug 1812 - Where taken: Mediterranean - Date received: 2 Sep 1813 - From what ship: HM Ship-of-the-Line Tremendous - Discharged on 25 Jan 1813 - How discharged: HM Ship-of-the-Line Sultan.

Braler, John - Seaman - Number: 504 - How taken: Gave himself up from HM Ship-of-the-Line Fame and HM Brig Philomel - Date taken: 2 Jan 1813 - Where taken: Gibraltar - Date received: 20 May 1813 - From what ship: HMS Ephegema - Discharged on 22 May 1813 - How discharged: HM Brig Zephyr.

Brant, Solomon - Seaman - Number: 281 - Prize name: Maria - Ship type: MV - Discharged on 25 Jan 1813 - How discharged: HM Ship-of-the-Line Sultan.

Bristol, Nicholas - Mate - Number: 463 - Prize name: Amphitrite - Ship type: MV - From what ship: Amphitrite - Discharged on 19 Mar 1813 - How discharged: HM Schooner Sylvia.

Brockelman, William - Seaman - Number: 243 - Prize name: Conde Mary - Ship type: MV - How taken: HM Ship-of-the-Line Grampus - Date taken: 24 Oct 1812 - Where taken: On passage to Cadiz - Date received: 21 Nov 1812 - From what ship: HM Ship-of-the-Line Grampus - Discharged on 31 Dec 1812 - How discharged: Being a licensed vessel.

Brown, Elisha - Seaman - Number: 401 - How taken: Gave himself up from HM Frigate Franchise - Date taken: 12 Feb 1812 - Where taken: Gibraltar - Date received: 13 Feb 1813 - From what ship: HM Frigate Franchise - Discharged on 6 Mar 1813 - How discharged: HM Ship-of-the-Line Blake.

Brown, George - Seaman - Number: 336 - Prize name: San Joseph Volorado - Ship type: MV - How taken: HM Brig Desperate - Date taken: 15 Jan 1813 - Where taken: near Cadiz - Date received: 27 Jan 1813 - From what ship: HM Brig Basilisk - Discharged on 18 Feb 1813 - How discharged: Being a licensed vessel.

Brown, George - Seaman - Number: 658 - How taken: HM Ship-of-the-Line Ocean - Date taken: 28 May 1813 - Where taken: Mahon (Island of Minorca) - Date received: 1 Jul 1813 - From what ship: HMT Royal Boston No. 344 - Discharged on 21 Jul 1813 - How discharged: HM Brig Savage.

Brown, Isaac - Seaman - Number: 680 - How taken: HM Brig Shearwater - Date taken: 3 Jun 1813 - Where taken: Mahon (Island of Minorca) - Date received: 1 Jul 1813 - Discharged on 21 Jul 1813 - How discharged: HM Brig Savage.

Brown, James - Seaman - Number: 372 - Prize name: George - Ship type: MV - How taken: HM Brig Columbine - Date taken: 13 Jan 1813 - Where taken: off Lisbon - Date received: 22 Jan 1813 - From what ship: HM Sloop Comet - Discharged on 15 Apr 1813 - How discharged: Being a licensed vessel.

Brown, James - Seaman - Number: 351 - Prize name: Pallas - Ship type: MV - How taken: HM Brig Rebuff - Date taken: 24 Dec 1812 - Where taken: near Cadiz - Date received: 19 Jan 1813 - From what ship: HM Brig Rebuff - Discharged on 19 Feb 1813 - How discharged: HM Brig Protector.

Brown, John - Seaman - Number: 417 - Prize name: Charlotte - Ship type: MV - How taken: HM Brig Charger - Date taken: 14 Jan 1813 - Where taken: near Cadiz - Date received: 18 Feb 1813 - From what ship: HM Brig Charger - Discharged on 14 Apr 1813 - How discharged: Being a licensed vessel.

Brown, John - Seaman - Number: 317 - Prize name: Concordia - Ship type: MV - How taken: HM Brig Basilisk - Date taken: 6 Jan 1813 - Where taken: near Cadiz - Date received: 12 Jan 1813 - From what ship: HM Brig Basilisk - Discharged on 14 Apr 1813 - How discharged: Being a licensed vessel.

Brown, John - Seaman - Number: 664 - How taken: HM Ship-of-the-Line Ocean - Date taken: 28 May 1813 - Where taken: Mahon (Island of Minorca) - Date received: 1 Jul 1813 - From what ship: HMT Royal Boston No. 344 - Discharged on 28 Jun 1813 - How discharged: HMT Minstraele.

Brown, Reuben - Seaman - Number: 604 - How taken: HM Ship-of-the-Line Berwick - Date taken: 28 May 1813 - Where taken: Mahon (Island of Minorca) - Date received: 1 Jul 1813 - From what ship: HMT Royal Boston No. 344 - Discharged on 28 Jun 1813 - How discharged: HMT Minstraele.

Brown, Samuel - Seaman - Number: 495 - How taken: Gave himself up from HM Ship-of-the-Line Malta - Date taken: 2 Jan 1813 - Where taken: Gibraltar - Date received: 9 Apr 1813 - From what ship: HM Bomb Vessel Strombolo - Discharged on 22 May 1813 - How discharged: HM Brig Zephyr.

Brown, Samuel - Seaman - Number: 730 - Prize name: Engenia - Ship type: MV - How taken: HM Brig Papillion - Date taken: 17 Jul 1813 - Where taken: near Cadiz - Date received: 10 Aug 1813 - From what ship: Eugenia Brig - Discharged on 7 Oct 1813 - How discharged: Eugenia.

Brown, Sawyer - Number: 740 - How taken: Taken off the HM Ship-of-the-Line Invincible - Discharged on 27 Oct 1813 - How discharged: HMT Sir John Borlair Warren No. 183 for England.

Brown, Silvanus - Seaman - Number: 221 - Prize name: Topaz - Ship type: MV - How taken: HM Ship-of-the-Line Grampus - Date taken: 19 Oct 1812 - Where taken: On passage to Cadiz - Date received: 21 Nov 1812 - From what ship: HM Ship-of-the-Line Grampus - Discharged on 14 Dec 1812 - How discharged: Being a licensed vessel.

Brown, Silvester - Seaman - Number: 297 - Prize name: George & Albert - Ship type: MV - How taken: HMS Myrtle - Date taken: 5 Jan 1813 - Where taken: off Cape St. Mary (Portugal) - Date received: 10 Jan 1813 - From what ship: HMS Myrtle - Discharged on 14 Apr 1813 - How discharged: Being a licensed vessel.

Brown, Thomas - Number: 593 - How taken: Taken off the HMS Bombay - Discharged on 28 Jun 1813 - How discharged: HMT Minstraele.

Brownman, Benjamin - Mate - Number: 269 - Prize name: Argus - Ship type: MV - How taken: HM Ship-of-the-Line Grampus - Date taken: 19 Oct 1812 - Where taken: On passage to Cadiz - Date received: 22 Nov 1812 - From what ship: Argus - Discharged on 14 Dec 1812 - How discharged: Being a licensed vessel.

Bruce, Peter - Seaman - Number: 274 - Prize name: Topaz - Ship type: MV - How taken: HM Ship-of-the-Line Grampus - Date taken: 19 Oct 1812 - Date received: 23 Nov 1812 - From what ship: Topaz - Discharged on 14 Dec 1812 - How discharged: Being a licensed vessel.

Buchanan, Christopher - Seaman - Number: 619 - How taken: HM Ship-of-the-Line Prince of Wales - Date taken: 28 May 1813 - Where taken: Mahon (Island of Minorca) - Date received: 1 Jul 1813 - From what ship: HMT Royal Boston No. 344 - Discharged on 12 Jul 1813 - How discharged: HM Sloop Bacchus.

Buchanan, James - Seaman - Number: 313 - Prize name: John L. Kees - Ship type: MV - How taken: HM Brig Basilisk - Date taken: 6 Jan 1813 - Where taken: near Cadiz - Date received: 12 Jan 1813 - From what ship: HM Brig Basilisk - Discharged on 14 Apr 1813 - How discharged: Being a licensed vessel.

Bullock, John (see prisoner number 140) - Seaman - Number: 92 - Prize name: Commerce - Ship type: MV - How taken: HM Brig Rebuff - Date taken: 28 Aug 1812 - Where taken: near Cadiz - Date received: 2 Sep 1813 - From what ship: HM Ship-of-the-Line Tremendous.

Bullock, John - Seaman - Number: 140 - Prize name: Commerce - Ship type: MV - How taken: HM Brig Rebuff -

Date taken: 28 Aug 1812 - Where taken: near Cadiz - Discharged on 28 Jan 1813 - How discharged: Being a licensed vessel.

Burey, Brook - Seaman - Number: 37 - Prize name: Allegany - Ship type: MV - How taken: HM Ship-of-the-Line San Juan - Date taken: 10 Aug 1812 - Where taken: Gibraltar Bay - Date received: 12 Aug 1812 - From what ship: Allegany - Discharged on 15 Jan 1813 - How discharged: HM Frigate Andromeda.

Burns, William - Seaman - Number: 62 - Prize name: Howard - Ship type: MV - How taken: HM Brig Scout - Date taken: 23 Jun 1812 - Where taken: Minorca - Date received: 15 Aug 1812 - Discharged on 15 Jan 1813 - How discharged: HM Frigate Andromeda.

Burton, John - Seaman - Number: 345 - Prize name: Pallas - Ship type: MV - How taken: HM Brig Rebuff - Date taken: 24 Dec 1812 - Where taken: near Cadiz - Date received: 19 Jan 1813 - From what ship: HM Brig Rebuff - Discharged on 19 Feb 1813 - How discharged: HM Sloop Dauntless.

Butler, John - Seaman - Number: 319 - Prize name: Eliza - Ship type: MV - How taken: HM Brig Basilisk - Date taken: 6 Jan 1813 - Where taken: near Cadiz - Date received: 12 Jan 1813 - From what ship: HM Brig Basilisk - Discharged on 14 Apr 1813 - How discharged: Being a licensed vessel.

Butterfield, Edward - Seaman - Number: 75 - Prize name: Pallas - Ship type: MV - How taken: HM Brig Papillion - Date taken: 7 Aug 1812 - Where taken: off Sanlucar (Spain) - Date received: 26 Aug 1812 - From what ship: HMS Lavinia - Discharged on 22 Jan 1813 - How discharged: HM Sloop Comet.

Cadwell, Abraham - Seaman - Number: 574 - Prize name: Hendosten - Ship type: MV - How taken: Gave himself up from HM Corvette Scipio - Date taken: 28 May 1813 - Where taken: Mahon (Island of Minorca) - Date received: 1 Jul 1813 - From what ship: HMT Royal Boston No. 344 - Discharged on 21 Jul 1813 - How discharged: HM Brig Savage.

Campbell, John - Passenger - Number: 311 - Prize name: Eliza - Ship type: MV - How taken: HM Brig Basilisk - Date taken: 6 Jan 1813 - Where taken: near Cadiz - Date received: 12 Jan 1813 - From what ship: HM Brig Basilisk - Discharged on 6 Mar 1813 - How discharged: HM Ship-of-the-Line Blake.

Campbell, John - Seaman - Number: 198 - Prize name: Meser - Ship type: MV - How taken: Not mentioned - Where taken: Unknown - Discharged on 13 Nov 1813 - How discharged: Being a licensed vessel.

Campbell, Nicholas - Seaman - Number: 597 - How taken: HM Frigate Bombay - Date taken: 28 May 1813 - Where taken: Mahon (Island of Minorca) - Date received: 1 Jul 1813 - From what ship: HMT Royal Boston No. 344 - Discharged on 21 Jul 1813 - How discharged: HM Brig Savage.

Canning, James - Seaman - Number: 626 - How taken: HM Ship-of-the-Line Prince of Wales - Date taken: 28 May 1813 - Where taken: Mahon (Island of Minorca) - Date received: 1 Jul 1813 - From what ship: HMT Royal Boston No. 344 - Discharged on 12 Jul 1813 - How discharged: HM Sloop Bacchus.

Cannon, Charles D. - Seaman - Number: 224 - Prize name: Topaz - Ship type: MV - How taken: HM Ship-of-the-Line Grampus - Date taken: 19 Oct 1812 - Where taken: On passage to Cadiz - Date received: 21 Nov 1812 - From what ship: HM Ship-of-the-Line Grampus - Discharged on 14 Dec 1812 - How discharged: Being a licensed vessel.

Caren, Thomas - Seaman - Number: 124 - Prize name: Albion - Ship type: MV - How taken: HM Frigate Cossack - Date taken: 8 Aug 1812 - Where taken: Cape Spartel (Morocco) - Date received: 2 Sep 1813.

Carr, James (see prisoner number 143) - Seaman - Number: 94 - Prize name: Commerce - Ship type: MV - How taken: HM Brig Rebuff - Date taken: 28 Aug 1812 - Where taken: near Cadiz - Date received: 2 Sep 1813 - From what ship: HM Ship-of-the-Line Tremendous.

Carr, James - Seaman - Number: 143 - Prize name: Commerce - Ship type: MV - How taken: Not mentioned - Discharged on 28 Jan 1813 - How discharged: Being a licensed vessel.

Cars, Bartlett - Master - Number: 115 - Prize name: John - Ship type: MV - How taken: HM Sloop Blossom - Date taken: 10 Aug 1812 - Where taken: Mediterranean - Date received: 2 Sep 1813 - From what ship: HM Ship-of-the-Line Tremendous - Discharged on 25 Jan 1813 - How discharged: HM Ship-of-the-Line Sultan.

Ceasar, Joseph - Seaman - Number: 206 - Prize name: Paulina - Ship type: MV - How taken: HMS Lavinia - Date taken: 19 Aug 1812 - Where taken: near Cadiz - Date received: 28 Oct 1812 - From what ship: Pauline -

Discharged on 19 Feb 1813 - How discharged: HM Sloop Dauntless.

Caesar, Julian - Seaman - Number: 276 - Prize name: Julian Mary - Ship type: MV - How taken: HM Ship-of-the-Line Grampus - Date taken: 21 Oct 1812 - Where taken: On passage to Cadiz - Date received: 23 Nov 1812 - From what ship: Topaz - Discharged on 14 Dec 1812 - How discharged: Being a licensed vessel.

Cela, Lewis - Seaman - Number: 438 - Prize name: Essex - Ship type: MV - How taken: HM Gunboat No. 22 - Date taken: 12 Jan 1813 - Where taken: near Cadiz - Date received: 5 Mar 1813 - From what ship: Essex Prize - Discharged on 16 Apr 1813 - How discharged: Being a licensed vessel.

Chambers, Thomas (see prisoner number 145) - Seaman - Number: 96 - Prize name: Commerce - Ship type: MV - How taken: HM Brig Rebuff - Date taken: 28 Aug 1812 - Where taken: near Cadiz - Date received: 2 Sep 1813 - From what ship: HM Ship-of-the-Line Tremendous.

Chambers, Thomas - Seaman - Number: 145 - Prize name: Commerce - Ship type: MV - How taken: HM Brig Desperate - Date taken: 22 Aug 1812 - Where taken: near Cadiz - Discharged on 28 Jan 1813 - How discharged: Being a licensed vessel.

Chapman, Joseph - Mate - Number: 181 - Prize name: Sally - Ship type: MV - How taken: HM Brig Badger - Date taken: 10 Sep 1812 - Where taken: Mediterranean - Date received: 22 Nov 1812 - From what ship: Sally - Discharged on 25 Jan 1813 - How discharged: HM Ship-of-the-Line Sultan.

Chase, Josiah - Seaman - Number: 508 - How taken: Gave himself up from HM Ship-of-the-Line Fame and HM Brig Philomel - Date taken: 2 Jan 1813 - Where taken: Gibraltar - Date received: 20 May 1813 - From what ship: HMS Ephegema - Discharged on 22 May 1813 - How discharged: HM Brig Zephyr.

Chase, Matthew - Seaman - Number: 6 - Prize name: Margaret - Ship type: MV - How taken: HM Ship-of-the-Line San Juan - Date taken: 10 Aug 1812 - Where taken: Gibraltar Bay - Date received: 12 Aug 1812 - From what ship: Margaret - Discharged on 15 Jan 1813 - How discharged: HM Brig Derwent.

Chasse, Jacob - Seaman - Number: 631 - How taken: HM Ship-of-the-Line Prince of Wales - Date taken: 28 May 1813 - Where taken: Mahon (Island of Minorca) - Date received: 1 Jul 1813 - From what ship: HMT Royal Boston No. 344 - Discharged on 12 Jul 1813 - How discharged: HM Sloop Bacchus.

Cherry, D. - Seaman - Number: 207 - Prize name: Meser - Ship type: MV - How taken: Not mentioned - Where taken: Unknown - Discharged on 13 Nov 1813 - How discharged: Being a licensed vessel.

Christian, Joseph - Seaman - Number: 245 - Prize name: Conde Mary - Ship type: MV - How taken: HM Ship-of-the-Line Grampus - Date taken: 24 Oct 1812 - Where taken: On passage to Cadiz - Date received: 21 Nov 1812 - From what ship: HM Ship-of-the-Line Grampus - Discharged on 31 Dec 1812 - How discharged: Being a licensed vessel.

Cin, James - 1st Mate - Number: 16 - Prize name: Horace - Ship type: MV - How taken: HM Ship-of-the-Line San Juan - Date taken: 10 Aug 1812 - Where taken: Gibraltar Bay - Date received: 12 Aug 1812 - From what ship: Horace - Discharged on 29 Aug 1812 - How discharged: Being a licensed vessel.

Clark, John - Master - Number: 135 - Prize name: Commerce - Ship type: MV - How taken: HM Brig Rebuff - Date taken: 28 Aug 1812 - Where taken: near Cadiz - Date received: 2 Sep 1813 - Discharged on 28 Jan 1813 - How discharged: Being a licensed vessel.

Clarke, Francoise M. - Passenger - Number: 782 - Prize name: Leo - Ship type: P - How taken: HM Ship-of-the-Line Grampus - Date taken: 2 Dec 1814 - Where taken: off Lisbon - Date received: 9 Dec 1814 - From what ship: HM Frigate Granicus - Discharged on 15 Dec 1814 - How discharged: HMS Eurasso.

Clasp, Silas - Seaman - Number: 376 - Prize name: George - Ship type: MV - How taken: HM Brig Columbine - Date taken: 13 Jan 1813 - Where taken: off Lisbon - Date received: 22 Jan 1813 - From what ship: HM Sloop Comet - Discharged on 15 Apr 1813 - How discharged: Being a licensed vessel.

Clayson, Laurence - Seaman - Number: 548 - Prize name: Isabella - Ship type: MV - How taken: HM Brig Zenoha - Date taken: 27 Jun 1813 - Where taken: off Cape St. Mary (Portugal) - Date received: 1 Jul 1813 - From what ship: HM Brig Protection - Discharged on 4 Sep 1813 - How discharged: HM Brig Teazer.

Clifford, S. L. - Seaman - Number: 381 - How taken: Gave himself up at Gibraltar - Date taken: 30 Jan 1813 - Date received: 30 Jan 1813 - From what ship: HM Frigate Brune - Discharged on 6 Mar 1813 - How discharged:

HM Ship-of-the-Line Blake.

Cock, Isaac - Seaman - Number: 618 - How taken: HM Ship-of-the-Line Royal George - Date taken: 28 May 1813 - Where taken: Mahon (Island of Minorca) - Date received: 1 Jul 1813 - From what ship: HMT Royal Boston No. 344 - Discharged on 21 Jul 1813 - How discharged: HM Brig Savage.

Coffin, James - Seaman - Number: 538 - Prize name: Sampson - Ship type: MV - Discharged on Aug 1813 - How discharged: HM Ship-of-the-Line Achille.

Coffin, Joseph - Number: 737 - How taken: Taken off the HM Ship-of-the-Line Invincible - Discharged on 27 Oct 1813 - How discharged: HMT Sir John Borlair Warren No. 183 for England.

Cole, E. - Seaman - Number: 208 - Prize name: Meser - Ship type: MV - How taken: Not mentioned - Where taken: Unknown - Discharged on 13 Nov 1813 - How discharged: Being a licensed vessel.

Cole, John - Seaman - Number: 753 - Prize name: Adeline - Ship type: LM - How taken: HM Frigate Magiciene - Date taken: 14 Mar 1814 - Where taken: at sea - Date received: 14 Apr 1814 - From what ship: HM Frigate Magiciene - Discharged on 22 Apr 1814 - How discharged: HM Store Ship Tortoise.

Cole, Thomas - Steward - Number: 130 - Prize name: Eliza - Ship type: MV - How taken: HM Sloop Hyacinth and HM Frigate Argo - Date taken: 27 Aug 1812 - Where taken: Straits of Gibraltar - Date received: 2 Sep 1813.

Colefax, William - Seaman - Number: 342 - Prize name: Pallas - Ship type: MV - How taken: HM Brig Rebuff - Date taken: 24 Dec 1812 - Where taken: near Cadiz - Date received: 19 Jan 1813 - From what ship: HM Brig Rebuff - Discharged on 19 Feb 1813 - How discharged: HM Sloop Dauntless.

Coleman, William (see prisoner number 144) - Seaman - Number: 95 - Prize name: Commerce - Ship type: MV - How taken: HM Brig Rebuff - Date taken: 28 Aug 1812 - Where taken: near Cadiz - Date received: 2 Sep 1813 - From what ship: HM Ship-of-the-Line Tremendous.

Coleman, William - Seaman - Number: 144 - Prize name: Commerce - Ship type: MV - How taken: HM Brig Desperate - Date taken: 22 Aug 1812 - Where taken: near Cadiz - Discharged on 28 Jan 1813 - How discharged: Being a licensed vessel.

Combs, Richard - Seaman - Number: 11 - Prize name: Margaret - Ship type: MV - How taken: HM Ship-of-the-Line San Juan - Date taken: 10 Aug 1812 - Where taken: Gibraltar Bay - Date received: 12 Aug 1812 - From what ship: Margaret - Discharged on 15 Jan 1813 - How discharged: HM Brig Derwent.

Conklin, Edward - Seaman - Number: 757 - Prize name: Adeline - Ship type: LM - How taken: HM Frigate Magiciene - Date taken: 14 Mar 1814 - Where taken: at sea - Date received: 14 Apr 1814 - From what ship: HM Frigate Magiciene - Discharged on 22 Apr 1814 - How discharged: HM Store Ship Tortoise.

Conner, John - Number: 741 - How taken: Taken off the HM Ship-of-the-Line Invincible - Discharged on 27 Oct 1813 - How discharged: HMT Sir John Borlair Warren No. 183 for England.

Conway, William - Seaman - Number: 38 - Prize name: Allegany - Ship type: MV - How taken: HM Ship-of-the-Line San Juan - Date taken: 10 Aug 1812 - Where taken: Gibraltar Bay - Date received: 12 Aug 1812 - From what ship: Allegany - Discharged on 15 Jan 1813 - How discharged: HM Frigate Andromeda.

Coody, William - Mate - Number: 386 - Prize name: Veroni - Ship type: MV - How taken: HM Sloop Comet - Date taken: 14 Jan 1813 - Where taken: near Cadiz - Date received: 8 Feb 1813 - From what ship: HMS Brig Desperate - How discharged: Taken to the ship on 9 Feb 1813, in charge of ship.

Cooke, John - Seaman - Number: 581 - Where taken: Mahon (Island of Minorca) - Discharged on 28 Jun 1813 - How discharged: HMT Minstraele.

Cormick, Henry - Seaman - Number: 322 - Prize name: Essex - Ship type: MV - How taken: HM Gunboat No. 22 - Date taken: 12 Jan 1813 - Where taken: near Cadiz - Date received: 12 Jan 1813 - From what ship: HM Gunboat No. 22 - Discharged on 16 Apr 1813 - How discharged: Being a licensed vessel.

Couan, John - Master - Number: 406 - Prize name: John L. Kees - Ship type: MV - How taken: HM Brig Basilisk - Date taken: 6 Jan 1813 - Where taken: near Cadiz - Date received: 13 Feb 1813 - From what ship: John L. Kees - Discharged on 14 Apr 1813 - How discharged: Being a licensed vessel.

Cox, Abraham - Seaman - Number: 561 - Prize name: Hendosten - Ship type: MV - How taken: Gave himself up from HM Corvette Scipio - Date taken: 28 May 1813 - Where taken: Mahon (Island of Minorca) - Date received: 1 Jul 1813 - From what ship: HMT Royal Boston No. 344 - Discharged on 12 Jul 1813 - How discharged: HM Sloop Bacchus.

Crafts, Jonathan - Seaman - Number: 69 - Prize name: Albion - Ship type: MV - How taken: HM Frigate Cossack - Date taken: 8 Aug 1812 - Where taken: Cape Spartel (Morocco) - Date received: 21 Aug 1812 - From what ship: HM Brig Rebuff - Discharged on 3 Nov 1812 - How discharged: Being a licensed vessel.

Craig, William - Seaman - Number: 280 - Prize name: Maria - Ship type: MV - Discharged on 25 Jan 1813 - How discharged: HM Ship-of-the-Line Sultan.

Crawford, James - Seaman - Number: 672 - How taken: HM Ship-of-the-Line Barfleur - Date taken: 28 May 1813 - Where taken: Mahon (Island of Minorca) - Date received: 1 Jul 1813 - Discharged on 3 Jul 1813 - How discharged: HM Frigate Thames.

Cromwell, Oliver - Seaman - Number: 763 - Prize name: Adeline - Ship type: LM - How taken: HM Frigate Magiciene - Date taken: 14 Mar 1814 - Where taken: at sea - Date received: 14 Apr 1814 - From what ship: HM Frigate Magiciene - Discharged on 24 Apr 1814.

Croomdie, John - Seaman - Number: 294 - Prize name: George & Albert - Ship type: MV - How taken: HMS Myrtle - Date taken: 5 Jan 1813 - Where taken: off Cape St. Mary (Portugal) - Date received: 10 Jan 1813 - From what ship: HMS Myrtle - Discharged on 14 Apr 1813 - How discharged: Being a licensed vessel.

Cunningham, S. - Seaman - Number: 82 - Prize name: Eliza - Ship type: MV - How taken: HM Brig Desperate - Date taken: 22 Aug 1812 - Where taken: near Cadiz - Date received: 30 Aug 1812 - From what ship: HM Frigate Argo - Discharged on 22 Jan 1813 - How discharged: HM Sloop Comet.

Dalby, Owen - 2nd Mate - Number: 99 - Prize name: Margaret - Ship type: MV - How taken: HM Ship-of-the-Line San Juan - Date taken: 10 Aug 1812 - Where taken: Gibraltar Bay - Date received: 2 Sep 1813 - From what ship: HM Ship-of-the-Line Tremendous.

Daniels, Bradley - Seaman - Number: 77 - Prize name: Eliza - Ship type: MV - How taken: HM Sloop Hyacinth and HM Frigate Argo - Date taken: 27 Aug 1812 - Where taken: Straits of Gibraltar - Date received: 30 Aug 1812 - From what ship: HM Frigate Argo - Discharged on 22 Jan 1813 - How discharged: HM Sloop Comet.

Daniels, John (see prisoner number 112) - Mate - Number: 53 - Prize name: Phoenix - Ship type: MV - How taken: HM Ship-of-the-Line San Juan - Date taken: 10 Aug 1812 - Where taken: Gibraltar Bay - Date received: 12 Aug 1812 - From what ship: Tiger - Discharged on 22 Jan 1813 - How discharged: HM Sloop Comet.

Daniels, John - Mate - Number: 112 - Prize name: Phoenix - Ship type: MV - How taken: HM Ship-of-the-Line San Juan - Date taken: 10 Aug 1812 - Where taken: Gibraltar Bay - Date received: 2 Sep 1813 - From what ship: HM Ship-of-the-Line Tremendous.

Davidson, Andrew - Seaman - Number: 73 - Prize name: Pallas - Ship type: MV - How taken: HM Brig Papillion - Date taken: 7 Aug 1812 - Where taken: off Sanlucar (Spain) - Date received: 26 Aug 1812 - From what ship: HMS Lavinia - Discharged on 22 Jan 1813 - How discharged: HM Sloop Comet.

Davidson, Henry - Seaman - Number: 407 - Prize name: Thrasher - Ship type: MV - How taken: HM Frigate Magiciene - Date taken: 17 Jan 1813 - Where taken: Western Isles - Date received: 14 Feb 1813 - From what ship: Thrasher - Discharged on 19 Mar 1813 - How discharged: Being a licensed vessel.

Davidson, John - Seaman - Number: 694 - Prize name: Hendosten - Ship type: MV - How taken: HM Brig Zenoha - Date taken: 25 Jun 1813 - Where taken: near Lisbon - Date received: 2 Jul 1813 - From what ship: HM Brig Protector - Discharged on 22 Aug 1813 - How discharged: HM Brig Imogen.

Davis, Charles (see prisoner number 101) - Seaman - Number: 13 - Prize name: Margaret - Ship type: MV - How taken: HM Ship-of-the-Line San Juan - Date taken: 10 Aug 1812 - Where taken: Gibraltar Bay - Date received: 12 Aug 1812 - From what ship: Margaret - Discharged on 15 Jan 1813 - How discharged: HM Brig Derwent.

Davis, Charles - Boy - Number: 101 - Prize name: Margaret - Ship type: MV - How taken: HM Ship-of-the-Line San Juan - Date taken: 10 Aug 1812 - Where taken: Gibraltar Bay - Date received: 2 Sep 1813 - From what ship: HM Ship-of-the-Line Tremendous.

Davis, Elias - Master - Number: 271 - Prize name: Topaz - Ship type: MV - How taken: HM Ship-of-the-Line Grampus - Date taken: 19 Oct 1812 - Date received: 23 Nov 1812 - From what ship: Topaz - Discharged on 14 Dec 1812 - How discharged: Being a licensed vessel.

Davis, John - Seaman - Number: 505 - How taken: Gave himself up from HM Ship-of-the-Line Fame and HM Brig Philomel - Date taken: 2 Jan 1813 - Where taken: Gibraltar - Date received: 20 May 1813 - From what ship: HMS Ephegema - Discharged on 22 May 1813 - How discharged: HM Brig Zephyr.

Davis, Joseph - Seaman - Number: 227 - Prize name: Topaz - Ship type: MV - How taken: HM Ship-of-the-Line Grampus - Date taken: 19 Oct 1812 - Where taken: On passage to Cadiz - Date received: 21 Nov 1812 - From what ship: HM Ship-of-the-Line Grampus - Discharged on 14 Dec 1812 - How discharged: Being a licensed vessel.

Davis, Osborn - Seaman - Number: 714 - Discharged on Aug 1813 - How discharged: HM Ship-of-the-Line Achille.

Davis, Thomas - Seaman - Number: 230 - Prize name: Argus - Ship type: MV - How taken: HM Ship-of-the-Line Grampus - Date taken: 19 Oct 1812 - Where taken: On passage to Cadiz - Date received: 21 Nov 1812 - From what ship: HM Ship-of-the-Line Grampus - Discharged on 14 Dec 1812 - How discharged: Being a licensed vessel.

Dean, Moses - Seaman - Number: 744 - Prize name: Mary English - Ship type: MV - How taken: HM Post Ship Crocodile - Date taken: 6 Aug 1813 - Where taken: off Cape Finisterre (Spain) - Date received: 8 Dec 1813 - From what ship: HMS Brig Desperate - Discharged on 7 Feb 1814 - How discharged: HMT Fanny No. 186.

Dean, Samuel - Seaman - Number: 25 - Prize name: Horace - Ship type: MV - How taken: HM Ship-of-the-Line San Juan - Date taken: 10 Aug 1812 - Where taken: Gibraltar Bay - Date received: 12 Aug 1812 - From what ship: Horace - Discharged on 29 Aug 1812 - How discharged: Being a licensed vessel.

Delany, M. - Seaman - Number: 432 - How taken: Gave himself up from HMT Leopard - From what ship: HMT Leopard - Discharged on 19 Mar 1813 - How discharged: HM Schooner Sylvia.

Depeyster, Pierre - 1st Officer - Number: 780 - Prize name: Leo - Ship type: P - How taken: HM Ship-of-the-Line Grampus - Date taken: 2 Dec 1814 - Where taken: off Lisbon - Date received: 9 Dec 1814 - From what ship: HM Frigate Granicus - Discharged on 15 Dec 1814 - How discharged: HMS Eurasso.

Dewell, A. D. - Seaman - Number: 695 - Prize name: Hendosten - Ship type: MV - How taken: HM Brig Zenoha - Date taken: 25 Jun 1813 - Where taken: near Lisbon - Date received: 2 Jul 1813 - From what ship: HM Brig Protector - Discharged on 22 Aug 1813 - How discharged: HM Brig Imogen.

Dewick, James - Seaman - Number: 66 - Prize name: John - Ship type: MV - How taken: HM Sloop Blossom - Date taken: 16 Aug 1812 - Where taken: Mediterranean - Date received: 18 Aug 1812 - From what ship: HM Sloop Blossom - Discharged on 22 Jan 1813 - How discharged: HM Sloop Comet.

Diamond, William - Seaman - Number: 747 - Prize name: Mary English - Ship type: MV - How taken: HM Post Ship Crocodile - Date taken: 6 Aug 1813 - Where taken: off Cape Finisterre (Spain) - Date received: 8 Dec 1813 - From what ship: HMS Brig Desperate - Discharged on 7 Feb 1814 - How discharged: HMT Fanny No. 186.

Dickenson, Thomas - Seaman - Number: 475 - Prize name: John Buckley - Ship type: MV - How taken: HMT Druid - Date taken: 21 Feb 1813 - Where taken: near Lisbon - Date received: 8 Mar 1813 - From what ship: HM Ketch Gleamer - Discharged on 10 Apr 1813 - How discharged: Being a licensed vessel.

Doak, Nathaniel - Mate - Number: 190 - Prize name: Meser - Ship type: MV - How taken: Not mentioned - Where taken: Unknown - Discharged on 13 Nov 1813 - How discharged: Being a licensed

Dockerson, Thomas - Seaman - Number: 455 - Prize name: John Buckley - Ship type: MV - How taken: HMT Druid - Date taken: 21 Feb 1813 - Where taken: near Lisbon - Date received: 7 Mar 1813 - From what ship: HMT Pererserance.

Dodridge, M. - Seaman - Number: 286 - Prize name: John - Ship type: MV - How taken: HM Battery Gorgon - Date taken: 16 Aug 1812 - Where taken: Mediterranean - Discharged on 22 Jan 1813 - How discharged: HM Sloop Comet.

Dolbert, Owen - Seaman - Number: 287 - Prize name: Maria - Ship type: MV - Discharged on 18 Dec 1812.

Dolby, Owen - 2nd Mate - Number: 3 - Prize name: Margaret - Ship type: MV - How taken: HM Ship-of-the-Line San Juan - Date taken: 10 Aug 1812 - Where taken: Gibraltar Bay - Date received: 12 Aug 1812 - From what ship: Margaret.

Dolinson, Andrew (see prisoner number 104) - Mate - Number: 28 - Prize name: Allegany - Ship type: MV - How taken: HM Ship-of-the-Line San Juan - Date taken: 10 Aug 1812 - Where taken: Gibraltar Bay - Date received: 12 Aug 1812 - From what ship: Allegany - Discharged on 19 Feb 1813 - How discharged: HM Sloop Dauntless.

Dolinson, Andrew - Mate - Number: 104 - Prize name: Allegany - Ship type: MV - How taken: HM Ship-of-the-Line San Juan - Date taken: 10 Aug 1812 - Where taken: Gibraltar Bay - Date received: 2 Sep 1813 - From what ship: HM Ship-of-the-Line Tremendous.

Donaldson, Nathaniel - Seaman - Number: 321 - Prize name: Essex - Ship type: MV - How taken: HM Gunboat No. 22 - Date taken: 12 Jan 1813 - Where taken: near Cadiz - Date received: 12 Jan 1813 - From what ship: HM Gunboat No. 22 - Discharged on 16 Apr 1813 - How discharged: Being a licensed vessel.

Douglas, John - Seaman - Number: 636 - How taken: HM Ship-of-the-Line Prince of Wales - Date taken: 28 May 1813 - Where taken: Mahon (Island of Minorca) - Date received: 1 Jul 1813 - From what ship: HMT Royal Boston No. 344 - Discharged on 24 Jul 1813 - How discharged: HM Store Ship Tortoise.

Dourdick, Matthew - Seaman - Number: 277 - Prize name: John - Ship type: MV - How taken: HM Sloop Blossom - Date taken: 16 Aug 1812 - Where taken: Mediterranean - Date received: 22 Nov 1812 - From what ship: John.

Dousty, Angelo - Seaman - Number: 347 - Prize name: Pallas - Ship type: MV - How taken: HM Brig Rebuff - Date taken: 24 Dec 1812 - Where taken: near Cadiz - Date received: 19 Jan 1813 - From what ship: HM Brig Rebuff - Discharged on 19 Feb 1813 - How discharged: HM Brig Protector.

Downs, Isaac - Number: 459 - Discharged on 15 Mar 1813 - How discharged: Being a licensed vessel.

Drake, Peter - Seaman - Number: 726 - Prize name: Engenia - Ship type: MV - How taken: HM Brig Papillion - Date taken: 17 Jul 1813 - Where taken: near Cadiz - Date received: 10 Aug 1813 - From what ship: HM Brig Papillion - Discharged on 7 Oct 1813 - How discharged: Eugenia.

Dubois, Alexander - Seaman - Number: 543 - Prize name: Isabella - Ship type: MV - How taken: HM Brig Zenoha - Date taken: 27 Jun 1813 - Where taken: off Cape St. Mary (Portugal) - Date received: 1 Jul 1813 - From what ship: HM Brig Protection - Discharged on 4 Sep 1813 - How discharged: HM Brig Teazer.

Durham, G. D. - Seaman - Number: 445 - Prize name: Catharine - Ship type: MV - How taken: HMT Druid - Date taken: 21 Feb 1813 - Where taken: near Lisbon - Date received: 5 Mar 1813 - From what ship: HMT Pererserance - Discharged on 10 Apr 1813 - How discharged: Being a licensed vessel.

Durham, William - Seaman - Number: 732 - Prize name: Engenia - Ship type: MV - How taken: HM Brig Papillion - Date taken: 17 Jul 1813 - Where taken: near Cadiz - Date received: 10 Aug 1813 - From what ship: Eugenia Brig - Discharged on 7 Oct 1813 - How discharged: Eugenia.

Dyer, Thomas - Master - Number: 132 - Prize name: Louisa - Ship type: MV - How taken: HM Brig Columbine - Date taken: 11 Aug 1812 - Where taken: near Cadiz - Date received: 2 Sep 1813 - Discharged on 15 Nov 1813 - How discharged: Being a licensed vessel.

Ealy, Robert - Seaman - Number: 385 - Prize name: George - Ship type: MV - How taken: HM Brig Columbine - Date taken: 15 Jan1813 - Where taken: off Lisbon - Date received: 6 Feb 1813 - From what ship: HM Ship-of-the-Line San Juan.

Eames, D. - Seaman - Number: 428 - Prize name: Mark & Abigail - Ship type: MV - How taken: HM Brig Basilisk - Date taken: 9 Jan 1813 - Where taken: off Cape St. Vincent (Portugal) - Date received: 19 Feb 1813 - From what ship: HM Gunboat No. 22 - Discharged on 16 Apr 1813 - How discharged: Being a licensed vessel.

Eaton, James - Seaman - Number: 497 - How taken: Gave himself up from HM Ship-of-the-Line Malta - Date taken: 2 Jan 1813 - Where taken: Gibraltar - Date received: 9 Apr 1813 - From what ship: HM Bomb Vessel Strombolo - Discharged on 23 Apr 1813 - How discharged: HM Sloop Helena.

Edgar, William - Seaman - Number: 692 - Prize name: Hepsey - Ship type: MV - Discharged on 4 Sep 1813 - How discharged: HM Brig Teazer.

Edwards, John - Seaman - Number: 382 - How taken: Gave himself up at Gibraltar - Date taken: 30 Jan 1813 - Date received: 30 Jan 1813 - From what ship: HM Frigate Brune - Discharged on 6 Mar 1813 - How discharged: HM Ship-of-the-Line Blake.

Edwards, Punie - Seaman - Number: 350 - Prize name: Pallas - Ship type: MV - How taken: HM Brig Rebuff - Date taken: 24 Dec 1812 - Where taken: near Cadiz - Date received: 19 Jan 1813 - From what ship: HM Brig Rebuff - Discharged on 19 Feb 1813 - How discharged: HM Brig Protector.

Eldridge, Nathaniel - Seaman - Number: 431 - How taken: Gave himself up from HMT Leopard - From what ship: HMT Leopard - Discharged on 19 Mar 1813 - How discharged: HM Schooner Sylvia.

Elf, James - Seaman - Number: 702 - Prize name: Hendosten - Ship type: MV - How taken: HM Brig Zenoha - Date taken: 25 Jun 1813 - Where taken: near Lisbon - Date received: 2 Jul 1813 - From what ship: HM Brig Protector - Discharged on 22 Aug 1813 - How discharged: HM Brig Imogen.

Ellis, George - Mate - Number: 238 - Prize name: Conde Mary - Ship type: MV - How taken: HM Ship-of-the-Line Grampus - Date taken: 24 Oct 1812 - Where taken: On passage to Cadiz - Date received: 21 Nov 1812 - From what ship: HM Ship-of-the-Line Grampus - Discharged on 31 Dec 1812 - How discharged: Being a licensed vessel.

Ellis, Lewis - Seaman - Number: 487 - How taken: 487A - Discharged on 20 Mar 1813 - How discharged: Being a licensed vessel.

Erwigg, John - Seaman - Number: 554 - Prize name: Hendosten - Ship type: MV - How taken: HM Brig Zenoha - Date taken: 23 Jun 1813 - Where taken: near Lisbon - Date received: 7 Jul 1814 - From what ship: HM Naval Hospital - Discharged on 7 Feb 1814 - How discharged: HMT Fanny No. 186.

Evans, Robert - Number: 285 - Prize name: Maria - Ship type: MV - Discharged on 25 Jan 1813 - How discharged: HM Ship-of-the-Line Sultan.

Eveleth, Ebenezer (see prisoner number 103) - Master - Number: 27 - Prize name: Allegany - Ship type: MV - How taken: HM Ship-of-the-Line San Juan - Date taken: 10 Aug 1812 - Where taken: Gibraltar Bay - Date received: 12 Aug 1812 - From what ship: Allegany.

Eveleth, Ebenezer - Master - Number: 103 - Prize name: Allegany - Ship type: MV - How taken: HM Ship-of-the-Line San Juan - Date taken: 10 Aug 1812 - Where taken: Gibraltar Bay - Date received: 2 Sep 1813 - From what ship: HM Ship-of-the-Line Tremendous - How discharged: To America on parole.

Eveleth, William (see prisoner number 105) - Boy - Number: 29 - Prize name: Allegany - Ship type: MV - How taken: HM Ship-of-the-Line San Juan - Date taken: 10 Aug 1812 - Where taken: Gibraltar Bay - Date received: 12 Aug 1812 - From what ship: Allegany - Discharged on 1 Dec 1812 - How discharged: By request of Colonel Leantz.

Eveleth, William - Boy - Number: 105 - Prize name: Allegany - Ship type: MV - How taken: HM Ship-of-the-Line San Juan - Date taken: 10 Aug 1812 - Where taken: Gibraltar Bay - Date received: 2 Sep 1813 - From what ship: HM Ship-of-the-Line Tremendous.

Falanda, John - Seaman - Number: 7 - Prize name: Margaret - Ship type: MV - How taken: HM Ship-of-the-Line San Juan - Date taken: 10 Aug 1812 - Where taken: Gibraltar Bay - Date received: 12 Aug 1812 - From what ship: Margaret - Discharged on 15 Jan 1813 - How discharged: HM Brig Derwent.

Feldean, John - Seaman - Number: 292 - Prize name: George & Albert - Ship type: MV - How taken: HMS Myrtle - Date taken: 5 Jan 1813 - Where taken: off Cape St. Mary (Portugal) - Date received: 10 Jan 1813 - From what ship: HMS Myrtle - Discharged on 14 Apr 1813 - How discharged: Being a licensed vessel.

Fenn, John - Mate - Number: 136 - Prize name: Commerce - Ship type: MV - How taken: HM Brig Rebuff - Date taken: 28 Aug 1812 - Where taken: near Cadiz - Date received: Returned to ship on 8 Sep 1812 - Discharged on 28 Jan 1813 - How discharged: Being a licensed vessel.

Fernald, Edmund - Seaman - Number: 19 - Prize name: Horace - Ship type: MV - How taken: HM Ship-of-the-Line San Juan - Date taken: 10 Aug 1812 - Where taken: Gibraltar Bay - Date received: 12 Aug 1812 - From what ship: Horace - Discharged on 29 Aug 1812 - How discharged: Being a licensed vessel.

Fernand, John - Seaman - Number: 356 - Prize name: Pallas - Ship type: MV - How taken: Gave himself up at Gibraltar - Date taken: 20 Jan 1813 - Date received: 20 Jan 1813 - From what ship: HMS Leyden - Discharged on 19 Feb 1813 - How discharged: HM Brig Protector.

Field, F. - Seaman - Number: 205 - Prize name: Meser - Ship type: MV - How taken: Not mentioned - Where taken: Unknown - Discharged on 13 Nov 1813 - How discharged: Being a licensed vessel.

Fitch, William - Seaman - Number: 394 - Prize name: Pallas - Ship type: MV - How taken: HMS Rebuff - Date taken: 24 Dec 1812 - Where taken: near Cadiz - Date received: 9 Feb 1813 - From what ship: Pallas Prize - Discharged on 6 Mar 1813 - How discharged: HM Ship-of-the-Line Blake.

Fito, Gaspo - Seaman - Number: 216 - Prize name: Dolphin - Ship type: MV - How taken: HM Ship-of-the-Line Invincible - Date taken: 24 Aug 1812 - Where taken: Meg'n (Unknown) - Date received: 28 Nov 1812 - From what ship: HM Ship-of-the-Line Invincible - Discharged on 25 Jan 1813 - How discharged: HM Ship-of-the-Line Sultan.

Flage, William - Seaman - Number: 555 - Prize name: Hendosten - Ship type: MV - How taken: HM Brig Zenoha - Date taken: 25 Jun 1813 - Where taken: near Lisbon - Date received: 21 Jul 1813 - From what ship: Hepsey Prize - Discharged on 22 Aug 1813 - How discharged: HM Brig Imogen.

Flexon, Charles - Seaman - Number: 418 - Prize name: Charlotte - Ship type: MV - How taken: HM Brig Charger - Date taken: 14 Jan 1813 - Where taken: near Cadiz - Date received: 18 Feb 1813 - From what ship: HM Brig Charger - Discharged on 14 Apr 1813 - How discharged: Being a licensed vessel.

Flood, John - Seaman - Number: 609 - How taken: HM Ship-of-the-Line Berwick - Date taken: 28 May 1813 - Where taken: Mahon (Island of Minorca) - Date received: 1 Jul 1813 - From what ship: HMT Royal Boston No. 344 - Discharged on 3 Jul 1813 - How discharged: HM Frigate Thames.

Floyd, John - Seaman - Number: 304 - Prize name: Concordia - Ship type: MV - How taken: HM Brig Basilisk - Date taken: 6 Jan 1813 - Where taken: near Cadiz - Date received: 12 Jan 1813 - From what ship: HM Brig Basilisk - Discharged on 14 Apr 1813 - How discharged: Being a licensed vessel.

Folger, Frederick - Seaman - Number: 707 - Discharged on Aug 1813 - How discharged: HM Ship-of-the-Line Achille.

Follansbee, William - Mate - Number: 447 - Prize name: John Buckley - Ship type: MV - How taken: HMT Druid - Date taken: 21 Feb 1813 - Where taken: near Lisbon - Date received: 7 Mar 1813 - From what ship: HMT Pererserance - Discharged on 10 Apr 1813 - How discharged: Being a licensed vessel.

Forbes, Thomas - Seaman - Number: 519 - Prize name: Tyber - Ship type: MV - How taken: HM Sloop Comet - Date taken: 6 Jun 1813 - Where taken: near Lisbon - Date received: 15 Jun 1813 - From what ship: HM Ship-of-Line San Josef.

Forrest, James - Seaman - Number: 496 - How taken: Gave himself up from HM Ship-of-the-Line Malta - Date taken: 2 Jan 1813 - Where taken: Gibraltar - Date received: 9 Apr 1813 - From what ship: HM Bomb Vessel Strombolo - Discharged on 23 Apr 1813 - How discharged: HM Sloop Helena.

Foster, Joseph - Seaman - Number: 56 - Prize name: Phoenix - Ship type: MV - How taken: HM Ship-of-the-Line San Juan - Date taken: 10 Aug 1812 - Where taken: Gibraltar Bay - Date received: 12 Aug 1812 - From what ship: Tiger - Discharged on 15 Jan 1813 - How discharged: HM Frigate Andromeda.

Foster, Thomas - Seaman - Number: 560 - Prize name: Hendosten - Ship type: MV - How taken: Gave himself up from HM Corvette Scipio - Date taken: 28 May 1813 - Where taken: Mahon (Island of Minorca) - Date received: 1 Jul 1813 - From what ship: HMT Royal Boston No. 344 - Discharged on 21 Jul 1813 - How discharged: HM Brig Savage.

Foster, William - Seaman - Number: 367 - Prize name: Mentor - Ship type: MV - How taken: HM Brig Columbine - Date taken: 13 Jan 1813 - Where taken: near Cadiz - Date received: 22 Jan 1813 - From what ship: HM Sloop Comet - Discharged on 14 Apr 1813 - How discharged: Being a licensed vessel.

Freberg, Charles (see prisoner number 474) - Seaman - Number: 454 - Prize name: John Buckley - Ship type: MV - How taken: HMT Druid - Date taken: 21 Feb 1813 - Where taken: near Lisbon - Date received: 7 Mar 1813 -

From what ship: HMT Pererserance.

Freberg, Charles - Seaman - Number: 474 - Prize name: John Buckley - Ship type: MV - How taken: HMT Druid - Date taken: 21 Feb 1813 - Where taken: near Lisbon - Date received: 8 Mar 1813 - From what ship: HM Ketch Gleamer - Discharged on 10 Apr 1813 - How discharged: Being a licensed vessel.

Fredericks, John - Passenger - Number: 310 - Prize name: Eliza - Ship type: MV - How taken: HM Brig Basilisk - Date taken: 6 Jan 1813 - Where taken: near Cadiz - Date received: 12 Jan 1813 - From what ship: HM Brig Basilisk - Discharged on 6 Mar 1813 - How discharged: HM Ship-of-the-Line Blake.

Fredericks, John - Seaman - Number: 193 - Prize name: Meser - Ship type: MV - How taken: Not mentioned - Where taken: Unknown - Discharged on 13 Nov 1813 - How discharged: Being a licensed vessel.

French, Samuel - Seaman - Number: 391 - Prize name: Veroni - Ship type: MV - How taken: HM Sloop Comet - Date taken: 14 Jan 1813 - Where taken: near Cadiz - Date received: 8 Feb 1813 - From what ship: HMS Brig Desperate - Discharged on 14 Apr 1813 - How discharged: Being a licensed vessel.

Frisque, William - Seaman - Number: 380 - How taken: Gave himself up at Gibraltar - Date taken: 30 Jan 1813 - Date received: 30 Jan 1813 - From what ship: HM Frigate Brune - Discharged on 6 Mar 1813 - How discharged: HM Ship-of-the-Line Blake.

Frost, Michael - Seaman - Number: 766 - Prize name: Adeline - Ship type: LM - How taken: HM Frigate Magiciene - Date taken: 14 Mar 1814 - Where taken: at sea - Date received: 14 Apr 1814 - From what ship: HM Frigate Magiciene - Discharged on 24 Apr 1814.

Frytucker, D. - Seaman - Number: 443 - Prize name: Catharine - Ship type: MV - How taken: HMT Druid - Date taken: 21 Feb 1813 - Where taken: near Lisbon - Date received: 5 Mar 1813 - From what ship: HMT Pererserance - Discharged on 10 Apr 1813 - How discharged: Being a licensed vessel.

Fuller, William - Seaman - Number: 68 - Prize name: Albion - Ship type: MV - How taken: HM Frigate Cossack - Date taken: 8 Aug 1812 - Where taken: Cape Spartel (Morocco) - Date received: 21 Aug 1812 - From what ship: HM Brig Rebuff - Discharged on 3 Nov 1812 - How discharged: Being a licensed vessel.

Furguson, John - Seaman - Number: 201 - Prize name: Meser - Ship type: MV - How taken: Not mentioned - Where taken: Unknown - Discharged on 13 Nov 1813 - How discharged: Being a licensed vessel.

Gamel, Josiah - Seaman - Number: 332 - Discharged on 20 Jan 1813 - How discharged: Being a licensed vessel.

Gaues, Richard - Seaman - Number: 334 - Prize name: San Joseph Volorado - Ship type: MV - How taken: HM Brig Desperate - Date taken: 15 Jan 1813 - Where taken: near Cadiz - Date received: 27 Jan 1813 - From what ship: HM Brig Basilisk - Discharged on 18 Feb 1813 - How discharged: Being a licensed vessel.

Gavel, S. B. - Seaman - Number: 437 - Prize name: Essex - Ship type: MV - How taken: HM Gunboat No. 22 - Date taken: 12 Jan 1813 - Where taken: near Cadiz - Date received: 5 Mar 1813 - From what ship: Essex Prize - Discharged on 16 Apr 1813 - How discharged: Being a licensed vessel.

Gerris, William - Seaman - Number: 731 - Prize name: Engenia - Ship type: MV - How taken: HM Brig Papillion - Date taken: 17 Jul 1813 - Where taken: near Cadiz - Date received: 10 Aug 1813 - From what ship: Eugenia Brig - Discharged on 7 Oct 1813 - How discharged: Eugenia.

Gerrish, Timothy - Seaman - Number: 18 - Prize name: Horace - Ship type: MV - How taken: HM Ship-of-the-Line San Juan - Date taken: 10 Aug 1812 - Where taken: Gibraltar Bay - Date received: 12 Aug 1812 - From what ship: Horace - Discharged on 29 Aug 1812 - How discharged: Being a licensed vessel.

Gibson, Samuel - Seaman - Number: 683 - How taken: Taken off the HMS Undaunted - Discharged on 28 Jun 1813 - How discharged: HMT Minstraele.

Gilbert, George - Cook - Number: 270 - Prize name: Argus - Ship type: MV - How taken: HM Ship-of-the-Line Grampus - Date taken: 19 Oct 1812 - Where taken: On passage to Cadiz - Date received: 22 Nov 1812 - From what ship: Argus - Discharged on 14 Dec 1812 - How discharged: Being a licensed vessel.

Giles, William - Seaman - Number: 223 - Prize name: Topaz - Ship type: MV - How taken: HM Ship-of-the-Line Grampus - Date taken: 19 Oct 1812 - Where taken: On passage to Cadiz - Date received: 21 Nov 1812 - From what ship: HM Ship-of-the-Line Grampus - Discharged on 14 Dec 1812 - How discharged: Being a licensed vessel.

Gilpin, John - Seaman - Number: 398 - How taken: Gave himself up from HM Frigate Franchise - Date taken: 12 Feb 1812 - Where taken: Gibraltar - Date received: 13 Feb 1813 - From what ship: HM Frigate Franchise - Discharged on 6 Mar 1813 - How discharged: HM Ship-of-the-Line Blake.

Glover, John - Seaman - Number: 54 - Prize name: Phoenix - Ship type: MV - How taken: HM Ship-of-the-Line San Juan - Date taken: 10 Aug 1812 - Where taken: Gibraltar Bay - Date received: 12 Aug 1812 - From what ship: Tiger - Discharged on 15 Jan 1813 - How discharged: HM Frigate Andromeda.

Glover, Samuel - Seaman - Number: 708 - Discharged on Aug 1813 - How discharged: HM Ship-of-the-Line Achille.

Goff, John - Seaman - Number: 471 - Prize name: Amphitrite - Ship type: MV - How taken: HM Ketch Gleamer - Date taken: 27 Feb 1813 - Where taken: Bay of Biscay - Date received: 8 Mar 1813 - From what ship: HM Ketch Gleamer - Discharged on 5 Apr 1813 - How discharged: HM Frigate Ethalion.

Goodridge, R. - Seaman - Number: 470 - Prize name: Amphitrite - Ship type: MV - How taken: HM Ketch Gleamer - Date taken: 27 Feb 1813 - Where taken: Bay of Biscay - Date received: 8 Mar 1813 - From what ship: HM Ketch Gleamer - Discharged on 5 Apr 1813 - How discharged: HM Frigate Ethalion.

Goodwin, R. C. - Supercargo, permitted to stay on shore 16 Feb 1813 - Number: 361 - Prize name: George - Ship type: MV - How taken: HM Brig Columbine - Date taken: 13 Jan 1813 - Where taken: off Lisbon - Date received: 22 Jan 1813 - From what ship: HM Sloop Comet - Discharged on 15 Apr 1813 - How discharged: Being a licensed vessel.

Goodwin, William - Master - Number: 275 - Prize name: Julian Mary - Ship type: MV - How taken: HM Ship-of-the-Line Grampus - Date taken: 21 Oct 1812 - Where taken: On passage to Cadiz - Date received: 23 Nov 1812 - From what ship: Topaz - Discharged on 14 Dec 1812 - How discharged: Being a licensed vessel.

Gordon, Abraham - Seaman - Number: 635 - How taken: HM Ship-of-the-Line Prince of Wales - Date taken: 28 May 1813 - Where taken: Mahon (Island of Minorca) - Date received: 1 Jul 1813 - From what ship: HMT Royal Boston No. 344 - Discharged on 12 Jul 1813 - How discharged: HM Sloop Bacchus.

Gordon, James - Seaman - Number: 571 - Prize name: Hendosten - Ship type: MV - How taken: Gave himself up from HM Corvette Scipio - Date taken: 28 May 1813 - Where taken: Mahon (Island of Minorca) - Date received: 1 Jul 1813 - From what ship: HMT Royal Boston No. 344 - Discharged on 28 Jun 1813 - How discharged: HMT Minstraele.

Gordon, William - Seaman - Number: 481 - Discharged on 22 Mar 1813 - How discharged: Being a licensed vessel.

Gore, John - Seaman - Number: 31 - Prize name: Allegany - Ship type: MV - How taken: HM Ship-of-the-Line San Juan - Date taken: 10 Aug 1812 - Where taken: Gibraltar Bay - Date received: 12 Aug 1812 - From what ship: Allegany - Discharged on 15 Jan 1813 - How discharged: HM Brig Derwent.

Gore, Thomas - Seaman - Number: 260 - Prize name: Lydia - Ship type: MV - How taken: HM Ship-of-the-Line Grampus - Date taken: 2 Nov 1812 - Where taken: On passage to Cadiz - Date received: 21 Nov 1812 - From what ship: HM Ship-of-the-Line Grampus - Discharged on 14 Dec 1812 - How discharged: Being a licensed vessel.

Gow, Henry - Number: 739 - How taken: Taken off the HM Ship-of-the-Line Invincible - Discharged on 27 Oct 1813 - How discharged: HMT Sir John Borlair Warren No. 183 for England.

Graham, David - Seaman - Number: 218 - Prize name: Topaz - Ship type: MV - How taken: HM Ship-of-the-Line Grampus - Date taken: 19 Oct 1812 - Where taken: On passage to Cadiz - Date received: 21 Nov 1812 - From what ship: HM Ship-of-the-Line Grampus - Discharged on 14 Dec 1812 - How discharged: Being a licensed vessel.

Graves, Frederick - Seaman - Number: 329 - Prize name: Essex - Ship type: MV - How taken: HM Gunboat No. 22 - Date taken: 12 Jan 1813 - Where taken: near Cadiz - Date received: 12 Jan 1813 - From what ship: HM Gunboat No. 22 - Discharged on 16 Apr 1813 - How discharged: Being a licensed vessel.

Greaves, John - Seaman - Number: 605 - How taken: HM Ship-of-the-Line Berwick - Date taken: 28 May 1813 - Where taken: Mahon (Island of Minorca) - Date received: 1 Jul 1813 - From what ship: HMT Royal Boston

No. 344 - Discharged on 12 Jul 1813 - How discharged: HM Sloop Bacchus.

Green, George - Seaman - Number: 723 - Discharged on Aug 1813 - How discharged: HM Ship-of-the-Line Achille.

Gregory, Cornelius - Seaman - Number: 323 - Prize name: Essex - Ship type: MV - How taken: HM Gunboat No. 22 - Date taken: 12 Jan 1813 - Where taken: near Cadiz - Date received: 12 Jan 1813 - From what ship: HM Gunboat No. 22 - Discharged on 16 Apr 1813 - How discharged: Being a licensed vessel.

Griffin, Evan - Mate - Number: 217 - Prize name: Topaz - Ship type: MV - How taken: HM Ship-of-the-Line Grampus - Date taken: 19 Oct 1812 - Where taken: On passage to Cadiz - Date received: 21 Nov 1812 - From what ship: HM Ship-of-the-Line Grampus - Discharged on 14 Dec 1812 - How discharged: Being a licensed vessel.

Grimes, George - Seaman - Number: 413 - Prize name: Thomas Wilson - Ship type: MV - How taken: HM Sloop Comet - Date taken: 14 Jan 1813 - Where taken: near Cadiz - Date received: 18 Feb 1813 - From what ship: HM Brig Charger - Discharged on 10 Apr 1813 - How discharged: Being a licensed vessel.

Grimes, James - Seaman - Number: 749 - How taken: Gave himself up from HM Sloop Volentaire - Date taken: 19 Jan 1814 - Date received: 19 Jan 1814 - From what ship: HM Sloop Volentaire - Discharged on 7 Feb 1814 - How discharged: HMT Fanny No. 186.

Guenls, Henry - Boy - Number: 134 - Prize name: Louisa - Ship type: MV - How taken: HM Brig Columbine - Date taken: 11 Aug 1812 - Where taken: near Cadiz - Date received: 2 Sep 1813 - Discharged on 15 Nov 1813 - How discharged: Being a licensed vessel.

Guilder, Jacob - Seaman - Number: 420 - Prize name: Charlotte - Ship type: MV - How taken: HM Brig Charger - Date taken: 14 Jan 1813 - Where taken: near Cadiz - Date received: 18 Feb 1813 - From what ship: HM Brig Charger - Discharged on 14 Apr 1813 - How discharged: Being a licensed vessel.

Hadden, Felix - Mate - Number: 237 - Prize name: Julian Mary - Ship type: MV - How taken: HM Ship-of-the-Line Grampus - Date taken: 21 Oct 1812 - Where taken: On passage to Cadiz - Date received: 21 Nov 1812 - From what ship: HM Ship-of-the-Line Grampus - Discharged on 14 Dec 1812 - How discharged: Being a licensed vessel.

Halbrook, David - Number: 592 - How taken: Taken off the HMS Bombay - Discharged on 28 Jun 1813 - How discharged: HMT Minstraele.

Hall, Henry - Seaman - Number: 522 - Prize name: Tyber - Ship type: MV - How taken: HM Sloop Comet - Date taken: 6 Jun 1813 - Where taken: near Lisbon - Date received: 15 Jun 1813 - From what ship: HM Ship-of-Line San Josef.

Hall, Henry - Master - Number: 180 - Prize name: Sally - Ship type: MV - How taken: HM Brig Badger - Date taken: 10 Sep 1812 - Where taken: Mediterranean - Date received: 22 Nov 1812 - From what ship: Sally - Discharged on 25 Jan 1813 - How discharged: HM Ship-of-the-Line Sultan.

Hall, James - Seaman - Number: 607 - How taken: Gave himself up from HM Ship-of-the-Line Berwick - Date taken: 28 May 1813 - Where taken: Mahon (Island of Minorca) - Date received: 1 Jul 1813 - From what ship: HMT Royal Boston No. 344 - Discharged on 12 Jul 1813 - How discharged: HM Sloop Bacchus.

Hall, John - Seaman - Number: 616 - How taken: HM Ship-of-the-Line Royal George - Date taken: 28 May 1813 - Where taken: Mahon (Island of Minorca) - Date received: 1 Jul 1813 - From what ship: HMT Royal Boston No. 344 - Discharged on 24 Jul 1813 - How discharged: HM Store Ship Tortoise.

Hall, Robert - Seaman - Number: 762 - Prize name: Adeline - Ship type: LM - How taken: HM Frigate Magiciene - Date taken: 14 Mar 1814 - Where taken: at sea - Date received: 14 Apr 1814 - From what ship: HM Frigate Magiciene - Discharged on 22 Apr 1814 - How discharged: HM Store Ship Tortoise.

Hall, Stephen - Seaman - Number: 452 - Prize name: John Buckley - Ship type: MV - How taken: HMT Druid - Date taken: 21 Feb 1813 - Where taken: near Lisbon - Date received: 7 Mar 1813 - From what ship: HMT Pererserance - Discharged on 10 Apr 1813 - How discharged: Being a licensed vessel.

Hall, William - Seaman - Number: 402 - How taken: Gave himself up from HM Frigate Franchise - Date taken: 12 Feb 1812 - Where taken: Gibraltar - Date received: 13 Feb 1813 - From what ship: HM Frigate Franchise - Discharged on 6 Mar 1813 - How discharged: HM Ship-of-the-Line Blake.

Hamilton, John - Seaman - Number: 194 - Prize name: Meser - Ship type: MV - How taken: Not mentioned - Where taken: Unknown - Discharged on 13 Nov 1813 - How discharged: Being a licensed vessel.

Hammond, Joseph - Seaman - Number: 263 - Prize name: Lydia - Ship type: MV - How taken: HM Ship-of-the-Line Grampus - Date taken: 2 Nov 1812 - Where taken: On passage to Cadiz - Date received: 22 Nov 1812 - From what ship: Lydia - Discharged on 14 Dec 1812 - How discharged: Being a licensed vessel.

Handshaw, Spruce (see prisoner number 142} - Seaman - Number: 85 - Prize name: Taken in an open boat formerly belonging to American ship Fame which was captured by the French - How taken: HM Brig Desperate - Date taken: 22 Aug 1812 - Where taken: near Cadiz - Date received: 31 Aug 1812 - From what ship: HM Frigate Argo.

Handshaw, Spruce - Number: 142 - Prize name: Taken in an open boat formerly belonging to American ship Fame which was captured by the French - How taken: HM Brig Desperate - Date taken: 22 Aug 1812 - Where taken: near Cadiz - Date received: 31 Aug 1812, sent to hospital, released on 7 Nov 1812.

Hanna, Edward - Seaman - Number: 485 - Discharged on 20 Mar 1813 - How discharged: Being a licensed vessel.

Harding, John - Seaman - Number: 279 - Prize name: Maria - Ship type: MV - How taken: HM Sloop Blossom - Date taken: 16 Aug 1812 - Discharged on 25 Jan 1813 - How discharged: HM Ship-of-the-Line Sultan.

Harding, Samuel - Seaman - Number: 364 - Prize name: Mentor - Ship type: MV - How taken: HM Brig Columbine - Date taken: 13 Jan 1813 - Where taken: near Cadiz - Date received: 22 Jan 1813 - From what ship: HM Sloop Comet - Discharged on 14 Apr 1813 - How discharged: Being a licensed vessel.

Hardwick, James - Seaman - Number: 128 - Prize name: Eliza - Ship type: MV - How taken: HM Sloop Hyacinth and HM Frigate Argo - Date taken: 27 Aug 1812 - Where taken: Straits of Gibraltar - Date received: 2 Sep 1813 - Discharged on 22 Jan 1813 - How discharged: HM Sloop Comet.

Hardy, Jonathan - Seaman - Number: 327 - Prize name: Essex - Ship type: MV - How taken: HM Gunboat No. 22 - Date taken: 12 Jan 1813 - Where taken: near Cadiz - Date received: 12 Jan 1813 - From what ship: HM Gunboat No. 22 - Discharged on 16 Apr 1813 - How discharged: Being a licensed vessel.

Harman, William - Mate - Number: 409 - Prize name: Thomas Wilson - Ship type: MV - How taken: HM Sloop Comet - Date taken: 14 Jan 1813 - Where taken: near Cadiz - Date received: 18 Feb 1813 - From what ship: HM Brig Charger - Discharged on 10 Apr 1813 - How discharged: Being a licensed vessel.

Harnford, John - Seaman - Number: 611 - How taken: HM Ship-of-the-Line Berwick - Date taken: 28 May 1813 - Where taken: Mahon (Island of Minorca) - Date received: 1 Jul 1813 - From what ship: HMT Royal Boston No. 344 - Discharged on 23 Jul 1813 - How discharged: HM Frigate Unicorn.

Harper, John - Seaman - Number: 257 - Prize name: Lydia - Ship type: MV - How taken: HM Ship-of-the-Line Grampus - Date taken: 2 Nov 1812 - Where taken: On passage to Cadiz - Date received: 21 Nov 1812 - From what ship: HM Ship-of-the-Line Grampus - Discharged on 14 Dec 1812 - How discharged: Being a licensed vessel.

Harris, Charles - Seaman - Number: 423 - Prize name: Mark & Abigail - Ship type: MV - How taken: HM Brig Basilisk - Date taken: 9 Jan 1813 - Where taken: off Cape St. Vincent (Portugal) - Date received: 19 Feb 1813 - From what ship: HM Gunboat No. 22 - Discharged on 16 Apr 1813 - How discharged: Being a licensed vessel.

Harris, John - Seaman - Number: 419 - Prize name: Charlotte - Ship type: MV - How taken: HM Brig Charger - Date taken: 14 Jan 1813 - Where taken: near Cadiz - Date received: 18 Feb 1813 - From what ship: HM Brig Charger - Discharged on 14 Apr 1813 - How discharged: Being a licensed vessel.

Harris, William - Seaman - Number: 494 - How taken: Gave himself up from HM Ship-of-the-Line Malta - Date taken: 2 Jan 1813 - Where taken: Gibraltar - Date received: 9 Apr 1813 - From what ship: HM Bomb Vessel Strombolo - Discharged on 23 Apr 1813 - How discharged: HM Sloop Helena.

Harrison, Henry - Seaman - Number: 507 - How taken: Gave himself up from HM Ship-of-the-Line Fame and HM Brig Philomel - Date taken: 2 Jan 1813 - Where taken: Gibraltar - Date received: 20 May 1813 - From what ship: HMS Ephegema - Discharged on 22 May 1813 - How discharged: HM Brig Zephyr.

Harrison, Joseph - Seaman - Number: 127 - Prize name: Eliza - Ship type: MV - How taken: HM Sloop Hyacinth and HM Frigate Argo - Date taken: 27 Aug 1812 - Where taken: Straits of Gibraltar - Date received: Returned to ship on 1 Sep 1812 - Discharged on 22 Jan 1813 - How discharged: HM Sloop Comet.

Hartfield, James - Seaman - Number: 572 - Prize name: Hendosten - Ship type: MV - How taken: Gave himself up from HM Corvette Scipio - Date taken: 28 May 1813 - Where taken: Mahon (Island of Minorca) - Date received: 1 Jul 1813 - From what ship: HMT Royal Boston No. 344 - Discharged on 1 Jul 1813 - How discharged: HM Brig Protector for England.

Hartfield, John - Seaman - Number: 569 - Prize name: Hendosten - Ship type: MV - How taken: Gave himself up from HM Corvette Scipio - Date taken: 28 May 1813 - Where taken: Mahon (Island of Minorca) - Date received: 1 Jul 1813 - From what ship: HMT Royal Boston No. 344.

Harvey, John - Seaman - Number: 585 - Where taken: Mahon (Island of Minorca) - Date received: 1 Jul 1813 - From what ship: HMT Royal Boston No. 344.

Harvey, Joseph - Seaman - Number: 55 - Prize name: Phoenix - Ship type: MV - How taken: HM Ship-of-the-Line San Juan - Date taken: 10 Aug 1812 - Where taken: Gibraltar Bay - Date received: 12 Aug 1812 - From what ship: Tiger - Discharged on 15 Jan 1813 - How discharged: HM Frigate Andromeda.

Harvey, Peter - Seaman - Number: 716 - Prize name: America - Ship type: MV - Discharged on Aug 1813 - How discharged: HM Ship-of-the-Line Achille.

Hawkins, John - Seaman - Number: 354 - Prize name: Pallas - Ship type: MV - How taken: Gave himself up at Gibraltar - Date taken: 20 Jan 1813 - Date received: 20 Jan 1813 - From what ship: HMS Leyden - Discharged on 19 Feb 1813 - How discharged: HM Brig Protector.

Hayden, Fuller - Seaman - Number: 483 - Prize name: Polly - Discharged on 20 Mar 1813 - How discharged: Being a licensed vessel.

Hayes, Edward - Seaman - Number: 440 - Prize name: Catharine - Ship type: MV - How taken: HMT Druid - Date taken: 21 Feb 1813 - Where taken: near Lisbon - Date received: 5 Mar 1813 - From what ship: HMT Pererserance - Discharged on 16 Apr 1813 - How discharged: Being a licensed vessel.

Hazard, Thomas - Seaman - Number: 610 - How taken: HM Ship-of-the-Line Berwick - Date taken: 28 May 1813 - Where taken: Mahon (Island of Minorca) - Date received: 1 Jul 1813 - From what ship: HMT Royal Boston No. 344 - Discharged on 26 Jul 1813 - How discharged: HM Store Ship Weymouth.

Heady, Lindy - Seaman - Number: 627 - How taken: HM Ship-of-the-Line Prince of Wales - Date taken: 28 May 1813 - Where taken: Mahon (Island of Minorca) - Date received: 1 Jul 1813 - From what ship: HMT Royal Boston No. 344 - Discharged on 3 Jul 1813 - How discharged: HM Frigate Thames.

Heaton, H. J. - Seaman - Number: 715 - Prize name: America - Ship type: MV - Discharged on Aug 1813 - How discharged: HM Ship-of-the-Line Achille.

Hendecott, N. H. - Mate - Number: 439 - Prize name: Catharine - Ship type: MV - How taken: HMT Druid - Date taken: 21 Feb 1813 - Where taken: near Lisbon - Date received: 5 Mar 1813 - From what ship: HMT Pererserance - Discharged on 16 Apr 1813 - How discharged: Being a licensed vessel.

Henderson, Henry - Seaman - Number: 579 - Where taken: Mahon (Island of Minorca) - Date received: 1 Jul 1813 - From what ship: HMT Royal Boston No. 344 - Discharged on 24 Jul 1813 - How discharged: HM Store Ship Tortoise.

Heywood, Alexander - Seaman - Number: 414 - Prize name: Thomas Wilson - Ship type: MV - How taken: HM Sloop Comet - Date taken: 14 Jan 1813 - Where taken: near Cadiz - Date received: 18 Feb 1813 - From what ship: HM Brig Charger - Discharged on 10 Apr 1813 - How discharged: Being a licensed vessel.

Heywood, John - Seaman - Number: 588 - Where taken: Mahon (Island of Minorca) - Date received: 1 Jul 1813 - From what ship: HMT Royal Boston No. 344 - Discharged on 24 Jul 1813 - How discharged: HM Store Ship Tortoise.

Higgins, George - Seaman - Number: 40 - Prize name: Allegany - Ship type: MV - How taken: HM Ship-of-the-Line San Juan - Date taken: 10 Aug 1812 - Where taken: Gibraltar Bay - Date received: 12 Aug 1812 - From what ship: Allegany - Discharged on 15 Jan 1813 - How discharged: HM Frigate Andromeda.

Hill, James - Number: 736 - How taken: Taken off the HM Ship-of-the-Line Invincible - Discharged on 27 Oct 1813 - How discharged: HMT Sir John Borlair Warren No. 183 for England.

Hill, Timothy - Seaman - Number: 625 - How taken: HM Ship-of-the-Line Prince of Wales - Date taken: 28 May 1813 - Where taken: Mahon (Island of Minorca) - Date received: 1 Jul 1813 - From what ship: HMT Royal Boston No. 344 - Discharged on 3 Jul 1813 - How discharged: HM Frigate Thames.

Hoaton, Stephen - Seaman - Number: 473 - Prize name: Amphitrite - Ship type: MV - How taken: HM Ketch Gleamer - Date taken: 27 Feb 1813 - Where taken: Bay of Biscay - Date received: 8 Mar 1813 - From what ship: HM Ketch Gleamer - Discharged on 5 Apr 1813 - How discharged: HM Frigate Ethalion.

Hobbart, William - Seaman - Number: 638 - How taken: HM Ship-of-the-Line Prince of Wales - Date taken: 28 May 1813 - Where taken: Mahon (Island of Minorca) - Date received: 1 Jul 1813 - From what ship: HMT Royal Boston No. 344 - Discharged on 26 Jul 1813 - How discharged: HM Store Ship Weymouth.

Hockman, William - Seaman - Number: 349 - Prize name: Pallas - Ship type: MV - How taken: HM Brig Rebuff - Date taken: 24 Dec 1812 - Where taken: near Cadiz - Date received: 19 Jan 1813 - From what ship: HM Brig Rebuff - Discharged on 19 Feb 1813 - How discharged: HM Brig Protector.

Holbrook, Elias - Seaman - Number: 767 - Prize name: Adeline - Ship type: LM - How taken: HM Frigate Magiciene - Date taken: 14 Mar 1814 - Where taken: at sea - Date received: 14 Apr 1814 - From what ship: HM Frigate Magiciene - Discharged on 22 Apr 1814 - How discharged: HM Store Ship Tortoise.

Holcom, George - Seaman - Number: 315 - Prize name: John L. Kees - Ship type: MV - How taken: HM Brig Basilisk - Date taken: 6 Jan 1813 - Where taken: near Cadiz - Date received: 12 Jan 1813 - From what ship: HM Brig Basilisk - Discharged on 14 Apr 1813 - How discharged: Being a licensed vessel.

Holmes, Zechariah - Seaman - Number: 278 - Prize name: John - Ship type: MV - How taken: HM Sloop Blossom - Date taken: 16 Aug 1812 - Where taken: Mediterranean - Date received: 22 Nov 1812 - From what ship: John - Discharged on 25 Jan 1813 - How discharged: HM Ship-of-the-Line Sultan.

Holstean, Samuel - Seaman - Number: 388 - Prize name: Veroni - Ship type: MV - How taken: HM Sloop Comet - Date taken: 14 Jan 1813 - Where taken: near Cadiz - Date received: 8 Feb 1813 - From what ship: HMS Brig Desperate - Discharged on 14 Apr 1813 - How discharged: Being a licensed vessel.

Hopburn, R. - Seaman - Number: 416 - Prize name: Thomas Wilson - Ship type: MV - How taken: HM Sloop Comet - Date taken: 14 Jan 1813 - Where taken: near Cadiz - Date received: 18 Feb 1813 - From what ship: HM Brig Charger - Discharged on 10 Apr 1813 - How discharged: Being a licensed vessel.

Hopkins, Lewis - Seaman - Number: 231 - Prize name: Argus - Ship type: MV - How taken: HM Ship-of-the-Line Grampus - Date taken: 19 Oct 1812 - Where taken: On passage to Cadiz - Date received: 21 Nov 1812 - From what ship: HM Ship-of-the-Line Grampus - Discharged on 14 Dec 1812 - How discharged: Being a licensed vessel.

Hopkins, Thomas - Seaman - Number: 228 - Prize name: Argus - Ship type: MV - How taken: HM Ship-of-the-Line Grampus - Date taken: 19 Oct 1812 - Where taken: On passage to Cadiz - Date received: 21 Nov 1812 - From what ship: HM Ship-of-the-Line Grampus - Discharged on 14 Dec 1812 - How discharged: Being a licensed vessel.

Horsham, Samuel - Number: 460 - Discharged on 15 Mar 1813 - How discharged: Being a licensed vessel.

Hough, Ebenezer - Boy - Number: 42 - Prize name: Allegany - Ship type: MV - How taken: HM Ship-of-the-Line San Juan - Date taken: 10 Aug 1812 - Where taken: Gibraltar Bay - Date received: 12 Aug 1812 - From what ship: Allegany - Discharged on 15 Jan 1813 - How discharged: HM Frigate Andromeda.

Houston, Henry - Seaman - Number: 296 - Prize name: George & Albert - Ship type: MV - How taken: HMS Myrtle - Date taken: 5 Jan 1813 - Where taken: off Cape St. Mary (Portugal) - Date received: 10 Jan 1813 - From what ship: HMS Myrtle - Discharged on 14 Apr 1813 - How discharged: Being a licensed vessel.

Howard, John - Seaman - Number: 291 - Prize name: George & Albert - Ship type: MV - How taken: HMS Myrtle - Date taken: 5 Jan 1813 - Where taken: off Cape St. Mary (Portugal) - Date received: 10 Jan 1813 - From what ship: HMS Myrtle - Discharged on 14 Apr 1813 - How discharged: Being a licensed vessel.

Howell, John - Seaman - Number: 682 - How taken: HM Brig Paulina - Date taken: 5 Jun 1813 - Where taken:

Mahon (Island of Minorca) - Date received: 1 Jul 1813 - Discharged on 24 Jul 1813 - How discharged: HM Store Ship Tortoise.

Howell, H. C. - Seaman - Number: 693 - Prize name: Hepsey - Ship type: MV - Discharged on 8 Aug 1813 - How discharged: HM Sloop Kingfisher.

Howland, William - Seaman - Number: 570 - Prize name: Hendosten - Ship type: MV - How taken: Gave himself up from HM Corvette Scipio - Date taken: 28 May 1813 - Where taken: Mahon (Island of Minorca) - Date received: 1 Jul 1813 - From what ship: HMT Royal Boston No. 344 - Discharged on 28 Jun 1813 - How discharged: HMT Minstraele.

Hubbard, John - Seaman - Number: 49 - Prize name: Tiger - Ship type: MV - How taken: HM Ship-of-the-Line San Juan - Date taken: 10 Aug 1812 - Where taken: Gibraltar Bay - Date received: 12 Aug 1812 - From what ship: Tiger - Discharged on 15 Jan 1813 - How discharged: HM Frigate Andromeda.

Hubbard, John - Seaman - Number: 589 - How taken: HM Frigate Bombay - Date taken: 28 May 1813 - Where taken: Mahon (Island of Minorca) - Date received: 1 Jul 1813 - From what ship: HMT Royal Boston No. 344 - Discharged on 1 Jul 1813 - How discharged: HM Brig Protector for England.

Hudgety, George - Seaman - Number: 343 - Prize name: Pallas - Ship type: MV - How taken: HM Brig Rebuff - Date taken: 24 Dec 1812 - Where taken: near Cadiz - Date received: 19 Jan 1813 - From what ship: HM Brig Rebuff - Discharged on 19 Feb 1813 - How discharged: HM Sloop Dauntless.

Hudson, John - Seaman - Number: 632 - How taken: Taken off the HMS Unicorn - Date taken: 28 May 1813 - Where taken: Mahon (Island of Minorca) - Date received: 1 Jul 1813 - From what ship: HMT Royal Boston No. 344 - Discharged on 28 Jun 1813 - How discharged: HMT Minstraele.

Huff, Ebenezer - Boy - Number: 106 - Prize name: Allegany - Ship type: MV - How taken: HM Ship-of-the-Line San Juan - Date taken: 10 Aug 1812 - Where taken: Gibraltar Bay - How discharged: Return to ship on 17 Aug 1812.

Hughes, Aaron - Mate - Number: 133 - Prize name: Louisa - Ship type: MV - How taken: HM Brig Columbine - Date taken: 11 Aug 1812 - Where taken: near Cadiz - Date received: 2 Sep 1813 - Discharged on 15 Nov 1813 - How discharged: Being a licensed vessel.

Hughes, John - Seaman - Number: 759 - Prize name: Adeline - Ship type: LM - How taken: HM Frigate Magiciene - Date taken: 14 Mar 1814 - Where taken: at sea - Date received: 14 Apr 1814 - From what ship: HM Frigate Magiciene - Discharged on 29 Apr 1814 - How discharged: HM Store Ship Hindostan.

Hughes, John - Seaman - Number: 335 - Prize name: San Joseph Volorado - Ship type: MV - How taken: HM Brig Desperate - Date taken: 15 Jan 1813 - Where taken: near Cadiz - Date received: 27 Jan 1813 - From what ship: HM Brig Basilisk - Discharged on 18 Feb 1813 - How discharged: Being a licensed vessel.

Hundling, John - Seaman - Number: 674 - How taken: HM Ship-of-the-Line Repulse - Date taken: 28 May 1813 - Where taken: Mahon (Island of Minorca) - Date received: 1 Jul 1813 - Discharged on 3 Jul 1813 - How discharged: HM Frigate Thames.

Huntley, Charles - Seaman - Number: 502 - How taken: Gave himself up from HM Ship-of-the-Line Fame and HM Brig Philomel - Date taken: 2 Jan 1813 - Where taken: Gibraltar - Date received: 20 May 1813 - From what ship: HMS Ephegema - Discharged on 22 May 1813 - How discharged: HM Brig Zephyr.

Husband, Joseph - Seaman - Number: 713 - Discharged on Aug 1813 - How discharged: HM Ship-of-the-Line Achille.

Hussard, John K. - Seaman - Number: 226 - Prize name: Topaz - Ship type: MV - How taken: HM Ship-of-the-Line Grampus - Date taken: 19 Oct 1812 - Where taken: On passage to Cadiz - Date received: 21 Nov 1812 - From what ship: HM Ship-of-the-Line Grampus - Discharged on 14 Dec 1812 - How discharged: Being a licensed vessel.

Hutchison, James - Seaman - Number: 129 - Prize name: Eliza - Ship type: MV - How taken: HM Sloop Hyacinth and HM Frigate Argo - Date taken: 27 Aug 1812 - Where taken: Straits of Gibraltar - Date received: 2 Sep 1813 - Discharged on 22 Jan 1813 - How discharged: HM Sloop Comet.

Jackson, William - Seaman - Number: 646 - How taken: HM Battery Gorgon - Date taken: 28 May 1813 - Where taken: Mahon (Island of Minorca) - Discharged on 28 Jun 1813 - How discharged: HMT Minstraele.

Jacob, Thomas - Seaman - Number: 93 - Prize name: Commerce - Ship type: MV - How taken: HM Brig Rebuff - Date taken: 28 Aug 1812 - Where taken: near Cadiz - Date received: 2 Sep 1813 - From what ship: HM Ship-of-the-Line Tremendous.

Jacobs, Thomas - Number: 141 - Prize name: Commerce - Ship type: MV - How taken: HM Brig Rebuff - Date taken: 28 Aug 1812 - Where taken: near Cadiz - Discharged on 28 Jan 1813 - How discharged: Being a licensed vessel.

James, John - Seaman - Number: 621 - How taken: HM Ship-of-the-Line Prince of Wales - Date taken: 28 May 1813 - Where taken: Mahon (Island of Minorca) - Date received: 1 Jul 1813 - From what ship: HMT Royal Boston No. 344 - Discharged on 21 Jul 1813 - How discharged: HM Brig Savage.

Jameson, John - Seaman - Number: 511 - How taken: Gave himself up from HM Ship-of-the-Line Fame and HM Brig Philomel - Date taken: 2 Jan 1813 - Where taken: Gibraltar - Date received: 20 May 1813 - From what ship: HMS Ephegema - Discharged on 22 May 1813 - How discharged: HM Brig Zephyr.

Jennings, John - Seaman - Number: 324 - Prize name: Essex - Ship type: MV - How taken: HM Gunboat No. 22 - Date taken: 12 Jan 1813 - Where taken: near Cadiz - Date received: 12 Jan 1813 - From what ship: HM Gunboat No. 22 - Discharged on 16 Apr 1813 - How discharged: Being a licensed vessel.

Jennings, John - Seaman - Number: 204 - How taken: Gave himself up from HM Ship-of-the-Line San Juan - Date taken: 24 Oct 1812 - Where taken: Gibraltar Bay - Date received: 24 Oct 1812 - From what ship: HM Ship-of-the-Line San Juan - Discharged on 22 Jan 1813 - How discharged: HM Sloop Comet.

Johnson, George - Seaman - Number: 499 - How taken: Gave himself up from HM Ship-of-the-Line Malta - Date taken: 2 Jan 1813 - Where taken: Gibraltar - Date received: 9 Apr 1813 - From what ship: HM Bomb Vessel Strombolo - Discharged on 23 Apr 1813 - How discharged: HM Sloop Helena.

Johnson, Henry - Seaman - Number: 318 - Prize name: Eliza - Ship type: MV - How taken: HM Brig Basilisk - Date taken: 6 Jan 1813 - Where taken: near Cadiz - Date received: 14 Jan 1813 - From what ship: HM Brig Basilisk - Discharged on 14 Apr 1813 - How discharged: Being a licensed vessel.

Johnson, Thomas - Seaman - Number: 448 - Prize name: John Buckley - Ship type: MV - How taken: HMT Druid - Date taken: 21 Feb 1813 - Where taken: near Lisbon - Date received: 7 Mar 1813 - From what ship: HMT Pererserance - Discharged on 10 Apr 1813 - How discharged: Being a licensed vessel.

Johnston, Edward - Seaman - Number: 379 - How taken: Gave himself up at Gibraltar - Date taken: 30 Jan 1813 - Date received: 30 Jan 1813 - From what ship: HM Frigate Brune - Discharged on 6 Mar 1813 - How discharged: HM Ship-of-the-Line Blake.

Johnston, Matthew - Seaman - Number: 503 - How taken: Gave himself up from HM Ship-of-the-Line Fame and HM Brig Philomel - Date taken: 2 Jan 1813 - Where taken: Gibraltar - Date received: 20 May 1813 - From what ship: HMS Ephegema - Discharged on 22 May 1813 - How discharged: HM Brig Zephyr.

Johnston, Nathaniel - Seaman - Number: 65 - Prize name: John - Ship type: MV - How taken: HM Sloop Blossom - Date taken: 16 Aug 1812 - Where taken: Mediterranean - Date received: 18 Aug 1812 - From what ship: HM Sloop Blossom - Discharged on 22 Jan 1813 - How discharged: HM Sloop Comet.

Johnston, Rock - Seaman - Number: 666 - How taken: HM Ship-of-the-Line Ocean - Date taken: 28 May 1813 - Where taken: Mahon (Island of Minorca) - Date received: 1 Jul 1813 - From what ship: HMT Royal Boston No. 344 - Discharged on 12 Jul 1813 - How discharged: HM Sloop Bacchus.

Johnston, Samuel - Seaman - Number: 565 - Prize name: Hendosten - Ship type: MV - How taken: Gave himself up from HM Corvette Scipio - Date taken: 28 May 1813 - Where taken: Mahon (Island of Minorca) - Date received: 1 Jul 1813 - From what ship: HMT Royal Boston No. 344 - Discharged on 1 Jul 1813 - How discharged: HM Brig Protector for England.

Johnston, Stephen - Seaman - Number: 298 - Prize name: George & Albert - Ship type: MV - How taken: HMS Myrtle - Date taken: 5 Jan 1813 - Where taken: off Cape St. Mary (Portugal) - Date received: 10 Jan 1813 - From what ship: HMS Myrtle - Discharged on 14 Apr 1813 - How discharged: Being a licensed vessel.

Johnston, William - Seaman - Number: 752 - Prize name: Adeline - Ship type: LM - How taken: HM Frigate

Magiciene - Date taken: 14 Mar 1814 - Where taken: at sea - Date received: 14 Apr 1814 - From what ship: HM Frigate Magiciene - Discharged on 22 Apr 1814 - How discharged: HM Store Ship Tortoise.

Jones, Peter - Seaman - Number: 202 - Prize name: Meser - Ship type: MV - How taken: Not mentioned - Where taken: Unknown - Discharged on 13 Nov 1813 - How discharged: Being a licensed vessel.

Jones, Richard - Seaman - Number: 446 - Prize name: John Buckley - Ship type: MV - How taken: HMT Druid - Date taken: 21 Feb 1813 - Where taken: near Lisbon - Date received: 5 Mar 1813 - From what ship: HMT Pererserance - Discharged on 10 Apr 1813 - How discharged: Being a licensed vessel.

Jones, Thomas - Number: 735 - How taken: Taken off the HMS Buzzard - Discharged on 27 Oct 1813 - How discharged: HMT Sir John Borlair Warren No. 183 for England.

Jones, Uriah - Seaman - Number: 184 - Prize name: Draper - Ship type: MV - How taken: HM Brig Fearly - Date taken: 18 Sep 1812 - Where taken: near Cadiz - Date received: 22 Nov 1812 - From what ship: Draper - Discharged on 22 Jan 1813 - How discharged: HM Sloop Comet.

Jordan, Artenius - Seaman - Number: 647 - How taken: HM Battery Gorgon - Date taken: 28 May 1813 - Where taken: Mahon (Island of Minorca) - Date received: 1 Jul 1813 - From what ship: HMT Royal Boston No. 344 - Discharged on 23 Jul 1813 - How discharged: HM Frigate Unicorn.

Kellum, Smith - Seaman - Number: 669 - How taken: Taken off the HMS Barfleur - Discharged on 28 Jun 1813 - How discharged: HMT Minstraele.

Kelly, John - Seaman - Number: 506 - How taken: Gave himself up from HM Ship-of-the-Line Fame and HM Brig Philomel - Date taken: 2 Jan 1813 - Where taken: Gibraltar - Date received: 20 May 1813 - From what ship: HMS Ephegema - Discharged on 22 May 1813 - How discharged: HM Brig Zephyr.

Kemp, William - Seaman - Number: 239 - Prize name: Conde Mary - Ship type: MV - How taken: HM Ship-of-the-Line Grampus - Date taken: 24 Oct 1812 - Where taken: On passage to Cadiz - Date received: 21 Nov 1812 - From what ship: HM Ship-of-the-Line Grampus - Discharged on 31 Dec 1812 - How discharged: Being a licensed vessel.

King, John B. - Seaman - Number: 469 - Prize name: Amphitrite - Ship type: MV - How taken: HM Ketch Gleamer - Date taken: 27 Feb 1813 - Where taken: Bay of Biscay - Date received: 8 Mar 1813 - From what ship: HM Ketch Gleamer - Discharged on 5 Apr 1813 - How discharged: HM Frigate Ethalion.

Lacemo, Larey - Seaman - Number: 308 - Prize name: Eliza - Ship type: MV - How taken: HM Brig Basilisk - Date taken: 6 Jan 1813 - Where taken: near Cadiz - Date received: 12 Jan 1813 - From what ship: HM Brig Basilisk - Discharged on 14 Apr 1813 - How discharged: Being a licensed vessel.

Lakeman, Asa - Mate - Number: 360 - Prize name: Mentor - Ship type: MV - How taken: HM Brig Columbine - Date taken: 14 Jan 1813 - Where taken: near Cadiz - Date received: 22 Jan 1813 - From what ship: HM Sloop Comet - Discharged on 14 Apr 1813 - How discharged: Being a licensed vessel.

Lamb, Jack - Seaman - Number: 698 - Prize name: Hendosten - Ship type: MV - How taken: HM Brig Zenoha - Date taken: 25 Jun 1813 - Where taken: near Lisbon - Date received: 2 Jul 1813 - From what ship: HM Brig Protector - Discharged on 22 Aug 1813 - How discharged: HM Brig Imogen.

Lang, Samuel - Seaman - Number: 123 - Prize name: Albion - Ship type: MV - How taken: HM Frigate Cossack - Date taken: 8 Aug 1812 - Where taken: Cape Spartel (Morocco) - Date received: 2 Sep 1813 - From what ship: HM Ship-of-the-Line Tremendous.

Larrounas, Elias - Boy - Number: 138 - Prize name: Commerce - Ship type: MV - How taken: HM Brig Rebuff - Date taken: 28 Aug 1812 - Where taken: near Cadiz - Date received: Returned to ship on 11 Sep 1812.

Lathan, John - Seaman - Number: 688 - How taken: HM Brig Shearwater - Date taken: 3 Jun 1813 - Where taken: Mahon (Island of Minorca) - Date received: 1 Jul 1813 - Discharged on 3 Jul 1813 - How discharged: HM Frigate Thames.

Latimer, John (see prisoner number 102) - Seaman - Number: 14 - Prize name: Margaret - Ship type: MV - How taken: HM Ship-of-the-Line San Juan - Date taken: 10 Aug 1812 - Where taken: Gibraltar Bay - Date received: 12 Aug 1812 - From what ship: Margaret - Discharged on 15 Jan 1813 - How discharged: HM Brig Derwent.

Latimer, John - Boy - Number: 102 - Prize name: Margaret - Ship type: MV - How taken: HM Ship-of-the-Line San Juan - Date taken: 10 Aug 1812 - Where taken: Gibraltar Bay - Date received: 2 Sep 1813 - From what ship: HM Ship-of-the-Line Tremendous.

Lattour, Armeda - Seaman - Number: 252 - Prize name: Apollo - Ship type: MV - How taken: HM Ship-of-the-Line Grampus - Date taken: 29 Oct 1812 - Where taken: On passage to Cadiz - Date received: 21 Nov 1812 - From what ship: HM Ship-of-the-Line Grampus - Discharged on 14 Dec 1812 - How discharged: Being a licensed vessel.

Lawler, Matthew - Seaman - Number: 487 - Discharged on 20 Mar 1813 - How discharged: Being a licensed vessel.

Lawrence, Clark - Seaman - Number: 547 - Prize name: Isabella - Ship type: MV - How taken: HM Brig Zenoha - Date taken: 27 Jun 1813 - Where taken: off Cape St. Mary (Portugal) - Date received: 1 Jul 1813 - From what ship: HM Brig Protection - Discharged on 7 Oct 1813 - How discharged: Isabella.

Layland, John - Seaman - Number: 78 - Prize name: Eliza - Ship type: MV - How taken: HM Sloop Hyacinth and HM Frigate Argo - Date taken: 27 Aug 1812 - Where taken: Straits of Gibraltar - Date received: 30 Aug 1812 - From what ship: HM Frigate Argo - Discharged on 22 Jan 1813 - How discharged: HM Sloop Comet.

Lea, Joseph - Seaman - Number: 295 - Prize name: George & Albert - Ship type: MV - How taken: HMS Myrtle - Date taken: 5 Jan 1813 - Where taken: off Cape St. Mary (Portugal) - Date received: 10 Jan 1813 - From what ship: HMS Myrtle - Discharged on 14 Apr 1813 - How discharged: Being a licensed vessel.

Leach, James - Seaman - Number: 24 - Prize name: Horace - Ship type: MV - How taken: HM Ship-of-the-Line San Juan - Date taken: 10 Aug 1812 - Where taken: Gibraltar Bay - Date received: 12 Aug 1812 - From what ship: Horace - Discharged on 29 Aug 1812 - How discharged: Being a licensed vessel.

Leach, John (see prisoner number 110) - Seaman - Number: 46 - Prize name: Tiger - Ship type: MV - How taken: HM Ship-of-the-Line San Juan - Date taken: 10 Aug 1812 - Where taken: Gibraltar Bay - Date received: 12 Aug 1812 - From what ship: Tiger - Discharged on 4 Jan 1813 - How discharged: An Englishman.

Leach, John - Seaman - Number: 110 - Prize name: Tiger - Ship type: MV - How taken: HM Ship-of-the-Line San Juan - Date taken: 10 Aug 1812 - Where taken: Gibraltar Bay - Date received: 2 Sep 1813 - From what ship: HM Ship-of-the-Line Tremendous.

Leeds, Leon - Seaman - Number: 50 - Prize name: Tiger - Ship type: MV - How taken: HM Ship-of-the-Line San Juan - Date taken: 10 Aug 1812 - Where taken: Gibraltar Bay - Date received: 12 Aug 1812 - From what ship: Tiger - Discharged on 15 Jan 1813 - How discharged: HM Frigate Andromeda.

Leonard, Edward - Seaman - Number: 375 - Prize name: George - Ship type: MV - How taken: HM Brig Columbine - Date taken: 13 Jan 1813 - Where taken: off Lisbon - Date received: 22 Jan 1813 - From what ship: HM Sloop Comet - Discharged on 15 Apr 1813 - How discharged: Being a licensed vessel.

Leonard, Robert - Seaman - Number: 535 - Prize name: Sampson - Ship type: MV - Discharged on Aug 1813 - How discharged: HM Ship-of-the-Line Achille.

Leonard, Robert (see prisoner number 114) - Seaman - Number: 59 - Prize name: Horace - Ship type: MV - How taken: HM Ship-of-the-Line San Juan - Date taken: 10 Aug 1812 - Where taken: Gibraltar Bay - Date received: 13 Aug 1812 - From what ship: Horace.

Leonard, Robert - Seaman - Number: 114 - Prize name: Phoenix - Ship type: MV - How taken: HM Ship-of-the-Line San Juan - Date taken: 10 Aug 1812 - Where taken: Gibraltar Bay - Date received: 2 Sep 1813 - From what ship: HM Ship-of-the-Line Tremendous.

Leslie, Henry - Master - Number: 125 - Prize name: Eliza - Ship type: MV - How taken: HM Sloop Hyacinth and HM Frigate Argo - Date taken: 27 Aug 1812 - Where taken: Straits of Gibraltar - Date received: 2 Sep 1813 - Discharged on 8 Feb 1813.

Levant, Thomas - Number: 742 - How taken: Taken off the HM Ship-of-the-Line Invincible - Discharged on 27 Oct 1813 - How discharged: HMT Sir John Borlair Warren No. 183 for England.

Lewis, Edward - Seaman - Number: 353 - Prize name: Pallas - Ship type: MV - How taken: HM Brig Rebuff - Date taken: 24 Dec 1812 - Where taken: near Cadiz - Date received: 19 Jan 1813 - From what ship: HM Brig Rebuff - Discharged on 19 Feb 1813 - How discharged: HM Brig Protector.

Lewis, William - Seaman - Number: 426 - Prize name: Mark & Abigail - Ship type: MV - How taken: HM Brig Basilisk - Date taken: 9 Jan 1813 - Where taken: off Cape St. Vincent (Portugal) - Date received: 19 Feb 1813 - From what ship: HM Gunboat No. 22 - Discharged on 16 Apr 1813 - How discharged: Being a licensed vessel.

Libby, Nathaniel - Seaman - Number: 22 - Prize name: Horace - Ship type: MV - How taken: HM Ship-of-the-Line San Juan - Date taken: 10 Aug 1812 - Where taken: Gibraltar Bay - Date received: 12 Aug 1812 - From what ship: Horace - Discharged on 29 Aug 1812 - How discharged: Being a licensed vessel.

Lightfoot, Sharp - Seaman - Number: 357 - Prize name: Concordia - Ship type: MV - How taken: HM Brig Basilisk - Date taken: 20 Jan 1813 - Where taken: near Cadiz - Date received: 20 Jan 1813 - From what ship: HM Brig Basilisk - Discharged on 14 Apr 1813 - How discharged: Being a licensed vessel.

Lindon, John - Seaman - Number: 365 - Prize name: Mentor - Ship type: MV - How taken: HM Brig Columbine - Date taken: 13 Jan 1813 - Where taken: near Cadiz - Date received: 22 Jan 1813 - From what ship: HM Sloop Comet - Discharged on 14 Apr 1813 - How discharged: Being a licensed vessel.

Line, Latony - Seaman - Number: 268 - Prize name: Apollo - Ship type: MV - How taken: HM Ship-of-the-Line Grampus - Date taken: 29 Oct 1812 - Where taken: On passage to Cadiz - Date received: 22 Nov 1812 - From what ship: Apollo - Discharged on 14 Dec 1812 - How discharged: Being a licensed vessel.

Linsey, Samuel - Number: 591 - How taken: Taken off the HMS Bombay - Discharged on 28 Jun 1813 - How discharged: HMT Minstraele.

Litchfield, Foster - Seaman - Number: 373 - Prize name: George - Ship type: MV - How taken: HM Brig Columbine - Date taken: 13 Jan 1813 - Where taken: off Lisbon - Date received: 22 Jan 1813 - From what ship: HM Sloop Comet - Discharged on 15 Apr 1813 - How discharged: Being a licensed vessel.

Littlefield, Isaac - Seaman - Number: 467 - Prize name: Amphitrite - Ship type: MV - How taken: HM Ketch Gleamer - Date taken: 27 Feb 1813 - Where taken: Bay of Biscay - Date received: 8 Mar 1813 - From what ship: HM Ketch Gleamer - Discharged on 5 Apr 1813 - How discharged: HM Frigate Ethalion.

Lochely, William - Mate - Number: 384 - Prize name: Pallas - Ship type: MV - How taken: HMS Rebuff - Date taken: 24 Dec 1812 - Where taken: near Cadiz - Date received: 4 Feb 1813 - From what ship: Pallas - Discharged on 6 Mar 1813 - How discharged: HM Ship-of-the-Line Blake.

Lonekin, Charles - Seaman - Number: 468 - Prize name: Amphitrite - Ship type: MV - How taken: HM Ketch Gleamer - Date taken: 27 Feb 1813 - Where taken: Bay of Biscay - Date received: 8 Mar 1813 - From what ship: HM Ketch Gleamer - Discharged on 5 Apr 1813 - How discharged: HM Frigate Ethalion.

Lopez, James - Seaman - Number: 312 - Prize name: Eliza - Ship type: MV - How taken: HM Brig Basilisk - Date taken: 6 Jan 1813 - Where taken: near Cadiz - Date received: 12 Jan 1813 - From what ship: HM Brig Basilisk - Discharged on 8 Feb 1813.

Lopez, John - Seaman - Number: 203 - Prize name: Meser - Ship type: MV - How taken: Not mentioned - Where taken: Unknown - Discharged on 13 Nov 1813 - How discharged: Being a licensed vessel.

Lounge, Thomas - Seaman - Number: 760 - Prize name: Adeline - Ship type: LM - How taken: HM Frigate Magiciene - Date taken: 14 Mar 1814 - Where taken: at sea - Date received: 14 Apr 1814 - From what ship: HM Frigate Magiciene - Discharged on 22 Apr 1814 - How discharged: HM Store Ship Tortoise.

Love, Peter - Seaman - Number: 5 - Prize name: Margaret - Ship type: MV - How taken: HM Ship-of-the-Line San Juan - Date taken: 10 Aug 1812 - Where taken: Gibraltar Bay - Date received: 12 Aug 1812 - From what ship: Margaret - Discharged on 15 Jan 1813 - How discharged: HM Brig Derwent.

Lovett, Israel - Mate - Number: 518 - Prize name: Tyber - Ship type: MV - How taken: HM Sloop Comet - Date taken: 6 Jun 1813 - Where taken: near Lisbon - Date received: 15 Jun 1813 - From what ship: HM Ship-of-Line San Josef.

Lovett, Peter - Seaman - Number: 177 - Prize name: Sally - Ship type: MV - How taken: Not mentioned - Date taken: 22 Aug 1812 - Discharged on 30 Sep 1812 - How discharged: Either a Moor or a Spaniard.

Low, Frederick G. - Mate - Number: 362 - Prize name: George - Ship type: MV - How taken: HM Brig Columbine - Date taken: 13 Jan 1813 - Where taken: off Lisbon - Date received: 22 Jan 1813 - From what ship: HM Sloop

Comet - Discharged on 15 Apr 1813 - How discharged: Being a licensed vessel.

Lowe, Thomas - Seaman - Number: 641 - How taken: HM Ship-of-the-Line Prince of Wales - Date taken: 28 May 1813 - Where taken: Mahon (Island of Minorca) - Date received: 1 Jul 1813 - From what ship: HMT Royal Boston No. 344 - Discharged on 23 Jul 1813 - How discharged: HM Frigate Unicorn.

Lubeck, James - Seaman - Number: 516 - Prize name: John Barnes - Ship type: MV - How taken: HM Sloop Comet - Date taken: 14 May 1813 - Where taken: near Lisbon - Date received: 15 Jun 1813 - From what ship: HM Ship-of-Line San Josef.

Lucas, Mas. - Seaman - Number: 705 - How taken: Taken off the HM Ship-of-the-Line Swiftsure - Discharged on Aug 1813 - How discharged: HM Ship-of-the-Line Achille.

Luce, Abijah - Commander - Number: 784 - Prize name: Sine Qua Non - Ship type: P - How taken: HMS Eske - Date taken: 20 Feb 1815 - Where taken: off Madeira - Date received: 14 Mar 1815 - From what ship: HMS Eske - Discharged on 14 Mar 1815 - How discharged: HMT Ann No. 124 for England.

Luschaw, John - Seaman - Number: 580 - Where taken: Mahon (Island of Minorca) - Date received: 1 Jul 1813 - From what ship: HMT Royal Boston No. 344 - Discharged on 21 Jul 1813 - How discharged: HM Brig Savage.

Lynch, Charles - Seaman - Number: 532 - Prize name: Spanish MV - How taken: HM Brig Papillion - Date taken: Jun 1813 - Where taken: near Cadiz - Date received: 7 Jun 1813 - From what ship: HMS Brig Papillion.

Mackay, James - Seaman - Number: 673 - How taken: HM Ship-of-the-Line Repulse - Date taken: 28 May 1813 - Where taken: Mahon (Island of Minorca) - Date received: 1 Jul 1813 - Discharged on 3 Jul 1813 - How discharged: HM Frigate Thames.

Madden, Isaac - Seaman - Number: 489 - How taken: HM Frigate Brune - Date taken: 14 Mar 1813 - Date received: 7 Mar 1813 - From what ship: HM Frigate Brune - Discharged on 5 Apr 1813 - How discharged: HM Frigate Ethalion.

Madellon, Peter - Seaman - Number: 214 - Prize name: Dolphin - Ship type: MV - How taken: HM Ship-of-the-Line Invincible - Date taken: 24 Aug 1812 - Where taken: Meg'n (Unknown) - Date received: 22 Nov 1812 - From what ship: Dolphin - Discharged on 25 Jan 1813 - How discharged: HM Ship-of-the-Line Sultan.

Magee, Charles - Master - Number: 189 - Prize name: Meser - Ship type: MV - How taken: Not mentioned - Where taken: Unknown - Discharged on 13 Nov 1813 - How discharged: Being a licensed vessel.

Malbon, Evan - Mate - Number: 512 - Prize name: John Barnes - Ship type: MV - How taken: HM Sloop Comet - Date taken: 14 May 1813 - Where taken: near Lisbon - Date received: 15 Jun 1813 - From what ship: HM Ship-of-Line San Josef - Discharged on 1 Jul 1813 - How discharged: HM Brig Protector for England.

Malling, James - Seaman - Number: 378 - How taken: Gave himself up at Gibraltar - Date taken: 30 Jan 1813 - Date received: 30 Jan 1813 - From what ship: HM Frigate Brune - Discharged on 6 Mar 1813 - How discharged: HM Ship-of-the-Line Blake.

Manby, Rooth - Seaman - Number: 539 - Prize name: Sampson - Ship type: MV - Discharged on Aug 1813 - How discharged: HM Ship-of-the-Line Achille.

Manley, James (see prisoner number 488) - Seaman - Number: 330 - How taken: Taken off the HMT Druid - Discharged on 8 Feb 1813 - How discharged: Return to HMT Druid.

Manley, James - Seaman - Number: 488 - How taken: Gave himself up from HMT Druid - Date taken: 9 Mar 1813 - Date received: 9 Mar 1813 - From what ship: HMT Druid - Discharged on 5 Apr 1813 - How discharged: HM Frigate Ethalion.

Manlove, Roberts - Seaman - Number: 530 - Prize name: Spanish MV - How taken: HM Brig Papillion - Date taken: Jun 1813 - Where taken: near Cadiz - Date received: 7 Jun 1813 - From what ship: HMS Brig Papillion.

Manuel, Dio - Seaman - Number: 514 - Prize name: John Barnes - Ship type: MV - How taken: HM Sloop Comet - Date taken: 14 May 1813 - Where taken: near Lisbon - Date received: 15 Jun 1813 - From what ship: HM Ship-of-Line San Josef - Discharged on 1 Jul 1813 - How discharged: HM Brig Protector for England.

Marshall, Thomas - Seaman - Number: 653 - How taken: HM Ship-of-the-Line Pompee - Date taken: 28 May 1813 - Where taken: Mahon (Island of Minorca) - Date received: 1 Jul 1813 - From what ship: HMT Royal Boston No. 344 - Discharged on 1 Jul 1813 - How discharged: HM Brig Protector for England.

Marten, John - Seaman - Number: 64 - Prize name: John - Ship type: MV - How taken: HM Sloop Blossom - Date taken: 16 Aug 1812 - Where taken: Mediterranean - Date received: 18 Aug 1812 - From what ship: HM Sloop Blossom - Discharged on 22 Jan 1813 - How discharged: HM Sloop Comet.

Martin, John - Seaman - Number: 187 - Prize name: Draper - Ship type: MV - How taken: HM Brig Fearless - Date taken: 18 Sep 1812 - Where taken: near Cadiz - Date received: 22 Nov 1812 - From what ship: Draper - Discharged on 22 Jan 1813 - How discharged: HM Sloop Comet.

Mason, Charles (see prisoner number 100) - Seaman - Number: 12 - Prize name: Margaret - Ship type: MV - How taken: HM Ship-of-the-Line San Juan - Date taken: 10 Aug 1812 - Where taken: Gibraltar Bay - Date received: 12 Aug 1812 - From what ship: Margaret - Discharged on 15 Jan 1813 - How discharged: HM Brig Derwent.

Mason, Charles - Seaman - Number: 100 - Prize name: Margaret - Ship type: MV - How taken: HM Ship-of-the-Line San Juan - Date taken: 10 Aug 1812 - Where taken: Gibraltar Bay - Date received: 2 Sep 1813 - From what ship: HM Ship-of-the-Line Tremendous.

Mathell, Benjamin - Seaman - Number: 369 - Prize name: Mentor - Ship type: MV - How taken: HM Brig Columbine - Date taken: 13 Jan 1813 - Where taken: near Cadiz - Date received: 22 Jan 1813 - From what ship: HM Sloop Comet - Discharged on 14 Apr 1813 - How discharged: Being a licensed vessel.

Matlock, Abraham - Mate - Number: 429 - Prize name: Charlotte - Ship type: MV - How taken: HM Brig Charger - Date taken: 14 Jan 1813 - Where taken: near Cadiz - Date received: 20 Feb 1813 - From what ship: Charlotte - Discharged on 14 Apr 1813 - How discharged: Being a licensed vessel.

Matten, Norman - Seaman - Number: 84 - Prize name: Taken in an open boat formerly belonging to American ship Fame which was captured by the French - How taken: HM Brig Desperate - Date taken: 22 Aug 1812 - Where taken: near Cadiz - Date received: 31 Aug 1813 - From what ship: HM Frigate Argo.

Matthews, John - Seaman - Number: 686 - How taken: HM Frigate Undaunted - Date taken: 5 Jun 1813 - Date received: 1 Jul 1813 - From what ship: HMT Royal Boston No. 344 - Discharged on 23 Jul 1813 - How discharged: HM Frigate Unicorn.

Maver, John - Seaman - Number: 89 - Prize name: Louisa - Ship type: MV - How taken: HM Brig Columbine - Date taken: 16 Aug 1812 - Where taken: near Cadiz - Date received: 31 Aug 1813 - From what ship: HM Frigate Argo - Discharged on 15 Nov 1812 - How discharged: Being a licensed vessel.

Mazel, James - Seaman - Number: 434 - How taken: Gave himself up from HMT Leopard - From what ship: HMT Leopard - Discharged on 19 Mar 1813 - How discharged: HM Schooner Sylvia.

McIntyre, Samuel - Seaman - Number: 477 - Prize name: Catharine - Ship type: MV - Discharged on 22 Mar 1813 - How discharged: Being a licensed vessel.

McKensey, George - Seaman - Number: 606 - How taken: HM Ship-of-the-Line Berwick - Date taken: 28 May 1813 - Where taken: Mahon (Island of Minorca) - Date received: 1 Jul 1813 - From what ship: HMT Royal Boston No. 344 - Discharged on 28 Jun 1813 - How discharged: HMT Minstraele.

McKenzie, John - Seaman - Number: 671 - Discharged on 28 Jun 1813 - How discharged: HMT Minstraele.

McKenzie, William - Seaman - Number: 690 - Prize name: Hepsey - Ship type: MV - Discharged on 8 Aug 1813 - How discharged: HM Sloop Kingfisher.

McMilledge, James - Seaman - Number: 249 - Prize name: Apollo - Ship type: MV - How taken: HM Ship-of-the-Line Grampus - Date taken: 29 Oct 1812 - Where taken: On passage to Cadiz - Date received: 21 Nov 1812 - From what ship: HM Ship-of-the-Line Grampus - Discharged on 31 Dec 1812 - How discharged: Being a licensed vessel.

Metcalf, Anthony - Seaman - Number: 390 - Prize name: Veroni - Ship type: MV - How taken: HM Sloop Comet - Date taken: 14 Jan 1813 - Where taken: near Cadiz - Date received: 8 Feb 1813 - From what ship: HMS Brig Desperate - Discharged on 14 Apr 1813 - How discharged: Being a licensed vessel.

224 Gibraltar Depot

Miller, John - Seaman - Number: 614 - How taken: HM Ship-of-the-Line Royal George - Date taken: 28 May 1813 - Where taken: Mahon (Island of Minorca) - Date received: 1 Jul 1813 - From what ship: HMT Royal Boston No. 344 - Discharged on 24 Jul 1813 - How discharged: HM Store Ship Tortoise.

Miller, Juan - Seaman - Number: 567 - Date received: 1 Jul 1813 - From what ship: HMT Royal Boston No. 344 - Discharged on 28 Jun 1813 - How discharged: HMT Minstraele.

Mitchell, Fairley - Seaman - Number: 544 - Prize name: Isabella - Ship type: MV - How taken: HM Brig Zenoha - Date taken: 27 Jun 1813 - Where taken: off Cape St. Mary (Portugal) - Date received: 1 Jul 1813 - From what ship: HM Brig Protection - Discharged on 4 Sep 1813 - How discharged: HM Brig Teazer.

Molineuse, Charles - Seaman - Number: 122 - Prize name: Albion - Ship type: MV - How taken: HM Frigate Cossack - Date taken: 8 Aug 1812 - Where taken: Cape Spartel (Morocco) - Date received: Returned to ship on 24 Aug 1812 - Discharged on 3 Nov 1812 - How discharged: Being a licensed vessel.

Molyneaux, William - Seaman - Number: 513 - Prize name: John Barnes - Ship type: MV - How taken: HM Sloop Comet - Date taken: 14 May 1813 - Where taken: near Lisbon - Date received: 15 Jun 1813 - From what ship: HM Ship-of-Line San Josef - Discharged on 1 Jul 1813 - How discharged: HM Brig Protector for England.

Mones, Peter - Seaman - Number: 255 - Prize name: Apollo - Ship type: MV - How taken: HM Ship-of-the-Line Grampus - Date taken: 29 Oct 1812 - Where taken: On passage to Cadiz - Date received: 21 Nov 1812 - From what ship: HM Ship-of-the-Line Grampus - Discharged on 14 Dec 1812 - How discharged: Being a licensed vessel.

Moody, Samuel - Mate - Number: 183 - Prize name: Draper - Ship type: MV - How taken: HM Brig Fearly - Date taken: 18 Sep 1812 - Where taken: near Cadiz - Date received: 22 Nov 1812 - From what ship: Draper - Discharged on 25 Jan 1813 - How discharged: HM Ship-of-the-Line Sultan.

Moor, Lawrence - Seaman - Number: 352 - Prize name: Pallas - Ship type: MV - How taken: HM Brig Rebuff - Date taken: 24 Dec 1812 - Where taken: near Cadiz - Date received: 19 Jan 1813 - From what ship: HM Brig Rebuff - Discharged on 19 Feb 1813 - How discharged: HM Brig Protector.

Moore, Francis - Seaman - Number: 261 - Prize name: Lydia - Ship type: MV - How taken: HM Ship-of-the-Line Grampus - Date taken: 2 Nov 1812 - Where taken: On passage to Cadiz - Date received: 21 Nov 1812 - From what ship: HM Ship-of-the-Line Grampus - Discharged on 14 Dec 1812 - How discharged: Being a licensed vessel.

Morgan, James - Seaman - Number: 265 - Prize name: Lydia - Ship type: MV - How taken: HM Ship-of-the-Line Grampus - Date taken: 2 Nov 1812 - Where taken: On passage to Cadiz - Date received: 22 Nov 1812 - From what ship: Lydia - Discharged on 14 Dec 1812 - How discharged: Being a licensed vessel.

Moro, Henry - Number: 490 - Prize name: Paul Jones - How taken: HMS Rebuff - Date taken: 7 Mar 1813 - Where taken: off Cape St. Vincent (Portugal) - Date received: 20 Mar 1813 - From what ship: MV Little Jones - Died on 20 Jun 1813 from fever.

Morrell, John - Seaman - Number: 395 - How taken: Gave himself up from HM Frigate Mermaid - Date taken: 11 Feb 1813 - Where taken: Gibraltar - Date received: 12 Feb 1813 - From what ship: HM Frigate Mermaid - Discharged on 6 Mar 1813 - How discharged: HM Ship-of-the-Line Blake.

Morris, Isaac- Seaman - Number: 750 - Prize name: Adeline - Ship type: LM - How taken: HM Frigate Magiciene - Date taken: 14 Mar 1814 - Where taken: at sea - Date received: 14 Apr 1814 - From what ship: HM Frigate Magiciene - Discharged on 22 Apr 1814 - How discharged: HM Store Ship Tortoise.

Morris, Robert - Seaman - Number: 63 - Prize name: Howard - Ship type: MV - How taken: HM Brig Scout - Date taken: 23 Jun 1812 - Where taken: Minorca - Date received: 15 Aug 1812 - Discharged on 15 Jan 1813 - How discharged: HM Frigate Andromeda.

Morrison, John - Seaman - Number: 397 - How taken: Gave himself up from HM Frigate Mermaid - Date taken: 11 Feb 1813 - Where taken: Gibraltar - Date received: 12 Feb 1813 - From what ship: HM Frigate Mermaid - Discharged on 6 Mar 1813 - How discharged: HM Ship-of-the-Line Blake.

Morton, Pliny - Surgeon - Number: 785 - Prize name: Sine Qua Non - Ship type: P - How taken: HMS Eske - Date taken: 20 Feb 1815 - Where taken: off Madeira - Date received: 14 Mar 1815 - From what ship: HMS Eske - Discharged on 14 Mar 1815 - How discharged: HMT Ann No. 124 for England.

Morton, Seth - Mate - Number: 116 - Prize name: John - Ship type: MV - How taken: HM Sloop Blossom - Date taken: 10 Aug 1812 - Where taken: Mediterranean - Date received: 2 Sep 1813 - From what ship: HM Ship-of-the-Line Tremendous - Discharged on 25 Jan 1813 - How discharged: HM Ship-of-the-Line Sultan.

Moses, John - Seaman - Number: 17 - Prize name: Horace - Ship type: MV - How taken: HM Ship-of-the-Line San Juan - Date taken: 10 Aug 1812 - Where taken: Gibraltar Bay - Date received: 12 Aug 1812 - From what ship: Horace - Discharged on 29 Aug 1812 - How discharged: Being a licensed vessel.

Moss, Nathaniel P. - Seaman - Number: 371 - Prize name: George - Ship type: MV - How taken: HM Brig Columbine - Date taken: 13 Jan 1813 - Where taken: off Lisbon - Date received: 22 Jan 1813 - From what ship: HM Sloop Comet - Discharged on 15 Apr 1813 - How discharged: Being a licensed vessel.

Mulch, James - Seaman - Number: 681 - How taken: HM Brig Shearwater - Date taken: 3 Jun 1813 - Where taken: Mahon (Island of Minorca) - Date received: 1 Jul 1813 - Discharged on 3 Jul 1813 - How discharged: HM Frigate Thames.

Mulde, Sebron - Seaman - Number: 253 - Prize name: Apollo - Ship type: MV - How taken: HM Ship-of-the-Line Grampus - Date taken: 29 Oct 1812 - Where taken: On passage to Cadiz - Date received: 21 Nov 1812 - From what ship: HM Ship-of-the-Line Grampus - Discharged on 14 Dec 1812 - How discharged: Being a licensed vessel.

Mullen, John B. - Seaman - Number: 250 - Prize name: Apollo - Ship type: MV - How taken: HM Ship-of-the-Line Grampus - Date taken: 29 Oct 1812 - Where taken: On passage to Cadiz - Date received: 21 Nov 1812 - From what ship: HM Ship-of-the-Line Grampus - Discharged on 14 Dec 1812 - How discharged: Being a licensed vessel.

Muller, Samuel - Number: 458 - Discharged on 15 Mar 1813 - How discharged: Being a licensed vessel.

Mulleus, Joseph - 1st Mate - Number: 2 - Prize name: Margaret - Ship type: MV - How taken: HM Ship-of-the-Line San Juan - Date taken: 10 Aug 1812 - Where taken: Gibraltar Bay - Date received: 12 Aug 1812 - From what ship: Margaret - Discharged on 15 Jan 1813 - How discharged: HM Brig Derwent.

Murray, James - Number: 577 - Where taken: Mahon (Island of Minorca) - Discharged on 28 Jun 1813 - How discharged: HMT Minstraele.

Murray, Peter - Seaman - Number: 656 - How taken: HM Ship-of-the-Line Ocean - Date taken: 28 May 1813 - Where taken: Mahon (Island of Minorca) - Date received: 1 Jul 1813 - From what ship: HMT Royal Boston No. 344 - Discharged on 3 Jul 1813 - How discharged: HM Frigate Thames.

Murray, Richard - Seaman - Number: 389 - Prize name: Veroni - Ship type: MV - How taken: HM Sloop Comet - Date taken: 14 Jan 1813 - Where taken: near Cadiz - Date received: 8 Feb 1813 - From what ship: HMS Brig Desperate - Discharged on 14 Apr 1813 - How discharged: Being a licensed vessel.

Mutch, Thomas T. - Seaman - Number: 586 - Where taken: Mahon (Island of Minorca) - Date received: 1 Jul 1813 - From what ship: HMT Royal Boston No. 344 - Discharged on 3 Jul 1813 - How discharged: HM Frigate Thames.

Myers, James - Seaman - Number: 703 - How taken: Taken off the HM Frigate Ganymede - Discharged on Aug 1813 - How discharged: HM Ship-of-the-Line Achille.

Navari, Peter - Seaman - Number: 8 - Prize name: Margaret - Ship type: MV - How taken: HM Ship-of-the-Line San Juan - Date taken: 10 Aug 1812 - Where taken: Gibraltar Bay - Date received: 12 Aug 1812 - From what ship: Margaret - Discharged on 15 Jan 1813 - How discharged: HM Brig Derwent.

Nearl, William - Seaman - Number: 745 - Prize name: Mary English - Ship type: MV - How taken: HM Post Ship Crocodile - Date taken: 6 Aug 1813 - Where taken: off Cape Finisterre (Spain) - Date received: 8 Dec 1813 - From what ship: HMS Brig Desperate - Discharged on 7 Feb 1814 - How discharged: HMT Fanny No. 186.

Nelson, James - Seaman - Number: 200 - Prize name: Meser - Ship type: MV - How taken: Not mentioned - Where taken: Unknown - Discharged on 13 Nov 1813 - How discharged: Being a licensed vessel.

Newel, Noah - Seaman - Number: 325 - Prize name: Essex - Ship type: MV - How taken: HM Gunboat No. 22 - Date taken: 12 Jan 1813 - Where taken: near Cadiz - Date received: 12 Jan 1813 - From what ship: HM Gunboat No. 22 - Discharged on 16 Apr 1813 - How discharged: Being a licensed vessel.

Newell, John - Seaman - Number: 47 - Prize name: Tiger - Ship type: MV - How taken: HM Ship-of-the-Line San Juan - Date taken: 10 Aug 1812 - Where taken: Gibraltar Bay - Date received: 12 Aug 1812 - From what ship: Tiger - Discharged on 15 Jan 1813 - How discharged: HM Frigate Andromeda.

Newman, Daniel - Seaman - Number: 755 - Prize name: Adeline - Ship type: LM - How taken: HM Frigate Magiciene - Date taken: 14 Mar 1814 - Where taken: at sea - Date received: 14 Apr 1814 - From what ship: HM Frigate Magiciene - Discharged on 22 Apr 1814 - How discharged: HM Store Ship Tortoise.

Nichett, Pierre - Passenger - Number: 783 - Prize name: Leo - Ship type: P - How taken: HM Ship-of-the-Line Grampus - Date taken: 2 Dec 1814 - Where taken: off Lisbon - Date received: 9 Dec 1814 - From what ship: HM Frigate Granicus - Discharged on 15 Dec 1814 - How discharged: HMS Eurasso.

Nicholas, John - Seaman - Number: 676 - How taken: HM Ship-of-the-Line Repulse - Date taken: 28 May 1813 - Where taken: Mahon (Island of Minorca) - Date received: 1 Jul 1813 - Discharged on 3 Jul 1813 - How discharged: HM Frigate Thames.

Nixon, Charles - Number: 595 - Where taken: Mahon (Island of Minorca) - Discharged on 12 Jul 1813 - How discharged: HM Sloop Bacchus.

Noble, Charles - Seaman - Number: 582 - Where taken: Mahon (Island of Minorca) - Date received: 1 Jul 1813 - From what ship: HMT Royal Boston No. 344 - Discharged on 21 Jul 1813 - How discharged: HM Brig Savage.

Oden, John - Seaman - Number: 35 - Prize name: Allegany - Ship type: MV - How taken: HM Ship-of-the-Line San Juan - Date taken: 10 Aug 1812 - Where taken: Gibraltar Bay - Date received: 12 Aug 1812 - From what ship: Allegany - Discharged on 15 Jan 1813 - How discharged: HM Brig Derwent.

Oliver, Robert - Seaman - Number: 191 - Prize name: Meser - Ship type: MV - How taken: Not mentioned - Where taken: Unknown - Discharged on 13 Nov 1813 - How discharged: Being a licensed vessel.

Olsen, Henry - Seaman - Number: 289 - Prize name: George & Albert - Ship type: MV - How taken: HMS Myrtle - Date taken: 5 Jan 1813 - Where taken: off Cape St. Mary (Portugal) - Date received: 10 Jan 1813 - From what ship: HMS Myrtle - Discharged on 14 Apr 1813 - How discharged: Being a licensed vessel.

Osborn, Ebenezer - Seaman - Number: 301 - Prize name: Concordia - Ship type: MV - How taken: HM Brig Basilisk - Date taken: 6 Jan 1813 - Where taken: near Cadiz - Date received: 12 Jan 1813 - From what ship: HM Brig Basilisk - Discharged on 14 Apr 1813 - How discharged: Being a licensed vessel.

Osborne, Lewis - Seaman - Number: 564 - Prize name: Hendosten - Ship type: MV - How taken: Gave himself up from HM Corvette Scipio - Date taken: 28 May 1813 - Where taken: Mahon (Island of Minorca) - Date received: 1 Jul 1813 - From what ship: HMT Royal Boston No. 344 - Discharged on 21 Jul 1813 - How discharged: HM Brig Savage.

Overstock, Peter - Seaman - Number: 523 - Prize name: Tyber - Ship type: MV - How taken: HM Sloop Comet - Date taken: 6 Jun 1813 - Where taken: near Lisbon - Date received: 15 Jun 1813 - From what ship: HM Ship-of-Line San Josef.

Owen, Burden - Seaman - Number: 660 - How taken: HM Ship-of-the-Line Ocean - Date taken: 28 May 1813 - Where taken: Mahon (Island of Minorca) - Date received: 1 Jul 1813 - From what ship: HMT Royal Boston No. 344 - Discharged on 21 Jul 1813 - How discharged: HM Brig Savage.

Parker, John - Seaman - Number: 486 - Discharged on 20 Mar 1813 - How discharged: Being a licensed vessel.

Parks, Richard - Seaman - Number: 80 - Prize name: Eliza - Ship type: MV - How taken: HM Sloop Hyacinth and HM Frigate Argo - Date taken: 27 Aug 1812 - Where taken: Straits of Gibraltar - Date received: 30 Aug 1812 - From what ship: HM Frigate Argo - Discharged on 22 Jan 1813 - How discharged: HM Sloop Comet.

Parto, Pero - Seaman - Number: 244 - Prize name: Conde Mary - Ship type: MV - How taken: HM Ship-of-the-Line Grampus - Date taken: 24 Oct 1812 - Where taken: On passage to Cadiz - Date received: 21 Nov 1812 - From what ship: HM Ship-of-the-Line Grampus - Discharged on 31 Dec 1812 - How discharged: Being a licensed vessel.

Passino, Thomas - Seaman - Number: 179 - Prize name: Sally - Ship type: MV - How taken: Not mentioned - Date taken: 22 Aug 1812 - Discharged on 30 Sep 1812 - How discharged: Either a Moor or a Spaniard.

Patterson, John (1) - Seaman - Number: 751 - Prize name: Adeline - Ship type: LM - How taken: HM Frigate Magiciene - Date taken: 14 Mar 1814 - Where taken: at sea - Date received: 14 Apr 1814 - From what ship: HM Frigate Magiciene - Discharged on 24 Apr 1814.

Patterson, John (2) - Seaman - Number: 754 - Prize name: Adeline - Ship type: LM - How taken: HM Frigate Magiciene - Date taken: 14 Mar 1814 - Where taken: at sea - Date received: 14 Apr 1814 - From what ship: HM Frigate Magiciene - Discharged on 24 Apr 1814.

Paul, Dempey - Mate - Number: 212 - Prize name: Dolphin - Ship type: MV - How taken: HM Ship-of-the-Line Invincible - Date taken: 24 Aug 1812 - Where taken: Meg'n (Unknown) - Date received: 22 Nov 1812 - From what ship: Dolphin - Discharged on 25 Jan 1813 - How discharged: HM Ship-of-the-Line Sultan.

Paul, Mark - Seaman - Number: 485 - How taken: 485A - Discharged on 20 Mar 1813 - How discharged: Being a licensed vessel.

Pearson, William - Master - Number: 119 - Prize name: Albion - Ship type: MV - How taken: HM Frigate Cossack - Date taken: 8 Aug 1812 - Where taken: Cape Spartel (Morocco) - Date received: 2 Sep 1813 - From what ship: HM Ship-of-the-Line Tremendous - Discharged on 3 Nov 1812 - How discharged: Being a licensed vessel.

Peckham, Isaac - Seaman - Number: 534 - How taken: Taken off the Spanish MV Maydock - Discharged on 26 Jul 1813 - How discharged: HM Store Ship Weymouth.

Penerson, Hance - Boy - Number: 58 - Prize name: Phoenix - Ship type: MV - How taken: HM Ship-of-the-Line San Juan - Date taken: 10 Aug 1812 - Where taken: Gibraltar Bay - Date received: 12 Aug 1812 - From what ship: Tiger - Discharged on 15 Jan 1813 - How discharged: HM Frigate Andromeda.

Penny, Richard - Seaman - Number: 573 - Prize name: Hendosten - Ship type: MV - How taken: Gave himself up from HM Corvette Scipio - Date taken: 28 May 1813 - Where taken: Mahon (Island of Minorca) - Date received: 1 Jul 1813 - From what ship: HMT Royal Boston No. 344 - Discharged on 28 Jun 1813 - How discharged: HMT Minstraele.

Penny, Samuel - Seaman - Number: 393 - Prize name: Pallas - Ship type: MV - How taken: HMS Rebuff - Date taken: 24 Dec 1812 - Where taken: near Cadiz - Date received: 9 Feb 1813 - From what ship: Pallas Prize.

Penrose, Abraham - Seaman - Number: 655 - How taken: HM Ship-of-the-Line Pompee - Date taken: 28 May 1813 - Where taken: Mahon (Island of Minorca) - Date received: 1 Jul 1813 - From what ship: HMT Royal Boston No. 344 - Discharged on 28 Jun 1813 - How discharged: HMT Minstraele.

Perry, Samuel - Seaman - Number: 720 - Discharged on Aug 1813 - How discharged: HM Ship-of-the-Line Achille.

Peters, Thomas - Seaman - Number: 602 - How taken: HM Ship-of-the-Line Berwick - Date taken: 28 May 1813 - Where taken: Mahon (Island of Minorca) - Date received: 1 Jul 1813 - From what ship: HMT Royal Boston No. 344 - Discharged on 26 Jul 1813 - How discharged: HM Store Ship Weymouth.

Peters, William - Seaman - Number: 307 - Prize name: Eliza - Ship type: MV - How taken: HM Brig Basilisk - Date taken: 6 Jan 1813 - Where taken: near Cadiz - Date received: 12 Jan 1813 - From what ship: HM Brig Basilisk - Discharged on 6 Mar 1813 - How discharged: HM Ship-of-the-Line Blake.

Peterson, Hance - Seaman - Number: 113 - Prize name: Phoenix - Ship type: MV - How taken: HM Ship-of-the-Line San Juan - Date taken: 10 Aug 1812 - Where taken: Gibraltar Bay - How discharged: Returned to ship on 29 Aug 1812.

Peterson, William - Number: 662 - How taken: HM Ship-of-the-Line Ocean - Date taken: 28 May 1813 - Where taken: Mahon (Island of Minorca) - Discharged on 28 Jun 1813 - How discharged: HMT Minstraele.

Peverly, Henry - Seaman - Number: 594 - Where taken: Mahon (Island of Minorca) - Date received: 1 Jul 1813 - From what ship: HMT Royal Boston No. 344 - Discharged on 3 Jul 1813 - How discharged: HM Frigate Thames.

Phaesenton, Robert - Seaman - Number: 74 - Prize name: Pallas - Ship type: MV - How taken: HM Brig Papillion - Date taken: 7 Aug 1812 - Where taken: off Sanlucar (Spain) - Date received: 26 Aug 1812 - From what ship: HMS Lavinia - Discharged on 22 Jan 1813 - How discharged: HM Sloop Comet.

Phillips, William (2) - Seaman - Number: 578 - Where taken: Mahon (Island of Minorca) - Date received: 1 Jul 1813 - From what ship: HMT Royal Boston No. 344 - Discharged on 24 Jul 1813 - How discharged: HM Store Ship Tortoise.

Phyney, William - Seaman - Number: 305 - Prize name: Eliza - Ship type: MV - How taken: HM Brig Basilisk - Date taken: 6 Jan 1813 - Where taken: near Cadiz - Date received: 12 Jan 1813 - From what ship: HM Brig Basilisk - Discharged on 14 Apr 1813 - How discharged: Being a licensed vessel.

Pinkhorn, Allan - Seaman - Number: 403 - How taken: Gave himself up from HM Frigate Franchise - Date taken: 12 Feb 1812 - Where taken: Gibraltar - Date received: 13 Feb 1813 - From what ship: HM Frigate Franchise - Discharged on 6 Mar 1813 - How discharged: HM Ship-of-the-Line Blake.

Pirman, John - Seaman - Number: 415 - Prize name: Thomas Wilson - Ship type: MV - How taken: HM Sloop Comet - Date taken: 14 Jan 1813 - Where taken: near Cadiz - Date received: 18 Feb 1813 - From what ship: HM Brig Charger - Discharged on 10 Apr 1813 - How discharged: Being a licensed vessel.

Pitt, Charles - Seaman - Number: 533 - How taken: Taken off the Spanish MV Maydock - Discharged on 26 Jul 1813 - How discharged: HM Store Ship Weymouth.

Pitt, William - Number: 738 - How taken: Taken off the HM Ship-of-the-Line Invincible - Discharged on 27 Oct 1813 - How discharged: HMT Sir John Borlair Warren No. 183 for England.

Pitts, James - Seaman - Number: 225 - Prize name: Topaz - Ship type: MV - How taken: HM Ship-of-the-Line Grampus - Date taken: 19 Oct 1812 - Where taken: On passage to Cadiz - Date received: 21 Nov 1812 - From what ship: HM Ship-of-the-Line Grampus - Discharged on 14 Dec 1812 - How discharged: Being a licensed vessel.

Pope, William - Seaman - Number: 400 - How taken: Gave himself up from HM Frigate Franchise - Date taken: 12 Feb 1812 - Where taken: Gibraltar - Date received: 13 Feb 1813 - From what ship: HM Frigate Franchise - Discharged on 6 Mar 1813 - How discharged: HM Ship-of-the-Line Blake.

Poppins, John - Seaman - Number: 87 - Prize name: Louisa - Ship type: MV - How taken: HM Brig Columbine - Date taken: 16 Aug 1812 - Where taken: near Cadiz - Date received: 31 Aug 1813 - From what ship: HM Frigate Argo - Discharged on 15 Nov 1812 - How discharged: Being a licensed vessel.

Porter, Josiah - Seaman - Number: 651 - How taken: HM Ship-of-the-Line Pompee - Date taken: 28 May 1813 - Where taken: Mahon (Island of Minorca) - Date received: 1 Jul 1813 - From what ship: HMT Royal Boston No. 344 - Discharged on 28 Jun 1813 - How discharged: HMT Minstraele.

Potter, John - Seaman - Number: 654 - How taken: HM Ship-of-the-Line Pompee - Date taken: 28 May 1813 - Where taken: Mahon (Island of Minorca) - Date received: 1 Jul 1813 - From what ship: HMT Royal Boston No. 344 - Discharged on 21 Jul 1813 - How discharged: HM Brig Savage.

Pottingale, John - Seaman - Number: 757 - Prize name: Adeline - Ship type: LM - How taken: HM Frigate Magiciene - Date taken: 14 Mar 1814 - Where taken: at sea - Date received: 14 Apr 1814 - From what ship: HM Frigate Magiciene - Discharged on 22 Apr 1814 - How discharged: HM Store Ship Tortoise.

Powel, Joseph - Seaman - Number: 600 - How taken: HM Ship-of-the-Line Berwick - Date taken: 28 May 1813 - Where taken: Mahon (Island of Minorca) - Date received: 1 Jul 1813 - From what ship: HMT Royal Boston No. 344 - Discharged on 23 Jul 1813 - How discharged: HM Frigate Unicorn.

Pratts, Samuel - Seaman - Number: 328 - Prize name: Essex - Ship type: MV - How taken: HM Gunboat No. 22 - Date taken: 12 Jan 1813 - Where taken: near Cadiz - Date received: 12 Jan 1813 - From what ship: HM Gunboat No. 22 - Discharged on 16 Apr 1813 - How discharged: Being a licensed vessel.

Price, John - Seaman - Number: 663 - How taken: HM Ship-of-the-Line Ocean - Date taken: 28 May 1813 - Where taken: Mahon (Island of Minorca) - Discharged on 3 Jul 1813 - How discharged: HM Frigate Thames.

Puffer, John - Carpenter - Number: 422 - Prize name: Mark & Abigail - Ship type: MV - How taken: HM Brig Basilisk - Date taken: 9 Jan 1813 - Where taken: off Cape St. Vincent (Portugal) - Date received: 19 Feb

1813 - From what ship: HM Gunboat No. 22 - Discharged on 16 Apr 1813 - How discharged: Being a licensed vessel.

Quann, Sim. - Seaman - Number: 430 - Prize name: Charlotte - Ship type: MV - How taken: HM Brig Charger - Date taken: 14 Jan 1813 - Where taken: near Cadiz - Date received: 20 Feb 1813 - From what ship: Charlotte - Discharged on 14 Apr 1813 - How discharged: Being a licensed vessel.

Quarterruaun, William - Seaman - Number: 657 - How taken: HM Ship-of-the-Line Ocean - Date taken: 28 May 1813 - Where taken: Mahon (Island of Minorca) - Date received: 1 Jul 1813 - From what ship: HMT Royal Boston No. 344 - Discharged on 21 Jul 1813 - How discharged: HM Brig Savage.

Randolph, Horace - Seaman - Number: 685 - How taken: HM Frigate Undaunted - Date taken: 5 Jun 1813 - Date received: 1 Jul 1813 - Discharged on 3 Jul 1813 - How discharged: HM Frigate Thames.

Ratoon, Thomas - Seaman - Number: 341 - Prize name: Pallas - Ship type: MV - How taken: HM Brig Rebuff - Date taken: 24 Dec 1812 - Where taken: near Cadiz - Date received: 19 Jan 1813 - From what ship: HM Brig Rebuff - Discharged on 19 Feb 1813 - How discharged: HM Sloop Dauntless.

Ray, David - Seaman - Number: 746 - Prize name: Mary English - Ship type: MV - How taken: HM Post Ship Crocodile - Date taken: 6 Aug 1813 - Where taken: off Cape Finisterre (Spain) - Date received: 8 Dec 1813 - From what ship: HMS Brig Desperate - Discharged on 7 Feb 1814 - How discharged: HMT Fanny No. 186.

Raymond, Cable - Seaman - Number: 557 - Date received: 2 Jul 1813 - From what ship: HM Brig Protection - Discharged on 22 Aug 1813 - How discharged: HM Brig Imogen.

Read, John - Seaman - Number: 684 - How taken: HM Frigate Undaunted - Date taken: 5 Jun 1813 - Date received: 1 Jul 1813 - From what ship: HMT Royal Boston No. 344 - Discharged on 23 Jul 1813 - How discharged: HM Frigate Unicorn.

Reed, Bartholomew - Seaman - Number: 484 - Discharged on 20 Mar 1813 - How discharged: Being a licensed vessel.

Reid, John - Seaman - Number: 645 - How taken: HM Battery Gorgon - Date taken: 28 May 1813 - Where taken: Mahon (Island of Minorca) - Date received: 1 Jul 1813 - From what ship: HMT Royal Boston No. 344 - Discharged on 23 Jul 1813 - How discharged: HM Frigate Unicorn.

Renkins, Henry - Number: 282 - Prize name: Maria - Ship type: MV - Discharged on 5 Jan 1813 - How discharged: Being a licensed vessel.

Reunie, David - Seaman - Number: 756 - Prize name: Adeline - Ship type: LM - How taken: HM Frigate Magiciene - Date taken: 14 Mar 1814 - Where taken: at sea - Date received: 14 Apr 1814 - From what ship: HM Frigate Magiciene - Discharged on 22 Apr 1814 - How discharged: HM Store Ship Tortoise.

Rianoer, Anthony - Seaman - Number: 346 - Prize name: Pallas - Ship type: MV - How taken: HM Brig Rebuff - Date taken: 24 Dec 1812 - Where taken: near Cadiz - Date received: 19 Jan 1813 - From what ship: HM Brig Rebuff - Discharged on 19 Feb 1813 - How discharged: HM Sloop Dauntless.

Rich, William - Seaman - Number: 433 - How taken: Gave himself up from HMT Leopard - From what ship: HMT Leopard - Discharged on 19 Mar 1813 - How discharged: HM Schooner Sylvia.

Richards, Edward - Seaman - Number: 500 - How taken: Gave himself up from HM Ship-of-the-Line Malta - Date taken: 2 Jan 1813 - Where taken: Gibraltar - Date received: 9 Apr 1813 - From what ship: HM Bomb Vessel Strombolo - Discharged on 23 Apr 1813 - How discharged: HM Sloop Helena.

Richards, Henry - Seaman - Number: 661 - How taken: HM Ship-of-the-Line Ocean - Date taken: 28 May 1813 - Where taken: Mahon (Island of Minorca) - Date received: 1 Jul 1813 - From what ship: HMT Royal Boston No. 344 - Discharged on 3 Jul 1813 - How discharged: HM Frigate Thames.

Richardson, Joel - Seaman - Number: 97 - Prize name: Pallas - Ship type: MV - How taken: HM Brig Papillion - Date taken: 7 Aug 1812 - Where taken: off Sanlucar (Spain) - Date received: 2 Sep 1813 - From what ship: HM Ship-of-the-Line Tremendous.

Richardson, Robert - Seaman - Number: 710 - Discharged on Aug 1813 - How discharged: HM Ship-of-the-Line Achille.

Richmond, James G. - Seaman - Number: 229 - Prize name: Argus - Ship type: MV - How taken: HM Ship-of-the-Line Grampus - Date taken: 19 Oct 1812 - Where taken: On passage to Cadiz - Date received: 21 Nov 1812 - From what ship: HM Ship-of-the-Line Grampus - Discharged on 14 Dec 1812 - How discharged: Being a licensed vessel.

Ricker, Elijah - Number: 456 - Prize name: Mariner - Ship type: MV - Discharged on 15 Mar 1813 - How discharged: Being a licensed vessel.

Robarts, Samuel - Seaman - Number: 421 - Prize name: Charlotte - Ship type: MV - How taken: HM Brig Charger - Date taken: 14 Jan 1813 - Where taken: near Cadiz - Date received: 18 Feb 1813 - From what ship: HM Brig Charger - Discharged on 14 Apr 1813 - How discharged: Being a licensed vessel.

Roberts, John - Seaman - Number: 326 - Prize name: Essex - Ship type: MV - How taken: HM Gunboat No. 22 - Date taken: 12 Jan 1813 - Where taken: near Cadiz - Date received: 12 Jan 1813 - From what ship: HM Gunboat No. 22 - Discharged on 16 Apr 1813 - How discharged: Being a licensed vessel.

Roberts, Joseph - Seaman - Number: 240 - Prize name: Conde Mary - Ship type: MV - How taken: HM Ship-of-the-Line Grampus - Date taken: 24 Oct 1812 - Where taken: On passage to Cadiz - Date received: 21 Nov 1812 - From what ship: HM Ship-of-the-Line Grampus - Discharged on 31 Dec 1812 - How discharged: Being a licensed vessel.

Roberts, Moses - Seaman - Number: 779 - Prize name: Adeline - Ship type: LM - How taken: HM Frigate Magiciene - Date taken: 14 Mar 1814 - Where taken: at sea - Date received: 14 Apr 1814 - From what ship: HM Frigate Magiciene - Discharged on 22 Apr 1814 - How discharged: HM Store Ship Tortoise.

Roberts, Nathaniel - Seaman - Number: 777 - Prize name: Adeline - Ship type: LM - How taken: HM Frigate Magiciene - Date taken: 14 Mar 1814 - Where taken: at sea - Date received: 14 Apr 1814 - From what ship: HM Frigate Magiciene - Discharged on 29 Apr 1814 - How discharged: HM Store Ship Hindostan.

Roberts, Thomas - Seaman - Number: 314 - Prize name: John L. Kees - Ship type: MV - How taken: HM Brig Basilisk - Date taken: 6 Jan 1813 - Where taken: near Cadiz - Date received: 12 Jan 1813 - From what ship: HM Brig Basilisk - Discharged on 14 Apr 1813 - How discharged: Being a licensed vessel.

Robinson, Ebenezer - Seaman - Number: 339 - Prize name: Pallas - Ship type: MV - How taken: HM Brig Rebuff - Date taken: 24 Dec 1812 - Where taken: near Cadiz - Date received: 19 Jan 1813 - From what ship: HM Brig Rebuff - Discharged on 19 Feb 1813 - How discharged: HM Sloop Dauntless.

Robinson, Henry - Seaman - Number: 608 - How taken: HM Ship-of-the-Line Berwick - Date taken: 28 May 1813 - Where taken: Mahon (Island of Minorca) - Date received: 1 Jul 1813 - From what ship: HMT Royal Boston No. 344 - Discharged on 12 Jul 1813 - How discharged: HM Sloop Bacchus.

Robinson, John - Seaman - Number: 197 - Prize name: Meser - Ship type: MV - How taken: Not mentioned - Where taken: Unknown - Discharged on 13 Nov 1813 - How discharged: Being a licensed vessel.

Robinson, John - Seaman - Number: 718 - Prize name: America - Ship type: MV - Discharged on Aug 1813 - How discharged: HM Ship-of-the-Line Achille.

Robinson, William - Seaman - Number: 344 - Prize name: Pallas - Ship type: MV - How taken: HM Brig Rebuff - Date taken: 24 Dec 1812 - Where taken: near Cadiz - Date received: 19 Jan 1813 - From what ship: HM Brig Rebuff - Discharged on 19 Feb 1813 - How discharged: HM Sloop Dauntless.

Roderecus, R. - Seaman - Number: 247 - Prize name: Conde Mary - Ship type: MV - How taken: HM Ship-of-the-Line Grampus - Date taken: 24 Oct 1812 - Where taken: On passage to Cadiz - Date received: 21 Nov 1812 - From what ship: HM Ship-of-the-Line Grampus - Discharged on 31 Dec 1812 - How discharged: Being a licensed vessel.

Roding, Abraham - Seaman - Number: 449 - Prize name: John Buckley - Ship type: MV - How taken: HMT Druid - Date taken: 21 Feb 1813 - Where taken: near Lisbon - Date received: 7 Mar 1813 - From what ship: HMT Pererserance - Discharged on 10 Apr 1813 - How discharged: Being a licensed vessel.

Roebuck, John - Seaman - Number: 88 - Prize name: Louisa - Ship type: MV - How taken: HM Brig Columbine - Date taken: 16 Aug 1812 - Where taken: near Cadiz - Date received: 31 Aug 1813 - From what ship: HM Frigate Argo - Discharged on 15 Nov 1812 - How discharged: Being a licensed vessel.

Rogers, John - Mate - Number: 478 - Prize name: S. Crew Packet - Discharged on 22 Mar 1813 - How discharged: Being a licensed vessel.

Rogers, Jonathan - Seaman - Number: 453 - Prize name: John Buckley - Ship type: MV - How taken: HMT Druid - Date taken: 21 Feb 1813 - Where taken: near Lisbon - Date received: 7 Mar 1813 - From what ship: HMT Pererserance - Discharged on 10 Apr 1813 - How discharged: Being a licensed vessel.

Rose, Andrew - Seaman - Number: 242 - Prize name: Conde Mary - Ship type: MV - How taken: HM Ship-of-the-Line Grampus - Date taken: 24 Oct 1812 - Where taken: On passage to Cadiz - Date received: 21 Nov 1812 - From what ship: HM Ship-of-the-Line Grampus - Discharged on 31 Dec 1812 - How discharged: Being a licensed vessel.

Rose, Stanley - Seaman - Number: 331 - Prize name: San Juan - Ship type: MV - Discharged on 20 Jan 1813 - How discharged: Being a licensed vessel.

Rosenby, Magnus - Number: 461 - Discharged on 15 Mar 1813 - How discharged: Being a licensed vessel.

Ross, Philip - Seaman - Number: 541 - Prize name: Isabella - Ship type: MV - How taken: HM Brig Zenoha - Date taken: 27 Jun 1813 - Where taken: off Cape St. Mary (Portugal) - Date received: 1 Jul 1813 - From what ship: HM Brig Protection - Discharged on 4 Sep 1813 - How discharged: HM Brig Teazer.

Row, Simon - Seaman - Number: 491 - How taken: Gave himself up from HM Ship-of-the-Line Malta - Date taken: 2 Jan 1813 - Where taken: Gibraltar - Date received: 9 Apr 1813 - From what ship: HM Bomb Vessel Strombolo - Discharged on 23 Apr 1813 - How discharged: HM Sloop Helena.

Rush, Laten (see prisoner number 383) - Seaman - Number: 4 - Prize name: Margaret - Ship type: MV - How taken: HM Ship-of-the-Line San Juan - Date taken: 10 Aug 1812 - Where taken: Gibraltar Bay - Date received: 12 Aug 1812 - From what ship: Margaret.

Rush, Laten - Seaman - Number: 383 - How taken: Taken up in Gibraltar - Date taken: 4 Feb 1813 - Date received: 4 Feb 1813 - Discharged on 18 Feb 1813 - How discharged: Being a licensed vessel.

Russell, Henry - Seaman - Number: 196 - Prize name: Meser - Ship type: MV - How taken: Not mentioned - Where taken: Unknown - Discharged on 13 Nov 1813 - How discharged: Being a licensed vessel.

Russel, Thomas - Boy - Number: 71 - Prize name: Albion - Ship type: MV - How ltaken: HM Frigate Cossack - Date taken: 8 Aug 1812 - Where taken: Cape Spartel (Morocco) - Date received: 21 Aug 1812 - From what ship: HM Brig Rebuff - Discharged on 3 Nov 1812 - How discharged: Being a licensed vessel.

Rust, Zebulun - Seaman - Number: 81 - Prize name: Eliza - Ship type: MV - How taken: HM Sloop Hyacinth and HM Frigate Argo - Date taken: 27 Aug 1812 - Where taken: Straits of Gibraltar - Date received: 30 Aug 1812 - From what ship: HM Frigate Argo - Discharged on 22 Jan 1813 - How discharged: HM Sloop Comet.

Ryercraft, William - Seaman - Number: 232 - Prize name: Julian Mary - Ship type: MV - How taken: HM Ship-of-the-Line Grampus - Date taken: 21 Oct 1812 - Where taken: On passage to Cadiz - Date received: 21 Nov 1812 - From what ship: HM Ship-of-the-Line Grampus - Discharged on 14 Dec 1812 - How discharged: Being a licensed vessel.

Saffion, John - Seaman - Number: 444 - Prize name: Catharine - Ship type: MV - How taken: HMT Druid - Date taken: 21 Feb 1813 - Where taken: near Lisbon - Date received: 5 Mar 1813 - From what ship: HMT Pererserance - Discharged on 10 Apr 1813 - How discharged: Being a licensed vessel.

Salis, Peter - Seaman - Number: 634 - How taken: HM Ship-of-the-Line Prince of Wales - Date taken: 28 May 1813 - Where taken: Mahon (Island of Minorca) - Date received: 1 Jul 1813 - From what ship: HMT Royal Boston No. 344 - Discharged on 12 Jul 1813 - How discharged: HM Sloop Bacchus.

Salkor, Abel - Seaman - Number: 563 - Prize name: Hendosten - Ship type: MV - How taken: Gave himself up from HM Corvette Scipio - Date taken: 28 May 1813 - Where taken: Mahon (Island of Minorca) - Date received: 1 Jul 1813 - From what ship: HMT Royal Boston No. 344 - Discharged on 3 Jul 1813 - How discharged: HM Frigate Thames.

Samuels, Samuel - Seaman - Number: 472 - Prize name: Amphitrite - Ship type: MV - How taken: HM Ketch Gleamer - Date taken: 27 Feb 1813 - Where taken: Bay of Biscay - Date received: 8 Mar 1813 - From what ship: HM Ketch Gleamer - Discharged on 5 Apr 1813 - How discharged: HM Frigate Ethalion.

Sarouna, Charles - Seaman - Number: 147 - Prize name: Commerce - Ship type: MV - How taken: HM Brig Desperate - Date taken: 22 Aug 1812 - Where taken: near Cadiz - Discharged on 28 Jan 1813 - How discharged: Being a licensed vessel.

Saunders, Elijah - Seaman - Number: 701 - Prize name: La Guera - Ship type: MV - How taken: Sophia, Letter of Marque - Date taken: 25 Jun 1813 - Where taken: near Lisbon - Date received: 2 Jul 1813 - From what ship: HM Brig Protector.

Saunders, Richard - Mate - Number: 248 - Prize name: Apollo - Ship type: MV - How taken: HM Ship-of-the-Line Grampus - Date taken: 29 Oct 1812 - Where taken: On passage to Cadiz - Date received: 21 Nov 1812 - From what ship: HM Ship-of-the-Line Grampus - Discharged on 31 Dec 1812 - How discharged: Being a licensed vessel.

Saverick, John - Seaman - Number: 546 - Prize name: Isabella - Ship type: MV - How taken: HM Brig Zenoha - Date taken: 27 Jun 1813 - Where taken: off Cape St. Mary (Portugal) - Date received: 1 Jul 1813 - From what ship: HM Brig Protection - Discharged on 7 Oct 1813 - How discharged: Isabella.

Scauk, William - Seaman - Number: 598 - How taken: HM Frigate Bombay - Date taken: 28 May 1813 - Where taken: Mahon (Island of Minorca) - Date received: 1 Jul 1813 - From what ship: HMT Royal Boston No. 344 - Discharged on 3 Jul 1813 - How discharged: HM Frigate Thames.

Schnider, John - Seaman - Number: 300 - Prize name: Concordia - Ship type: MV - How taken: HM Brig Basilisk - Date taken: 6 Jan 1813 - Where taken: near Cadiz - Date received: 12 Jan 1813 - From what ship: HM Brig Basilisk - Discharged on 14 Apr 1813 - How discharged: Being a licensed vessel.

Scott, William - Number: 649 - How taken: Taken off the HMS Tarmedor - Discharged on 28 Jun 1813 - How discharged: HMT Minstraele.

Sears, Isaac - Seaman - Number: 549 - Prize name: Isabella - Ship type: MV - How taken: HM Brig Zenoha - Date taken: 27 Jun 1813 - Where taken: off Cape St. Mary (Portugal) - Date received: 1 Jul 1813 - From what ship: HM Brig Protection - Discharged on 7 Oct 1813 - How discharged: Isabella.

Sebastian, Joseph - Boy - Number: 131 - Prize name: Eliza - Ship type: MV - How taken: HM Sloop Hyacinth and HM Frigate Argo - Date taken: 27 Aug 1812 - Where taken: Straits of Gibraltar - Date received: Returned to ship on 1 Sep 1812 - Discharged on 22 Jan 1813 - How discharged: HM Sloop Comet.

Sentar, Noah - Seaman - Number: 769 - Prize name: Adeline - Ship type: LM - How taken: HM Frigate Magiciene - Date taken: 14 Mar 1814 - Where taken: at sea - Date received: 14 Apr 1814 - From what ship: HM Frigate Magiciene - Discharged on 29 Apr 1814 - How discharged: HM Store Ship Hindostan.

Severleach, Anthony - Seaman - Number: 425 - Prize name: Mark & Abigail - Ship type: MV - How taken: HM Brig Basilisk - Date taken: 9 Jan 1813 - Where taken: off Cape St. Vincent (Portugal) - Date received: 19 Feb 1813 - From what ship: HM Gunboat No. 22 - Discharged on 16 Apr 1813 - How discharged: Being a licensed vessel.

Seville, Robert - 2nd Mate - Number: 121 - Prize name: Albion - Ship type: MV - How taken: HM Frigate Cossack - Date taken: 8 Aug 1812 - Where taken: Cape Spartel (Morocco) - Date received: Returned to ship on 24 Aug 1812 - Discharged on 3 Nov 1812 - How discharged: Being a licensed vessel.

Seymore, Samuel - Seaman - Number: 303 - Prize name: Concordia - Ship type: MV - How taken: HM Brig Basilisk - Date taken: 6 Jan 1813 - Where taken: near Cadiz - Date received: 12 Jan 1813 - From what ship: HM Brig Basilisk - Discharged on 14 Apr 1813 - How discharged: Being a licensed vessel.

Shairs, Samuel - Seaman - Number: 464 - Prize name: Amphitrite - Ship type: MV - From what ship: Amphitrite - Discharged on 19 Mar 1813 - How discharged: HM Schooner Sylvia.

Sharpe, George - Seaman - Number: 67 - Prize name: Albion - Ship type: MV - How taken: HM Frigate Cossack - Date taken: 8 Aug 1812 - Where taken: Cape Spartel (Morocco) - Date received: 21 Aug 1812 - From what ship: HM Brig Rebuff - Discharged on 3 Nov 1812 - How discharged: Being a licensed vessel.

Shaw, Daniel - Mate - Number: 288 - Prize name: George & Albert - Ship type: MV - How taken: HMS Myrtle - Date taken: 5 Jan 1813 - Where taken: off Cape St. Mary (Portugal) - Date received: 10 Jan 1813 - From what ship: HMS Myrtle - Discharged on 14 Apr 1813 - How discharged: Being a licensed vessel.

Sheas, Jonathan - Number: 457 - Discharged on 15 Mar 1813 - How discharged: Being a licensed vessel.

Shepherd, Thomas - Seaman - Number: 521 - Prize name: Tyber - Ship type: MV - How taken: HM Sloop Comet - Date taken: 6 Jun 1813 - Where taken: near Lisbon - Date received: 15 Jun 1813 - From what ship: HM Ship-of-Line San Josef.

Sheppard, James - Seaman - Number: 613 - How taken: HM Ship-of-the-Line Royal George - Date taken: 28 May 1813 - Where taken: Mahon (Island of Minorca) - Date received: 1 Jul 1813 - From what ship: HMT Royal Boston No. 344 - Discharged on 24 Jul 1813 - How discharged: HM Store Ship Tortoise.

Sheridan, Henry - Seaman - Number: 583 - Where taken: Mahon (Island of Minorca) - Date received: 1 Jul 1813 - From what ship: HMT Royal Boston No. 344 - Discharged on Aug 1813 - How discharged: HM Ship-of-the-Line Achille.

Shrine, Edward - Master - Number: 182 - Prize name: Draper - Ship type: MV - How taken: HM Brig Fearly - Date taken: 18 Sep 1812 - Where taken: near Cadiz - Date received: 22 Nov 1812 - From what ship: Draper - Discharged on 8 Feb 1813.

Silbey, James (see prisoner number 98) - Master - Number: 1 - Prize name: Margaret - Ship type: MV - How taken: HM Ship-of-the-Line San Juan - Date taken: 10 Aug 1812 - Where taken: Gibraltar Bay - Date received: 12 Aug 1812 - From what ship: Margaret - Discharged on 15 Jan 1813 - How discharged: HM Brig Derwent.

Silbey, James - Master - Number: 98 - Prize name: Margaret - Ship type: MV - How taken: HM Brig Papillion - Date taken: 10 Aug 1812 - Where taken: Gibraltar Bay - Date received: 2 Sep 1813 - From what ship: HM Ship-of-the-Line Tremendous.

Silvy, John - Seaman - Number: 358 - Prize name: Thomas Wilson - Ship type: MV - How taken: HM Sloop Comet - Date taken: 14 Jan 1813 - Where taken: near Cadiz - Discharged on 18 Feb 1813 - How discharged: Being a licensed vessel.

Simmonds, William - Seaman - Number: 509 - How taken: Gave himself up from HM Ship-of-the-Line Fame and HM Brig Philomel - Date taken: 2 Jan 1813 - Where taken: Gibraltar - Date received: 20 May 1813 - From what ship: HMS Ephegema - Discharged on 22 May 1813 - How discharged: HM Brig Zephyr.

Sims, Clement - Seaman - Number: 396 - How taken: Gave himself up from HM Frigate Mermaid - Date taken: 11 Feb 1813 - Where taken: Gibraltar - Date received: 12 Feb 1813 - From what ship: HM Frigate Mermaid - Discharged on 6 Mar 1813 - How discharged: HM Ship-of-the-Line Blake.

Sirucus, William (alias Sims) - Seaman - Number: 603 - How taken: HM Ship-of-the-Line Berwick - Date taken: 28 May 1813 - Where taken: Mahon (Island of Minorca) - Date received: 1 Jul 1813 - From what ship: HMT Royal Boston No. 344 - Discharged on 12 Jul 1813 - How discharged: HM Sloop Bacchus.

Skinner, Johnston - Master - Number: 210 - Prize name: Dolphin - Ship type: MV - How taken: HM Ship-of-the-Line Invincible - Date taken: 24 Aug 1812 - Where taken: Meg'n (Unknown) - Date received: 22 Nov 1812 - From what ship: Dolphin - Discharged on 25 Jan 1813 - How discharged: HM Ship-of-the-Line Sultan.

Small, Enoch - Seaman - Number: 540 - Prize name: Isabella - Ship type: MV - How taken: HM Brig Zenoha - Date taken: 27 Jun 1813 - Where taken: off Cape St. Mary (Portugal) - Date received: 1 Jul 1813 - From what ship: HM Brig Protection - Discharged on 4 Sep 1813 - How discharged: HM Brig Teazer.

Smith, George - Seaman - Number: 195 - Prize name: Meser - Ship type: MV - How taken: Not mentioned - Where taken: Unknown - Discharged on 13 Nov 1813 - How discharged: Being a licensed vessel.

Smith, George - Seaman - Number: 348 - Prize name: Pallas - Ship type: MV - How taken: HM Brig Rebuff - Date taken: 24 Dec 1812 - Where taken: near Cadiz - Date received: 19 Jan 1813 - From what ship: HM Brig Rebuff - Discharged on 19 Feb 1813 - How discharged: HM Brig Protector.

Smith, George - Seaman - Number: 366 - Prize name: Mentor - Ship type: MV - How taken: HM Brig Columbine - Date taken: 13 Jan 1813 - Where taken: near Cadiz - Date received: 22 Jan 1813 - From what ship: HM Sloop Comet - Discharged on 14 Apr 1813 - How discharged: Being a licensed vessel.

Smith, Henry - Seaman - Number: 711 - Discharged on Aug 1813 - How discharged: HM Ship-of-the-Line Achille.

Smith, Jacob - Number: 462 - Discharged on 15 Mar 1813 - How discharged: Being a licensed vessel.

Smith, Jacob (see prisoner number 188) - Seaman - Number: 176 - Prize name: Sally - Ship type: MV - How taken: Not mentioned - Date taken: 22 Aug 1812 - Discharged on 28 Jan 1813 - How discharged: Being an Englishman.

Smith, Jacob - Seaman - Number: 188 - Prize name: Sally - Ship type: MV.

Smith, James - Number: 644 - How taken: Taken off the HM Battery Gorgon - Discharged on 28 Jun 1813 - How discharged: HMT Minstraele.

Smith, James - Seaman - Number: 76 - Prize name: Pallas - Ship type: MV - How taken: HM Brig Papillion - Date taken: 7 Aug 1812 - Where taken: off Sanlucar (Spain) - Date received: 26 Aug 1812 - From what ship: HMS Lavinia - Discharged on 22 Jan 1813 - How discharged: HM Sloop Comet.

Smith, John - Seaman - Number: 630 - How taken: HM Ship-of-the-Line Prince of Wales - Date taken: 28 May 1813 - Where taken: Mahon (Island of Minorca) - Date received: 1 Jul 1813 - From what ship: HMT Royal Boston No. 344 - Discharged on 3 Jul 1813 - How discharged: HM Frigate Thames.

Smith, John - Seaman - Number: 733 - Prize name: Engenia - Ship type: MV - How taken: HM Brig Papillion - Date taken: 17 Jul 1813 - Where taken: near Cadiz - Date received: 10 Aug 1813 - From what ship: Eugenia Brig - Discharged on 7 Oct 1813 - How discharged: Eugenia.

Smith, John - Seaman - Number: 479 - Discharged on 22 Mar 1813 - How discharged: Being a licensed vessel.

Smith, John - Seaman - Number: 33 - Prize name: Allegany - Ship type: MV - How taken: HM Ship-of-the-Line San Juan - Date taken: 10 Aug 1812 - Where taken: Gibraltar Bay - Date received: 12 Aug 1812 - From what ship: Allegany - Discharged on 15 Jan 1813 - How discharged: HM Brig Derwent.

Smith, John - Seaman - Number: 427 - Prize name: Mark & Abigail - Ship type: MV - How taken: HM Brig Basilisk - Date taken: 9 Jan 1813 - Where taken: off Cape St. Vincent (Portugal) - Date received: 19 Feb 1813 - From what ship: HM Gunboat No. 22 - Discharged on 16 Apr 1813 - How discharged: Being a licensed vessel.

Smith, Obadiah - Seaman - Number: 32 - Prize name: Allegany - Ship type: MV - How taken: HM Ship-of-the-Line San Juan - Date taken: 10 Aug 1812 - Where taken: Gibraltar Bay - Date received: 12 Aug 1812 - From what ship: Allegany - Discharged on 15 Jan 1813 - How discharged: HM Brig Derwent.

Smith, Thomas - Seaman - Number: 90 - Prize name: Louisa - Ship type: MV - How taken: HM Brig Columbine - Date taken: 16 Aug 1812 - Where taken: near Cadiz - Date received: 31 Aug 1813 - From what ship: HM Frigate Argo - Discharged on 15 Nov 1812 - How discharged: Being a licensed vessel.

Smith, Thomas - Seaman - Number: 306 - Prize name: Eliza - Ship type: MV - How taken: HM Brig Basilisk - Date taken: 6 Jan 1813 - Where taken: near Cadiz - Date received: 12 Jan 1813 - From what ship: HM Brig Basilisk - Discharged on 14 Apr 1813 - How discharged: Being a licensed vessel.

Smith, William - Seaman - Number: 283 - Prize name: Maria - Ship type: MV - Discharged on 18 Dec 1812.

Smith, William - Seaman - Number: 309 - Prize name: Eliza - Ship type: MV - How taken: HM Brig Basilisk - Date taken: 6 Jan 1813 - Where taken: near Cadiz - Date received: 12 Jan 1813 - From what ship: HM Brig Basilisk - Discharged on 6 Mar 1813 - How discharged: HM Ship-of-the-Line Blake.

Snow, Joseph (see prisoner number 108) - Mate - Number: 44 - Prize name: Tiger - Ship type: MV - How taken: HM Ship-of-the-Line San Juan - Date taken: 10 Aug 1812 - Where taken: Gibraltar Bay - Date received: 12 Aug 1812 - From what ship: Tiger - Discharged on 15 Jan 1813 - How discharged: HM Frigate Andromeda.

Snow, Joseph - Mate - Number: 108 - Prize name: Tiger - Ship type: MV - How taken: HM Ship-of-the-Line San Juan - Date taken: 10 Aug 1812 - Where taken: Gibraltar Bay - Date received: 2 Sep 1813 - From what ship: HM Ship-of-the-Line Tremendous.

Sole, Edward - Seaman - Number: 765 - Prize name: Adeline - Ship type: LM - How taken: HM Frigate Magiciene - Date taken: 14 Mar 1814 - Where taken: at sea - Date received: 14 Apr 1814 - From what ship: HM Frigate Magiciene - Discharged on 22 Apr 1814 - How discharged: HM Store Ship Tortoise.

Sole, Elias - Seaman - Number: 768 - Prize name: Adeline - Ship type: LM - How taken: HM Frigate Magiciene - Date taken: 14 Mar 1814 - Where taken: at sea - Date received: 14 Apr 1814 - From what ship: HM Frigate Magiciene - Discharged on 22 Apr 1814 - How discharged: HM Store Ship Tortoise.

Sole, Thomas - Seaman - Number: 773 - Prize name: Adeline - Ship type: LM - How taken: HM Frigate Magiciene - Date taken: 14 Mar 1814 - Where taken: at sea - Date received: 14 Apr 1814 - From what ship: HM Frigate Magiciene - Discharged on 22 Apr 1814 - How discharged: HM Store Ship Tortoise.

Solley, William - Seaman - Number: 368 - Prize name: Mentor - Ship type: MV - How taken: HM Brig Columbine - Date taken: 13 Jan 1813 - Where taken: near Cadiz - Date received: 22 Jan 1813 - From what ship: HM Sloop Comet - Discharged on 14 Apr 1813 - How discharged: Being a licensed vessel.

Somerville, Charles - Seaman - Number: 408 - Prize name: Thrasher - Ship type: MV - How taken: HM Frigate Magiciene - Date taken: 17 Jan 1813 - Where taken: Western Isles - Date received: 14 Feb 1813 - From what ship: Thrasher - Discharged on 19 Mar 1813 - How discharged: Being a licensed vessel.

Soutter, John - Seaman - Number: 562 - Prize name: Hendosten - Ship type: MV - How taken: Gave himself up from HM Corvette Scipio - Date taken: 28 May 1813 - Where taken: Mahon (Island of Minorca) - Date received: 1 Jul 1813 - From what ship: HMT Royal Boston No. 344 - Discharged on 1 Jul 1813 - How discharged: HM Brig Protector for England.

Sparkes, Samuel - Seaman - Number: 748 - Prize name: Mary English - Ship type: MV - How taken: HM Post Ship Crocodile - Date taken: 6 Aug 1813 - Where taken: off Cape Finisterre (Spain) - Date received: 8 Dec 1813 - From what ship: HMS Brig Desperate - Discharged on 7 Feb 1814 - How discharged: HMT Fanny No. 186.

Spear, Francis - Seaman - Number: 412 - Prize name: Thomas Wilson - Ship type: MV - How taken: HM Sloop Comet - Date taken: 14 Jan 1813 - Where taken: near Cadiz - Date received: 18 Feb 1813 - From what ship: HM Brig Charger - Discharged on 10 Apr 1813 - How discharged: Being a licensed vessel.

Stanley, Timothy - Seaman - Number: 441 - Prize name: Catharine - Ship type: MV - How taken: HMT Druid - Date taken: 21 Feb 1813 - Where taken: near Lisbon - Date received: 5 Mar 1813 - From what ship: HMT Pererserance - Discharged on 10 Apr 1813 - How discharged: Being a licensed vessel.

Stanwood, Wenthoop - Mate - Number: 363 - Prize name: George - Ship type: MV - How taken: HM Brig Columbine - Date taken: 13 Jan 1813 - Where taken: off Lisbon - Date received: 22 Jan 1813 - From what ship: HM Sloop Comet - Discharged on 15 Apr 1813 - How discharged: Being a licensed vessel.

Starbord, John - Seaman - Number: 20 - Prize name: Horace - Ship type: MV - How taken: HM Ship-of-the-Line San Juan - Date taken: 10 Aug 1812 - Where taken: Gibraltar Bay - Date received: 12 Aug 1812 - From what ship: Horace - Discharged on 29 Aug 1812 - How discharged: Being a licensed vessel.

Stegman, Christopher - Seaman - Number: 699 - Prize name: Hendosten - Ship type: MV - How taken: HM Brig Zenoha - Date taken: 25 Jun 1813 - Where taken: near Lisbon - Date received: 2 Jul 1813 - From what ship: HM Brig Protector - Discharged on 22 Aug 1813 - How discharged: HM Brig Imogen.

Stephenson, J, - Seaman - Number: 199 - Prize name: Meser - Ship type: MV - How taken: Not mentioned - Where taken: Unknown - Discharged on 13 Nov 1813 - How discharged: Being a licensed vessel.

Stephenson, Levy - Seaman - Number: 624 - How taken: HM Ship-of-the-Line Prince of Wales - Date taken: 28 May 1813 - Where taken: Mahon (Island of Minorca) - Date received: 1 Jul 1813 - From what ship: HMT Royal Boston No. 344 - Discharged on 3 Jul 1813 - How discharged: HM Frigate Thames.

Stetson, Daniel - Seaman - Number: 436 - Prize name: Essex - Ship type: MV - How taken: HM Gunboat No. 22 - Date taken: 12 Jan 1813 - Where taken: near Cadiz - Date received: 5 Mar 1813 - From what ship: Essex Prize - Discharged on 16 Apr 1813 - How discharged: Being a licensed vessel.

Steward, Henry - Seaman - Number: 466 - Prize name: Amphitrite - Ship type: MV - How taken: HM Ketch Gleamer - Date taken: 27 Feb 1813 - Where taken: Bay of Biscay - Date received: 8 Mar 1813 - From what ship: HM Ketch Gleamer - Discharged on 5 Apr 1813 - How discharged: HM Frigate Ethalion.

Steward, John - Seaman - Number: 492 - How taken: Gave himself up from HM Ship-of-the-Line Malta - Date taken: 2 Jan 1813 - Where taken: Gibraltar - Date received: 9 Apr 1813 - From what ship: HM Bomb Vessel Strombolo - Discharged on 23 Apr 1813 - How discharged: HM Sloop Helena.

Stone, Henry - Seaman - Number: 642 - How taken: HM Ship-of-the-Line Prince of Wales - Date taken: 28 May 1813 - Where taken: Mahon (Island of Minorca) - Date received: 1 Jul 1813 - From what ship: HMT Royal Boston No. 344 - Discharged on 23 Jul 1813 - How discharged: HM Frigate Unicorn.

Stone, John - 2nd Mate - Number: 772 - Prize name: Adeline - Ship type: LM - How taken: HM Frigate Magiciene - Date taken: 14 Mar 1814 - Where taken: at sea - Date received: 14 Apr 1814 - From what ship: HM Frigate Magiciene - Discharged on 22 Apr 1814 - How discharged: HM Store Ship Tortoise.

Storm, John - Seaman - Number: 410 - Prize name: Thomas Wilson - Ship type: MV - How taken: HM Sloop Comet - Date taken: 14 Jan 1813 - Where taken: near Cadiz - Date received: 18 Feb 1813 - From what ship: HM Brig Charger - Discharged on 10 Apr 1813 - How discharged: Being a licensed vessel.

Stow, Jeremiah - Seaman - Number: 355 - Prize name: Pallas - Ship type: MV - How taken: Gave himself up at Gibraltar - Date taken: 20 Jan 1813 - Date received: 20 Jan 1813 - From what ship: HMS Leyden - Discharged on 19 Feb 1813 - How discharged: HM Brig Protector.

Styles, Israel - Seaman - Number: 517 - Prize name: John Barnes - Ship type: MV - How taken: HM Sloop Comet - Date taken: 14 May 1813 - Where taken: near Lisbon - Date received: 15 Jun 1813 - From what ship: HM Ship-of-Line San Josef - Discharged on 1 Jul 1813 - How discharged: HM Brig Protector for England.

Summers, Arthur - Seaman - Number: 302 - Prize name: Concordia - Ship type: MV - How taken: HM Brig Basilisk - Date taken: 6 Jan 1813 - Where taken: near Cadiz - Date received: 12 Jan 1813 - From what ship: HM Brig Basilisk - Discharged on 14 Apr 1813 - How discharged: Being a licensed vessel.

Swan, Peter - Seaman - Number: 450 - Prize name: John Buckley - Ship type: MV - How taken: HMT Druid - Date taken: 21 Feb 1813 - Where taken: near Lisbon - Date received: 7 Mar 1813 - From what ship: HMT Pererserance - Discharged on 10 Apr 1813 - How discharged: Being a licensed vessel.

Taggart, John - Seaman - Number: 771 - Prize name: Adeline - Ship type: LM - How taken: HM Frigate Magiciene - Date taken: 14 Mar 1814 - Where taken: at sea - Date received: 14 Apr 1814 - From what ship: HM Frigate Magiciene - Discharged on 22 Apr 1814 - How discharged: HM Store Ship Tortoise.

Talbot, Joseph - Seaman - Number: 320 - Prize name: Eliza - Ship type: MV - How taken: HM Brig Basilisk - Date taken: 6 Jan 1813 - Where taken: near Cadiz - Date received: 12 Jan 1813 - From what ship: HM Brig Basilisk - Discharged on 14 Apr 1813 - How discharged: Being a licensed vessel.

Tatem, George W. - 1st Mate - Number: 778 - Prize name: Adeline - Ship type: LM - How taken: HM Frigate Magiciene - Date taken: 14 Mar 1814 - Where taken: at sea - Date received: 14 Apr 1814 - From what ship: HM Frigate Magiciene - Discharged on 29 Apr 1814 - How discharged: HM Store Ship Hindostan.

Taylor, George - Seaman - Number: 451 - Prize name: John Buckley - Ship type: MV - How taken: HMT Druid - Date taken: 21 Feb 1813 - Where taken: near Lisbon - Date received: 7 Mar 1813 - From what ship: HMT Pererserance - Discharged on 10 Apr 1813 - How discharged: Being a licensed vessel.

Taylor, William - Seaman - Number: 599 - How taken: HM Frigate Bombay - Date taken: 28 May 1813 - Where taken: Mahon (Island of Minorca) - Date received: 1 Jul 1813 - From what ship: HMT Royal Boston No. 344 - Discharged on 12 Jul 1813 - How discharged: HM Sloop Bacchus.

Thayer, Abner - Seaman - Number: 86 - Prize name: Louisa - Ship type: MV - How taken: HM Brig Columbine - Date taken: 16 Aug 1812 - Where taken: near Cadiz - Date received: 31 Aug 1813 - From what ship: HM Frigate Argo - Discharged on 15 Nov 1812 - How discharged: Being a licensed vessel.

Thayer, James - Seaman - Number: 640 - How taken: HM Ship-of-the-Line Prince of Wales - Date taken: 28 May 1813 - Where taken: Mahon (Island of Minorca) - Date received: 1 Jul 1813 - From what ship: HMT Royal Boston No. 344 - Discharged on 23 Jul 1813 - How discharged: HM Frigate Unicorn.

Thomas, Charles - Seaman - Number: 399 - How taken: Gave himself up from HM Frigate Franchise - Date taken: 12 Feb 1812 - Where taken: Gibraltar - Date received: 13 Feb 1813 - From what ship: HM Frigate Franchise - Discharged on 6 Mar 1813 - How discharged: HM Ship-of-the-Line Blake.

Thomas, J. - Seaman - Number: 387 - Prize name: Veroni - Ship type: MV - How taken: HM Sloop Comet - Date taken: 14 Jan 1813 - Where taken: near Cadiz - Date received: 8 Feb 1813 - From what ship: HMS Brig Desperate - Discharged on 14 Apr 1813 - How discharged: Being a licensed vessel.

Thomas, James - Seaman - Number: 775 - Prize name: Adeline - Ship type: LM - How taken: HM Frigate Magiciene - Date taken: 14 Mar 1814 - Where taken: at sea - Date received: 14 Apr 1814 - From what ship: HM Frigate Magiciene - Discharged on 24 Apr 1814.

Thomas, John - Seaman - Number: 520 - Prize name: Tyber - Ship type: MV - How taken: HM Sloop Comet - Date taken: 6 Jun 1813 - Where taken: near Lisbon - Date received: 15 Jun 1813 - From what ship: HM Ship-of-Line San Josef.

Thomas, John (see prisoner number 623) - Seaman - Number: 559 - Prize name: Hendosten - Ship type: MV - How taken: Gave himself up from HM Corvette Scipio - Date taken: 28 May 1813 - Where taken: Mahon (Island of Minorca) - Date received: 1 Jul 1813 - From what ship: HMT Royal Boston No. 344 - Discharged on 3 Jul 1813 - How discharged: HM Frigate Thames.

Thomas, John - Seaman - Number: 623 - How taken: HM Ship-of-the-Line Prince of Wales - Date taken: 28 May 1813 - Where taken: Mahon (Island of Minorca) - Date received: 1 Jul 1813 - From what ship: HMT Royal Boston No. 344 - Discharged on 12 Jul 1813 - How discharged: HM Sloop Bacchus.

Thomas, Moses - Seaman - Number: 706 - Discharged on Aug 1813 - How discharged: HM Ship-of-the-Line Achille.

Thomas, Stephen - Seaman - Number: 770 - Prize name: Adeline - Ship type: LM - How taken: HM Frigate Magiciene - Date taken: 14 Mar 1814 - Where taken: at sea - Date received: 14 Apr 1814 - From what ship: HM Frigate Magiciene - Discharged on 22 Apr 1814 - How discharged: HM Store Ship Tortoise.

Thomas, William - Seaman - Number: 424 - Prize name: Mark & Abigail - Ship type: MV - How taken: HM Brig Basilisk - Date taken: 9 Jan 1813 - Where taken: off Cape St. Vincent (Portugal) - Date received: 19 Feb 1813 - From what ship: HM Gunboat No. 22 - Discharged on 16 Apr 1813 - How discharged: Being a licensed vessel.

Thompson, James - Seaman - Number: 679 - How taken: HM Brig Shearwater - Date taken: 3 Jun 1813 - Where taken: Mahon (Island of Minorca) - Date received: 1 Jul 1813 - Discharged on 3 Jul 1813 - How discharged: HM Frigate Thames.

Thompson, John - Cook - Number: 213 - Prize name: Dolphin - Ship type: MV - How taken: HM Ship-of-the-Line Invincible - Date taken: 24 Aug 1812 - Where taken: not readable - Date received: 22 Nov 1812 - From what ship: Dolphin - Discharged on 25 Jan 1813 - How discharged: HM Ship-of-the-Line Sultan.

Thompson, Robert - Seaman - Number: 667 - How taken: HM Ship-of-the-Line Aboukir - Date received: 1 Jul 1813 - From what ship: HMT Royal Boston No. 344 - Discharged on 12 Jul 1813 - How discharged: HM Sloop Bacchus.

Thompson, William - Seaman - Number: 404 - How taken: Gave himself up from HM Frigate Franchise - Date taken: 12 Feb 1812 - Where taken: Gibraltar - Date received: 13 Feb 1813 - From what ship: HM Frigate Franchise - Discharged on 6 Mar 1813 - How discharged: HM Ship-of-the-Line Blake.

Thornton, David (see prisoner number 527) - Seaman - Number: 524 - Prize name: Sampson - Ship type: MV - Discharged on 26 Jul 1813 - How discharged: HM Store Ship Weymouth.

Thornton, David - Number: 527 - Prize name: Sampson - Ship type: MV - Discharged on Aug 1813 - How discharged: HM Ship-of-the-Line Achille.

Thoroughgood, Anthony - Seaman - Number: 370 - Prize name: Mentor - Ship type: MV - How taken: HM Brig Columbine - Date taken: 13 Jan 1813 - Where taken: off Lisbon - Date received: 22 Jan 1813 - From what ship: HM Sloop Comet - Discharged on 14 Apr 1813 - How discharged: Being a licensed vessel.

Till, Samuel - Seaman - Number: 476 - Prize name: John Buckley - Ship type: MV - How taken: HMT Druid - Date taken: 21 Feb 1813 - Where taken: near Lisbon - Date received: 8 Mar 1813 - From what ship: HM Ketch Gleamer - Discharged on 10 Apr 1813 - How discharged: Being a licensed vessel.

Tombolin, Thomas - Seaman - Number: 515 - Prize name: John Barnes - Ship type: MV - How taken: HM Sloop Comet - Date taken: 14 May 1813 - Where taken: near Lisbon - Date received: 15 Jun 1813 - From what ship: HM Ship-of-Line San Josef.

Toole, Gannet - Seaman - Number: 717 - Prize name: America - Ship type: MV - Discharged on Aug 1813 - How discharged: HM Ship-of-the-Line Achille.

Traphagn, Peter - Seaman - Number: 566 - Date received: 1 Jul 1813 - From what ship: HMT Royal Boston No. 344 - Discharged on 28 Jun 1813 - How discharged: HMT Minstraele.

Tronia, Richard - Seaman - Number: 192 - Prize name: Meser - Ship type: MV - How taken: Not mentioned - Where taken: Unknown - Discharged on 13 Nov 1813 - How discharged: Being a licensed vessel.

Tucker, Arthur - Seaman - Number: 23 - Prize name: Horace - Ship type: MV - How taken: HM Ship-of-the-Line San Juan - Date taken: 10 Aug 1812 - Where taken: Gibraltar Bay - Date received: 12 Aug 1812 - From what ship: Horace - Discharged on 29 Aug 1812 - How discharged: Being a licensed vessel.

Tucker, Nathaniel (see prisoner number 528) - Number: 525 - Prize name: Sampson - Ship type: MV - Discharged on 26 Jul 1813 - How discharged: HM Store Ship Weymouth.

Tucker, Nathaniel - Number: 528 - Prize name: Sampson - Ship type: MV - Discharged on Aug 1813 - How discharged: HM Ship-of-the-Line Achille.

Truesdell, William - Seaman - Number: 359 - Prize name: Thomas Wilson - Ship type: MV - How taken: HM Sloop Comet - Date taken: 14 Jan 1813 - Where taken: near Cadiz - Date received: 22 Jan 1813 - From what ship: HM Sloop Comet - Discharged on 10 Apr 1813 - How discharged: Being a licensed vessel.

Turner, Thomas - Seaman - Number: 552 - Prize name: Hepsey - Ship type: MV - How taken: HM Brig Zenoha - Date taken: 23 Jun 1813 - Where taken: near Lisbon - Date received: 1 Jul 1813 - From what ship: Hepsey Prize.

Valentine, James - Seaman - Number: 10 - Prize name: Margaret - Ship type: MV - How taken: HM Ship-of-the-Line San Juan - Date taken: 10 Aug 1812 - Where taken: Gibraltar Bay - Date received: 12 Aug 1812 - From what ship: Margaret - Discharged on 15 Jan 1813 - How discharged: HM Brig Derwent.

Valentine, John - Seaman - Number: 724 - Discharged on Aug 1813 - How discharged: HM Ship-of-the-Line Achille.

Vancouver, David - Seaman - Number: 234 - Prize name: Julian Mary - Ship type: MV - How taken: HM Ship-of-the-Line Grampus - Date taken: 21 Oct 1812 - Where taken: On passage to Cadiz - Date received: 21 Nov 1812 - From what ship: HM Ship-of-the-Line Grampus - Discharged on 14 Dec 1812 - How discharged: Being a licensed vessel.

Vandervenier, John - Seaman - Number: 576 - Where taken: Mahon (Island of Minorca) - Date received: 1 Jul 1813 - From what ship: HMT Royal Boston No. 344 - Discharged on 12 Jul 1813 - How discharged: HM Sloop Bacchus.

Van Kirke, Joseph - Seaman - Number: 57 - Prize name: Phoenix - Ship type: MV - How taken: HM Ship-of-the-Line San Juan - Date taken: 10 Aug 1812 - Where taken: Gibraltar Bay - Date received: 12 Aug 1812 - From what ship: Tiger - Discharged on 15 Jan 1813 - How discharged: HM Frigate Andromeda.

Varney, John (see prisoner number 139) - 2nd Mate - Number: 91 - Prize name: Commerce - Ship type: MV - How taken: HM Brig Rebuff - Date taken: 28 Aug 1812 - Where taken: near Cadiz - Date received: 2 Sep 1813 - From what ship: HM Ship-of-the-Line Tremendous.

Varney, John - 2nd Mate - Number: 139 - How taken: Not mentioned - Date received: 2 Sep 1813 - Discharged on 28 Jan 1813 - How discharged: Being a licensed vessel.

Vincent, Henry (see prisoner number 529) - Number: 526 - Prize name: Sampson - Ship type: MV - Discharged on 26 Jul 1813 - How discharged: HM Store Ship Weymouth.

Vincent, Henry - Number: 529 - Prize name: Sampson Maydock - Ship type: MV - Discharged on 8 Aug 1813 - How discharged: HM Sloop Kingfisher.

Vous, Philip - Seaman - Number: 482 - Discharged on 22 Mar 1813 - How discharged: Being a licensed vessel.

Waggoner, John - Seaman - Number: 728 - Prize name: Engenia - Ship type: MV - How taken: HM Brig Papillion - Date taken: 17 Jul 1813 - Where taken: near Cadiz - Date received: 10 Aug 1813 - From what ship: HM Brig Papillion - Discharged on 7 Oct 1813 - How discharged: Eugenia.

Waite, Nathaniel - Boy - Number: 118 - Prize name: John - Ship type: MV - How taken: HM Sloop Blossom - Date taken: 10 Aug 1812 - Where taken: Mediterranean - Date received: 2 Sep 1813 - From what ship: HM Ship-of-the-Line Tremendous.

Walker, John - Seaman - Number: 677 - How taken: HM Ship-of-the-Line Prince George - Date taken: 28 May 1813 - Where taken: Mahon (Island of Minorca) - Date received: 1 Jul 1813 - Discharged on 3 Jul 1813 - How discharged: HM Frigate Thames.

Walker, William - Seaman - Number: 79 - Prize name: Eliza - Ship type: MV - How taken: HM Sloop Hyacinth and HM Frigate Argo - Date taken: 27 Aug 1812 - Where taken: Straits of Gibraltar - Date received: 30 Aug 1812 - From what ship: HM Frigate Argo - Discharged on 22 Jan 1813 - How discharged: HM Sloop Comet.

Walkington, George - Mate - Number: 126 - Prize name: Eliza - Ship type: MV - How taken: HM Sloop Hyacinth and HM Frigate Argo - Date taken: 27 Aug 1812 - Where taken: Straits of Gibraltar - Date received: 2 Sep 1813 - Discharged on 22 Jan 1813 - How discharged: HM Sloop Comet.

Warner, Henry - Seaman - Number: 36 - Prize name: Allegany - Ship type: MV - How taken: HM Ship-of-the-Line San Juan - Date taken: 10 Aug 1812 - Where taken: Gibraltar Bay - Date received: 12 Aug 1812 - From what ship: Allegany - Discharged on 15 Jan 1813 - How discharged: HM Frigate Andromeda.

Warner, John - Seaman - Number: 689 - Prize name: Hepsey - Ship type: MV - Discharged on 8 Aug 1813 - How discharged: HM Sloop Kingfisher.

Warner, John - Seaman - Number: 622 - How taken: HM Ship-of-the-Line Prince of Wales - Date taken: 28 May 1813 - Where taken: Mahon (Island of Minorca) - Date received: 1 Jul 1813 - From what ship: HMT Royal Boston No. 344 - Discharged on 3 Jul 1813 - How discharged: HM Frigate Thames.

Warnock, Robert - Seaman - Number: 612 - How taken: HM Ship-of-the-Line Royal George - Date taken: 28 May 1813 - Where taken: Mahon (Island of Minorca) - Date received: 1 Jul 1813 - From what ship: HMT Royal Boston No. 344 - Discharged on 3 Jul 1813 - How discharged: HM Frigate Thames.

Washburn, Albert - Seaman - Number: 776 - Prize name: Adeline - Ship type: LM - How taken: HM Frigate Magiciene - Date taken: 14 Mar 1814 - Where taken: at sea - Date received: 14 Apr 1814 - From what ship: HM Frigate Magiciene - Discharged on 22 Apr 1814 - How discharged: HM Store Ship Tortoise.

Waters, Philip - Seaman - Number: 774 - Prize name: Adeline - Ship type: LM - How taken: HM Frigate Magiciene - Date taken: 14 Mar 1814 - Where taken: at sea - Date received: 14 Apr 1814 - From what ship: HM Frigate Magiciene - Discharged on 22 Apr 1814 - How discharged: HM Store Ship Tortoise.

Watson, Daniel - Seaman - Number: 709 - Discharged on Aug 1813 - How discharged: HM Ship-of-the-Line Achille.

Watson, James - Seaman - Number: 264 - Prize name: Lydia - Ship type: MV - How taken: HM Ship-of-the-Line Grampus - Date taken: 2 Nov 1812 - Where taken: On passage to Cadiz - Date received: 22 Nov 1812 - From what ship: Lydia - Discharged on 14 Dec 1812 - How discharged: Being a licensed vessel.

Watson, John - Seaman - Number: 764 - Prize name: Adeline - Ship type: LM - How taken: HM Frigate Magiciene - Date taken: 14 Mar 1814 - Where taken: at sea - Date received: 14 Apr 1814 - From what ship: HM Frigate Magiciene - Discharged on 29 Apr 1814 - How discharged: HM Store Ship Hindostan.

Watson, Stephen - Seaman - Number: 617 - How taken: HM Ship-of-the-Line Royal George - Date taken: 28 May 1813 - Where taken: Mahon (Island of Minorca) - Date received: 1 Jul 1813 - From what ship: HMT Royal Boston No. 344 - Discharged on 24 Jul 1813 - How discharged: HM Store Ship Tortoise.

Watson, William - Seaman - Number: 596 - How taken: HM Frigate Bombay - Date taken: 28 May 1813 - Where taken: Mahon (Island of Minorca) - Date received: 1 Jul 1813 - From what ship: HMT Royal Boston No. 344 - Discharged on 12 Jul 1813 - How discharged: HM Sloop Bacchus.

Wedgwood, John - Mate - Number: 120 - Prize name: Albion - Ship type: MV - How taken: HM Frigate Cossack - Date taken: 8 Aug 1812 - Where taken: Cape Spartel (Morocco) - Date received: 2 Sep 1813 - From what ship: HM Ship-of-the-Line Tremendous - Discharged on 3 Nov 1812 - How discharged: Being a licensed vessel.

Weekhams, Thaddeus - Seaman - Number: 377 - How taken: Gave himself up at Gibraltar - Date taken: 30 Jan 1813 - Date received: 30 Jan 1813 - From what ship: HM Frigate Brune - Discharged on 6 Mar 1813 - How discharged: HM Ship-of-the-Line Blake.

Welse, James - Seaman - Number: 734 - Prize name: Engenia - Ship type: MV - How taken: HM Brig Papillion -

Date taken: 17 Jul 1813 - Where taken: near Cadiz - Date received: 10 Aug 1813 - From what ship: Eugenia Brig - Discharged on 7 Oct 1813 - How discharged: Eugenia.

Wendall, Isaac - Seaman - Number: 340 - Prize name: Pallas - Ship type: MV - How taken: HM Brig Rebuff - Date taken: 24 Dec 1812 - Where taken: near Cadiz - Date received: 19 Jan 1813 - From what ship: HM Brig Rebuff - Discharged on 19 Feb 1813 - How discharged: HM Sloop Dauntless.

West, George - Seaman - Number: 493 - How taken: Gave himself up from HM Ship-of-the-Line Malta - Date taken: 2 Jan 1813 - Where taken: Gibraltar - Date received: 9 Apr 1813 - From what ship: HM Bomb Vessel Strombolo - Discharged on 23 Apr 1813 - How discharged: HM Sloop Helena.

West, Reuben (see prisoner number 109) - Seaman - Number: 45 - Prize name: Tiger - Ship type: MV - How taken: HM Ship-of-the-Line San Juan - Date taken: 10 Aug 1812 - Where taken: Gibraltar Bay - Date received: 12 Aug 1812 -From what ship: Tiger - Discharged on 15 Jan 1813 - How discharged: HM Frigate Andromeda.

West, Reuben - Seaman - Number: 109 - Prize name: Tiger - Ship type: MV - How taken: HM Ship-of-the-Line San Juan - Date taken: 10 Aug 1812 - Where taken: Gibraltar Bay - Date received: 2 Sep 1813 - From what ship: HM Ship-of-the-Line Tremendous.

Where, John - Seaman - Number: 41 - Prize name: Allegany - Ship type: MV - How taken: HM Ship-of-the-Line San Juan - Date taken: 10 Aug 1812 - Where taken: Gibraltar Bay - Date received: 12 Aug 1812 - From what ship: Allegany - Discharged on 15 Jan 1813 - How discharged: HM Frigate Andromeda.

White, Isaac - Boy - Number: 26 - Prize name: Horace - Ship type: MV - How taken: HM Ship-of-the-Line San Juan - Date taken: 10 Aug 1812 - Where taken: Gibraltar Bay - Date received: 12 Aug 1812 - From what ship: Horace - Discharged on 29 Aug 1812 - How discharged: Being a licensed vessel.

White, John - Mate - Number: 186 - Prize name: Draper - Ship type: MV - How taken: HM Brig Fearly - Date taken: 18 Sep 1812 - Where taken: near Cadiz - Date received: 27 Sep 1812 - From what ship: HM Brig Fearless - Discharged on 22 Jan 1813 - How discharged: HM Sloop Comet.

White, Martin - Seaman - Number: 251 - Prize name: Apollo - Ship type: MV - How taken: HM Ship-of-the-Line Grampus - Date taken: 29 Oct 1812 - Where taken: On passage to Cadiz - Date received: 21 Nov 1812 - From what ship: HM Ship-of-the-Line Grampus - Discharged on 14 Dec 1812 - How discharged: Being a licensed vessel.

White, R. N. - Seaman - Number: 687 - Prize name: Confounder - Discharged on 28 Jun 1813 - How discharged: HMT Minstraele.

Whitton, Reuben - Seaman - Number: 233 - Prize name: Julian Mary - Ship type: MV - How taken: HM Ship-of-the-Line Grampus - Date taken: 21 Oct 1812 - Where taken: On passage to Cadiz - Date received: 21 Nov 1812 - From what ship: HM Ship-of-the-Line Grampus - Discharged on 14 Dec 1812 - How discharged: Being a licensed vessel.

Wicky, Timothy - Seaman - Number: 536 - How taken: Taken off the Spanish MV Maydock - Discharged on 8 Aug 1813 - How discharged: HM Sloop Kingfisher.

Williams, David - Seaman - Number: 70 - Prize name: Albion - Ship type: MV - How taken: HM Frigate Cossack - Date taken: 8 Aug 1812 - Where taken: Cape Spartel (Morocco) - Date received: 21 Aug 1812 - From what ship: HM Brig Rebuff - Discharged on 3 Nov 1812 - How discharged: Being a licensed vessel.

Williams, John - Seaman - Number: 678 - Prize name: Eslair - Discharged on 28 Jun 1813 - How discharged: HMT Minstraele.

Williams, John - Seaman - Number: 60 - How taken: Gave himself up from HM Brig Sabine - Date received: 15 Aug 1812 - From what ship: HM Brig Sabine - Discharged on 5 Sep 1812 - How discharged: Returned to HM Brig Sabine.

Williams, John - Seaman - Number: 620 - How taken: HM Ship-of-the-Line Prince of Wales - Date taken: 28 May 1813 - Where taken: Mahon (Island of Minorca) - Date received: 1 Jul 1813 - From what ship: HMT Royal Boston No. 344 - Discharged on 21 Jul 1813 - How discharged: HM Brig Savage.

Williams, Richard - Seaman - Number: 442 - Prize name: Catharine - Ship type: MV - How taken: HMT Druid - Date taken: 21 Feb 1813 - Where taken: near Lisbon - Date received: 5 Mar 1813 - From what ship: HMT

Pererserance - Discharged on 10 Apr 1813 - How discharged: Being a licensed vessel.

Williams, Robert (see prisoner number 637) - Seaman - Number: 584 - Where taken: Mahon (Island of Minorca) - Date received: 1 Jul 1813 - From what ship: HMT Royal Boston No. 344 - Discharged on 21 Jul 1813 - How discharged: HM Brig Savage.

Williams, Robert - Seaman - Number: 637 - How taken: HM Ship-of-the-Line Prince of Wales - Date taken: 28 May 1813 - Where taken: Mahon (Island of Minorca) - Date received: 1 Jul 1813 - From what ship: HMT Royal Boston No. 344 - Discharged on 21 Jul 1813 - How discharged: HM Brig Savage.

Williams, Thomas - Seaman - Number: 551 - Discharged on 8 Aug 1813 - How discharged: HM Sloop Kingfisher.

Williamson, Richard - Seaman - Number: 254 - Prize name: Apollo - Ship type: MV - How taken: HM Ship-of-the-Line Grampus - Date taken: 29 Oct 1812 - Where taken: On passage to Cadiz - Date received: 21 Nov 1812 - From what ship: HM Ship-of-the-Line Grampus - Discharged on 14 Dec 1812 - How discharged: Being a licensed vessel.

Wills, Hugh - Seaman - Number: 727 - Prize name: Engenia - Ship type: MV - How taken: HM Brig Papillion - Date taken: 17 Jul 1813 - Where taken: near Cadiz - Date received: 10 Aug 1813 - From what ship: HM Brig Papillion - Discharged on 7 Oct 1813 - How discharged: Eugenia.

Willson, John - Seaman - Number: 587 - Where taken: Mahon (Island of Minorca) - Date received: 1 Jul 1813 - From what ship: HMT Royal Boston No. 344 - Discharged on 3 Jul 1813 - How discharged: HM Frigate Thames.

Wilson, Francis - Seaman - Number: 465 - Prize name: Amphitrite - Ship type: MV - From what ship: Amphitrite - Discharged on 19 Mar 1813 - How discharged: HM Schooner Sylvia.

Wilson, James (see prisoner number 601) - Seaman - Number: 316 - Prize name: John L. Kees - Ship type: MV - How taken: HM Brig Basilisk - Date taken: 6 Jan 1813 - Where taken: near Cadiz - Date received: 12 Jan 1813 - From what ship: HM Brig Basilisk - Discharged on 14 Apr 1813 - How discharged: Being a licensed vessel.

Wilson, James - Seaman - Number: 601 - How taken: HM Ship-of-the-Line Berwick - Date taken: 28 May 1813 - Where taken: Mahon (Island of Minorca) - Date received: 1 Jul 1813 - From what ship: HMT Royal Boston No. 344 - Discharged on 12 Jul 1813 - How discharged: HM Sloop Bacchus.

Wilson, John - Seaman - Number: 72 - Prize name: Pallas - Ship type: MV - How taken: HM Brig Papillion - Date taken: 7 Aug 1812 - Where taken: off Sanlucar (Spain) - Date received: 26 Aug 1812 - From what ship: HMS Lavinia - Discharged on 22 Jan 1813 - How discharged: HM Sloop Comet.

Wilson, Robert - Seaman - Number: 722 - Discharged on Aug 1813 - How discharged: HM Ship-of-the-Line Achille.

Wingate, David - Seaman - Number: 643 - How taken: HM Ship-of-the-Line Prince of Wales - Date taken: 28 May 1813 - Where taken: Mahon (Island of Minorca) - Date received: 1 Jul 1813 - From what ship: HMT Royal Boston No. 344 - Discharged on 21 Jul 1813 - How discharged: HM Brig Savage.

Wood, James - Master - Number: 435 - Prize name: Essex - Ship type: MV - How taken: HM Gunboat No. 22 - Date taken: 12 Jan 1813 - Where taken: near Cadiz - Date received: 5 Mar 1813 - From what ship: Essex Prize - Discharged on 16 Apr 1813 - How discharged: Being a licensed vessel.

Woods, William - Seaman - Number: 665 - How taken: HM Ship-of-the-Line Ocean - Date taken: 28 May 1813 - Where taken: Mahon (Island of Minorca) - Date received: 1 Jul 1813 - From what ship: HMT Royal Boston No. 344 - Discharged on 23 Jul 1813 - How discharged: HM Frigate Unicorn.

Wort, William - Seaman - Number: 220 - Prize name: Topaz - Ship type: MV - How taken: HM Ship-of-the-Line Grampus - Date taken: 19 Oct 1812 - Where taken: On passage to Cadiz - Date received: 21 Nov 1812 - From what ship: HM Ship-of-the-Line Grampus - Discharged on 14 Dec 1812 - How discharged: Being a licensed vessel.

Wright, John - Seaman - Number: 284 - Prize name: Maria - Ship type: MV - Discharged on 18 Dec 1812.

Yeaton, John - Seaman - Number: 21 - Prize name: Horace - Ship type: MV - How taken: HM Ship-of-the-Line San

Juan - Date taken: 10 Aug 1812 - Where taken: Gibraltar Bay - Date received: 12 Aug 1812 - From what ship: Horace - Discharged on 29 Aug 1812 - How discharged: Being a licensed vessel.

Young, John (see prisoner number 650) - Seaman - Number: 337 - Prize name: San Joseph Volorado - Ship type: MV - How taken: HM Brig Desperate - Date taken: 15 Jan1813 - Where taken: near Cadiz - Date received: 27 Jan 1813 - From what ship: HM Brig Basilisk - Discharged on 18 Feb 1813 - How discharged: Being a licensed vessel.

Young, John - Seaman - Number: 650 - How taken: Gave himself up from HMS Tarmendor - Date taken: 28 May 1813 - Where taken: Mahon (Island of Minorca) - Date received: 1 Jul 1813 - From what ship: HMT Royal Boston No. 344 - Discharged on 1 Jul 1813 - How discharged: HM Brig Protector for England.

Young, Richard D. - Seaman - Number: 215 - Prize name: Dolphin - Ship type: MV - How taken: HM Ship-of-the-Line Invincible - Date taken: 24 Aug 1812 - Where taken: Meg'n (Unknown) - Date received: 22 Nov 1812 - From what ship: Dolphin - Discharged on 25 Jan 1813 - How discharged: HM Ship-of-the-Line Sultan.

Young, Thomas - Seaman - Number: 668 - How taken: HM Ship-of-the-Line Barfleur - Date taken: 28 May 1813 - Where taken: Mahon (Island of Minorca) - Date received: 1 Jul 1813 - From what ship: HMT Royal Boston No. 344.

Younger, Levi - Seaman - Number: 652 - How taken: HM Ship-of-the-Line Pompee - Date taken: 28 May 1813 - Where taken: Mahon (Island of Minorca) - Date received: 1 Jul 1813 - From what ship: HMT Royal Boston No. 344 - Discharged on 21 Jul 1813 - How discharged: HM Brig Savage.

Numeric listing by prisoner number

1	Silbey, James		48	Atkens, Uriah
2	Mulleus, Joseph		49	Hubbard, John
3	Dolby, Owen		50	Leeds, Leon
4	Rush, Laten		51	Blanchard, Calvin
5	Love, Peter		52	Batchelor, Nathaniel
6	Chase, Matthew		53	Daniels, John
7	Falanda, John		54	Glover, John
8	Navari, Peter		55	Harvey, Joseph
9	Affan, John		56	Foster, Joseph
10	Valentine, James		57	VanKirke, Joseph
11	Combs, Richard		58	Penerson, Hance
12	Mason, Charles		59	Leonard, Robert
13	Davis, Charles		60	Williams, John
14	Latimer, John		61	Barton, Matthew
15	Appleton, William		62	Burns, William
16	Cin, James		63	Morris, Robert
17	Moses, John		64	Marten, John
18	Gerrish, Timothy		65	Johnston, Nathaniel
19	Fernald, Edmund		66	Dewick, James
20	Starbord, John		67	Sharpe, George
21	Yeaton, John		68	Fuller, William
22	Libby, Nathaniel		69	Crafts, Jonathan
23	Tucker, Arthur		70	Williams, David
24	Leach, James		71	Russel, Thomas
25	Dean, Samuel		72	Wilson, John
26	White, Isaac		73	Davidson, Andrew
27	Eveleth, Ebenezer		74	Phaesenton, Robert
28	Dolinson, Andrew		75	Butterfield, Edward
29	Eveleth, William		76	Smith, James
30	Borne, John		77	Daniels, Bradley
31	Gore, John		78	Layland, John
32	Smith, Obadiah		79	Walker, William
33	Smith, John		80	Parks, Richard
34	Allen, William		81	Rust, Zebulun
35	Oden, John		82	Cunningham, S.
36	Warner, Henry		83	Bhovey, Josiah
37	Burey, Brook		84	Matten, Norman
38	Conway, William		85	Handshaw, Spruce
39	Not used		86	Thayer, Abner
40	Higgens, George		87	Poppins, John
41	Where, John		88	Roebuck, John
42	Hough, Ebenezer		89	Maver, John
43	Bartlett, John		90	Smith, Thomas
44	Snow, Joseph		91	Varney, John
45	West, Reuben		92	Bullock, John
46	Leach, John		93	Jacob, Thomas
47	Newell, John		94	Carr, James

95	Coleman, William	144	Coleman, William
96	Chambers, Thomas	145	Chambers, Thomas
97	Richardson, Joel	146	Bentley, Samuel
98	Silbey, James	147	Sarouna, Charles
99	Dalby, Owen	148	Not used
100	Mason, Charles	149	Not used
101	Davis, Charles	150	Not used
102	Latimer, John	151	Not used
103	Eveleth, Ebenezer	152	Not used
104	Dolinson, Andrew	153	Not used
105	Eveleth, William	154	Not used
106	Huff, Ebenezer	155	Not used
107	Bartlett, John	156	Not used
108	Snow, Joseph	157	Not used
109	West, Reuben	158	Not used
110	Leach, John	159	Not used
111	Batchelor, Nathaniel	160	Not used
112	Daniels, John	161	Not used
113	Peterson, Hance	162	Not used
114	Leonard, Robert	163	Not used
115	Cars, Bartlett	164	Not used
116	Morton, Seth	165	Not used
117	Braizer, William	166	Not used
118	Waite, Nathaniel	167	Not used
119	Pearson, William	168	Not used
120	Wedgwood, John	169	Not used
121	Seville, Robert	170	Not used
122	Molineuse, Charles	171	Not used
123	Lang, Samuel	172	Not used
124	Caren, Thomas	173	Not used
125	Leslie, Henry	174	Not used
126	Walkington, George	175	Not used
127	Harrison, Joseph	176	Smith, Jacob
128	Hardwick, James	177	Lovett, Peter
129	Hutchison, James	178	Aroid, Aaron
130	Cole, Thomas	179	Passino, Thomas
131	Sebastion, Joseph	180	Hall, Henry
132	Dyer, Thomas	181	Champman, Joseph
133	Hughes, Aaron	182	Shrine, Edward
134	Guenls, Henry	183	Moody, Samuel
135	Clark, John	184	Jones, Uriah
136	Fenn, John	185	Bellar, John
137	Bentley, Samuel	186	White, John
138	Larrounas, Elias	187	Martin, John
139	Varney, John	188	Smith, Jacob
140	Bullock, John	189	Magee, Charles
141	Jacobs, Thomas	190	Doak, Nathaniel
142	Handshaw, Spruce	191	Oliver, Robert
143	Carr, James	192	Tronia, Richard

193	Fredericks, John	242	Rose, Andrew
194	Hamilton, John	243	Brockelman, William
195	Smith, George	244	Parto, Pero
196	Russel, Henry	245	Christian, Joseph
197	Robinson, John	246	Biera, Manuel
198	Campbell, John	247	Roderecus, R.
199	Stephenson, J,	248	Saunders, Richard
200	Nelson, James	249	McMilledge, James
201	Furguson, John	250	Mullen, John B.
202	Jones, Peter	251	White, Martin
203	Lopez, John	252	Lattour, Armeda
204	Jennings, John	253	Mulde, Sebron
205	Field, F.	254	Williamson, Richard
206	Casar, Joseph	255	Mones, Peter
207	Cherry, D.	256	Andrews, John
208	Cole, E.	257	Harper, John
209	Bert, R.	258	Ashbourne, Luke
210	Skinner, Johnston	259	Ash, Luke
211	Not used	260	Gore, Thomas
212	Paul, Dempsey	261	Moore, Francis
213	Thompson, John	262	Birket, James
214	Madellon, Peter	263	Hammond, Joseph
215	Young, Richard D.	264	Watson, James
216	Fito, Gaspo	265	Morgan, James
217	Griffin, Evan	266	Bell, Peter (1)
218	Graham, David	267	Bell, Peter (2)
219	Anbeck, John A.	268	Line, Latony
220	Wort, William	269	Brownman, Benjamin
221	Brown, Silvenus	270	Gilbert, George
222	Bain, Daniel	271	Davis, Elias
223	Giles, William	272	Bennett, Thomas
224	Cannon, Charles D.	273	Begnall, Charles
225	Pitts, James	274	Bruce, Peter
226	Hussard, John K.	275	Goodwin, William
227	Davis, Joseph	276	Casar, Julian
228	Hopkins, Thomas	277	Dourdick, Matthew
229	Richmond, James G.	278	Holmes, Zechariah
230	Davis, Thomas	279	Harding, John
231	Hopkins, Lewis	280	Craig, William
232	Ryercraft, William	281	Brant, Solomon
233	Whitton, Reuben	282	Renkins, Henry
234	Vancorue, David	283	Smith, William
235	Ashwood, Ralph	284	Wright, John
236	Bennett, William	285	Evans, Robert
237	Hadden, Felix	286	Dodridge, M.
238	Ellis, George	287	Dolbert, Owen
239	Kemp, William	288	Shaw, Daniel
240	Roberts, Joseph	289	Olsen, Henry
241	Armshell, John	290	Amens, John

291	Howard, John	340	Wendall, Isaac
292	Feldean, John	341	Ratoon, Thomas
293	Anderson, Peter	342	Colefax, William
294	Croomdie, John	343	Hudgety, George
295	Lea, Joseph	344	Robinson, William
296	Houston, Henry	345	Burton, John
297	Brown, Silvester	346	Rianoer, Anthony
298	Johnston, Stephen	347	Dousty, Angelo
299	Berroy, John	348	Smith, George
300	Schnider, John	349	Hockman, William
301	Osborn, Ebenezer	350	Edwards, Punie
302	Summers, Arthur	351	Brown, James
303	Seymore, Samuel	352	Moor, Lawrence
304	Floyd, John	353	Lewis, Edward
305	Phyney, William	354	Hawkins, John
306	Smith, Thomas	355	Stow, Jeremiah
307	Peters, William	356	Fernand, John
308	Lacemo, Larey	357	Lightfoot, Sharp
309	Smith, William	358	Silvy, John
310	Fredericks, John	359	Tuesdell, William
311	Campbell, John	360	Lakeman, Asa
312	Lopez, James	361	Goodwin, R. C.
313	Buchanan, James	362	Low, Frederick G.
314	Roberts, Thomas	363	Stanwood, Wenthoop
315	Holcom, George	364	Harding, Samuel
316	Wilson, James	365	Lindon, John
317	Brown, John	366	Smith, George
318	Johnson, Henry	367	Foster, William
319	Butler, John	368	Soley, William
320	Talbot, Joseph	369	Mathell, Benjamin
321	Donaldson, Nathaniel	370	Thoroughgood, Anthony
322	Cormick, Henry	371	Moss, Nathaniel P.
323	Gregory, Cornelius	372	Brown, James
324	Jennings, John	373	Litchfield, Foster
325	Newel, Noah	374	Booth, John
326	Roberts, John	375	Leonard, Edward
327	Hardy, Jonathan	376	Clasp, Silas
328	Pratts, Samuel	377	Weekhams, Thaddeus
329	Graves, Frederick	378	Malling, James
330	Manley, James	379	Johnston, Edward
331	Rose, Stanley	380	Frisque, William
332	Gamel, Josiah	381	Clifford, S. L.
333	Alford, Edward	382	Edwards, John
334	Gaues, Richard	383	Rush, Laten
335	Hughes, John	384	Lochely, William
336	Brown, George	385	Ealy, Robert
337	Young, John	386	Coody, William
338	Babcock, John	387	Thomas, J.
339	Robinson, Ebenezer	388	Holstean, Samuel

Gibraltar Depot 247

389	Murray, Richard	438	Cela, Lewis
390	Metcalf, Anthony	439	Hendecott, N. H.
391	French, Samuel	440	Hayes, Edward
392	Benjamin, Vallasky	441	Stanley, Timothy
393	Penny, Samuel	442	Williams, Richard
394	Fitch, William	443	Frytucker, D.
395	Morrell, John	444	Saffion, John
396	Sims, Clement	445	Durham, G. D.
397	Morrison, John	446	Jones, Richard
398	Gilpin, John	447	Follousbie, William
399	Thomas, Charles	448	Johnson, Thomas
400	Pope, William	449	Roding, Abraham
401	Brown, Elisha	450	Swan, Peter
402	Hall, William	451	Taylor, George
403	Pinkhorn, Allan	452	Hall, Stephen
404	Thompson, William	453	Rogers, Jonathan
405	Archibald, Robert	454	Freberg, Charles
406	Couan, John	455	Dockerson, Thomas
407	Davidson, Henry	456	Ricker, Elijah
408	Somerville, Charles	457	Sheas, Jonathan
409	Harman, William	458	Muller, Samuel
410	Storm, John	459	Downs, Isaac
411	Arthurs, Williams	460	Horsham, Samuel
412	Spear, Francis	461	Rosenby, Magnus
413	Grimes, George	462	Smith, Jacob
414	Heywood, Alexander	463	Bristol, Nicholas
415	Pirman, John	464	Shairs, Samuel
416	Hopburn, R.	465	Wilson, Francis
417	Brown, John	466	Steward, Henry
418	Flexon, Charles	467	Littlefield, Isaac
419	Harris, John	468	Lonekin, Charles
420	Guilder, Jacob	469	King, John B.
421	Robarts, Samuel	470	Goodridge, R.
422	Puffer, John	471	Goff, John
423	Harris, Charles	472	Samuels, Samuel
424	Thomas, William	473	Hoaton, Stephen
425	Severleach, Anthony	474	Freberg, Charles
426	Lewis, William	475	Dickenson, Thomas
427	Smith, John	476	Till, Samuel
428	Eames, D.	477	McIntyre, Samuel
429	Matlock, Abraham	478	Rogers, John
430	Quann, Sim.	479	Smith, John
431	Eldridge, Nathaniel	480	Arnold, Alfred
432	Delany, M.	481	Gordon, William
433	Rich, William	482	Vous, Philip
434	Mazel, James	483	Hayden, Fuller
435	Wood, James	484	Reed, Bartholomew
436	Stetson, Daniel	485	Hanna, Edward
437	Gavel, S. B.	485	Paul, Mark

Gibraltar Depot

486	Parker, John		534	Peckham, Isaac
487	Ellis, Lewis		535	Leonard, Robert
487	Lawler, Matthew		536	Wicky, Timothy
488	Manley, James		537	Barber, John
489	Madden, Isaac		538	Coffin, James
490	Moro, Henry		539	Manby, Rooth
491	Row, Simon		540	Small, Enoch
492	Steward, John		541	Ross, Philip
493	West, George		542	Not used
494	Harris, William		543	Dubois, Alexander
495	Brown, Samuel		544	Mitchell, Fairley
496	Forrest, James		545	Andrews, George
497	Eaton, James		546	Saverick, John
498	Benn, William		547	Lawrence, Clark
499	Johnson, George		548	Clayson, Laurence
500	Richards, Edward		549	Sears, Isaac
501	Avery, Charles		550	Boyd, Andrew
502	Huntley, Charles		551	Williams, Thomas
503	Johnston, Matthew		552	Turner, Thomas
504	Braler, John		553	Bateman, Ely
505	Davis, John		554	Erwigg, John
506	Kelly, John		555	Flage, William
507	Harrison, Henry		556	Boyd, Stephen
508	Chase, Josiah		557	Raymond, Cable
509	Simmonds, William		558	Not used
510	Bird, James		559	Thomas, John
511	Jameson, John		560	Foster, Thomas
512	Malbon, Evan		561	Cox, Abraham
513	Molyneaux, William		562	Soutter, John
514	Manuel, Dio		563	Salkor, Abel
515	Tombolin, Thomas		564	Osborne, Lewis
516	Lubeck, James		565	Johnston, Samuel
517	Styles, Israel		566	Traphagn, Peter
518	Lovett, Israel		567	Miller, Juan
519	Forbes, Thomas		568	Alexander, George
520	Thomas, John		569	Hartfield, John
521	Shepherd, Thomas		570	Howland, William
522	Hall, Henry		571	Gordon, James
523	Overstock, Peter		572	Hartfield, James
524	Thornton, David		573	Penny, Richard
525	Tucker, Nathaniel		574	Cadwell, Abraham
526	Vincent, Henry		575	Allen, William
527	Thornton, David		576	Vandervenier, John
528	Tucker, Nathaniel		577	Murry, James
529	Vincent, Henry		578	Phillips, William (2)
530	Manlove, Roberts		579	Henderson, Henry
531	Blackloch, John		580	Luschaw, John
532	Lynch, Charles		581	Cooke, John
533	Pitt, Charles		582	Noble, Charles

Gibraltar Depot 249

583	Sherridan, Henry		632	Hudson, John
584	Williams, Robert		633	Bailey, William
585	Harvey, John		634	Salis, Peter
586	Mutch, Thomas T.		635	Gordon, Abraham
587	Willson, John		636	Douglas, John
588	Heywood, John		637	Williams, Robert
589	Hubbard, John		638	Hobbart, William
590	Boyd, John		639	Boswell, James
591	Linsey, Samuel		640	Thayer, James
592	Halbrook, David		641	Lowe, Thomas
593	Brown, Thomas		642	Stone, Henry
594	Peverly, Henry		643	Wingate, David
595	Nixon, Charles		644	Smith, James
596	Watson, William		645	Reid, John
597	Campbell, Nicholas		646	Jackson, William
598	Scauk, William		647	Jordan, Artenius
599	Taylor, William		648	Adams, Thomas
600	Powel, Joseph		649	Scott, William
601	Wilson, James		650	Young, John
602	Peters, Thomas		651	Porter, Josiah
603	Sirucus, William		652	Younger, Levi
604	Brown, Reuben		653	Marshall, Thomas
605	Greaves, John		654	Potter, John
606	McKensey, George		655	Penrose, Abraham
607	Hall, James		656	Murray, Peter
608	Robinson, Henry		657	Quarterruaun, William
609	Flood, John		658	Brown, George
610	Hazard, Thomas		659	Bond, Samuel
611	Harnford, John		660	Owen, Burden
612	Warnock, Robert		661	Richards, Henry
613	Sheppard, James		662	Peterson, William
614	Miller, John		663	Price, John
615	Augustus, Benjamin		664	Brown, John
616	Hall, John		665	Woods, William
617	Watson, Stephen		666	Johnston, Rock
618	Cock, Isaac		667	Thompson, Robert
619	Buckanan, Christopher		668	Young, Thomas
620	Williams, John		669	Kellum, Smith
621	James, John		670	Bordley, George
622	Warner, John		671	McKenzie, John
623	Thomas, John		672	Crawford, James
624	Stephenson, Levy		673	Mackay, James
625	Hill, Timothy		674	Hundling, John
626	Canning, James		675	Blake, William
627	Heady, Lindy		676	Nicholes, John
628	Baker, Daniel		677	Walker, John
629	Austin, James		678	Williams, John
630	Smith, John		679	Thompson, James
631	Chasse, Jacob		680	Brown, Isaac

Gibraltar Depot

681	Mulch, James		730	Brown, Samuel
682	Howel, John		731	Gerris, William
683	Gibson, Samuel		732	Durham, William
684	Read, John		733	Smith, John
685	Randolph, Horace		734	Welse, James
686	Matthews, John		735	Jones, Thomas
687	White, R. N.		736	Hill, James
688	Lathan, John		737	Coffin, Joseph
689	Warner, John		738	Pitt, William
690	McKenzie, William		739	Gow, Henry
691	Bissell, Samuel F.		740	Brown, Sawyer
692	Edgar, William		741	Conner, John
693	Howell, H. C.		742	Levant, Thomas
694	Davidson, John		743	Not used
695	Dewell, A. D.		744	Dean, Moses
696	Not used		745	Nearl, William
697	Not used		746	Ray, David
698	Lamb, Jack		747	Diamond, William
699	Stegman, Christopher		748	Sparkes, Samuel
700	Beates, John		749	Grimes, James
701	Saunders, Elijah		750	Morrice, Isaac
702	Elf, James		751	Patterson, John (1)
703	Myers, James		752	Johnston, William
704	Adams, Thomas		753	Cole, John
705	Lucas, Mas.		754	Patterson, John (2)
706	Thomas, Moses		755	Newman, Daniel
707	Folger, Frederick		756	Reunie, David
708	Glover, Samuel		757	Conklin, Edward
709	Watson, Daniel		757	Pottingale, John
710	Richardson, Robert		759	Hughes, John
711	Smith, Henry		760	Lounge, Thomas
712	Bates, Joseph		761	Bartoll, Samuel
713	Husband, Joseph		762	Hall, Robert
714	Davis, Osborn		763	Cromwell, Oliver
715	Heaton, H. J.		764	Watson, John
716	Harvey, Peter		765	Sole, Edward
717	Toole, Ganet		766	Frost, Michael
718	Robinson, John		767	Holbrook, Elias
719	Andrews, John (1)		768	Sole, Elias
720	Perry, Samuel		769	Sentar, Noah
721	Andrews, John (2)		770	Thomas, Stephen
722	Wilson, Robert		771	Taggart, John
723	Green, George		772	Stone, John
724	Valentine, John		773	Sole, Thomas
725	Not used		774	Waters, Philip
726	Drake, Peter		775	Thomas, James
727	Wills, Hugh		776	Washburn, Albert
728	Waggoner, John		777	Roberts, Nathaniel
729	Barclay, D. William		778	Tatem, George W.

779 Roberts, Moses
780 Depeyster, Pierre
781 Allen, Henry
782 Clarke, Francoise M.
783 Nichett, Pierre
784 Luce, Abijah
785 Morton, Pliny
786 Beard, Richard

Crew listing

Unknown ship

- Adams, Thomas
- Alexander, George
- Allen, William
- Andrews, John (1)
- Andrews, John (2)
- Arnold, Alfred
- Augustus, Benjamin
- Austin, James
- Avery, Charles
- Baker, Daniel
- Bailey, William
- Barber, John
- Barton, Matthew
- Bates, Joseph
- Benn, William
- Bird, James
- Blake, William
- Bond, Samuel
- Bordley, George
- Boswell, James
- Boyd, John
- Boyd, Stephen
- Braler, John
- Brown, Elisha
- Brown, George
- Brown, Isaac
- Brown, John
- Brown, Reuben
- Brown, Samuel
- Brown, Sawyer
- Brown, Thomas
- Buckanan, Christopher
- Campbell, Nicholas
- Canning, James
- Chase, Joriah
- Chasse, Jacob
- Clifford, S. L.
- Cock, Isaac
- Coffin, Joseph
- Conner, John
- Cooke, John
- Crawford, James
- Davis, John
- Davis, Osborn
- Delany, M.
- Douglas, John
- Downs, Isaac

Unknown ship

- Eaton, James
- Edwards, John
- Eldridge, Nathaniel
- Ellis, Lewis
- Flood, John
- Folger, Frederick
- Forrest, James
- Frisque, William
- Gamel, Josiah
- Gibson, Samuel
- Gilpin, John
- Glover, Samuel
- Gordon, Abraham
- Gordon, William
- Gow, Henry
- Greaves, John
- Green, George
- Grimes, James
- Halbrook, David
- Hall, James
- Hall, John
- Hall, William
- Hanna, Edward
- Harnford, John
- Harris, William
- Harrison, Henry
- Harvey, John
- Hazard, Thomas
- Heady, Lindy
- Henderson, Henry
- Heywood, John
- Hill, James
- Hill, Timothy
- Hobbart, William
- Horsham, Samuel
- Howel, John
- Hubbard, John
- Hudson, John
- Hundling, John
- Huntley, Charles
- Husband, Joseph
- Jackson, William
- James, John
- Jameson, John
- Jennings, John
- Johnson, George
- Johnston, Edward

Unknown ship	Johnston, Matthew
Johnston, Rock
Jones, Thomas
Jordan, Artenius
Kellum, Smith
Kelly, John
Lathan, John
Lawler, Matthew
Levant, Thomas
Linsey, Samuel
Lowe, Thomas
Lucas, Mas.
Luschaw, John
Mackay, James
Madden, Isaac
Malling, James
Manley, James
Marshall, Thomas
Matthews, John
Mazel, James
McKensey, George
McKenzie, John
Miller, John
Miller, Juan
Morrell, John
Morrison, John
Mulch, James
Muller, Samuel
Murray, Peter
Murry, James
Mutch, Thomas T.
Myers, James
Nicholes, John
Nixon, Charles
Noble, Charles
Owen, Burden
Parker, John
Paul, Mark
Peckham, Isaac
Penrose, Abraham
Perry, Samuel
Peters, Thomas
Peterson, William
Peverly, Henry
Phillips, William (2)
Pinkhorn, Allan
Pitt, Charles
Pitt, William
Pope, William

Unknown ship	Porter, Josiah
Potter, John
Powel, Joseph
Price, John
Quarterruaun, William
Randolph, Horace
Raymond, Cable
Read, John
Reed, Bartholomew
Reid, John
Rich, William
Richards, Edward
Richards, Henry
Richardson, Robert
Robinson, Henry
Rosenby, Magnus
Row, Simon
Rush, Laten
Salis, Peter
Scauk, William
Scott, William
Sheas, Jonathan
Sheppard, James
Sherridan, Henry
Simmonds, William
Sims, Clement
Sirucus, William
Smith, Henry
Smith, Jacob
Smith, James
Smith, John
Stephenson, Levy
Steward, John
Stone, Henry
Taylor, William
Thayer, James
Thomas, Charles
Thomas, John
Thomas, Moses
Thompson, James
Thompson, Robert
Thompson, William
Traphagn, Peter
Valentine, John
Vandervenier, John
Varney, John
Vous, Philip
Walker, John
Warner, John

Gibraltar Depot

Ship	Name
Unknown ship	Warnock, Robert
	Watson, Daniel
	Watson, Stephen
	Watson, William
	Weekhams, Thadeus
	West, George
	Wicky, Timothy
	Williams, John
	Williams, Robert
	Williams, Thomas
	Willson, John
	Wilson, James
	Wilson, Robert
	Wingate, David
	Woods, William
	Young, John
	Young, Thomas
	Younger, Levi
Adeline	Bartoll, Samuel
	Cole, John
	Conklin, Edward
	Cromwell, Oliver
	Frost, Michael
	Hall, Robert
	Holbrook, Elias
	Hughes, John
	Johnston, William
	Lounge, Thomas
	Morrice, Isaac
	Newman, Daniel
	Patterson, John (1)
	Patterson, John (2)
	Pottingale, John
	Reunie, David
	Roberts, Moses
	Roberts, Nathaniel
	Sentar, Noah
	Sole, Edward
	Sole, Elias
	Sole, Thomas
	Stone, John
	Taggart, John
	Tatem, George W.
	Thomas, James
	Thomas, Stephen
	Washburn, Albert
	Waters, Philip
	Watson, John
Albion	Caren, Thomas
	Crafts, Jonathan
	Fuller, William
	Lang, Samuel
	Molineuse, Charles
	Pearson, William
	Russel, Thomas
	Seville, Robert
	Sharpe, George
	Wedgwood, John
	Williams, David
Allegany	Allen, William
	Borne, John
	Burey, Brook
	Conway, William
	Dolinson, Andrew
	Eveleth, Ebenezer
	Eveleth, William
	Gore, John
	Higgens, George
	Hough, Ebenezer
	Huff, Ebenezer
	Oden, John
	Smith, John
	Smith, Obediah
	Warner, Henry
	Where, John
America	Harvey, Peter
	Heaton, H. J.
	Robinson, John
	Toole, Ganet
Amphitrite	Bristol, Nicholas
	Goff, John
	Goodridge, R.
	Hoaton, Stephen
	King, John B.
	Littlefield, Isaac
	Lonekin, Charles
	Samuels, Samuel
	Shairs, Samuel
	Steward, Henry
	Wilson, Francis
Apollo	Andrews, John
	Bell, Peter (1)
	Bell, Peter (2)

Apollo	Lattour, Armeda	Concordia	Lightfoot, Sharp
	Line, Latony		Osborn, Ebenezer
	McMilledge, James		Schnider, John
	Mones, Peter		Seymore, Samuel
	Mulde, Sebron		Summers, Arthur
	Mullen, John B.		
	Saunders, Richard	Conde Mary	Armshell, John
	White, Martin		Biera, Manuel
	Williamson, Richard		Brockelman, William
			Christian, Joseph
Argus	Brownman, Benjamin		Ellis, George
	Davis, Thomas		Kemp, William
	Gilbert, George	Conde Mary	Parto, Pero
	Hopkins, Lewis		Roberts, Joseph
	Hopkins, Thomas		Roderecus, R.
	Richmond, James G.		Rose, Andrew
Catharine	Durham, G. D.	Confounder	White, R. N.
	Frytucker, D.		
	Hayes, Edward	Dolphin	Fito, Gaspo
	Hendecott, N. H.		Madellon, Peter
	McIntyre, Samuel		Paul, Dempey
	Saffion, John		Skinner, Johnston
	Stanley, Timothy		Thompson, John
	Williams, Richard		Young, Richard D.
Charlotte	Brown, John	Draper	Bellar, John
	Flexon, Charles		Jones, Uriah
	Guilder, Jacob		Martin, John
	Harris, John		Moody, Samuel
	Matlock, Abraham		Shrine, Edward
	Quann, Sim.		White, John
	Robarts, Samuel		
		Eliza	Butler, John
Commerce	Bentley, Samuel		Campbell, John
	Bullock, John		Cole, Thomas
	Carr, James		Cunningham, S.
	Chambers, Thomas		Daniels, Bradley
	Clark, John		Fredericks, John
	Coleman, William		Hardwick, James
	Fenn, John		Harrison, Joseph
	Jacob, Thomas		Hutchison, James
	Jacobs, Thomas		Johnson, Henry
	Larrounas, Elias		Lacemo, Larey
	Sarouna, Charles		Layland, John
	Varney, Jo		Leslie, Henry
			Lopez, James
Concordia	Brown, John		Parks, Richard
	Floyd, John		Peters, William

Eliza	Phyney, William	George	Stanwood, Wenthoop
	Rust, Zebulun		
	Sebastion, Joseph	George & Albert	Amens, John
	Smith, William		Anderson, Peter
	Smith, Thomas		Berroy, John
	Talbot, Joseph		Brown, Silvester
	Walker, William		Croomdie, John
	Walkington, George		Feldean, John
			Houston, Henry
Engenia	Barclay, D. William		Howard, John
	Brown, Samuel		Johnston, Stephen
	Drake, Peter		Lea, Joseph
	Durham, William		Olsen, Henry
	Gerris, William		Shaw, Daniel
	Smith, John		
	Waggoner, John	Hendosten	Cadwell, Abraham
	Welse, James		Cox, Abraham
	Wills, Hugh		Davidson, John
			Dewell, A. D.
Eslair	Williams, John		Elf, James
			Erwigg, John
Essex	Babcock, John		Flage, William
	Cela, Lewis		Foster, Thomas
	Cormick, Henry		Gordon, James
	Donaldson, Nathaniel		Hartfield, James
	Gavel, S. B.		Hartfield, John
	Graves, Frederick		Howland, William
	Gregory, Cornelius		Johnston, Samuel
	Hardy, Jonathan		Lamb, Jack
	Jennings, John		Osborne, Lewis
	Newel, Noah		Penny, Richard
	Pratts, Samuel		Salkor, Abel
	Roberts, John		Soutter, John
	Stetson, Daniel		Stegman, Christopher
	Wood, James		Thomas, John
Fame	Bhovey, Josiah	Hepsey	Bateman, Ely
	Handshaw, Spruce		Bissell, Samuel F.
	Matten, Norman		Boyd, Andrew
			Edgar, William
George	Booth, John		Howell, H. C.
	Brown, James		McKenzie, William
	Clasp, Silas		Turner, Thomas
	Ealy, Robert		Warner, John
	Goodwin, R. C.	Horace	Appleton, William
	Leonard, Edward		Cin, James
	Litchfield, Foster		Dean, Samuel
	Low, Frederick G.		Fernald, Edmund
	Moss, Nathaniel P.		Gerrish, Timothy

Horace	Leach, James	John Buckley	Swan, Peter
	Leonard, Robert		Taylor, George
	Libby, Nathaniel		Till, Samuel
	Moses, John		
	Starbord, John	John L. Kees	Alford, Edward
	Tucker, Arthur		Buchanan, James
	White, Isaac		Couan, John
	Yeaton, John		Holcom, George
			Roberts, Thomas
Howard	Burns, William		Wilson, James
	Morris, Robert		
		Julian Mary	Ashwood, Ralph
Isabella	Andrews, George		Bennett, William
	Clayson, Laurence		Casar, Julian
	Dubois, Alexander		Goodwin, William
	Lawrence, Clark		Hadden, Felix
	Mitchell, Fairley		Ryercraft, William
	Ross, Philip		Vancorue, David
	Saverick, John		Whitton, Reuben
	Sears, Isaac		
	Small, Enoch	La Guera	Beates, John
			Saunders, Elijah
John	Braizer, William		
	Cars, Bartlett	Leo	Allen, Henry
	Dewick, James		Clarke, Francoise M.
	Dodridge, M.		Depeyster, Pierre
	Dourdick, Matthew		Nichett, Pierre
	Holmes, Zechariah		
	Johnston, Nathanel	Louisa	Dyer, Thomas
	Marten, John		Guenls, Henry
	Morton, Seth		Hughes, Aaron
	Waite, Nathaniel		Maver, John
			Poppins, John
John Barnes	Lubeck, James		Roebuck, John
	Malbon, Evan		Smith, Thomas
	Manuel, Dio		Thayer, Abner
	Molyneaux, William		
	Styles, Israel	Lydia	Ash, Luke
	Tombolin, Thomas		Ashbourne, Luke
			Birket, James
John Buckley	Dickenson, Thomas		Gore, Thomas
	Dockerson, Thomas		Hammond, Joseph
	Follousbie, William		Harper, John
	Freberg, Charles		Moore, Francis
	Hall, Stephen		Morgan, James
	Johnson, Thomas		Watson, James
	Jones, Richard		
	Roding, Abraham	Margaret	Affan, John
	Rogers, Jonathan		Chase, Matthew

Margaret	Combs, Richard	Meser	Campbell, John
	Dalby, Owen		Cherry, D.
	Davis, Charles		Cole, E.
	Dolby, Owen		Doak, Nathaniel
	Falanda, John		Field, F.
	Latimer, John		Fredericks, John
	Love, Peter		Furguson, John
	Mason, Charles		Hamilton, John
	Mulleus, Joseph		Jones, Peter
	Navari, Peter		Lopez, John
	Rush, Laten		Magee, Charles
	Silbey, James		Nelson, James
	Valentine, James		Oliver, Robert
			Robinson, John
Maria	Brant, Solomon		Russel, Henry
	Craig, William		Smith, George
	Dolbert, Owen		Stephenson, J,
	Evans, Robert		Tronia, Richard
	Harding, John		
Maria	Renkins, Henry	Pallas	Benjamin, Vallasky
	Smith, William		Brown, James
	Wright, John		Burton, John
			Butterfield, Edward
Mariner	Ricker, Elijah		Colefax, William
			Davidson, Andrew
Mark & Abigail	Eames, D.		Dousty, Angelo
	Harris, Charles		Edwards, Punie
	Lewis, William		Fernand, John
	Puffer, John		Fitch, William
	Severleach, Anthony		Hawkins, John
	Smith, John		Hockman, William
	Thomas, William		Hudgety, George
			Lewis, Edward
Mary English	Dean, Moses		Lochely, William
	Diamond, William		Moor, Lawrence
	Nearl, William		Penny, Samuel
	Ray, David		Phaesenton, Robert
	Sparkes, Samuel		Ratoon, Thomas
			Rianoer, Anthony
Mentor	Foster, William		Richardson, Joel
	Harding, Samuel		Robinson, William
	Lakeman, Asa		Robinson, Ebenezer
	Lindon, John		Smith, George
	Mathell, Benjamin		Smith, James
	Smith, George		Stow, Jeremiah
	Soley, William		Wendall, Isaac
	Thoroughgood, Anthony		Wilson, John
Meser	Bert, R.	Paul Jones	Moro, Henry

Ship	Name
Paulina	Casar, Joseph
Phoenix	Batchelor, Nathaniel
	Daniels, John
	Foster, Joseph
	Glover, John
	Harvey, Joseph
	Leonard, Robert
	Penerson, Hance
	Peterson, Hance
	VanKirke, Joseph
Polly	Hayden, Fuller
S. Crew Packet	Rogers, John
Sally	Aroid, Aaron
	Champman, Joseph
	Hall, Henry
	Lovett, Peter
	Passino, Thomas
	Smith, Jacob
Sampson	Coffin, James
	Leonard, Robert
	Manby, Rooth
	Thornton, David
	Tucker, Nathaniel
Sampson Maydock	Vincent, Henry
San Joseph Volorado	Brown, George
	Gaues, Richard
	Hughes, John
	Young, John
San Juan	Rose, Stanley
Sine Qua Non	Beard, Richard
	Luce, Abijah
	Morton, Pliny
Spanish MV	Blackloch, John
	Lynch, Charles
	Manlove, Roberts
Thomas Wilson	Arthurs, Williams
	Grimes, George
	Harman, William
Thomas Wilson	Heywood, Alexander
	Hopburn, R.
	Pirman, John
	Silvy, John
	Spear, Francis
	Storm, John
	Tuesdell, William
Thrasher	Davidson, Henry
	Somerville, Charles
Tiger	Atkens, Uriah
	Bartlett, John
	Blanchard, Calvin
	Hubbard, John
	Leach, John
	Leeds, Leon
	Newell, John
	Snow, Joseph
	West, Reuben
Topaz	Anbeck, John A.
	Bain, Daniel
	Begnall, Charles
	Bennett, Thomas
	Brown, Silvenus
	Bruce, Peter
	Cannon, Charles D.
	Davis, Elias
	Davis, Joseph
	Giles, William
	Graham, David
	Griffin, Evan
	Hussard, John K.
	Pitts, James
	Wort, William
Tyber	Forbes, Thomas
	Hall, Henry
	Lovett, Israel
	Overstock, Peter
	Shepherd, Thomas
	Thomas, John
Veroni	Archibald, Robert
	Coody, William
	French, Samuel
	Holstean, Samuel
	Metcalf, Anthony

Veroni   Murray, Richard
                   Thomas, J.

Malta

Akerman, William - Seaman - Number: 1 - How taken: Gave himself up from unknown ship - Date received: 17 Nov 1812 - From what ship: HM Frigate Havannah - Discharged on 4 Mar 1814 - How discharged: HMS Repulse for England.

Brown, Thomas - Seaman - Number: 5 - How taken: Gave himself up from unknown ship - Date received: 23 Nov 1812 - From what ship: HM Ship-of-the-Line Trident - Discharged on 4 Mar 1814 - How discharged: HM Ship-of-the-Line Repulse for England.

Browne, Jesse - Seaman - Number: 7 - How taken: Gave himself up from unknown ship - Date received: 2 Dec 1812 - From what ship: HM Ship-of-the-Line Trident - Discharged on 4 Mar 1814 - How discharged: HM Ship-of-the-Line Repulse for England.

Chace, Joseph - Seaman - Number: 49 - How taken: Gave himself up from unknown ship - Date received: 22 May 1813 - From what ship: HMT Cleveland - Discharged on 4 Mar 1814 - How discharged: HM Ship-of-the-Line Repulse for England.

Chapman, Enoch - Seaman - Number: 36 - How taken: Gave himself up from HM Frigate Alcmene - Date received: 26 Jan 1813 - From what ship: HM Frigate Alcmene - Died on 6 Apr 1813 from small pox.

Charles, Philip - Seaman - Number: 41 - How taken: Gave himself up from HM Ship-of-the-Line Elizabeth - Date received: 21 Mar 1813 - From what ship: HM Ship-of-the-Line Elizabeth - Discharged on 5 Mar 1814 - How discharged: Onboard a transport for England.

Connor, William - Master - Date received: 10 Mar 1814 - From what ship: General Green - Discharged on 3 May 1814 - How discharged: HM Ship-of-the-Line Milford for England.

Cox, John - Seaman - Number: 43 - How taken: Gave himself up from HM Ship-of-the-Line Elizabeth - Date received: 21 Mar 1813 - From what ship: HM Ship-of-the-Line Elizabeth - Discharged on 4 Mar 1814 - How discharged: HM Ship-of-the-Line Repulse for England.

Craig, William - Seaman - Number: 32 - How taken: Gave himself up from HM Frigate Alcmene - Date received: 26 Jan 1813 - From what ship: HM Frigate Alcmene - Discharged on 4 Mar 1814 - How discharged: HM Ship-of-the-Line Repulse for England.

Dalton, Samuel - Seaman - Number: 39 - How taken: Gave himself up from HM Frigate Bacchante - Date received: 12 Mar 1813 - From what ship: HM Frigate Bacchante - Discharged on 3 May 1814 - How discharged: HM Ship-of-the-Line Milford for England.

Daniels, Robert - Seaman - Number: 40 - How taken: Sent to prison by the master of the MV Eurydice - Date received: 17 Mar 1813 - From what ship: MV Eurydice - Discharged on 4 Mar 1814 - How discharged: HM Ship-of-the-Line Repulse for England.

Day, John - Seaman - Number: 37 - How taken: Gave himself up from HM Sloop Guadeloupe - Date received: 3 Feb 1813 - From what ship: HM Sloop Guadeloupe - Discharged on 4 Mar 1814 - How discharged: HM Ship-of-the-Line Repulse for England.

Dexter, Thomas - Mate - Number: 28 - Prize name: L'Endymion - Type of Ship: MV - How taken: HM Brig Eclair - Date taken: 13 Jan 1813 - Where taken: off Goleta (La Goulette, Tunisia) - Date received: 21 Jan 1813 - From what ship: MV L'Endymion - Discharged on 23 Jan 1813 - How discharged: Not readable.

Dorchester, Preston - Seaman - Number: 44 - How taken: Gave himself up from HM Ship-of-the-Line Elizabeth - Date received: 21 Mar 1813 - From what ship: HM Ship-of-the-Line Elizabeth - Discharged on 3 May 1814 - How discharged: HM Ship-of-the-Line Milford for England.

Drives, John - Seaman - Number: 47 - How taken: Gave himself up from unknown ship - Date received: 22 May 1813 - From what ship: HMT Cleveland - Discharged on 4 Mar 1814 - How discharged: HM Ship-of-the-Line Repulse for England.

Elmy, John - Seaman - Number: 45 - How taken: Gave himself up from MV Eurydice - Date received: 1 May 1813 - From what ship: MV Eurydice - Discharged on 4 Apr 1814 - How discharged: Fox Packet for England.

Enochs, Joseph - Seaman - Number: 54 - How taken: Gave himself up from unknown ship - Date received: 7 Mar 1814 - From what ship: HM Sloop Badger - Discharged on 3 May 1814 - How discharged: HM Ship-of-the-Line Milford for England.

Eyres, John - Seaman - Number: 30 - How taken: Gave himself up from HM Frigate Alcmene - Date received: 26 Jan 1813 - From what ship: HM Frigate Alcmene - Discharged on 4 Mar 1814 - How discharged: HM Ship-of-the-Line Repulse for England.

Ford, Charles - Seaman - Number: 51 - How taken: Gave himself up from unknown ship - Date received: 22 May 1813 - From what ship: HMT Cleveland - Discharged on 4 Mar 1814 - How discharged: HM Ship-of-the-Line Repulse for England.

Ford, Philip - Seaman - Number: 24 - How taken: Gave himself up from HM Ship-of-the-Line Trident - Date received: 15 Jan 1813 - From what ship: HM Ship-of-the-Line Trident - Discharged on 4 Mar 1814 - How discharged: HM Ship-of-the-Line Repulse for England.

Frizzle, David - Seaman - Number: 23 - How taken: Gave himself up from unknown ship - Date received: 31 Dec 1812 - From what ship: HM Frigate Thames - Discharged on 3 May 1814 - How discharged: HM Ship-of-the-Line Milford for England.

Govet, Charles - Seaman - Number: 9 - Prize name: Nebrophenus - Type of Ship: P - How taken: HM Frigate Furieuse - Date taken: 9 Nov 1812 - Where taken: off Ponza (Italy) - Date received: 7 Dec 1812 - From what ship: HM Frigate Furieuse - Discharged on 4 Mar 1814 - How discharged: HM Ship-of-the-Line Repulse for England.

Green, Solomon - Seaman - Number: 19 - How taken: Gave himself up from unknown ship - Date received: 29 Dec 1812 - From what ship: HM Frigate Thames - Discharged on 4 Mar 1814 - How discharged: HM Ship-of-the-Line Repulse for England.

Halback, Emanuel - Seaman - Number: 48 - How taken: Gave himself up from unknown ship - Date received: 22 May 1813 - From what ship: HMT Cleveland - Discharged on 4 Mar 1814 - How discharged: HM Ship-of-the-Line Repulse for England.

Halstead, Joseph - Seaman - Number: 2 - How taken: Gave himself up from unknown ship - Date received: 17 Nov 1812 - From what ship: HM Frigate Havannah - Discharged on 4 Mar 1814 - How discharged: HMS Repulse for England.

Hartwell, Barney - Seaman - Number: 22 - How taken: Gave himself up from unknown ship - Date received: 31 Dec 1812 - From what ship: HM Frigate Thames - Discharged on 4 Mar 1814 - How discharged: HM Ship-of-the-Line Repulse for England.

Hooper, William - Seaman - Number: 42 - How taken: Gave himself up from HM Ship-of-the-Line Elizabeth - Date received: 21 Mar 1813 - From what ship: HM Ship-of-the-Line Elizabeth - Discharged on 4 Mar 1814 - How discharged: HM Ship-of-the-Line Repulse for England.

Howes, Ensign E. - Seaman - Number: 35 - How taken: Gave himself up from HM Frigate Alcmene - Date received: 26 Jan 1813 - From what ship: HM Frigate Alcmene - Discharged on 3 May 1814 - How discharged: HM Ship-of-the-Line Milford for England.

Hudson, Thomas - Seaman - Number: 3 - How taken: Gave himself up from unknown ship - Date received: 17 Nov 1812 - From what ship: HM Frigate Havannah - Discharged on 30 Apr 1813 - How discharged: HM Ship-of-the-Line Leviathan.

Jarvis, James - Seaman - Number: 6 - How taken: Gave himself up from unknown ship - Date received: 24 Nov 1812 - From what ship: HM Brig Haughty - Discharged on 4 Mar 1814 - How discharged: HM Ship-of-the-Line Repulse for England.

Johnson, Andrew - Seaman - Number: 29 - How taken: Taken from unknown ship - Date received: 23 Jan 1813 - From what ship: HM Ship-of-the-Line Agar - Discharged on 4 Mar 1814 - How discharged: HM Ship-of-the-Line Repulse for England.

Keep, Alexander - Seaman - Number: 14 - How taken: Gave himself up from unknown ship - Date received: 29 Dec 1812 - From what ship: HM Sloop Nautilus - Discharged on 3 May 1814 - How discharged: HM Ship-of-the-

Line Milford for England.

Kinder, Alexander - Seaman - Number: 8 - Prize name: Nebrophenus - Type of Ship: P - How taken: HM Frigate Furieuse - Date taken: 9 Nov 1812 - Where taken: off Ponza (Italy) - Date received: 7 Dec 1812 - From what ship: HM Frigate Furieuse - Discharged on 4 Mar 1814 - How discharged: HM Ship-of-the-Line Repulse for England.

Lane, John - Seaman - Number: 12 - How taken: Gave himself up from unknown ship - Date received: 28 Dec 1812 - From what ship: HM Sloop Sparrowhawk - Discharged on 3 May 1814 - How discharged: HM Ship-of-the-Line Milford for England.

Marsh, James - Seaman - Number: 26 - Prize name: L'Endymion - Type of Ship: MV - How taken: HM Brig Eclair - Date taken: 13 Jan 1813 - Where taken: off Goleta (La Goulette, Tunisia) - Date received: 21 Jan 1813 - From what ship: MV L'Endymion - Discharged on 23 Jan 1813 - How discharged: Not readable.

Marshall, John - Seaman - Number: 34 - How taken: Gave himself up from HM Frigate Alcmene - Date received: 26 Jan 1813 - From what ship: HM Frigate Alcmene - Discharged on 3 May 1814 - How discharged: HM Ship-of-the-Line Milford for England.

McCarty, John - Seaman - Number: 18 - How taken: Gave himself up from unknown ship - Date received: 29 Dec 1812 - From what ship: HM Sloop Nautilus - Discharged on 4 Mar 1814 - How discharged: HM Ship-of-the-Line Repulse for England.

Merchant, William - Seaman - Number: 38 - How taken: Gave himself up from HM Sloop Guadeloupe - Date received: 3 Feb 1813 - From what ship: HM Sloop Guadeloupe - Discharged on 4 Mar 1814 – How discharged: HM Ship-of-the-Line Repulse for England.

Moore, James - Seaman - Number: 31 - How taken: Gave himself up from HM Frigate Alcmene - Date received: 26 Jan 1813 - From what ship: HM Frigate Alcmene - Discharged on 3 May 1814 - How discharged: HM Ship-of-the-Line Milford for England.

Musick, Joseph - Seaman - Number: 10 - How taken: Gave himself up from unknown ship - Date received: 10 Dec 1812 - From what ship: HM Frigate Furieuse - Discharged on 4 Mar 1814 - How discharged: HM Ship-of-the-Line Repulse for England.

Parker, Richard - Seaman - Number: 46 - How taken: Gave himself up from unknown ship - Date received: 22 May 1813 - From what ship: HMT Cleveland - Discharged on 3 May 1814 - How discharged: HM Ship-of-the-Line Milford for England.

Rice, William - Seaman - Number: 20 - How taken: Gave himself up from unknown ship - Date received: 29 Dec 1812 - From what ship: HM Frigate Thames - Discharged on 3 May 1814 - How discharged: HM Ship-of-the-Line Milford for England.

Rose, William - Seaman - Number: 13 - How taken: Gave himself up from unknown ship - Date received: 29 Dec 1812 - From what ship: HM Sloop Nautilus.

Silverlock, John - Seaman - Number: 21 - How taken: Gave himself up from unknown ship - Date received: 29 Dec 1812 - From what ship: HM Frigate Thames - Discharged on 3 May 1814 - How discharged: HM Ship-of-the-Line Milford for England.

Smith, William - Seaman - Number: 17 - How taken: Gave himself up from unknown ship - Date received: 29 Dec 1812 - From what ship: HM Sloop Nautilus - Discharged on 4 Mar 1814 - How discharged: HM Ship-of-the-Line Repulse for England.

Stephens, Obadiah - Seaman - Number: 33 - How taken: Gave himself up from HM Frigate Alcmene - Date received: 26 Jan 1813 - From what ship: HM Frigate Alcmene - Discharged on 4 Mar 1814 - How discharged: HM Ship-of-the-Line Repulse for England.

Steward, Scorpio - Seaman - Number: 52 - How taken: Gave himself up from unknown ship - Date received: 22 May 1813 - From what ship: HMT Cleveland - Discharged on 3 May 1814 - How discharged: HM Ship-of-the-Line Milford for England.

Taylor, William - Seaman - Number: 15 - How taken: Gave himself up from unknown ship - Date received: 29 Dec 1812 - From what ship: HM Sloop Nautilus - Discharged on 4 Mar 1814 - How discharged: HM Ship-of-the-

Line Repulse for England.

Taylor, William - Seaman - Number: 25 - Prize name: L'Endymion - Type of Ship: MV - How taken: HM Brig Eclair - Date taken: 13 Jan 1813 - Where taken: off Goleta (La Goulette, Tunisia) - Date received: 21 Jan 1813 - From what ship: MV L'Endymion - Discharged on 23 Jan 1813 - How discharged: Not readable.

Thomas, Henry - Seaman - Number: 27 - Prize name: L'Endymion - Type of Ship: MV - How taken: HM Brig Eclair - Date taken: 13 Jan 1813 - Where taken: off Goleta (La Goulette, Tunisia) - Date received: 21 Jan 1813 - From what ship: MV L'Endymion - Discharged on 23 Jan 1813 - How discharged: Not readable.

Tuxen, Peter - Mate - Date received: 10 Mar 1814 - From what ship: General Green - Discharged on 3 May 1814 - How discharged: HM Ship-of-the-Line Milford for England.

Wampo, Nathaniel - Seaman - Number: 53 - How taken: Gave himself up from unknown ship - Date received: 22 May 1813 - From what ship: HMT Cleveland – Died on 22 Jan 1814 from consumption (tuberculosis).

Warner, Samuel - Seaman - Number: 11 - How taken: Gave himself up from unknown ship - Date received: 10 Dec 1812 - From what ship: HM Frigate Furieuse - Discharged on 4 Mar 1814 - How discharged: HM Ship-of-the-Line Repulse for England.

Williams, James - Seaman - Number: 55 - How taken: Gave himself up from unknown ship - Date received: 7 Mar 1814 - From what ship: HM Sloop Badger - Discharged on 3 May 1814 - How discharged: HM Ship-of-the-Line Milford for England.

Williams, William - Seaman - Number: 16 - How taken: Gave himself up from unknown ship - Date received: 29 Dec 1812 - From what ship: HM Sloop Nautilus - Discharged on 3 May 1814 - How discharged: HM Ship-of-the-Line Milford for England.

Wilson, Thomas - Seaman-Cook - Number: 4 - How taken: Gave himself up from unknown ship - Date received: 18 Nov 1812 - From what ship: HM Frigate Havannah – Died on 14 Jul 1813 from consumption (tuberculosis).

Wilson, Thomas - Seaman - Number: 50 - How taken: Gave himself up from unknown ship - Date received: 22 May 1813 - From what ship: HMT Cleveland - Discharged on 4 Mar 1814 - How discharged: HM Ship-of-the-Line Repulse for England.

Numeric listing by prisoner number

1	Akerman, William		29	Johnson, Andrew
2	Halstead, Joseph		30	Eyres, John
3	Hudson, Thomas		31	Moore, James
4	Wilson, Thomas		32	Craig, William
5	Brown, Thomas		33	Stephens, Obadiah
6	Jarvis, James		34	Marshall, John
7	Browne, Jesse		35	Howes, Ensign E.
8	Kinder, Alexander		36	Chapman, Enoch
9	Govet, Charles		37	Day, John
10	Musick, Joseph		38	Merchant, William
11	Warner, Samuel		39	Dalton, Samuel
12	Lane, John		40	Daniels, Robert
13	Rose, William		41	Charles, Philip
14	Keep, Alexander		42	Hooper, William
15	Taylor, William		43	Cox, John
16	Williams, William		44	Dorchester, Preston
17	Smith, William		45	Elmy, John
18	McCarty, John		46	Parker, Richard
19	Green, Solomon		47	Drives, John
20	Rice, William		48	Halback, Emanuel
21	Silverlock, John		49	Chace, Joseph
22	Hartwell, Barney		50	Wilson, Thomas
23	Frizzle, David		51	Ford, Charles
24	Ford, Philip		52	Steward, Scorpio
25	Taylor, William		53	Wampo, Nathaniel
26	Marsh, James		54	Enochs, Joseph
27	Thomas, Henry		55	Williams, James
28	Dexter, Thomas			

Prisoner numbers not assigned

Connor, William

Tuxen, Peter

Crew listing

Unknown ship	Akerman, William	Unknown ship	Keep, Alexander
	Brown, Thomas		Lane, John
	Browne, Jesse		Marshall, John
	Chace, Joseph		McCarty, John
	Chapman, Enoch		Merchant, William
	Charles, Philip		Moore, James
	Connor, William		Musick, Joseph
	Cox, John		Parker, Richard
	Craig, William		Rice, William
	Dalton, Samuel		Rose, William
	Daniels, Robert		Silverlock, John
	Day, John		Smith, William
	Dorchester, Preston		Stephens, Obadiah
	Drives, John		Steward, Scorpio
	Elmy, John		Taylor, William
	Enochs, Joseph		Tuxen, Peter
	Eyres, John		Wampo, Nathaniel
	Ford, Charles		Warner, Samuel
	Ford, Philip		Williams, James
	Frizzle, David		Williams, William
	Green, Solomon		Wilson, Thomas
	Halback, Emanuel		
	Halstead, Joseph	MV L'Endymion	Dexter, Thomas
	Hartwell, Barney		Marsh, James
	Hooper, William		Taylor, William
	Howes, Ensign E.		Thomas, Henry
	Hudson, Thomas		
	Jarvis, James	MV Nebrophenus	Govet, Charles
	Johnson, Andrew		Kinder, Alexander